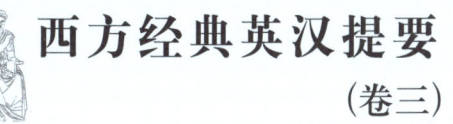

西方经典英汉提要
（卷三）

(奥) 雷立柏 (Leopold Leeb) 著

中世纪经典100部

English-Chinese Summaries of Western Classics Volume III
100 Classics of the Middle Ages

(650年到1450年)

世界图书出版公司
北京·广州·上海·西安

目 录
CONTENTS

《西方经典英汉提要》总序 / 1
序 / 4
大事年表 / 9

第一篇
中世纪早期
（650 年到 780 年）

CHAPTER 1
The Early Middle Ages
(650—780 AD)

阿达梅南 2
  001.《圣科伦班传》.......................................2
阿尔德海姆 4
  002.《赞美独身生活》...................................4
  003.《致阿基求斯的信》...............................4
约翰内斯 6
  004.《巴兰和约沙法特》...............................6
  005.《智慧的泉源》.......................................6
比德 10
  006.《英格兰教会史》................................10
博尼法修斯 14
  007.《信集》...14

Adamnanus 3
  001. *Vita Columbae* 3
Aldhelmus 5
  002. *De laudibus virginitatis* 5
  003. *Epistola ad Acircium* 5
Iōannēs Damaskēnos 7
  004. *Barlaam et Joasaph* 7
  005. *Pēgē Gnōseōs* 7
Beda Venerabilis 11
  006. *Historia Ecclesiastica gentis Anglorum* 11
Bonifatius 15
  007. *Epistulae* 15

第二篇
卡洛琳文艺复兴时期
（780 年到 900 年）

CHAPTER 2
The Age of the Carolingian Renaissance
(780—900 AD)

保禄（保罗）...20
  008.《伦巴第人的历史》...........................20
阿尔库因 24

Paulus Diaconus 21
  008. *Historia Langobardorum* 21
Alcuin 25

1

009.《约克教会历代主教和圣人》..............24	009. *De pontificibus et sanctis Eboracensis ecclesiae*......25

基涅武甫 26
010.《埃琳娜》..............................26

Kynewulf 27
010. *Elene* 27

艾因哈德 28
011.《查理大帝传》..........................28

Eginhardus 29
011. *Vita Caroli Magni* 29

拉班努 32
012.《论教士的培养》........................32

Flavius Arrianus 33
012. *De institutione clericorum* 33

奥特弗里德 36
013.《福音之书》............................36

Otfrid von Weissenburg 37
013. *Evangelienbuch* 37

瓦拉夫瑞德 38
014.《园艺之书》............................38
015.《维提的神视》..........................40

Walahfridus Strabo 39
014. *Liber de cultura hortorum* 39
015. *Visio Wettini* 41

艾利基纳 42
016.《论自然的区分》........................42

Ioannes Scotus Eriugena 43
016. *De divisione naturae* 43

佛提乌斯 46
017.《万书之书》............................46

Phōtios 47
017. *Myrobiblion* 47

诺特克尔 50
018.《查理大帝言行录》......................50

Notkerus Balbulus 51
018. *Gesta Caroli Magni imperatoris* 51

第三篇
民族大迁移的结束和城市文明的开始
（900 年到 1080 年）

CHAPTER 3
The End of the Migrations and the Emergence of Urban Centers (900－1080 AD)

埃克哈德 54
019.《瓦尔塔里乌斯之诗》....................54

Ekkehard I 55
019. *Waltharii Poiesis* 55

阿德索 58
020.《论反基督的诞生和时期》................58

Adso Dervensis 59
020. *De ortu et tempore Antichristi* 59

赫若斯维塔 60
021.《隐修者亚巴郎》........................60
022.《杜启修斯》............................62
023.《德欧斐路斯》..........................62

Hrotsvita Gandeshemensis 61
021. *Abraham eremita* 61
022. *Dulcitius* 63
023. *Theophilus* 63

阿维森纳 …… 64
024.《康复书》…… 64

维波 …… 66
025.《康拉德二世皇帝传》…… 66

赫尔曼 …… 68
026.《编年史》…… 68
027.《八宗罪》…… 68

额我略七世 …… 70
028.《教宗的规定》…… 70

第四篇
大学的形成和 12 世纪的复兴
（1080 年到 1200 年）

安瑟伦 …… 76
029.《上主为什么降生成人？》…… 76
030.《独白篇》…… 76
031.《对话篇》…… 78

布拉格的科斯玛斯 …… 80
032.《波希米亚人的历史》…… 80

涅斯托尔 …… 82
033.《往年故事》…… 82

阿伯拉尔 …… 84
034.《是与否》…… 84

马梅斯布里 …… 88
035.《英国史》…… 88

阿纳·康尼纳 …… 90
036.《阿历克塞亚斯》…… 90

伯尔纳德 …… 92
037.《论反省》…… 92
038.《论爱神》…… 94

Avicenna …… 65
024. *Kitab as-sifa* …… 65

Wipo …… 67
025. *Gesta Chuonradi II imperatoris* …… 67

Hermannus …… 69
026. *Chronicon* …… 69
027. *De octo vitiis principalibus* …… 69

Gregorius VII …… 71
028. *Dictatus Papae* …… 71

CHAPTER 4
The Formation of Universities and the Renaissance of the 12th Century (1080－1200 AD)

Anselmus Cantuariensis …… 77
029. *Cur Deus Homo* …… 77
030. *Monologion* …… 77
031. *Proslogion* …… 79

Cosmas Pragensis …… 81
032. *Chronica Bohemorum* …… 81

Nestorius …… 83
033. *Povest' vremennykh let* …… 83

Petrus Abaelardus …… 85
034. *Sic et non* …… 85

Guilelmus Malmesburiensis …… 89
035. *Gesta regum Anglorum* …… 89

Anna Komnēnē …… 91
036. *Alexias* …… 91

Bernardus …… 93
037. *De consideratione* …… 93
038. *De diligendo Deo* …… 95

伯铎禄	96	Petrus Venerabilis	97
039.《反驳萨拉森人》	96	039. *Contra Saracenos*	97
圣维克多的雨果	98	Hugo	99
040.《学问之阶》	98	040. *Didascalicon*	99
圣希尔德加德	102	Hildegardis de Alemannia	103
041.《诸病因和治疗》	102	041. *Causae et curae*	103
格拉狄安	106	Gratianus	107
042.《教会法汇编》	106	042. *Concordantia discordantium canonum*	107
蒙默思的杰弗里	108	Galfridus	109
043.《不列颠诸王纪》	108	043. *Historia regum Britanniae*	109
彼得·隆巴	112	Petrus Lombardus	113
044.《四部语录》	112	044. *Sententiarum libri quattuor*	113
奥托	114	Otto Frisingensis	115
045.《编年史或两个社会的历史》	114	045. *Chronica sive Historia de duabus civitatibus*	115
索尔兹伯里的约翰	116	Johannes Saresberiensis	117
046.《论政治》	116	046. *Policraticus*	117
阿维罗伊	120	Averroes	121
047.《论灵魂注》	120	047. *Tafsir kitab an-nafs*	121
阿兰	124	Alanus ab Insulis	125
048.《反克劳蒂安》	124	048. *Anticlaudianus*	125
约亚敬	128	Joachim de Flore	129
049.《象征之书》	128	049. *Liber figurarum*	129
克里蒂安·德·特鲁瓦	132	Chretien de Troyes	133
050.《艾莱克与艾尼德》	132	050. *Erec et Enide*	133
迈蒙尼德	136	Moses Maimonides	137
051.《迷途指津》	136	051. *More nevukhim*	137
萨克索	140	Saxo Grammaticus	141
052.《丹麦历史》	140	052. *Gesta Danorum*	141
哈特曼	142	Hartmann von Aue	143
053.《可怜的亨利》	142	053. *Der arme Heinrich*	143

第五篇
中世纪盛期和经院哲学的黄金时期
（1200 年到 1320 年）

CHAPTER 5
The High Middle Ages and the Golden Age of Scholasticism（1200—1320 AD）

依诺森三世 148
   054.《论人生的悲惨情况》................. 148
沃尔夫拉姆·冯·埃申巴赫 150
   055.《帕尔齐法尔》.............................. 150
斯诺里·斯图鲁松 156
   056.《埃达》.. 156
托马斯 160
   057.《圣方济各传》.............................. 160
博韦的樊尚 164
   058.《知识宝鉴》.................................. 164
费德利希二世 168
   059.《论用鸟去打猎》.......................... 168
布拉克顿 172
   060.《英格兰的法律与习惯》.............. 172
大阿尔伯特 174
   061.《受造界大全》.............................. 174
西班牙的伯多禄（彼得）..................... 178
   062.《逻辑学大全》.............................. 178
罗里斯 182
   063.《玫瑰传奇》.................................. 182
罗吉尔·培根 186
   064.《伟大著作》.................................. 186
鲁布鲁克 188
   065.《东方游记》.................................. 188
波那文图拉 190
   066.《灵魂迈向天主的路程》.............. 190
托马斯·阿奎那 194
   067.《反驳异教大全》.......................... 194
   068.《神学大全》.................................. 196

Innocens III 149
   054. *De miseria humanae conditionis* 149
Wolfram von Eschenbach 151
   055. *Parzival* 151
Snorri Sturluson 157
   056. *Edda* 157
Thomas de Celano 161
   057. *Vita sancti Francisci* 161
Vincentius Bellovacensis 165
   058. *Speculum maius* 165
Fredericus II 169
   059. *De arte venandi cum avibus* 169
Bracton 173
   060. *De legibus et consuetudinibus Angliae* ...173
Albertus Magnus 175
   061. *Summa de creaturis* 175
Petrus Hispanus 179
   062. *Summulae logicales* 179
Guillaume de Lorris 183
   063. *Le Roman de la rose* 183
Rogerius Baco 187
   064. *Opus maius* 187
Rubruk 189
   065. *Itinerarium ad partes orientales* ... 189
Bonaventura 191
   066. *Itinerarium mentis in Deum* 191
Thomas Aquinas 195
   067. *Summa contra gentiles* 195
   068. *Summa Theologiae* 197

沃拉吉纳的雅各 204	Jacobus de Voragine 205
069.《金传》......204	069. *Legenda Aurea* 205
卢尔 208	Raimundus Lullus 209
070.《宏大的技术》......208	070. *Ars magna* 209
071.《巴奎纳》......210	071. *Blanquerna* 211
马可·波罗 214	Marco Polo 215
072.《马可·波罗游记》......214	072. *Il Milione* 215
格尔特儒德 218	Gertrudis de Helfta 219
073.《神爱的使者》......218	073. *Legatus divinae pietatis* 219
艾克哈特 222	Johannes Eckehart 223
074.《神慰之书》......222	074. *Liber benedictus* 223
但丁 226	Dante Alighieri 227
075.《神曲》......226	075. *Commedia Divina* 227
076.《论俗语》......234	076. *De vulgari eloquentia* 235

第六篇

中世纪晚期和文艺复兴的开端
（1320年到1450年）

CHAPTER 6

The Late Middle Ages and the Beginnings of the Renaissance（1320—1450 AD）

利尔的尼古拉斯 240	Nicolaus de Lyra 241
077.《全部〈圣经〉注解集》......240	077. *Postilla litteralis super totam Bibliam* 241
威廉·奥康 242	Occam 243
078.《语录注集》......242	078. *Sententiae* 243
布里吉特 246	Birgitta 247
079.《诸神视》......246	079. *Revelationes* 247
彼特拉克 248	Petrarca 249
080.《两种不同命运之道》......248	080. *De remediis utriusque fortunae* 249
081.《歌集》......250	081. *Rime* 251
薄伽丘 252	Giovanni Boccaccio 253
082.《十日谈》......252	082. *Decamerone* 253
083.《名人之堕落》......256	083. *De casibus virorum illustrium* 257
俄瑞斯梅的尼古拉斯 258	Nicolaus Oresmensis 259
084.《货币论》......258	084. *De origine monetarum* 259

威克利夫	262	Johannes Wyclif	263
085.《论世俗政权》	262	085. *De civili dominio*	263
兰格朗	266	Langland	267
086.《耕者皮尔斯的梦》	266	086. *Piers Plowman*	267
傅华萨	270	Jean Froissart	271
087.《闻见录》	270	087. *Chroniques*	271
杰弗里·乔叟	272	Geoffrey Chaucer	273
088.《坎特伯雷故事集》	272	089. *The Canterbury Tales*	273
若望	276	Johannes de Tepla	277
089.《波希米亚的耕夫》	276	089. *Der Ackermann aus Boehmen*	277
杰尔松	280	Johannes Carlerius de Gerson	281
090.《神秘神学》	280	090. *De mystica theologia*	281
托马斯·肯璧斯	284	Thomas a Kempis	285
091.《师主篇》	284	091. *De imitatione Christi*	285
库撒的尼古拉	288	Nicolaus Cusanus	289
092.《论有学识的无知》	288	092. *De docta ignorantia*	289
贝萨里翁	292	Bessarion	293
093.《反驳柏拉图的诽谤者》	292	093. *In calumniatorem Platonis*	293
皮科罗米尼	294	Enea Silvio de Piccolomini	295
094.《回忆录》	294	094. *Commentarii rerum memorabilium*	295
格雷邦	300	Arnoul Greban	301
095.《巴黎受难剧》	300	095. *Passion de Paris*	301

附录 Appendix

无名作者	306	Anonymus	307
096.《古兰经》	306	096. *Qur'an*	307
097.《亚历山大传奇》	308	097. *Alexandreis*	309
098.《一千零一夜》	310	098. *Alf lailah wa-lailah*	311
099.《贝奥武夫》	312	099. *Beowulf*	313
100.《救世主》	314	100. *Heliand*	315
101.《罗兰之歌》	314	101. *Chanson de Roland*	315
102.《熙德之歌》	316	102. *Poema de mio Cid*	317

103.《列那狐传奇》..................316	103. *Roman de Renard* 317
104.《布拉纳歌集》..................318	104. *Carmina Burana* 319
105.《尼伯龙根之歌》..................320	105. *Nibelungenlied* 321
106.《英国大宪章》..................324	106. *Magna Charta Libertatum* 325
107.《黄金诏书》..................326	107. *Bulla aurea* 327
108.《每一个人》..................328	108. *Elkerlijk* 329

拉—英—德（法、意等）—汉索引 Latin–English–German(French, Italian etc.)–Chinese Index / 332

出版后记 / 438

西方经典英汉提要
总 序

就早期的来龙去脉而言,欧洲文化的根源在埃及、巴勒斯坦、叙利亚和波斯地区,因此"西方文化"和"西方经典"是有争论的概念。然而从文学和思想来看,古希腊的传统在人类思想史上形成了一种很关键的新开端。因此,本系列从荷马开始梳理欧洲经典的悠久传统,其目标是提供关于一些重要著作及其作者的基本知识。当然,仅仅轮廓性地描述一部经典的内容是远远不够的,应该还要鉴定每一部经典在文学史及思想史上的位置和影响,又要提供一些分析和解释,以及关于该著作的研究书目。不过,这一切都超出本系列的范围。

欧洲文化以及西方思想史应该被视为一个整体。这就意味着人们应该研究每一个时代的作者以及前后著作之间的关联。一种比较全面的角度也应该注意到不同的知识领域,因为一些作者可能通过诗歌表达一些哲学理念或他们会将神话与历史结合起来。因此,文学、历史、哲学、法律和宗教在很多古代经典中是分不开的。比如奥古斯丁的《上帝之城》谈论历史、伦理、政治、神话学、宗教信仰以及解释学的问题。

本系列分为五卷:《古希腊罗马经典100部》(公元前800年到公元150年)、《古代晚期经典100部》(公元150年到650年)、《中世纪经典100部》(650年到1450年)、《文艺复兴和巴罗克时期经典100部》(1450到1750年)、《近现代经典100部》(1750年到1950年)。每一卷都可以充当一部独立的文集,因此在每一卷附加索引,其中罗列作者、著作和重要概念的原名、英语及汉语的翻译。本系列的经典主要属于文学、历史学、哲学、法学和宗教学的领域,但也包括一些著名的自然科学著作和百科全书式的著作。在选择经典时我们优先收录那些形成比较完整叙事的著作,因此残片式的著作、"诗歌集"、"信集"和"讲演集"类型的著作比较少。一些重要的作者在正文中被忽略,但在索引中仍然有关于他们的基本资料。因为本系列特别注重经典的原文,在汉语的叙述中仍然使用ABC写出西文的人名、地名和书名。"关于专名,除有惯译者外,一般均不译成汉语对音。因为单是《荷马史诗》中的英雄Achilleus就有阿喀琉斯、阿基琉斯、阿戏留、阿溪里等许多译名,难定取舍,所以都不采用,一概使用原文。"(参见罗念生,《古希腊语汉语词典》,商务印书馆,2004年,前言)。西文专名的汉译能在索引中查获。

希望本系列能够帮助读者更好地了解和欣赏西方文学及思想的高度、深度和广度!

编者雷立柏
2009年于北京

The Series of "English–Chinese Summaries of Western Classics"

General Preface

The more ancient origins of European culture are in Egypt, Palestine, Syria and Persia, and thus the expressions "western culture" and "western classics" are debatable. However, as far as literature and thought are concerned, the tradition of ancient Greece forms a decisive new beginning in the intellectual history of mankind. Thus this series starts with Homer and from there follows the long stream of European classics. The purpose of the collection is to provide basic knowledge about some important classical works and about their authors. Of course, a simple summary of the contents of a classic is not enough, it would also be necessary to assess the position and influence of each work in the history of literature and thought, to offer analysis and possible interpretations, and to add a short bibliography of the studies on each of the classics. However, this exceeds the scope of this series.

European culture and the intellectual history of the West should be understood as a whole. This implies that we should be acquainted with the scholars of every period and with the continuity that links earlier and later works. A more wholistic approach will also pay attention to different fields of knowledge, because many authors may use poetry to express philosophical ideas or combine myth and history. Thus literature, history, philosophy, law, and religion are intertwined in many of the classical writings. For example, Augustine's *The City of God* discusses questions of history, ethics, politics, mythology, religious faith, and hermeneutical questions.

This series is divided into five volumes: "100 Classics of Ancient Greece and Rome" (800 BC —150 AD), "100 Classics of Late Antiquity" (150 AD—650 AD), "100 Classics of the Middle Ages" (650—1450 AD), "100 Classics of Renaissance and Baroque" (1450—1750), "100 Classics of the Modern Age" (1750—1950). Each volume is designed as an independent collection and thus has an index which contains the original names of the authors, important works and ideas, and the English and Chinese transcriptions. The classical works chosen in this series are mainly taken from the areas of literature, history, philosophy, law, and religion, but there are also some famous scientific works and encyclopedic collections. Preference was given to those works who present a complete narrative, thus collections of fragments, poems, letters, and speeches have been somewhat neglected. Some important authors may not be mentioned in the text, but they appear in the index. Since this series pays special attention to the original languages of the classics, the Chinese text uses the ABC for western personal names, place names, and book titles. "Proper names are generally not transliterated into Chinese, except for commonly used translations. Take for example the different Chinese translations for the hero Achilles in Homer's epic, it will be hard to choose between 'A-ka-liu-si', 'A-ji-liu-si', 'A-xi-liu','A-xi-li' and many other different translations. Thus we do not use any of these transliterations and keep the original way of writing." (Luo Niansheng, *Classical Greek–Chinese Dictionary*, Shangwu, 2004, preface). The Chinese transliterations of western names can be found in the index.

May this series help the reader to better understand and enjoy the height, depth, and width of western literature and thought!

Leopold Leeb, Beijing 2009

序

  大体来看，欧洲中世纪历史可以分为一个衰退期和一个建设期，但在不同地区这两个阶段的表现有所差异。从375年(匈奴入侵)到955年(匈牙利人定居)的时期被称为"民族大迁移"，而在这个阶段中也同时伴随着穆斯林军的扩展和维京人(诺曼人)的侵略，因此欧洲始终处于一种不安定的状态之中。大约在950年后，在英、德、法国地区出现了越来越多隐修院、城镇、大教堂和学校。人口的增长、经济和文化的繁荣意味着西欧各国已走上稳定发展的道路，而在文化和政治上，则由800年在罗马被加冕的查理曼指出了这种发展的基本路线：他在自己学习拉丁语和希腊语、推动使用拉丁语为共同的学术语言和宗教语言的同时，积极从外面引进新知识，建立了一个国际性的学院，不仅接受基督信仰和罗马教会为具有约束力的共同宗教，而且让各地的贵族和领主相当自由地发展和领导他们的采邑、封地以建国，以此塑造了欧洲那典型的联邦制的封建主义。

  就文学、历史、哲学和宗教而言，欧洲中世纪继承了古希腊罗马的文化并且创造性地改造和超越了这些传统：古代的英雄颂歌和史诗转化为中世纪的骑士文学和圣人传奇。从古代的诗歌和抒情诗中发展出了教育诗、庄严的赞美诗以及热烈的神秘文学。古代的历史记载发展成为中世纪的世界史、民族史、国史和教会史，古代的皇帝传成为中世纪的帝王传，而《圣经》的相关文献则塑造了圣人传记。古代的文集成为中世纪的百科全书、各种"大全"、词典和教科书。古代的相对主义和那些彼此互不兼容的哲学流派转化为中世纪的共同形而上学和具有权威性的宗教哲学和神学。古代的多神论和非权威性宗教发展到一神论和具有道德约束力的共同信仰。古代以内心平安和自我为中心的人生观转化为一种以神和社会为核心的世界观。在古代的法律思想基础上，中世纪的政治权力和宗教权力开始分立并存，双方都有自己的法律体系，而在这种多元化的环境中甚至出现了一些保障公民权利的文献(如《英国大宪章》)。古代那些比较单一的文化发展到多语的社会和持久的翻译工作，即从拉丁语到本地语，或从阿拉伯语和希腊语到拉丁语。古代的精英文化变成一种知识和文化普及的现代教育模式；各地的隐修院、大教堂学校和大学的教育极大地推动了教育制度的改善。根据古代的自然科学知识，中世纪的欧洲人培养了一个跨国性的科学家共同体，其成员始终互相学习和竞争。古代的话剧和音乐发展成了中世纪的宗教话剧与和声圣乐。古代的美术和建筑则发展到中世纪的宗教艺术和宗教建筑以及贵族们的碉堡。

根据这些发展,可以说中世纪在很多方面为近现代的思想模式和文化作了准备,它是一个不容忽略或蔑视的时代。由于许多原因,中世纪曾被称为"黑暗的时代",而这种说法尤其针对前面提到的"衰退时期"。毫无疑问,在1000年的悠久过程中发生了很多灾难性的事件(外族的侵略、经济的衰退、饥荒、动乱、教会内部的冲突、异端邪教的传播、十字军运动的失败及它所造成的损失、君士坦丁堡和西欧的长期冲突、妇女的镇压和巫婆热,法院中的拷打、残酷的刑法等)。然而,从总体来看,中世纪的西欧(拜占庭经历了另一种发展)相当稳定地走向新文化的建设、社会的普遍发展,乃至多元化和现代化。

本书参鉴的主要书目如下:

Max Manitius, *Geschichte der lateinischen Literatur des Mittelalters*, Beck, Muenchen, 1911—1931 (3 vols.);

Ernst Robert Curtius, *Europaeische Literatur und lateinisches Mittelalter*, Francke, Bern, 1948;

Kindlers Literaturlexikon, Muenchen 1971 (12 vols.);

Joseph Dahmus, *Dictionary of Medieval Civilization*, Macmillan, New York, 1984;

Franz Brunhoelzl, *Geschichte der lateinischen Literatur des Mittelalters*, Fink, Muenchen, 1975, 1992 (2 vols);

Karl Langosch, *Mittellatein und Europa: Fuehrung in die Hauptliteratur des Mittelalters*, Wiss. Buchges., Darmstadt, 1990;

Marcia L. Colish, *Medieval Foundations of the Western Intellectual Tradition, 400—1400*, Yale University Press, London, 1997;

杨慧林,黄晋凯,《欧洲中世纪文学史》,译林出版社,南京 2001 年。

我希望这本提要集能帮助读者更好地了解欧洲中世纪的复杂性以及其至今在很多方面仍然存在的贡献。

编者雷立柏
2009 年于北京

Preface

Seen from a wider perspective the history of the European Middle Ages can be divided into two periods, namely a period of decline and a period of positive construction, although these two stages were intertwined and took place at different times in different places. From the arrival of the Huns (375 AD) to the final settlement of the Madyars in Hungary (955 AD) Europe underwent the period known as "Migration of Peoples", and in this period also fell the expansion of the Muslims and the invasion of the Vikings (Normans). Therefore Europe was constantly facing unrest and harassment. Since around 950 AD in the area of modern England, France and Germany there emerged ever more monasteries, cities, cathedrals and schools. The increase of the population, florishing of the economy and culture implied that Western Europe had already embarked on a course of stable development, and in the area of culture and politics, Charlemagne who was crowned in Rome in the year 800 AD, set out the course of development for the next centuries: he learned Latin and Greek himself and promoted Latin as the common academic and ecclesiastical language, he introduced knowledge from abroad and established an academy with scholars from many lands; he accepted the Christian faith and the Roman Church as the obligatory religion, and he allowed the nobles to develop their fiefdoms and duchies in considerable freedom, thus creating the typical European federalist form of feudalism.

As to literature, historiography, philosophy, and religion, it may be said that the European Middle Ages inherited the classical Greek and Roman culture and creatively transformed this tradition and superseded it. The heroic poems of antiquity were transformed into the medieval literature of courtly knightship and legends of saints. The songs and lyric poetry of antiquity developed into medieval didactic poetry, dignified hymns, and expressions of mystical enthusiasm. The historiography of antiquity was transformed into medieval world histories, national histories, and ecclesiastical historiography. Classical biographies of emperors became models for medieval biographies of kings and emperors, and Biblical motives shaped lifes of saints. The collections of antiquity became medieval lexica, sums, textbooks, and dictionaries. The mutually exclusive philosophical schools of antiquity and their relativism were replaced by the medieval common metaphysics, an authoritative philosophy of religion, and theology. The polytheistic mythology and non-authoritative religions of antiquity developed into monotheism and a common faith with obligatory moral force. The old world view that centered on the peace of the mind and on the self was transformed into a world view that put God and society in the first place. Based on the legal thought of antiquity, the medievals could separate secular and ecclesiastical power, develop the legal systems of each, and in this pluralist environment there emerged documents that protected the rights of the citizens (like the "Magna Charta"). The rather uniform cultures of antiquity grew into the multilingual medieval societies and their long-term translation efforts, from Latin into the vernacular languages, or from Arab and Greek into Latin. The elitist culture of antiquity became a culture where knowledge and education were made available to wider circles. The educational efforts at monastery schools, cathedral schools, and universities led to improvements in the education system. The ancient world saw many great scientists and inventors, but the Middle Ages nurtured an international scientific community, and the scholars of this academic body constantly learned from each other and competed with each other. The drama and music of antiquity became the medieval religious plays and polyphonic music. The classical features of architecture and the fine arts developed into ecclesiastical architecture and into the palaces of aristocratic families.

Regarding these developments it may be said that the Middle Ages prepared modern thought and culture in many ways. The medieval period should not be treated with neglect or despise. For some reasons the European Middle Ages have been called the "Dark Ages", and this particularly with regard to the "period of decline" mentioned above. It cannot be denied that in the long stretch of a millenium many disasters and calamities befell Europe (invasions of foreign tribes, decline of economy, famine, plague, unrest, great conflicts within the Church, spread of heresies and evil sects, failure of the crusades and the damage they inflicted, protracted conflicts between Constantinople and the West, the suppression of women and the witch craze, torture in the courts, harsh legal procedures etc.) However, seen as a whole, the peoples of Western Europe (Byzantine went a special course) steadily marched toward the construction of a common new culture, toward the general development of society, even toward pluralism and modernity.

The reference books I used for the compilation of this short outline of medieval literature are mainly the following:

Max Manitius, *Geschichte der lateinischen Literatur des Mittelalters*, Beck, Muenchen, 1911—1931 (3 vols.);

Ernst Robert Curtius, *Europaeische Literatur und lateinisches Mittelalter*, Francke, Bern, 1948;

Kindlers Literaturlexikon, Muenchen 1971 (12 vols.);

Joseph Dahmus, *Dictionary of Medieval Civilization*, Macmillan, New York, 1984;

Franz Brunhoelzl, *Geschichte der lateinischen Literatur des Mittelalters*, Fink, Muenchen, 1975, 1992 (2 vols);

Karl Langosch, *Mittellatein und Europa: Fuehrung in die Hauptliteratur des Mittelalters*, Wiss. Buchges., Darmstadt, 1990;

Marcia L. Colish, *Medieval Foundations of the Western Intellectual Tradition, 400—1400*, Yale University Press, London, 1997;

Yang Huilin, Huang Jinkai, *Ouzhou Zhongshiji Wenxue Shi* (*A History of Medieval European Literature*), Yilin, Nanjing, 2001;

I hope that this book may help the reader to better understand the complexity and many lasting contributions of the European Middle Ages.

Leopold Leeb, Beijing 2009

Table of Important Events
大事年表

568	伦巴第人侵入意大利	Lombards enter Italy
590—604	教宗格列高利派遣传教士到英国	Pope Gregory the Great sends missionaries to England
591—615	爱尔兰人科伦巴在欧洲大陆传播文化	Columban from Ireland brings culture to continental Europe
630	穆罕默德占领麦加并建立伊斯兰教	Muhammad occupies Mecca and establishes Islam
636	穆斯林战胜拜占庭军队	Arab forces defeat the Byzantine army
650—950	隐修院成为西欧的文化中心	Monasteries become cultural centers of western Europe
711	穆斯林军进入西班牙	Muslim forces enter Spain
716—754	博尼法修斯组织德国地区的教会	Boniface organizes the Church in Germany
726—843	拜占庭的皇帝发起破坏圣像运动	Byzantine emperors launch iconoclasm
732	查理·马特在普瓦捷交战阻拦穆斯林军侵入	Charles Martell stops Muslim invasion at Poitiers
756	丕平三世将意大利中部地区交给教宗	Pepin III hands the central region of Italy over to the Pope
781	查理曼邀请各地学者进行教育改革	Charlemagne invites foreign scholars for education reforms
800	查理曼在罗马加冕	Charlemagne crowned in Rome
800—950	维京人(诺曼人)侵略海岸地区	Vikings (Normans) raid coastal areas of western Europe
843	凡尔登协议分裂卡洛琳帝国	Treaty of Verdun divides the Carolingian empire
911	诺曼人定居在诺曼底(法国)	Normans settle in Normandy (France)
936—1002	奥托时期的文化复兴	Ottonian Renaissance
1000	匈牙利王斯德望被加冕	Stephen, King of Hungary, is crowned
1054	拉丁教会和希腊教会分裂	Schism divides the Latin and Greek halves of Christendom
1066	征服者威廉统治英国	William the Conqueror rules England
1071	突厥(土耳其)人歼灭拜占庭军队	Seljuk Turks crush the Byzantine army
1096—1270	八次十字军运动的目标是解放圣地	Eight Crusades are organized to liberate the Holy Land
1098	熙笃会被创立并获得迅速的发展	Cistercians are founded and soon develop fast
1122	沃尔姆斯协议解决授权争论	Concordat of Worms ends the Investiture Controversy
1150	哥特的建筑和艺术传到西欧各地	Gothic architecture and art spreads in western Europe
1152—1190	红胡子腓特烈任德国国王	Frederick I Barbarossa is King of Germany
1200	菲利普·奥古斯都批准巴黎大学	Philip II Augustus of France charters the University of Paris
1215	依诺森三世召开第四次拉特兰会议	Innocent III convokes the Fourth Lateran Council
1226	圣方济各·亚西西去世	St. Francis of Assisi passes away
1235—1246	蒙古人侵略俄罗斯和东欧地区	Mongols invade Russia and Eastern Europe

年份	事件	Event
1245	教宗的使者来华与蒙古人进行谈判	Papal emissaries reach China and negotiate with Mongols
1285—1314	菲利普统治法国,镇压圣殿骑士团	Philip the Fair rules France; suppression of Knights Templars
1309—1377	教廷在阿维农	Popes reside in Avignon
1321	但丁去世;彼特拉克研究古代文学	Dante passes away; Petrarch starts to read classical poetry
1337—1453	英法百年战争	Hundred Years' War between France and England
1347—1351	瘟疫席卷欧洲	Plague sweeps across Europe
1348	查理四世皇帝创立布拉格大学	Emperor Charles IV founds the University of Prague
1378—1415	西方教会处于分裂状态	Schism divides Christians in western Europe
1397	佛洛伦萨开始吸引希腊学者和教师	Florence begins to attract Greek scholars and teachers
1415—1434	胡斯战争	Hussite Wars
1438—1439	菲拉拉-佛洛伦萨主教会议追求合一	Council of Ferrara-Florence aims at union of the Church
1445	德国人古腾贝格发明活字印刷技术	Gutenberg develops printing with movable metal types
1447—1520	文艺复兴时代的教宗资助艺术和学术	Renaissance Popes patronize the arts and support scholars
1453	土耳其人围攻和占领拜占庭	Turks besiege and conquer Constantinople
1492	哥伦布发现美洲。穆斯林退出西班牙	Columbus discovers America. Muslims withdraw from Spain

第一篇

中世纪早期
The Early Middle Ages

(650—780 AD)

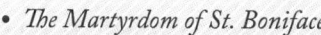
The Martyrdom of St. Boniface

阿达梅南（624—704）

爱尔兰隐修者，679年任苏格兰地区Hy(=Iona)隐修院院长，与Hy的创立人Columba有亲戚关系。

著作：《阿达梅南之法》(697年的爱尔兰主教会议规定要改进妇女的生活状况，使她们免于军役，以及在战争中要保护孩子和圣职人员)，《诸圣地》(旅游记，描述各地的教堂等)，《圣科伦班传》

001.《圣科伦班传》

早期中世纪文学最著名的传记之一 *Vita Columbae*（《圣科伦班传》）共分3卷（预言、奇迹、神视），大约成书于680年。作者很熟悉古典拉丁语文学传统，他曾引用一些来自Gregorius Magnus、Sulpicius Severus、Vergilius等人的语句。

本传记描述Sanctus Columba（亦称"Columcille"、"Columbanus"或"老科伦班"，约521—597年）的生活与行动。他曾是一位爱尔兰隐修者和司铎，约于560年前往苏格兰西部的海岸地区，在一个小岛上创立了一所隐修院。该海岛的名称有不同的写法："Hy"、"Io"、"Eo"、"Iona"等。这所隐修院成为爱尔兰隐修者在苏格兰地区的传教中心与文化基地。在30多年的不懈传教工作后，Columba在Hy隐修院去世（约于594年或597年）。他是一位诗人、书法家，又因其预言和奇迹著名。与St. Patrick一样，他是爱尔兰最受尊敬的圣徒之一。另一个有类似称号的爱尔兰传教士是所谓的Younger Columban（"小科伦班"或"高隆班"），他于591年前往法兰克地区并在今天的法国、德国、瑞士和意大利地区成为一个成功的传教士和隐修院的创立人。值得注意的是，爱尔兰的基督信仰和古典文化是从英国与法国南部传入的。因此早期的爱尔兰的基督宗教在礼仪和复活节时期方面与罗马教会有所差别。爱尔兰的隐修院比本笃会的传统更严格，但它们也同样成为教育中心与艺术基地。

Adamnanus de Iona / Adomnan (Adamnan) of Hy

Opera: *Cain Adomnain (Lex Innocentium), De locis sanctis, Vita Columbae (=Vita Sancti Columbani)*
Works: *Law of Adamnan, Sacred Places, Life of Saint Columba*

001. *Vita Columbae / Life of Saint Columba*

One of the most famous biographies of early medieval literature is *the Life of Saint Columba*, written around 680 and divided into three books (prophecies, miracles, visions). The author is well acquainted with the classical tradition of Latin literature, he uses phrases from the works of Gregory the Great, Sulpicius Severus, Virgil and other earlier writers.

The biography gives an account of the life of St. Columba (also known as "Columcille", "Columbanus", "the Elder Columba", ca. 521—597 AD). He was an Irish monk and priest who went to a small island off the west coast of Scotland and founded a monastery there around 560 AD. The name of the island is variously given as "Hy", "Io", "Eo", "Iona". This monastery became the cultural basis and the center of the mission activities of the Irish monks in Scotland. After more than 30 years of restless mission work St. Columba died in Hy around 597 (or 594). He was also a poet, a calligrapher and was famous for his prophetic gift and his miracles. Together with St. Patrick he is one of the most venerated saints of Ireland. He should not be confused with the "Younger Columban", an Irish monk who went to the kingdom of the Franks in 591 and was a successful missionary and founder of monasteries in what is today France, Germany, Switzerland, and Italy, until his death in 615. It is remarkable that the Christian faith and the classical learning entered Ireland by way of England and southern France. Thus early Irish Christianity differed from Rome in its liturgy and the date of Easter. Irish monasteries were much more ascetic than the Benedictine tradition, but they likewise became educational and artistic centers.

阿尔德海姆(约639—709)

他曾在 Malmesbury 隐修院(在 West Saxon 即 Wessex 地区)中接受拉丁文学及 Celtic-Irish 语言方面的教育,又在 Canterbury(坎特伯雷)的著名学校学习希腊语和拉丁语诗歌、数学和天文学。大约于675年他成为 Malmesbury 隐修院的院长,705年被祝圣为 Sherborne 的主教。他推动教育,成为一个学术赞助者和拉丁文诗人,又被称为7世纪最有学问的西萨克逊人,也是最早的英国作者之一。通过 Bonifatius 等传教士,他的著作也影响了欧洲大陆。他的晦涩文风和渊博知识深受当时教会读者的欢迎。

著作:《教会诸歌》(428行)、《赞美独身生活》(在当时隐修院很流行的著作,包括 De octo principalibus vitiis《论八个主要的恶习》)、《致阿基求斯的信》(一部韵律学著作,其中包括100个谜语)

002. 《赞美独身生活》

本著作大约成书于690年,Aldhelmus 将它分为两个部分。第1部分是用散文写成的,偶尔插入一些诗句,共60章,介绍了一些贞洁的典范人物。第2部分是一首很长的诗(2848六韵步诗行),赞美贞洁和谦逊的美德。本作品是献给 Barking 隐修院的修女们以及她们的院长修女 Hildelitha 的。

作者介绍那些过着独身生活和贞洁生活的著名男女圣徒。因为 Aldhelmus 描述修女们的生活方式和教育,他的著作保存了一些涉及宗教历史和文化史的细节。比如,在第58章中,他劝勉修女们不要在服装和清洁工作方面浪费太多时间,但同时他全面地描述不同的衣服与豪华的服装。在他的诗中(1327~1391行),他攻击古典神话。他使用《旧约》中 Samson 的叙述来解释 Heracles 的故事。Aldhelmus 的拉丁语在词汇上相当丰富,也没有什么语法错误。他熟悉 Vergilius、Horatius、Lucanius 和 Statius 等人的著作,而他自己的作品则影响了卡洛琳时期的创作者们。

003. 《致阿基求斯的信》

约成书于695年的 Epistola ad Acircium(《致阿基求斯的信》)是一篇关于格律的论文。Aldhelmus 将它送给自己的朋友 Aldfrith(亦称 Aelfrith),即 Northumbria 的国王。作者在开始部分谈论数字"七"的神秘意义,此后一位老师和一位学生谈论拉丁文学中的格律,尤其是 hexameter(六韵步)的种种规律。这部著作的核心是100个谜语(aenigmata, enigmata)。大部分谜语的长度在4到16诗行之间,它们描述一个词语或一件事物。读者要猜想的事物基本上是动物、植物、金属、星星、家里使用的工具或基督宗教的象征。他在关于动物方面的描述暗示他受到了 Physiologus 的影响。

Aldhelmus / Aldhelm (Ealdhelm)

Opera: *Carmina ecclesiastica, De laude virginitatis, Epistola ad Acircium (=De metris et enigmatibus ac pedum regulis)*
Works: *Church Hymns, In Praise of Virginity, Letter to Acircius (On Metric Rules)*

002. *De laudibus virginitatis / In Praise of Virginity*

Written around 690, Aldhelm's treatise is divided into two parts. The first part in prose and occasional verse presents models of chastity in 60 chapters. The second part is a long poem (2848 hexameters) in praise of virginity and modesty. The work was written for the nuns of the monastery of Barking and for their abbess Hildelitha.

Aldhelm presents the most famous Christian saints, men and women, who led a life in celibate chastity. Since the author describes the life style and the education of the nuns, his book preserves important details from the history of religious life and cultural history. For example, in chapter 58 he exhorts the nuns not to waste time with appearances and cleanliness, giving at the same time a thorough description of different clothes and splendid garments. In the poem (verses 1327~1391) the author attacks classical mythology. He reinterprets the narrative of Heracles as the story of Samson in the Old Testament. Aldhelm's Latin is rich in vocabulary and without grammar mistakes. He knew Virgil, Horace, Lucan, Statius, and his own works in turn influenced the Carolingians.

003. *Epistola ad Acircium / Letter to Acircius*

The *Epistola ad Acircium* (*Letter to Acircius*, written around 695) is a treatise on metrics. It was sent to Aldhelm's friend Aldfrith (or "Aelfrith"), king of Northumbria. At the beginning the author ponders about the mystical meaning of the number seven, then follows a dialogue between teacher and student on Latin metres, especially on the rules of the hexameter. The core of the work is a collection of 100 riddles (aenigmata, enigmata). Each riddle is a poetic circumscription of a word or a thing, usually in the length of 4 to 16 lines. The things the reader should find out are animals, plants, minerals, stars, household tools or symbols of the Christian world. Many descriptions of animals show the influence of the *Physiologus*.

约翰内斯(约 650—753)

东方 Damaskos 的教会作者,教父,约 700 年在耶路撒冷的一座隐修院内被祝圣司铎;享年 104 岁。

著作:《巴兰和约沙法特》、《阐明正教信仰》、《智慧的泉源》;还有很多其他的关于圣像、异端、伦理道德和宗教生活的著作;他也写过圣诗(kanōn)并帮助修补东正教的《圣歌集》(Oktōēchos)。

004.《巴兰和约沙法特》

该故事保存在一篇希腊文的手抄本中,并被归于 Johannes Damaskenos,但也有一个格鲁吉亚语文本以及很多拉丁语译本,其中一个在 *Legenda aurea*(《金传》)之中。在 17 世纪的巴罗克歌剧中,这个故事也多次出现,比如在 Lope de Vega 的 *Barlaam y Josafa*(1618 年)。拉丁语中的 Josaphat(约沙法特)是希腊语的 Ioasaph 和阿拉伯语中的 Judasaf,其根源是 Budasaf 即 Bodhisattva(菩萨)。

该故事的主题是整个中世纪最流行的论题之一,即皈依。印度的国王 Abenner 大权在握,他有一个非常英俊的儿子 Josaphat(约沙法特)。Josaphat 多才多艺,拥有一切美德。一个占星家曾经预言说王子有一天将会皈依基督信仰,而因为这个预言国王为儿子建立了一座非常豪华的宫殿,以此阻止儿子皈依基督信仰。在宫殿那种完美的幸福和充满享乐的环境中,王子应该可以过一种不受干扰的、圆满的生活,他可以远离平常生活中的种种危险和困难。然而,有一天 Josaphat 见到了一个麻风病人和一个瞎子,不久后他又遇到一个老人,甚至见到一个死人。这些体验开启了王子的眼睛,使他认识到生活的真实情况——他的父亲恰恰想隐瞒他,使他看不到这些。一位名叫 Barlaam 的基督徒隐修士与 Josaphat 谈话并向王子说明他的使命,即远离人间的享乐并过一种克修的、灵性的生活。国王想方设法劝勉儿子不要皈依基督宗教,他甚至要赐给儿子王国的一半领土,以此使他牢牢地与"真正的"世界相牵连,但 Josaphat 不久后放弃了他的权力。他放下一切王家的尊荣并开始过一种宗教性的和克修的独处生活。

005.《智慧的泉源》

作者 Iōannēs 是当时最伟大的希腊神学家。他的著作分为三个部分:*Kephalaia philosophika*(《哲学文章》)、*Peri haireseōn*(《论异端》)和 *Ekdosis akribēs tēs orthodoxou pisteōs*(《正统信仰的详细解释》)。该文集为 Iōannēs 赢得了"最后的教父"的美名,该著作于 1151 年被译成拉丁语并以 *De fide orthodoxa*(《正统信仰》)的书名发行。很多

Iōannēs Damaskēnos / St. John of Damascus

Opera: *Barlaam et Joasaph, Ekthesis tēs orthodoxu pisteōs (Expositio fidei = De fide), Pēgē gnōseōs*
Works: *Barlaam and Josaphat, An Exposition of the Faith, Fountain of Knowledge*

004. *Barlaam et Joasaph / Barlaam and Josaphat*

This story is extant in an early Greek manuscript attributed to Johannes Damascenus, but there is also a Georgian version and many Latin translations, one of them in the *Legenda aurea*. In the Baroque dramas of the 17th century the theme was very common, confer for example Lope de Vega, *Barlaam y Josafa* (1618). The name Josaphat (Latin) is the same as the Greek Ioasaph and the Arab Judasaf, it comes from Budasaf = Bodhisattva (from Buddha).

The theme of the story was one of the most popular of the Middle Ages: conversion. The powerful Indian King Abenner has an extremely handsome son, Josaphat, who is endowed with many talents and possesses all virtues. An astrologer has predicted that the king's son will one day convert to Christianity, and because of this prophecy the king builds a magnificent palace for his son in order to prevent his conversion. In the luxury and unstained joy of this palace the son should lead a life of undisturbed happiness, far away from the dangers and the misery of ordinary life. However, one day Josaphat sees a leper and a blind man, and some time later he also encounters an old man and even a dead person. These encounters open the prince's eyes to the reality of life, which his father always wanted to hide from him. A Christian hermit named Barlaam talks to Josaphat and tells him about his inner vocation, namely to lead an ascetic and spiritual life far from worldly pleasures. The king tries to dissuade his son from converting to Christianity. He even offers him half of the kingdom, hoping to attach him firmly to the "real" world, but Josaphat soon retreats from power. He leaves behind all royal honours and starts to lead a life in pious and ascetic solitude.

005. *Pēgē Gnōseōs / Fountain of Wisdom*

The work of the greatest Greek theologian of his day is divided into three parts: *Kephalaia philosophika* (*Philosophical Chapters*), *Peri haireseōn* (*On Heresies*), and *Ekdosis akribēs tēs orthodoxou pisteōs* (*Exact Explanation of the Orthodox Faith*). The compilation earned John the title "Last Father of the Church"; it was translated into Latin in 1151 and published under the title *De fide orthodoxa* (*The Orthodox Faith*).

思想家,比如 Albertus Magnus 和 Thomas Aquinas 多次引用了这部著作。

第 1 部分(68 章)试图阐述从哲学到神学的道路。古典哲学家的逻辑学和本体论能够为神学体系的建构提供一些基本的要素。作者尤其重视 Aristotelēs 的思想概念和清晰语言。在 Iōannēs 的眼中,神学是一切学科的女王。哲学和其他学科只是神学的有力"助手"。这种观点——即哲学是"神学的婢女"(ancilla theologiae)——也影响了后来的经院思想。

第 2 部分谈论了大约 100 种异端邪说,包括多神论的教导以及犹太人和穆斯林的错误思想。作者感觉到伊斯兰教的压倒性影响,所以他强调基督宗教的传统信仰,即关于基督神性和三位一体的信仰。Iōannēs 多次引用了 Salamis 的 Epiphanios(约315—403 年)的著作 Panarion(《种种补救之道》)以及来自 Byzantium 的 Leontios(约475—543 年)的相关著作。

第 3 部分是关于基督信仰的全面性解释,而这种解释符合宗徒/使徒信经的顺序。该论述分为 100 章,后来的编者将它分成 4 部书卷,而这种结构成为许多经院思想家的"基督信仰大全"之类著作的典范。首先,Iōannēs 谈论神的存在和可知性,此后他论及创世论,包括天使、人心等人类学问题。下面的部分则分析基督论的种种问题,而第四部分说明教会的圣事。在附录中,Iōannēs 讨论《圣经》中的圣母论、圣洗、基督的十字架、圣像的崇拜、恶的来源、复活以及反基督(antichristos)。Iōannēs 种种观点的基础是《圣经》、最权威的教父们的论断以及历代主教会议的种种决定。对他产生深厚影响的人是 Kappadokia 的教父们、Byzantion 的 Leontios 以及 Maximos Homologētēs。在当时构成政治争论的"圣像敬拜"的问题上,Iōannēs 反对那些破坏圣像的做法。

Thinkers like Albert the Great, and Thomas of Aquinas quoted from it repeatedly.

The first part (68 chapters) attempts to show the way from philosophical insight to theology. The logical and ontological knowledge of the classical philosophers can provide basic elements for the construction of theological systems. In a special way the author emphasizes the concepts and lucid language of Aristotle. In John's eyes theology is the queen of all sciences. Philosophy and the other sciences are helpful "servants" of theology. This conception of philosophy being the "handmaid of theology" (ancilla theologiae) influenced later scholasticism.

The second part discusses about 100 heresies, including the teachings of polytheist paganism, and the errors of Jews and Muslims. Feeling the overwhelming influence of Islam the author emphasizes the traditional Christian tenets concerning the divinity of Christ and the Holy Trinity. John quotes much from the *Panarion* (*Remedies*) of Epiphanius of Salamis (c. 315—403 AD) and from the works of Leontius of Byzantium (c. 475—543).

The third part is a comprehensive explanation of the Christian faith according to the order of the Apostolic Creed. This treatise is divided into 100 chapters and was later edited in four separate books, it became a model for many scholastic sums on the Christian faith. First John discusses the existence and knowability of God, then the doctrine of Creation, including theories concerning angels, the human heart, and other anthropological issues. The next part treats the questions of Christology, and the fourth part explains the sacraments. John continues with an appendix in which he discusses issues like Mariology in the Bible, baptism, the cross of Christ, the veneration of images, the origin of evil, the resurrection, and the Antichrist. John bases his considerations on the Bible, the most respected Fathers of the Church and on the decisions of the synods. He is mainly influenced by the Cappadocian Fathers, by Leontius of Byzantium, and by Maximus Confessor. Responding to a very political and controversial issue of his time — the veneration of images—he opposed iconoclasm.

比德(672—735)

英国 Northumberland 人，本笃会会士，6 岁入隐修院（puer oblatus），一生在 Wearmouth / Jarrow 隐修院任写作、教学的工作。他曾被视为当时欧洲西部最有学问的人。

著作：《论韵律学》、《论诸事物的本性》、《论语文》、《论典故》、《论诸时期》(附有《小历史表》)、《论时间的计算法》(附有《大历史表》)、《诸隐修院院长的历史》、《英格兰教会史》(5 卷，早期英国史最重要的资料，陈述从公元前 55 年 Caesar 的侵略到公元 597 年 Augustinus 等传教士的到来期间的历史；作者引用可靠的资料，想写一部客观的历史书)、《解释福音的讲道集》、《赞美诗集》(只保存部分)、《向上主的祈祷》、《格言集》、《Cuthbertus 传记》；还有一些赞美诗等；Beda 在晚年还开始将《约翰福音》译成自己的母语。

006.《英格兰教会史》

这部分为 5 卷的历史书完成于 731 年，后来成为整个中世纪最流行的著作之一，至今保存 160 多部手抄本，而 Alfredus Magnus 王曾把它译成古英语。关于英国早期的历史，Beda 的《英格兰教会史》是主要的、甚至在某些方面是唯一的资料来源。作者将本书献给 Northumbria 的国王 Ceowulf。他也说，他曾经邀请英国各地的主教帮助他搜集资料，以编写一部详细的"英国教会史"。这部书包括很多关于主教和圣人/圣徒的报告，但也包含许多重要的政治事件和文化生活方面的因素。作者首次使用"主降生之年"来确定某一个年代，这样他为今天通用的"公元纪年"奠定了基础（"公元"即是以"主基督诞生"为元年）。

第 1 卷首先描述了英国和爱尔兰的自然环境、这些地区的气候和早期的居民。从公元前 55 年起，英国就受到罗马文化的影响。作者叙述 Gaius Iulius（=Caesar 恺撒）的到来，也提到 Claudius 皇帝和 Vespasianus 皇帝(第 3 章)。不列颠人的王 Lucius 向 Eleutherius（公元 175—189 年）教宗写信，信中说他愿意成为基督徒(第 4 章)。爱尔兰的凯尔特人和 Pictes（皮克特）人侵略英国，所以英国人向罗马人求助，而罗马人从东到西建立一道"长城"（所谓的 Hadrianus 长城，第 12 章）。不列颠人后来邀请德国北部地区的 Angli（盎格鲁人）前往他们的海岛，但这些外来的民族不久后占领部分地区并"反对原来的同盟"（第 15 章）。在英国的 Germanus 主教和 Alban（一位圣人/圣徒）领导英国的教会，他们治好很多人的病，又施行很多奇迹（第 17~21 章）。罗马的教宗 Gregorius Magnus（590—604 年）于 597 年派遣一位 Benedictus（本笃）会的会士，即 Augustinus 去英国传教（第 23、24 章）。这位 Augustinus 向 Kent 的国王讲道，后来成为 Kent 的主教。他向罗马教宗写一个报告，而教宗也写给他很多信，其中劝告那

Beda Venerabilis / Bede (Baeda) the Venerable

Opera: *De arte metrica, De natura rerum, De orthographia, De schematibus et tropis, De temporibus (Chronica minora), De temporibus ratione (Chronica maiora), Historia abbatum, Historia Ecclesiastica gentis Anglorum, Homiliae evangelii, Liber hymnorum (diverso metro sive rhythmo), Oratio ad Deum, Proverbia, Vita Cuthberti*

Works: *On Metric, The Nature of Things, On Orthography, On Tropes, On Times (Chronicle), On the Reckoning of Time (longer Chronicle), Lives of the Abbots, Ecclesiastical History of England, Homilies to the Gospel, Book of Hymns, Prayers to God, Collection of Proverbs, Life of Cuthbert*

006. *Historia Ecclesiastica gentis Anglorum / Ecclesiastical History of England*

This historical work in 5 books was finished in 731 and became one of the most popular books of the Middle Ages—more than 160 manuscripts of the work have been preserved, and it was translated into Old English by King Alfred the Great. Bede's *History* is the main source for the early history of England. It is dedicated to King Ceowulf of Northumbria. The author says that he asked Church leaders in the country to help him in the task to write a detailled history of the Church of England. Bede's account of the Church history of England comprises the actions and miracles of bishops and saints but also contains important information about events of political and cultural life. The author for the first time uses "the year of the incarnation" to determine the events, and in this way he laid the basis for our modern chronology ("AD = anno Domini", in the year of Christ's birth).

The first book starts with a short geographical description of England and Ireland, their climate and their early inhabitants. Since the arrival of the Romans in 55 BC, England was influenced by their culture, and Bede tells how "Gaius Iulius" (=Caesar) came to England, he also mentions Emperor Claudius and Vespasianus (chapter 3). Lucius, king of the Britanni, asks in a letter to Pope Eleutherius (175—189 AD) to become a Christian (c. 4). The Celts of Ireland and the Pictes devastate England, and therefore the Brites ask the Romans for help, whereupon a wall is built across the island (the so-called Hadrian's Wall, c. 12). The tribe of the Angles is invited by the Brites to come over from Germany, but they soon occupy parts of the island, "turning their weapons against their former allies" (c. 15). Bishop Germanus and St. Alban lead the Church of Britain, they heal many sick and work miracles (cc. 17~21). Chapters 23~24

些传教士不要太突然地改变本地人的宗教生活，而是要使他们一步步地接受信仰，"因为不能使那些迟钝的心灵一下子失去一切东西"（第 30 章）。

　　第 2 卷（共 20 章）一开始叙述 Gregorius Magnus（在 604 年）的逝世，后来报告几个不列颠国王的皈依过程，其中最著名的是真福 Paulinus 的讲道和 Edwinus 王（约于 626 年？）的皈依。在开会时，国王的一个顾问用"麻雀飞过屋子"的比喻来说明人生的短暂，并说接受这个新信仰也许是很合理的："一只麻雀很快地飞过这一屋子……而人生也是这样的短暂。我们根本不知道死亡以后的事或生前的事。因此，如果这个新的教导（指基督信仰）能够提供一些比较确切的观点，那么应该接受它。"（第 2 章 13 节）

　　第 3 卷（共 30 章）包含关于"最重视基督的"国王 Oswaldus 的资料，还有关于 Aidanus 主教和"东撒克逊人"的皈依的叙述。第 4 卷（共 32 章）描述第 7 世纪的发展，其中一个事件是 Theodorus 总主教于 668 年前往英国，他向本地人介绍世俗和神圣的知识和教育，又教导他们学习拉丁语和古希腊语（第 2 章）。在第 5 卷中，西撒克逊王 Caedwalla 前往罗马以接受圣洗（第 7 章），而英国人 Willibrordus 则在德国北部的 Frisia 地区传教（第 10 章）。第 24 章总结了整部著作并提供了一些关于作者的资料："我始终全心全意地阅读《圣经》，遵守会规，每天在教堂中唱歌，并且始终喜爱学习、教书以及撰写书籍。"自 6 岁起，Beda 就生活在一个本笃会的隐修院中。

tell of the mission efforts directed by Pope Gregory the Great (590—604), who sent the Benedictine monk Augustine to Britain in 597. Augustine preaches to the king of Kent, is made bishop of Kent, writes a report to the Pope in Rome and receives many letters from Rome, one of them exhorting the missionary to convert the local people step by step, not by sudden radical changes, since "it is impossible to take away everything at once from sluggish minds" (c. 30).

Book 2(20 chapters) begins with the death of Pope Gregory the Great (in 604) and continues with the conversion stories of several British kings, among whom the narrative about Blessed Paulinus and the conversion of King Edwin (in the year 626?) is most famous. One of the nobles of the king tells the parable comparing human life to a sparrow quickly flying through a room and adds that it might be reasonable to receive the new faith: "Adveniens unus passerum domum citissime pervolaverit… Ita haec vita hominum ad modicum apparet, quid autem sequatur, quidve praecesserit, prorsus ignoramus. Unde, si haec nova doctrina certius aliquid attulit, merito esse sequenda videtur." (chapter 2, 13: One of the sparrows flies quickly through the house… and this human life seems to be very short in the same way; what follows and what was before, we do not know at all. Therefore, if this new teaching can tell us something more certain, it could duly be followed.)

Book 3 (30 chapters) contains information about "Christianissimus" King Oswald, Bishop Aidan and the slow conversion of the East-Saxons (Orientales Saxones). Book 4 (32 chapters) narrates (among many other events) how Archbishop Theodore is sent to Britain (in 668) and how he brings secular and divine sciences and the knowledge of Greek and Latin to Britain (c. 2). Book 5 tells of the West-Saxon King Caedwalla who travels to Rome to be baptized (c. 7) and of the mission activities of Willibrord in Frisia (c. 10). Chapter 24 recapitulates the whole work and tells about the author: Omnem meditandis scripturis operam dedi, atque inter observantiam disciplinae regularis et cotidianam cantandi in ecclesia curam semper aut discere aut docere aut scribere dulce habui. (All energy I spent in meditating the scriptures, observing the rule and singing daily in the church, and I always felt joy in learning, teaching or writing.) Since the age of 6, Bede lived in a Benedictine monastery.

博尼法修斯（673—754）

  Wynfrith 生于英国 Wessex 的贵族家庭，曾在 Exeter 和 Nursling 的本笃会修院获得杰出的教育，入本笃会，30 岁被祝圣司铎，并于 716 年开始在德国北部的 Frisia 地区传教，但因当地的 Saxon 王不支持他而影响不大。他于 718 年陪同一些 Anglo-Saxon 的朝圣者前往罗马，而教宗 Gregorius II 给他起名 Bonifatius 并派遣他到 Rhein 东部地区传教，又要求他采纳罗马式的圣洗经文。Bonifatius 于 722 年从 Frisia 转入 Hessen 地区，同年再次奔赴罗马，被祝圣为传教主教。教宗向法兰克王 Carolus Martellus 推荐 Bonifatius，而 Martellus 支持他的传教工作。因此，Bonifatius 成功地在 Hessen 开教并在 Geismar 附近砍倒了一棵献给 Thor 神的橡树（著名的 Donareiche）。725 至 735 年间他在 Thuringia 活动，此后又组织 Bavaria 地区的教务，于 732 年成为总主教（获得了 pallium，白披肩）。总主教的权力包括祝圣主教以及召集主教会议的权力。Bonifatius 于 737 年第三次到罗马报告教务，并于 740 年后召开了几次主教会议，借此改进本地圣职人员的教育和整顿教务。在 744 年他创立了 Fulda 隐修院，并于 747 年召开了全法兰克地区的主教会议。Martellus 的儿子们 Carloman 和 Pepin 将主教会议的规定列入了法兰克人的法典（即所谓的 Capitularia）。80 多岁的老主教再次前往 Frisia 传教，但于 754 年 6 月 5 日在 Dokkum 被一帮外教人打死。这位圣人曾被称为"德国的宗徒/使徒"，其墓地位于 Fulda。

  著作：《谜语》（关于德性和恶习的谜语，受 Aldhelm 的影响）、《语法书》、《格律书》、《信集》（提供宝贵的史料）

007.《信集》

  Bonifatius 的信使我们可以窥视到当时的教会生活以及传教士的工作情况。这部文集也包含教宗向 Bonifatius 写的信，比如第 12 封信，其中要求 Bonifatius 遵守罗马的洗礼仪式和罗马的洗礼信经。第 28 封信谈论教宗送给 Bonifatius 的 pallium（白披肩）。根据其他一些信件可以了解 Bonifatius 和英国的本笃会修士和修女之间的密切来往。家乡的会士以寄书、写一些鼓励他的信和其他礼物来支持他，而一些会士也去了欧洲大陆，在由 Bonifatius 创立的四所德国隐修院中组成核心团体。这些隐修院成为有修养的基督徒生活的基地，这样就提高了法兰克王国中的生活水平。

  第 78 封信包含这样一种劝勉："教会像一条很大的船只那样航过这个世界的大海，而海浪的漩涡也使教会之船转向——海浪是生活中的危险和挑战。我们不可以放弃这只船，而应该要致力于引导它。在这项任务上，我们的榜样是早期的教父，罗马的

Bonifatius / Boniface / Wynfrith

Opera: *Aenigmata, Ars Grammatica, Ars metrica, Epistulae*
Works: *Enigmata, Grammar, Metrics, Letters*

007. *Epistulae / Letters*

Boniface's letters provide unique insights into the life of the Church and of the missionaries of that time. The collection also contains papal letters to Boniface, for example Ep. 12 which demands that Boniface observes the Roman baptismal liturgy and baptism formula. Letter 28 is concerned with the pallium sent to Boniface. Other letters show that Boniface kept close contact with Benedictine monks and sisters in England. They supported him with books, encouraging letters and other gifts, and some of them went to the continent where they became the core group of the four monasteries Boniface had founded on German soil. These monasteries became centers of cultured Christian life and so improved the quality of life in the Frankish kingdom.

Letter 78 contains this exhortation: "The Church travels through the sea of this world like a large ship and is tossed around by the waves—these waves are the dangers and challenges of this life. We must not forsake the ship but should try to direct it. Our

Clemens 和 Cornelius 以及很多其他的罗马主教,迦太基的 Cyprianus,以及 Alexandria 的 Athanasius。他们在一些外教皇帝的统治下引导了该船只。他们曾指导、教导和保卫教会,曾为她工作,为教会受苦,乃至为她牺牲性命。"

models in this calling are the early Fathers, Clement and Cornelius of Rome, and many other bishops of Rome, Cyprian of Carthage, and Athanasius of Alexandria. They steered the ship under pagan emperors. They directed the Church, taught and defended her, worked for her, and they have suffered for her even up to the point of shedding their blood for her."

第二篇

卡洛琳文艺复兴时期
The Age of the Carolingian Renaissance
(780—900 AD)

• *The Bust of Charlemagne*

保禄（保罗）(约 720—799)

出生于意大利北部，来自伦巴第人的贵族家庭。在法兰克人攻击伦巴第国后，他进入了 Monte Cassino 的本笃会隐修院并成为一名隐修者(774 年)。从 784 年至 788 年他生活在法兰克人的朝廷，而查理曼友好地对待他。回到意大利的隐修院后，他编写了他的历史著作。

著作：《梅茨主教史》、《伦巴第人的历史》(主要的著作，在史学史有影响)、《罗马史》(世界史，到 Iustinianus 的时代，在意大利很有影响)、《讲道集》、《额我略传》，还有赞美诗

008.《伦巴第人的历史》

Paulus Diaconus 来自伦巴第人的贵族家庭。在伦巴第王国崩溃(774 年)后，他进入了 Monte Cassino 的隐修院并成为一名隐修者。从 784 年至 788 年他生活在 Carolus Magnus 的朝廷，但后来他回到隐修院并在那里编写了他的巨著（共 6 卷）。与 Beda 的《英格兰教会史》以及 Gregorius Turonensis 的《法兰克人史》一样，这部著作是中世纪早期阶段最出色的历史书之一。中世纪的学者曾多次引用它，而其中有部分传说和故事在 Grimm 兄弟的《童话集》中再次出现。

第 1 卷记载伦巴第人在北欧的半传奇性起源。作者告诉我们关于 566 年以前的早期英雄和国王的故事。第 2 卷开始了比较详细的历史叙述，以伦巴第人在他们的王 Alboinus(566—572 年)的率领下于 568 年进入意大利北部开始。第 3 卷记载 Authari 王(584—590 年)时期所发生的事——他与巴伐利亚公主 Theodelinde 结婚。伦巴第人本来信奉的是 Arius 派，而这一点导致与当地的某些公教主教的摩擦。因为 Theodelinde 是一位公教公主，所以她能够改善伦巴第人与罗马教宗的关系以及与意大利的公教居民的关系。

第 4 卷叙述最后的 Arius 派的统治者的时期，即 Rothari 王(636—652 年)的时期。第 5 卷的核心是 Grimuald 王(661—671 年)——他统一了伦巴第人的老地区和意大利南部的 Benevento(贝内文托)地区。第 6 卷报告 Liutprand 王(712—744 年)任期内的进一步扩展——这位国王将拜占庭人从意大利驱逐，他甚至想占领 Ravenna 和罗马，最后仅仅因宗教的考虑而放弃这个计划。Paulus 的叙述在 744 年突然停止，就是 Liutprand 王去世的那一年。作者谴责后期各王的扩张思想，认为这种扩张导致了整个伦巴第王国的崩溃，但他没有描述自己民族的衰落和毁灭。(773 至 781 年，Carolus Magnus 在一系列的战争中消灭了伦巴第人的王国，而在 787 年他也征服了 Benevento 地区。)

Paulus Diaconus / Paul the Deacon

Opera: *Gesta episcoporum Mettensium, Historia Langobardorum, Historia Romana, Homiliarium, Vita Gregorii*

Works: *History of the Bishops of Metz, History of the Lombards, History of Rome, Collection of Homilies, Life of Gregory the Great*

008. *Historia Langobardorum / History of the Lombards*

Paulus Diaconus came from Lombard nobility. After the collapse of the Lombard kingdom (774) he entered Monte Cassino and became a monk. From 784 to 788 he lived at Charlemagne's court, but later he returned to the monastery and compiled this monumental history in 6 books. Together with Bede's *Ecclesiastical History of England* and Gregory of Tours' *History of the Franks* it is one of the outstanding chronicles of the early Middle Ages. It was often quoted by medieval scholars, and some of the stories and legends reappear in *Grimm's Fairy Tales*.

The first book records the semi-legendary origins of the Lombards in Scandinavia. The author imparts to us stories about the early heroes and kings up to the year 566 AD. With the second book begins a more detailed historical narrative, starting from the migration of the Lombards into the northern parts of Italy in 568 under their king Alboin (566—572 AD). The third book contains the developments during the reign of king Authari (584—590 AD) who married the Bavarian princess Theodelinde. The Lombards adhered to Arianism which caused some friction with the Catholic bishops. Being a Catholic Christian queen Theodelinde improved the relations of the Lombards with the Pope and with the Catholic population of their lands.

Book 4 narrates the events at the time of the last Arianist ruler, king Rothari (636—652 AD). Book 5 centers on king Grimuald (661—671 AD) who united the traditional area of the Lombards with possessions in Benevento in southern Italy. Book 6 reports about further expansions under king Liutprand (712—744 AD) who expelled the Byzantines from Italy. He even intended to occupy Ravenna and Rome and only gave up his plans because of religious considerations. Paulus' narrative stops abruptly in the year 744 with the death of Liutprand. He blamed the expansionism of the later kings for the eventual destruction of the Lombard empire, but he did not describe the decline and destruction of his own people until the end. (In a series of wars Charlemagne subdued the Lombard kingdom between 773 and 781 AD and in 787 AD also conquered Benevento.)

Paulus 引用了很多著作，其中有 *Liber pontificalis*（《历代教宗之书》）以及 Plinius, Justinus, Eugippius, Gregorius Turonensis, Venantius Fortunatus, Gregorius Magnus, Isidorus de Sevilla 和 Beda 的著作。就伦巴第人的历史而言，作者的叙述是最主要的，而在某些方面是唯一的历史资料来源，但这部著作也包含许多有关法兰克人、巴伐利亚人、拜占庭人与阿拉伯人的观察。作者对教会历史和教宗史有兴趣，他关于 Gregorius Magnus（590—604 年）和 Benedictus de Nursia 有很多记载。第 4 卷包含关于罗马万神殿的一个段落："皇帝 Focas 回应了教宗 Bonifatius 并规定罗马和从宗徒传下来的教会的圣座等于是一切地方教会的元首，因为 Constantinopolis 的教会曾经认为自己有首要的地位。回应教宗 Bonifatius 的要求，他也命令那座被称为 Pantheon 的古老神殿应该消除偶像，使之成为一个奉献给童贞圣母玛利亚和众圣人的教堂，这样，那个原来敬拜众鬼怪而不是真神的地方可以成为一个纪念圣人的圣堂。在这个时期中，波斯人攻击了国度并夺取了许多罗马帝国的行省，包括耶路撒冷。他们破坏了诸教堂，亵渎了诸圣所，并且带走了圣所的事物以及主的十字架的标记。"

Paulus quotes from many sources, among them the *Liber pontificalis* (*Book of the Popes*), and the works of Plinius, Justinus, Eugippius, Gregory of Tours, Venantius Fortunatus, Gregory the Great, Isidore of Sevilla and Bede. His narrative is the main and in many respects the only source for the history of the Lombards, but it contains also many observations concerning the Franks, Bavarians, Byzantines, and Arabs. The author was also interested in ecclesiastical and papal history and wrote quite extensively about Pope Gregory the Great (590—604 BC) and about Benedict of Nursia. Book 4 contains a passage about the Pantheon in Rome: "The emperor (of Constantinople) Focas was asked by Pope Bonifatius (607—615) to declare that the See of the Roman and apostolic Church is the head of all churches (caput omnium ecclesiarum), since the church of Constantinople claimed the first place among all churches for herself. Responding to the requests of Pope Bonifatius, he (Focas) also ordered that in the ancient temple which is called Pantheon, the idols should be removed and that it should be turned into a church dedicated to Mary and to all martyrs, so that in the place where before the worship of demons was performed, hereafter should be a memorial of all the saints. In those times the Arabs (Persae) attacked the republic and occupied many Roman provinces and even Jerusalem. Destroying churches and secularizing holy places, they not only took away the artefacts and ornaments of the holy places but also the signs of the cross of the Lord." (4,36)

阿尔库因（约 730—804）

英国 Northumbria 的贵族，778 年主持 York 的教会学校，781 年后到法国，在 Carolus Magnus 的学院任教。最后在 Tours 的 St. Martin 隐修院建立了一个书法学校，抄录圣书，发明或推广 minuscula（Carolingian minuscule 小体字，即现在通用的字体）。

著作：《反驳 Felix》、《论圣三唯一天主的信仰》（成了第 9 世纪最有影响的信理书之一）、《约克教会历代主教和圣人》、《论真正的哲学》（视学习为进步的过程，有 gradus 阶层）、《约翰福音注解》、《罗马弥撒经本》（只进行修订）、《圣马丁传》、《圣维理博传》、《维达传》。他重新修订了拉丁文《圣经》译本（主要修改其中的语法错误），有神学、教育（语文、普通知识）、哲学（逻辑学）、圣人传记等方面的著作，但有时候只改进前人的书。他留下 300 多封拉丁文书信（宝贵的史料），其中也有很多诗歌。

009. 《约克教会历代主教和圣人》

拉丁语诗歌（六韵步），大约在 782—798 年间写成，献给 Echternach 隐修院的 Beornrad 院长。

这首诗叙述作者家乡城市 York（约克，拉丁语：Eboracum）的历史。当时的约克是一个重要的政治和教会中心。最早，罗马人是这个城市的奠基人。几百年后，盎格鲁人和撒克逊人到来了。作者认为"撒克逊"的名字来自拉丁语的 saxum（磐石），因为撒克逊人的性格很坚定不移。在后来的时期中，很多航海者民族从外面攻击约克。依赖于许多圣人主教的协助，本地的领导者完成了伟大的事业，比如 Eduinus 王率领他的人民接受基督信仰。圣 Oswaldus 勇敢地抵抗侵略者。大部分的历史事件都是根据 Beda（比德）的 *Historia ecclesiastica*（《教会史》）撰写的。最后的部分包括一些关于约克近代（第 8 世纪）的记载，而这个部分是一个重要的、很有价值的历史文献。

Alcuin (Alchuine, Alcuinus, Albinus, Alkuin)

Opera: *Adversus Felicem, De fide sanctae et individuae trinitatis, De pontificibus et sanctis Eboracensis ecclesiae (=Versus de sanctis Eboricensis ecclesiae), Disputatio de vera philosophia, Expositio super Johannem, Missale Romanum, Vita Martini Turonensis, Vita S. Willibrordi, Vita Vedastis Atrebatensis*

Works: *Against Felix, On the Holy Life of the Trinity, The Bishops and Saints of the Church in York, Disputation on True Philosophy, Explanation to John, Roman Missal, Life of Martin of Tours, Life of Saint Willibrord, Life of Vedastis*

009. *De pontificibus et sanctis Eboracensis ecclesiae / The Bishops and Saints of the Church in York*

This Latin poem in hexameters was probably written between 782—798 and dedicated to abbot Beornrad of Echternach.

The poem tells the history of the home city of the author, York (Latin: Eboracum), an important political and ecclesiastical center. The report starts with the founding of York by the Romans. Centuries later the Angles and Saxons arrive. The author derives the name of the Saxons from the Latin "saxum" (=rock) because of their unwavering firmness and solidity. Througout the following period many seafaring people come from abroad in their fragile barks and attacked York. Relying on the help of saintly bishops, local leaders accomplish great achievements, for example King Edwin who leads his people to accepting Christianity. St. Oswald resisted invaders courageously. These and other historical events are mainly based on Bede's *Historia ecclesiastica*. The last part of the poem deals with the events of recent history, and this part is a valuable and important historical document.

基涅武甫（约 750—800）

他是一位具有神学修养的英格兰诗人，可能生活在 Northumbria 或 Mercia 地区，但关于他的资料甚少。他的著作是用古英语写成的。

著作：《基督升天》、《埃琳娜》（1321 行，圣 Helena 发现真十字架的故事）、《宗徒们的命运》、《朱利亚娜》（一位女殉道者的故事）

010.《埃琳娜》

在意大利 Vercelli 发现的古老手抄本（所谓的 *Codex Vercellensis*）包含这部来自 8 世纪下半叶的史诗传说。该史诗长达 1321 行，使用头韵法的诗律并被称为 Cynewulf 的最好著作。在 Jacobus de Voragine 的 *Legenda Aurea*（《金传》）中有关于 Helena 故事的相似叙述。在史诗中有一些盎格鲁—萨克逊的因素，比如对于军队和交战的漫长描述以及陪同军队的 Odin 神的象征动物（老鹰、乌鸦、狼）。

该叙述被分为 15 章，以描述一个由匈奴人、哥特人和法兰克人共同组成的庞大军队开始。这些民族正准备侵略罗马帝国。Constantinus 皇帝率军抵抗这个庞大的军事力量。他在一次神视中见到基督的十字架。他下令为自己的军队做军旗，在旗子上要有十字架这个符号，因此他鼓励他的士兵们并打败了对手。Constantinus 从教宗 Silvester 手中接受了洗礼。此后他派遣他的母亲 Helena 在军队的陪同下到以色列去，让她寻找真正的十字架。然而，在耶路撒冷没有人知道基督的十字架在哪里。只有 Simon 的儿子 Judas 想起一个古老的预言：当人们开始寻找基督的十字架时，犹太人的王国就要走向衰落。Judas 自己也不知道十字架的所在地。通过一个奇迹 Helena 被引到 Golgota 山，在那里她发现三个十字架——基督和两个囚徒一起被钉在十字架上。当一个亡者接触到真正的十字架，他就复活过来，这样人们就知道了哪一个是基督的十字架。此后 Judas 接受洗礼，而教宗 Eusebius 指定他为耶路撒冷的主教。人们通知 Constantinus 皇帝，而他规定 Helena 要在耶路撒冷建造一座教堂。通过来自上天的记号，Helena 甚至能找到十字架的钉子，并且在耶路撒冷城内建立一座教堂。她回到罗马去，但在离开耶城之前，她还吩咐犹太人听从他们的新主教。在结束语中有关于 Cynewulf 的一些自传式的信息。

Kynewulf / Cynewulf

Opera: *Crist II, Elene, Fata apostolorum, Juliana*
Works: *Christ, Helena, The Fate of the Apostles, Juliana*

010. *Elene / Helena*

An old manuscript found in Vercelli (Italy), the *Codex Vercellensis*, contains this epic legend from the second half of the 8th century. The poem in 1321 alliterating verses is considered to be the best of Cynewulf's four works. A similar version of the story of Helena is found in Jacobus de Voragine's *Legenda Aurea*. Among the Anglosaxon elements of the epic are the long description of armies and battles and Odin's animals (eagle, crow, wolf) which accompany the armies.

The narrative is divided into 15 chapters and starts with the description of a huge army made up of Huns, Goths, and Franks. They are about to invade the Roman Empire. Constantine the Great marches against this overwhelming power and in a vision sees the cross of Christ. He gives orders to have military flags made for his army, displaying the sign of the cross on the flags, thus he inspires his soldiers and defeats the enemy. Constantine receives baptism from the hand of Pope Silvester. Then he sends his mother Helena to Israel, accompanied by an army, in order to find the real cross. However, in Jerusalem nobody knows anything about the cross of Christ. Only Judas, son of Simon, remembers an old oracle predicting the decline of the Jewish kingdom on the day when someone should search for Christ's cross. Judas does not know about the location of the cross either. Through a miracle Helena is led to Mt. Golgotha where she finds three crosses—Christ was crucified between two criminals. A dead person is resurrected as he touches one of these crosses, thus indicating that this is the true cross of Christ. Now Judas receives baptism and is made bishop of Jerusalem by Pope Eusebius. Emperor Constantine is informed and he orders that Helena should build a church in Jerusalem. Through a sign from Heaven Helena even manages to find the nails of the cross, and she sets up a church in the city. Before leaving for Rome she exhorts the Jews to obey their new bishop. The epilogue contains some autobiographical information about Cynewulf.

艾因哈德(约 770—840)

出生于德国 Maingau 地区,曾在 Fulda 的隐修院接受教育,于 794 年来到查理曼在 Aachen(亚琛)的宫庭,不久后成为国王的顾问,受命监督一些建筑项目,又奉命管理几所隐修院。查理曼于 806 年派遣他去罗马。当查理曼于 814 年去世后,Eginhardus 退隐,并于 826 年在德国的 Seligenstadt 创立了一所本笃会隐修院,他的墓也在那里,墓碑的碑文是他的朋友 Hrabanus Maurus 撰写的。

著作:《圣咏注解》、《论敬拜十字架》、《圣 Marcellinus 和 Petrus 墓的迁移及其奇迹》、《查理大帝传》

011.《查理大帝传》

查理曼的传记大约在 830—836 年间成书,保存有 80 多种手抄本,由此可见,它是整个中世纪最流行的传记之一。法兰克人的国王(自从 800 年以来,他也是"皇帝")查理曼的传记不长,但从几个角度值得注意:它是中世纪第一个"非圣徒"形式的传记,因为它的主要目标不是表明一个人的诚心或神圣生活,或描述他的神奇能力,而是仅仅赞美查理曼的 magnanimitas(慷慨的心,崇高的精神)。它模仿 Suetonius 的 *De vita Caesarum*,但它并不包含该著作的轶事或微不足道的谣言。查理曼的传记很可靠,甚至在一些细节上也符合实际情况。Eginhardus 时代的人已经赞美这部传记,而整个中世纪的人也很喜欢阅读这本书。Walahfried Strabo 后来将这部书编排为 33 章。

作者在开始(第 1~3 章)谈论查理曼的祖先,他们曾经在 Merovingi(梅洛温格)王朝(481—751 年)当过宫相,最有名的是查理曼的祖父 Carolus Martellus,他的父亲 Pippinus,以及他的弟兄 Carolomannus。这部传记提到查理曼的童年时期,后来转向他的战争和征服:在法国南部的战争(769—772 年,第 5 章),抵抗伦巴第人的战争(773—781 年,第 6 章),针对萨克逊的战争(772—804 年,第 7、8 章),在西班牙的活动(778 年,第 9 章),反对意大利的 Benevento 的战争(787 年,第 10 章),在巴伐利亚的战争(787 年,第 11 章),反对斯拉夫人的战争(787、788 年,第 12 章),抵抗匈奴人的战争(797—799 年,第 13 章),以及针对丹麦人的战争(810 年,第 14 章)。第 16 章描述查理曼和其他国度的关系,还有他建筑方面的成就(第 17 章),他的私人生活(他的妻子们,第 18 章),他的孩子所受的教育(第 19 章),785 年和 792 年的阴谋(第 20 章),他对宫殿的外国人的友好态度(第 21 章),查理曼的外貌("高大堂皇",第 22 章),他的服装(第 23 章),他的习惯(在饮食方面有节制,他喜欢在吃饭时听音乐或听一些人阅读有益的文献,第 24 章),他的学习(他在拉丁语和古希腊语方面达到相当高的水平,但写作能力不强,第 25 章),他的宗教情怀(第 26 章),他的慷慨态度

Eginhardus / Einhard

Opera: *Libellus de psalmis, Quaestio de adoranda cruce, Translatio et miracula ss. Marcellini et Petri, Vita Caroli Magni* (= *Vita Karoli Magni*)

Works: *Booklet on the Psalms, On the Veneration of the Cross, The Relocation and the Miracles of the Saints Marcellinus and Peter, Life of Charles the Great*

011. *Vita Caroli Magni / Life of Charles the Great*

This biography of Charlemagne was written between 830 and 836, and there are more than 80 manuscripts extant, thus it was one of the most popular biographies of the Middle Ages. The small account of the life of the Frankish king (and since 800 "emperor") is remarkable in several aspects: it is the first non-hagiographical biography of the Middle Ages, it has no spiritual intention to show the holiness or miraculous powers of a person but rather extols Charlemagne's "magnanimitas" (nobility of mind). It is modeled after Sueton's *De vita Caesarum*, but does not contain any of Sueton's trifles and anecdotes. The vita of Charlemagne is reliable even in details, it was praised by Eginhard's contemporaries and much read throughout the Middle Ages. Walahfried Strabo edited the work in 33 chapters.

The biography starts from Charlemagne's ancestors who served in the dynasty of the Merovingians (481—751), his grandfather Charles Martell, his father Pippin, and his brother Karlmann (Carolomannus, chapters 1~3). After a few remarks about Charlemagne's childhood, the wars of the king and his conquests are reported: the wars in Aquitania (Southern France, 769—772, chapter 5), wars against the Lombards (773—781, c. 6), against the Saxons (772—804, chapters 7~8), the campaign in Spain (778, c. 9), against Benevent (787, c. 10), wars in Bavaria (787, c. 11), against the Slavs (787, 788, c. 12), against the Huns (797—799, c. 13), and against the Danes (810, c. 14). Chapter 16 tells of Charlemagne's relations to other countries, chapter 17 about his building activities, then follow his private life (his wives c. 18), the education of his children (c. 19), the conjurations of 785 and 792 (c. 20), his friendly treatment of foreigners at court (c. 21), his physical appearance ("tall and dignified", c. 22), his dress (c.23), his habits (moderation in food and drink, listening to music or readings during meals, c. 24), his studies (learned Latin and Greek quite well, but had limited writing abilities, c. 25), his piety (c. 26), his generosity (c. 27) etc. Outstanding in the report is the coronation at Christmas 800 in Rome (chapter 28). The author says that Charles did not know that he would be crowned emperor, which is different from the account of Anastasius Bibliothecarius in his *Vita Leonis III*.

(第27章)等。第28章报告一个非常重要的事件:他在800年的圣诞节在罗马被加冕为皇帝。作者说,查理曼事先并不知道教宗将要宣布他为罗马人的君王,但 Anastasius Bibliothecarius 在他的 *Vita Leonis III* 有与此不同的说法。

第29章报告说查理曼命令萨克逊人、弗里西亚人和图林根人记载他们那些口述的法律,这样导致一些法典的形成。国王也使人记载一些德语的赞美歌和诗歌(但这些文献没有被保存)。第30章描述查理曼儿子 Ludovicus 的加冕礼(814—840年)以及查理曼的逝世(814年1月28日)。他的葬礼(第31章),他去世之前发生的预兆(第32章),他的遗嘱(第33章)是这部著作的结尾。

Chapter 29 reports that Charlemagne ordered the codification of the (oral) laws of the Saxons, Frisians and Thuringians, also the recording of hymns and songs in the German language (however, there are no extant collections of these songs). Chapter 30 narrates the coronation of his son Louis (Louis the Pious 814—840) and the death of Charles on Jan 28th of 814. His funeral (c. 31), omens before his death (c. 32) and his testament (c. 33) conclude the book.

拉班努(784—856)

生于德国 Moguntia(Mainz)的贵族家庭,约于791年被父母送到Fulda的本笃会隐修院;他成为修士,于801年被祝圣执事,曾一度在Charlemagne的宫廷生活,后在Tours成为Alcuinus的学生,814年升司铎,开始任教并成为著名的隐修院老师。很多人闻名而来,比如Walahfried Strabo、Otfried de Weissenburg和Lupus Ferreires。822—842年间他任Fulda隐修院院长,当时大约领导了600名隐修者,推动教育、学术、艺术和牧灵工作。由于政治原因(法兰克国的分裂),他退位,但于847年成为Mainz的总主教,提高了德国教会和社会的学术水平。

著作:《论灵魂》、《语法学》(对中世纪逻辑学的发展有贡献)、《论赞美上主》(关于日课祈祷的意义)、《论教会的纪律》、《论教士的培养》(重要的散文著作,呼吁人们学习教父们和世俗学者的著作)、《论十字架的赞美》(28首诗,"形象诗",一种特殊的书法方式:Figurengedichte, technopaigneia)、《论诸事物的性质》(《论宇宙》,22卷,一部百科全书,根据Isidorus的 *Etymologiae* 写的)、《论儿子们的孝道》、《论诸美德和诸恶习》、《计算之书》(论数字、历史计算、8个历史时期);还有关于《圣经》的注解、书信、诗歌(carmina);他主持 *Diatessaron*(《四部福音合参》)与萨克逊语叙事诗 *Heliand*(《救世主》)的翻译工作。

012. 《论教士的培养》

这部教育性手册分为3卷,成书时间是819年。作者将它献给德国Fulda的隐修者以及Mainz总主教Haistulf。因为该书结合古典和基督宗教的知识,它成为中世纪的规范性工具书之一。Hrabanus引用很多古代基督徒作者的作品,包括Cyprianus、Hieronymus、Augustinus、Isidorus de Sevilla。

本著作的目标是帮助圣职人员完成他们的任务。他们应该按规定举行礼仪,同时为教徒们提供道德教育和宗教教育。第1卷谈论教会的圣统制、司铎们的正当服装和礼仪服装、洗礼、坚振以及感恩祭诸圣事。

第2卷的主要内容是日课(圣职人员的正式祈祷)、忏悔礼(告解圣事)的意义、守斋规定、教会的节庆、读经的制度以及教会的诗歌和赞美诗。作者也列出"信经"中的信条以及各种异端邪说的主张——这些异端违背教会的正统教导。

第3卷是一种研究《圣经》的导论,又介绍《圣经》的正当理解和解释。基督宗教的诗人应该被注意,但非基督教作者的作品也值得研究,因为他们的修辞学才华能够丰富司铎们的讲道方式。然而,如果这些著作中出现一些有害的因素——偶像崇拜、仅

Flavius Arrianus / Arrianos

Opera: *De anima, De arte grammatica, De benedictionibus Dei, De ecclesiasticis disciplinis, De institutione clericorum, De laudibus sanctae crucis, De rerum naturis seu (De universo), De reverentia filiorum erga patres, De virtutibus et vitiis, Liber de computo*

Works: *On the Soul, On Grammar, On the Praise of God, On Church Disciplines, The Formation of Clerics, On the Praises of the Holy Cross, On the Nature of Things (On the Universe), On the Reverence of Sons to the Fathers, On Virtues and Vices, Book of Computation*

012. *De institutione clericorum / The Formation of Clerics*

Written in 819 this educational compendium in 3 books is dedicated to the monks in Fulda (Germany) and to the Archbishop Haistulf of Mainz. Blending classical and Christian scholarship Hrabanus' masterpiece became one of the standard handbooks of the Middle Ages. Hrabanus incorporates many of the Christian authors of antiquity, including Cyprianus, Jerome, Augustine, and Isidore of Sevilla.

The work is intended to help the clergy to fulfill their duties as they regularly perform the liturgy and thereby provide moral and religious education for the people of God. The first book discusses the hierarchy of the Church, the proper dress and liturgical garments of the priests, the sacraments of baptism, confirmation and the Eucharist.

The main contents of the second book are the office of the hours, the meaning of the sacrament of reconciliation (confession, sacrament of penitence), the fasting regulations, the ecclesiastical feasts, the order of the readings and ecclesiastical songs and hymns. The author also lists up the articles of the faith and the tenets of the heresies opposed to the orthodox teaching of the Church.

Book 3 presents an introduction to the study of the Holy Scriptures and the proper understanding and interpretation of the Word of God. Not only the Christian poets should receive attention, but also the works of pagan authors are to be studied, since their rhetorical exuberance enriches the preaching of the priests. However, harmful and secular elements in these works—idolatry, mere concern for worldly matters, passages centered on love and desire—should be "removed or trimmed down, according to the sug-

仅看重世俗事物、以爱情和欲望为核心的章节——应该"除掉或改写它们,这样才符合 *Dtn* 21:11(《申命记》)的建议"。

和 Augustinus 一样(参见其 *De doctrina christiana* 4,2),Hrabanus 也鼓励人们学习七门自由学科:修辞学有益于讲道者的说服力,逻辑学指导人们的思考和学习。算术学帮助人们理解《圣经》中的神秘数字,依靠几何学的技术人们能建立一座大殿或一个隐修院,而如果没有音乐就无法进行教会的礼仪。天文学的研究测定诸行星与恒星的轨道,又认定时间的划分,以此帮助人们鉴定复活节的日期以及其他教会节日的日期计算。诸哲学家的著作应该被尊敬,尤其 Plato 学派的书,因为这些著作包含一些宝贵的道德教训,甚至包含关于唯一真神的洞察。与其老师 Alcuin 一样,Hrabanus 强调世俗的学科也是有用的,如果它们可以为基督徒们的新目标服务,即理解《圣经》并培养教会的生活。

gestion of *Dtn* 21:11".

Like Augustine (*confer De doctrina christiana* 4,2) Hrabanus recommends the study of the seven liberal arts: Rhetoric is useful for persuasive preaching, logical thinking teaches how to think and how to study. Arithmetics is helpful for the understanding of the mystical numbers in the Bible, geometry provides skills for the construction of the temple or for a monastery, and liturgical worship cannot do without music. The study of astronomy determines the course of planets and stars and the division of time, therefore this science is indispensable for the determination of the date of Easter and for the computation of the other ecclesiastical feastdays. The works of the philosophers deserve respect, especially the writings of the Platonists, since they contain precious moral teachings and even some insights concerning the one and true God. Following the footsteps of his teacher Alcuin, Hrabanus emphasizes that the secular arts are useful, as long as they serve the modern Christian purpose of understanding the Bible and cultivating Church life.

奥特弗里德（约 800—870）

大约 800 年生于德国 Alsatia 地区的 Weissenburg，于 807 年被送到本笃会的隐修院，830 年后在 Fulda 学习；他的老师是 Hrabanus Maurus。在 845 年后 Otfrid 是 Weissenburg 隐修院的抄书员和语文老师。他进行《圣经》研究，曾想对全部《圣经》撰写一些注解。他是第一位资料比较多的德语诗人，867 年（或 870 年）在 Weissenburg 去世。

著作：《福音之书》

013. 《福音之书》

在公元 863 年和 870 年间 Otfrid 使用古高德语来编写这部福音诗，将它分为 5 卷、140 章和 7104 行。Otfrid 的努力没有引起很大共鸣（只有 4 个手抄本被保存），而在他死后，德语诗歌归于沉寂长达 150 年之久。虽然如此，Otfrid 仍是欧洲韵律诗歌的奠基人之一。他为 Franci 的语言创造了一种写作风格，而在他之前这种语言基本上没有什么文学作品。

在序言中 Otfrid 说明他为什么使用日耳曼方言（theotisce，即"德语"）来编写这部福音书。他指出神是一切语言之主，因此圣言能够弥补法兰克语的缺陷。无论是在军事、经济或文化方面，法兰克人并不落后于希腊人或罗马人，因此"法兰克语"（frenkisga zunga）可以被提升加入那些"高尚语言"（edilzungun，即希伯来语、希腊语、拉丁语）的行列。因此他这样开始写："Nu will ih scriban unser heil … in frenkisga zungun."（"我在此要写我们的救恩，用法兰克语……"）Otfrid 观察到拉丁语和德语在语法上有很多相同之处，而他使用 Ambrosius 那种八步韵的"短长格"来写他的德语诗；他忽略雅韵和德语的传统头韵法。Otfrid 了解关于解释《圣经》的一些原则，他读过 Hrabanus 的一些注解书，并且以 spiritaliter（"精神性地"）、moraliter（"道德上地"）和 mystice（"神秘地"）等拉丁词为部分章节的标题。

第 1 卷描述耶稣的诞生和童年，第 2 卷叙述门徒们的召唤以及耶稣的教导和宣教。第 3 卷形容耶稣所行的奇迹，而第 4 卷涉及基督的受难和死亡。第 5 卷论及耶稣的复活和升天。最后几章（5,19~23）指向基督将来的审判以及天上的永远福乐。作者是一个学者，他很谨慎地反思他的著作的结构和内涵，但在这部杰出的作品中也有很多诗意的、动人的段落。学者有时候将 *Evangelienbuch* 与 *Heliand* 作比较——这是一部以古萨克逊语写的福音书，作者不明，大约成书于 840 年。*Heliand* 使用头韵法并且利用一些日耳曼文化因素来阐述《圣经》的意义。

Otfrid von Weissenburg / Otfried

Opera: *Evangelium (Liber evangeliorum)*
Works: *Book of the Gospels*

013.   *Evangelienbuch / Book of the Gospels*

Between 863 and 870 Otfrid created this Old High German Gospel poem in 5 books, 140 chapters, and 7104 verses. Otfrid's efforts did not find much resonance (only 4 manuscripts are known), and after his death German poetry fell into a period of silence which lasted for 150 years. Nevertheless, Otfrid is one of the founders of European rhyme poetry. He creatively developed a way of writing for the Frankish language that had practically no literature before him.

In the preface Otfrid explains why he used the vernacular German (theotisce) to write the Gospel. He points out that God is the Lord of all languages, thus the shortcomings of the Frankish tongue would be healed by the Divine Word. In terms of military prowess, economy and culture the Franks are not inferior to the Greeks or Romans, thus the "Frankish tongue" (frenkisga zunga) can be elevated to the rank of the "noble tongues" (edilzungun), namely Hebrew, Greek, and Latin. Thus he begins: "Nu will ih scriban unser heil ⋯ in frenkisga zungun." ("Now shall I write about our salvation⋯ in Frankish language") Otfrid notices that Latin and German have many grammatical similarities, and he uses an iambic meter in the style of Ambrose's eight-legged verses to write his German poem, neglecting the traditional German alliteration. Otfrid knew about the rules of Biblical interpretation, he had read some of Hrabanus' commentaries and entitled some chapters of his work with the Latin words "spiritaliter" (in a spiritual understanding), "moraliter" (morally) and "mystice" (mystically).

The first book describes the birth and childhood of Jesus, book 2 the calling of the disciples and Jesus' teaching and preaching. Book 3 narrates the miracles which Jesus worked, and book 4 comes to the passion and death of Christ. Book 5 tells of the resurrection and of Jesus' ascension to Heaven. The final chapters (5,19~23) point to the coming of Christ as judge and to the eternal joys of Heaven. The whole work is written by a scholar who carefully reflects on the structure and meaning of his narrative, but there are also many poetic and moving passages in this outstanding work. The *Evangelienbuch* is sometimes compared to the *Heliand*, a Gospel epic in Old Saxon by an unknown author, dating from ca. 840. The *Heliand* makes use of alliteration and tries to employ some elements of German culture to express the meaning of the Bible.

瓦拉夫瑞德(808—849)

808 年(或 807 年)生于德国的 Alamannia 地区,曾在 Reichenau 隐修院作 Wetti 的学生,15 岁时已经写过一些拉丁语的诗歌,827 年被派到 Fulda 隐修院,在那里受 Hrabanus Maurus 的影响并开始写《圣经》的注解著作,829 年被召前往 Aachen 朝廷,他也曾描述宫廷生活和文化,838 年被指定为 Reichenau 隐修院院长,但于 842 年才就职。他于 848 年出使法国地区,想与 Carolus Glaber 谈话,但途中在 Loire 河里淹死。

著作:《Blaithmaic 传记》、《论 Theoderich 的雕像》、《起源和发展》(欧洲历史上第一部"教会礼仪史")、《隐修士 Mamma 的生与死》、《园艺之书》、《Wetti 的神视》(945 行,Hexameter)、《圣 Gallus 传》、《圣 Otmarus 传》,还为部分《圣经》书卷写过注解。

014. 《园艺之书》

这首诗长达 444 行六韵步,大概在 Reichenau 或 Fulda 的隐修院写成(这两个本笃会的隐修院都有一些花园,参见 *Regula Benedicti*《本笃会会规》66 章)。

头 75 行是一种导论,正文列出一些花草的特征。作者认为,园艺是"默观生活"的表现。应该注意到土壤的质量,也必须加肥料。诗人说他的知识不仅仅来自别人的书,也来自自己种花的经验(15~18 行)。在春天必须除掉野草,需要准备田地,才能够播种或种植。虽然某一个地方的位置不理想,但灌溉能够弥补这些缺点(62~69 行)。

第 76~428 行描述花园中大约 25 种不同的花草或蔬菜,它们的特征和药用。第一个是 salvia(鼠尾草,撒尔维亚),它能够治很多病。其他的药草和植物是:ruta(芸香),cucurbita(南瓜),absinthium(洋艾,苦艾),foeniculum(茴香,它对眼睛有好处,能治疗咳嗽),lilium(百合花,被毒蛇咬的人可以使用它),papaver(罂粟花,它能治疗忧郁症,会带来"渴望的遗忘"),menta(薄荷,它清凉嗓子),apium(芹菜,它治疗胃病,而胃被称为"身体之王"),rafanum(萝卜)和 rosa(蔷薇,玫瑰花)。诗人将玫瑰花与圣母 Maria(玛利亚)以及"殉道"联系起来。玫瑰花的象征意义是"给予自己的生命",而百合花象征"信仰"。基督结合了这两种美德("花",426~427 行)。

最后几行(429~444 行)包含一个祝福语以及本书献给"最有学问的"Grimaldus 的话。本"教育诗"的资料来源是古代和中世纪早期的著作,如 Vergilius 的 *Georgica*,Plinius 的 *Historia Naturalis*,Columella 的 *De cultu hortorum*,Quintus Serenus 的 *Liber medicinalis*,Carolus Magnus(查理曼)的 *Capitulare de villis* 等等。

Walahfridus Strabo / Walafried

Opera: *De beati Blaithmaic vita et fine, De imagine Tetrici, De exordiis et incrementis, De vita et fine Mammae monachi, Liber de cultura hortorum* (*=Hortulus*), *Visio Wettini, Vita Sancti Galli, Vita Sancti Otmari*

Works: *Life and Death of Blessed Blaithmaic, The Monument of Theoderich, Origins and Developments, Life and Death of the Monk Mamma, On the Cultivation of Gardens, The Vision of Wetti, The Life of St. Gallus, The Life of St. Othmar*

014. *Liber de cultura hortorum / On the Cultivation of Gardens*

Poem in 444 Latin hexameters, written either in the monastery of Reichenau or in Fulda (both Benedictine monasteries with gardens, see *Regula Benedicti*, 66).

The first 75 verses are a kind of introduction to the following list of herbs. The author sees gardening as a part of contemplative life. One must pay attention to the quality of the soil and fertilizing. The poet says he himself did not only rely on books for his knowledge but he has experience in keeping a garden himself (vv. 15~18). In spring the weeds must be removed, the ground must be prepared for planting and sowing. Watering can make up for a bad location (vv. 62~69).

Verses 76 to 428 describe 25 different herbs in the garden, their qualities, characteristics and their medical usefulness. First comes sage (salvia), which can cure many ailments. Other herbs and vegetables are: rue (ruta), gourd (cucurbita), wormwood (absinthium), fennel (foeniculum, which is good for the eyes and can cure cough), lily (lilium, which can cure the bite of a poisonous snake), poppy (papaver, which can cure depression and brings sweet oblivion "optata oblivia"), mint (menta, which clears the voice), celeriac (apium, which is good for the "rex corporis", the stomach), radish (rafanum), and finally the rose (rosa). The poet connects the rose with Mary and martyrdom. The symbolic value of the rose is giving one's life, and the lily symbolizes faith. Christ combined these two (vv. 426~427).

The last verses (429~444) contain a blessing and the dedication of the book to Grimaldus, the "pater doctissime" (most learned father). This "didactic poem" is based on the works of Vergilius (*Georgica*), Plinius (*Hist. Nat.*), Columella (*De cultu hortorum*), Quintus Serenus (*Liber medicinalis*), Charlemagne (*Capitulare de villis*) and others.

015. 《维提的神视》

　　这首长达945行的诗写成于828年(当时作者才18岁),是根据Reichenau隐修院的Heito院长对Wetti(维提)的神视所作的记载撰写的——Wetti当时是隐修院学校的校长,在临终时有这样的神秘体验(visio"神视")。Walahfried第一次以诗的形式写出一个"神视",因此它的著作成了Dante(但丁)*Commedia*(《神曲》)的原型。

　　在第一个神视中,魔鬼向Wetti显现并向他宣布将要在第二天惩罚他。然而,Wetti的护守天使能够拯救他。在第二个神视中,Wetti的护守天使带他来到地狱,在那里他看到那些被审判的灵魂以及他们遭受的永恒折磨。在那些处于地狱的灵魂中,Wetti也认出一些在人间和他有关系的人。后来他被带到"炼狱",在那里他看到一些教会人士和社会上的贵族。一些国君也在这个地区为他们的罪作补赎,其中有法兰克人的王查理曼。最终,Wetti被引到上面,他升天并在天堂中见到幸福的灵魂的永恒喜乐。通过圣母玛利亚的求情,他自己的罪也被赦免。

015. *Visio Wettini / The Vision of Wetti*

This is a poem in 945 hexameters, written in 828 (at the age of 18), based on the script of abbot Heito of Reichenau who recorded the vision which Wetti, the rector of the monastery school, had before he died. Walahfried Strabo's poem is the first vision in a lyric form and became the archetype of Dante's *Commedia*.

In the first vision the devil appears to Wetti and announces that he will punish him the next day. However, Wetti's guardian angel can save him. In a second vision Wetti is led by his guardian angel first into hell, where he sees the condemned souls and their painful sufferings. Among the souls in hell he also recognizes some people he knows. Then he is led to the purgatory, where he sees some famous people from Church and society. By doing penitence some kings are freed from their sins in this area, among them the king of the Franks, Charlemagne. Finally Wetti is taken up to heaven where he sees the eternal joys of the souls in heaven. Through the intercession of Mary his sins are forgiven.

艾利基纳(810—877)

这位来自爱尔兰的学者于845年任法国地区 Laon 大教堂学校的老师,曾使用 Martianus Capella 的名著为"自由学科"的教材。他于847年后生活在法兰克王 Carolus Glaber 的朝廷,而法兰克王 Carolus 要求他修订 Hilduinus 于834年对 *Corpus Dionysiacum* 作的翻译。(*Corpus Dionysiacum* 是 Dionysius Areopagita 的著作集。东方的皇帝于827年将这个文集赠送给法兰克王 Ludovicus Pius。)Eriugena 也曾翻译 Gregorius Nyssenus 的 *Peri kataskeuēs anthrōpou* 和 Maximos Confessor 的 *Ambigua* 等希腊语著作。Eriugena 的哲学和神学思想后来影响了 Berengar、Llullus、Eckhart、Nicolaus Cusanus、Giordano Bruno 等人。

著作:《论自然的区分》(本书试图结合新柏拉图主义和基督信仰,具有泛神论的倾向,因此在13世纪受到谴责)、《论预定论》;他还将 Pseudo-Dionysius(Dionysios Areiopagita)、Gregorios de Nyssa(*De hominis opificio*)、Maximus Confessor(*Ambigua, Quaestiones ad Thalassum*)等希腊著作译成拉丁语,为许多著作写注解,为《若望福音》*Jn* 作注解。

016. 《论自然的区分》

本著名论文创作于862—866年间,这是一个很少产生伟大哲学著作的时代。

Eriugena 将万物区分为(1)创造的而不受造的(natura creans, non creata),(2)创造的而受造的(natura creans creata),(3)不创造的而受造的(natura non creans creata),以及(4)不创造的不受造的(natura non creans non creata)。第一个和第四个是神,即在万物的开始和万物终末的神。第二个是可以理解的世界,即理念的世界;第三个是可以通过感官认识的物质世界。在庞大的宇宙当中,人是一个微小的世界(microcosmos),因为人可以通过感官认识物质世界,通过理性能了解宇宙的合理结构,而通过理解能力人可以默想神。由于人类的堕落,人较多受其兽性的支配,但由于基督的救赎,人可以再次与神合一。这个体系中的新柏拉图主义因素是很明显的:神是万物的第一个原因,一切事物是借着理念而受造的,宇宙被区分为存在的几个层次,而这种区分也包含一种价值判断。最终一切万物将会归于神。

神是一切万物的来源,他不是被创造的。受造而创造的物是第二等级的存在物,它们是揭示神的存在的理念,构成了万物。当神默想自己时,永恒的理念就会出现。这些理念展示出神的存在并构成万物。他们是一切可见的现象的原因和原型(causae primordiales, prototypae)。虽然 Eriugena 说理念是"永恒地"被创造的,它们的"永恒"不及神的"永恒",因为它们是神的心意中的思念。

Ioannes Scotus Eriugena / John Scottus Erigena

Opera: *De divisione naturae (Periphyseon), De divina praedestinatione*
Works: *On the Division of Nature, On Divine Providence*

016. *De divisione naturae / On the Division of Nature*

This famous work was written in 862—866 during a period which produced only few great works of philosophy.

Eriugena classifies nature into (1) that which creates and is not created (natura creans, non creata), (2) that which creates and is created (natura creans creata), (3) that which does not create and is created (natura non creans creata), and (4) that which does not create and is not created (non creans non creata). The first and the fourth are God at the beginning and at the end of all things. The second is the intelligible world, the world of ideas, and the third is the material world that is perceived by the senses. Man is a small world (microcosmos) within the greater universe because he has senses to perceive the material world, reason to understand the intelligible features of the universe, and intellect to contemplate God. Because of the fall of mankind the animal nature dominates, but through redemption man may reunite with God. The Neoplatonist elements of this system are obvious: God is the first cause of all things, through the ideas all things are created, the universe is divided into certain levels of being, and this classification implies a value judgment. In the end all things will return to God.

God, the uncreated origin of all contemplates Himself and thereby the eternal ideas come into existence. Things created and creating are the second class of beings, they are the ideas which unfold God's being and constitute all things. They are the causes and principles (causae primordiales, prototypae) of all visible phenomena. Although Eriugena says that the ideas are created "eternally" they are conceived as somewhat less eternal than God, since they are the thoughts of God's mind.

根据这些理念,第三种存在出现,就是按时、空受支配的物质世界。因此,这个宇宙是神的表现。有形的世界要表达和反映理念的世界,虽然这种反映受一定的限制。这种"归于理念"的倾向引发出第四个阶段("不创造,不受造的世界")。一切存在归于其来源和源头,即神,他将在末日引导万有归向他。由于这些泛神论因素,Honorius III 于 1225 年谴责 Eriugena 的著作,因为 Amalric de Bena 曾在 Eriugena 的思想基础上建立了他的异端教导。然而,Eriugena 那种泛神论形式并不想消除神的概念,他更多想阐明神在创造界中的伟大。Eriugena 基本上重复 Gregorios Nyssenos、Dionysios Areiopagita 和 Maximus Confessor 的观点。对 Eriugena 来说,哲学和宗教是一回事:信仰的目标是心智的理解;信仰和理性拥有同样的来源,所以它们从不可能是矛盾的。

According to these ideas the third reality comes into existence, namely the material world that is ordered according to time and space. This visible universe is therefore a manifestation of God. The sensible world intends to express and mirror the world of ideas, even if this is only possible within certain limitations. The tendency to return to the world of ideas leads to the fourth stage (the uncreated and not creating nature). All being returns to its principle and origin, namely God, Who leads the universe to a consummation at the end of time. These pantheistic implications induced Pope Honorius III to condemn the work in 1225, after Amalric of Bena had built his heresy on Eriugena's thought. However, Eriugena's version of pantheism did not intend to eliminate the idea of God, he rather wanted to show God's greatness in creation. Eriugena basically repeats the tenets of Gregory of Nyssa, Dionysius Areopagita, and Maximus Confessor. For Eriugena philosophy and religion are the same: the aim of faith is the understanding of the intellect, faith and reason have the same origin and can thus never be contradictory.

佛提乌斯(约 819—893)

约于 819 年生于 Constantinopolis 的贵族家庭，获得优良的古典教育，20 岁在 Constantinopolis 的皇家学院任哲学老师，约于 845 年出使 Baghdad，与 Al-Wathik 哈里发进行谈判，于 856 年被任命为皇帝秘书处主任。皇后 Theodora 的弟兄 Bardas 于 858 年驱逐 Ignatios 宗主教并支持 Phōtios 被祝圣为其接班人。Phōtios 原来发誓承认 Ignatios 和他所祝圣的主教，但于 859 年就开始镇压支持 Ignatios 的宗派，这样引起教会内的分裂和与 Roma 教会的冲突。Phōtios 于 863 年派遣 Kyrillos 和 Methodios 到斯拉夫地区传教，又与 Armenia 的教会达成合一，但罗马教宗于 863 年谴责和开除了 Phōtios。因为 Bulgaria 地区脱离 Constantinopolis 的控制并转向 Roma(866 年)，Phōtios 进一步反对 Roma 在东方的影响。他于 867 年召开会议并宣布开除罗马教宗，但同年他自己因政变而被迫退位。新的皇帝于 877 年又肯定 Phōtios 为宗主教，但他原来的学生 Leon VI 皇帝于 886 年再次强迫他退位，所以 Phōtios 晚年在一所隐修院生活。他的著作很多，大部分被保存，但他的思想深化了东方与西方教会之间的冲突。

著作：《安菲罗基亚》、《论文》、《问答》(谈论 300 多神学问题)、《词语汇编》(一部以 ABC 排列的古典希腊语词典)、《关于圣神/圣灵的教导》、《万书之书》，还有 220 封信。

017.《万书之书》

本文集的别名是 *Myrobiblos*、*Bibliotheca* 或 *Bibliothecae codices*，它在 280 章中囊括 386 部希腊语著作的提要，其中有 56% 来自基督教传统，其他的是历史性著作，大部分的著作来自公元 5 到 9 世纪。其中有很多书仅仅是在 Phōtios 的提要中保存的，因此这个文集是关于早期基督教文学以及早期拜占庭文献的最重要资料来源之一。法国学者 R. Henry 出版的希腊语—法语版本（巴黎，1959—1978 年）分为 8 卷。Phōtios 这部百科全书表明作者很渊博、读过很多书，但对于所介绍的著作没有提供太多原创性的想法。学者曾经说，这部著作反映拜占庭学术界在 9、10、11 世纪的普遍倾向，因为当时的马其顿王朝鼓励学者编写一些标准性的工具书，但阻碍创造性的著作。Phōtios 的 *Myrobiblion* 曾被称为 Byzantion 第一部百科全书式的著作。在 10 世纪出现了 *Suda*(亦写 *Souda*)，即是一个包含 3 万条目的巨大百科全书。这部大工具书的词条是根据 ABC 编排的，而在后来的几百年中这种编排方式逐渐被西方的拉丁语手册采纳。

一般的人大概不太了解 Phōtios 的学术贡献，而更多地注意他在教会分裂方面的

Phōtios / Photius

Opera: *Amphilochia, Diēgēsis (=Tractatus), Erōtapokriseis, Lexeōn synagōgē, Logos peri tēs tou Hagiou Pneumatos Mystagōgias, Myrobiblion (=Bibliothēkē, Bibliothecae codices)*

Works: *Amphilochia, Treatise (against Neo-Manichaeism), Answers to Questions, Compilation of Sayings, Treatise concerning the Teachings about the Holy Spirit, Myrobiblion*

017. *Myrobiblion*

The name of this collection is variously given as *Myrobiblos*, *Bibliotheca*, or *Bibliothecae codices*. In 280 chapters it contains the abstracts of 386 Greek books, 56% of them belong to Christian literature, the rest are historical works. Most of the books are from the 5th to 9th centuries AD. Many of the books are only known from Photius' excerpts, therefore this is one of the most important sources for our knowledge about early Christian literature and early Byzantine texts. The Greek-French edition of the work by R. Henry (Paris, 1959—1978) runs up to 8 volumes. Photius' encyclopedia displays extraordinary erudition and wide reading but not much original insight into the works reviewed. It has been observed that the work reflected the general trend of Byzantine scholarship between the ninth and eleventh centuries, when the dynasty of the Macedonians encouraged the production of standard reference works but discouraged creativity. Photius' *Myrobiblion* is sometimes regarded as the first Byzantine encyclopedic work. In the tenth century there appeared the *Suda* (*Souda*), a huge encyclopedia with 30,000 entries. This big reference book was arranged alphabetically, and in the following centuries this way of ordering knowledge slowly also became more widespread in the Latin handbooks in the West.

Photius is probably better known for his influence on the split within the Church than for his scholarly achievements. In the conflict between the Greek and the Roman Church in

影响。在9世纪希腊教会和罗马教会的分裂过程中，关于Filioque("及由圣子"，即圣神/圣灵是由圣父"及圣子"共发的)的教导是一个核心的因素。西方的教会4世纪时曾经在《信经》中加上了"及由圣子"，但东方的教会拒绝这种"新的信经"。当Phōtios于886年第二次被罢免时，他编写了一篇谈论"圣神/圣灵"的论文，这篇以信件的形式编写的论文的题目是 *Logos peri tēs tou Hagiou Pneumatos Mystagōgias*（《关于圣神/圣灵的神秘教导的文章》），其中找出一切论点来反对Filioque("及由圣子")并指出圣神/圣灵唯独是从圣父出发的。

部分的《圣经》章节看来表明圣神/圣灵仅仅是从圣父出发的。在研究《圣经》文献后，Phōtios使用逻辑性的论点并且很巧妙地说明如果认为圣神/圣灵有两个根源，这就会导致很奇怪的后果，甚至无法保持神的合一性。拉丁语的神学家也引用一些《圣经》章节来肯定自己的立场，而Phōtios分析他们的观点。他也研究拉丁教父们的看法（比如Augustinus、Hieronymus、Ambrosius），最终向历代教宗——从Petros的时期一直到当时代的教宗——发出呼吁，因为他们应该是正统信仰的保卫者。Phōtios的信后来成为其他的反对罗马文献的基础。他的口才和尖锐分析也受了一些充满攻击情绪和夸大的说法的影响，所以他的信没能促进教会的合一精神。

the 9th century the teaching about the "Filioque" (=the procession of the Holy Spirit from the Father "and from the Son") played a decisive part. The western Church had added the formulation "and from the Son" to the creed in the fourth century, but the Eastern Church rejected this "new creed". After having been deposed the second time in 886, Photius wrote a treatise on the teaching about the Holy Spirit in the form of a polemic letter entitled *Logos peri tēs tou Hagiou Pneumatos Mystagōgias* (*Treatise on the Mysterious Teaching About the Holy Spirit*). He tries to gather all arguments against the "Filioque" so as to show that the Spirit proceeds from the Father alone.

Some Biblical passages seem to show that the Spirit proceeds from the Father alone. After this Biblical studies Photius continues in logical argumentation and with great eloquence to explain that a double origin of the Holy Spirit would lead to absurd consequences, it would even imply that the unity of God could not be preserved. In the further discussion some Biblical passages that were used by the Latin theologians to support their views are analyzed. Photius examines the opinions of the great Latin Fathers of the Church (Augustine, Jerome, Ambrose) and finally calls upon the Popes from Peter up to his own time as witnesses for the orthodox faith. Photius' letter became the basis for later polemical writings against Rome. His elegant and sharp argumentation is marred by aggressive and exaggerating overtones and thus worked against the ecumenical spirit.

诺特克尔(约 840—912)

出生于德国,曾在 St. Gallen(圣伽伦)隐修院接受教育。他说话有一些结巴(因此被称为 Balbulus "结结巴巴者"),然而他成为一个杰出的教师和拉丁文学中的 sequencia(福音前唱的赞美歌)的创始者。当查理曼的曾孙子 Carolus III 于 883 年经过 St. Gallen 隐修院时,他建议 Notkerus 写一部关于查理曼的著作,这就是作者那部名著的缘起。

著作:《查理大帝言行录》、《赞美歌集》(大约包括 40 首赞美歌)、《殉道者列传》、《提要》(教父学纲要)、《圣伽卢斯传》

018. 《查理大帝言行录》

这部著作包含很多有趣的轶事和小故事,都围绕着 Carolus Magnus(查理曼)以及他在朝廷中的生活。在中世纪和现代,这部作品都很受欢迎。这些关于那位伟大的领袖的故事所描绘的图景已经包括一些传奇虚构的因素。Carolus Magnus(查理曼)被描写为一个好的基督徒和正义的国王,他试图奠定社会的秩序。他经常遇到贵族们和臣民的缺陷和局限性,但都以智慧和清楚的辨别能力面对这些挑战。比如,在第 1 卷 Carolus Magnus 去探访一群小孩子,他曾经将这些孩子交给一个老师,要求他好好地教导他们。他发现那些来自贵族家庭的孩子并没有认真写作业,但很多来自穷困家庭的孩子反而有良好的成绩。因此,Carolus Magnus 将孩子们分为两个小组,一个在他的左边,一个在他的右边,并且"以模仿神的审判的形式"赞美好学生并严厉谴责懒惰的学生。

Notkerus Balbulus / Notker the Stammerer

Opera: *Gesta Caroli Magni imperatoris, Liber (h)ymnorum, Martyrologium, Notatio, Vita S. Galli*

Works: *The Deeds of Charles the Great, Book of Hymns, Martyology, Notation, Life of Gallus*

018. *Gesta Caroli Magni imperatoris / The Deeds of Charles the Great*

This entertaining chain of short narratives and anecdotes concerning Charlemagne and the life at his court was very popular in the Middle Ages and even in modern times. The stories create a picture of the great ruler that in some places betrays the touch of legendary fiction already. Charlemagne is presented as a good Christian and just king who tries to bring order into society. He faces the many shortcomings and mediocrities of the nobles and of his subjects with wisdom and clear discernment. For example, in book 1 Charlemagne visits a group of children whom he entrusted to a teacher to be educated. He discovers that the children of the nobles did not write their homework well, but many children coming from poor families could boast good results. Seeing this Charlemagne divides the children in two groups, one to his right and one to his left, and "in imitation of the divine judgment" he praises the good students and fiercely scolds the lazy students.

第三篇

民族大迁移的结束和城市文明的开始
The End of the Migrations and the Emergence of Urban Centers

(900—1080 AD)

• *Antichrist*

埃克哈德（约 910—973）

瑞士 Thurgau 地区人，在 St. Gallen 隐修院修道。

著作：《瓦尔塔里乌斯之诗》

019.《瓦尔塔里乌斯之诗》

在瑞士 St. Gallen 隐修院的 Ekkehard 修士的著作名单上出现一部 *Vita Waltharii manu fortis*（《瓦尔塔里乌斯英雄传》），而这部著作也许是 *Waltharius*（亦称 *Waltharii poiesis*），一部长达 1456 六韵步行的拉丁史诗。然而，一般都认为该史诗书写于 850—950 年间。它是一个日耳曼故事的唯一拉丁语版本，深受 Vergilius、Statius 和 Prudentius 风格的影响。其历史根据是匈奴人的攻击——他们在 Attila 王的领导下约于 450 年跨越了莱茵河并毁灭了勃艮第国，那个传奇的日耳曼王国。

《瓦尔塔里乌斯之诗》是关于 Waltharius de Aquitania 的诗，他是 Aquitania 王的儿子。他的爱人是 Hiltgunt（亦写 Hildgundi），即勃艮第王的女儿。因为匈奴人威胁各地的日耳曼国，这些部落的国王们决定要向匈奴人纳贡并送给他们自己的子女作为人质。因此，在孩童时期已经订婚的 Waltharius 与 Hiltgunt 一起在匈奴人的王宫中长大。法兰克人的王决定要送给匈奴人自己的忠臣 Hagano。因为 Waltharius 与 Hagano 都是匈奴人的人质，他们的共同命运也使双方产生了友谊。然而，当法兰克人的老王去世后，新的领导 Guntharius（亦称 Gunther）停止向匈奴人纳税，而 Hagano 也偷偷地骑马逃回自己的国王那里。Attila 王想让 Waltharius 长期留在匈奴人那里，所以要他与一个匈奴公主结婚，但 Waltharius 与 Hiltgunt 得以逃跑，并且他们带走了 Attila 的宝藏——这个宝藏原来委托给 Hiltgunt 照管。

当两个逃难者跨过莱茵河并接近 Worms（沃尔姆斯）城时，Hagano 认出了他们并礼貌地迎接他们，但 Guntharius 王要从 Waltharius 的手里夺取他的宝藏。因此 Waltharius 与 Hiltgunt 不得不再次逃跑，Guntharius 王和他的战士们追赶他们。在 Vogesen 山区中，Waltharius 在一个非常狭窄的山隘等待他的对手们——他们在那里只能一个个地攻击他。在一系列决斗中 Waltharius 杀死 Guntharius 的 11 位战士，其中包括 Hagano 的侄子 Patafried。Hagano 在一个小讲演中诅咒贪财（avaritia）的害处（857~874 行）并劝勉他的亲戚不要参与战争，但毫无效果。在傍晚时 Waltharius 感到很累，他为那些被杀的人的灵魂祈祷（1161~1168 行）并去找他们的马。

Ekkehard I / Ekkehard the Elder

Opera: *Vita Waltharii manu fortis* (=*Waltharii poiesis?*)
Works: *Life of Waltharius* (=*Waltharius?*)

019. *Waltharii Poiesis* / *Waltharius*

In a list of the works of Ekkehard, a monk of St. Gall, Switzerland, there appears the title *Vita Waltharii manu fortis* (*Life of the Valiant Fighter Waltharius*), but it is debatable whether this is identical with the Latin poem variously known as *Waltharius* or *Waltharii poiesis*, an epic in 1456 hexameter verses. However, it is generally assumed that the epic was written between 850 and 950. It is the only extant Latin version of a Germanic narrative and was influenced by the style of Vergil, Statius and Prudentius. The historical basis of the poem is the attack of the Huns who crossed the Rhine under their king Attila and destroyed the legendary Germanic kingdom of the Burgundians around 450.

The *Waltharius* is the story of Walter of Aquitania, the son of the king of Aquitania, and of Hiltgunt, the daughter of the Burgundian king. As the Huns threaten the Germanic kingdoms the kings of these peoples decide to pay tribute and send their sons and daughters as hostages to the Huns. Thus Waltharius and Hiltgunt who have been betrothed as children grow up together at the court of the Huns. The king of the Franks decides to send his loyal vassal Hagano as hostage to the Huns, and their common destiny as hostages forges bonds of friendship between Hagano and Waltharius. However, as the old king of the Franks dies and the new ruler Gunther (Guntharius) stops paying tribute to the Huns, Hagano manages to ride off secretly and returns to his king. With the intention to bind Waltharius to the Hunnic court, Attila suggests that he should marry one of the princesses of the Hun realm, but Waltharius and Hiltgunt are able to escape together, taking with them the rich treasure of Attila which had been entrusted to the care of Hiltgunt.

As the two refugees cross the Rhine River and approach the city of Worms, Hagano recognizes them and wants to receive his old friends cordially, but king Guntharius plans to seize the treasure from Waltharius. Thus Waltharius and Hiltgunt have to flee again, pursued by Guntharius and his men. Waltharius takes up his position in a narrow ravine in the Vosges, where only one man can attack him at a time. In a series of single combats he kills eleven of Guntharius' men, among them Hagano's nephew Patafried. Hagano unsuccessfully tries to dissuade his nephew from the fight, cursing the crave for gold (avaritia, vv. 857~874) in a short speech. As evening approaches, Waltharius is tired from the fights. He prays for the souls of the men he killed (1161~1168) and collects their horses.

第二天 Waltharius 与 Hiltgunt 想继续他们的旅程。此时国王 Guntharius 要求 Hagano 帮助他战胜 Waltharius。此前 Hagano 一直没有用武力来对付他的老朋友 Waltharius，但现在他被迫表现他对国王的忠诚。另外，他也要为其侄子的死亡报仇。Guntharius 与 Hagano 在一个平原中攻击 Waltharius 并开始激烈的交战（1280~1395 行）。Waltharius 砍掉 Guntharius 的脚，但正在他准备杀死国王时，Hagano 用自己的头盔保护了国王的性命，而 Waltharius 的剑被打碎。Hagano 割下 Waltharius 的右手，但这个 Aquitania 英雄用左手攻击 Hagano，结果 Hagano 的一只眼睛和几颗牙齿被打掉。三个人都受如此严重的创伤后，他们停止作战并和好。最终 Waltharius 回到 Aquitania 去，他与 Hiltgunt 结婚并成为一个幸福的国王，统治自己的国民达 30 年之久。日耳曼人 Waltharius 代表一个基督徒英雄，他结合美德(virtus)和智慧(sapientia)，但 Guntharius 反过来是一个贪婪的、傲慢的和固执的领导人物的化身。

The next morning Waltharius and Hiltgunt want to continue their journey. King Guntharius demands that Hagano helps him to overcome Waltharius. Up to this moment Hagano has avoided taking up arms against his old friend, but now he feels compelled to show his loyalty to the king. He is also eager to avenge his nephew. Guntharius and Hagano attack Waltharius together in open terrain which results in fierce fighting (vv. 1280~1395). Waltharius lops off Guntharius' leg, but just as he is about to kill the king, Hagano with his helmet protects the king's life, and Waltharius' sword breaks. Hagano cuts off Waltharius' right hand, but the Aquitanian attacks Hagano with his left hand. Hagano loses one eye and several teeth. Being wounded so severely the three men stop the combat and are reconciled. Waltharius finally returns to Aquitania, he marries Hiltgunt and reigns happily for thirty years. The Germanic image of Waltharius embodies the ideal Christian hero who combines virtue (virtus) and wisdom (sapientia), whereas Guntharius is the personification of a greedy, conceited and stubborn ruler.

阿德索（约920—992）

约于920年生于法国东部的Jura地区的贵族家庭，幼年被送到Luxeuil的本笃会隐修院，曾在Toul任教，935年以来在Montier-en-Der修道，968年任院长，他的朋友包括Adalbero de Rheims、Gerbertus de Aurillac和Abbo de Fleury。他去以色列朝圣，中途去世。

著作：《论反基督的诞生和时期》、《Frodobertus传》、《Bercharius传》

020. 《论反基督的诞生和时期》

这篇散文叙述大约于950年成书，作者Adso Dervensis当时回应了西法兰克人女王Gerberga（她是德国王Henricus I的女儿）的要求并写出这部著作。大约在1160年某一诗人根据这个故事写了一出话剧，剧名为Ludus de Antichristo（《反基督的话剧》）。关于"反基督"来临的想法是根据《新约》最后的书卷中的一些章节而来的（参见Rev 11:7; 2 Thess 2:8-10），而由于这种思想很多中世纪的人也怀着某种忧虑和期待意识。

这个故事的结构反映了当时的反穆斯林斗争并且实际上围绕着"统治世界"的概念。德国皇帝试图征服东部地区，而Babylon的王和一些非基督教的军队攻击他。皇帝战胜那些非基督徒，他进入耶路撒冷的圣殿并把自己的冕冠和权杖置于祭坛之上，这样他表示他为了信仰的缘故而放弃皇帝的尊严。耶路撒冷的王提醒德国皇帝不要忘记他的任务是将非基督徒引向信仰。基督徒统治的内在敌人是虚荣心和世俗化，而当这些力量逐渐增强时，Antichristus（反基督）出现。他开始取代皇帝的地位并建立自己的帝国。在话剧里拟人化的"谄媚"和"异端"围绕着他。反基督征服很多地区并战胜很多国王。在开始德国国王抵抗反基督，但通过三个奇迹德国皇帝也拥护反基督。现在连皇帝都服务于反基督并为反基督征服全世界。耶路撒冷和Babylon也沦陷于反基督，而犹太人敬拜反基督为弥赛亚/默西亚。此时Enoch和Elijah出现并揭露反基督的真面目，所以一些犹太人再次转向基督。此后反基督压迫犹太人并杀死他们很多人。他统治全世界，但"最终他将屈服于上主的审判，而通过主耶稣基督的力量，他将被杀"。

Adso Dervensis / Adso of Montier-en-Der (Adso of Toul)

Opera: *De ortu et tempore Antichristi, Vita Frodoberti, Vita Bercharii*
Works: *On the Birth and Time of the Antichrist, Life of Frodobertus, Life of Bercharius*

020. *De ortu et tempore Antichristi / On the Birth and Time of the Antichrist*

This prose narrative was written around 950 by Adso of Toul in response to a request of Gerberga, daughter of the German king Henry I, the queen of the Western Franks. Around 1160 some unknown poet elaborated the story into a play entitled "Ludus de Antichristo". The idea of the "coming of the Antichrist" is based on certain passages from the last book of the New Testament (*Revelations, Rev* 11:7, confer 2 *Thess* 2:8-10), and because of it many people in the Middle Ages may have lived in an atmosphere of anxious expectation.

The structure of the story mirrors certain historical developments in the time of the struggle against Muslim forces and is actually centered on the idea of world domination. As the German Emperor attempts to conquer some regions in the East, the king of Babylon attacks him together with pagan forces. The Emperor defeats the heathens, he enters the temple of Jerusalem and puts his crown and scepter on the altar, showing that he relinquishes imperial power for the sake of the faith. The king of Jerusalem reminds the German Emperor that he must not neglect the task of leading the pagans to Christ. As vanity and secularization, the inner enemies of the Christian reign, grow stronger, the Antichrist appears. He begins to replace the Emperor and establishes his own empire. In the play the allegories of flattering and heresy surround him. The Antichrist conquers Christian regions and defeats many kings. After initial resistance the German Emperor is won over through three miracles. Now even the Emperor serves the Antichrist and conquers the world for the Antichrist. Jerusalem and Babylon fall to the Antichrist as well, and the Jews adore the Antichrist as the Messiah. As Enoch and Elijah appear and unmask the Antichrist, some Jews turn back to Christ, whereupon the Antichrist persecutes the Jews and kills many of them. His reign is universal, but finally "he will be subjected to God's judgment, and through the power of the Lord Jesus Christ he will be killed."

赫若斯维塔(约 935—975)

第一位德国女诗人,来自撒克逊的贵族,曾在 Gandersheim 隐修院接受教育。(德国贵族人士于 856 年建立 Gandersheim 隐修院,其中的修女来自王家贵族、中下层贵族和城民。)Hrotsvita 的老师是 Rikkardis 修女和 Gerberga 院长(940—1001年),而后者是 Otto I 皇帝的侄女。Hrotsvita 后来也任 Gandersheim 女隐修院的院长。她的著作是用拉丁文写成的,其中有 8 首传奇诗和 6 出话剧,还有两篇历史诗(关于 Gandersheim 的历史和关于 Otto 皇帝的行动)。她的思想围绕着基督信仰和道德生活,她尤其歌颂贞洁的美德,经常以幽默的言辞描述具有纯洁情操和哲学知识的女性。

著作:《隐修者亚巴郎》、《阿格内斯》、《巴西略》、《卡立马库斯》、《论主的升天》、《狄奥尼修斯》、《杜启修斯》、《伽立卡奴斯》、《奥托皇帝之武功》、《贡勾夫斯》、《玛利亚》、《巴夫奴修斯》、《佩拉修斯》、《甘德斯海姆隐修院的创立》(从 856 年建立到 919 年的历史)、《智慧》、《德欧斐路斯》。

021. 《隐修者亚巴郎》

隐修者 Abraham 来探访他的朋友 Ephraim,他们谈论 Abraham 侄女 Maria 的未来。这个侄女的父母去世了,所以她是一个孤儿。两个男人和 Maria 谈话——她的名字被解释为"海星",而这个女青年就很愿意成为修女,过一种严格克修的生活。

20 年后,Abraham 再一次去拜访 Ephraim。他很担心 Maria 的生活,因为他听说她放弃了原先的崇高理想,现在在妓院过日子。Abraham 说一定要找到她并劝她离开那种可耻的生活。然而,这个隐修者发过圣愿,所以他不可以去那些地方找一个女子。Ephraim 劝勉 Abraham 说,如果只是为了拯救一位女性而去那些地方应该不算犯罪。

不久后,Abraham 获知他的亲戚 Maria 在什么地方。他穿上一个士兵的服装,骑着马前往那里。他进入一家餐馆,在那里假装客人的样子。有人给他介绍一位妇女(实际上就是 Maria),她与这个客人一起吃饭,后来他们进入一个房间。在那里 Maria 认出她的叔叔,她非常感动地痛哭,又承诺她将要作补赎,要改变她的生活。Abraham 和 Maria 一起回到隐修院那里去。

在最后的部分,Abraham 又来到 Ephraim 的小屋,与他的朋友交谈。他报告了 Maria 悔改的过程。她和她的榜样将来也能够帮助别人改进自己的生活。这部剧的结尾引用《圣经》的一句话:"一个罪人的悔改,天上的喜乐胜过拥有 99 个不需悔改的义人。"(参见古罗马 Terentius 的剧 *Heauton timoroumenos*,在那里有两个年龄比

Hrotsvita Gandeshemensis / Roswitha of Gandersheim

Opera: *Abraham eremita, Agnes, Basilius, Calimachus, De ascensione Domini, Dionysius, Dulcitius, Gallicanus, Gesta Ottonis* (*Gesta Oddonis*), *Gongolfus* (*Passio Gongolfi*), *Maria, Pafnutius* (=*Conversio Thaidis meretricis*), *Pelagius, Primordia coenobii Gandeshemensis, Sapientia, Theophilus* (*Lapsus et conversio Theophili vicedomini*)

Works: *Abraham the Hermit, Agnes, Basilius, Calimachus, The Ascension of the Lord, Dionysius, Dulcitius, Gallicanus, The Labours of Otto I, Gongolfus, Mary, Pafnutius, Pelagius, On the Foundation of the Monastery of Gandesheim, Sapientia, Theophilus*

021. *Abraham eremita / Abraham the Hermit*

The hermit Abraham visits his friend Ephraim, and they plan the future of Abraham's niece Maria, who lost her parents and is an orphan now. The men talk to Maria (her name is interpreted as stella maris = star of the sea), and the girl is enthusiastic to become a religious sister, leading a strict life as a recluse.

After 20 years Abraham meets Ephraim again. He is very worried about Maria, since he heard that she has abandoned her pious ideals and has become a prostitute. Abraham wants to find her and to persuade her to give up the shameful life of prostitution. However, it would be against the vows of a monk to go to a brothel and look for a woman. Ephraim convinces Abraham that it is no sin to go to these places in order to rescue a woman.

Soon Abraham receives a message about Maria's whereabouts. He puts on a soldier's dress, gets on a horse and rides off. He enters the inn, where he must play a customer. A woman (Maria) is introduced to him. He eats and drinks with her and enters the bedroom. There Maria recognizes her uncle, she is moved to tears and promises to do penitence and to change her life. Abraham and Maria go back to the eremitage together.

In a last scene, Abraham visits Ephraim's hut again. He reports about the conversion of Maria. She and her example will move other people to change their lives, too. The play ends with a quotation from the Bible: There is more joy in heaven about one sinner who is converted than about 99 just people. (Confer Terentius' *Heauton timoroumenos*:

较大的男人,Menedemus 和 Chremes,担心他们儿子们——Clinia 和 Clitipho——的不洁生活。)

022. 《杜启修斯》

本话剧的原名是 *Passio sanctarum virginum Agapes, Chioniae et Hirenae*(《神圣贞女阿格佩、基欧尼阿和艾瑞纳的受难》),这是关于三位在 Diocletianus 皇帝(284—305 年在位)时代殉道的基督徒女性的故事。

前言告诉我们这件事发生在 Makedonia 的 Thessalonike。三个基督徒姐妹,即 Agape(爱慕)、Chionia(雪白)和 Hirene(和平)被迫前往法庭,因为她们的信仰违背皇帝新颁布的法律。Diocletianus 皇帝亲自审问她们。他劝她们放弃她们的信仰,许诺让她们与一些朝廷贵族人士结婚,又威胁她们,但都不能改变这三个贞女的坚定态度。因此她们被交给 Dulcitius 总督(praeses),让他用拷打和虐待的方式强迫她们。

然而,Dulcitius 钦慕于三个姑娘的美丽并下令不在监狱而在自己的房子监禁她们。他想她们可以成为自己的奴隶并把她们禁闭在一个位于厨房旁边的贮藏室里。夜里他悄悄地来到这个地方,因为他渴望与他的俘虏合欢,但他的欲火使他失去方向,他在黑暗中进入厨房,他什么也看不清,所以他在黑屋里并没有拥抱这些女孩子,反而抱住一些肮脏的锅子和工具。三个姐妹通过墙里的窟窿窥视 Dulcitius 的疯狂表现。当他第二天离开厨房时他的脸和衣服非常肮脏,以至于他的仆人没有认出他们的主人,一见他就跑掉。此后这种尴尬的情况被揭露。无法控制自己欲望的 Dulcitius 获得应有的惩罚,但在这个幽默的插曲后三个基督徒贞女仍然被杀害。她们以坚定的信仰和圣人般的虔诚迎接她们的殉道。

023. 《德欧斐路斯》

那位年轻的 Theophilus(名字的意思是"爱神者")是一个很虔诚的人。他在教区担任一名管理人,既有地位,又很富裕。然而,一天有人诽谤他,因此他失去了原来的职位。由于这个打击,他的信仰变得脆弱,所以魔鬼来引诱他:如果他在一个文献上签名,魔鬼可以恢复他的职位,又可以让他变得比以前更富有、更有威望,但这件将要签的文献就表示 Theophilus 放弃他对耶稣和对 Maria(玛利亚)的信仰。Theophilus 在文件上签名并放弃原有的信仰,但不久后,他又后悔这个决定,因为他背离了基督信仰。他请求 Maria 帮助自己;他说,David 王,Niniveh 的人民和 Petrus 也都获得他们罪的赦免,所以他也希望自己还会有一个机会。他祈祷了 40 天,此后童贞女 Maria 回应了他的祈求。她从魔鬼那里索回那个不幸的"契约",将它交给 Theophilus。他又将文献带到教堂里,那里的主教将它焚毁。这样,Theophilus 得以安祥地死去。(这个故事在 Goethe 的 *Faust* 中获得了更全面的表述。)

two elderly men, Menedemus and Chremes, are worried about the unchaste life of their sons, Clinia and Clitipho.)

022. *Dulcitius*

The original title of this play is *Passio sanctarum virginum Agapes, Chioniae et Hirenae* (*The Passion of the Saintly Virgins Agape, Chionia and Hirene*), it is the story of three Christian women who were martyred during the persecution of the Roman Emperor Diocletian (in power 284—305 AD).

The prologue tells us that the events take place in the Macedonian city of Thessalonica. The three Christian sisters Agape (Love), Chionia (Snow) and Hirene (Peace) are summoned to court because their faith contradicts the new laws issued by the emperor. Diocletian personally leads the interrogation. He tries to persuade them to give up their faith by promising them that they would be married to noble Romans at court. Then the emperor threatens them, but nothing can change the steadfastness of the three virgins. Thus they are handed over to the proconsul (praeses) Dulcitius who is supposed to force them into submission by torture.

However, Dulcitius is enraptured by the beauty of the three young women and has them detained in his own house instead of sending them to prison. He wants to enslave them and locks them up in a store-room beside the kitchen. Longing for the caresses of the captives he secretly makes his way to that room at night, but his lust makes him blind, and in the darkness he enters the kitchen and embraces sooty pans and rusty tools instead of the girls. Through a hole in the wall the three sisters watch the madness of Dulcitius. The next morning he leaves the kitchen, but his face and dress are soiled and so dirty that the servants do not recognize their master and run away as they see him. Then the embarrassing reality comes to light. Dulcitius receives the due reward for his immodest desires, but after this humorous episode the Christian virgins are nevertheless put to death. With steadfast faith and saintly piety they welcome their martyrdom.

023. *Theophilus*

Theophilus ("lover of God") is a pious and learned young man, who holds a respected and lucrative position as administrator of a diocese. However, one day some accusations are brought up against him, and he loses his office. His faith is weakened by this blow, and now the devil tries to seduce him: if he signs a document in which he denies faith in Jesus and Mary, the devil can reinstate him in his rights and will make him even more respected and richer than he was before. Theophilus signs the document and renounces his faith, but later he feels very sorry for this apostasy. He asks Mary for help, arguing that David, the people of Niniveh and Peter were forgiven their sins, therefore he hopes that he will be given another chance. After 40 days of prayer the Virgin Mary responds to his pleas. She gets the contract back from the devil and gives it to Theophilus. He takes the devilish document to the church where the bishop burns it, and so Theophilus can die in peace. (The story was later elaborated by Goethe in his *Faust*.)

阿维森纳（约 980—1037）

生于 Bukhara（伊朗地区），是伊斯兰教那些科学家兼哲学家中最著名的、最有影响的人物。他始终生活在波斯，10 岁时就背熟《古兰经》，21 岁时精通伊斯兰教正式教育的一切领域（伊斯兰教法律、医学、哲学）。突厥人于 1000 年的入侵迫使他离开家乡，到各处行医并写作。后来他成为统治波斯中部地区 Buyid 王朝的宫廷医生。

著作：《医学大全》、《教导与注解之书》、《康复书》、《拯救书》（即《康复书》的提要）、《阿拉伯语》等

024. 《康复书》

波斯的医生 Ibn Sina / Avicenna 于 1016 年开始编写这部巨大的哲学和科学百科全书，在晚年才结束它。它是阿拉伯世界那种 Aristoteles 和 Neoplatonismus 传统中最有影响的哲学著作。自从 9 世纪以来，阿拉伯的学者形成了这种被称为 falsafah（"哲学"）的传统，但正统的伊斯兰教神学（即 kalam）从来没有正式接受这种哲学思维。Avicenna 的著作的一部分在 12 世纪由 Dominicus Gundissalinus 等人译成拉丁语并深深影响了 12、13 世纪的经院思想（参见 Averroes）。

这部 Kitab 分为四部分：1）逻辑学（包括修辞学和诗学）；2）物理学（宇宙论、自然哲学、心理学）；3）数学（包括天文学和音乐）；4）形而上学。Avicenna 的哲学依赖于 Aristoteles 的文献、Plotinos（205—270 年）以及 Al Farabi（875—950 年）。作者认为神是绝对的存在，而一切其他的存在都是从他那里一层一层流溢而成的。这种永恒的流溢不是一个意志行动的结果，而更多的是一种自然且必然的事件。最高的有限理智是纯粹的理智（spiritus purus），而从它流出来的是比较低级的理智，一层一层符合天界的层次。最下面的层次是"主动的理智"（intelligentia agens），它为月亮以下的物质世界提供形式和生命。与这种理智相对应的是人的"物质理智"（intelligentia materialis），它需要从"主动理智"那里接受很多东西，正如物质需要接受形式和形状。每一个人都有自己的"物质理智"，即一种不依赖于身体的精神实体，这个精神实体是不死的。

Avicenna / Ibn Sina

Opera: *Al-Qanun fi at-tibb, Kitab al-isharat wa attanbihat, Kitab as-sifa, Kitab an-najat, Lisan al-'arab*

Works: *The Canon of Medicine, Book of Directives and Remarks, Book of Healing, Book of Salvation, The Arabic Language*

024. *Kitab as-sifa / Book of Healing*

The Persian physician Ibn Sina (=Avicenna) wrote this vast philosophical and scientific encyclopedia from 1016 to the end of his life. It is the most influential philosophical document of the Aristotelian-Neoplatonist tradition that flourished in the Arab world since the 9th century under the name "falsafah" (philosophy) and which was never fully accepted by the orthodox theology of Islam ("kalam"). Avicenna's book was partly translated into Latin early in the 12th century by Dominicus Gundissalinus and others and deeply influenced scholastic thought in the 12th and 13th centuries (confer Averroes).

The Kitab is divided into four parts: 1) logic (including rhetoric and poetics), 2) physics (cosmology, philosophy of nature, psychology), 3) mathematics (including astronomy and music), and 4) metaphysics. Avicenna's philosophy depends on Aristotle's texts, on Plotinus (205—270 AD) and on Al Farabi (875—950 AD). The author understands God as the absolute being from which all other beings emanate in a sequence of steps. This eternal emanation is not the result of a willed act but rather a natural and necessary event. The highest finite intelligence is pure intellect (pure spirit), and from this pure spirit proceed the lower intellects which correspond to the heavenly spheres. The lowest level is the active intellect (intelligentia agens) which acts upon passive matter and provides form and life for the bodies of the sublunar world. This intellect corresponds to the "material intellect" (intelligentia materialis) of man which receives insight from the active intellect like matter receives form and shape. Every person has a proper material intellect, namely a spiritual substance that is independent of the body and thus immortal.

维波（约 1000—1046）

约于 1000 年出生于勃艮第的 Alemannia 地区，被祝圣为司铎，曾是 Conradus II 朝廷中的司铎与 Henricus III 皇帝的老师。他一生身体欠佳，大概在 1046 年后不久去世。

著作：《康拉德二世皇帝传》、《格言集》、《四人对话》、《复活节歌》

025. 《康拉德二世皇帝传》

这部历史学著作分为 39 章，在 1046 年前成书，并献给 Wipo 的学生 Henricus III，后者于 1046 年被加冕为皇帝。Wipo 要求皇帝"像在一面镜子里那样观望和默想你父亲的美德"。他描述 Conradus 的理想风度；Conradus 曾是一位公正的国王，他被称为 vicarius Christi（基督的代言人）并领导一个 Christianum imperium（基督徒王国）。作者的文笔优雅流畅，他对书中事情的了解也很深入，因为他与皇帝家庭的关系很密切。

Wipo 的 *Tetralogus*（《四人对话》）是一首长达 326 行的教育诗。作者以典型的中世纪方式描述"文艺女神"、"法律"和"恩典"三位女士。诗人与她们谈论，而这种谈论的目标是劝勉和赞美皇帝。Wipo 于 1041 年的圣诞节将这首诗献给 Henricus III 皇帝。

Wipo

Opera: *Gesta Chuonradi II imperatoris, Proverbia, Tetralogus, Victimae paschali laudes*
Works: *Biography of Emperor Conrad II, Proverbs, Tetralogus (Conversation of Four Persons), Victimae paschali Laudes*

025. *Gesta Chuonradi II imperatoris / Biography of Emperor Conrad II*

This historical work in 39 chapters was written in the years before 1046 and dedicated to the student of Wipo, Henry III, who was crowned emperor in 1046. Wipo wants the emperor to "contemplate the virtues of your father like in a mirror". He describes the ideals of Conrad, the just ruler, whom he views as "vicarius Christi" (vicar of Christ) in a "Christianum imperium" (Christian empire). The refined and clear language and entertaining narrative are complemented by a good command of the subject matter, since the author had close contacts to the imperial family.

Wipo's *Tetralogus* (*Conversation of Four Persons*) is a didactic poem in 326 hexameters. In typical medieval fashion it presents the allegories of the Muses, of Law and Grace. The poet's conversation with the three symbolic ladies is meant to exhort and praise the Emperor. Wipo submitted the poem to the Emperor Henry III at the Christmas celebration of the year 1041.

赫尔曼（1015—1054）

生于德国 Althausen 的贵族家庭，约于 1020 年被送到 Reichenau 隐修院，在那里接受了良好的教育；他从童年起就患有一种痉挛病，因此被称为 Contractus（"瘫痪者"）。他于 1043 年被祝圣司铎，成为当时最渊博的、多才多艺的学者之一，特别喜欢研究天文学、音乐、数学、算数学、历史、教会礼仪和文学，具有全面的知识。他的主要著作是一部《世界史》。

著作：《大哉，救主之母》（作者不完全确定）、《编年史》（从基督诞生到 1054 年的世界史）、《雅韵之冲突》、《论咎的衡量》、《八宗罪》、《论算盘的乘法》、《母后，万福》（作者不完全确定；著名的歌曲，"母后"也代表"教会"）；还有关于音乐的著作等。

026.《编年史》

这部"世界史"是以编年体撰写的；它可能是 Hermannus 最有影响的著作。他的学生 Berthold 后来续写了这部书，并且它是很多其他历史性著作的基础。

《编年史》的叙述是从基督的诞生开始的，很详细地描写每一个时代的历史事件直到作者去世的那一年（1054 年），甚至在 500 年到 800 年这段时期中也保持编年的方法。作者并没有掌握很多关于法兰克人早期历史的资料，所以写这方面的编年史无疑非常艰难。Hermannus 第一次结合了德国帝国的历史与世界史。《编年史》的文笔很清晰，而作者的评价非常公正；他追求的是表达上的准确和观点上的客观。

027.《八宗罪》

这篇道德诗长达 1722 行，是写给一个修女团体的。在导论后有 20 篇诗歌，每一篇都是根据不同的韵律编写的，这也许受了 Boethius 的 *Consolatio* 的影响。Hermannus 描述八个主要罪行（宗罪）的负面影响。在这些宗罪中，骄傲（Superbia）占首位。她被描述为一个妇女，而这个妇女有七个女儿，即其他的主要罪恶（如贪婪、嫉妒、愤怒等）。这部诗的许多地方是以对话体编写的，在对话中 Melpomene（一个文艺女神）劝勉读者。

在基督宗教世界中最流行的赞美诗之一是 *Salve Regina*，而这首诗也曾被归于 Hermannus，但学者们似乎无法证明这首诗的作者是谁。其内容是对基督的母亲 Maria 的问候，Maria 是"天上的皇后"，而信徒们向她呼吁，因为她是"仁慈的母亲"（mater misericordiae），也是信徒们在一个充满考验和困难的世界中的希望。这首诗使用著名的 lacrimarum vallis（泪谷）比喻来描绘人生的困境。怀着怜悯和同情的 Maria 俯视着教会的挣扎，而信徒们祈求使她显现出她的儿子耶稣。这首赞美诗的最后部分颂扬 Maria 的虔诚、温和与甘饴。

Hermannus Contractus / Herman the Lame

Opera: *Alma Redemptoris Mater, Chronicon, De conflictu rithmimachiae, De mensura astrolabii, De octo vitiis principalibus, Qualiter multiplicationes fiant in abaco, Salve regina*

Works: *Loving Mother of the Redeemer, Chronicle, On the Conflicts of Rhythmimachia, On the Measure of the Astriolabe, On the Eight Capital Sins, How Multiplications Happen in the Abacus, Salve regina*

026. *Chronicon / Chronicle*

This "world history" arranged in the form of annalist records is probably the most famous and influential work of Herman. It was later continued by his student Berthold and became the basis of other historical works.

The *Chronicle* starts with the birth of Christ and meticulously leads the narrative up to the year of the death of the author (1054), even keeping the annalistic method for the period from ca. 500 to 800. The author did not have many records covering the early history of the Franks, thus writing a chronicle about those centuries was doubtless very difficult. For the first time Herman combined the history of the German empire with a history of the world. The Chronicle is also remarkable for the sober and balanced judgment of the author who pursued clarity of expression and objectivity in his views.

027. *De octo vitiis principalibus / On the Eight Capital Sins*

This moral poem in 1722 verses was written for a group of nuns. After an introduction follow 20 songs, each arranged according to a different metre, possibly influenced by Boethius' *Consolation*. Herman describes the negative influences of the eight main sins. Among the sins Pride (Superbia) takes the first place. She is depicted as a woman who has seven daughters, namely the seven other main sins or capital sins (greed, envy, wrath etc.). Many parts of the poem are a dialogue, in which Melpomene (one of the Muses) exhorts the reader.

One of the most popular hymns of the Christian world, the *Salve Regina*, has been ascribed to Herman, although it is difficult to prove his authorship. The hymn greets Mary, the mother of Christ and heavenly queen, and calls upon her, since she is the "mother of mercy" (mater misericordiae) and hope of the Christians in a world of trials and calamities described with the famous word "valley of tears" (lacrimarum vallis). Full of pity and compassion, Mary looks on the struggles of the Church, and the Christians pray that she may show them Jesus, her son. The final passage of the hymn praises the piety, clemency and sweetness of Mary.

额我略七世(约 1015—1085)

约于 1015 年生于意大利 Toscana 地区的平民家庭,原名 Hildebrand;他早年在罗马修道并在 Lateranum 接受教育,曾于 1047 年陪同 Gregorius VI 教宗前往德国,但于 1049 年回罗马,1054 年到 1058 年间在法国和德国朝廷担任教宗大使(legatus),1058 年后大力支持 Nicolaus II 教宗和 Alexander II 教宗的改革工作。罗马民众和枢机们于 1073 年宣布他为教宗,他取名为 Gregorius VII,致力于教会的改革,强化教会的管理制度并肯定教宗的权威。德国国王 Henricus VI 于 1076 年拒绝承认 Gregorius VII 并同时强化对意大利北部的控制。此时 Gregorius 开除 Henricus 并有效地弹劾这位皇帝。因为 Henricus 需要德国贵族人士的支持,他去意大利朝圣,于 1077 年 1 月 28 日在意大利北部的 Canossa 堡垒里请求教宗的宽恕,而教宗恢复了皇帝的教籍。然而,教宗于 1080 年更多地支持 Henricus 在德国的对手 Rudolphus,所以 Henricus 于 1081 年前后率军入侵意大利,1084 年甚至攻克了罗马城,而 Gregorius 被迫逃难,一年后他在 Salerno 去世。

著作:《教宗的规定》(27 条规定,认为教宗有很高的权力,而皇帝的权威也来自教宗),《信集》(360 封信)

028. 《教宗的规定》

教宗 Gregorius VII 的信件集包含一个由 27 条规定组成的文件,通常称之为 *Dictatus Papae*,虽然该文献并没以这种书名问世。它大概于 1075 年成书;一些专家曾认为这些原则是一部计划的教会法典的章节标题。内容反映出当时 Gregorius 和教会的改革者眼中对教宗权柄的崇高理想。应该注意的是这一点:在 1000 年到 1200 年的两个世纪中,大部分的原则逐渐被落实,但在 Gregorius 教宗的时期其中有很多要求仍是一种不现实的理想,远远无法执行。部分的原则针对 1054 年和 Constantinopolis 教会发生的冲突和教会的分裂。

教宗的规定包括:1)主基督创立了罗马教会。2)只有罗马的主教正当地被称为"普世的"主教。3)只有他(教宗)能罢免主教或恢复主教的职位。4)即使教宗特使本身的地位不高,但在一个主教会议上,他应该有首要的地位并可以审判或罢免主教们。5)教宗可以罢免那些不在场的人。6)信徒们不应该和教宗所开除的人居住在同一个房子内。7)只有教宗能够合法地宣布一些新的、回应时代需要的法律,只有他能组织新的修会或将司铎团改成隐修院;只有他能分开一个富有的教区或合并一些穷的教区。8)(在一切圣职人员中)只有教宗可以使用帝王的象征(Quod solus possit uti im-

Gregorius VII / Gregory VII

Opera: *Dictatus Papae, Epistulae*
Works: *The Dictate of the Pope, Letters*

028. *Dictatus Papae / The Dictate of the Pope*

The collection of the letters of Pope Gregory VII contains a list of 27 short principles commonly known as *Dictatus Papae*, although the document was never published as such. It was probably composed in spring of 1075. Scholars have suggested that they might have been the headings of a planned collection of canon law. The declarations represent the high view of papal power which was dominant among Gregory and the Church reformers of that period. It is important to know that in the period from 1000 to 1200 most of the declarations became gradually true, but in Gregory's own day many of the demands were wishful thinking and far from being implemented. Some of the declarations aim at the schism with Constantinople that had taken place in 1054.

The declarations are: 1.That the Roman Church was founded by the Lord alone. 2. That only the Roman bishop is rightly called "universal". 3. That he [the Pope] alone can depose or reinstate bishops. 4. That his legate, even if of lower grade, takes precedence in a council over all bishops and can give sentence of deposition against them. 5. That the Pope can depose those who are absent. 6. That, among other things, we should not stay in the same house with those excommunicated by him. 7. That for him alone it is lawful to enact new laws for the need of the time, to assemble together new congregations, to make an abbey of a canonry and vice versa; and to divide a rich bishopric and unite poor ones. 8. That only the Pope [among other clerics] can use imperial symbols (Quod solus possit uti imperialibus insigniis.) 9. That only the feet of the pope should be kissed by all kings (Quod solius papae pedes omnes principes deosculentur). 10. That his name alone is to be recited in churches. 11. That his title is unique in the world. 12. That he may depose emperors (Quod illi liceat imperatores deponere.) 13. That he may transfer bishops from one see to another, if necessity requires it.

perialibus insigniis)。9)只有教宗的脚可以获得一切国王的亲脚礼(Quod solius papae pedes omnes principes deosculentur)。10)只有他的名字可以在各地教堂中宣读。11)教宗的尊号在全世界中是独一无二的。12)教宗可以弹劾皇帝(Quod illi liceat imperatores deponere)。13)如果需要这样做,教宗可以命令主教离开自己的教区并前往其他教区。

14)教宗有权利随意祝圣任何地方教会的圣职人员。15)任何由教宗祝圣的人可以领导某地方的教会,但不应该在该地方教会有服从性的职位;任何由教宗祝圣的人不应该从另一个主教接受更高的铎品。16)除非有教宗的命令,没有任何主教会议可以说自己是"普世的"。17)除非有教宗的批准,没有法规或书本可以被称为是"属教规的"。18)没有人可以纠正教宗的决定,而只有他能纠正一切其他人的决定。19)没有人可以审判教宗。20)没有人可以审判一个向圣座申诉的人。21)任何地方教会的比较重大案件应该向圣座提交。22)正如《圣经》所记载,罗马教会从来没有犯错误,将来也不会犯错误。23)如果罗马的主教是根据教规而祝圣的,他无疑因圣Petrus的功劳而被圣化……24)依赖教宗的命令和允许,臣民可以控诉(他们的领导者)。25)教宗不需要召开主教会议就可以罢除或恢复某一个主教的职位。26)那些不支持罗马教会的人不应该被视为公教徒。27)如果臣民必须服从一些不公正的领导者,教宗可以解开他们服从的义务(Quod a fidelitate iniquorum subjectos potest absolvere)。

14. That he has power to ordain a cleric of any church he wishes. 15. That anyone ordained by the Pope may preside over another church but may not be a subordinate in it; and that one ordained by the Pope should not accept a higher order from another bishop. 16. That no synod should be called "general" without his order. 17. That no law and no book may be regarded canonical without his authority. 18. That his decision ought to be reconsidered by no one and he alone can reconsider the decisions of everyone. 19. That he himself should be judged by no one. 20. That no one should dare to condemn a person appealing to the Apostolic See. 21. That the more important cases of every church should be submitted to it [i. e. the Roman Church]. 22. That the Roman Church has never erred nor will it ever err, as the scripture testifies. 23. That if he has been ordained according to the canons, the Roman bishop is undoubtedly made holy by the merits of blessed Peter, […]. 24. That by his order and permission subjects may accuse [their leaders]. 25. That without a synod he can depose and reinstate bishops. 26. That he should not be considered as Catholic who does not agree with the Roman Church. 27. That he can absolve subjects from their oath of loyalty if they must obey unjust rulers. (Quod a fidelitate iniquorum subjectos potest absolvere.)

第四篇

大学的形成和12世纪的复兴
The Formation of Universities and the Renaissance of the 12th Century
(1080—1200 AD)

• *The Three Philosophers*

安瑟伦（1033—1109）

于 1033 年生于意大利北部 Piemont 地区的 Aosta。他曾在法国地区的几所学校求学，后在法国西北部 Normandie 的 Bec 隐修院成为本笃会会士（1060 年），1079 年被选为院长。他的同乡和老师是 Lanfrancus。在 1093 年 Anselmus 接替 Lanfrancus 之位并担任 Canterbury 的总主教，这样他领导了整个英国教会。当时的英国国王想全面控制教会，所以 Anselmus 需要长期应付来自政治的压力。他两次被迫离开英国，而 1107 年的政教协定才结束了双方的冲突。教会尊称 Anselmus 为圣人和 doctor ecclesiae（圣师）。

著作：《上主为什么降生成人？》、《论恶魔的堕落》、《论神的预知、预先安排、恩典与自由意志的和谐》、《论语文老师》、《以比喻讲述人类的习惯》、《论意志自由》、《论真理》、《信集》、《反驳高尼罗的书》、《独白篇》、《祈祷或默想文集》、《对话篇》（亦译《论道篇》）

029. 《上主为什么降生成人？》

Anselmus 的神学论文成书于 1094—1098 年，旨在为基督论寻找一些理性论证。

作者描述与 Boso 的对话，其中阐述自己的思想，这样他强调那些可以沟通的、合理的论点的重要性超过权威性的论述。第 1 卷勾勒出传统的救恩论：魔鬼控制堕落的人类。人们都有罪，因为他们拒绝上主，而他们的罪要求某种补赎（satisfactio）。然而，任何符合上主旨意的人类行为都是一种取决于上主的行为，所以它无法弥补什么罪责。因此人类无法为 Adam 的犯罪而作出什么补赎：Monstratur, quod secundum mensuram peccati oporteat esse satisfactionem, nec homo eam per se facere possit.（应该说明，补赎应该符合罪恶的严重性，而人类自己无法作这种补赎。）

第 2 卷的开头指出人生的使命：人将要与神合一。只有上主的自由行动能使罪人与上主和好。上主派遣他的儿子耶稣基督，他的死亡和复活是一种补赎，这样他恢复神和人之间的合一。

Anselmus 的论述还包括几个新的因素：救恩被视为神和人之间的事，所有的天使和魔鬼都被排除。Anselmus 并没有引用《圣经》的语句。他那种理性的方法很清楚地强调法律的观点，而根据这个观点正义比仁慈更重要。这些新的层面曾多次受批评，但它们仍然是一种可以参考的思路，与此相反的是一种过分模糊的、主观的思维，一种否认一切先定标准的思想。

030. 《独白篇》

本著作成书于 1076 年，可称为经院哲学的第一部著作，因为它没有提到《圣经》

Anselmus Cantuariensis / Anselm of Canterbury

Opera: *Cur Deus homo, De casu diaboli, De concordia praescientiae, praedestinationis et gratiae Dei cum libero arbitrio, De grammatico, De humanis moribus per similitudines, De libertate arbitrii, De veritate, Epistulae, Liber apologeticus contra Gaunilonem, Monologion, Orationes sive Meditationes, Proslogion*

Works: *Why was God made Man? On the Devil's Fall, On the Harmony of Divine Prescience, Predestination and Grace with the Free Will, On the Grammarian, On Morals, On the Free Will, On Truth, Letters, Letter against Gaunilo, Monologion, Prayers or Meditations, Proslogion*

029. *Cur Deus Homo / Why Was God Made Man?*

Anselm's theological treatise was written in the years 1094—1098 and tries to place Christology on reasonable arguments.

In a dialogue with Boso, Anselm unfolds his thoughts, thus emphasizing the role of communicable and reasonable arguments over against the use of authority. Book 1 outlines the traditional doctrine of salvation: the devil has power over fallen mankind. Human beings are guilty since they rejected God. Their guilt demands some kind of satisfaction. However, any human action that is in accord with the divine will is an action depending on God and thus cannot recompensate guilt. Therefore mankind is unable to give satisfaction for Adam's offence: Monstratur, quod secundum mensuram peccati oporteat esse satisfactionem, nec homo eam per se facere possit. (It is to be shown that according to the measure of sin there should be some satisfaction, and that man could not do this by himself.)

Book 2 starts from the destiny of man: to achieve union with God. Only God's free action can reconcile God and the sinner. He sends His son Jesus Christ whose death and resurrection give satisfaction and restore the unity of God and man.

Anselm's argumentation includes several new elements: salvation is viewed as an event between God and man and excludes angels and devils. Anselm does not quote the Bible. His rational method clearly emphasizes the juridical aspect, according to which justice prevails over mercy. These new dimensions were often criticized but nevertheless offer a remarkable alternative to an overly vage and subjective mode of thought which denies the existence of any preordained standards.

030. *Monologion*

Written in 1076, this work may be called the first treatise of scholasticism since it

和教父们,而是想依靠理性为基督信仰中的一神论和三位一体的教导建立一个基础。这种努力的前提是:人心能够通过思辨而达到信仰的基本真理。因此,Anselmus 使用一些简单的逻辑推理来引导读者达到最高深的形而上学真理:体验到不同程度的完美导致最高的存在(最高的实体),它是自立的并照亮一切其他事物。这个最高的实体创造一切事物。本论文的主要部分讨论三位一体,而三位一体的奥迹反映人心的三个主要活动:意识或记忆力(memoria)、理智或理解的能力(intellectus),以及意志力(voluntas)或爱(amor)。人们都应该发展这种内在的形象,并对于最高的存在(神)怀着纯粹的爱。这种爱应该是永恒的,而因此人的心灵也应该是永恒的。为了转向最高的美善,人的灵魂需要有希望(spes)与信仰(fides)。最终 Anselmus 解释说,"最高的存在"就是上主,即宇宙的创造者和统治者。

031. 《对话篇》

本神学论文是 Anselmus 大约在 1077 年写成的,即在写 Monologion 不久之后。该著作的目标是证明上主的存在,而这种证明依赖于一个特殊的论点。正如"前言"所说,这种推理是"寻求理解的信仰"(fides quaerens intellectum)的表现。

Anselmus 从基督信仰的基本原则入手:上主的伟大超越一切万在,而我们无法想象出一个比上主更伟大的实在:Credimus te esse aliquid quo nihil maius cogitari potest.(我们相信你是一种不能设想更大的实在。)Anselmus 的观点是这样的:如果有这样的概念,那么它不可能是一种纯粹在想象中存在的实在,而必须有现实上的存在,因为如果它没有真正的存在等于说这是一种缺点或可以超越的因素。任何实在的东西都超越一个虚构的东西。

根据同样的论点 Anselmus 还试图肯定神的其他特征:上主是最高的存在,他是独立的自立体,他是万有的创造者,是全知的,爱一切的,又是正义的。上主是正义的,而因为他的正义是完美的,他甚至可以拯救那些应受惩罚的灵魂们。他的权力能使恶人成为好人。因为上主的美善也是完美的,他对一切存在都是善良的,不仅仅对好人是善的。

Anselmus 关于神的存在的证明只依赖于"神的概念"而不需要对物质世界的任何观察。这种证论曾被称为"上主存在的本体论证明"。与他同时代的人,比如隐修者 Gaunilo 已经试图反驳这种思想并认为某个事物的理念并不能证明这个事物的现实存在。在他的回答中 Anselmus 说上主的存在与其他事物的存在是不同的,因为上主是一种必然的存在。在哲学史上,Thomas Aquinas 和 Kant 反对了 Anselmus 的论点,但 Franciscani 学派(比如 Bonaventura 等人)以及 Descartes、Leibniz 和 Hegel 的立场比较多地支持"本体论证明"。

sets aside Biblical and patristic authorities and tries to employ reason in order to find a basis for the Christian doctrine of God and the Trinity. The premise is that the human mind is able to arrive at the basic truths of the faith through speculation. Thus Anselm uses simple logical conclusions to lead the reader to an understanding of the highest metaphysical truths: the experience of different degrees of perfection leads to the highest being (a highest substance) which is self-supportive and enlightens all other things. This highest substance creates all things. The main part of the treatise discusses the Trinity, which reflects the three main activities of the soul: consciousness or memory (memoria), intellect or the capacity of understanding (intellectus) and will (voluntas) or love (amor). The task of any person is to develop this inner image towards the pure love of the highest being (God). This love must be eternal and thus the human soul must be eternal. In order to be oriented towards the highest good, the soul must have hope (spes) and faith (fides). Finally Anselm reveals that the "highest being" is identical with God, the creator and ruler of the universe.

031. *Proslogion*

Anselm wrote this theological treatise ca. in 1077, shortly after the *Monologion*. The purpose of the work is to prove the existence of God relying on only one special argument. As the prooemium formulates, this kind of reasoning is "faith searching for understanding" (fides quaerens intellectum).

Anselm starts from a basic tenet of the Christian faith: God surpasses all things in His greatness, and it is impossible to conceive of anything greater: Credimus te esse aliquid quo nihil maius cogitari potest. (We believe that you are something of which it is not possible to think something greater.) The argument raised by Anselm is that such an idea cannot only be a pure mental concept but must also exist in reality, since anything that does not exist in reality is somewhat imperfect and surpassable. Any fiction can be outshined by something real.

Anselm uses this same argument to confirm all other qualities of God. God is the highest being, He exists in Himself, He is the creator of all, omnipotent and all-loving and just. God is just, and since His justice is perfect he can even save those who deserve punishment. His power can even change evil people into good ones. Since God's goodness is perfect, He is good to all, not only to the good.

Anselm's proof of the existence of God is only based on the idea of God and does not need any observation of the material world; this proof has been called "ontological proof of the existence of God". Already contemporaries like the monk Gaunilo attacked this kind of thinking by raising the objection that the idea of a thing cannot prove its existence in reality. In his reply Anselm says that God's existence is different from other beings, since God is a necessary being. In the history of philosophy Thomas Aquinas and Kant rejected Anselm's argument, whereas the Franciscan School (Bonaventure and others), Descartes, Leibnitz and Hegel took a more supportive stance towards the "ontological proof".

布拉格的科斯玛斯(1045—1125)

这位大概属于捷克民族的学者是第一位捷克历史学家。他有妻子但与 Praga 大教堂的圣职团有关系,曾为 Praga 的主教工作,他也是 canonicus(大教堂圣职团团员)。

著作:《波希米亚人的历史》

032. 《波希米亚人的历史》

作者曾是 Praga 的圣职人员,但并没有成为如部分书籍所说的 Praga 的主教。在他的晚年他编写了波希米亚(今天的捷克地区)的第一部历史书。他没有很仔细地搜集早期的文献,但更多地想编写那些和他祖国有关系的传说和故事。他完全忽略某些重要的事件,比如 Henricus IV 皇帝和 Gregorius VII 教宗之间的冲突。这部著作没有遵守历史学的严格规则,因此也出现一些时代记载的错误,所以整部书在某些方面很不可靠。Cosmas 有一次写道:"就这一段落而言,希望读者自己决定这是虚构的还是真实的。"然而,因为 Cosmas 的著作是波希米亚早期历史方面的第一部研究,所以后来的一切相关的著作都必须提到它。

本著作使用一篇《圣经》故事作为开端,即人类在建立 Babylon 塔后解散的事件。某一位 Croccos(他的名字来自 Cracovia / Cracow 城,在今天的波兰)有三个女儿,她们将魔术和占卜方面的知识传入波希米亚。她们中最聪明的是 Libussa,而她和当地的君王 Przemysl 结婚,这样他们共同奠定了波希米亚国的基础。本著作的论述包含许多有关教会、一些主教、隐修者、殉道者的资料。很多章节揭露出一种反对德国人的态度。Cosmas 说德国人是骄傲的,他们始终看不起斯拉夫人和斯拉夫人的语言。

第 2 卷记载从 1038 年到 1092 年所发生的事。在他们的公爵 Bretislav I 的领导之下,波希米亚人攻击波兰,但在另一方面德国国王 Henricus III 率军入侵波希米亚地区。第 3 卷叙述后来所发生的事,一直到作者自己的时代(到 1125 年为止),其中描述 Bretislav II 王的统治和他与别的斯拉夫国度及匈牙利的关系。Bretislav 的继承人是 Borivoy、Wladislav 和 Sobieslav。

Cosmas Pragensis / Cosmas of Prague

Opera: *Chronica Bohemorum*
Works: *Chronicle of the Bohemians*

032. *Chronica Bohemorum / Chronicle of the Bohemians*

The author was a clergyman in Prague but was never bishop of Prague as some sources say. In his old age he wrote this first history of Bohemia. He did not carefully collect earlier records but rather wants to compile the legends and stories connected with his fatherland. Some important events are not even mentioned, for example the conflict between emperor Henry IV and Pope Gregory VII. The work does not follow the strict rules of historiography and there are some chronological mistakes, thus it is not very reliable in some regards. At one passage Cosmas writes: "May the reader decide whether the lines above are fiction or reality." However, since Cosmas' work is the first account of the early history of Bohemia, all later studies were bound to at least mention it.

The first book starts with the Biblical story of the dispersion of mankind after building the tower of Babylon. The three daughters of a certain Croccos (derived from the city of Cracow, now in Poland) introduce divination and magic to Bohemia. Finally the cleverest of them (Libussa) marries the local king Przemysl, and together they lay the foundations of the kingdom of Bohemia. The narrative contains much material about the Church, about bishops, monks and martyrs. Many passages betray an anti-German attitude. Cosmas says that the Germans are proud and always have looked down on the Slavs and their languages.

The second book records the events from 1038 to 1092 AD. Under their Duke Bretislav I the Bohemians attack Poland, but the German king Henry III on the other hand leads campaigns against Bohemia. The third book leads the story up to the last years of the author himself (until the year 1125). The narrative describes the reign of king Bretislav II and his relations to other Slavic states and to Hungary. The successors of Bretislav are Borivoy, Wladislav, and Sobieslav.

涅斯托尔（约 1056—1113）

Nestorius 曾是（今俄罗斯）Kiova（基辅）地区的"山洞隐修院"中的隐修士，他编写了几部圣人传记。根据 13 世纪的传统说法，他是 *Povest'* 的作者，但实际上，这部东斯拉夫最早的历史书来自 11 世纪 30 年代，而 Nestorius 仅仅编修了其中的部分文献。

著作：《往年故事》（《俄罗斯编年史》，约 1112 年完成，关于斯拉夫人早期历史的最重要文献，在 Kiev 编写的，叙述 Kiev 的创立，Rus 于 988 年接受基督信仰等；语言：古教会斯拉夫语，古俄语）；还有 Boris、Gleb 和隐修院院长 St. Theodosius 的传记。

033. 《往年故事》

本作品的语言部分是古俄罗斯语，部分是古教会斯拉夫语，并与 Kiova 总教区的创立（1039 年）有关系。因此，该作品的基本态度是脱离 Byzantion 并确保独立，而 Kiova 国的建立是该著作的重点关注。

编年体的元年是世界的创造，而这个事件的年代被规定为公元前 5508 年。（俄罗斯人的历史学一直到彼得大帝都保持了这种编年写法。）本历史书在开始描述 Noah 的儿子们 Shem、Ham 与 Japheth 如何划分世界各地的地区。斯拉夫民族是 Japheth 的后代。在公元一世纪，Andreias 宗徒/使徒曾来过俄罗斯地区并首次在那里传播基督信仰。这种传说很明显表达一种反拜占庭的态度。三个俄罗斯兄弟，即 Kij、Scek 和 Choriv 建立了 Kiova 城，这是最古老的俄罗斯国。根据这部历史书，Kiova 城的奠立发生在 Varangii（北方民族）的到来之前，即是 850 年之前。俄罗斯人于 852 年开始攻击 Constantinopolis，后来与该城签订了一些条约。Rus 国与其首都 Kiova 于 988 年转向基督信仰，当时的国王 Vladimir Svjatoslavic 接受洗礼并与 Constantinopolis 的公主 Anna 结婚。一个比较重要的国王是"智慧的"Yaroslav（1019—1054 年），他曾抵抗突厥人的游牧部落并引导自己的国度走向一个文化繁荣的时期。

这部历史书的一个版本包含 Vladimir Monomachos 大公的自传，而这个文献反映出一个强大的基督徒国王的政治理想。国王应该是一个有责任感的人，他需要为民众的政治性和精神性需要服务。Vladimir 强调说一个领导需要有军事力量、精力与恒心，但他也必须有诚心，必须爱慕真理，他应该遵守誓言和契约，同时也应该是一位公道的、温和的与仁慈的统治者，因为这才符合一个基督徒国王的风度。除此之外，一个统治者要获得良好的教育，他也必须会外语，这样才能够良好地为自己的国度服务。

Nestorius / Nestor

Opera: *Povest' vremennykh let*
Works: *Tale of Bygone Years*

033. *Povest' vremennykh let / Tale of Bygone Years*

This work is written partly in Old Russian language, partly in Old Church Slavonic and is connected to the establishment of the metropolitan diocese of Kiova (Kiev) in 1039, thus the general attitude is centered on the securing of independence from Byzanz, and emphasis is laid on the foundation of the state of Kiova.

The chronology starts from the creation of the world in the year 5508 BC. (The Russian calendar kept this traditional chronology until the time of Peter the Great.) The chronicle sets out with the partition of the regions of the world among the sons of Noah, Shem, Ham, and Japheth. The Slavic nations are descendents of the tribe of Japhet. The apostle Andrew visits the country in the first century and thereby introduces Christianity for the first time. This legend clearly betrays an anti–Byzantine attitude. The Russian brothers Kij, Scek and Choriv found Kiev, the oldest Russian state. According to the chronicle this happened even before the invasion of the Varangians (Norsemen) who arrived around 850. The Russians start to carry on wars against Constantinople in 852 and sign treaties with that city. The country of Rus with its capital in Kiova is converted to Christianity in 988, when king Vladimir Svjatoslavic is baptized and marries princess Anna from Constantinople. One of the more important kings was Yaroslav the Wise of Kiev (1019—1054) who fought wars against the Turkic nomads and led his country to cultural prosperity.

One edition of the chronicle contains an autobiography of Grand Duke Vladimir Monomachos which reflects the political ideal of a powerful Christian ruler: a king living up to this ideal should be a dutiful servant of the political and spiritual needs of his people. Vladimir emphasizes that a leader needs military strength, energy and perseverance, but he must also cherish honesty and truthfulness, he is bound to keep oaths and treaties, must be just, mild, and merciful as is fitting for a Christian king. Besides that a ruler has to get a good education and needs to know foreign languages in order to serve his nation well.

阿伯拉尔(1079—1142)

他于 1079 年生于法国北部 Nantes 地区的 Le Pallet 的骑士家庭，曾在 Paris 学习逻辑学，其老师是 Roscellinus de Compiegne 和 Guilelmus de Champeaux。在 1102—1109 年间他自己成为教师，1113 年向 Anselmus de Laon 学习神学，1114 年后在 Paris 的 Notre-Dame 大教堂学校任教，大概也是该学院的校长。同时他也担任家庭教师并爱上了他的学生 Heloise(1100—1164 年)，与她有一个孩子(名为 Astrolabius)并于 1118 年秘密与其结婚，但她的叔叔 Fulbertus 反对这种关系并唆使人阉割了 Abaelardus。此后 Abaelardus 进入 St.Denis 隐修院，并劝 Heloise 也进入了 Argenteuil 修女院。Abaelardus 继续任教，但 1121 年在 Soissons 召开的主教会议谴责他的著作 *Theologia summi boni*。他在 Nogent-sur-Seine 创立了 Le Paraclet 学校和隐修院团体（后来 Heloise 从 1135 年到 1164 年任该团体的院长）。Abaelardus 从 1127 年到 1133 年任 St. Gildas 隐修院(在 Bretagne 地区)的院长，后又回 Paris 任教，但于 1140 年他的思想再次被谴责，因为 Bernardus 反对他的观点。在 1140 年 Abaelardus 进入 Cluny 隐修院，在那里的院长 Petrus Venerabilis 很友善地照顾了他。

著作:《致儿子 Astrolabius》、《反驳 Bernardus 的表白》、《犹太和基督徒哲学家的对话》、《伦理学"认识你自己"》、《自传》、《逻辑学》、《是与否》、《神学体系》、《至善的神学》(改写为《基督宗教神学》)

034.《是与否》

这部神学论文在 1121 年和 1140 年间被修改多次。Abaelardus 的研究方法对后来的经院思想家产生很大的影响。

这本书的 158 个论题(quaestiones)分为三个部分:第 1~105 点涉及到信仰的问题，第 106~135 点谈论诸圣事(sacramenta)，而 136~158 点解释基督徒的爱。作者从《圣经》和教父文献列出很多"语句"(sententiae)，他引用了 1800 多个这样的格言。因为不同的作者或不同的圣经语句似乎对同样的问题给予不同的回答，Abaelardus 在前言提出一些重要的诠释学(解释学)原则，根据这些原则可以在不一致的甚至矛盾的语句中辨认真理:同样的言辞(voces)可以有不同的意义(significatio);有的作者使用一种比较通俗的表达方式来适应某些读者;某些无名的著作被归于古代的权威性人物;有的作者在晚年收回早期的著作(比如 Augustinus 与他的 *Retractationes*);特殊的时期或特殊的情况导致特殊的说话方式等等。如果某些语句呈现出一种直接的矛盾，逻辑学的分析就必须让步，必须用"权威"(一般指《圣经》)来解决该问题。《圣经》

Petrus Abaelardus /Abelard (Abailard)

Opera: *Ad Astrolabium filium, Apologia contra Bernardum, Dialogus inter philosophum Judaeum et Christianum, Ethica seu Liber "Scito te ipsum", Historia calamitatum, Logica "ingredientibus", Sic et non, Theologia "Scholarium", Theologia Summi boni(Theologia christiana)*

Works: *To my Son Astrolabius, Apology against Bernard, Dialog between a Jewish and a Christian philosopher, Ethics or "Know thyself", History of Calamities, Logic, Yes and No, Theology "Scholarium", Theology of the Highest Good* (reworked under the title *Christian Theology*)

034. *Sic et non* / Yes and No

This theological treatise was reworked several times in the years between 1121 and 1140. Abelard's method became very important for later scholastic thinkers.

The 158 quaestiones (points to be debated) of the book are divided into three groups: 1~105 pertain to the matters of faith, 106~135 are concerned with the sacraments, and the quaestiones 136~158 are about Christian love. The author lists up many statements (sententia) from the Bible and from patristic literature, he quotes more than 1800 of these authoritative sentences. Since different authors or different Bible quotations seem to give different answers to the same questions, Abelard presents in the prologue a number of important hermeneutic rules to discern the truth of diverging or even contradictory statements: the same words (voces) can have different meanings (significationes); some authors used more colloquial expressions in order to be understood by a certain group of readers; apocryphal writings were ascribed to ancient authorities; some authors revoked in their later life what they had written formerly (like Augustinus in his *Retractationes*); special times or occasions allow for exceptions. If the sentences are in a clear contradiction, the dialectical method and logical analysis must cede to an authority (especially the Bible) for a decision. The Bible cannot be treated like later commentaries to Biblical texts, because the Bible itself is sacred and must never be doubted,

本身与其他的著作不同,它是神圣的,不能怀疑的;《圣经》的文本错误,也许是因为后人的传授有问题,翻译者的翻译不全面或者读者的理解能力有限。

  早期的作者也曾使用这种"并列"方式,即将一些表面上是矛盾的语句并列,比如Augustinus、Gregorius Magnus、Charlemagne时代的作者、Abaelardus同时代的人Anselmus de Laon、Guilelmus de Saint-Thierry（后来成为Abaelardus的对手）。然而Abaelardus的著作第一次很系统地罗列"是"与"否"、"正"和"反",而且他也第一次全面使用"辩证的方式",这样他可以指出这一点:如果那些auctoritates(权威性的作者或文献)导致一种aporia(思想上的疑难),那么人的理性(ratio)需要作出最后的决定,包括在信仰的问题上也是这样。毫无疑问,Abaelardus并不想传播一种怀疑主义或理性主义的态度。他并不怀疑神圣的启示,但他想表明《圣经》和基督宗教传统的文献中的语句记载的多样性。然而,这种询问、怀疑、比较和相对化的过程也激发了一些反对他的观点。

there is only the possibility of a faulty transmission of the text, of a mistake made by a translator or of a limited understanding of the reader.

Earlier authors used the juxtaposition of seemingly contrary sentences, for example Augustine, Gregory the Great, authors of Charlemagne's time or Abelards contemporaries, his teacher Anselm of Laon and William of Saint-Thierry, his later opponent. However, Abelard's work is the first that systematically lists up "yes" and "no", thesis and antithesis, and he is also the first to consistently use the dialectical method, thereby showing that if the auctoritates (authoritative authors or texts) lead to an aporia, human reason (ratio) is the last resort, also in matters of faith. Abelard's intention is certainly not to promote an attitude of skepticism and rationalism. He does not doubt the truth of divine revelation but wants to show the plurality of verbal expressions in Bible and Christian tradition. However the necessary process of questioning, doubting, comparing and relativizing incited opposition against his method.

马梅斯布里(约 1080—1142)

　　1080 年生于英国南部,后进入 Malmesbury 的本笃会隐修院,在那里获得教育并成为修士,曾任图书馆的馆长。他循从 Beda 的传统编写了一些包含丰富历史资料的历史学著作。他受过古典教育,知识很渊博,文笔优美简明,因此被视为当时最重要的英国史学家。

　　著作:《Glastonia 教会的历史》、《英国诸主教历史》、《英国史》、《Dunstanus 传记》

035. 《英国史》

　　这部具有重大影响的著作分为 5 卷,保存有 3 个版本(1120 年、1128 年和 1140 年的版本),这些版本陆续叙述最近几年所发生的事件。作者引用 Beda 的著作和其他比较可靠的文献来编写自己关于英国历史的著作。

　　第 1 卷在开头描述 Anglosaxones 于 449 年到达英国的事,并叙述英国历史一直到 Egbertus 王的统治(802—839 年)。第 2 卷继续谈论英国史到征服者 William,他于 1066 年在 Hastings 交战中战胜了 Anglosaxones。第 2 卷也包含很多关于德国、法国、意大利等欧洲地区的资料。本卷提供很多有关 Gerbertus de Aurillac(即后来的教宗 Silvester II,999—1003 年在位)的故事,他曾是当时最优秀的数学家和非常渊博的学者。他与德国皇帝的关系很好,并且支持波兰和匈牙利的基督徒国王(比如匈牙利的 Stephanus 王)。因为他的知识很渊博,他被视为一个魔术家,与古代的"学者、先知和预言家"Vergilius 有点相似。

　　第 3 卷覆盖征服者 William 的统治(1066—1087 年)。他必须镇压很多反对诺曼人的起义并且逐渐以诺曼底地区的教士取代了 Anglosaxoni 的教会领导。他与 Canterbury 总主教 Lanfranc 一起试图改革社会和教会,比如他落实了教宗法院和世俗法院的分开。

　　第 4、5 卷描述作者生活的时代。他深入地叙述了第一次十字军运动(1097—1099 年)。拜占庭的皇帝 Alexios I 曾于 1095 年要求教宗 Urbanus II 协助东方的信徒,而教宗劝勉人们去解放耶路撒冷。因此一些贵族人士率领几个骑士队前往东方,他们于 1097 年在拜占庭聚集,此后一起向圣地以色列迈进。他们于 1099 年攻克了耶路撒冷并建立了四个十字军国度,又与本地的人口结合。(这些十字军国都在一段时间后归于穆斯林的统治:Edessa 于 1144 年,Antiochia 于 1268 年,Tripolis 于 1289 年,而 Jerusalem 于 1291 年。)

Guilelmus Malmesburiensis / Wilhelm of Malmesbury

Opera: *De antiquitate Glastoniensis ecclesiae, Gesta pontificum Anglorum, Gesta regum Anglorum, Vita s. Dunstani*

Works: *On the History of the Church of Gloucester, The Achievements of the English Bishops, History of English Kings, Life of Saint Dunstan*

035. *Gesta regum Anglorum / History of English Kings*

This monumental work in 5 books is preserved in 3 versions (of 1120, 1128, and of 1140) which successively lead the narrative up to the latest events. The author used Beda and other quite reliable sources for his own account of English history.

Book 1 starts with the arrival of the Anglosaxons in England in the year 449 AD and ends with the reign of king Egbertus (802—839 AD). Book 2 continues the progress of events until the victory of William the Conqueror in 1066 who defeated the Anglosaxons at the battle of Hastings. The second book also contains information about events in Germany, France, Italy and other European regions. This volume reports many stories and legends about Gerbert of Aurillac (= Pope Silvester II, 999—1003), who was the leading mathematician of his time and a scholar of universal erudition. He had very good connections to the German Emperor and as Pope supported the Catholic rulers in Poland and Hungary (King Stephen). Because of his profound learning he was regarded as a kind of wizard, similar to Vergilius, the scholarly wise man and diviner of antiquity.

Book 3 covers the reign of William the Conqueror (1066—1087) who had to suppress many rebellions against the Normans and gradually replaced Anglosaxon Church leaders with those from the Normandy. Together with Lanfranc, the Archbishop of Canterbury, he reformed society and Church of England, for example he implemented the separation of ecclesiastical and secular courts.

Books 4 and 5 describe the times of the author himself. He gives a broad account of the first crusade (1097—1099). Emperor Alexios I of Byzanz had asked the Pope Urbanus II in 1095 to support the Christians of the East, and the Pope urged the liberation of Jerusalem. Thus groups of knights under aristocratic leadership met in Constantinople in 1097 and from there advanced toward the Holy Land. They managed to conquer Jerusalem in 1099 and established four crusader states, mixing with the local population. (All these crusader states fell back to Muslim rule after some time: Edessa in 1144, Antioch in 1268, Tripolis in 1289, and Jerusalem in 1291).

阿纳·康尼纳(1083—1148)

这位女作家是拜占庭皇帝 Alexios Komnēnos（阿历克塞·康尼努斯,1048—1118 年,在位 1081—1118 年）的女儿。她曾学习文学、哲学、历史学以及地理学,受过良好的教育。她与 Bryennium 的领导 Nikēphoros Bryennios(1062—1138 年)结婚并曾经与自己的母亲 Irēnē 一起致力于劝阻 Alexios 不让他的儿子 Iōannēs II Komnēnos 继承皇位,因为她认为她的丈夫 Nikēphoros 应该成为皇帝。当她的弟兄 Iōannēs 于 1118 年登基时,她还组织人们推翻他的政权,但被发现,因此她失去了一切财产并退隐到一所隐修院,在那里编写了她的名著。

著作：《阿历克塞亚斯》

036. 《阿历克塞亚斯》

这部分为 15 卷的历史研究是由 Alexios Komnēnos I（1081—1118 年间任拜占庭皇帝）的女儿 Anna Komnēnē 编写的。Anna Komnēnē 想颂扬其父的丰功伟业。这部著作写成于 1148 年并就拜占庭帝国 1069—1118 年间的历史阶段而言它是最重要的历史资料。Anna 的丈夫 Nikēphoros Bryennios(1062—1138 年)曾经撰写了关于 1070—1079 年时期的著作,而 Anna 继续了他的工作。

正如书名所暗示的那样,Anna 想强调其父亲 Alexios 的贡献——他曾经引导拜占庭走向相当的繁荣与和平。本著作描述拜占庭在 11 世纪末和 12 世纪初的文化和学术生活,尤其注意到宗教的领域和当时的十字军运动。Anna 因自己的文化遗产而感到很自豪,她居高临下地对待那些从西方来的骑士们。她认为唯独拜占庭可以算作古典文化传统的真正继承者,而她的优越感大概也代表着东方人对于拉丁地区的人的普遍态度。Anna 曾获得了非常高级的教育,所以她的文笔试图模仿古典雅典的希腊语。她经常引用 Homēros、Aristotelēs、Thoukydidēs 等古代作家。

Anna Komnēnē / Anna Comnene

Opera: *Alexias*
Works: *Alexiad*

036. *Alexias / Alexiad*

This historical narrative in 15 books was written by Anna Comnene, the daughter of Alexius Comnenus I, Emperor of Byzanz from 1081 to 1118. Anna Comnene wanted to glorify the achievements of her father. The work was finished in 1148 and counts as the most important historical source for the history of the Byzantine Empire in the period from 1069 to 1118. Anna's husband Nicephorus Bryennius (1062—1138) had compiled a detailed account of the years from 1070 to 1079, and Anna continued his study.

As the title suggests, Anna wants to highlight the merits of her father Alexius who led Byzanz into an era of relative prosperity and peace. The narrative depicts the cultural and intellectual life of Byzanz at the late 11th and early 12th centuries. The developments in the area of religion and the crusades receive special attention. Anna is proud of her own cultural heritage and looks with disdain on the barbarian knights coming from the western regions to the East. She thinks that only Byzanz is to be seen as the true heir of the riches of the classical tradition, and her feeling of superiority most probably mirrors the general attitude of the people in the East towards the Latin speaking world. Having received excellent education Anna writes in a style imitating classical Attic Greek. She often quotes from Homer, Aristotle, Thucydides and many other authors.

伯尔纳德(1091—1153)

他于 1090 年或 1091 年在 Burgund 贵族的家庭出生(出生地是 Fontaines-les-Dijon),还有 5 个弟兄和 1 个姐姐。他曾在 Chatillon 的隐修院上学,在 1111 年聚集了 30 个朋友并于 1112 年和他们一起进入 Citeaux 的隐修院(Cistercians 即"熙笃"会这个名称来自 Citeaux)。因为此时有很多人加入修会,所以他们能够建立一些新的分院:La Ferte(1113 年)、Pontigny(1114 年)、Morimond(1115 年);Bernardus 自己成为 Clairvaux(拉丁语 Claravallis"明谷")隐修院的院长,后来一直到晚年他继续建立了一些分院,他总共创立了 68 处隐修院,引导熙笃会的快速发展。通过一些书信他推动了隐修院生活和教会生活的改革,曾保卫正统教会,反对 antipope(对立教宗)。他曾前往法国南部、意大利、德国,在各地和教会的长上会谈。1135 年他参与 Pisa 的主教会议,在 Aquitania(法国南部)反对清洁派,1146 年在德国宣讲和鼓励第二场十字军运动,1148 年参与 Reims 的主教会议。他的一切作品都是以优美的拉丁语写的,因为他的语气充满感情和感召力,他获得了 doctor mellifluus ("流蜜博士")的尊称。他对圣母 Maria(玛利亚)也怀有特别的尊敬,并根据新 Plato 主义和 Augustinus 的思想强调人需要爱神,需要(通过隐修生活和灵修)上升到神的面前,而不应该使用理性的分析将神拉下到人间。因此,他反对 Abelardus 等人的经院思想。他的思想影响曾对 Wolfram de Eschenbach、Joachim de Fiore、Bonaventura、Jan Hus、Dante、Gerson、Eckhart、Luther、Calvin 等人产生了影响。

著作:《反驳 Abaelardus 的错误》、《论反省》(5 卷,给教宗写的,论教会的情况)、《论皈依》、《论爱神》、《论谦虚和骄傲的等级》、《论恩宠和自由意志》、《论圣殿军团》、《论主教的职务》、《讲演》(包括关于 Canticum canticorum《雅歌》的讲演,即上主与灵魂之间的爱情);还有讲道稿和 500 多封信。

037. 《论反省》

这部伦理道德和政治性文章曾经被称为 Bernardus 最伟大的著作。它于 1149—1153 年间成书并是一种"完美教会领导者"的手册。Bernardus 针对的人是他原先的学生和朋友,现在他成了教宗(即 Eugenius III,1145—1153 年在位),而 Bernardus 劝勉他。

一个教宗不可以忘记自己的局限性,他必须是一个谦逊的人。他需要始终记得自己灵魂的拯救(consideratio),这样他才能够帮助别人。一个教宗应该想起古代教会的伟大教会领袖,比如 Gregorius Magnus 教宗——这些伟人能够成为自己的榜样。最关键的是,一个教宗必须选择一些有能力的、虔诚的人作为他的助手和枢机主教。Petrus 的继承人(即教宗)需要始终为信徒们服务。"你当领导应该是为了服务,而不

Bernardus Claravallensis / Bernard de Clairvaux

Opera: *Contra errores Abaelardi, De consideratione (De consideratione libri V ad Eugenium Papam), De conversione, De diligendo Deo, De gradibus humilitatis et superbiae, De gratia et libero arbitrio, De laude novae militiae ad milites templi, De moribus et officio episcoporum, Sermones*

Works: *Against the Errors of Abaelard, On Consideration, On Conversion, On Divine Love, On the Stages of Humility and Pride, On Grace and the Free Will, On the Knights of the Temple, On the Office of Bishops, Sermons*

037. *De consideratione / On Consideration*

This moral and political treatise has been called the most important of Bernard's works. It was written between 1149 and 1153 and is a kind of "manual of a perfect ecclesiastical leader". Bernard addresses his former student and friend who has become Pope now (Eugene III, 1145—1153) and admonishes him.

A pope must not forget his own limitations, he needs to be humble. Only if he keeps the salvation of his soul in mind (consideratio), he will be able to help others. A pope should remember the great Church leaders of antiquity, for example Pope Gregory the Great, and take them as models for his own actions. It is crucial that a pope selects able and pious people to be his co-workers and cardinals. The successor of Peter should always be serving the faithful. "You should be a leader in order to serve, not to dominate." (Praeses ut prosis non ut imperes. 2,6) The pope should also know that he has to fulfill certain duties towards non-Christians, for example preaching the gospel to them. Bernard thinks that violence from the side of the Muslims might be resisted or repelled by violence. However, the conversion of the infidels should be brought about "by the word rather than by the sword".

是为了控制人们。"(Praeses ut prosis non ut imperes, 2,6)教宗应该知道他也对那些非基督徒需要承担一些责任,比如需要向他们宣布福音。Bernardus 认为可以使用暴力来抵抗穆斯林军的攻击,但非基督徒的皈依"更多取决于言辞,而不依赖于刀剑"。

Bernardus 首次使用"两把剑"的比喻来说明教宗的权柄:教宗从神那里获得了两把剑,即精神性的权力和世俗性的权力。然而,教宗自己应该仅仅使用言辞的权柄(即精神性的力量)。在需要的情况下,教宗可以请求皇帝来保卫教会的权利,而这时皇帝可以运用世俗的(军事)力量。然而,如果皇帝侵犯教会的权利,教宗应该要勇敢地和坚定地抵抗他。因为 Bernardus 也批评教宗的奢侈生活——教宗"身穿丝绸,以宝石和黄金为装饰,瑞士卫兵将他的轿子抬来抬去"——曾有人将他比作 Martin Luther。Luther 在 400 年后曾写过类似的语句,但他的基本态度是不一样的。

038.《论爱神》

这部教义性的文章完成于 1126 年。

在开头 Bernardus 提出他最喜欢的原则之一:"对神的爱是从哪里来的?是从神来的。而爱神的程度是什么?无限度的爱。"(Causa diligendi Deum Deus est, modus sine modo diligere. 1,1)对 Bernardus 来说,感情性的爱是最核心的问题,而理性上的掌握是从这个基本态度的延伸:"人们在什么程度上爱一件事就是在这样的程度上理解它。"(Res in tantum intelligitur, in quantum amatur.)基督成为人并被钉在十字架上,这都是为了表现神对我们的爱。因为神在人性中受苦,他赢得了被爱的完美权利。神完全应当获得我们的爱,而他自己是神圣灵魂们的食粮,即拯救那些被俘虏的人的祭品。神不仅仅给予生命,他还给予救恩,这样应该"无限地"(sine modo)被爱。每一个活的人都应该对神表达来自内心的感恩。如果一个人爱神,他一般会经过这几个步骤:首先一个人靠自己的感性欲望爱自己;在这个阶段中对神的爱是隐藏的,这是一种准备阶段。第二个阶段是一种比较有意识的神爱,但这种爱的基础仍然是一个人的自私或世俗的利益。第三种爱是比较纯洁的,是对神的无私敬拜。在第四个阶段中,一个人仅仅通过神的爱而爱自己。在这种阶段中人的灵魂消融在神内,正如葡萄酒中的一滴水。正如一滴水在一杯葡萄酒中接受葡萄酒的颜色和味道,一个圣徒也放弃他的一切世俗感情并完全地消融在神的旨意当中。

在他的其他著作中 Bernardus 将爱神区分为三个阶段。爱神是从专心寻求神的人心开始的(即 consideratio 的阶段),经过一种信赖和奉献的态度和一种瞻望(contemplatio),最后达到与神的神秘结合(ecstasis)。因为任何一个人都是"按照神的肖像"(ad imaginem Dei)而被创造的,每一个人都有可能掌握"上面的种种事"(superna)以及永恒。这种可能性也意味着人的灵魂的伟大和尊严(celsitudo),因为这种能力始终存在,虽然某些灵魂没有追求精神性的世界,并且保持一种自私的、委屈的或自我中心的状态(所谓的 anima curva)。

Bernard is the first to use the symbol of the two swords given to the successor of Peter: the Pope received from God the two "swords" of spiritual and secular power. However, the pope himself should only use the power of the word (spiritual power). If necessary the pope can ask the emperor to defend the rights of the Church, and then the emperor may make use of secular (military) powers. But if the emperor violates the rights of the Church, then the pope should have the courage to resist him resolutely. Since Bernard also criticizes papal luxuries—the pope "decorated with silk, jewels and clad in gold, carried around by the Swiss Guards"—he has been compared to Martin Luther who wrote similar things some 400 years later, albeit in a different spirit.

038. *De diligendo Deo / On Divine Love*

This dogmatic treatise was written in 1126.

At the beginning of the work Bernard places one of his favorite maxims: "Whence arises the love of God? From God. And what is the measure of this love? To love without measure." (Causa diligendi Deum Deus est, modus sine modo diligere. 1,1) For Bernard emotional love is the central idea, and intellectual understanding follows from this basic attitude: "A matter is understood insofar as it is loved." (Res in tantum intelligitur, in quantum amatur.) Christ became man and was crucified so as to show us God's love. By suffering as a human person, God won a perfect right to be loved by His creature. He fully deserves our love, and He Himself is the food of the holy souls, the sacrifice that redeems those in captivity. God not only gives life, He also gives redemption and thus is to be loved "beyond measure" (sine modo). Every living person must express a deep gratitude towards God. If a man loves God, he usually passes through several steps: In a first stage man loves himself with the desire of his own sensual nature; in this stage the love of God is hidden and somehow in preparation. The second degree is a kind of more conscientious divine love where man loves God, but this love is still based on a person's own worldly interest. A third type of love is a more purified and selfless adoration of God, and in the fourth level a person will love himself only through God. In this highest form of divine love the human soul is lost in God like a drop of water in a glass of wine. Just like a drop of water in a glass of wine accepts the colour and taste of the wine, a saintly person dissolves all human feeling and is dispersed in the will of God alone.

In his other writings Bernard divides the development of divine love into three steps. It starts from the recollection of the heart that searches for God (consideratio), passes through an attitude of trusting dedication and vision (contemplatio) and arrives at a mystical union with God (ecstasis). Since any human person is created "according to the image of God" (ad imaginem Dei) they have the possibility to grasp "the things above" (superna) and eternity. This capacity is what signifies the greatness and majesty (celsitudo) of the human soul, a capacity that is always there, even if the human soul does not reach out to the spiritual world and remains bent and self-centered (anima curva).

伯铎禄（约 1094—1156）

1094 年（或 1092 年）生于法国 Auvergne 的 de Montboissier 贵族家庭中，1109 年入本笃会，而 Cluny 隐修院的 Hugo I 接受他进入隐修院；他先在 Vezelay、Domene 等地的隐修院生活，于 1122 年被选为 Cluny 的院长。他曾去过意大利、西班牙、英国等地，因为他需要为隐修院办事。在 1147 年和 1148 年他想进行一些改革，所以 Bernardus 谴责他说他放弃原来会规的标准，但 Petrus 很完美地回应 Bernardus 的疑问。在 1140 年他接受那位受谴责的 Abaelardus 到 Cluny 隐修院。Petrus 与许多教会领导和贵族人士有来往。

著作：《诸奇迹》（主要的著作，赞扬 Cluny 隐修院的生活）、《反驳萨拉森人》、《萨拉森异端大全》，还有圣诗、讲演稿。

039. 《反驳萨拉森人》

法国南部 Cluny 隐修院的院长的这篇论文首次被提到是在 1143 年。该著作分 4 卷，但至今存留的只有两卷。作者曾于 1141 年去西班牙旅游，在那里他试图使 Alfonso de Castilia 与 Alfonso de Aragon 和好。在西班牙他接触到伊斯兰教的世界，并且劝勉人们要将《古兰经》译成拉丁语。他的论文旨在理解伊斯兰教的教导并从基督信仰的角度作出一种评论。

Petrus 深信，根据教会教导的传统权威（即教父们）可以获得关于伊斯兰教的正确评论。然而，Petrus 自己的态度相当温和与宽容。比如说他认为十字军运动是不合理的。他试图推动与伊斯兰教的对话，且认为哲学是两个宗教之间的桥梁。视哲学为一种媒介和中介者这种观点与 Abaelardus 的经院哲学方法有类似之处，因为 Abaelardus 强调逻辑思维能够帮助决定信仰的问题或传统权威之间的冲突。Petrus 鼓励穆斯林敞开他们的心，要他们意识到他们的信仰也许有一些缺陷。他们也应该对基督宗教的教导有兴趣。Petrus 探讨 Muhammad 是否是先知的问题并将他与《旧约》的先知进行比较。最终他说不应该将 Muhammad 称为先知。

Petrus 的论文是历史上第一部严肃地从基督信仰的角度谈论伊斯兰教信仰的著作，而学者们普遍认为他的态度基本上很宽容（比如 Manitius）。作者曾与很多教宗、宗主教、总主教、国王和皇帝有联系，他与 Bernardus Claravallensis 有良好的关系，但当 Abaelardus 的教导受到官方教会的谴责后，他仍接受 Abaelardus 来到他的隐修院。这一切表明 Petrus 是一位具有学问和经验的人物，人们普遍尊敬他是因为他尊敬别人。德国皇帝 Fredericus I 首次给他 Venerabilis（"可敬的"）的尊号。

Petrus Venerabilis / Peter the Venerable

Opera: *De Miraculis, Contra Saracenos* (=*Liber contra sectam sive haeresim Saracenorum*), *Summa totius haeresis Saracenorum*

Works: *Miracles, Against the Saracenes* (=*Book against the Sect of the Saracenes*), *Sum of the Heresy of the Saracenes*

039. *Contra Saracenos* / *Against the Saracenes*

This treatise of the Abbot of Cluny (southern France) was first mentioned in 1143. It has four books, but only two of them have been preserved. The author traveled to Spain in 1141, where he tried to reconcile Alfonso of Castile and Alfonso of Aragon. In Spain he had contacts to the world of Islam, and he urged that the *Qur'an* should be translated into Latin. His treatise attempts to understand and to evaluate the teachings of Islam from a Christian perspective.

Peter is convinced that the Church and the traditional authorities of ecclesiastical teaching (the Fathers of the Church) are sufficient to arrive at a sound judgment on the questions of Islam. However, Peter's attitude is quite mild and tolerant. For example he criticizes the crusades as unjustified. He tries to promote a dialogue with Islam by relying on philosophy as mediating link between the two religions. This view of the intermediating function of philosophy is somewhat similar to Abaelard's scholastic method, because Abaelard emphasizes the role of logical reasoning in order to decide questions of faith and conflicting views of traditional authorities. Peter exhorts the Muslims to be open to the possibility that their own faith has some shortcomings. They should also show interest in the teachings of Christianity. Peter explores the question whether Muhammad was a prophet and tries to compare him to the prophets of the Old Testament, finally arriving at the conclusion that Muhammad was no prophet.

Peter's treatise is the very first serious discussion of the faith of Islam from a Christian point of view, and scholars agree that his attitude was basically quite tolerant (Manitius). The author was in contact with many Popes, patriarchs, archbishops, kings and Emperors, he had good relations with Bernard of Clairvaux, but he also received Abaelard into the monastery of Cluny, after the latter's teachings had been condemned by the official Church. All this shows that Peter was a learned and experienced man who enjoyed respect because he respected others. Emperor Frederick I was the first to give him the title "Venerable" (Venerabilis).

圣维克多的雨果(约 1096—1141)

德国学者，大概来自 Sachsen 的贵族家庭，曾在 Halberstadt 附近的 Hamersleben 隐修院中受教育，大约于 1113 年进入 Paris 的 St.-Victor 隐修院，1118 年后在 St. Victor 任教，始终过一种虔诚的修士学者式的生活，他没有参与当时的教会和政治生活，而是进行研究和写作(studium quaerendi)。在他的指导下，St.-Victor 的神学派成为 12 世纪最有影响力的学派之一。他们比较多的受 Augustinus 思想的影响并倾向于神秘主义。Hugo 的著作很多，可以分为四类：1)哲学；2)对《圣经》、教父著作的注解；3)百科全书式的著作；4)灵修书。

著作：《诺亚方舟的道德意义和神秘意义》、《论灵魂的奇妙》、《默想及其种类》、《论肉身和精神的果实》、《论基督信仰的圣事》(一种神学百科全书，与 Thomas《神学大全》有类似之处)、《论世界的虚伪》(表达他的灵修思想)、《关于诸圣事的对话》、《学问之阶》、《关于神的命题》等

040. 《学问之阶》

这部非常简明的小百科全书分为 7 卷；另一个书名是 *Eruditionis didascalicae libri septem*(《学术教导七卷》)，成书于 1137 年。它在基督宗教百科全书的传统中是一个环节。

当时反对逻辑学的人说："学习哲学是没有用的"，但 Hugo 鼓励人们学习世俗的学科："你们应该学习一切，你将会发现没有一个无用处的东西。"与 Augustinus 的 *De doctrina christiana*、Isidorus 的 *Etymologiae* 以及 Hrabanus 的 *De institutione clericorum* 一样，Hugo 也结合世俗的学科与《圣经》研究。因此，*Didascalicon* 前三卷献给七个自由学科，后面的三卷讨论《圣经》的问题和神学的难题，而最后一卷(卷名为 *De meditatione*)论及灵修问题。

根据 Hugo 的说法，各种学科可以分为四个领域：理论学科(artes theoreticae)、实践性的学科(artes practicae)、技术性的知识(artes mechanicae)以及逻辑学(logica)。理论性的学科是神学、数学、物理学；实践性的学科包括伦理学、经济学、政治学。技术性学科是织布、铸铁的技术、航海、农业、医学、剧院中的设施等等；逻辑学则包含语文学和那些与修辞学有关系的学科。

在另一部著作(*De fructibus carnis et spiritus*)中，Hugo(或他的学生)描述一棵"美德之树"，而在其中"谦逊"(humilitas)是一切美德的根源。树在下部的树枝是 Plato 的"四枢德"，而树冠是三个神学性美德，即信德、望德、爱德。这七个树枝每一个都结

Hugo / Hugh of Saint-Victor

Opera: *De arca Noe morali et mystica, De arrha animae, De contemplatione et eius speciebus, De fructibus carnis et spiritus, De sacramentis christianae fidei, De vanitate mundi, Dialogus de sacramentis, Didascalicon, Sententiae de divinitate*

Works: *The Ark of Noah, its Moral and Mystical Meaning; The Ineffability of the Soul, On different kinds of Contemplation, Fruits of the Flesh and of the Spirit, The Sacraments of the Christian Faith, The Vanity of the World, Dialogue on the Sacraments, Didascalicon, Sentences on the Divine*

040. *Didascalicon*

This remarkably comprehensive encyclopedia in 7 books is also known under the title *Eruditionis didascalicae libri septem* (*Seven Books of Scholarly Teaching*). It was written around 1137 and continues the tradition of Christian encyclopedias.

In a time when those opposed to logic said: "The study of philosophy is useless", Hugh encouraged the study of secular sciences: "Learn everything, and you will soon see that nothing is useless." Following Augustine's *De doctrina christiana*, Isidore's *Etymologiae*, and Hrabanus' *De institutione clericorum*, Hugh combines secular science with the study of the Holy Scriptures. Thus the first three books of the *Didascalicon* are dedicated to the seven liberal arts, another three books expound biblical and theological questions, and the last book, entitled *De meditatione*, treats spirituality.

According to Hugh the sciences can be divided into four areas: theoretical sciences (artes theoreticae), practical sciences (artes practicae), technical knowledge (artes mechanicae), and logic (logica). The theoretical sciences are theology, mathematics, physics. As practical sciences he enlists ethics, economy, politics. The mechanical sciences are weaving, forging, navigation, agriculture, medicine, technical devices of the theater, and many others. Logic is divided into grammar and rhetorical sciences.

In some other work (*De fructibus carnis et spiritus*) Hugh (or one of his students) depicts a "tree of virtues", in which humility (humilitas) is the root of all virtues. The lower branches of the tree are the four cardinal virtues of Plato, and the crown of the tree are faith, hope, and love, the three theological virtues. Each of these seven branches

了七个果子，只有"爱德"的树枝结出了十个果子。每一个果子都是某种道德价值，而这幅图画为每一种价值下了一个简明的定义。在 *Didascalicon* 中，Hugo 也强调伦理道德的重要性；如果一个人没有德性，他无法获得知识，无法走近科学。一个好的学生需要有一颗纯洁的心以及俭朴和节制（控制欲望），他也需要有能力来评价世俗事物的价值。

bears seven fruits, only the branch of love bears ten fruits, and each fruit is a certain value, explained by a concise definition. Also in the *Didascalicon* Hugh emphasizes the importance of ethical values and moral attitudes. If they are missing it is impossible to attain knowledge and approach the sciences. A good student needs purity, frugality, temperance (control of the desires), and the ability to assess the value of secular things.

圣希尔德加德(1098—1179)

她是德国贵族人士 Hildebert von Bermersheim 的第 10 个孩子,8 岁时就被交给 Disibodenberg 的本笃会(Benedictines)修女院,在那里师从 Jutta 修女(1084—1136 年),后者于 1112 年在 Disibodenberg 的男修院附近创立了一个修女院并成为其院长(magistra)。在她去世后,Hildegardis 被选为院长(1136 年),而在 1151 年 Hildegardis 在 Bingen 附近创立了她自己的隐修院。根据她自己的说法,Hildegardis 从幼年就有接受 visiones(神视)的特恩,而在 1141 年后她开始记载她所见到的景象。Bernardus 认为她的神视很有价值,而 1146 年在德国 Trier 举行的主教会议上,教宗 Eugenius III 正式肯定她的"神视"。在该会议上也曾宣读她的 Scivias 的部分章节。很多人曾去找她,愿意听她的劝勉或警告。她也曾四次进行"宣讲旅游",公开在各地教堂讲道。虽然她身体健康欠佳,但仍然编写很多著作,并与许多贵族人士和教宗有信件来往。在她的拉丁著作中也有德语的语句。

著作:《诸病因和治疗》(医学和药物学著作,很理性地谈论性欲的问题)、《福音的注解》、《普通人诸神功之书》(描述人、宇宙和神之间的神秘关系,宇宙中的一切事物都有象征意义,人是一个小宇宙,应该通过一切感官认出上主的伟大)、《诸功劳之书》、《物理学》(包括 1000 多种植物和动物的名称和许多药物学知识)、《知道路》(包括世界的创造和拯救,即救恩的历史);还有其他的著作、圣诗、信等。

041.《诸病因和治疗》

这部著作写成于 1150—1160 年,又被称为 *Liber compositae medicinae*。

Hildegardis 的 *Physica*(《物理学》)从医生的角度描述自然界,但她的第二部医学著作 *Causae et curae*(《诸病因和治疗》)则是从患病者的观点提供一些观察。Hildegardis 的医学知识和治病经验都是很著名的。她也从民间医学和隐修院医学那里继承很多知识。19 世纪和 20 世纪的理性主义人士曾讽刺她的医学著作,比如参见 Manitius 的评价:"她为种种疾病提出非常奇怪的医药及一些施用这些药品的更怪异的方式。"然而,她的医学著作在 20 世纪末的德国又变得非常流行。

从 Hildegardis 的宇宙论和宗教形而上学的角度来看,她的医学很有道理。人们能够从这些方面来理解它:患病者始终是上主的受造物,他和其他的受造物一样都依赖于神对世界所规定的秩序。神是第一个存在,也是最完满的存在,而一切人的生活都应该指向这个最高级的存在。人们应该意识到,身体上的疾病和道德上的恶习是一样的:它们自己本身不存在,因为它们只是一种缺陷,比如健康上的缺陷,或存在上

Hildegardis de Alemannia / St. Hildegard of Bingen

Opera: *Causae et curae, Expositiones quorundam evangeliorum, Liber divinorum operum simplicis hominis, Liber vitae meritorum, Physica, Scivias*

Works: *Causes and Cures, Exposition of the Gospels, Book of Spiritual Works of a Simple Person, Book of a Life of Merits, Physics, Know the Ways*

041. *Causae et curae / Causes and Cures*

This work was written ca. in 1150—1160 and is also known under the title *Liber compositae medicinae*.

Hildegard's *Physica* describes nature from the point of a physician, but her second medical book *Causae et curae* presents many observations from the perspective of a sick person. Hildegard was famous for her medical knowledge and experience. She also learned much from popular medicine and monastery medicine. The book was ridiculed in the rationalist era of the 19th and early 20th century as naming the "most curious medicines for the diseases and even more strange ways of applying these" (Manitius). However, her medical writings became very popular in Germany at the end of the 20th century.

Within the cosmology and religious metaphysics of Hildegard her medicine makes sense and can be understood in this way: the patient is always one of God's creatures, and like all other creatures he depends on God's world order. God is the first being and the fullness of all being, and human beings are ordered towards this fullness. They should realize that physical evils are similar to moral deficiencies: they do not exist in themselves, they are only a lack of health or a lack of being, an omission like vices are a lack of virtue. The healing process relies on medical herbs that are God-given, on a healthy life-style and diet that are divinely ordained, and on the help of a doctor who is inspired by divine mercy and compassion. Based on this outlook, Hildegard describes all kinds of diseases, emotional disorders, digestion problems, diets and different life-styles. She almost always emphasizes the interplay of body and soul (psycho-somatic correlation) and is remarkably modern-minded. For example she describes sexuality as some-

的缺陷,正如恶习是美德上的缺陷。一个人的治疗过程取决于一些来自神的药品或药草,依赖于一种很有秩序的生活方式或特殊的食品,这些也是来自神的,以及取决于医生的慈悲心和同情心,医生这种态度也受宗教信仰的启发。根据这种观点,Hildegardis 描述各种疾病、心理的烦乱、消化问题、食品和生活方式的影响。她都提到身体和心灵之间的互相影响(身心相互影响),并且在某些方面有相当现代的思想。比如她描述性生活为一种基本上是好的、纯洁的和积极的事。上主创造了 Adam(亚当),而当 Adam 见到 Eva 时,他是充满智慧的,因为他意识到 Eva 将是他们的孩子的母亲。另外,Hildegardis 也具体谈论刷牙和剪指甲的事,她说体育、骑马、游泳和按摩都有一些好处。

在她的神学著作 *Scivias*、*Liber vitae meritorum* 和 *Liber divinae operum* 当中,Hildegardis 也同样在 actio(行动)和 contemplatio(默想)之间寻找一种平衡点。她阐述自己的独特神学思路,其中的核心概念是三位一体的神、创造论、降生成人(道成肉身)的原则、诸圣事、诸美德、教会论和终末论。她经常使用"rationalitas"(理性)、"viriditas"(新鲜性)和"virginitas"(贞洁)这样的词语,因此强调丰富的生命和人的潜力的发挥。她指向神的"praescientia"(预先认识)和"operatio"(历史中的行动)并认为随从基督应该是在这种知识和行动方面效法神。Hildegardis 的著作在宇宙论和人性论方面呈现出一种普遍的、开放的精神,而这种精神在现代仍然有吸引力。

thing good, pure and positive. God created Adam, and when Adam saw Eve he was filled with wisdom because he perceived Eve as the mother of their children. Hildegard gives detailed orders for the cleaning of teeth, for the cultivation of fingernails, she sees the benefits of gymnastics, horse-riding, swimming and massage.

Hildegard's balance of "actio" (action) and "contemplatio" (contemplation) is also found in her theological works *Scivias*, *Liber vitae meritorum*, and *Liber divinae operum*. She develops an independent theological train of thought that is centered on the Trinity, creation, the incarnation, the sacraments, virtues, ecclesiology, and eschatology. She often uses the terms "rationalitas" (rationality), "viriditas" (freshness), and "virginitas" (chastity), thus emphasizes the fullness of life and the unfolding of the different dimensions of human talents. She points to God's "praescientia" (prescience) and "operatio" (action in history) and shows that following Christ should be a kind of imitation of God in knowledge and activity. The cosmology and anthropology of Hildegard's writings breath a universal and open spirit that has remained fascinating also in the modern era.

格拉狄安（约 1100—1150）

意大利人，Camaldoli 隐修会的会士，在 Bologna 的 St. Felix 隐修院担任神学教师。他肯定在 1179 年之前去世。关于他的生平没有很多资料，但他是教会法学的奠基人。

著作：《教会法汇编》（约 1140 年，4000 章，第一部比较系统的教会法典）

042.《教会法汇编》

大约于 1142 年本著作由 Gratianus 以讲课稿的形式编写，而 Gratianus 曾是在 Bologna 修道的、属于 Camaldolesi 修会的隐修士。后来这部书成为中世纪最重要的教科书之一并引起一个新学科的诞生：教会法律的学术性研究。

自从古代以来，教会那些大公会议（concilium oecumenicum）的规定以及历代教宗的敕令（所谓的 decreta 或 decretalia）管理着教会的生活，但一直没有一部系统的教会法典。Gratianus 试图整理那些不同的规定和敕令。他的著作向读者提供一些虚构的法案（causae）所引发的问题（quaestiones）的不同解决方案。根据经院思想的方法的清晰概念和区分，以及依赖于教宗文献及会议文献，Gratianus 的教科书能够相当一致地决定大部分的案件。作者很熟悉 Justinianus 的 *Corpus iuris civilis*（《民法大全》），但他从基督信仰的角度来解释这部法典。

另一位来自 Bologna 的法学家是 Irnerius，他曾于 1100 年恢复了罗马法的研究，因此 Bologna 大学在全欧洲的法学中都占有领先地位。Bologna 的法学专家们（legistae）为 *Corpus iuris civilis* 编写了很多"注解"（glossae）。大约半个世纪后 Gratianus 的著作很快导致"教会法学师"（canonistae）学派的形成，他们为教会权威文献编写了很多注解。在 1122 年的 *Concordatum de Wormatia* 中，教宗和德国皇帝在理论上解决了双方的冲突（所谓的"任命权争论"），而这个新的学科是非常需要的并受欢迎的，教会也很支持它。此后有很多中世纪的学者研究"两个法律"即世俗的法典和教会的法律，而且很多中世纪的教宗也是很有成就的法学家。

Gratianus / Gratian

Opera: *Concordia discordantium canonum (Decretum Gratiani)*
Works: *Concordance of Canons (Decret of Gratian)*

042. *Concordantia discordantium canonum / Concordance of Canons*

This work was compiled around 1142 as a textbook for lectures by Gratian, a Camaldolese monk at Bologna. Subsequently the work became one of the great textbooks of the Middle Ages and gave birth to the foundation of a new science: the scientific study of canon law.

Since antiquity the rulings of ecumenical councils and the edicts of Popes (the so-called decreta or decretals) had governed the Church, but there was no systematic code of ecclesiastical law (canon law). Gratian tries to bring order to the many different stipulations and decrees. His work confronts the reader with different solutions to the questions (quaestiones) of possible legal cases (causae). Relying on the clear distinctions of the scholastic method and on collections of papal and synodal documents, Gratians textbook is able to decide the cases in a coherent way. The author is well acquainted with Justinianus' *Code of Civil Law*, but he tries to interpret it in a Christian spirit.

Another great Bolognese scholar, Irnerius, had renewed the study of Roman law around 1100 and thus elevated the university of Bologna to a leadership role in the jurisprudence of Europe. The legal experts (legistae) of Bologna wrote commentaries (glossae) on the *Code of Civil Law*. About half a century later Gratians book soon led to the emergence of the school of the canonists (canonistae), who wrote commentaries on the decretals of the ecclesiastical authorities. After the controversy between the German Emperor and the Pope (the so-called investiture controversy) had been solved in theory by the *Concordate of Worms* of 1122, the new discipline was much needed and found vigorous support from the side of the Church. Many medieval scholars thenceforth studied "both laws", namely secular and ecclesiastical law, and many medieval popes were accomplished legal experts.

蒙默思的杰弗里（约 1100—1155）

约于 1100 年出生在英国 Wales 地区的 Normanni 居民家庭，曾在 1129 年和 1151 年间在 Oxford 任教，于 1152 年成为 St. Asaph 的主教，大概于 1154 年去世。

著作：《不列颠诸王纪》

043.《不列颠诸王纪》

分为 12 卷的 *Historia regum Britanniae* 成书于 1139 年。作者说他将这部书从一部"英语写的"古老书籍译成拉丁语，但即使他有这类的古代资料，他也非常自由地改写其中的内容，并且加上了各种神话、传说和奇妙的故事。他的虚构叙述受了《圣经》、Vergilius 和关于 Alexander 的传说的启发，比如他认为犹太人的命运是 Britannia 早期历史的模式。因此，他著作的历史资料价值很低，虽然它成为中世纪最流行的、影响最广泛的著作之一。不久之后，一些历史学家已经指出 Galfridus 的书是不可靠的。无论如何，*Historia* 迅速地从拉丁语被译成法语、中古英语和威尔士语，后来也出现西班牙语及荷兰语版本。

第 1 卷报告 Britannia 人的来源——他们是 Troia 人的后裔。Troia 英雄 Aeneas 的曾孙子 Brutus 来到 Albion 岛，这样开始有人居住在这些地区，而 Brutus 为该地区起名 Britannia，将自己的妻子称为 Briti。另一个 Troia 人 Corineus 成为 Cornwall 的建立者，他帮助 Brutus 驱逐该地区的"巨人"。Troia 的移民建立了一个城市，即 Troia nova，但后来这个城市的名称变成"Kaerlud"、"Kaerlundein"和"London"。在罗马人到来之前有几代传奇性的国王，比如 Bladud 王是 Bath 的创立者，而 Leir 王建立了 Leicester 城。Leir（即 Lear）将国土分为两块交给他那两个忘恩负义的女儿，而这个故事后来启发 Shakespeare 创作了他的 *King Lear*。

5 世纪初，罗马军队从 Britannia 撤走，此后本地居民遭受 Scoti、Pictes 和 Saxones 等民族的侵略和骚扰。在僭君 Vortimer 的统治后，Aurelius 王和他的弟兄 Uther Pendragon 成为王。这就导致 Arthur 王的征服——他是 Uther Pendragon 的传奇性儿子。根据凯尔特作者 Nennius（9 世纪初）的 *Historia Britonum* 的记载，Arthur 曾是一位英勇的统治者，他约于 500 年率领 Wales 人抵抗 Saxones 的侵略。在 Galfridus 的叙述中，这个地方性酋长被描述为一个伟大的国王，他征服了全英国、周围的海岛以及高卢，他甚至想统治全欧洲并准备侵略罗马。与自己的侄子 Mordred 相战时，Arthur 遭受致命的伤害并奇妙地被带到 Avalon 海岛，这是一种凯尔特式的 elysium 岛，在那里

Galfridus / Geoffrey of Monmouth

Opera: *Historia regum Britanniae*
Works: *History of the Kings of Britain*

043. *Historia regum Britanniae / History of the Kings of Britain*

The *History of the Kings of Britain* in 12 books was finished in 1139. The author alleges that he translated it into Latin from a very old book "in the British tongue", but even if he had some sources of this kind, he elaborated them very freely, adding all kinds of myths, legends and miraculous stories. The Bible, Virgil, and the story of Alexander inspired his many fictions, for example he saw the fate of the Jews as a model for the early history of Britain. Thus the historical value of this work is neglegible although it was one of the most popular and influential pieces of literature in the Middle Ages. Soon some historians pointed to the historical unreliability of Geoffrey's work. However, the *History* was quickly translated from Latin into French, Middle English, and Welsh, and later translations produced versions in Spanish and Dutch.

Book 1 reports about the descent of the Britons from the Trojans. Brutus, the great-grandson of the Trojan hero Aeneas arrives on the island of Albion, thus starting the settlement of the region, giving it the name "Britannia". Accordingly, Brutus' wife is called "Briti". Another Trojan, Corineus, becomes the founder of Cornwall and helps Brutus to expel the race of giants that inhabitates the land. The Trojan settlers found a city with the name "Troia nova", but later on the place is called "Kaerlud", "Kaerlundein", and "London". Several generations of legendary kings pass before the Romans arrive King Bladud is the founder of Bath, and King Leir the founder of Leicester. Leir (Lear) divides the kingdom between his two ungrateful daughters, a story which inspired Shakespeare to write his *King Lear*.

After the Roman legions have left in the early fifth century the locals suffer from the invasions of the Scots, Pictes, and Saxons. After the reign of the usurper Vortimer, King Aurelius and his brother Uther Pendragon, rule the country. This leads the story to the conquests of King Arthur, the legendary son of Uther Pendragon. According to the *Historia Britonum* of the Celtic author Nennius (early 9th century), Arthur was a heroic ruler who led the people of Wales to resist Saxon invasions around 500 AD. In Geoffrey's narrative this local chieftain is developed into a great king who conquers all England, the surrounding islands and Gaul, he even aspires the control of all Europe and contemplates attacking Rome. Fighting against his nephew Mordred, Arthur is lethally wounded and mysteriously carried off to the legendary island of Avalon, a kind of Celtic elysium,

他的著名宝剑 Caliburn 被制造。不久后，关于 Arthur "圆桌"骑士们的优雅风度的报告以及关于 Ywain、Gawain、Perceval、Lancelot、Tristan 等人的英雄故事给很多其他诗人带去了灵感，这样就导致欧洲文学中的 Arthur 传统（即"Cycle breton"）的形成。通过 Chretien de Troyes 的努力，这些故事进入法语读者群体，而 Hartmann von Aue 在德国地区传播它。

　　第 7 卷介绍魔术家和哲人 Merlin，他曾是 Uther Pendragon 和 Arthur 王的顾问。他曾预言英国的政治发展，虽然他的预言是相当模糊的。这些章节后来导致一种新的文学类型，即"被归于 Merlin 的政治预言"。这些预言多半是针对某些统治者的偷袭，而教会当局多次禁止这类的书籍，将它们列入《禁书目录》(*Index librorum prohibitorum*)。Galfridus 也曾写过一首谈论 Merlin 的诗（即 *Vita Merlini*），其中借 Merlin 之口预言 Anglosaxones 将被迫离开 Britannia。

where his famous sword Caliburn has been produced. The stories about the fine manners of the knights at Arthur's "Round table", about the heroic deeds of Ywain, Gawain, Perceval, Lancelot, and Tristan soon inspired many other authors and led to the development of the Arthur-tradition ("Cycle breton") in European literature. Chretien of Troyes introduced these stories to French readers, and Hartmann of Aue spread them in Germany.

Book 7 introduces the enchanter and wise man Merlin, adviser to Uther Pendragon and King Arthur, who predicts the political fate of Britain, although many of his prophecies are rather obscure. These chapters later gave rise to the literary genre of "political prophecies attributed to Merlin". Many of these "prophecies" were hidden attacks of certain rulers, and the authorities of the Church repeatedly put some of these books on the *Index librorum prohibitorum* (*Index of Forbidden Books*). Geoffrey also wrote a poem about Merlin (*Vita Merlini*), in which he has Merlin predict the expulsion of the Anglosaxons from Britain.

彼得·隆巴(1100—1160)

约于 1100 年生于意大利北部 Lombardia 地区的 Novara。Bernardus Claravallensis 负责他的教育并支持他在 Rheims 上学,后来推荐他去 Paris 的 Saint-Victor 修院学习。他的老师可能是 Hugo de St.-Victor。大约在 1145 年 Petrus 开始在 Notre-Dame 大教堂学院任教,1159 年他被祝圣为 Paris 的主教,一年后去世。

著作:《圣 Paulus 书信解释文集》、《Psalmi 注释集》、《四部语录》

044. 《四部语录》

本著作经常简称 Sententiae,成书于 1158 年。

第 1 卷介绍关于圣三以及神的本性(永恒、美善、正义等)的教导。第 2 卷谈论被创造的世界和罪恶(人的堕落);第 3 卷提出耶稣基督的教导,他那种带来救恩的死亡及复活,又解释种种美德、恶习以及基督宗教伦理学的教导。第 4 卷说明教会的圣事(圣洗、坚振、圣体、忏悔等)以及最后的事(审判与永恒的赏报)。因此,这部著作的结构引导读者从神走向创造界、救恩以及到终末论。作者使用很多来自《圣经》或教父著作的名言(sententiae)来系统地阐述传统的基督宗教教导。最多的引语来自 Augustinus。Petrus 大概曾经当过 Abaelardus 的学生,但他和老师不同:他并不投入于一些哲学性的辩论,始终提出比较普遍被接受的或比较传统的观点。因此,他的著作没有创造性,但它成为一个很平衡的神学教科书,因为作者回避那些涉及基督信仰边缘性小问题的争论。愿意获得 magister theologiae(神学硕士学位)的人必须为 Sententiae 写注,还需要给《圣经》和 Historia scholastica 写注解——后者是 Petrus Comestor(1120—1178 年)编写的、普遍使用的历史教科书。1222 年 Alexander de Hales 选择 Sententiae 为 Paris 大学的教科书,而英国的 Oxford 于 1245 年模仿他的榜样。从此 Petrus 的著作成为普遍被阅读和使用的神学教科书。很多人编写一些说明《语录》的注释,而这种传统协助了神学的发展,一直到 16 世纪。

Petrus Lombardus / Peter Lombard

Opera: *Collectanea in omnes d. Pauli apostoli epistolas (=Magna glossatura), Commentaria in Psalmos, Sententiarum libri quattuor*

Works: *Explanations to the Pauline Letters, Commentary to the Psalms, Sentences in Four Books*

044. *Sententiarum libri quattuor / Sentences in Four Books*

This book is often simply called "*Sententiae*" and was finished in 1158.

Book one is a treatise on the Holy Trinity and the properties of God (eternity, goodness, justice etc.). The second book discusses creation and sin (the fall of man); book three presents the teachings of Jesus Christ, His salvific death and resurrection and treats the virtues, vices and commandments of Christian ethics. Book four explains the sacraments (Baptism, Confirmation, Holy Eucharist, Penitence, etc.) and the last things (judgment and eternal reward). The structure of the work leads therefore from God to creation, redemption and to eschatology. The author uses numerous quotations (sententiae) from the Bible and the writings of the Church Fathers in order to present the traditional Christian teachings in a systematic way. Most of his quotations come from Augustine. Peter probably was Abelard's student for some time, but in distinction to Abelard, he does not embark on philosophical speculations and always keeps to the more common or traditional opinion. Therefore his work displays no originality, but it became a very balanced textbook of theology, since the author avoided the many controversies that centered on minor tenets of the Christian doctrine. Those who wanted to attain the degree "magister theologiae" had to write commentaries to the *Sentences*, together with commentaries to the Bible and to the *Historia scholastica*, the popular historical textbook by Petrus Comestor (1120—1178). In 1222 Alexander of Hales chose the *Sentences* as textbook for his students in Paris, and Oxford followed this example in 1245. Since then Peter's work was the universally accepted and generally used textbook of theology, and the numerous commentaries to the *Sententiae* helped to develop theological thought, even up to the 16th century.

奥托（约 1111—1158）

生于奥地利 Babenberg 王家，其父亲是奥地利公爵 Leopoldus III，母亲是 Henricus IV 皇帝（1056—1106 年）的女儿 Agnes；因此他与 Fredericus I Barbarossa 皇帝（1122—1190 年，1155 年称帝）有亲戚关系。他于 1126 年进入 Klosterneuburg 隐修院，1127 年到 Paris 读书，在那里获得最高级的教育，他的老师包括 Abaelardus、Gilbertus Porretanus 以及 Hugo de St.-Victor 等人。他于 1132 年进入 Cistercienses（熙笃会）在 Morimond 的隐修院，但于 1138 年被提名为德国 Freising 的主教。

著作：《编年史或两个社会的历史》（一部影响深远的世界史，将人类历史分为 4 个阶段，最后的阶段从 Carolus Magnus 开始）、《Fridericus 皇帝的功绩》（描述 Fridericus Barbarossa 皇帝在 1256 年前的行动）

045. 《编年史或两个社会的历史》

这部世界史分为 8 卷，它在一些方面效法 Augustinus 的 *De civitate Dei*，因此结合历史事件的记载与受神学影响的历史哲学。作者表达世俗事物的变化无常，又强调"上主之城"的永恒理念。

作者 Otto 是首次向德国介绍经院思想的方法和知识的人，他对于 Aristoteles 的部分著作有一定的了解，虽然他自己没有学过希腊语。他很好地掌握教父们和古典诗人的著作。在他的历史编写方面他曾引用 Orosius、Eusebius、Hegesippus、Wipo、Hermannus de Reichenau 等作者的著作。

有人曾经指出 Otto 对于他的信息来源的辨别性态度以及他的客观性在很多方面都是令人敬佩的。当他发现不同历史资料的记载有所出入时，他指出这些差异。他也说出自己的看法，比如他并不支持教宗 Gregorius VII 于 1076 年将 Otto 的叔叔 Henricus IV 皇帝开除教籍。Otto 也批评关于伊斯兰教的夸大说法和谣言，他自己相当客观地描述这个宗教，甚至指明伊斯兰教和基督宗教之间的相似之处（7,7）。

前 4 卷是根据 Orosius 的著作而写的，因此构成一部世界史。在后面的部分中 Otto 描绘中世纪的世界，而他观察的宽广视野包括东欧的斯拉夫国度、意大利、希腊以及近东地区。第 8 卷涉及终末论（eschatologia）的种种问题，即反基督（Antichristus）的到来、世界的审判以及上主之国的最终实现。

Otto Frisingensis / Otto of Freising

Opera: *Chronica sive Historia de duabus civitatibus, Gesta Friderici*
Works: *Chronicle or a History of the Two Cities, The Achievements of Frederick*

045. *Chronica sive Historia de duabus civitatibus / Chronicle or a History of the Two Cities*

This universal history in 8 books follows the example of Augustine's *De civitate Dei* and is thus both a historical account of events and a theologically inspired philosophy of history. The author wants to show the transitoriness of worldly things and the eternal ideals of the City of God.

Otto was the first to introduce scholastic methods and knowledge to Germany, he was acquainted with some of Aristotle's works, although he did not know Greek. He had a good grasp of the patrological works and of the classical poets. For his historical compilation he used the works of Orosius, Eusebius, Hegesippus, Wipo, Hermann of Reichenau and many other authors.

It has been pointed out that Otto's critical attitude towards his sources and his objectivity are outstanding in many respects. Whenever he observes that historical sources are contradictory, he points out these differences. He also makes personal comments, for example he does not support the excommunication of his uncle Henry IV by Pope Gregory VII in 1076. He criticizes the exaggerated rumors about the Islam and presents a rather objective account of that religion, showing similarities and differences between the Islam and the Christian faith (7,7).

The first four books follow Orosius' account and are thus a universal history. In the later books Otto describes the medieval world, and the wide horizon of his observation includes the Slavic states in Eastern Europe, Italy, Greece, and the Orient. The eighth book is concerned with the themes of eschatology, namely the coming of the Antichrist, the Judgment of the world, and the final realization of God's reign.

索尔兹伯里的约翰(约 1115—1180)

约于 1115 年生于英国 Salisbury 附近的 Old-Sarum,1136—1147 年在 Paris 和 Chartres 求学,他的老师包括 Abaelardus、Gilbertus de Poitiers 和 Thierry de Chartres 等人,所以他也算是沙特尔学派的代表。1148 年以来他担任 Canterbury 总主教 Theobaldus 及其接班人 Thomas Beckett(1162—1170 年)的助手,后来撰写 Beckett 的传记。Johannes 热爱古代文化,他对当时的一切政治、教会和学术问题都有相当深入的了解,并与很多重要的人物有来往。

著作:《哲学导论》、《教廷史》(只保存开端)、《元逻辑》、《论政治》;还有一些人(Anselmus, Thomas Becket)的传记。

046. 《论政治》

《论政治》一书全名为《波利克瑞提库斯或论宫廷琐事和诸哲学家的思想》,献给 Thomas Becket(1118—1170 年)。作者 Johannes 曾经是 Henricus II(亨利二世,1133—1189 年)王以及他的宰相 Thomas Becket(贝克特)的顾问。后来 Becket 成为 Canterbury(坎特伯雷)的总主教并在 1170 年被暗杀;他曾经劝勉作者不要在宫廷里浪费他的时间,而要在哲学和文学研究中获得安慰。

本书的第一部包含对于宫廷生活的批评性描述,其中谈论贵族们的狩猎活动、音乐和戏剧表演、迷信和天文学。作者所用的语言表达他对古典文学的热切爱慕,又说明他对于整个人生的各个层面有深入的观察。

这部著作在政治思想史上有特殊的地位,因为作者在第四部分分析了国家的基本制度("宪法")、世俗权力和教会权力的关系以及统治者的权威基础。如果一个统治者的权威来自上主(神),那么一位缺少这种"神圣委托"的国王应该说是魔鬼的形象,而在这样的情况下,臣民们有权利不服从他,甚至可以审判和杀死他。作者大概还写过另一部著作来专门谈论"杀死暴君"的问题(*De exitu tyrannorum*《论暴君的死亡》)。

人的身体代表国度:脚等于是那些种地的农民,人的手臂代表那些保卫祖国的军人。眼睛和耳朵是官员们,而头部是国王。不同的肢体必须彼此帮助。"如果你要国度繁荣,高等的肢体要为低层的肢体服务。"任何一个身体还需要一个灵魂才能够生活,而宗教是这个"灵魂",即教会、罗马教宗和圣职人员。"国君是司铎们的仆人,必须服从他们。"世俗的统治者宣布法律,但他也宣布神圣的法律,因此他在神和自然之间有

Johannes Saresberiensis / John of Salisbury

Opera: *Entheticus, Historia pontificalis, Metalogicus (Metalogicon sive Apologia quasi pro arte dialectica), Policraticus (sive De nugis curialium et vestigiis philosophorum)*

Works: *Entheticus, Church History, Metalogicus, Polycraticus*

046. *Policraticus*

The whole title of the book is *Policraticus sive De nugis curialium et vestigiis philosophorum* (*Polycraticus or On the Trifles at Court and On Philosophical Investigations*), and it is dedicated to Thomas Becket (1118—1170). John had been the advisor of King Henry II (1133—1189) and of Thomas Becket at the English court. Becket who became Archbishop of Canterbury later and was murdered in 1170, had urged the author not to waste his time at court but to find consolation in philosophy and in studies.

The first part of the book contains a critical description of the life at the court, the hunting parties, music and theatrical performances, of superstitions and astrology. The language used shows the enthusiasm of the author for classical studies and his attentive observation of all aspects of human life.

The work has a special position in the history of political thought, since in the fourth book the author analyses the constitution of the state, relations between secular and ecclesiastical power and the basis of the authority of a ruler. If the ruler receives his authorization from God, then a king who lacks this divine mandate must be an image of the devil, and in this case the people are entitled to disobey him, they may even sentence him and kill him. The author probably wrote a separate work on the topic of tyrannicide (*De exitu tyrannorum*).

The human body is an image of the state: the feet are the people who till the soil, the arms are the soldiers who protect the fatherland. The eyes and the ears are the officials, and the head is the king. The different function of the members must complement each other. "If you want the state to prosper, the higher members must serve the lower ones." No body can live without a soul (religion), embodied by the servants of the Church, the Pope and the clergy. "The king is a servant of the priests, he must obey them." The divine law is promulgated by the ruler who has a mediating role between

某种"中介者"的角色。作者全面而平衡地评价宗教信仰，理性地观察社会关系，这就导致这部著作的成功，它不仅仅在中世纪，而且在文艺复兴时期也很受欢迎。*Policraticus* 是中世纪第一部伟大的涉及国度理论的著作。

God and nature. A healthy and balanced evaluation of religious faith and reasonable assessment of human social relations led to the lasting success of this work throughout the Middle Ages and the Renaissance. The *Policraticus* is the first great theory of a state written in the Middle Ages.

阿维罗伊（1126—1198）

生于西班牙 Cordoba 的律师家庭,在《古兰经》解释学、圣训、伊斯兰教法律（fiqh）、医学和哲学方面获得了良好的教育,后成为 Cordoba 的主任法官（quadi）,1182 年成为哈里发的随身大夫。在 1169—1195 年间,Averroes 回应了统治者 Abu Yaʻqub 的要求并编写了一系列注解著作,大部分针对 Aristoteles 的书。因为他没见过 Aristoteles 的 *Politika*,所以他给 Plato 的 *Politeia* 撰写了注解。

著作:《论宗教法律和哲学之间的协调》、《针对宗教教导的种种论证的考验》、《论灵魂注》、《不一致性的不一致性》

047. 《论灵魂注》

这部注解著作试图说明 Aristoteles 的名著 *Peri psychēs*（《论灵魂》）。对 Averroes 来说,Aristoteles 是最高的权威,人们都不应该对他提出怀疑或批评。Averroes 的书仅保存了 Michael Scottus 约于 1230 年作的拉丁语译本,阿拉伯语的原著失传。本注释本将 Aristoteles 的著作分为 325 个小段,并针对每一个段落作了详细的解释。

Averroes 的思想对西方哲学产生了深远的影响,尤其是他关于"人类只有一个共同的理智"的理论。Avicenna 曾说"主动的理智"（intellectus agens）是一切人的知识的共同来源。Averroes 进一步地认为连"被动的理智"（或"物质理智"intellectus materialis）也不是一种"个体化"的恒定原则;"被动理智"将与身体一同死去,所以人的个体灵魂没有不朽性,没有永恒的存在。对于 Averroes 来说,人的个体灵魂仅仅是一种高级的动物灵魂,在理智方面有局限性。感官认识是理性认识的前提和材料,而理智与个别人的存在只有很松散的关系。对 Averroes 来说,人的个体灵魂既不是理智性的,又不是永恒的。他认为只有"共同的理性灵魂"是永久存在的。通过这种理论 Averroes 想说明人的理解的普遍性,因为人的理解建立在一种不依赖于具体的个人的普遍原则之上。

因为这些教导贬低人的个体灵魂的价值和个体的不朽,那些基督徒学者就反驳它们。一方面,那些本来就反对 Aristoteles 的人可以很容易地指出 Averroes 主义中的危险之处,而另一方面,基督宗教的 Aristoteles 主义者（比如 Albertus Magnus 等人）被鼓励提出对 Aristoteles 思想的新解释（参见 Albertus 的 *De unitate intellectus* 和 Thomas Aquinas 的 *De unitate intellectus contra Averroem*）。在 Paris 的部分学者接受了 Averroes 的许多观点,同时他们肯定基督宗教的启示。因此,所谓的"拉丁语 Averroes 主义"形成宗教真理和哲学真理之间的隔阂。在 1277 年,Paris 的总主教

Averroes / Ibn Rushd

Opera: *Fasl, Manahij, Tafsir kitab an-nafs, Tahafut at-tahafut*
Works: *Decisive Treatise on the Agreement between Religious Law and Philosophy, Examination of the Methods of Proof Concerning the Doctrines of Religion, Great Commentary on The Soul, The Incoherence of the Incoherence*

047. *Tafsir kitab an-nafs / De anima*

This commentary explains Aristotle's work *Peri psychēs* (*On the Soul*). For Averroes Aristotle is the last authority which must never be doubted or criticized. Averroes' book is only extant in the Latin translation made by Michael Scottus around 1230. The Arab original is lost. The commentary divides Aristotle's work into 325 paragraphs and adds a detailed explanation to each of these paragraphs.

Averroes' thought deeply influenced Western philosophy, mainly through his theory that there is only one intellect for all human beings. Avicenna had said that the active intellect (intellectus agens) is the common source of knowledge for all men. Averroes goes one step further and holds that even the passive intellect (intellectus materialis) is not a permanent principle of individuation, it dies with the body, and thus there is no personal immortality of the human soul. For Averroes the individual souls are but highly developed animal souls which lack intellectual abilities. Sensual perceptions are precondition and material for intellectual insight, and the intellect is only loosely connected to the individual person. For Averroes the individual human soul is neither intellectual nor immortal. Only the "common intellectual soul" is immortal. With this theory Averroes wants to show the universality of human insight based on a universal principle that is independent of physical human beings.

Because these teachings disparage the value of the individual human soul and personal immortality, Christian thinkers objected to them. On the one hand those who rejected Aristotle found it easy to show the dangers of Averroism, on the other hand Christian Aristotelianists, like Albertus Magnus, were called forth to present a new interpretation of Aristotle's thought. (Confer Albertus' *De unitate intellectus*, and Thomas Aquinas' *De unitate intellectus contra Averroem.*) Some scholars in Paris accepted many of Averroes' teachings without denying the truths of Christian revelation. Thus this "Latin Averroism" maintained a dichotomy between religious and philosophical truth. In

Stephanus Tempier 正式谴责了 Aristoteles 思想中的部分观点，即一些与基督信仰有矛盾的观点，而这种谴责在学术界中有很大的影响，因为"伟大的哲学家"（即 Aristoteles）的权威性第一次被动摇。Averroes 主义在中世纪晚期、文艺复兴时期和现代时期继续影响了一些思想家，比如德国哲学家 Leibnitz。当 Kant 于 1781 年出版了他的 *Kritik der reinen Vernunft* 时，有人曾经说他的思想仅仅是 Averroes 主义的新版本。

1277 Stephen Tempier, the Archbishop of Paris, solemnly condemned some of the Aristotelian theses that contradict the faith, which had a great impact on academic circles, because the authority of "the Philosopher" was shaken for the first time. Averroism continued to influence thinkers in the late Middle Ages, in the Renaissance, and in modern times, for example Leibnitz. When Kant published his *Critique of Pure Reason* in 1781 it was remarked that his thought was just a new version of Averroism.

阿兰（约 1128—1202）

约于 1128 年生于法国北部的 Lille；他加入 Ordo Cisterciensium（熙笃会），曾在 Chartres、Tours、Paris 和 Orleans 求学，后在 Montpellier 和 Paris 担任哲学老师，也曾教过神学。他多次谈论作为学科的神学和其他学科的关系，也分析神学的术语和普通语言的差异。后来称这位百科全书式的神学家和学者为"doctor universalis"（"百科博士"）。

著作：《反克劳蒂安》（以比喻的方式陈列一切知识）、《论诸美德和诸恶习以及圣神的恩赐》、《神学术语》（一部按 ABC 字母编排的圣经学辞典）、《忏悔之书》、《诸比喻》、《自然的呻吟》（论人类的腐败）、《神学的规则》、《大全"因人类"》（一种神学大全的著作）

048. 《反克劳蒂安》

这部寓言式的史诗的全名是 *Anticlaudianus de Antirufino*（《反克劳蒂安论反儒菲诺斯》）。它成书于 1183 年，长达 4354 六韵步行。4 世纪末，诗人 Claudianus 曾经写了一首抨击 Rufinus 的诗——Rufinus 当时是 Theodosius 皇帝的大臣。这首 *In Rufinum*（《反儒菲诺斯》）将 Rufinus 描绘为一切邪恶的化身。黑暗的种种势力派遣了一个以人的形象出现的代表——即 Rufinus——到皇帝的王宫，其目的是为整个人类带来灾难。Alanus 的诗受了 Claudianus 的著作的启发，但他转化负面的因素，使之成为"创造新人"的乐观图景。

就像他的 *De planctu naturae*（《自然的呻吟》）一样，Alanus 的 *Anticlaudianus* 在开头也有自然（Natura）的哀叹和抱怨。自然看到人类离完美的状态非常远，所以她打算创造一个十全十美的人。她召集她的精神性姐妹们，即和谐（Concordia）、丰富（Plenitudo）、宠惠（Favor）、青春（Iuventus）、笑（Risus）、谦虚（Modestia）、羞耻（Pudicitia）、理性（Ratio）、道德（Honestia）、礼貌（Decorum）、明智（Prudentia）、虔诚（Pietas）、信仰（Fides）、慷慨（Generositas）和崇高（Nobilitas）来到她的花园——这个花园处于一种永恒的春天状态，花园的周围环绕着一片森林。自然的房子处于花园的正中间，在房子的墙上有古代文化奠基人或伟大英雄的图像，比如 Aristoteles、Plato、Seneca、Ptolemaeus、Cicero、Vergilius、Hercules、Odysseus 等人的图像。天上的种种美德在这个房子的大厅中聚会，而她自己宣布她的计划：她想创造一个新人，这个人既要有人性，也要有神圣的气质。明智赞美这个计划，但她说她要退出这个项目，因为人的灵魂需要有更高级的创造者。只有神能够创造一个人的灵魂。理性建议要征求 Phronesis（智慧，亦称 Sophia）的意见，因为她理解一切神圣的奥秘。和谐也同意，而现在所有的美德都

Alanus ab Insulis / Alain de Lille

Opera: *Anticlaudianus (sive De officiis viri boni et perfecti), De virtutibus et de vitiis et de donis Spiritus Sancti, Distinctiones dictionum theologicalium, Liber poenitentialis, Parabolae, Planctus naturae, Regulae de sacra theoliga (Theologiae Regulae), Summa "Quoniam Homines"*

Works: Anticlaudianus, On Virtues and Vices and the Gifts of the Holy Spirit, Distinctions of Theological Terms, Book of Penitence, Parables, The Plaint of Nature, Maxims of Theology, Sum "Quoniam homines"

048. *Anticlaudianus*

The full title of this allegorical epic is *Anticlaudianus de Antirufino*. It was written in 1183 and has the remarkable length of 4354 hexameter verses. At the end of the 4th century the poet Claudianus wrote a polemic poem against Rufinus, minister at the court of emperor Theodosius. This poem *In Rufinum (Against Rufinus)* depicts Rufinus as the embodiment of wickedness. The evil powers of darkness have sent a messenger in human shape to the imperial court so as to throw mankind into disaster, and this messenger is Rufinus. Alanus' poem is inspired by Claudian, but he turns it into a positive vision of the creation of a "new man".

Like his *De planctu naturae (The Plaint of Nature)*, Alanus' *Anticlaudianus* also starts with a complaint of Nature. Nature sees that humankind is far from perfection, and so she plans to create a perfect human being. She summons her heavenly sisters Concord, Plenitude, Favor, Youth, Laughter, Modesty, Bashfulness, Reason, Morality, Decorum, Prudence, Piety, Faith, Generosity, and Nobility to her garden of eternal spring, which is surrounded by a forest. In the middle of the garden there is the house of Nature, adorned with the paintings of Aristotle, Plato, Seneca, Ptolemy, Cicero, Virgil, Heracles, Odysseus, and other great heroes or originators of culture. In these halls the heavenly virtues hold an assembly, and Nature announces her plan: to create a new man who should be human and at the same time divine. Prudence (Prudentia) praises this plan but remarks she will retreat from the project since the soul must be created by a higher artist. Only God can create a human soul. Reason (Ratio) suggests to call in Wisdom (Phronesis, also named Sophia), because she understands all divine mysteries. Concord agrees, and now all support the plan to create a new man.

Phronesis orders seven virgins (the seven liberal arts) to build a chariot for the journey to Heaven. Grammar makes the shaft of the cart, Dialectica the axle, Rhetorica

支持创造新人的计划。

智慧命令七个贞女（即七个"自由学科"）来制造一辆车以走到天界。语法（Grammatica）制造车的辕，逻辑学（Dialectica）做轴承；修辞学（Rhetorica）用黄金包装整个车子，而其他的四个技艺生产四个轮子。五个感官等于是五匹马，它们负责拉这辆车。此后智慧、理性和明智启程，她们穿过一层一层的天界，直到来到神学（Theologia）那里。神学被描述为"吸取神圣的神灵"（haurit mente noym）。智慧说明自然的计划并请求神学带她们到最崇高的神的宫殿。神学带领智慧上去，但智慧必须留下马、车，甚至要放弃理性。

智慧经过水晶的天界，到达了"火天"（Empyreum），在这一层有天使的团体、享受真福的人和童贞玛利亚。在那些享受真福的人中有 Abraham、Petrus、Paulus、Laurentius、Vincentius de Lerin 等人。在神的宫殿那里有永恒的理念和一切万物的元素。三位一体的神被描述为结合为一的"泉源、溪流和大河"（fons, rivus, flumen），又被描述为光明（lumen）。神应允智慧的要求。他命令圣灵（Noys，亦译"圣神"）来创造一个完美的灵魂并将自己的封印打入这个灵魂，这样就使灵魂成为人的灵魂。智慧用一种药膏来保护灵魂，因为在回去的路上他们必须经过一层一层的行星天界。

此后自然着手于创造人的工作。她使用四种元素来创造一个美丽的身体，使这个人与 Narcissus 和 Adonis 有同样大的吸引力。每一个精神性的姐妹都在创造工程上有特殊的贡献，只有命运（Fortuna）被排除在外。当这个新人——其名字是 Juvenis（青年）——的创造被完成时，名誉（Fama）到处传播关于完美人的消息。Allecto，一个复仇女神，听到这个消息后就召集一切威胁着人类的恶习和灾难到阴间来。他们组织起来并攻击这个青年，但在另一方面，自然率领种种美德协助人。因此这个新人能够打败恶习和种种邪恶的力量，使它们撤退到阴间。这个胜利预示着一种充满爱与和谐的时期的开始；在这个新的时代，田地自愿地结果实，而玫瑰花没有刺。

Alanus 的诗并不属于什么特殊的哲学流派，它结合柏拉图思想因素（走向光明）和亚里士多德的思维（自然相当独立；一旦灵魂来到人间，神对灵魂就没有影响力）。理性不能引导人们完全理解神，而这个观点被视为对理性主义和亚里士多德主义的谴责。Alanus 第一次看到自然的力量在两个领域中发挥作用：在物理学的领域中以及在伦理道德和美德的领域中。Alanus 想结合宇宙中的一切力量和因素，使之成为一个神圣的制度，在这个系统中的最高顶点是神，但在另一方面他忽略基督的拯救的核心重要性——这一点在后来的文艺复兴思想中也是一个比较普遍的特征。

covers the chariot with gold, and the other four arts produce the four wheels. The five senses are the horses that draw the chariot. Now Wisdom, Ratio and Prudentia travel through the heavenly spheres until they reach Theology (Theologia). Theology is described as "imbibing the divine spirit" ("haurit mente noym"). Wisdom presents Natura's plan and asks Theology to lead her unto the fortress of the highest God. Theology leads her up, but Wisdom must leave behind horses, wagon, and even Reason.

Passing through the crystal heaven, Phronesis ascends to the Heaven of Fire (Empyreum), which is the location of the angelic choirs, the blessed, and the Virgin Mary. Among the blessed are Abraham, Peter, Paul, Lawrence, and Vincent of Lerins. At the palace of God one can see the eternal ideas and elements of all things. The Triune God is described as "fountain, stream and river" in one (fons, rivus, flumen), and as light (lumen). God grants Wisdom's request. He orders Noys (the Spirit) to create a perfect soul and then imprints His seal on her, thus making her human. Phronesis protects the soul with a kind of ointment, since they must pass the spheres of the planets on their way back.

Now Nature can start her work. She uses the four elements to create a beautiful body, equally attractive to Narcissus and Adonis. Each of the divine sisters contributes to the creation, only Fortuna is excluded from participation. As the new man, Juvenis ("Youth"), is completed, Fama (Fame) spreads the sensational news of the perfect man. Allecto, one of the Furies, hears about this new man and summons all vices and calamities that threaten mankind to the Tartarus. They organize themselves to attack the young man, but on the other side Nature commands the virtues in the fight. The new man defeats the vices and evil forces who retreat to the Tartarus. This victory inaugurates an era of love and harmony, where the fields yield their harvest spontaneously and roses have no thorns.

Alan's poem does not belong to any special philosophical school, it combines Platonic elements (ascent to the light) and Aristotelian thinking (Nature is quite independent, God has no influence on the soul, once it is released to the earthly sphere). The view that Reason cannot lead to a full understanding of God has been interpreted as a critique of rationalism and Aristotelianism. For the first time Alanus sees the functions of nature being at work in two realms: in the realm of physics, and in the realm of morality and virtue. Alanus wants to integrate all forces and elements of the universe into a divine order with God on the top, but on the other hand he neglects the central importance of the salvation of Christ, a trait that was rather common in later Renaissance thought.

约亚敬(约 1130—1202)

约生于 1130 年，家乡是意大利 Calabria 地区的 Celino，1177—1188 年成为 Corazzo 本笃会修院的院长，约于 1189 年离开了本笃会并创立 Fiore 的 San Giovanni 隐修院(在 Calabria 山区)，成为一个新的修会(Florenses)的创始人，但他的修会仅仅在意大利内传播，并在 17 世纪消失。Joachim 被视为一个伟大的修会改革者，但他的思想后来引起很多争论。第四届 Laterano 大会议(1215 年)曾谴责他的观点，因为 Joachim 的思想有"三位三神论"(tritheismus)的倾向。他的历史观影响了 Dante、Hegel、Solowjew 等人，"象征主义"的思维方式影响了 Bouvet(白晋)等人在清朝发展的"索隐派"(figurismus)。

著作：《反驳犹太人》、《新约和旧约的一致性》、《论信仰的信条》、《论七封印》、《圣 Benedictus 传记》、《默示录解读》、《象征之书》、《十条弦的圣咏集》、《论四福音》

049. 《象征之书》

这部著作大约于 12 世纪末写成，以两个非常优美的手抄本保存；也许其内容激发了 Dante 的想象力。

这部《象征之书》使用图画来解释 Joachim 的思想。在他的其他著作中(比如 *Concordia, Expositio in apocalypsim, Psalterium*)也能够找到一些图画，但在《象征之书》中，这些画图比较详细，并有比较全面的解释。这些图并不是一些神秘奥妙的"神视"，但它们的目标是以形象化的方式说明某些思想概念，比如通过"家谱之树"。这些"家谱"也表达 Joachim 的基本历史思想：42 代的人(每一代维持 30 年)形成一个阶段，先是"圣父的时期"(即犹太人的历史，从 Abraham 到基督，参见 *Mt* 1:17)，后来有"圣子"的时代(即教会的时期)，最后会有"圣神/圣灵"的时代(他认为，这个时代应该会在 1260 年开始)。作者认为，人类救恩史的第三个"状态"(所谓的 status)将是最后的时期，它将会带来一种"隐修式的教会"和"默观式的生活方式"。第三个时期将要维持到"基督第二次的降临"，这就意味着世界的末日。在"第三时期"到来之前，"反基督"会出现，而这个想法引起了很多人的恐惧。后来有一些 Franciscani 修会的作者认为圣 Franciscus 是"反基督"的伟大对手。

将历史分为三段的做法后来成为很普遍地被使用的分类方式(比如参见"古代—中世纪—近现代"或 Hegel 的思想等)。Joachim 认为，第一个时代的代表是"有过婚姻的人及老人"，第二个时代的代表是"圣职人员和青年"，而第三个时代的代表是"隐修者和婴儿"。历史的进展从"法律"(圣父)发展到"恩典"(圣子)，再走到"圣神/圣灵"内

Joachim de Flore / Joachim of Fiore

Opera: *Adversus Judaeos, Concordia novi ac veteris testamenti, De articulis fidei, De septem sigillis, De vita s. Benedicti et de officio divino secundum eius doctrinam, Expositio in apocalypsim, Liber figurarum, Psalterium decem chordarum, Tractatus super quatuor evangelia*

Works: *Against the Jews, The Unity of the New and Old Testament, On the Articles of the Faith, On the seven Seals, A Life of St. Benedict, Essay on the Book of Revelation, Book of Symbols, Psalter of the Ten Strings, An Essay on the Four Gospels*

049. *Liber figurarum / Book of Symbols*

This work was written at the end of the 12th century, it is extant in two magnificent manuscripts. Possibly it inspired Dante's visions.

The *Liber figurarum* is a collection of pictorial explanations of Joachim's thought. In his other main works (*Concordia, Expositio in apocalypsim, Psalterium*) one can also find occasional drawings. The *Book of Symbols* presents a comprehensive elaboration and explanation of the different drawings. These drawings are no mystical visionary pictures, but rather want to express certain ideas in a graphic way, for example by way of genealogical trees. These genealogies express Joachim's basic concept of history: 42 generations (each generation lasts for 30 years) form one era, first the era of God Father (Jewish history from Abraham to Christ, conf. *Mt* 1:17), then the era of God Son (the period of the Church), then the era of the Holy Spirit (expected to start in the year 1260). Joachim thinks that the third and last age (he calls it "status") in the history of salvation will bring about a monastic Church and a contemplative way of life. This era of the Holy Spirit would last until the coming of Christ, which is the end of the world. The arrival of the "Antichrist" would precede the beginning of the "Third Age", and this idea caused considerable fear. Later some Franciscan authors saw Saint Francis as the great counterpart of the "Antichrist".

The division of history into three ages became very popular (confer our "antiquity—Middle Ages— modernity", or Hegel's thought). Joachim identified the first age with married and old people, the second age with clerics and youths, and the third age with monks and infants. The progress of history goes from the law (Father), to grace (Son) to the freedom of the Holy Spirit. According to the last book of the Bible, the *Book of Revelations* (*Apocalypsis*), Joachim depicts the events or persons of the eschato-

的自由。根据《圣经》最后一部书卷(《默示录/启示录》),Joachim 描述"终末时期"的人物和事件,其中使用一个有七个头的大龙的形象。另一些形象意在解释"三位一体"的神:"十弦的琴"或三个互相渗透的圆圈(参见 Dante 的《神曲·天堂》33, 115)。

在后来几百年的时期内,Joachim 的思想产生了很深远的影响。那些支持隐修生活理想的人或反对世俗化的教会的人多传播或利用他的思想,因为他的著作似乎都肯定隐修院的生活是最完美的基督徒的生活。方济各会的"灵性派",那些"鞭策派"的人,清洁派和 Waldo(瓦尔多)派的人,都直接或间接受到 Joachim 那种反圣职主义和"千禧年"思想的影响。和许多中世纪学者一样,Joachim 试图在《旧约》中找一些暗示基督信仰的象征(所谓的 figurae,形象),比如以色列等于教会,红海的水暗示洗礼,沙漠代表试探,沙漠中的食粮代表感恩祭(圣体),火代表圣神/圣灵等等。这种"预示"的方法也影响了一些 17 世纪来华的传教士,他们想从基督宗教的角度来解释中国文化(比如解释汉字或一些"圣王")。这种思想学派被称为 figurismus(汉译为"索隐派"、"象征派"等等)。

logical time by using the image of a dragon with seven heads. Other images try to explain the Trinity: the ten-stringed psalter (lyre), or three inter-penetrating circles (conf. Dante, *Paradiso* 33,115).

Joachim's thought was very influential in the subsequent centuries. Many of those who embraced the monastic ideal or were opposed to a more secular Church, propagated or used his ideas, since his books suggested that monasticism is the most perfect Christian lifestyle. Spiritual Franciscans, flagellants, Cathars and Waldensians, all were directly or indirectly influenced by Joachim's anticlericalism and chiliasm (=millenarism). Like many other medieval scholars, Joachim tried to find symbols (figurae) in the Old Testament which suggested the truths of the Christian faith (Israel—Church, water of the Red Sea—baptism, desert—temptation, bread in the desert—eucharist, fire—spirit, etc). This method of "pre-figuration" also influenced some missionaries in China in the 17th century to interpret Chinese culture (for example Chinese characters or legendary rulers) in a Christian way (the so-called "figurists").

克里蒂安·德·特鲁瓦（约 1135—1190）

法国诗人，生活年代约为 1135—1190 年，生平不详。他可能在 Champagne 地区的女伯爵 Marie 的宫廷生活过一段时间，也许曾去过英国。他的文学作品（骑士文学）都是以本地语叙述的。Dante 曾经赞美他说法国因为 Chretien 的缘故在叙述诗学方面占有领导地位。

著作：《克里赛》、《伯斯华，或圣杯故事》（9000 多行，未完成）、《艾莱克与艾尼德》、《英国的威廉》、《兰斯洛特，或坐刑车的骑士》（骑士 Lancelot 追求 Guenievre 王后）、《伊万或带狮子的骑士》（关于骑士 Yvain 与 Laudine 的故事）

050. 《艾莱克与艾尼德》

这部宫廷小说长达 7000 行，约于 1165 年写成。它描述一个人失去骑士的荣誉，又失去爱情，并在一个漫长的过程中恢复它们。这种发展既可以视为"作补赎"，又可以解释为"寻找社会中的正当角色"。

在 Arthur（不列塔尼传奇中的亚瑟王）的圆桌骑士团体中，骑士们举行了一次狩猎活动。王子 Erec（他也是 Arthur 宫廷中的骑士之一）遇到了一个穿黑衣服的骑士和他的女士。陪同他们的有一个矮子，他用鞭子打了 Erec 一下，而 Arthur 王的妻子 Guinevere 也看到了这个重大的侮辱。Erec 失去了他的荣誉。他追赶那位"黑骑士"，要求他"赔罪"。在一次比武竞赛中，他克服了他的对手，获得了最高的奖品，同时又赢得 Enide 的欢心——她是他所在城市东道主的女儿。Erec 和他美丽的新娘 Enide 进入 Arthur 的宫廷，而 Arthur 王为他们准备了一场隆重的婚礼庆典。

年轻的夫妻沉迷在他们的爱中。他们的"蜜月"破坏了生活价值的平衡，因为 Erec 忽略了他的另一些身份：他也应该是一个骑士、统治者和公共生活的榜样。他的妻子 Enide 有一天在夜里自言自语地说她感到很悲伤，因为他的丈夫"太懒惰，不愿意拿起武器"，所以他失去了他的"骑士荣誉"。Erec 仅仅是假装睡觉的样子，因此听见了她的话并且感情上受到了深深的伤害。他决定要离开圆桌骑士团，他将妻子 Enide 带走，但中止与她的亲密来往，甚至禁止 Enide 和他说话。如果她敢说话，她将面临死刑！（不久后，他意识到这种态度过于极端，变得比较温和。）Enide 接受他的严厉对待并跟随他，通过这种方式表示她仍然爱他。

在他们的旅途中，Erec 和一些强盗、巨人、骑士进行决斗，充分表现了他的勇气和武力。他也遇到一些穷人或需要帮助的人，而他的行动证明他有同情心，愿意帮助

Chretien de Troyes / Chretien of Troyes

Opera: *Cliges, Conte del Gral (Perceval le Gallois, Perceval ou Le Conte du Graal), Erec et Enide, Guillaume d'Angleterre, Lancelot ou Le Chevalier de la charrette, Yvain ou Le Chevalier au lion*

Works: *Cliges, Perceval, Erec and Enide, Wilhelm of England, Lancelot, Yvain*

050. *Erec et Enide / Erec and Enide*

This court novel in ca. 7000 verses was written around the year 1165. It describes the loss of knightly honor, the loss of love and a restoration process which is at the same time a kind of penitence and the search for the proper role in society.

At the Round Table of King Arthur (a legendary King in Brittany), the knights meet for a festive hunting party. Erec, a prince and knight at Arthur's court, encounters a black knight and his lady. A dwarf who accompanies them strikes Erec with a whip, and Queen Guinevere, the wife of Arthur, witnesses this terrible insult. Erec has lost his honor. He pursues the black knight and demands satisfaction. At a tournament he can overcome his rival and together with the prize he also wins the hand of Enide, the daughter of his host in that city. Erec and his beautiful bride Enide enter Arthur's court, and a sumptuous wedding celebration is arranged by King Arthur.

The young couple is infatuated by their love. Their long honeymoon destroys the harmony of values, because Erec neglects his duties as knight, ruler and public model at Arthur's court. One night Enide complains in a sad monologue that her husband has lost his "chevalerie" (knightly honor), since he is "tired of bearing arms". Erec who has only pretended to be asleep hears her words and is deeply offended. He decides to leave the court and takes Enide with him but renounces the marital community with her, he even forbids her to talk to him. If she says a word she will be killed! (However after some time he realizes the egoism of this extreme attitude and becomes milder.) Enide bears this harsh treatment and accompanies him, which shows her continuing love for Erec.

On their journey Erec fights with robbers, giants and knights which gives him opportunity to show his courage and fighting capability. He also meets poor or needy people, and his actions prove his compassion and readiness to help those in need. Enide's

那些需要帮助的人。Enide 的忠诚爱情也经历了一些考验。Galoain 伯爵渴望拥有她，而 Enide 使用一个诡计来拯救她自己和 Erec。在另一个危险的情况中，Erec 看起来已经濒临死亡，但 Enide 仍然拒绝成为 Oringle 骑士的妻子。后来 Erec 还能克服危险并解救他的妻子。最后，他们来到一个神秘的花园，即所谓的"喜乐之园"。在那里巨大的红色骑士 Mabonagrin 守卫他的爱人。他曾经发誓说，永远不离开这个花园，除非有一个比他更强的骑士能够战胜他。在一次可怕的决斗中，Erec 能够征服这位巨大的骑士，这样也终结了他誓言的约束。因此，这两个骑士和他们的爱人一起回到 Arthur 的宫廷，那里的人隆重地欢迎 Erec 和 Enide。他们经历了种种外在的和情感上的考验，最终达到了一种 parfit amor（完美的爱，它也包括社会上的关心和博爱）。Erec 在 Nantes 被加冕为王的典礼结束了整部小说。

love is also put to the test. Count Galoain longs for her beauty, and Enide uses a trick to save Erec and herself. At one point Erec seems to be dead, but Enide still refuses to accept the offers of the brutal knight Oringle. Soon Erec manages to overcome the dangerous Oringle and frees his wife. Finally they arrive at the magic garden "Joie de la cort" (Joy of the court). The huge red knight Mabonagrin guards the garden and his lady. He has sworn never to leave his lady and never return to society unless a knight can defeat him. In a terrible duel Erec can subdue this mighty knight and thereby releases him from his oath. Both couples now return to Arthur's court where Erec and Enide are welcomed and honored. After undergoing so many physical and emotional tests and hardships they have arrived at "parfit amor" (perfect love, which includes also caritative concern, as shown above). The crowning ceremony of Erec at Nantes ends the novel.

迈蒙尼德(1138—1204)

犹太思想家,原名 Rabbi Moshe ben Maimon,缩写为 RaMBaM,生于西班牙 Cordoba;当 Almohades 征服西班牙时,他的家族移民到 Africa 北部。1159 到 1165 年他生活在 Morocco,后来迁居巴勒斯坦,后到埃及。从 1170 年起,他是开罗(埃及)苏丹的随身大夫,又是当地犹太人团体的会长。Maimonides 通常被视为中世纪最重要的犹太学者和思想家。

著作:《迷途指津》、《密西拿注解》(阿拉伯文)、《密西拿律法书》(希伯来文);还有别的哲学、法学和医学著作。

051.《迷途指津》

1190 年 Moses Maimonides 用阿拉伯语编写他的主要哲学著作(原名是 *Dalalat al-ha'irin*),而在作者去世的那一年(1204 年)Shemuel ibn Tibbon 将它译成希伯来语。不久后它又被译成拉丁语和其他语言。该著作的目标是调节哲学教导和律法书之间的种种冲突。有人曾说 Maimonides 的理性主义将"有位格神"的概念转换为一种哲学性的"神力"的概念,以永生不死的灵魂代替传统的终末论以及以哲学家的理想生活代替先知的风度。

作者阐述希腊和阿拉伯哲学历史发展的路线并指出他对于 Aristoteles、Al-Farabi 和 Averroes 的著作具有深入的了解。他认为古代的犹太人曾经培养宇宙论和形而上学方面的学问,但在流亡巴比伦后,犹太人的哲学传统被忽略。无论如何,因为哲学是犹太宗教的组成部分,犹太人不需要从希腊思想那里借来什么。希腊哲学和中世纪哲学"对于我们的律法并不陌生"(2,11),而哲学探讨"并不会破坏律法的基础"(1,33)。任何一位信徒都应该使用自己的理性来研究神和世界。Maimonides 提供的关于神存在的证明受了 Aristoteles 的启发,但也受 Al-Farabi 和 Avicenna 的影响。

Maimonides 所处理的问题是典型的中世纪哲学的问题:信仰和理性,《圣经》的哲学,神的存在,神的合一性与无形,神的意志和自由,作为神创造的世界,神对世界的指导,神和人之间的沟通以及启示的作用,伦理道德,人的自由意志和命运,不死和最终的事。作者反对使用任何人性的因素来描述神。在描写神方面只能使用一些否定性的说法。任何具体的肯定的说法都将限制神的存在,因此都是不可取的。在《圣经》中关于神的具体肯定的说法仅仅指向神的行动,它们并不描述神的本质。神是"第一个原因"(Aristoteles)和"一"(Plato)。通过神的种种显现,人知道神的存在,但人无法了解神,也不能具体地描写他的本性。

Moses Maimonides / Moshe Ben Maimon

Opera: *Dalalat al–ha'irin (More nevukhim), Kitab al–Siraj, Mishne Torah*
Works: *The Guide of the Perplexed, Commentary on the Mishna, The Torah Reviewed*

051. *More nevukhim / The Guide of the Perplexed*

The main philosophical work of Moses Maimonides was composed in Arabic (original title: *Dalalat al–ha'irin*) in 1190 and translated into Hebrew by Shemuel ibn Tibbon in 1204, the year of the author's death. Soon it was also translated into Latin and other languages. The aim of the work is to harmonize the contradictions between philosophical teachings and the text of the Tora. It has been said that Maimonides' rationalism transforms the personal God into a philosophical idea of the divine, substitutes the traditional eschatology with the immortal soul, and prophetic existence with the ideal life of a philosopher.

The author presents a thorough outline of the history of Greek and Arab philosophy, showing that he is well acquainted with the works of Aristotle, Al–Farabi, and Averroes. He believes that the Jews of antiquity cultivated the sciences of physics and metaphysics, but after the exile in Babylon, the Jewish philosophical tradition was somewhat neglected. However, since philosophy is an integral part of the Jewish religion, the Jews did not need to borrow from Greek thought. Greek and medieval philosophy is not "foreign to our Law" (2,11), and philosophical inquiry "will not undermine the foundations of the Law" (1,33). A believer even has the obligation to apply his intellect to the study of God and the world. Maimonides' proofs of the existence of God are inspired by Aristotle, but also by Al–Farabi and Avicenna.

Maimonides deals with the typical medieval questions of the philosophy of religion: faith and reason, philosophy of the Bible, the existence, unity, incorporality of God, His will and freedom, the world as created and guided by God, communication between God and man through revelation, ethics, free will and human fate, immortality and the last things. The author opposes any anthropomorphism in the description of God. Only negative attributes are suitable for God. Any positive descriptions would limit His being and are thus not admissible. The positive statements about God as they are found in the

根据律法书(Tora),神从无中创造这个世界(creatio ex nihilo),而如果 Aristoteles 知道《圣经》的启示,他也会接受这种 creatio ex nihilo。上主根据自己的意志和计划管理着这个世界。他以自己的方式知道将来的事,但这种"预先知道"并不排除人的自由。因此,神的全能和全知并不限制人的行为的伦理责任。Maimonides 的伦理学思想结合 Tora 中的法条和 Aristoteles 的"中间道路",即一种回避极端、追求和谐的生活方式。人们应该通过一种"对神的理性爱慕"而走向完美。人应该努力寻求认识神、渴望神以及与神的合一,而在过去 Moses、Aaron 和 Mirjam 都达到了这个层次。

Bible can only point to God's actions, not to His being. God is the "first cause" (Aristotle) and the "One" (Plato). Through His manifestations man knows about God's existence, but he cannot understand Him or positively describe His being.

According to the Tora, God created the world out of nothing (creatio ex nihilo), and even Aristotle would have accepted this creatio ex nihilo, had he known the revelation of the Bible. God governs the world He has created according to His will and providential plan. He knows the future in His own way, but this prescience does not preclude human freedom. Thus God's omnipotence and omniscience does not limit the ethical responsibility of human actions. Maimonides' ethical thought combines the laws of the Tora with the basic attitude of Aristotle's "middle way", a life-style that avoids extremes and pursues harmony. Humans should attain perfection through a kind of intellectual love for God. Man must strife to know God, to desire God and the union with Him, a union which was attained in the past by Moses, Aaron, and Mirjam.

萨克索（约 1150—1216）

丹麦人，生平不详；他曾在 Lund 总主教的宫廷工作。

著作：《丹麦历史》（包括神话以及关于 Amlet [Hamlet] 等国王的故事，启发了后世诗人的想象力）

052.《丹麦历史》

这是第一部丹麦历史的大篇幅著作，也是最有名的作品，是在 1185 年到 1222 年间以拉丁语写成的。整部著作分为 16 卷。关于作者没有很多资料，他曾经是 Lund 的总主教 Absalon 的秘书。Absalon 主教是 Copenhavn 城的创立人，他在 1201 年去世。Saxo 和 Absalon 都在法国受教育。*Gesta* 的拉丁语是很优雅的，这就表明 Saxo 很熟悉 Vergilius、Horatius、Ovidius、Curtius Rufus、Valerius Maximus、Martianus Capella、Beda、Paulus Diaconus 和 John of Salisbury 等人的著作。与 Snorri Sturluson 不同，Saxo 并不想保存自己民族的语言，而选择了欧洲通用的语言（拉丁语）来向许多欧洲的读者叙述自己民族的历史。

第 1 卷到第 9 卷涉及丹麦的早期历史，作者从 Dan 王开始叙述 60 多个有传奇色彩的国王的故事。这些传奇是珍贵的资料来源，因为它们描述在基督宗教到来之前的维京人的生活与神话。其中最著名的故事是丹麦王子 Hamlet 的故事，他后来成为 Shakespeare 悲剧中的主人翁。第 10 卷包含 Harald Bluetooth 的时期，而这位国王开始接触基督宗教。第 11 卷到 13 卷覆盖与 Svend Estridson 的统治有关系的事件以及 Niels 王的时期。第 14 卷很仔细地描述 Erik Emunes 登基的情况以及 Absalon 于 1177 年被选为总主教的过程。第 15 和 16 卷涉及 Valdemar 大王的统治和 Knut VI 的时期。

Saxo Grammaticus

Opera: *Gesta Danorum*
Works: *Danish History*

052. *Gesta Danorum / Danish History*

This first and most famous monumental work on the history of Denmark was written in Latin in the years from 1185 to 1222. It is divided into 16 books. Few things are known about the author who was secretary of Absalon, the archbishop of Lund. Being also the founder of Copenhavn, Absalon died in 1201. Both Saxo and Absalon received their education in France. The refined Latin text of the *Gesta* shows that Saxo was well acquainted with the works of Virgil, Horace, Ovid, Curtius Rufus, Valerius Maximus, Martianus Capella, Beda, Paulus Diaconus, and John of Salisbury. Unlike Snorri Sturluson who tried to preserve the national language, Saxo wanted to use the common language of Europe (Latin) to present the history of his people to many educated readers in Europe.

Books 1 to 9 treat the early period of Danish history, starting with king Dan and narrating the stories of around 60 legendary kings. These legends are a precious source of information concerning the life and mythology of the Vikings before the advent of Christianity. The most famous figure became the Danish prince Hamlet, who is the protagonist in Shakespeare's drama. Book 10 presents the era of Harald Bluetooth who came in contact with Christianity. Books 11 to 13 cover the events connected with the reign of Svend Estridson and King Niels. Book 14 describes in great detail the accession to the throne of Erik Emunes and the election of Absalon to the archbishopric in 1177. Books 15 and 16 are concerned with the rule of king Valdemar the Great and king Knut VI.

哈特曼(约1150—1220)

德国诗人,他曾在隐修院接受教育,后在 Swabia 宫廷任 ministerialis(高官);他参与1179年的十字军运动。他的著作继承 Chretien de Troyes 和 Henricus de Veldecke 的宫廷文学,后来成为 Wolfram de Eschenbach 和 Gottfried de Strasbourg 的榜样。他第一次向德语读者介绍 Arthur 王的传说,也是骑士传奇的创始人。他的语言是中古高地德语(mittelhochdeutsch)的典范,而他的道德观(以 maze [节制]为核心)成为宫廷风度的基本原则。

著作:《可怜的亨利》、《埃雷克》、《格列高利乌斯》、《伊万因》

053. 《可怜的亨利》

这部用中古高地德语写成的史诗大约于1195年完成(取决于作者是参与1189年的十字军运动还是1197年的十字军运动)。主题是一个骑士的苦恼和皈依。

年轻的 Herre Heinrich(亨利)代表宫廷骑士的理想,他很崇高、英俊、富有、在社会上受尊敬和爱慕。突然一种严重的皮肤病夺取了他的可爱外貌,同时也结束了他生活中的一切乐趣。这位原来很乐观的人现在无法理解或接受他的命运(作者称他为第二个 Job)。他的错误和罪在于这里:他不认为原来的成就是上主给予的恩典,而视之为自己的成就。他不愿意看到自己的命运是信仰的考验。他去了很多地方,花了很多钱,都是为了治好他的病,但都没有效果。最终,在 Salerno 有一个很著名的大夫告诉他,治好病的唯一办法是一个自由的、纯洁的贞女主动地为 Heinrich 牺牲自己的生命("心血")。现在 Heinrich 放弃一切希望,他离开社会,退隐到一个乡下农民的朴素家庭。农人、他的妻子和他们的女儿照顾这位可怜的骑士。尤其是年轻的女儿对这个悲伤的男人表现了热切的关心和同情。

三年后,Heinrich 逐渐发现,他的苦难本来是一种惩罚,因为他原先的生活态度过于世俗化和骄傲。他认为,社会的荣誉和财富是自己的成就,不是上主的礼物。有一次,照顾他的农夫问他如何治好他的疾病,他告诉他们那位大夫所说的话。当女儿听到这些,她就说她要为骑士牺牲自己的生命,这是她的热烈并坚定的渴望,因为这样她将获得天堂里的永远喜乐。她说服她的父母,而 Heinrich 仍然很自信地认为,别人应该替他作补赎。他们启程去大夫那里,而他就准备挖出这位女士的心。在最后的时刻,Heinrich 看到这个女孩子躺在医生面前,他比较她美丽的身体和自己的疾苦身体,突然转变态度并阻止医生杀害她。现在 Heinrich 愿意接受自己的疾病为一种来自

Hartmann von Aue

Opera: *Der arme Heinrich, Erec, Gregorius, Iwein*
Works: *Poor Henry, Erec, Gregory, Iwein*

053. *Der arme Heinrich / Poor Henry*

This epic in Middle High German about the sufferings and the conversion of a knight was written ca. in 1195 (depending on whether the author took part in the crusade of 1189 or of 1197).

The young Lord Henry ("Herre Heinrich") embodies the ideal of courtly knighthood, he is noble, handsome, rich, respected in society and beloved. Suddenly a severe skin disease takes away his amiability and his joy. The optimistic Henry turns into someone who just cannot understand his fate (he is compared to Job). His error and guilt is that he does not understand his former success as God-given grace but rather as his own achievement. He is far from seeing his calamity as a test of faith. He travels far and wide and spends much money to find a cure for his ailment, but it is all in vain. Finally a famous doctor in Salerno tells him that the only way to heal him is this: a free and pure virgin has to voluntarily sacrifice her life ("herzebluot" "blood of her heart") for him. Now Henry gives up and retreats to a house in the countryside where a tenant receives him. The simple farmer, his wife and their young daughter care for the poor knight. Especially the daughter shows much concern and affection for the sad man.

In the course of three years Henry gradually realizes that his suffering is a punishment for his secular and proud attitude. He only perceived honors and wealth as his own merits and not as a gift from God. Once the farmer asks him about a possible cure for his disease, and he tells them what the doctor said. As soon as the daughter hears this, she expresses the ardent and firm will to sacrifice her own life for the knight, since this would earn her eternal joy in heaven. She persuades her parents to let her go, and Henry is still proud enough to think that someone else has to do penance for him. They travel to the doctor who prepares to cut out the girl's heart. At the last moment, as Henry sees the girl lying before the doctor and as he compares the beauty of her naked young body with his own sick body he suddenly changes his mind and prevents the doctor from killing her. Now Henry is ready to accept his own sickness as God-sent punishment and

神的惩罚,愿意一生过补赎的生活。他愿意无条件地接受上主对他的安排,而在这个时刻,他的病也突然好了。他皈依的奇迹带来了治病的奇迹。他和那个女孩子结婚,恢复他的财富并生活在社会的世俗世界中,但现在对上主有一种新的态度。这个故事中的女孩的角色非常独特,她结合两种爱:一种"方济各式的"同情心(caritas)及一种个人的爱情(amor),参见 *Erec* 中的女士 Enide。

prepares to lead a life of penitence. He is willing to accept God's will totally, and in this moment he is cured. The miracle of his conversion leads to the miracle of his healing. He marries the girl, he becomes rich again and they lead a life in the secular world, but with a new orientation towards God. The image of the girl in the story uniquely combines a kind of "Franciscan" compassion (caritas) and personal love (amor), confer the role of Enide in *Erec*.

第五篇

中世纪盛期和经院哲学的黄金时期
The High Middle Ages and the Golden Age of Scholasticism

(1200—1320 AD)

- *Triumph of St. Thomas d'Aquin*

依诺森三世（1160—1216）

这位教宗的原名是 Lotario Segni，他于 1160 年出生在 Agnani 的 Scotti 贵族家庭中；他曾在 Paris 求学，后在 Bologna 学习法律，约于 1185 年开始为罗马教廷服务，1190 年成为执事枢机，并于 1198 年被选为罗马教宗，取名 Innocens III；他推动教会内部的改革并支持新兴的修会（比如"方济各会"和"道明会"），于 1215 年召开了"第四届 Lateran 会议"，即中世纪规模最大的教会会议（参与者 1200 位，其中 800 位是主教）；他面对德国皇帝给意大利的压力，承担 Fredericus II 的教育，又于 1209 年被迫开除英国国王 Johannes（即 John Lackland）。在学术上，Innocens III 编写了《第三法律论集》，于 1210 年将这部巨著送给 Bologna 大学，因此后人尊称他为 pater iuris（"法律之父"）。

著作：《第三法律论集》、《论人生的悲惨情况》、《书信集》（保存有 6000 封信，其中有很多法令）；还有一些神学著作和诗歌。

054. 《论人生的悲惨情况》

本著作的别名是 *De contemptu mundi*（《论蔑视世俗》），成书时间是 1195 年。作者 Lotario Segni 三年后被选为教宗，并取名 Innocens III。这本书在中世纪非常有名，它是流传最广泛的著作之一，保存有无数的手抄本，也很早被印刷（1473 年在 Colonia）。

第 1 卷描述人生的一切令人感到厌恶的现象：肉身的虚弱和诱惑，疾病和健康问题以及对死亡的恐惧。这些因素始终降低人生的美丽和幸福。无论是孩子、中年人或老年人，都遭受种种威胁，面对无数的忧虑。没有任何年龄段的人或任何社会地位的人能完全摆脱压力和忧患的困扰。一个人的生活从一开始就令人感到讨厌："人是尘土和灰尘的产物，甚至是那种不体面的精液的产物。人是由欲望和淫欲而生育的，甚至是在罪恶的枷锁中诞生的。人生活在世界上必须经历很多恐惧、忧患和痛苦，甚至要面对死亡。"

第 2 卷讨论人类的主要恶习。这些恶习容易消除幸福和安乐，其根源是人们对财富、荣誉和享受的追求。在人类历史上，对银子、地位和色情的渴望始终给无数的人带来灾难和痛苦。第 3 卷涉及最后的事，即死亡、最后的审判和地狱中的惩罚。

这部小论文的目的是向读者指出人生在一切情况和时期中面对的种种限制和不幸。对于人生处境（conditio humana）的描述是极其悲观、森严的，旨在压服人们的骄傲和自信。Innocens 在前言中说，他还想写另一部论文来赞美人生的尊严和美丽，然而因为他始终忙于教务，他无法写成与他的名著对应的一种比较乐观的作品。

Innocens III / Innocent III

Opera: *Compilatio tertia, De miseria humanae conditionis, Epistulae*
Works: *The Third Compilation of Legal Texts, On the Misery of the Human Life, Epistulae*

054. *De miseria humanae conditionis* / *On the Misery of the Human Life*

This book is also known under the title *De contemptu mundi* (*On the Contempt of the World*), it was written in 1195, three years before Lotario Segni was elected pope and took the name Innocent III. One of the most famous and popular books in the Middle Ages, it was copied innumerable times and printed very early (1473 in Cologne).

The first book describes in gloomy terms all the disgusting and repulsive aspects of life: the weaknesses and temptations of the human body, diseases and illnesses, the fear of death. All these inimical forces constantly impair the beauty and happiness of human life. Whether as child, adult or old man, a human person is threatened by many fears and dangers. No age of life and no social position is free from anxiety and pressure. The life of a human person is disgusting right from the beginning: "Man is made of dust and of ashes, even worse, he is made of the disgusting fluid of semen; he is born in the heat of desire, of lust, even worse, in the bonds of sin; he is born to face fear, anxiety and suffering, even worse, he must face death."

The second book discusses the main vices which threaten happiness and peace. These evils and bad habits grow out of the human pursuit of wealth, honor and pleasure. Greed for money, position, and sex have always brought about many calamities and sufferings upon innumerable people. The third book is concerned with the last things, namely with death, the last judgment, and eternal punishment in Hell.

The purpose of the short treatise in 3 books is to show the reader the precarious condition of human life which is surrounded by countless limitations and calamities in all situations and at all times. The utterly gloomy and pessimistic description of the state of man (*conditio humana*) wants to damp the pride and conceitedness of men. In the preface Innocent says he plans to write another treatise which would extol the dignity and beauty of the human existence. However, as he was busy with ecclesiastical duties he did not manage to write a more positive counterpart to his famous work.

沃尔夫拉姆·冯·埃申巴赫(约 1170—1220)

约于 1170 年生于德国 Ansbach 地区的 Eschenbach，他的家庭属于骑士阶层，而他没有受过高等教育。他曾为 Wertheim 伯爵服务，但除此以外没有更多关于他生平的资料。他曾在 Thuringia 结识 Walther von der Vogelweide，也通晓一些法国文学著作。

著作：《帕尔齐法尔》、《破晓歌》、《蒂图埃尔》、《威廉》(叙述十字军 Guillaume d'Orange 的故事)

055. 《帕尔齐法尔》

这部小说分为 16 卷，共 24812 行，用古高地德语写成。

主人翁的名字 Parzival 曾经被解释为"穿过山谷"或"纯粹的愚蠢人"或"经过考验的人"。Parzival 的父亲是 Gahmuret de Anjou 骑士，他既渴望爱情，又渴望完成一些伟大的事业，所以他的行动相当极端。他和东方女王 Belacane 结婚，而他们的儿子 Feirefiz("优美的脸色"或"好儿子")的脸部分是白的，部分是黑的。因为 Balacane 不是基督徒，Gahmuret 离开她，前往西方，在那里和另一位女王 Herzeloyde("受苦的心")结婚，这就是 Parzival 的母亲。不久后，Gahmuret 需要帮助东方的一个哈里发，必须离开 Herzeloyde。当他的妻子获悉丈夫在外面阵亡时，她感到极度的悲伤并崩溃了，但在那时她第一次感觉到腹中的胎儿。因为她失去了她的丈夫，她想方设法绝对不让他的儿子成为骑士和离开她。因此，她与孩子生活在偏僻的地方，不告诉 Parzival 他的名字，回避任何社会上的来往。

有一次她的儿子在森林中杀了一些小鸟，而 Herzeloyde 禁止他伤害"上主的造物"。Parzival 问她："什么是神？"他的母亲形容上主为一种很光耀的，有人面的存在。人应该向神祈祷，但她仅仅提到上主的 triuwe(忠实)，没有谈论神的 genade(恩典)。不久后 Parzival 遇到三个来自 Arthur 王圆桌骑士团的骑士，认为他们是"神"并马上自己想成为骑士。他的母亲再无法阻止他。母亲的教导不太充分，因此他无法理解这些简单的教导将会为别人造成伤害。他骑着一匹老马，身穿一个小丑的衣服，这样出发。当他走出家园时，他的母亲 Herzeloyde 因为太难过，当场就死去了，但因为儿子没有回头，他没有发现他的告别导致了母亲的丧亡。

Herzeloyde 曾经告诉他应该获得女士们的欢欣，使她们高兴。现在 Parzival 在路边看到正睡觉的 Jeschute 女士并直接吻她。他也夺走她的项链，而因此 Jeschute 那个充满嫉妒的丈夫 Orilus 怀疑她并命令她进行很长的补赎之旅，其间 Jeschute 受了很

Wolfram von Eschenbach

Opera: *Parzival, Tagelieder, Titurel, Willehalm*
Works: *Parzival, Dawn Songs, Titurel, Willehalm*

055. *Parzival*

This novel in 24812 verses is divided into 16 books; it was written in Old High German.

The name Parzival has been interpreted as "pierce the valley", "parseh fal = pure fool" (Arab) or as "peritor = quaeritor" (=testperson, adventurer). Parzival's father is the knight Gahmuret of Anjou whose desire for love and great honor induces him to do extreme things. He marries an oriental queen, Belacane, and they have a son called Feirefiz ("fair face" or "fair fils = good son"), whose face is speckled partly white and partly dark. Since Belacane is a pagan, Gahmuret does not stay with his wife and goes to the West, where he marries another queen, Herzeloyde ("suffering heart"), the mother of Parzival. Gahmuret is bound to help a caliph in the East and leaves Herzeloyde. As Herzeloyde receives the news that her husband has fallen, she is overwhelmed with sadness and has a breakdown, but at the same moment she feels her baby for the first time in her womb. Because she lost her husband so soon she wants to prevent by all means that her son leaves and becomes a knight too. Therefore she keeps him at home, hides his name and true identity from him and avoids contact with the society.

Once her son kills some sparrows in the forest, and Herzeloyde forbids him to harm "God's creation". "What is God?" Parzival asks, and his mother describes God as something bright with a human face. One should pray to God. However, she only mentions God's steadfastness (triuwe) and not His forgiving grace (genade). As Parzival encounters three knights from King Arthur's Round Table, he thinks they are "God" and is immediately attracted to become a knight. His mother can no longer hold him back. Her instructions are short and not very useful, and since he cannot fully understand them, they bring harm to others. Riding an old horse and clad in a fool's dress he departs. As he leaves Herzeloyde, his mother is so sad that she collapses and dies, but since he does not turn back he does not realize that his departure has caused his mother's death.

Herzeloyde has told him to win the favor of women and make them happy, and seeing the sleeping Jeschute on the way, Parzival forces a kiss on her. Since he also takes

多苦,都是 Parzival 那种愚蠢无知的行为造成的。后来 Parzival 遇到自己的表姐 Sigune,她才告诉他自己的名字。她也向 Parzival 述说自己对于已亡丈夫的留恋,而 Parzival 第一次听到什么是"痛苦",但无法有比较深入的了解。又过了一段时间,他看到"红色骑士"Ither 以及他的闪亮武器和盔甲。因为 Parzival 仅仅看到自己的需要,他从后面(以强盗的方式)杀死这个骑士并夺取他的武器和战马。由于这种行为,Arthur 王的骑士们都认为,Parzifal 根本没有资格成为他们圆桌团体中的骑士。

Parzival 的叔叔 Gurnemanz 仍然喜欢这个青年并在自己的堡垒中给予他一些教育。他教导 Parzival 宫廷贵族生活的礼貌和骑士们的道德价值,如荣誉、仁慈(不杀敌人)、谦虚、节制(maze)和克己(zuht)、勇气、耿直(不说谎)、对财富的责任心和卫生知识。Gurnemanz 又告诉这个青年,"不要问太多问题"。Parzival 开始他的骑士生活并拯救 Condwiramur("我们走到一起"),她本来是 Gurnemanz 的侄女。他与她结婚,但不久后又离开她,因为他想寻找自己的母亲,他始终认为母亲还活着。

在他的徘徊和远游中,Parzival 偶然地来到 Munsalvesche(即 mundi salvatio"世界的拯救"),就是圣杯堡。圣杯(grail)是一块神秘的石头(或杯爵,它也被称 lapis ex caelis"从天上来的石头"或 lapis electrix"有电的石头"),而这个圣杯具有激活或治愈的力量。在每年的圣周五(耶稣受难日)一只白鸽子(代表圣神/圣灵)从天上送来一块圣饼(基督的圣体)到圣杯那里。圣杯团体的成员都是一些过独身生活的骑士或贞女,他们形成一种宗教组织或修会(参见 1119 年成立的圣殿骑士团)。只有圣杯堡的王被允许结婚。然而,当 Parzival 来到 Munsalvesche(圣杯堡)时,他对圣杯的意义一点都不了解,而没有人告诉他这些事。当 Repanse de Schoye("喜乐的观念",即 Herzeloyde 的姐妹)在一次隆重的游行中抬来圣杯时,Parzival 见到了"天上的石头"的显现,也看到圣杯的治病作用。Parzival 也观察到 Amfortas(圣杯堡的王)因一种神秘的创伤而遭受痛苦,但 Parzival 想起了 Gurnemanz 的话,所以他不问圣杯王关于他疾病的事。这一点后来被认为是一种严重的错误:他没有表现同情。当 Parzival 第二天早上醒来时,他就是一个人,无法找到任何人。他感到迷惑并离开了这个神秘的地方。

过了一些时间 Sigune 向他说明他在圣杯堡犯下了什么错误。更糟糕的是,圣杯的使者 Cundrie 来到 Arthur 的宫殿并公开地诅咒 Parzival。这就使他陷入一种沮丧绝望的状态。在他的痛苦中他问:"神是什么?我为什么要服从于他呢?"他感觉到神给他安排的命运很不公平,所以他否定神,因为他从一种封建主义的"贡献—报酬"关系的概念来理解神。他离开人们的团体并用四年之久巡回各地,他要靠自己的能力寻找圣杯堡,但没有结果。他非常悲伤,但仍然意识不到自己的罪,始终远离人类社会的快乐,并且远离神。

很久以后,他再次遇到Sigune并告诉她自己的痛苦。她感觉到 Parzival 已经开始

away her necklace, her jealous husband Orilus becomes very suspicious and sends her away for a long journey of penitence, where the innocent Jeschute suffers a lot, only because of Parzival's foolish and ignorant behavior. Then Parzival meets his cousin Sigune who tells him his own name. She also shares with him how much she still loves her dead husband, and Parzifal is for the first time confronted with suffering, but his understanding of it is very limited. Some time later he sees a red knight, Ither, and since he wants to become a knight and needs weapons and armor, he just kills the red knight from behind and robs his armor and horse. This behavior makes it clear for the knights at Arthur's Table that Parzival is not qualified to be one of them.

Parzival's uncle Gurnemanz likes the young man and tries to educate him at his castle. He teaches him knightly and courtly manners and moral values like honor, clemency (spare enemies), humility, moderation (maze) and self-control (zuht), manliness, uprightness (no lies), responsible care for money and goods, cleanliness. Gurnemanz also tells the young man "not to ask many questions". Parzival starts a life as knight and saves Condwiramur ("We are brought together"), a niece of Gurnemanz. He marries her but soon leaves her again in order to look for his mother whom he believes to be still alive.

On his journeys Parzival also comes by chance to Munsalvesche (=mundi salvatio "salvation of the world"), the castle of the Grail. The Grail is a mysterious stone (or chalice, also called "lapis ex caelis" or "lapis electrix") which has a lifegiving and healing power. Every year on Good Friday a white dove (symbol of the Holy Spirit) brings a host (body of Christ) down from heaven to the Grail. The members of the Grail community are celibate knights and virgins, they form a kind of religious order (confer the Order of the Templars, founded in 1119). Only the king of the Grail is allowed to marry. However, as Parzival is received in Munsalvesche, he does not know anything about the meaning of the Grail and nobody tells him about it. He witnesses the appearance of the "heavenly stone" and its healing effects, as Repanse de Schoye ("Idea of Joy", Herzeloyde's sister) carries in the Grail in a ceremonial procession. Parzival also sees that Amfortas, the King of the Grail, suffers from a mysterious wound, but Parzival remembers Gurnemanz's words and does not ask about the King's ailment, which is later interpreted as a grave sin of omission: he fails to show sympathy. As Parzival wakes up the next morning, he is alone and cannot find anyone. Confused he leaves this mysterious castle.

Some time later Sigune tells him that he made a mistake at the castle of the Grail. Even worse, the messenger of the Grail, Cundrie, arrives at Arthur's court and openly casts a curse on Parzival which causes his despair. He asks in torment: "What is God? Why should I serve him?" He feels that his divinely ordained fate is unjust and denies God, whom he perceives in a kind of feudalistic "merit—reward" framework. He leaves the human community and travels around for more than four years in order to find the Grail on his own, but without result. He is utterly sad but still does not realize his own guilt, always living far from the joys of human company and far from God.

有改进并且安慰他。他继续骑着马寻找圣杯堡，甚至在圣周五那一天带着武器——这一点表明他离人们团体和宗教团体有多远。他的马带他到隐修士 Trevrizent（实际上他是 Amfortas 的弟兄和 Parzival 的叔叔）那里。与 Trevrizent 那种弟兄般的交谈为 Parzival 带来了一个伟大的转折点，因为他开始意识到一切人类的行动都以某种方式涉及到他人的痛苦，这样一切行动都意味着罪和罪责。现在 Parzival 看到他部分上要为他母亲早死的事实负责，并且他和 Cain 一样杀了自己的亲戚，即 Ither。他承认自己没有关心 Amfortas 的痛苦是一种忽略的罪。此后他不再抱怨神，而开始控诉自己，他成为一个新的人，开始忏悔和改变。

他和 Gawan 骑士进行一次决斗，此后再次被接纳到 Arthur 的圆桌团体，但不久后他又离开。他寻找自己的妻子并在路上遇到一个强大的骑士；这个骑士就开始和 Parzival 决斗。Parzival 的剑被折断，而在这个危险的情况中，两个人彼此认出对方：这位骑士原来是 Parzival 的弟兄 Feirefiz。那位非基督徒 Feirefiz 的态度表现非常高尚，而两个人都被接受进入 Arthur 的骑士团。现在圣杯的使者 Cundrie 宣布说圣杯石头上的文字表明 Parzival 将来要成为圣杯王。在 Feirefiz 的陪同下他再次进入 Munsalvesche。这个时候他问 Amfortas 这个具有救恩意义的问题："您有什么忧虑呢？"此后 Amfortas 的病就被治愈了。Parzival 也找到了他的妻子 Condwiramur 并发现她生了双胞胎。其中一个小男孩儿（Loherangrin）就被预定为圣杯团体的领导，即 Parzival 的继承人。Feirefiz 爱上了 Repanse de Schoye 并接受洗礼。他们结婚并前往印度。在那里他们的儿子 Johannes（约翰）将要成为一个具有传奇色彩的基督徒国王（所谓的 Prester John）。Parzival 在人格上的成长意味着他对社会的关怀扩大了，最后他达到一种包括东方和西方的基督徒式的制度，而在这种思想中圣杯堡的团体（即隐修者的宗教生活）比骑士的生活（Arthur 的圆桌）更有吸引力。在这种普遍的理想中一切人都是一个大家庭的成员——似乎一切重要的人物都是 Parzifal 的亲戚。

After a long time he meets Sigune again and tells her about his sorrows. She feels that he has begun to change already and consoles him. On his horse he continues his sad search, carrying arms even on a Good Friday, which shows how far he still is from human and religious community. The horse brings him to Trevrizent, a hermit (in fact Amfortas' brother and Parzival's uncle). The brotherly conversation with Trevrizent brings the great turning point in Parzival's life, because he starts to realize that all human action is somehow connected to the suffering of other people and therefore implies guilt. Parzival sees now that he is partly guilty of his mother's early death, that similar to Cain he killed Ither who was his relative. He also admits that not caring about Amfortas' suffering was a sin of omission. Now he does no longer accuse God but instead accuses himself, he is a new person, open for penitence and change.

After a fight with the knight Gawan, Parzival is accepted again in the company of Arthur, but soon he leaves again. He searches for his wife and on the way meets a mighty knight who starts to fight with Parzival. Parzival's sword breaks, and in this dangerous situation they recognize each other: it is Feirefiz, Parzival's brother. The pagan Feirefiz shows a noble spirit and both are received at Arthur's Table. Now Cundrie, the messenger of the Grail, announces that the inscription on the Grail stone shows Parzival to be the future king of the Grail. He enters Munsalvesche again, together with Feirefiz. This time he asks Amfortas the salvific question: "What worries you?" whereupon Amfortas is healed. Parzival also finds his wife Condwiramur and discovers that she has borne him twins. One of the two boys (Loherangrin) is designated as his successor in the Grail community. Feirefiz falls in love with Repanse de Schoye and is baptized. They marry and travel to India, where their son John is to become a legendary Christian king ("Prester John"). The personal growth of Parzival implies a growth of social ethical concern finally leading to the vision of a Christian order for East and West, in which the Grail community (religious life of monks) is more attractive than the knightly life (Arthur's Round Table). In this universal ideal all people are members of one family—almost all main figures are Parzival's relatives.

斯诺里·斯图鲁松(1179—1241)

1178年或1179年生于冰岛,他是一位富有的人,曾经在1215—1218年和1222—1231年间任冰岛最高官员。他曾两次前往挪威,曾是挪威王Haakon IV的朋友,但因为Haakon想占领冰岛,Snorri卷入政治斗争,因同情挪威王的舅舅而引起挪威王的反感,于1241年在冰岛被处决。Snorri Sturluson是基督徒,知识渊博,他也曾编写过挪威王的历史(即 *Heimskringla*)。

著作:《埃达》(《散文埃达》,一种诗学手册,包括对古代神话的解释)、《海姆斯克林拉》(挪威诸王史,从神话的开端到1184年)、《埃吉尔萨迦》

056.《埃达》

直到今天"埃达"这个名称的意义仍不确定,虽然一些学者曾经试图解释它。保存至今的有两个古冰岛语写成的文集,即《诗体埃达》(亦称《旧埃达》,800年以后1100年以前形成的),以及《散文埃达》(或称《新埃达》),即Snorri Sturluson在第13世纪编写的著作。

《诗体埃达》是一部记载北欧神话和英雄的民间诗歌文集,共有34篇不完整的诗。这些诗歌可以分为两个部分:一些诗歌涉及神话,另一些记载关于英雄的传说。那些具有人性特征的神明们强调勇气和忠诚,但他们也喜爱智慧、女性和远游。神明们的"大父"是Odin(或Wodan、Wotan),他的名称是英语Wednesday的来源。这位主神是战争的神,又是守护秩序的神,他是愤怒的神,但也有一些慈祥的因素,又是亡者的神、智慧和文学的神;他的象征动物是乌鸦和狼,他前往世界各地,进入人们的家庭来考验他们的好客态度。他的妻子是Freya(参见英语的Friday),即是婚姻与多产的女神。罗马人曾将Freya与Venus视为同一个神,虽然Freya几乎没有什么情欲方面的特征。Freya的儿子是Baldur(或Balder),他是太阳、光明与春天的神。Odin的另一个儿子是Thor,即雷神(参见英语的Thursday);他驾驶的马车的车轮是雷霆的来源。他的对手是一条大蛇(或龙),即Midgard蛇。一首诗歌(即 *Thrymskvida*)叙述这样的故事:巨人Thrym偷走Thor的锤子Miolnir并将它隐藏起来。Thrym要求以Freya来换,才肯交出这个锤子。因此Thor假装为一个妇女,前往巨人们那里并说自己是Freya。当巨人们还给他锤子时,Thor用这个武器打死了巨人们。一个相当狡猾的神是Loki;因为他太邪恶,其他的神明最终惩罚他。另一些诗歌叙述世界的创造和灭亡(*Voluspa, Hamaval*)。

关于英雄的诗歌(如 *Fafnir, Sigrdrifumal, Brynhild's Helfahrt, Gudrun*)构成Vol-

Snorri Sturluson

Opera: *Edda, Heimskringla, Yingling Saga*
Works: *Prose Edda, Heimskringla (World Circle), Egils Saga*

056. *Edda*

The meaning of the name "Edda" is not known until today, although several attempts were made to explain it. Two different compilations written in Old Icelandic have survived, namely the *Poetic Edda* (or *Elder Edda*), composed after 800 and before 1100, and the *Prose Edda* (or *Younger Edda*), written by Snorri Sturluson in the 13th century.

The *Poetic Edda* is a collection of 34 fragmentary poems containing Scandinavian mythological and heroic lore. These poems can be divided into two groups: those concerned with the gods and heroic poems. The humanized gods are motivated by the ideals of courage and loyalty, but also by the love of wisdom, women, and wandering. The Allfather of the gods is Odin (or Wodan, Wotan), whose name is the origin of "Wednesday", he is a god of war but also of order, a god of wrath but also of benign character, the god of the dead, of wisdom and poetry. Accompanied by his symbol animals, the raven and the wolf, he wanders through the world and enters the houses of men in order to test their hospitality. His wife is Freya (confer "Friday"), the goddess of marriage and fertility. The Romans identified her with Venus although Freya lacks erotic features. Freya's son is Baldur (Balder), the god of light, sun and spring. Another son of Odin is Thor, the god of Thunder (confer "Thursday") whose chariot causes the noise of thunder. His rival is the huge snake (or dragon) Midgard. One of the songs (the *Lay of Thrym*) tells how the giant Thrym steals Thor's hammer Miolnir and hides it. Thrym demands the hand of Freya in exchange for the hammer. In order to regain his hammer Thor disguises himself, goes to the giants and pretends to be Freya. As soon as the giants return the hammer to the "bride", Thor uses his weapon to kill the giants. A figure of considerable shrewdness is the god Loki who is punished by the other gods for his wickedness. Other poems tell of the creation and decline of the world (*Voluspa, Hamaval*).

The lays about the heroes (*The Death of Fafnir, The Lay of Sigurd, Brynhild's Hel-*

sung 家族的传说。这些故事后来被结合与统一，形成了 *Volsung Saga*(《沃尔松萨迦》，13 世纪的冰岛语散文传说)以及 *Nibelungenlied*(《尼伯龙根之歌》)。Volsung 家族的核心英雄是 Sigurd(德语中的 Siegfried)，他杀死 Fafnir 龙并获得了 Nibelung 的黄金。他拯救了 Brynhild——这位妇女曾经被关入一座城堡，被迫长期沉睡，而在城堡周围围绕着火焰(即所谓的 Waberlohe)。Brynhild 与 Sigurd 说将要结婚，但在 Burgundi 人的王宫中 Sigurd 因一杯有魔力的饮料而失去记忆并与 Giuki(Gunther)王的女儿 Gudrun (Kriemhild) 结婚。然而，一个亲戚杀害了 Sigurd。那个同时爱与恨 Sigurd 的 Brynhild 登上烧毁 Sigurd 尸体的柴堆，因为她想在死亡中与爱人结合为一。Volsung 家族在 Atli(即匈奴王 Attila, Etzel)的王宫中被全部杀死。在《诗体埃达》中，话剧式的对话和哀叹歌制造了深厚的情感张力。几个主人公很坚定地走向自己的灭亡，同时深深地意识到人生的苦恼和悲剧性。

　　Snorri Sturluson 所编写的《散文埃达》是一些年轻诗人(skald)的手册，它说明诗人的艺术语言和诗歌的韵律。它包括来自《诗体埃达》的许多诗的散文论述。第一个部分(Gylfaginning"Gylfis 王被弄瞎")提供古代北欧创造神话的总结。

Ride, The Lay of Gudrun) form the central events of the history of the Volsungs. These tales were later elaborated into the unified narrative of the *Volsung Saga* (a 13th century Icelandic prose narrative) and the *Nibelungenlied*. Sigurd (in German: Siegfried), the central hero of the Volsungs, slays the dragon Fafnir and wins the Nibelung gold. He rescues Brynhild who has been put to a long sleep in a castle surrounded by a circle of fire (Waberlohe). Brynhild and Sigurd exchange vows of love, but at the court of the Burgundians Sigurd loses his memory through a magic potion and marries Gudrun (=Kriemhild), the daughter of king Giuki (Gunther). However, he dies at the hands of his kinsman, and Brynhild who both hates and loves Sigurd throws herself onto the pyre to be united with him in death. The dynasty of the Volsungs is destroyed at the court of Atli (=Attila, Etzel). In the *Poetic Edda* dramatic dialogues and laments create emotional tension of great depth. The main figures persistently move toward their doom with a deep sense of grief and the tragedy of human existence.

Snorri Sturluson compiled the *Prose Edda* as a manual for apprentice poets (the scalds), explaining the language and metrical rules of poetry. It contains prose paraphrases of many of the verses in the *Poetic Edda*. The first part (Gylfaginning—"The Blinding of King Gylfis") presents a summary of the Old Norse creation mythology.

托马斯(约 1190—1260)

方济各会会士 Thomas 来自意大利 Abruzzi 地区的 Celano。1221 年 Franciscus 派遣他和 26 位修士一起前往德国,所以他曾在 Worms、Mainz 和 Speyer 工作。

著作:《审判之日》(描述最后审判的情况)、《圣加拉传》、《圣方济各神迹》、《圣方济各传》

057.《圣方济各传》

在圣 Franciscus(1181—1226 年)去世后,Gregorius IX 教宗让 Thomas de Celano 写下方济各会创始人的传记。因此 Thomas 编写了第一部传记,文风优雅通俗。这个传记流传很广,成为中世纪最有名的生传文献之一。19 年后,Thomas 又写了一部 Franciscus 传,因为方济各会的总会长要求他这样做。因为这两部传记几乎没有提到什么奇迹,Thomas 另外编写了一部关于圣 Franciscus 所行奇迹的书(即 *Liber miraculorum*),而回应教宗的命令他又编写了圣 Clara 的传记(*Legenda Sanctae Clarae*)。在后来几百年中,Bonaventura 的 *Legenda Sancti Francisci* 成为官方的、比较流行的传记,但现代的学者认为 Thomas 的传记是更符合实情的,也是更早的文献。

1181 年或 1182 年圣 Franciscus 出生在意大利中部的 Assisi(Umbria 地区)。他的父亲 Pietro Bernardone 是一个富商,但他的儿子并没有步其后尘。年轻的 Franciscus 过着一种雄心勃勃的、不稳定的生活,他有很多梦想,但一场病和其他的不幸的遭遇使他于 1206 年改变了世界观。他开始过一种补赎和刻苦的生活,他是一种特别的、新型的隐修者。他想服侍穷人和麻风病人,又开始在他的家乡重新建立一些被破坏的小教堂。因为他的父亲无法接受儿子这种奇怪的生活方式,Franciscus 离开了他的家人。在 1209 年他经历了一次神视,从中获得一种肯定:他的圣召是效法耶稣所派遣的使徒们的(参见 Mt 10:7 等),即过一种贫穷的讲道者的生活。这种新的生活方式是当一个在各地巡回的、独身的隐修者,而这个理想形成了一种新型的修道生活,即"托钵修会"。在这种新方式到来之前,隐修生活的核心是一个固定的、安全的隐修院,其中的修道团体依赖于一个围墙的保护,而他们享受一种很有规律的、文化水平很高的生活。

不久后很多人想效法 Franciscus 的生活,而他们创立了"小弟兄会"(Fratres minores, Franciscani)。Franciscus 为这个团体写了一个简单的会规,而教宗 Innocens III 在 1210 年口头上支持他们,这样他肯定这个发展中的小组织并允许他们去各地讲道。方济各会的会士们前往欧洲各地并影响了无数的人恢复他们的灵性生活或修道承诺。在 1212 年 Franciscus 帮助来自 Assisi 贵族的贞女 Clara 创立了一个修女团体,

Thomas de Celano / Thomas of Celano

Opera: *Dies irae, Legenda S. Clarae, Tractatus de miraculis S. Francisci (=Liber miraculorum), Vita S. Francisci*

Works: *That Day of Wrath, Life of St. Clare, On the Wonders of Saint Francis, Life of St. Francis*

057. *Vita sancti Francisci / Life of Saint Francis*

After the death of St. Francis (1181—1226) Pope Gregory IX asked Thomas of Celano to write a biography of the founder of the Franciscans. Thus Thomas wrote a first biography in a poetic and elegant style. This biography was very influential and became one of the most famous medieval biographies. 19 years later Thomas wrote a second biography of Francis in response to the demand of the general superior of the Franciscans. Since both biographies hardly mention any miracles, Thomas wrote a book on the miracles of St. Francis (*Liber miraculorum*), and following the command of the Pope, he also compiled the *Life of Saint Clare* (*Legenda Sanctae Clarae*). In the following centuries, Bonaventure's *Legenda Sancti Francisci* became the official and more popular biography, but modern scholarship has preferred Thomas' biography which is older and more authentic.

St. Francis was born in 1181 or 1182 in Assisi (Umbria, central Italy), his father, Pietro Bernardone, was a rich merchant, but his son did not follow in his footsteps. Francis led the ambitious and unstable life of a knight in his youth, and he had many dreams, but a disease and other calamities changed his view of life in 1206, so that he tried to lead a life of penitence and mortification as a special and new kind of monk. He served the poor and the lepers and began to restore delapidated chapels in his home town. He left his family as his father could not tolerate his strange life style. In 1209 he had a vision which confirmed his vocation to live in poverty as a preacher in imitation of the apostles who were sent out by Jesus (according to *Mt* 10:7ff). This ideal of a new lifestyle as a wandering celibate monk shaped the new type of religious life of the "mendicant orders". Before the emergence of this new way, monastic life was centered on the safe and practical stability of a community of monks, protected by cloister walls, who enjoyed a regular and cultured life.

Soon many other people joined Francis, and they formed the community of the Fratres minores (Minorites, Franciscans). Francis wrote a simple rule for his community, and Pope Innocent III gave an oral approval in 1210, thus confirming the crescent community and allowing them to wander around preaching the gospel. The Franciscans traveled to many other countries in Europe and inspired countless people to renew their spiritual life and religious commitment. In 1212 Francis supported Clare, a virgin from a noble family in Assisi, to found a community of strictly monastic sisters in the chapel of St. Damiano (the "Sisters of St. Clare"). Francis wanted to convert the Muslims and therefore he traveled to

她们在 St. Damiano 小教堂过一种很严格的隐修生活。Franciscus 还想皈依或感化伊斯兰教徒,所以他于 1214 年前往西班牙,又于 1219/1220 年到达埃及。Franciscus 本人仅仅被祝圣执事,他没有渴望成为一位司铎,而在开始的阶段中,Franciscani(方济各会)只是一个平信徒的布道团。在 1221 年 Franciscus 停止管理这个快速发展的团体。在 1224 年他在一次神视中接受了基督的五伤。在晚年他受了很多苦,于 1226 年去世,并早在 1228 年就被宣布为教会的圣人(圣徒)。

在他的传记中,Thomas 表达了 Franciscus 的精神状态和灵修方式:"谁能描述他对一切属于神的东西所怀的爱慕呢?每当他在受造界中发现创造主的智慧、权柄和美善时,他感到一种不可言传的喜乐。每当他观望太阳时,当他观察月亮或星星时,他都感到一种奇妙的、不可思议的幸福……花朵的美丽使他如此高兴,无论他在哪里看到它们的美貌或香味!他的眼睛很快就上升到那个从 Jesse 长出来的花朵那里,他马上默想基督,而这个精神性的花的香味曾经恢复那些冷冻的灵魂们的生命。而当他在一个地方找到了很多花时,他开始向它们讲道并呼吁它们赞美上主,好像它们是一些具有理性的东西。同样,他有时候提醒农田、葡萄园、岩石、森林、水泉和花园中的一切植物,还以最纯洁的心态提醒大地、火、空气和风并劝勉它们要心甘情愿地服从于他们的创造主。他称一切受造物为'弟兄'。通过一种独特的、不被知道的方式,他进入了一切受造物最内在的奥秘。他已经达到了上主子女的奇妙自由。"

根据 Thomas 墓碑上的碑文,他也是著名诗歌 *Dies irae* 的作者。虽然有人曾经提出这方面的置疑,但大多数学者肯定传统的观点。这首诗表达了对于最后审判的恐惧,因为在最后的日子里一切人都必须面对神的审判:

"末日来临,震怒之日,在这一天,世界将化为灰烬,正如大卫和西比尔所预言。
天翻地覆,人心震荡,当末日审判来临之时,是非善恶,件件分明。
号角响彻四方,发出令人震撼的声音,穿越各处的坟墓,将所有的灵魂召集到审判台前。
当人类再次起来时,死神和自然皆为之震惊,亡者会起来面对审判者。
在记事簿上件件桩桩记分明,审判即将据此进行。
审判官落座就位,一切隐秘即将显现,一切都会得到报应。
(……)
我跪在此,祈求主的怜悯,我的心就像灰尘,万念俱灰,请在最后的时刻拯救我。
那个日子充满眼泪。那时,应该受审判的罪人要从灰烬中再生;请可怜他,上主!"

Spain in 1214 and to Egypt in 1219/1220. Francis himself was only ordained deacon, he did not aspire priesthood, and in the beginning the Franciscans were a community of lay preachers. In 1221 Francis retired from the administration of the rapidly growing community. In 1224 he received the stigmata of Christ during a vision. After much suffering in his last years he died in 1226 and was already canonized in 1228.

Thomas tries to express Francis' spirituality: "Who could describe the love he had for all things that belong to God? Who could narrate the overflowing joy which he felt whenever he contemplated the wisdom, power and goodness of the Creator in His creation? Whenever he looked up to the sun, whenever he observed the moon or the stars he was filled with a wonderful, ineffable happiness… How the beauty of the flowers could delight his spirit, whenever he perceived their amiable shape and their fragrant smell! His observant eye was immediately elevated to the contemplation of that one flower which grew out of the root of Jesse, and whose fragrant smell called back to life the souls that were frozen in a spiritual death. And when he found many flowers at one place he preached to them and invited them to praise the Lord, as if they were rational beings. Likewise he would remind fields, vineyards, rocks and forests, the fresh fountains and all plants of the gardens, earth and fire, air and wind, reminded them in utmost purity of the Love of God and admonished them to a joyful obedience. He called all creatures 'brother'. By a unique way, hidden to others, he entered into the innermost mystery of all creatures, he was a man who had already arrived at the magnificent freedom of the children of God."

According to his tomb inscription, Thomas is also the author of the famous sequence *Dies irae*. Although his authorship has been contested, some scholars reconfirm the traditional view. The sequence expresses the fear of the last judgment when all souls will face the judgment of God:

"Dies irae, dies illa, / solvet saeclum in favilla, / teste David cum Sibylla.
Quantus tremor est futurus, / quando iudex est venturus / cuncta stricte discussurus!
Tuba mirum spargens sonum / per sepulcra regionum / coget omnes ante thronum.
Mors stupebit et natura, / cum resurget creatura, / iudicanti responsura.
Liber scriptus proferetur, / in quo totum continetur, / unde mundus iudicetur.
Iudex ergo cum sedebit / quidquid latet, apparebit, / nil inultum remanebit.
Oro supplex et acclinis / cor contritum quasi cinis: / gere curam mei finis.
Lacrimosa dies illa, / qua resurget ex favilla / iudicandus homo reus: / huic ergo parce, deus!"
(That day of Wrath, that dreadful day, / shall heaven and earth in ashes lay, / as David and the Sibyl say. / What horror must invade the mind, / when the approaching judge shall find / and sift the deeds of all mankind. / The mighty trumpet's wondrous tone / shall rend each tomb's sepulcral stone / and summon all before the throne. / Now death and nature with surprise / behold the trembling. Sinners rise / to meet the Judge's searching eyes. / Then shall with universal dread / the book of Conscience be read / to judge the lives of all the dead. / Once the judge will sit down there / all things hidden will appear, / reward and punishment to bear. / Before you, humbled, Lord, I lie / my heart like ashes, crushed and dry, / assist me when I die. / Full of tears and full of dread / is that day that wakes the dead, / calling all, with solemn blast / to be judged for their past.)

博韦的樊尚（约 1190—1264）

约生于 1190 年，家乡是法国北部的 Beauvais(Picardie 地区)，他加入道明会，在 1223 年之前他在 Paris 的 St.-Jacques 修院上学，1254—1260 年成为王家的 Ordo Cisterciensium(熙笃会)隐修院 Royaumont 中的老师，在那里与法国国王 Ludovicus IX 有密切关系，并将自己的著作献给国王。因为他编写了中世纪最大的百科全书，人们称他为 speculator omnis materiae scibilis("一切可知事物的观望者")。

著作：《论贵族子女的教育》、《论光荣贞女的赞美》、《论王子的道德教育》、《慰藉之书》、《恩典之书》、《知识宝鉴》(或译《大镜》，80 卷，三部：《自然宝鉴》、《教义宝鉴》、《历史宝鉴》)

058. 《知识宝鉴》

《知识宝鉴》写成于 1250 年代，于 1328 年被译成法语，首次印行于 1473—1485 年间。它继续被印刷出版，特别是在宗教改革和公教改革的时代。这部大百科全书的篇幅比它的一切前身著作（参见 Plinius Maius, Cassiodorus, Isidorus, Hrabanus, Albertus Magnus）都大，只有 18 世纪的那些巨著才超越了它。作者引用了 400 多个希腊语、拉丁语、阿拉伯语和犹太人作者的 2000 多部著作。最常被引用的是 Plinius Maior 和 Isidorus，但 Vincentius 也引用那些新发现的 Aristoteles 的著作以及阿拉伯语的书（特别是阿拉伯人的医学著作）以及一些比较近代的拉丁语作者，比如 Adelardus de Bath。

本著作被分为 *Speculum naturale*（《自然宝鉴》）、*Speculum doctrinale*（《教义宝鉴》）、*Speculum morale*（《伦理学宝鉴》）和 *Speculum historiale*（《历史宝鉴》）。其中的 *Speculum morale* 是后来的作者加上去的，但 Vincentius 曾经计划完成该部分。这部分主要汇集了 Thomas Aquinas 的种种著作，谈论各种美德和恶习以及神学的问题（比如基督的降生、天堂和地狱）。

关于大自然的 *Speculum naturale* 分为 32 卷（又分为 3718 章），它描述世界的创造，一个一个地谈论无形的世界（神、天使）以及可见的世界、大自然的种种现象（光、元素）、大地、矿石、宝石、植物、动物和人；人的使命是管理万物。Vincentius 使用了传统的框架（"六天内创造世界"）来整理无数的细节（参见 Basilios 和 Ambrosius 的 *Hexaemeron*《六天创造》）。

长达 18 卷的 *Speculum doctrinale*（《教义宝鉴》）谈论哲学、语法、修辞学、文学的问题，也包括法学和政治学这样的实践性学科，以及一些具体的活动，比如农业和

Vincentius Bellovacensis / Vincent de Beauvais

Opera: *De eruditione seu modo instruendorum filiorum nobilium, De laudibus virginis gloriosae, De morali principis institutione, Liber consolatiorius, Liber gratiae, Speculum maius (Speculum naturale, doctrinale, historiale)*

Works: *On the Education of Noble Sons, Praises of the Glorious Virgin, On the Moral Education of a Prince, Book of Consolation, Book of Grace, The Great Mirror (Mirror of Nature, Mirror of Teachings, Mirror of History)*

058. *Speculum maius / The Great Mirror*

The *Great Mirror* was written in the 1250s, translated into French in 1328 and first printed in the years 1473—1485. It continued to be reprinted, especially in the time of the reformation and counter-reformation. This great encyclopedia was more comprehensive than all its predecessors (conf. Plinius Maius, Cassiodorus, Isidorus, Hrabanus, Albertus Magnus) and was only surpassed by compilations made in the 18th century. The author draws from some 2000 works of more than 400 Greek, Latin, Arab and Jewish authors. Plinius Maior and Isidore are quoted frequently, but Vincentius also uses the new Aristotelian texts and Arab sources (especially the medical works) and some recent Latin authors, for example Adelard of Bath.

The work is divided into the *Speculum naturale, Speculum doctrinale, Speculum morale*, and *Speculum historiale*. The *Speculum morale* was added by a later author, but Vincentius had intended to write it. It is mainly a compilation of the works of Thomas Aquinas, a discussion of the virtues and vices, and of theological issues (incarnation of Christ, heaven and hell).

The *Speculum naturale* consists of 32 books (divided into 3718 chapters) and describes the creation of the world, the invisible realities (God, the angels) and the visible universe, the phenomena of nature (light, the elements), the earth, minerals, jewels, plants, animals and man who is destined to govern creation. Vincentius still uses the traditional framework of "creation in six days" to structure the countless details he reports (confer. Basilius' and Ambrosius' *Hexaemeron*).

The 18 books of the *Speculum doctrinale* are discussing the areas of philosophy, grammar, rhetoric, poetry and the practical sciences of law and politics. This part also comprises natural sciences like physics, mathematics, medicine, and practical activities like agriculture or hunting.

狩猎等。

在 Speculum historiale(《历史宝鉴》)的 31 卷中,作者叙述世界的历史,包括埃及的历史,巴比伦的历史、犹太人的历史、东方的历史和欧洲历史。作者的思想标准在很多方面是《圣经》;他不严格地分开教会的历史和世俗的历史,这和当时流行的史学论述有所区别。

The 31 books of the *Speculum historiale* are an account of world history, including the history of Egypt, Babylonia, Israel, Orient, and European history. In many ways the author is biblically oriented, and he does not separate Church history and profane history, which is contrary to the usual division used in his day.

费德利希二世(1194—1250)

1194年生于意大利Ancona地区的Iesi，是德国皇帝Henricus VI和Sicilia女王Constantia的儿子。他的父亲在遗嘱中要求教宗Innocens III照顾儿子的教育。在母亲于1198年去世后，四岁的Fredericus被宣布为Sicilia之王，而教宗于1209年安排他与Constantia de Aragon结婚。Fredericus于1211年被选为德国国王，1212年在Aachen举行加冕礼，但于1214年才战胜了他的对手，1220年被加冕为皇帝，此后让他的儿子Henricus VII管理德国地区，自己组织Sicilia国，使之成为一个现代化的官僚国度，并于1224年创立Napoli大学。因为皇帝承诺要参加十字军运动但后来很长时间推迟了这个项目，教宗根据双方的协议于1227年开除了他的教籍。Fredericus于1228年前往东方，并相当成功地与伊斯兰教的领导进行谈判。因为皇帝同时想控制意大利北部和南部地区，教宗无法信任他，并于1239年再次开除皇帝，此后教宗和皇帝彼此谴责对方是"反基督"，这样他们无法共同抵抗蒙古人于1241年的侵略(波兰的Legnica被攻击)。皇帝的儿子也反对父亲。在Fredericus II去世后，德国诸侯没有选出一个新王，直到1273年(所谓的interregnum"空位期")。对德国人来说，在意大利南部长大的Fredericus II是一个神秘的人物，关于他有很多故事，而同时代的人已经称他为"stupor mundi"("世界奇人")。

著作：《论用鸟去打猎》；还有一些法律文献。

059. 《论用鸟去打猎》

这部探讨"用鹰去打猎"的名著是鸟学领域中第一部科学性的著作。全书分为8个部分，但最后两段(涉及鸟类的疾病和养狗的知识)失传。Fredericus在晚年回应他的儿子Manfred的要求写下了这部论文，当时他已有30多年的养鹰经验。

养鹰的技艺是关于捕获鹰并训练它们去打猎的知识和技术。一种方法是用一个眼罩来盖住鹰的眼睛，这样它们就不会受到惊吓。鹰的训练是为了使它们捕获鹤、鸭子或其他生活在湖边的鸟类。Fredericus的部分观察来自Aristoteles的 *Hai peri tōn zōōn historiai*(《生物志》)——这部著作不久之前译成拉丁语。然而，皇帝也敢批评"哲学之王"："这样我们不能在所有的观点上都遵从哲学家之王的看法，因为他自己从来没有去打猎，而我们已有很多年的狩猎经验。"Fredericus强调说他对于鹰有一手的了解，而依赖于他的丰富经验他甚至敢谴责挑战那些古老且受敬仰的权威人物。用他的话来说，实验性观察的原则是"如其所是地显示那些存在的东西"(Manifestare ea quae

Fredericus II / Frederick II

Opera: *De arte venandi cum avibus*
Works: *On Falconry*

059. *De arte venandi cum avibus / On Falconry*

This famous book on the art of hunting with falcons is the first scientific book in the field of ornithology (the science of birds). The work had eight parts altogether, but the last two books (concerning diseases of birds and the raising of various kinds of dogs) are lost. Frederick wrote the treatise at the end of his life in response to the urges of his son Manfred, thus he looked back on more than 30 years of experience with falcons.

The art of falconry deals with the techniques of catching falcons and training them for hunting. One device is to cover their eyes with a cap so that nothing would frighten them. Falcons are trained to hunt for cranes, ducks or other birds living at lakes. Frederick bases some of his observations on Aristotle's *Zoology* (*Hai peri tōn zōōn historiai*)— that work had been translated into Latin not long ago. However, the emperor is ready to criticize the "prince of philosophy": "Thus we could not always follow the prince of philosophers, since he never went hunting himself, whereas we have been hunting for many years." Frederick emphasizes that he has firsthand experience with falcons, and relying on this experience he dares to challenge even time-honored authorities. In his words the principle of empirical observation is "To show reality as it is" (*Manifestare ea quae sunt sicut sunt*), and thus his book has been praised as marking the beginning of European empiricism. For example, Frederick tested whether falcons could recognize meat by smelling it when they are blindfolded: "We have tested this several times. If the falcons sunt sicut sunt)。因此,这本书曾经被赞扬为欧洲经验主义的开端。比如,Fredericus 曾检查瞎眼的鹰是否能闻到肉味:"我们曾有几次作了这种实验。如果完全盖住鹰的眼睛,他们不会发现向他们扔的肉块,虽然他们的嗅觉不受阻碍。"几百个栩栩如生的鸟类图画也证明皇帝是一个认真的观察者:他亲手绘制了鹰和其他的飞鸟。Fredericus II 也因他的讽刺语气而著名。有一次蒙古的大汗邀请 Fredericus 在蒙古朝廷出任高官,只要他接受蒙古人的统治。当时 Fredericus 皇帝微笑着说道:"如果我能成为鞑靼陛下的养鹰专家,我会感到这是无比的荣耀。"

are totally blindfolded they will not notice meat thrown to them, even if their sense of smell is not impaired." Several hundred realistic drawings of falcons and other birds are another proof of the Emperor's diligence and careful observation. Frederick II was also notorious for his sarcastic remarks. The Mongol Khan once offered him an office at his court, hoping that Frederick would submit to Mongol rule. The emperor remarked with a smile: "It would be a great honor for me to be a falconer of his Majesty the Tartar."

布拉克顿（约 1200—1268）

　　Henricus de Bracton 生于英国的 Devon，Bracton（亦写 Bretton, Bratton 等）曾在 Exeter 的教会学校求学，攻读神学、罗马法、教会法，与当时大部分律师一样，他也是司铎（圣职人员）。约于 1230 年，他开始担任王室法官 William de Raleigh 的文书，1247—1257 年任 Coram rege（王座法院，后称 King's Bench）法官。他是国王法律顾问圈中的一员，于 1264 年任 Exeter 教区的主教，1268 年去世。他被称为英国中世纪最优秀的法学家。

著作：《英格兰的法律与习惯》

060.《英格兰的法律与习惯》

　　这部著作是关于英国的"普通法"的最古老的论文之一，同时被视为中世纪最杰出的法学著作之一。按照罗马法的 *Institutiones*，这部书也分为三个部分：人法，财产法和程序法。其中大约有四分之三的内容涉及程序法。作者澄清普通法的不同类型法案和简明判决书（brevia, writ）。所谓的"普通法"（common law）指英国的法律传统，这个传统更多注重前例（stare decisis），超过立法机关的制定法。

　　作者介绍很多来自 Bologna 学派的教会法学家和注释者的术语和概念，尤其重视 Azo（Azzone 阿佐，1190—1220 年，参见他的 *Digestum*《学说汇编集》）。因此有人曾经说 Bracton 想结合英国的法律与罗马法（欧陆法律传统）。他一方面强调英国法院的判决以及英国法官所要求的程序，但同时他向这个"普通法"介绍一些来自"民法"（ius civile，即罗马法）和"教会法"（ius canonicum，教会的法律）的原则。一般来说，在中世纪时代，罗马法包括契约法，而教会法是婚姻法与继承法的基础。Bracton 使用 2000 多个来自 Coram Rege（王座法院）的判决为具有权威性的例子，这样他起先奠定了"使用前例来决定法案"的方法。这种"习惯性原则"就是普通法的基本规则。Bracton 想为那些在英国任职的法官提供一些实用的指南，因此他选择了最有代表性的王座法院法案来探讨法律的程序问题。

Bracton / Henry de Bratton

Opera: *De legibus et consuetudinibus Angliae*
Works: *On the Laws and Customs of England*

060. *De legibus et consuetudinibus Angliae / On the Laws and Customs of England*

This is one of the oldest systematic treatises of the common law and is regarded as one of the outstanding medieval works on jurisprudence. Following the *Institutiones* of Roman Law, the work is divided into three parts: law of persons, law of commodities and procedure law. More than 75% of the content is concerned with procedure law. The author elucidates the different forms of lawsuits and concise decisions (brevia, writ) of the common law. The term "common law" denotes the legal tradition of England that is based on precedents (stare decisis) rather than on statutory law.

The author introduces many concepts and terms from the ecclesiastical lawyers and glossators of the Bolognese school, notably from Azo (Azzone, 1190—1220, see his *Digestum*), so that it has been said that Bracton wanted to combine the English law with the Roman (continental) law. He emphasized the English judicial decisions and the methods of pleading required by English judges, but at the same time he also introduced into this "common law" principles derived from the tradition of the "civil law" (=Roman law) and canon law (=ecclesiastical law, the law of the Church). Roughly speaking, during the Middle Ages Roman law covered contract law, and canon law was the basis for marriage regulations and inheritance rules. Bracton used more than 2000 decisions of Coram Rege (King's Bench) court cases as authoritative examples and thus laid the first foundation for the method of using precedents for deciding lawsuits. This customary principle is the basis of common law (also called "customary law"). Bracton wanted to give a practical orientation for judges working in England and thus he chose the most authoritative and representative cases from the King's court in order to explore the rules of legal procedures.

大阿尔伯特（约1206—1280）

约1200年生于德国南部Lauingen地区的贵族家庭，1223年在Padova加入道明会，在Colonia获得神学教育，于1245年在Paris成为magister theologiae并教授神学。他于1248年与其学生Thomas Aquinas一同到Colonia，在那里创立道明会的学院（studium generale），1248—1254年任教，后成为道明会德国省的省长，1256年曾在Anagni的教廷替托钵修会进行辩护。他于1260年成为Regensburg的主教，于1263年奉Urbanus IV教宗之命在德国和波希米亚推广十字军运动，1270年到1280年间在Colonia，曾多次担任当地总主教和市政府之间的谈判者。他学识渊博，因此被称为Doctor universalis（"全面的博士"）并于1931年被宣布为Doctor Ecclesiae "教会圣师"。

著作：《约伯传注》、《论灵魂》、《论动物》、《论天和地》、《论主的身体》、《论人》（亦称《受造物大全》）、《论降生》、《论善的本质》、《论复活》、《论诸圣事》、《论弥撒圣祭》、《论心智的统一性》、《论植物》、《形而上学》、《依撒意来注》、《受造界大全》、《认识上主的奇妙学问大全》、《神学大全》（只写了开头）、《伦理学注释》（即Aristoteles《伦理学》的注解）

061.《受造界大全》

这个书名一般指两部著作，即《四个同样永恒的实在》（*De quattuor coaequaevis*）和《论人》（*De homine*），但有时也包括另外4部作品，即《论圣事》（*De sacramentis*）、《论降生成人》（*De incarnatione*）、《论复活》（*De resurrectione*）和《论善》（*De bono*）。这些著作都是1240年后不久编写的。当时Albertus在Paris生活和任教，而这些书暗示13世纪上半叶向Aristoteles的重大转变。Paris大学曾在1210年和1215年发表了禁止研究Aristoteles的形而上学和宇宙论著作的规定，但在1255年Paris大学的哲学系（artes）要求所有学生学习这些著作。在这个过程中，Albertus的工作起了很大的作用，而他的观点也表明Avicenna和Averroes的影响在当时是无所不在的。Albertus想在基督教的世界观中融入他们的思想，但他的著作属于早期的尝试。25年后，他的学生Thomas的思想和著作达到了更高层次的一致性和连贯性。

《受造界大全》第一部分处理四个"同样永恒的"实在（quattuor coaequaeva）。神同时创造了这四个基本条件，即(1)原始的物质（materia prima），这是一切物体的被动的、不定形的和无区分的物质基础；(2)时间，即一切变化的真实衡量标准；(3)最高的天（empyreum，即"火天"，参见Dante《神曲》的最高天），以及(4)天使们，他们是一些被创造的、精神性的实体。

Albertus Magnus / Albert the Great

Opera: *Commentarii in Job, De anima, De animalibus libri XXVI, De caelo et mundo, De corpore Domini, De homine (Summa de creaturis), De incarnatione, De natura boni, De resurrectione, De sacramentis, De sacrificio missae, De unitate intellectus contra Averroistas, De vegetabilibus et plantis libri VII, Metaphysica, Postilla super Isaiam, Summa de creaturis, Summa de mirabili scientia Dei, Summa theologiae, Super ethica commentum*

Works: *Commentary on Job, On the Soul, On Animals, On Heaven and Earth, On the Body of the Lord, On Man (Summa of the Creatures), On Incarnation, On the Nature of the Good, On Resurrection, On the Sacraments, On the Sacrifice of the Mass, On the Unity of the Intellect against the Averroists, On Plants, Metaphysics, Postilla on Isaiah, Sum on Creation, Sum on the Wonderful Knowledge of God, Summa Theologiae, A Summa of Ethics*

061. *Summa de creaturis / Sum on Creation*

This title usually denotes two books, namely De quattuor coaequaevis (*The Four Equally Ancient Realities*) and *De homine* (*On Man*), but sometimes four other works are also included: *De sacramentis* (*On the Sacraments*), *De incarnatione* (*On Incarnation*), *De resurrectione* (*On Resurrection*), and *De bono* (*On the Good*). These works were compiled soon after 1240 when Albert lived and taught in Paris, and they mark the great shift towards Aristotelianism that took place in the first half of the 13th century. The University of Paris had published prohibitions to study the metaphysical and physical (cosmological) works of Aristotle in 1210 and 1215, but in 1255 the faculty of the "artes" obliged all to the study of these same Aristotelian works. Albert's work was a significant step in this process, and his considerations show the ubiquitous impact of Avicenna and Averroes. Albert tries to integrate their thought into his Christian world view but at this early stage he could not yet reach the level of cogency and unity displayed in the works of his pupil Thomas some 25 years later.

The first part of the *Summa de creaturis* treats four "equally ancient" realities (quattuor coaequaeva). God created these four basic conditions at the same time. They are (1) the first matter (materia prima), which is the passive, undetermined, and undifferentiated principle of all bodies; (2) time, the real measurement of all changes; (3) the highest heaven (empyreum, confer Dante's highest heaven), and (4) the angels who are created immaterial substances.

第 2 部分（*De homine*）详细地论述人的灵魂的植物性、感觉性和精神性能力，包括意志的自由和良心的能力。根据 Albertus 的论述，人的理智的接纳性原则（intellectus possibilis）和掌握真理的主动能力（intellectus agens）都是个别心灵的部分（partes）。人心的理解是感官知识的抽象过程的果实。人们曾描写 Albertus 的人观比 Thomas 的人观更"二元化"，因为他给予身体和心灵比较大的独立性。换言之，他更多采纳阿拉伯思想家们的新 Plato 主义，而 Thomas 关于心灵和肉身的理解更多的受了 Aristoteles 的启发。

自 1254 年以来，Albertus 致力于完成几部注解 Aristoteles 著作的书，这样他在对 Aristoteles 主义在中世纪学术界的突破有很大的影响。其中一部注解书是 Albertus 的 *Metaphysica*（约 1265 年成书），这是对希腊文本的拉丁论述，也包含很多针对相关问题的讨论（digressiones）。Albertus 也曾写过一篇保卫个别灵魂的存在的论文，即 *De unitate intellectus, contra Averroem*（《论心智的统一性》），其中反驳 Averroes 的思想倾向，即 monopsychismus（认为一切人的心智是一个共同的理性心智），该书写于 1256 年。

Albertus 很坚定地认为哲学应该是一门具有自己独立方法体系的学科，但他也指出哲学家都有犯错误的可能性，始终强调基督信仰应该是真理的标准。因此他的思想对新的因素是开放的，无论这些新思想来自 Aristoteles 或新 Plato 主义或阿拉伯的思想家。他促使大学中的哲学系对 Aristoteles 采取一种科学的态度，但他也编写了一些谈论思辨神秘主义问题的著作。

The second part (*De homine*) contains a detailed discussion of the vegetative, sensitive and spiritual capacities of the human soul, including the freedom of the will and conscience. According to Albert both the receptive principle of human understanding (the intellectus possibilis) and the active capacity of grasping truth (intellectus agens) are parts (partes) of the individual soul. Human understanding is the result of an abstraction from sensual perception. Albert's view of man has been described as more dualistic than that of Thomas, since he attributes a greater degree of independence to both, soul and body. In other words, he more closely follows the Neo-Platonism of the Arab thinkers, whereas Thomas' interpretation of the unity of soul and body is more inspired by Aristotle.

Since ca. 1254 Albert worked hard to elaborate several profound commentaries to Aristotle's works and thus became a scholar who was of crucial importance for the breakthrough of Aristotelianism in the medieval world of thought. One of this commentaries is the *Metaphysica* (ca. 1265), which is a Latin paraphrase of the Greek text and contains many discussions (digressiones) of related problems. Albert also wrote a treatise defending the reality of the individual soul against Averroist tendencies (monopsychism, the tenet that all people have only one common rational soul), namely the polemic essay *De unitate intellectus contra Averroem* (*On the Unity of the Intellect, against Averroes*), written in 1256.

Albert was consequent in his tenet that philosophy must be treated as a science which has its own independent methods, but he also pointed to the possible errors of the philosophers and clinged to the Christian faith as the standard of truth. Thus his thinking was open to new elements coming from Aristoteles, Neo-Platonism or the Arab thinkers. He influenced the scientific approach to Aristoteles within the philosophical studies of the "artes", but he also wrote about questions of speculative mysticism.

西班牙的伯多禄（彼得）(1210—1277)

Pedro Juliao(=Petrus Juliani)约 1220 年生于葡萄牙 Lisboa，他是一位医生的儿子，曾在 Paris 大学学习哲学和医学，后在意大利 Siena 大学任教。他曾是德国皇帝和 Gregorius X 教宗(1271—1276 年)的医生，1273 年成为 Tusculum 的枢机主教，1276 年被选为教宗，取名为 Johannes XXI。他为 Rudolf von Habsburg 举行加冕礼，这样结束了多年的"空位期"(interregnum)。他在哲学和医学方面都有贡献，是最有学问的教宗之一。据说他因房屋倒塌而被压死(1277 年 5 月 20 日)。

著作：《手术研究》、《论眼睛》(他最有影响的医学著作之一)、《论保护健康》、《心理学》(《论灵魂》，根据 Aristoteles 的著作而编写的心理学著作)、《逻辑学大全》(亦译《论理学概要》，历史上最经常使用的逻辑学教科书)、《病者宝库》(《实验大全》，一部医学百科全书)

062. 《逻辑学大全》

这本非常流行的逻辑学教科书成书于 1245 年。作者当时正在 Paris 任教，作为 magister artium(哲学教师)。

这部书分为七篇论文，前六篇处理 Aristoteles 逻辑学的种种问题(称 parva logicalia)，第 7 篇则是最重要的，它说明语言逻辑学的主要问题；该学科自 1100 年以来在 Paris 得到发展，它被称为 scientia sermocinalis(语言表达的科学)或 dialectica nova(新逻辑)。因为经院派的逻辑学家使用逻辑来分析语言，他们的研究成果后来远远超过阿拉伯地区和拜占庭的逻辑学家。毫无疑问，Petrus 著作中最有影响力的理论是关于 suppositiones(指称)的教导，即某一个词(terminus 概念、名称)如何代表某一个东西(所谓 suppositum)。比如，在"人将死"这句话中，"人"有形式上的指称，但在"人是一个名词"这句话中"人"有实质上的指称。如果说"一切人都要死"，这就是"普遍的指称"，而说"这个人是我的父亲"就是"特殊的指称"。在最后的句子中的"这个"和"我的"这些词被称为 syncategoremata(即一些不指向语言以外事物的词，如代词)。有的指称是自然的，但如果一个词的意义来自人们的共同约定，这些词指称就是约定的。《逻辑学大全》的贡献是系统地罗列不同类型的指称，这样就为 14 世纪的逻辑学发展作了准备，即是"唯名论"(nominalismus，亦称 terminismus 观念论)的影响逐渐加强。

关于指称的理论引发了 13 世纪中期的 modismus(形式论)逻辑学派关于表称的教导。这个属于 Aristoteles 派的逻辑学派认为语言符号的意义是固定的，并来自语言所代表的事物的固定本质，无论是个别的或群体的。对于这些 Aristoteles 派的人来说，指称是真实的、准确的、可验证的和永不改变的。这种指称适用于思想以外的实

Petrus Hispanus / Peter of Spain

Opera: *Diaetae super chirurgiam, Liber de oculo, Liber de conservanda sanitate, Scientia libri de anima, Summulae logicales, Thesaurus pauperum* (*Summa experimentorum*)

Works: *Chirurgical Exercises, Concerning the Eye, On the Preservation of Health, The Science of the Soul* (*On the Soul*), *Small Logical Sums, A Sum of the Poor* (*Sum of Experiments*)

062. *Summulae logicales / Small Logical Sums*

This hugely popular textbook for the discipline of "dialectica" was written around 1245, when the author taught in Paris as "magister artium" (teacher of philosophy).

The book is divided into seven treatises; the first six parts deal with the themes of Aristotelian logic ("parva logicalia"), the seventh and most important chapter explains the main problems of the logic of language, a branch of knowledge that developed in Paris since ca. 1100 under the name "scientia sermocinalis" (science of conversation) or "dialectica nova" (new logic). The application of logic to the study of language made the scholastic logicians much more fruitful than their colleagues in the Arab lands and in Byzanz. The most influential theory of Peter's book is certainly the teaching concerning the suppositions (suppositiones), namely the way in which a word (terminus, term) represents something (the suppositum). For example, the word "man" has a formal supposition in the sentence "Man is mortal." and a material supposition in the sentence "Man is a noun." It has a common supposition in "Every man is mortal." and a discrete supposition in "This man is my father." In the last sentence the words "this" and "my" are called syncategoremata (expressions which do not designate anything outside the language). Some suppositions may be natural, but when the meanings of the terms derive from common agreements of their denotations, then the suppositions are conventional. The achievement of the *Summulae logicales* is to present a systematic outline of the different kinds of suppositions, thus preparing the way for the logical developments of the 14th century, namely the growing influence of "nominalism" (also called "terminism").

The theory of supposition led to the theory of signification of the modist school of logic in the middle of the 13th century. The Aristotelian school of the modists believed that verbal signs have fixed meanings derived from the fixed essences of the things which

体,同样也适用于纯思想性的东西。相反,唯名论(nominalismus, terminismus)的代表者认为,这种形式论的逻辑学太僵硬,没有弹性,而唯名论的逻辑则能更好地解释类比观念、同音不同义的词、同义词、描绘性的话、语义的复杂性,以及那些不符合事实但仍然可以思考的观念。

they represent, individually or in groups. For the Aristotelians the significance is real, accurate, verifiable, and immutable. It applies to extra-mental as well as to intra-mental realities. The exponents of terminism (nominalism) on the other hand held that this modist logic was too rigid and lacked the flexibility of terminist logic, which could better explain analogous, equivocal, and synonymous terms, circumlocutions, complex meanings, and ideas that are contrary to facts but are nevertheless thinkable.

罗里斯（约 1213—1237）

法国诗人，来自 Lorris（即 Orleans 附近的村子），生平不详。约于 1235 年撰写了 *Le Roman de la Rose* 的前半部分。

著作：《玫瑰传奇》

063. 《玫瑰传奇》

这个叙述的格律来自法语的 romance（罗曼斯诗歌），即是带雅韵的 8 音节双行诗。《玫瑰传奇》曾是一部流传很广的诗，在当时有相当大的影响。Guillaume de Lorris 大约于 1235 年写成 4000 多行，虽然他没有完成这部作品，但大概认为它已逼近尾声。大约 50 年后 Jean de Meun（或 Meung，1255—1305 年）加上了 18000 多行。从很多角度来看，两个作者的观点是相反的：第一部分符合一种感情上的理想主义，并描写一个具有骑士风度的爱人对他的贵族情人（玫瑰花代表女子）的追求。第二个部分则是针对骑士和宫廷爱情的那些不自然的习俗的讽刺，其中暴露出自然主义、感官主义、理性主义、粗糙的现实主义以及贬低女性主义的种种倾向。

在第一个部分中，一个情人在梦中见到一个花园，而花园中有一朵玫瑰花，她既代表爱情本身，又代表贵族女士。这位情人走入那个安逸宁静的花园。被拒绝进入花园的是虚伪、贪婪、忧伤、嫉妒、穷困和另一些恶习。情人被邀请参加一些拟人化的美德的舞蹈。她们是礼貌、爱欲（Cupid）、美丽、坦诚、青春和喜悦。Cupid 的箭射中情人的心，而 Cupid 教导情人应该采取什么行动来接近玫瑰花。Cupid 也告诉情人关于爱情的种种忧伤和它们的良药。此后，欢迎（Bel-Accueil）、闲逸、喜乐和美好的希望邀请情人去接近玫瑰。依赖 Venus 的协助，他与玫瑰接吻，但坏话、羞愧和嫉妒阻碍他进一步靠近玫瑰。羞愧的母亲理性劝情人拒绝 Cupid，回避欲望和那种愚蠢的惹情作风。此后，嫉妒把欢迎关入一个塔楼，而敌对的力量，即恐惧、羞愧和嫉妒在玫瑰周围建立起一座碉堡。

此时 Jean de Meun 继续叙述这个故事，而他插入很多长篇的讲演。玫瑰在碉堡中被关起来，一个老妇女看守她。理性重复那些反对爱情的论点：爱情是多变的、不坚定的，并使人们忘记追求永恒的价值。一些新的论点暴露出贬低女性的态度。情人的朋友出现，他劝情人通过贿赂、虚伪和欺骗攻克碉堡。情人不愿意接受这些建议，但他的朋友带来玫瑰的丈夫，他充满嫉妒，是一个残酷的贬低女性主义者并抱怨玫瑰的种种缺点和不足。朋友催促情人去奋斗，所以情人再次找到 Cupid。Cupid 宽恕情人曾经听从理性的建议的行为。Cupid 和他的协助者——虚伪的外表、勉强的刻苦、礼貌和奢侈——解放欢迎，此后他们允许情人摘取玫瑰。

Guillaume de Lorris / William Lorris

Opera: *Le Romam de la rose*
Works: *Romance of the Rose*

063. *Le Roman de la rose / Romance of the Rose*

This narrative, written in the verse form of French romances, eight-syllable rhymed couplets, was a widely read poem and very influential in its day. Guillaume de Lorris wrote about 4000 lines c. in 1235 and left the work incomplete but probably very close to its intended conclusion. Jean the Meun (or "Meung", ca. 1255—1305) added more than 18000 lines some fifty years later. In many ways the views of the two authors were antithetical: the first part, basically in the line of emotional idealism, is an allegorical description of a courtly lover's difficult pursuit of his lady, personified as the Rose. The second part is a satire on the unnatural conventions of courtly love and betrays attitudes of naturalism, sensualism, rationalism, hard realism as well as anti-feminism.

In the first part a lover dreams of a garden which encloses the Rose, symbol both of love and of the lady herself. He enters the idyllic garden, from which Hypocrisy, Avarice, Sorrow, Envy, Poverty and other vices are excluded. The lover accepts an invitation to join in a dance together with Courtesy, Cupid, Beauty, Candor, Youth, and Delight. Cupid's arrow pierces his heart, and Cupid teaches the lover that kind of behaviour which will make him acceptable to the Rose. Cupid also instructs him about the pains of love and their remedies. Fair Welcome (Bel-Accueil), Idleness, Joy, and Sweet Looks invite him to approach the Rose. With the help of Venus he manages to kiss the Rose, but Evil Tongue, Shame and Jealousy prevent him from further approaching the Rose. Reason, the mother of Shame, unsuccessfully advises the lover to abandon Cupid, to shun lust and the folly of unprocreative love. Then Jealousy locks Fair Welcome up in a tower, and the adverse forces of Fear, Shame and Jealousy build a castle around the Rose.

At this point Jean de Meun takes up the narrative and leads it on, inserting many long digressions. The Rose is locked up in the castle, guarded by an Old woman. Reason repeats her arguments against love: love is transient and fickle, it distracts from the pursuit of eternal goods. Some new arguments against love betray attitudes of anti-feminism. The lover's Friend appears, he advises the lover to storm the castle by bribery, hypocrisy and deceit. The lover is offended by this suggestion, but the Friend brings in the Rose's jealous Husband, who is a cruel anti-feminist and complains about the Rose. The Friend urges the lover to fight, and so the lover returns to Cupid who forgives the lover for giving Reason a hearing. Cupid and his allies—False Seeming, Forced Abstinence, Courtesy and Luxury—liberate Fair Welcome, and then the lover is allowed to pluck the Rose.

在整个过程中出现了几个演讲者：那个老妇女很刻薄地揭露了妇女们的那些所谓的美德。这个老妇女认为人们可以过一种放纵的、不忠于对象的生活，她说爱情只是一种自然的冲动，与道德价值无关。另一个发言的女士是自然，她肯定说科学知识能克服迷信。她抱怨人类的退化和堕落并说，在自然的一切创造物中只有人能抵抗自然律，即生育繁殖的性行为，因为人有自由意志。在自然的眼中，贞洁和独身生活并不值得赞美。自然派遣 Genius（生育神灵）到 Cupid 那里，而 Genius 这个使者再次强调自然的种种观点。Genius 要求 Cupid 将爱情和生育牢牢联结，又要求 Cupid 放弃虚假表现和勉强的刻苦，而 Cupid 接受这些条件。因此，自然能使 Cupid 与理性和好，但同时扩大不道德的自然主义和理想的宫廷爱情之间的鸿沟；用宗教的语言来说，这也就是《旧约》的多生理想与《新约》的贞洁理想之间的鸿沟。

In the course of events, several figures hold speeches. The Old Woman scathingly exposes woman's presumed virtues. She counsels frivolity, infidelity and views love as a natural urge without any moral considerations. Another outspoken woman is Nature who asserts that science prevails over superstition. She deplores the degeneration of mankind, saying that humans with their free will are the only one of her creatures who can withstand Nature's laws of procreative sexuality. Chastity and celibacy are not praiseworthy in her eyes. Nature sends Genius as messenger to Cupid, and Genius (the god of good birth) confirms Nature's views on love. He asks Cupid to yoke love to procreation and to dismiss his companions False Seeming and Forced Abstinence, conditions which Cupid accepts. Thus Nature can reconcile Reason and Cupid, but widens the gap between immoral naturalism and the courtly ideals of love; phrased in religious language, this is the distance between the fertility ideal of the Old Testament and the chastity ideal of the New Testament.

罗吉尔·培根(1214—1294)

英国人,约生于 1214—1220 年间,曾在英国 Oxford 大学求学(大约在 1228—1240 年),在那里受 Grosseteste 的影响,后在 Paris 教授哲学(1240—1247 年),后来又回到 Oxford 学习神学,于 1256 年加入 OFM(方济各会),他关心哲学研究、自然科学的问题(尤其是光学)、教育制度的改革,但于 1277 年由于不同的原因受方济各会的谴责。他的尊称是 doctor mirabilis(可钦博士)。

著作:《研读哲学概要》、《研读神学概要》、《伟大著作》;还有其他著作。

064. 《伟大著作》

1265 年 Bacon 的一位朋友 Clemens IV 被选为教宗,而他要求 Bacon 寄给他一些教育改革的建议,因为教宗考虑要改革神学、哲学和自然科学的教学制度。1266 至 1268 年间 Bacon 拟定了改革的初稿,即 *Opus maius*,后来他在 *Opus minus*(《小著作》)和 *Opus tertium*(《第三著作》)中进一步发挥了自己的观点。

Opus maius 分为 7 章,其中谈论不同知识领域的问题。第 1 章提到一些阻碍人们获得真正知识的障碍。第 2 章说明哲学和神学诸学科之间的关系。第 3 章鼓励人们多学习《圣经》的语言(希伯来语和希腊语)以纠正 *Vulgata* 拉丁本。Bacon 曾建议要组织一个学术委员会来修订 *Vulgata* 的版本。强调外语的重要性与当时的主流思想有冲突,因为大多数的学者满足于使用 Abaelardus 的经院思想方法来理解《圣经》。第 4 章属于数学、天文学和修历的工程。第 5 章包含涉及光学的问题。Bacon 非常重视光学研究,他曾经说一个瞎子"不会知道这个世界的任何东西"。第 6 章覆盖实验性的学科,而第 7 章探讨伦理学和道德哲学问题。

Bacon 的基本目标是让数学和自然科学支撑神学这个学科。神学是一切知识的指南,神学超越一切学科。Bacon 批评一些神学家说他们满足于拉丁语文学、修辞学、一点逻辑学和自然科学方面的肤浅知识。他希望他们对其他的语言(希腊语、希伯来语、阿拉伯语)有更多兴趣,并要求他们热切爱好自然现象的研究。他也要求进行长期的实验,以发现一些数学原理,而这些原理就是一切现象的核心与根源。

Rogerius Baco / Roger Bacon

Opera: *Compendium studii philosophiae, Compendium studii theologiae, Opus maius*
Works: *Introduction to the Study of Philosophy, Introduction to the Study of Theology, Greater Work*

064. *Opus maius / Greater Work*

In 1265 Clement IV, a friend of Bacon, became Pope and asked Bacon to send him some suggestions for the reform of the theological, philosophical and scientific studies. Between 1266 and 1268 Bacon elaborated a first draft for reforms (the *Opus maius*), which he further developed in the *Opus minus* (*Minor Work*) and *Opus tertium* (*Third Work*).

The *Opus maius* treats the different areas of knowledge in 7 chapters. The first chapter discusses some obstacles that prevent the searching mind from arriving at true knowledge. Chapter 2 explains the relationships between philosophical and theological disciplines. Chapter 3 exhorts the study of the Biblical languages (Hebrew and Greek) in order to be able to correct the Latin text of the *Vulgate*. One of Bacon's suggestions is to appoint a comittee of scholars who should revise the *Vulgate*. This emphasis on learning languages was against the mainstream of his time, since at his day most scholars were content with using Abaelard's scholastic method to understand the Bible. Chapter 4 is dedicated to the mathematical sciences, astronomy, and a reform of the calendar. Chapter 5 contains questions concerning optic, the science very dear to Bacon who once said that a blind man would "know nothing of this world". Part 6 covers the empirical sciences, and part 7 questions of ethics and moral philosophy.

The basic intention of Bacon is that the discipline of theology should be supported by mathematics and the natural sciences. Theology gives orientation to all knowledge and is above all the other sciences. Bacon criticizes the theologians for being satisfied only with Latin grammar, rhetoric, some logic and superficial knowledge of the sciences. He expects them to show more interest for other languages (Greek, Hebrew, and Arabic) and zeal for the study of the phenomena of nature. He also demands that continuous experiments should show the mathematical principles that are at the root of all phenomena.

鲁布鲁克(1215—1270)

Rubruk(亦写 Roebroeck, Rubruc 等)生于 1215 年,在今天的比利时地区加入 OFM(方济各会),曾陪同法国国王 Ludovicus IX 到圣地参与十字军运动(1248—1250 年),后在 Acco 的一所隐修院生活。Ludovicus 王派遣他去和蒙古人的领导 Sertach 谈判。Rubruk 于 1253 年 5 月从 Constantinopolis 启程,与 4 位同事前往东方,在俄罗斯地区跨越 Don 河,不久后和 Sertach 相遇,但 Sertach 说他们应该去见蒙古大汗 Mangu。四个月后他们到达和林附近的大汗宫廷;大汗说如果法国国王接受蒙古人的统治,蒙古王将会允许基督宗教在东方的传播。Rubruk 于 1255 年回到欧洲,他曾在 Paris 向 Roger Bacon 提供大量地理知识,而后者的 *Opus maius* 也提到 Rubruk。

著作:《东方游记》

065.《东方游记》

从东方回来之后 Rubruk 需要在 Acco 授课,所以他无法亲自前往法国向国王作报告。因此他以信件的形式编写这部游记,将它寄给 Ludovicus IX 王。Rubruk 描述他在中亚地区的旅程并讲述蒙古人和其他民族的习俗、文化、宗教和语言。他的《游记》被视为关于当时蒙古人的最可靠文献。

Rubruk 的报告包含关于中亚地区的地理知识,又描写鞑靼人(即蒙古人)的房子、他们的食物、他们狩猎和食用的动物、他们的衣服和妇女的装饰品、妇女的家庭工作、鞑靼人的法律、他们的丧礼、叙利亚教徒(景教徒)和穆斯林在中国的居住地、佛塔和佛教和尚、他们的礼仪和偶像、蒙古人的大汗在 Karakorum(和林,今天在外蒙古)附近的宫殿。当然,作为一个传教士的 Rubruk 对外国民族的宗教很有兴趣,所以他描绘占卜者、和尚和在中国举行的宗教谈论会。根据他的报告,在三个大的蒙古部族中都有叙利亚教会(景教)的信徒(在今天的外蒙古),而叙利亚教会的信徒分布在 Cathay(契丹,中国)的 15 个城市。景教的总主教在"西京"(可能在今天的山西省大同地区)。

Rubruk / Guilelmus de Roebroeck

Opera: *Itinerarium ad partes orientales*
Works: *A Journey to the East*

065. *Itinerarium ad partes orientales / A Journey to the East*

Because Rubruk had to give lectures in Acco after his return from the East he could not go to France personally to report on his journey to the east. Therefore he wrote this itinerary in the form of a letter adressed to King Louis IX. Rubruk describes his journey through the regions of Central Asia and reports on the customs, culture, religion and languages of the Mongols and other peoples. His *Itinerary* counts as the most reliable Western source concerning the Mongols at that time.

Rubruk's account contains information about the geography of Central Asia, the houses of the Tatars (=Mongols), their food, the animals they hunt and eat, their clothes and the adornments of women, the housework of the weaker sex, the laws of the Tatars, their way of burying the dead, the settlements of the Syrian Christians (Nestorians) and Saracenes (Muslims) in China, pagodas and Buddhist monks, their rituals and idols, the palace of the Mongol Khan close to Karakorum. Naturally the missionary Rubruk is interested in the religion of the foreign peoples, thus he writes about diviners, monks, religious controversies in China. According to his report there were Christians of the Syrian Church (Nestorians) among three big Mongolian tribes in today's Mongolia, and Christians of the Syrian Church lived in 15 cities of Cathay (China). Their archbishop had his seat in the "Western Capital" (possibly in the area of Datong, Shanxi Province).

波那文图拉(1217—1274)

生于意大利 Viterbo 地区的 Bagnoreggio，曾在 Paris 学习，1243 年入方济各会，在 Alexander of Hales 的指导下学习神学，1254 年毕业，1257 年和 Thomas Aquinas 一起成为教师，同年当选为方济各会的总会长，1274 年在 Lyon 的主教会议上去世。Bonaventura 的尊号是 doctor angelicus(天使博士)。

著作:《简论》、《圣灵七恩论集》、《论诸学科归于神学》、《论三条路》、《命题之书》、《灵魂迈向天主的路程》、《圣 Franciscus 传》、《神学集成讲解》、《讲道集》、《独白篇》、《圣母站在十字架》

066. 《灵魂迈向天主的路程》

这部神秘神学作品写于 1259 年并描述人心向神的上升——神是灵魂的主人，而灵魂始终渴望他、需要他。当 Bonaventura 前往意大利时，他编写这部著作，而在同样的旅途中他还写了关于科学理论的书(书名为 De reductione artium ad theologiam《论诸学科归于神学》)。

Bonaventura 受 Augustinus 和 Plato(尤其是新 Plato 主义)的启发，他认为，与其说科学(scientia)是了解宇宙的结构不如说科学是对神的爱。知识和智慧必须引导心灵面对神。人心应该借着三个步骤默观外在的世界、人心内在的世界以及围绕着我们的神秘世界。"在这种灵魂走向神的过程当中，人心具有三个基本的态度或角度。第一个是针对外在的物质性东西，而在这个层面上人心被称为感觉性的或感官的。第二个是人心进入自身并观看自己，这就是人的精神；第三个是人心转向上面并超越自己，这个层面被称为心神(mens)。在这三方面人心必须准备将自己提升到神那里，这样才能全意、全心、全灵地爱慕他(参见 Mk 12:30, ex toto corde tuo, ex tota anima tua, et ex tota mente tua)，因为这就是完成律法和基督信仰的最高智慧。"因为每一个步骤分为两段，本著作的开始部分被分为 6 章，这又效法 6 天创造的过程(参见 Bonaventura 于 1273 年完成的 Collationes in Hexaemeron《论六天创造》)。人心的 6 个能力符合 6 个精神阶段，它们是：感觉(sensus)、想象(imaginatio)、理性(ratio)、心智(intellectus)、领悟(intelligentia)和心灵的顶峰(apex mentis)。"这些能力是天然赋予我们的，但罪恶扭曲了他们，因此需要通过恩典改革他们，需要通过正义净化他们，以知识训练他们，又以智慧完善他们。"

在开始的时候，灵魂应该使用自己的理性和心智能力来寻觅神在世界中的痕迹(vestigia)。第 2 个步骤要求人寻找神在灵魂中的形象(imago, exemplar, effigies)，这里就需要使用反思和思辨性的思维。这种思辨(speculatio)可以形容为一种"映像式的默

Bonaventura (Giovanni di Fidanza) / Bonaventure

Opera: *Breviloquium, Collationes de septem donis Spiritus Sancti, De reductione artium ad theologiam, De triplici via, In libros sententiarum, Itinerarium mentis in Deum, Legenda Sancti Francisci, Quaestiones, Sermones, Soliloquium, Stabat mater*

Works: *Breviloquium, The Seven Gifts of the Holy Spirit, On the Reduction of the Sciences to Theology, On the Threefold Way, On the Sentences, The Mind's Road to God, Life of St. Francis, Questions, Sermons, Soliloquy, Stabat Mater*

066. *Itinerarium mentis in Deum / The Mind's Road to God*

This mystical work was written in 1259 and describes the ascension of the human soul to God, her master, whom she constantly desires and needs. Bonaventure wrote the treatise when he visited Italy, and during the same journey he also wrote on the theory of the sciences (*De reductione artium ad theologiam, Reduction of the Arts to Theology*).

Being inspired by Augustine and Platonism (especially Neoplatonism) Bonaventure emphasizes that science (scientia) is love of God rather than insight into the structure of the universe. Knowledge and wisdom must lead the soul to God. In three steps the soul should contemplate the outside world, the realities within the human heart and the mystical world surrounding us. "In relation with this threefold progress of the soul to God, the human mind has three fundamental attitudes or outlooks. The first is towards corporeal things without, and in this respect it is designated as animal or simply sensual. The next is where it enters in within itself to contemplate itself, and here it ranks as spirit; the third is where its upward glance is beyond itself, and then it is designated mind (mens). In all three ways the human soul must prepare to raise itself to God so that it may love Him with the whole mind, with all its heart, and with its whole soul (see *Mk* 12:30, ex toto corde tuo, ex tota anima, et ex tota mente tua), for in this consists the fullness of the Law and the highest Christian wisdom." Since each step is twofold the first part of the work is divided into six chapters, thus imitating the six days of creation (conf. Bonaventure's *Collationes in Hexaemeron* of 1273). The six capacities of the soul which correspond to the six mental stages are: sensus (sense), imaginatio (imagination), ratio (reason), intellectus (intellect), intelligentia (understanding), and the apex mentis (peak of the mind). "These powers we have implanted in us by nature; by sin deformed, they are reformed through grace; and they must be purified by justice, exercised by knowledge, and made perfect by wisdom."

In the beginning the soul should use its rational and intellectual abilities to find the traces (vestigia) of God in the world. The second step is centered on finding the image

想"(mirroring meditation,参见拉丁语的 speculum,即"镜子")。第 3 步骤使人意识到灵魂离神很近(similitudo),这是一种超理性的、神秘的领悟。Bonaventura 认为创造界是一种"美善的链子",一个能帮助灵魂上升到最高的善——即神——的梯子。这种教导是 Franciscus 那种自然神秘主义的哲学化版本,但它仍然保留默观的(contemplatio)和以基督为核心的特征。

在第 7 章里,灵魂终于获得一种内心的平安(requies datur intellectui),因为心灵和一切感受都因神的临在而经历一种超拔(affectu totaliter in Deum per excessum transeunte)。只有在那个时刻灵魂才能达到自己的目标,因为它离开了有形的、多变的世界并来到了万物的第一个来源,即神。因此,灵魂在走向神的过程中的后期阶段需要有一种神秘体验。

(imago, exemplar, effigies) of God within the soul by applying reflection and speculative ways of thinking. This "speculation" might be described as a kind of "mirroring meditation", confer the Latin speculum = mirror. The third step leads to a mystical and irrational realization of the soul's closeness (similitudo) to God. Bonaventure sees the creation as a chain of goodness, a ladder which can help the soul to ascend to the supreme good which is God. This doctrine is a more philosophical version of Franciscan nature mysticism while retaining its contemplative and Christocentric features.

In the seventh chapter the soul finally reaches a state of inner peace (requies datur intellectui), since the heart and the emotions are totally enraptured by God (affectu totaliter in Deum per excessum transeunte). Only then the soul reaches her aim, since she has left the mutable world of images and has arrived at the first origin of all, God. Therefore the final stages of the journey of the soul to God require mystical experience.

托马斯·阿奎那(多玛斯、多默)(1225—1274)

1225年生于意大利Neapolis附近的Roccasecca宫殿，父亲是Lombard贵族人士Landulfus de Aquino。因为他是最小的儿子，5岁的Thomas被送到本笃会的Monte Cassino隐修院，在那里接受教育，1239年入Neapolis大学，进而学习语文、逻辑学，并在Petrus de Hibernia的指导下学习自然科学，1244年决定加入Ordo Praedicatorum（道明会/多明我会）。他的母亲强烈反对这种想法，甚至命人在Roccasecca宫殿中监禁她的儿子。家人终于在1245年释放Thomas，而道明会的领导者不久后派遣他去Paris听Albertus Magnus的课。1248年他随Albertus来到Colonia(科隆)，成为老师的助手并开始任教。他于1252年回到Paris，在那里任教并写作，1257年（与Bonaventura一起）正式获得神学硕士(magister theologiae)的学位。1259年他回到意大利(也许是Neapolis)并开始编写 *Summa contra gentiles*（《反驳异教大全》）。1265年他被任命在Roma建立一所学院，同时开始编写 *Summa theologiae*(《神学大全》)以及很多别的著作（所谓的 *Quaestiones disputatae* 等等）。1268—1272年他又在Paris任教，1272年前往Neapolis，1273年因工作压力太大而休息。他被邀请参与1274年在法国Lyon举行的主教会议，但途中在Fossanova隐修院去世。他是最杰出的经院神学家和哲学家，对欧洲思想史有深厚的影响，后来他经常被视为正统公教思想的代表人物，其尊称是Doctor angelicus（"天使博士"）。

著作：《神学手册》(未完成)、《为修会辩护》、《反驳那些反对宗教和修会的人》、《论世界的永恒》、《论灵魂》、《论存有与本质》(1256年前，早期的哲学著作)、《论恶》、《论灵修生活的完善》、《论上主的能力》、《论自然诸原则》、《论灵性的受造物》、《论分离的本质，或论天使的本性》、《论降生圣言的合一》、《论心灵的合一性》、《论真理》、《论诸美德》、《宗徒信经阐释》、《小作品》、《关于诸命题之书》、《反驳异教大全》(提供很多论点以说明基督信仰的优越性)、《神学大全》(最有影响的著作，一种神学百科全书，部分于1654年由Buglio译成汉语，名为《超性学要》)、《论Boethius关于三位一体的书》、《论〈原因〉》、《论Dionysius关于神圣名称之书》、《论圣Paulus书信》、《论Jeremias之著作》、《论Job》、《论Isaias》、《论Matthaeus》、《论诗篇》(《论圣咏》)。

067. 《反驳异教大全》

回应Raymond de Penafort的要求，Thomas在1259年到1267年间编写了这部著作。Thomas要为那些在伊斯兰教地区宣教的人提供一种导论。在欧洲的基督教国家中，这部著作很快流传开来，甚至被译成好几种东方语言。本著作的恒久贡献是它使用自然哲学的概念来阐述基督信仰而仍然没有放弃信仰的核心教义。

Thomas Aquinas

Opera: *Compendium theologiae, Contra doctrinam retrahentium a religione, Contra impugnantes dei cultum et religionem, De aeternitate mundi, De anima, De ente et essentia, De malo, De perfectione spiritualis vitae, De potentia Dei, De principiis naturae, De spiritualibus creaturis, De substantiis separatis seu de angelorum natura, De unione verbi incarnati, De unitate intellectus contra Averroistas, De veritate, De virtutibus, Expositio in symbolum apostolicum, Opuscula, Scriptum super libros Sententiarum, Summa contra gentiles, Summa theologiae, Super Boethium De Trinitate, Super de causis, Super Dionysium De divinis nominibus, Super Epistolas Pauli Apostoli, Super Ieremiam et Threnos, Super Iob, Super Ioannem, Super Isaiam, Super Matthaeum, Super Psalmos*

Works: *A Compendium of Theology, An Apology for the Religious Orders, Against those who fight against Divine Worship and Religious Orders, On the Eternity of the World, On the Soul, On Being and Essence, On Evil, On the Perfection of Spiritual Life, On the Power of God, On the Principles of Nature, On Spiritual Creatures, On Separate Substances, On the Unity of the Incarnated Word, On the Unicity of the Intellect, against the Averroists, On Truth, On the Virtues, Exposition of the Creed, Smaller Works, Script on the Books of the Sentences, Summa Against the Heathens (On the Truth of the Catholic Faith), Summa Theologiae, Concerning Boetius on the Trinity, On de Causis, Concerning Dionysius on the Divine Names, On the Letters of St. Paul, On Jeremy, On Job, On John, On Isaia, On Matthew, On the Psalms*

067. *Summa contra gentiles / Summa Against the Heathens*

Responding to the requests of Raymond de Penafort Thomas wrote this work in the years between 1259 and 1267. It was meant as an introduction to mission sermons in Muslim regions. This Summa spread fast in Christian lands and was even translated into several oriental languages. It's lasting contribution is the effort to present the faith in terms of natural philosophy without sacrificing the central tenets of the Christian tradition.

全书分为 4 部分：(1)论神的本性，(2)论受造的宇宙的本性，(3)一切受造物走向他们的终极目标(这个部分包括伦理问题和神的预先照顾 providentia)；(4)说明那些纯粹的理性无法理解的信条，即三位一体、降生成人的奥迹、诸圣事，以及肉身的复活等。每一卷用简短的章节来阐明这些内容，而不采用 Summa theologiae(《神学大全》)的对话风格。

作者没有预先设想读者是基督徒，所以他的理论基础是自然理性，因为所有人都分享这种理性。作者要寻求真理并排除某些错误。他也致力于说明基督信仰很符合理性。自然和启示有彼此相应的关系。人的本性向无限者是开放的，任何受造物都无法满足人心。人的爱慕的对象必须是无限的；一个理性存在者的完美幸福不可能是对于一个有限物体的沉思和向往。只有当人观望无限的神时，他才能找到真正的喜乐。因此人的本性指向一种超自然的目标，即神。这种来自第 3 卷的论点试图表明这一点：如果非基督徒想获得真正的喜乐，他们需要神的启示。

基督信仰的一个奥迹是基督降生成人(道成肉身)。作者解释说这个事件是在寻求真福的道路上的协助以及反抗罪恶的良药。这样，信仰的奥迹不是依赖理性而受到"证明"，而被解释为一些可信的、可理解的事。关于圣事的部分(第 4 卷)说明为什么教会的圣事是可见的、物质性的记号。基督取得了肉身，而他是一切圣事的来源，因此这些圣事也是可见的，可触摸的事件。人的罪意味着人远离神并以无序的方式转向可见的受造界，而因为诸圣事愿意治疗罪恶的创伤，这些圣事也必须是物质性的。在自然的领域中，一切领悟是以感官为媒介的，而因此灵性的知识也必须要从物质体验开始。根据这一切理由可以说明为什么诸圣事很正当地是可见的、可触摸的标记。

068. 《神学大全》

《神学大全》(缩写为 STh)写成于 1267—1273 年，但没有完成。整个巨著的结构是这样的：I. 神和受造界；II.I. 伦理道德问题和其他问题；II.II. 种种美德；III. I. 基督论，诸圣事和终末论的问题。Thomas 的同事 Reginaldus de Priverno 加上了一个 Supplementum("附录"，III.II.)。

作者在几千"章"(articuli)中澄清 611 个"论题"(quaestiones)，这些论题涉及到神学、哲学、伦理学和法学的种种问题。谈论这些问题的过程都是一样的：每一章(1)提出一个问题，(2)列出一些观点——这些观点或论点来自《圣经》、教父文献或 Aristoteles(亚里士多德)，并且好像要给予反面的答案(videtur…)；此后，(3)作者提出问题的正确答案(通常用 Respondeo, quod)，这样就权威性地回答疑问，并(4)一个一个地解释和反驳那些在前面列出的反对观点。只有通过这种严谨的和仔细的讨论，新兴的神学才能够成为一种科学。Thomas 在开头分析神学(sacra doctrina)作为科学的

The work is divided into four parts: (1) the nature of God; (2) the nature of the created universe; (3) the movement of created things to their last aim (this part includes ethical questions and divine Providence); (4) those central doctrines of Christianity which are not intelligible by mere reason, namely the Trinity, Incarnation, the sacraments and the resurrection of the body. Every book presents these tenets in short chapters without using the style of debate known from the *Summa theologiae*.

The author does not presuppose that the reader is a Christian and thus bases his explanations on natural reason which is common to all people. He wants to search for the truth and thus exclude certain errors. He also tries to show that the Christian faith is in harmony with reason. Nature and revelation correspond to each other. Human nature is open to the infinite and cannot be satisfied by any created being. The object of human love must be infinite; the perfect happiness of a reasonable being cannot consist in the contemplation of a limited object. Only the vision of the infinite Good will enable human persons to find true happiness. Thus human nature itself points to a supernatural aim, namely God. This argumentation from book 3 tries to show the non-Christians that they need divine revelation in order to find true joy.

One of the mysteries of the Christian faith is the incarnation of Christ. This event is explained as a help on the way to beatitude and a remedy against sin. In this way the mysteries of the faith are not "proven" by reason but made credible and accessible to the understanding of the human mind. The section covering the sacraments (book 4) explains why the sacraments of the Church are visible and material signs. Christ who appeared in the flesh is the origin of the sacraments which are thus also visible and tangible events. The sin of man means that a person turns away from God and turns to the visible creation in a disorderly way, and since the sacraments want to heal the wounds of sin they also need to be visible. Just like in the realm of nature all insight is mediated by the senses, also spiritual knowledge must start from physical experience. For all these reasons it is obvious that the sacraments rightly are visible and tangible effective signs.

068. *Summa Theologiae / Sum of Theology*

The *Summa Theologiae* (abbreviated as S.Th. or STh), written in 1267—1273, was left unfinished. The structure of the huge work is: I. God and creation; II.I. moral and other questions; II.II. the virtues; III.I. Christology, the sacraments and the last things. A *Supplementum* (III. II.) by Thomas' co-worker Reginald de Priverno completes the masterpiece.

In several thousand articles (articuli) Thomas discusses 611 theological, philosophical, ethical and legal questions (quaestiones). The procedure of disputing the questions is always the same: every article (1) presents a question (2) lists up several arguments (from the Bible, the Church fathers, or Aristotle etc.) that seem to support a negative answer ("videtur⋯"), then (3) the thesis is affirmed (usually with the words "Respondeo, quod⋯"), and this thesis answers the question in an authoritative way; finally (4) the contradictory arguments of the question are explained and refuted one by one. Only through this meticulous and diligent discussion of every detail it was possible to establish the new science of theology. Right in the beginning Thomas analyzes the possibility of scientific theology (sacra doctrina), asking (1) whether it is necessary to have

可能性并提出这些问题：(1)在各种哲学学科以外还需要神学的知识体系吗？(2)神学能成为一个学科吗？(3)它是一个学科还是很多学科呢？(4)神学属于实践性的学科吗？(5)神学比其他学科更有尊严吗？(6)这种知识是一种智慧吗？(7)这个学科的主题(subiectum)是神吗？(8)神学是否是一个辩论性的学科？(9)《圣经》需要使用比喻性的说法吗？(10)《圣经》中的一句话能有不同层次的意义(plures sensus)吗？值得注意的是这一点：Thomas 的学术性出发点成了公教的主流思想，而神学的探讨是按照他的原则发展的；与此不同，伊斯兰教的思想没走这条路。

同样，Thomas 以精耕细作的精神试图澄清一些涉及法律和伦理学的难题。比如，II.II.部分第 64 个论题的标题是"论杀人"(de homicidio)，分为 8 个 articuli(章)：(1)杀生物是否合法？(2)杀犯人是否合法？(3)私人是否可以杀犯人？(4)圣职人员是否可以杀恶人？(5)自杀是否合法？(6)在某些特殊条件下是否可以杀无辜的人？(7)在自卫过程中杀人是否是允许的？(8)在事故中无意杀人是否被认为有杀人的罪？ 第 1 章开始提出 3 种反对杀动物的观点，又罗列 3 种支持杀害生物的论点，此后是 Thomas 的回答和针对一些论点的反驳。

在《神学大全》I. 2 中，Thomas 提出五种证明神存在的道路(quinque viae)。第一条路建立在"运动"(motus)的原则之上。"运动"也被广泛地解释为"从可能到实现"的过程。一切运动导致一个最后的推动者(第一个推动者)，他自身不动。第二种思路建立在 causa efficiens(原因)的原则之上，这种思想最后导致万物的 prima causa(第一个原因)。第三种论证指出"可能性"和"必然性"之间的差别。如果宇宙是必然存在的，就需要有一个完全必然的实体——神。第四种思路受了 Plato 的影响：一切事物的存在都体现出一种"多"和"少"或"高"与"低"的秩序，所以必须有一个最完美，最现实的存在。第五个思路来自万物的安排和管理秩序(ex gubernatione rerum)。如果甚至那些没有思考的东西都指向一种目的，那么应该存在一个理性的引导它们的力量，这个力量给予自然万物一种目的和秩序。对于神的存在的五个论点或证据的出发点都是人的经验和对物质世界的观察，这就和 Augustinus 的思维方式有一定的差别(参见 Noli foras ire, in interiore homine habitat veritas! "不要出去，真理在人心之中！"*De vera religione*)

Thomas 深深受 Aristoteles 思想的影响，因此他认为世俗的学科是一些独立的学科，不仅仅是神学的支撑工具。正如国度是一个"自然的现象"，而其权威并不依赖于教会，哲学也是一门独立自主的学科。类似于他的老师 Albertus Magnus，Thomas 想了解一切东西，他的兴趣是探讨整个宇宙中的一切存在，而他想"描述整个宇宙及它的一切原因"。这就是科学的任务，而知识的两个根源，即自然理性(lumen naturale)和启示(lumen supernaturale)需要在这方面进行合作。在神学的框架中，一切其他的学科都能获得自己的正当位置(参见 I. 1，其中谈论神学，即 sacra doctrina this branch of knowledge in addition to the philosophical disciplines. (2) Can theology be a science? (3) Is it one discipline or many? (4) Does theology belong to the practical sciences? (5) Is theology more dignified than the other sciences? (6) Is that science a kind of wisdom? (7) Is God the subject (subiectum) of this science? (8) Is theology an argumentative science? (9) Is it necessary that the Holy Scriptures make use of metaphors? (10) Can a Biblical word have different layers of meaning (plures sensus)? It is noteworthy that Thomas' scholarly approach became the mainstream of Catholic thought, and theological inquiry developed along these lines, a development that did not take place in the world of Islam.

With the same precision and fervor Thomas tries to clarify questions concerning law and ethics. For example the question (quaestio) 64 of part II.II. is entitled "De homicidio" (on homicide) and is divided into these articles: (1) whether the killing of any living being (animals) may be admitted; (2) whether killing of criminals is licit; (3) whether a private person may kill a criminal; (4) whether clerics may kill an evildoer; (5) whether suicide is licit; (6) whether innocent people might be killed under certain circumstances; (7) whether killing in self-defence is allowed; (8) whether killing someone accidentally is to be considered having the guilt of homicide. Article 1 starts with presenting three arguments that seem to forbid the killing of animals and continues with three arguments that support the killing of living beings. Then follow Thomas' answer and the refutations of some arguments.

In S. Th. I. 2 Thomas tries to show in five ways (quinque viae) the existence of God. The first way is based on the principle of "movement" (motus), which is interpreted in a wider sense as the change from possibility to reality. All movement leads to a first moving force which in itself is unmoved. The second argumentation is based on the principle of the causa efficiens (effective cause) which leads to the first origin (prima causa) of all things. The third way points out the difference between possible and necessary things. If the universe is to have reality, then there should be a first, absolutely necessary entity—God. The fourth way is inspired by Plato and shows that all beings exist in a hierarchy of degrees. If there is a "more" and "less" in the levels of existence, then there should be a principle which is real and perfect in the highest sense. The fifth way argues from the ordinance of all things (ex gubernatione rerum). If even those things that have no intellect are ordered towards an aim, then there must be a rational force which directs all things in nature and imbues them with purpose. All five arguments or proofs for the existence of God proceed from our experience and from the observation of the material world, which is quite different from Augustine's way of thinking ("Noli foras ire, in interiore homine habitat veritas! Do not go out, the truth is in your heart!" *De vera religione*).

Thomas is deeply influenced by Aristotelian thought, thus he acknowledges that the secular sciences are independent disciplines and not only a supportive tool of theology. Just like the state is a "natural" phenomenon whose authority does not depend on the Church, philosophy too is a science in its own right. Similar to his teacher Albert the Great, Thomas wants to know all things, his interests encompass the whole universe of beings, and he wants to "describe the whole order of the universe with all its causes". This is the task of science, and both sources of knowledge, natural reason (lumen naturale) and revelation (lumen supernaturale) work together in this effort. All sciences find their proper place within the framework of theology (confer I. 1, on theology, the "sacra

和其他学科的关系)。

就知识论而言,Thomas 脱离 Augustinus 的教导,他不再认为我们的一切知识都来自永恒的理念。Thomas 同意说人的"自然理性之光"是"对于神性光明的某种参与",但他基本上远离"照明"(illuminatio)的观点并强调 Aristoteles 关于感官认识的观点:"对人来说,通过可以感觉的东西达到可理解的东西是自然的,因为我们的一切知识是从感官而开始的。"(omnis nostra cognitio a sensis initium habet, I. 1, 9) Plato 主义者说我们如果参与永恒的理念(rationes aeternae)可以知道一切东西,而在"太阳"的光内我们才知道一切(参见 *Psalmus* 35:10 In lumine tuo videbimus lumen "在你的光内我们见到光明")。然而 Thomas 认为仅仅观望太阳的光而不去观察具体的物体(res materiales)是不足够的。我们也需要感官上的认识(cognitio sensibilis,见 I. 84, 6)。

我们认识的秩序符合一个三阶段的过程:首先我们从具体的事物(res corporeas et materiales, ens mobile)走向一种数学上的抽象概念,这样从广袤和数量(ens quantum)的角度描述世界。此后我们再次抽象一些能够脱离物质而存在的原则,比如"存在"(ens)、"一"(unum)、"实现"(actus)和"可能性"(potentia)。这就是形而上的世界(I. 85, 1)。这样我们可以得到最基本的原理,这些是自明的原则(judicia per se nota)。"人们先知道的是存在,而第一个原则是这个:我们不能同时肯定和否定(……)正如我们第一个认出的东西是'存有'(ens),实践理性(ratio practica)认出的第一个概念是'善'(bonum)"(II. I. 94, 2)。

当然,感官认识是不足够的,它仅提供引发理性认识的资料,而这种更高级的知识必须超越感官(intellectualis cognitio ultra sensitivam se extendit, I. 84, 6)。"主动理性"(intellectus agens)是人理解的根本,而这种理性能够达到真实的、普遍的和具有说服力的领会。Thomas 缺乏现代人的怀疑态度,他认为我们从感官体验获得的抽象概念是可靠的,因为他肯定一切东西都有自己的真理,都有它们的形式和本质,而人的灵魂(anima, mens)能够反映出这些真理"如同一面镜子那样"(sicut in speculo, I. 16, 6)。"主动理性"的抽象概念等于是对东西本质的认识。根据 Aristoteles 的一个原则,即"一个人能生另一个人"(est in homine virtus generativa hominis),Thomas 说人的灵魂能够发现物质世界中隐藏的永恒形式(possit phantasma illustrare, I. 79, 4)。

人的心灵需要对事物作出一些判断,而"真理是思想与存在之间的相符相合"(veritas est adaequatio rei et intellectus, I. 16, 1)。这个定义来自 Avicenna 的著作。这种真理是可靠的,因为各种事物和他们的本质都是根据某种固定的秩序安排的,而这个秩序是永恒的、稳定的,并且对伦理问题也是有效的(自然法,lex naturae)。

在一个章节中(I. 85, 2)Thomas 提出一个现代性的问题,即:是否我们的一切思想仅仅是主观的创造。他说如果是这样的,我们的知识不可能涉及任何心灵以外之

doctrina" and the other disciplines).

As to the theory of knowledge, Thomas turns away from Augustine's teaching that we know everything from the eternal ideas. Thomas agrees that the "natural light of reason" is a "certain participation in the divine light", but basically he distances himself from the way of "illumination" (illuminatio) and emphasizes the Aristotelian concept of sensual perception: "It is natural for man to reach the intelligible through the perceptible, because all our knowledge starts from the senses" (omnis nostra cognitio a sensis initium habet, I. 1, 9). The Platonists say that we can know all things if we participate in the eternal ideas (rationes aeternae), and in this light of the "sun" we can know all things (See *Psalm* 35:10: In lumine tuo videbimus lumen. "In your light we see the light"). However, Thomas holds that it would not be enough just to gaze at the sunlight without observing the material objects (res materiales). Sensual perception (cognitio sensibilis) is also needed (I. 84, 6).

The order of our understanding follows a process of three stages: first we proceed from the concrete things (res corporeas et materiales, ens mobile) to a mathematical abstraction which gives us a picture of the world under the aspect of extension (ens quantum). Then we abstract again from the material world and arrive at principles which can exist without matter, like "being" (ens), "unity" (unum), "act" (actus) and "potence" (potentia). This is the metaphysical world (I. 85, 1). In this way we come to first principles, to the norms of knowledge (logical rules) and to the rules of all sciences. These basic rules are self-evident, they are obvious principles (judicia per se nota). "What humans know first is the being, and the first principle is that we cannot at the same time affirm and negate, … and just as the first thing which we perceive is the being (ens), the first thing of practical reason (ratio practica) is the good (bonum)." (II. I. 94, 2).

Of course, sensual perception is not enough, it is only the material that causes intellectual understanding, and this higher knowledge must transcend the senses (intellectualis cognitio ultra sensitivam se extendit. I. 84, 6). The "active intellect" (intellectus agens) is the cause of human insight and can arrive a real, universal and cogent insights. Thomas lacks the skeptical attitude of modernity, he believes that our abstractions of sensual experiences are reliable, because he confirms that all things have their truths, their forms and essences, and the human soul (anima, mens) can reflect and mirror these truths "like in a mirror" (sicut in speculo, I. 16, 6). The abstractions of the active intellect are insights into the essences of the things. Based on the Aristotelian principle that a man can give birth to a human being (est in homine virtus generativa hominis), Aquinas states that the human soul can reveal eternal forms hidden in the material world (possit phantasmata illustrare, I. 79, 4).

The human soul needs to approach truth by making statements about things, and "truth is the congruence between thinking and being" (veritas est adaequatio rei et intellectus, I. 16, 1), a definition which is derived from Avicenna's works. This truth is reliable because the things and their essences are arranged according to a certain order, and this order is eternal, stable and valid also for moral questions (law of nature, lex naturae).

In one article (I. 85, 2) Thomas asks the modern question whether all our thinking is only a subjective creation. He says that in this case our knowledge would not reach anything

物,而一切科学将是不可能的。因此,存在必须是超越主体的,它是客观存在的。各种事物决定(mensurant)我们的思想,而人的思维不可能"塑造"实在(比如根据 Kant 的"先验原则")。

对 Thomas 来说,个别事物是"第一实体"(I. 84, 7)。这种观点受了 Aristoteles、Stoa 学派和基督信仰中的创造论的影响。然而,Thomas 也使用来自 Plato 和 Augustinus 的"形而上的存在概念"。形而上学是关于存在本身的知识,这是关于无形的东西的学科。一切东西来自一个"普遍的根源"(a causa universali, I. 45, 1)。因此,一切事物具有某种联结,他们都参与第一个存在:"Aristoteles 说至高的存在和最真实的存在也是一切存在物和一切真理的根源。"(Aristoteles dicit quod id, quod est maxime ens et maxime verum, est causa omnis entis et omnis veri. I. 44, 1)这种思想结合 Plato 和 Aristoteles 的观点,而一个顺理成章的结果是"存有类比"(analogia entis)。

"存有类比"的原则来自 Aristoteles 的 *Metaphysica*(Gamma 卷),这种原则是"同义"和"同声"之间的中间路线("同义"的例子是"家"="居所","同声"的例子是头"发"和出"发")。一切事物参与共同的"存在"(esse),但是以一种类比的方式,而创造主与受造物之间的关系是这种类比关系的模式(et haec analogia est creaturae ad Deum, Sent. I, 35, 1, 4)。Thomas 接受了 Aristoteles 的范畴,但他的宇宙是 Plato 式的——由不完美走向完美的阶层。对 Thomas 来说,普遍概念存在于个别事物之先,这些理念决定事物的存在,因为理念是事物的内在特性(intrinseca natura rei)。普遍理念也存在"于个别事物当中"(in re)以及"在事物之后"(post rem),因为我们事物的概念留在我们心中,虽然事物本身已经消失,不复存在。物质是个体化的原则,而形式与存在的关系也可以和可能性与现实的关系相类比。

神学大师 Thomas 的语言表达没有修辞学的装饰。他的表达方式很透明、清楚,同时也比较易懂。在他的老师 Albertus Magnus 后,Thomas 第一次利用 Aristoteles 的术语和观念来解释神学问题。比如,Thomas 视人的灵魂为 forma corporis(肉身的形式)。其他的思想家,比如 Plato 和 Augustinus 等教父也影响了 Thomas 的思想。《神学大全》包含无数的来自基督宗教传统的格言或论题,其中讨论的问题涉及到伦理学、法律哲学、科学哲学、对《圣经》的解释等。在哲学史上,Thomas 也拥有关键的地位。

《神学大全》在后来成为一部权威性的、具有影响力的神学教科书。当耶稣会的传教士在 16、17 世纪进入中国时,他们试图介绍西方思想,而其中一个传教士是意大利人 Luigi Buglio(利类思,1606—1682 年),他开始将托马斯的名作译成汉语,1654 年后以《超性学要》为名发行。这种翻译向中国学术界介绍很多新的概念,比如"性学"(即"哲学")、"天学"(即"神学")、"性法"(即"自然法"),而 Buglio 等人当时创造的部分术语在今天的汉语中仍然被使用,比如"人类"、"行为"、"选择"等。某些人名的翻译(比如"亚里士多德")也和 Buglio 的工作有关系。

outside the mind, and all science would be impossible. Thus being must be beyond the subject, it is objective. The things determine (mensurant) our thinking, and human thought is far from shaping reality (according to "transcendental principles", as Kant would say).

For Thomas the concrete individual being is the first substance (I. 84, 7). This view of reality is influenced by Aristotle, the Stoics, and the Christian idea of creation. However, Thomas also uses the "metaphysical concept of reality" that comes from the tradition of Plato and Augustine. Metaphysics is the science of being as such, it is the science of imperceptible things. All things are created, they come from a "universal cause" (a causa universali, I. 45, 1). Thus all beings are somehow connected, and they participate in the first being: "Aristotle says that the highest and most true being is also the cause of all being and of all truth" (Aristoteles dicit quod id, quod est maxime ens et maxime verum, est causa omnis entis et omnis veri. I. 44, 1). This thinking combines the traditions of Plato and Aristotle, and a logical consequence of it is the principle of the "analogy of being" (analogia entis).

The principle of the "analogy of being" is based on Aristotle's *Metaphysics* (Book Gamma) as the middle way between synonymy and homonymy (example of synonymy: residence = domicile, example of homonymy: plane = even surface, plane = aeroplane). All things participate in the one "esse" (being), but in an analogical way, and this analogy is outlined by the relationship between the Creator and created things (et haec analogia est creaturae ad Deum, Sent. I, 35, 1, 4). Thomas accepts Aristotle's categories, but at the same time his universe is also Platonically structured by grades of perfection. For Thomas the universal ideas exist before the individual things, the ideas are the intrinsic nature of each phenomenon (intrinseca natura rei) which determine the things. Furthermore the universal ideas also exist "in the things" (in re), and they also exist "after the things" (post rem), since we have abstract concepts of the things in our mind even after the things have already ceased to exist. Matter is the principle of individuation, and the relation of form and being is analogous to the relation of potency and reality.

Thomas' language is devoid of rhetoric ornaments. His way of expression is transparent, very exact and at the same time easy to understand. After his teacher Albert the Great, Thomas is one of the first to use Aristotle's terms and concepts to explain theological questions. For example, Thomas sees the human soul as the "forma corporis". Plato, Augustine and other Church fathers also influenced Thomas' thought. The Summa is a rich gold mine for quotations from the Christian tradition and covers a huge range of topics, including ethics, philosophy of law, theory of science, interpretation of the Bible etc. In the history of philosophy Thomas also has a crucial position.

The *Summa Theologiae* became an authoritative and influential textbook for the study of theology. When Jesuit missionaries entered China in the 16th and 17th centuries, they tried to introduce Western thought to China, and one of them, the Italian Luigi Buglio (1606—1682) started to translate Thomas' masterpiece into Chinese, publishing it after 1654 under the title Chao Xing Xue Yao. This unfinished translation already introduced many new concepts to the Chinese academic world, like xingxue (philosophy), tianxue (theology), xingfa (natural law), and some of the words created by Buglio and his companions are still in use today, for example the terms renlei (humanity, human race), xingwei (behaviour), xuanze (choice) etc. The Chinese translation of certain names (for example "Aristotle") is also connected to Buglio's work.

沃拉吉纳的雅各（约 1228—1298）

生于意大利的 Varazze（在 Genoa 附近），1244 年入道明会（多明我会），1260 年成为院长，1267—1286 年间任道明会在 Lombardia（意大利北部）地区的区长，1286 年被选为 Genoa 的总主教，但他于 1292 年才接受这个职位。他致力于圣职人员生活的改革，要协调 Genoa 城的争论，为此写了一部 Chronica Januense（《Genoa 历史》）。

著作：《Genoa 历史》、《金传》（中世纪最流行的著作之一，按教会历逐日编排，它也曾被译成欧洲各国语言）

069.《金传》

本书的原名是 Legenda sanctorum《圣人列传》或 Legenda nova《新传》，但因为它成为一部非常流行的书，自从中世纪晚期以来就被称为《金传》。道明会会士 Jacobus de Voragine 约于 1263—1273 年间编写了这部"传集"。该书分为 184 章并包含很多关于圣人/圣徒的故事，这些故事主要不是历史性的叙述，而是一些有"振作精神"作用或教育作用的记载。

作者自己说他的故事来自《圣经》以及许多其他作者的书，比如来自 Augustinus、Eusebius、Hieronymos、Cassiodorus、Beda、Bernardus Claravallensis 等人。除此之外，他也引用很多民间传说来说明基督徒的美德。关于圣人/圣徒的道德榜样和他们施行的奇迹的故事第一次按照教会的礼仪年被排列，所以开始有"降临期"（圣诞节以前的时期）。因此，独特的历史事件被列入教会礼仪那种一年复一年的"永恒循环"。作者解释一切教会节日和圣人/圣徒的名字的意义。他的故事呈现出中世纪人那种渴望"奇迹"的典型爱好，但作者有时候也表达他的怀疑，他想纠正某些文献的错误记载。比如，在"七个青年长眠"的故事中，他记载这样的事：七位男青年在古罗马教难的时期被封闭在一个山洞里，他们几百年后才醒过来。作者加上了这样一句评论："据说他睡眠了 372 年，但这是可怀疑的，因为他们于 448 年醒过来了，而 Decius（德西乌）在公元 255 年成为皇帝，所以他们只能睡眠 196 年之久。"

这些小故事的拉丁语简明易懂。许多故事描述圣人/圣徒如何面对酷刑、穷困、自我折磨、诱惑（比如魔鬼变成一个美女来引诱某男人）等。由于这些特殊的"欲望和暴力"因素，这些叙述都很有娱乐价值。它成了中世纪流传最广泛的著作之一（有 1000 多部手抄本被保存至今），被译成很多其他的语言。

Jacobus de Voragine / Jacob of Voragine

Opera: *Chronicon Januense, Legenda Aurea*
Works: *Chronicle of Genoa, Golden Legend*

069. *Legenda Aurea / Golden Legend*

The original title of this famous book was *Legenda sanctorum* or *Legenda nova*, but due to it's popularity it was called *Golden Legend* since the late Middle Ages. The Dominican Jacobus de Voragine / Varazze wrote this collection in the years between 1263—1273. The 184 chapters of stories about saints are meant to be edifying and didactic narratives, not primarily historical descriptions.

The author himself says he bases his stories on the Bible and on the works of Augustinus, Eusebius, Hieronymus, Cassiodorus, Beda, Bernardus of Clairvaux etc. He also uses many popular legends to exemplify Christian virtues. The anecdotes about the moral ideals and the miracles of the saints are (for the first time) arranged according to the liturgical year of the Church, beginning with Advent (the time before Christmas). Therefore unique historical experiences are integrated into the "eternal recurrence" of the ecclesiastical calendar. The author explains all ecclesiastical feasts and the meaning of the names of the saints. The stories show the typical medieval desire to believe miracles, but the author sometimes also expresses doubts and corrects certain texts, for example in the story about the seven young men who are immured during the period of persecutions in ancient Rome and wake up two or three centuries later: "But it is doubtful whether they slept, as they say, for 372 years, because they woke up in 448 AD, and Decius' reign was in 255, therefore they could only have slept for a period of 196 years."

The narratives are written in plain Latin and easy to understand. They also describe how the saints face torture, deprivation, self-castigations, temptations (for example seduction of the devil who appears as a beautiful woman) and are very entertaining due to this mixture of eroticism and violence ("sex and crime"). The book became one of the most popular books in the Middle Ages (more than 1000 manuscripts are extant) and was translated into many languages.

在众多故事中最著名的也许是这些：圣 Andreias（安德列）的奇迹和他被钉十字架；Myra 城的主教圣 Nicolaus（尼古拉斯）的慈善工作，圣 Lucia（路西亚）女士的美貌、她的坚定信仰和她的殉道；在教难时期成为罗马主教（教宗）的圣 Silvester（西尔物斯德勒）；圣 Georgius（乔治）杀死一条龙，因此解放了一座城；圣 Christophorus（克里斯托夫）想当最强大主人的仆人，先找到魔鬼，后来转到耶稣。其中一个故事在中世纪有深远的影响，它影响了托钵修会的发展，同时也影响了 Waldenses（瓦尔多派）的人，这就是关于 Alexius（阿雷克修斯）的故事。他是一位非常富裕的罗马官员的儿子，但他离开他的家乡，后在叙利亚的 Edessa 的一座教堂附近乞讨为生。他将自己所有的财产分给穷人，又回避一切社会上的荣誉。17 年后，他回到罗马，但他不愿意让他的父母认出他来。这样，他在自己的家乡又当了乞丐 17 年之久，一生守斋作祈祷。家里的仆人们经常嘲笑和侮辱他。在他去世后（398 年），他的父母终于认出他来，他们充满忏悔的精神。这位苦修者的尸体能够治好那些触摸他的人的种种疾病。

生于 Syracuse（西西里）一个贵族家庭的美丽贞女 Lucia 具有坚定的信仰和完美贞洁的美德。她的名称也是贞洁的象征：正如光明（lux）在照耀肮脏事物时不受污染，她的贞洁在一种很不洁的环境中也没有受污染。有一次 Lucia 和她的母亲在圣 Agatha 的坟墓祈祷，而由于女儿的坚定信仰，母亲的长期疾病得到治疗。此后 Lucia 要求母亲不要谈论她将来的婚姻并且建议把嫁妆送给穷人。当 Lucia 的新郎发现嫁妆都已送给穷人时，他带 Lucia 到省总督 Paschasius 衙门那里并控诉她说她违背了皇帝的法律。Lucia 早就准备付出自己的性命并勇敢地拒绝总督的要求，因为 Paschasius 要她向偶像举行祭祀。她说："你遵守你的皇帝的法律，但我要遵守我神的法律。（Tu principum tuorum decreta custodis et ego Deo mei legem custodiam.）" 她说她将会保持她的童贞，没有任何威胁和折磨能改变她的意志。Paschasius 命人带她到一个妓院，使她在那里受侮辱并被折磨致死，但圣灵使她变得很重，以至于一千个人都无法移动她。她这种坚定不移的态度引起总督的愤恨。他使用火和剑来虐待她。在她死亡之前，Lucia 预言教难不久后将会结束。这事发生在公元 310 年。

Among the more famous stories are these: the miracles and crucifixion of St. Andrew the Apostle, the charity work of St. Nicolaus, Bishop of Myra, the beauty and steadfastness of St. Lucia and her martyrdom, how St. Silvester became Pope after the time of persecutions, how St. George frees a city by killing a dragon, how St. Christopher wants to serve the most powerful lord and finds first the devil, but then serves Jesus. One legend was very influential for the mendicant movement but also for the Waldenses, namely the story of Alexius, the son of a very wealthy Roman official who leaves his rich home to live as a beggar at a church in Edessa in Syria. All his possessions he gives to the poor, and he avoids all secular honors. After 17 years he returns to Rome to live incognito in the house of his father for another 17 years, again fasting and praying as beggar who earns much mockery and scorn from the servants of the house. After his death (in the year 398) he is finally recognized by his sorrowful parents. The dead body of the ascet heals all who touch it.

Born into a noble family in Syracuse (Sicily), the beautiful virgin Lucia has a strong faith and the virtue of pure chastity. Already her name is a symbol of her chastity: like light (lux) suffers no pollution when shining on dirty things, her chastity remains pure even in an immodest environment. Once Lucia and her mother pray at the tomb of St. Agatha, and the long-lasting disease of Lucia's mother is healed by the strong faith of the daughter. Then Lucia demands that her mother stops to talk about her marriage and to give her dowry to the poor. As Lucia's bridegroom hears that the dowry has been given to the poor, he drags Lucia to the provincial governor Paschasius and accuses her of offending the imperial laws. Lucia is ready to sacrifice her life and courageously rejects Paschasius' demand to sacrifice to the idols. She says: "You keep the decrees of your emperors, but I will keep the law of my God. (Tu principum tuorum decreta custodis et ego Deo mei legem custodiam.)" She explains that no threats and no tortures will change her will to remain a chaste virgin. Paschasius orders to bring her to a brothel in order to humiliate her and harass her until death, but the Holy Spirit makes her so heavy that even a thousand men are unable to move her from the spot. Her immovable steadfastness enrages the governor, and he tortures her with fire and the sword. Before her death Lucia predicts that the end of the persecutions is at hand. It is the year 310 AD.

卢尔(约 1232—1316)

Lullus(亦写 Llull, Lull)是 Catalan(加泰隆)人,1232 年生于 Palma de Mallorca,于 1263 年经历了神秘的体验(他五次见到基督),并因此改变自己的生活,此后终生追求三个目标:(1)去穆斯林地区传教,(2)针对不信者写一部力著(即他的 Ars magna)以及(3)劝勉教宗和国王建立很多隐修院和语言学校(教授希腊语、希伯来语和阿拉伯语的学校)。在 1263—1274 年间他单独学习哲学、神学和阿拉伯语,编写阿语著作,1275 年在 Montpellier 大学任教,1276 年创立 Miramar 学院,曾去 Africa 传教(1281 年、1292 年、1307 年、1314 年),曾到 Roma、Barcelona、Cyprus、Genoa、Pisa、Lyon、Paris,于 1311—1312 年参与法国 Vienne 的主教会议并推动教会支持东方语言的研究,可能于 1316 年在 Tunis 去世(传统的说法是他被穆斯林杀死)。他的 300 多部著作包括拉丁语的、西班牙语的和阿拉伯语的,他被称为"加泰隆文学之父"。在他的思想中有 Cabbala 的数字神秘主义,而他后来影响 Giordano Bruno、Gassendi、Athanasius Kircher、Leibniz 等人。

著作:《宏大的技术》(包括《知识之树》、《理智的上升和下降之书》;"宏大的技术"指从一些基本的概念可以推想到一切真理),《巴奎纳》、《论理性的灵魂》、《论理智》、《以对话方式编写的宣言以反驳错误的观点》、《费利克斯》(小说)、《爱情哲学之树》(其中说,"爱"和"认识"需要互补)、《外邦人和三个哲人之书》、《默观之书》、《爱者和被爱者之书》(强调不同的精神力量的合作,比如"意志力"、"记忆力"和"理智"的合作:"三个力量各尽其能,都想观看被爱者的光耀。")、《圣玛利亚之书》、《绝望》;共有 250 部著作,包括拉丁语、卡塔兰语和阿拉伯语的,涉及哲学、护教学、信理学、神秘神学、法学和教育学各领域。

070.《宏大的技术》

这部 Ars magna(亦称 Ars magna et ultima)成书于 1274 年至 1308 年间。作者写了几个版本,从早期的 Ars compendiosa inveniendi veritatem(《寻得真理的技术》,1274 年)到 Ars generalis ultima(《最普遍的和终极的技术》,1308 年)。

Lullus 认为通过信仰和理解(credere et intellegere)崇敬神超过仅仅通过信仰(credere)崇拜神。他要理解并通过哲学引导其他人走向信仰。他试图说明真理的统一性,又要证明"三位一体"、"降生成人"、"创造"、"宇宙的开端"等原则(rationes necessariae, dignitates divinae),因为他认为这些原则可以向任何理性的人说明。他的著作都想证明基督信仰的真理,而 Ars magna 的发现是这种证明的有力工具。它被称为"伟大的"或"终极的"技术,因为它提供最高的和最普遍的规则和原则,这些原则囊括一切其他学科的原则和知识。Lullus 将这些最高的概念分为 9 组,每一组有一个字母

Raimundus Lullus / Ramon Lull

Opera: *Ars magna* (*Ars generalis, Arbor scientiae, Liber de ascensu et descensu intellectus*), *Blanquerna, De anima rationali, De intellectu, Declaratio per modum dialogi edita contra opiniones erroneas, Felix de les meravelles del mon, L'arbre de filosofia d'amor, Liber de gentili et tribus sapientibus* (*Libre del gentil e los tres savis*), *Liber contemplationis* (*Libre de contemplacio en Dieu*), *Libre d'amic e amat, Libre de sancta Maria, Lo desconhort*

Works: *The Great Art* (*The Tree of Knowledge, The Book of the Ascent and Descent of the Intellect*), *Blanquerna, The Rational Soul, On the Intellect, Declaration against Errors in the form of a Dialogue, Felix, The Tree of the Philosophy of Love, Book of the Gentile and the Three Wise Men, Book of Contemplation, Book of the Lover and the Beloved, Book of Holy Mary, Despondency*

070. *Ars magna* /*The Great Art*

The *Ars magna* (also known as *Ars magna et ultima*) was written between 1274 and 1308 and developed in several versions, from the *Ars compendiosa inveniendi veritatem* (*The Comprehensive Art of Finding Truth*, 1274) until the *Ars generalis ultima* (*The General and Last Art*, 1308).

Lullus thought that to worship God by believing and understanding (credere et intellegere) would be more meritorious than to worship God only by faith (credere). He wants to understand and to lead others to the faith by way of philosophy. He intends to show that there is only one truth and that Trinity, Incarnation, Creation and the beginning of the universe are principles (rationes necessariae, dignitates divinae) which can be demonstrated to any reasonable mind. His works want to prove the truths of the Christian faith, and the *Ars magna* was invented as a useful instrument for this proof. It is called the "great" or "ultimate" art, because it presents the highest and most general rules and principles which in nuce contain the principles and insights of all other disci-

符号(从"B"到"K")。系统地结合这些原则将可以表达一切事物的原则和一切科学的知识。

Lullus 试图在一个逻辑的体系中整理一切理念,而人心可以在这个体系中像在一个梯子上升降。Ars magna 也包含两篇论文,即 Arbor scientiae(《知识之树》)和 Liber de ascensu et descensu intellectus(《理智的上升和下降之书》)。各种言词和数字的逻辑性结合也给了后来的思想家,比如 Athanasius Kircher(1602—1680 年)很多启迪。Leibnitz 的虚构语言以及他那种代表种种概念和判断的符号体系也受 Lullus 的影响。

071. 《巴奎纳》

本作品是 Catalan(加泰隆)语最早期的文学著作之一,因此具有深远的影响。该乌托邦式的教育性小说分为 5 卷,全名是 Blanquerna, qui tracta de sinch estaments de persones: de Matrimonio, de Religio, de Prelatura, de Apostolical Senyoria y del etat de vida Hermitana contemplativa(《巴奎纳,其中描述人的五种身份:婚姻、隐修生活、教会中的管理职位、宗徒式的领导职位以及独修者的默观生活》)。成书时间在 1278 年和 1289 年,它反映作者对教会和传教工作的一些理想。

第 1 卷描述夫妻 Evast 和 Alona 的和睦与他们的虔诚精神。他们的儿子 Blanquerna 应该要结婚,但他劝勉他的配偶 Natana 放弃世俗生活。Blanquerna 自己离开他的父母并走遍很多森林和山谷,似乎像一个骑士一样,但他并不寻求英雄的荣誉。他追求的是独处和默观。在他的旅程中他遇到一些需要他帮助的人。他安慰很多人,同时克服一切诱惑。在第 2 卷中他进入一所隐修院并因他的高尚德行被选为院长。他成为这个隐修团体的领导并开始改进修道生活。人们都知道他是一位德才兼备的人。在第 3 卷中他被祝圣主教,而因为他如此完美地完成一切任务,他甚至被选为教宗(第 4 卷)。当他参与教会领导和管理的高层生活时,Blanquerna 试图完成传教的任务,而他能吸引很多犹太人、穆斯林和非基督徒人士进入教会。最后的书卷描述最后的生活阶段:Blanquerna 辞去他的职位并开始一个独修者的生活,这样他获得独处与安宁。

这部小说的最后部分是一种几乎独立的、具有神秘主义因素的论文,标题是 Libre d'Amic e Amat(《爱者和被爱者之书》)。Blanquerna 过一个独修的隐修士的生活,他为每一天选择一个座右铭。这些"带给生活方向的话"的核心是"怀爱者"(Amic,即人或人的灵魂)和"爱人"(Amat,"被爱者",即神)。这部书的灵感来自《旧约》的 Canticum Canticorum(《雅歌》),但它不包含《雅歌》中的情感性描述。怀爱者寻觅爱人,他必须经过一种净化过程才可以与神结合。此时,他的"自我"融入爱人的伟大的"你"。这种过程是给予和接纳、赢得和失去的旅途。爱的渴望既保存怀爱

plines. Lullus arranges these highest ideas in 9 groups and assigns a letter of the ABC to each group (from "B" to "K"). Systematic combinations of the principles will lead to conclusions which express the principles of all things and the knowledge of all sciences.

Lullus tries to order all ideas into a certain logical system, in which the mind can climb up and down like on a ladder. The *Ars magna* contains the treatises *Arbor scientiae* (*Tree of knowledge*) and *Liber de ascensu et descensu intellectus* (*The Book of the Ascent and Descent of the Intellect*). The logical combinations of words and numbers inspired later thinkers like Athanasius Kircher (1602—1680) and the artificial language of Leibnitz who developed a system of symbols representing ideas and sentences.

071. *Blanquerna*

This is one of the first pieces of literature in the Catalan language and thus of considerable impact. The full name of this utopian educational novel in 5 books is *Blanquerna, qui tracta de sinch estaments de persones: de Matrimonio, de Religio, de Prelatura, de Apostolical Senyoria y del etat de vida Hermitana contemplativa.* (*Blanquerna, which treats the five estates of a person: Marriage, religious life, ecclesiastical administration, apostolic leadership, and the contemplative life of a hermit*). It was written between 1278 and 1289 and reflects the author's ideals of the Church and mission work.

The first book describes the harmonious and pious matrimonial life of Evast and Alona. Their son Blanquerna is supposed to marry, but he persuades his bride Natana to flee the secular world. Blanquerna himself leaves his parents and wanders through many forests and valleys like a knight, but he does not strive for the secular glory of a victorious hero. He searches for solitude and contemplation. On his journey he encounters people who need his help. He consoles many and resists all temptations. In the second book he enters a monastery and due to his virtuous life is elected abbot. Being the leader of the community he is in a position to start a reform of the monastic life. He is known to be a man of virtue and great capability. In book 3 he is ordained bishop, and because he is doing so well, he is even elected Pope (book 4). Being in the higher levels of Church leadership and administration, Blanquerna tries to fulfill the missionary mandate and manages to convert many Jews, Moslems and infidels. The fifth book shows the last stage of his life: Blanquerna resigning from his office and starting a life as hermit in solitude and peace.

The last part of the novel is a virtually independent mystical treatise entitled *Libre d'Amic e Amat* (*The Book of the Lover and the Beloved*). Living as solitary hermit, Blanquerna finds an aphorism for every day of the year. These "words to live by" are centered on the lover (Amic, namely the human person, the soul), and the beloved (Amat, i.e. God). The book is inspired by the *Song of Songs* (Old Testament), but it does not make use of erotic descriptions such as to be found in the *Song of Songs*. The lover searches for the beloved, he must undergo a process of purification before he can

者的生命,又耗尽它。爱需要想象力、理智和意志力。这部著名的关于怀爱者和被爱者的书也接受了 Sufi(伊斯兰教泛神论神秘主义)的影响,因此以某种特殊的方式结合东、西方的传统。

作者使用"爱者"和"被爱者"的形象来说明神和人之间的关系:"有一次怀爱者遇见他的爱人并看到了爱人的尊威和权柄;他向爱人说他感到很惊讶很少有人了解、爱慕与尊敬爱人,虽然爱人应该被爱、应该被尊敬。此时爱人回答说人类使他感到很失望,因为他创造了人是为了要人认识、爱慕和尊敬他,但在一千人中只有一百个人敬畏和爱慕他,而在这一百个人当中有 90 个只是因为害怕惩罚才爱他,而留下的 10 个人主要是因为想得到赏报而爱他,但几乎没有人因为他的仁爱与伟大本身爱慕他。当爱人听到了这些话时,他流泪,因为爱人被如此忽视。他说:我的爱人,你给予了人们如此多东西,又如此尊敬人们,但他们为什么忘记了你?"

Lullus 描述 Blanquerna 隐修者的默想:"当 Blanquerna 进行默观时,他流泪,而他的记忆力、理解力和意志力在他的灵魂内彼此谈论并非常欢悦于神的种种美德。记忆、理解与意志彼此同意说他们想要默观至高的善的美德、真理和荣誉。记忆回忆无限美善的美德,即在真理和荣誉内的无限美德。此后理解在内心中掌握了那些记忆所回忆的东西,而意志爱慕那些被记忆回忆的、被理解掌握的东西。"

achieve union with God. Then his ego is merged into the great "You" of the beloved. The process is a journey of giving and receiving, winning and losing. The desire of love at the same time preserves and consumes the life of the lover. Love involves imagination, intellect, and the will. The famous booklet of the lover and the beloved was also inspired by the Sufi poetry of Islam mystics and in a unique way combines traditions from the East and the West.

The author uses the image of the lover and the beloved to speak about the relationship between God and man: "The lover once encountered his Beloved and saw the nobility and power of the Beloved, and he told the Beloved that he was surprised that the people would know, love and honor the Beloved so little, although the Beloved deserved all love and honor and respect. And the Beloved answered him saying that he was very disappointed of the human person which he created in order to be known, loved and honored by him. Of one thousand people only one hundred would fear and love him, and ninety of these hundred would only fear his punishment, whereas the other ten would love him in order to get some reward, but there is hardly anyone who loves him for his benevolence and greatness. As the lover heard these words he wept about the dishonor which the Beloved suffered, and he said: Beloved One, you gave so much to humankind and have honored mankind so much, why have the people forgotten you like this?"

Lullus describes how the hermit Blanquerna meditates: "While Blanquerna contemplated and wept, his memory, understanding and will conversed mentally with each other within his soul, and they found great delight in the virtues of God. Memory, Understanding and Will agreed among themselves that they would contemplate the Sovereign Good in His virtue, truth and glory. Memory recalled the virtue of the Infinite Good, His virtue being infinite in truth and glory. Understanding comprehended that which Memory recalled, and Will loved that which Memory recalled and Understanding comprehended."

马可·波罗（1254—1324）

意大利商人、旅行家，1271年来到东方，1275年到上都（今内蒙古多伦西北），此后在元朝担任官职17年，游历中国各地。1291年经过东南亚、马来西亚、印度、波斯、小亚细亚回国。由他人记录的游记描述东方的富裕，对欧洲人力求发现通往亚洲的新航路很有影响。

著作：《马可·波罗游记》

072.《马可·波罗游记》

意大利商人 Marco Polo（马可·波罗）的游记以意大利语—法语的混合语记载于1298—1299年（Polo大概不能用这种语言写书），记录者是 Rusticiano da Pisa，一个职业作家。他和 Polo 一起参加了 Curzola 的海战（1298年）后在 Genoa 入狱。Rusticiano 的文本失传，但它是140个"原始手抄本"的基础，这些文本大约有10多种语言，而且有不同的书名（比如《世界的分界》，《世界的奇迹》等）。

意大利商人 Marco Polo、他的父亲 Nicolo Polo 和他的叔叔 Matteo Polo 在1271年到1295年的十几年间游历了许多东方的地区。他们经过波斯、阿富汗、帕米尔、喀什、敦煌、甘州（=张掖）、宁夏，与他们的随从到达了大汗的夏宫（上都，今内蒙古多伦西北，冬宫是"大都"，即北京）。他们通过交趾支那、马来西亚、印度、斯里兰卡、波斯和小亚细亚回去。他们陪同一位蒙古公主前往波斯并从泉州与14条船一起离开了中国（大约是1291年或1292年）。

马可·波罗不会说汉语，但他会用土耳其语（突厥语）、一种阿拉伯化的波斯语，也许还会说蒙古语和维吾尔人的突厥语。忽必烈（1215—1294年，1264年迁都燕京，即北京）喜欢并重用 Polo，派遣他在中国南部任职。因此，Marco 曾经在江南省当大汗的代表几年之久。由于他的种种任务，Polo 必须去中国很多地方，这就帮助了他观察各地的风俗和一些少数民族的生活习惯。他的游记包含一些来自别人讲述的故事，涉及一些他自己并没有去过的地方。这些插入的故事中也有一些传奇性的因素，比如一些戴狗头的人种等。Polo 记录一些有意思的细节，比如大汗宫廷使用"纸币"（钞票）。他也描述北京西南地区的卢沟桥（因此西方人将它称为"马可·波罗桥"）。

在"大发现"的时期，这种关于东方世界的方方面面的报告对欧洲人起了很大的作用。比如 Columbus（哥伦布）也阅读了这部游记并加上了自己的注释。Polo 描述了东方人用的种种调料，这就吸引了很多西方商人到东方去。游记的叙述基本上是以事

Marco Polo

Opera: *Il Milione (Divisament dou monde, Le meraviglie del mondo)*
Works: *The Travels of Marco Polo (The Division of the World, The Miracles of the World)*

072. *Il Milione / The Travels of Marco Polo*

This itinerary report of the Italian merchant Marco Polo was recorded in 1298—1299 in the Franco-Italian language (which Polo probably did not know well enough to write) by Rusticiano da Pisa, a professional writer. He and Polo had been imprisoned in Genoa following the naval battle of Curzola (1298). Rusticiano's text is lost, but it became the basis of ca. 140 "original manuscripts" in about ten different languages and with different titles (for example *Divisament dou monde, Le meraviglie del mondo*).

Marco Polo, his father Nicolo and his uncle Matteo Polo traveled through unknown countries in the East during the years from 1271 to 1295. They passed through Persia, Afghanistan, Pamir, then via Kashgar, Dunhuang, Ganzhou (=Zhangye), Ningxia they arrived with their entourage at the summer residence of the Khan (at Shangdu, the winter residence was Dadu, that is today's Beijing). They returned via Indochina, Malaysia, India, Ceylon, Persia and Asia Minor. On their way back they accompanied a Mongol princess to Persia and left China with 14 ships from Quanzhou, Fujian (probably in 1291 or 1292).

Marco Polo did not speak Chinese, but he knew Turkish, an Arabized Persian language, and perhaps Mongol and Uighur Turkish. Kublai Khan (1215—1294, he moved the capital to Yanjing = Beijing in 1264) liked him and sent him on missions to South China. For several years Marco stayed in Jiangnan Province as representative of the Mongol ruler. Being an official, Polo had to journey to many places in China, which helped him to observe the country's customs, and the special life style of some minorities. His itinerary contains some digressions, that is descriptions of people and places he did not visit himself. These passages are based on what other people told him, and these narratives contain some legendary elements, for example human beings with dog's heads etc. Polo describes interesting details, for example the use of paper money at the Khan's court and a bridge South-West of Beijing, the so-called "Marco-Polo Bridge" ("Lugou Qiao" in Chinese).

The multifaceted report about the Far East was very influential for the geographical and ethnological conceptions of Europeans in the time of discoveries. Columbus owned

物为核心的（Polo 没有提到自己个人的事！），既描述战争，又形容一些黄金的或白银的宫殿、隆重的礼仪和国君的伟大堂皇。在早期的意大利文学上，这部著作很独特，但它与法国的十字军游记、骑士文学和探险故事有类似之处。对某些人来说，Polo 对于别的民族的灿烂和富裕的描述看来是一种不可信的夸张。也有人曾说，这部游记没有提到中国人喝茶的习惯，没有提到汉字（象形文字）和长城。汉语的文献也没有提到 Polo。虽然如此，人们普遍认为，Polo 真去过 Cathay（契丹，即中国），而他的报告的大部分内容是有历史根据的。

one copy of the book and added many notes. Polo's description of spices used in the East was an incentive for European merchants. The basically pragmatic narrative (silence about Polo's personal matters!) also includes descriptions of battles, of golden and silver palaces, of solemn ceremonies and of the grandeur of kings. In early Italian literature the work is unique, but it bears many resemblances to French crusade chronicles and the narratives about knights and their adventures. To some people the descriptions of the splendor of other countries in Polo's account seemed to be wild exaggerations and incredible. Others have observed that the book does not mention the use of tea in China, the ideographic script (Chinese characters) or the Great Wall. Chinese sources do not mention Marco Polo either. However, the general assumption is that Polo was really in Cathay (China) and that most parts of his report are based on historical reality.

格尔特儒德(1256—1302)

生于德国 Thuringia,5 岁成为孤儿,被交给 Helfta 的 Cistercienses 修女院(在德国的 Eisleben 附近),在那里获得全面的知识性教育和灵修培养,一生在 Helfta 当隐修会修女。她的老师是 Mechtildis de Hackeborn 和 Mechtildis de Magdeburga。这三个修女的著作构成中世纪德国妇女学术运动的高峰。Gertrudis 热衷于哲学知识(artes liberales),但于 1281 年她在一次神视中见到基督,此后转向《圣经》和教父们的作品。她听从神圣的吩咐并开始记载她的灵修体验。因此,她成为德国最伟大的女神秘神学家,后被宣布为圣人。

著作:《精神性的神操》、《神爱的使者》(包括灵魂与基督的结合,对于耶稣圣心的敬拜)、《特恩之书》(记载 Mechtild 的神视)

073. 《神爱的使者》

这部文集分为 5 卷,其核心是圣 Gertrudis 的生活与她的神视。部分的内容是她自己写的,另一些章节是别的修女记录她的口述。与 *Liber specialis gratiae* 一起,这部著作在后来几百年中深深地影响了公教的灵修并形成了对于"耶稣圣心"的敬拜,因为很多其他的作者后来传播和发挥了 Gertrudis 的思想,比如 Petrus Canisius、Martin von Cochem、Jean Eudes、Maria Alacoque 等等。

第 1 卷写在 Gertrudis 去世后并包含一些关于她的生活、性格的资料,其中也叙述她的特殊圣召的表现和她所行的奇迹。

文集的核心部分是第 2 卷,这是由 Gertrudis 自己在 1289 年以后写的。她叙说自己与基督的神秘关系。救世主生活在她的心内,而因此她的灵魂安息在神内。基督的爱使她一步步接近神,直到达成一种神秘的合一,即神圣的新郎(基督)和他的纯洁配偶交换他们的心(2,23)。第 3 卷(以第三人称编写的)也同样围绕着与耶稣圣心的神秘友谊。耶稣打开他的心并接受 Gertrudis。对于 Gertrudis 充满光明的灵魂来说,进入主基督的心带来最大的喜乐和幸福。耶稣的心是上主对人类所怀的爱的最高尚象征。与 Mechtildis de Magdeburga 一样,Gertrudis 也同样认为自愿地受苦(主动牺牲自己)是真正的基督徒的标记。因此,在信徒的心中也应该有基督的伤痕。基督自己将他的母亲 Maria(玛利亚)介绍给信徒们,要他们效法玛利亚的榜样。所以 Gertrudis 称 Maria(玛利亚)为"神秘的玫瑰花"(rosa mystica)。

Gertrudis de Helfta / Gertrude the Great

Opera: *Exercitia spiritualia, Legatus divinae pietatis, Liber specialis gratiae*
Works: *Spiritual exercises, The Messenger of Divine Love, Book of Special Grace*

073. *Legatus divinae pietatis / The Messenger of Divine Love*

This work in 5 books is a collection centered on the life and the revelations of St. Gertrude. Some of the passages were written by her, others were recorded by other nuns in the form of a dictation. Together with the *Liber specialis gratiae* this work profoundly influenced Catholic spirituality in the following centuries and helped to shape the devotion to the Sacred Heart, as Gertrude's ideas were spread and developed by many other authors like Petrus Canisius, Martin von Cochem, Jean Eudes, Maria Alacoque etc.

The first book was written after Gertrude's death and contains information about her life, her character, and signs of her special calling. There are also stories about miracles she worked.

The most important part of the collection is the second book which was written by Gertrude herself in the years after 1289. She reports about her mystical relationship to Christ. The Redeemer lives in her heart, and thus her soul rests in God. Christ's love brings her ever closer to the divine, until a mystical union is achieved, and exchange of hearts between the divine Bridegroom (Christ) and His chaste spouse (2,23). Also the third book (written in the third person) is centered on the special mystical relationship to the Heart of Jesus. Jesus opens His heart and receives Gertrude. Entering the sacred Heart of her Lord means the greatest joy and beatitude to the enlightened soul of Gertrude. The Heart of Jesus is the highest symbol of God's love for mankind. Like Mechtild of Magdeburg, Gertrude also accepts the gift of voluntary suffering (self-sacrifice) as the hallmark of true discipleship of Christ. Thus the heart of the believer must also bear the wounds of Christ. Christ Himself presents His mother Mary as a model for the faithful. Thus for Gertrude Mary becomes the "mystical rose" (rosa mystica).

第4卷描述一些神视和基督、玛利亚以及一些圣人的显现,这些都与教会礼仪年中的节庆有关系。教会的庆日纪念耶稣或玛利亚的一些生活经历,另一些纪念日献给某些圣人。Gertrudis 在长达好几年的时期体验到了这些神视,现在她与读者分享这些神秘经验。第5卷包含一些 Helfta 隐修院的 Cistercienses(熙笃会)修女的讣告,包括 Gertrudis of Hackeborn,她曾是 Helfta 的院长,于1292年去世,还有 Mechtildis de Magdeburga 的讣告。Gertrudis 也描写她如何准备接受死亡,而其他修女加上了关于她临终情况的报告。

The fourth book describes visions and apparitions of Christ, Mary, and some saints in connection with the celebrations of ecclesiastical feastdays throughout the liturgical year, because these feastdays commemorate certain episodes of the life of Mary or Jesus or the feasts are dedicated to a saint. Gertrude has experienced these visions over a span of several years and shares them now with her readers. Book five contains obituaries of several Cistercian nuns from Helfta, including Gertrude of Hackeborn, the abbess of Helfta, who died in 1292, and Mechtild of Magdeburg. Gertrude also writes about her own preparation for death, and other nuns added a report about her last hour.

艾克哈特（约 1260—1327）

约于 1260 年生于德国 Gotha 或 Erfurt 地区的骑士家庭，在 Erfurt 进入 Ordo Praedicatorum（道明会），1296 年成为院长，1302 年在 Paris 任教，1303 年成为 Saxonia 省的道明会会长，1311—1313 年在 Paris，1314—1322 年间在 Strasbourg，后返回德国；他于 1326 年面对宗教裁判所的控诉（他是唯一的受这种指控的著名神学家），因为在他的书中有 108 个句子（12 个拉丁语的，96 个德语的）引起争论。Eckhart 向圣座申诉，最后有 28 个句子被谴责，但 Eckhart 自己并没有被审判为"持异端的人"。他始终追求正统的信仰。他第一次完成了一批用本地语（德语）创作的神学著作。

著作：《神慰之书》、《论诸命题》、《三部书》、《讲道稿》、《教导集》、《论独处》

074.《神慰之书》

这部德语著作成书于 1308 年和 1314 年间并献给匈牙利女王 Agnes。书名来自《新约》2 *Cor* 1:3："上主，仁慈的父和施予各种安慰的神……，他在我们的各种磨难中安慰我们……"

Eckhart 分析这些"磨难"和人心中的种种忧郁和悲伤。此后他提出 30 个例子和比喻来说明对一个基督徒来说没有任何完全缺乏希望或安慰的情况或困境。他的故事大多是一些《圣经》名言的解释，但他偶尔也引用一些来自 Stoa 学派（尤其 Seneca）和其他古代人物的道德格言或原则。

安慰在于这一点：人应该了解到在世界上没有任何纯粹的邪恶或纯粹的痛苦。任何痛苦只是暂时的并且早晚会导致某种美好的结果。然而，每一个人也应该意识到人生中有痛苦，这是人的命运的部分，而乐意地接受痛苦将能解放和鼓励人心。痛苦的根源是某人想念一个他所珍惜的但被夺取的东西，而这种情况应该使人理解到，他不应该过分爱惜世俗的世界。太多依赖于物质的或暂时的财富将会造成很大的痛苦。一个人应该放弃自己的意愿并转向神，这样他能够分享神性的恩典并能神秘地与主结合。本书的结尾部分描述一些曾面临灾难的、具有智慧的人（weise Leute）的言辞和行动（Werke und Worte）。

在 Eckhart 的思想中，一切事物的神秘合一是一个核心概念，而这种概念也受了 Augustinus 和 Dionysius Areopagita 的新 Plato 主义的影响，同时也吸收了一些犹太哲学和阿拉伯思想的因素。神是"一"，而因为他是"存在"，所以他临在于一切存在物之

Johannes Eckehart / Meister Eckhart

Opera: *Buch der göttlichen Tröstungen (Liber benedictus), Collationes in libros sententiarum, Opus tripartitum (Opus propositionum, Opus quaestionum, Opus expositionum), Predigten, Reden der Unterweisung, Von Abgeschiedenheit*

Works: *Book of Divine Consolation, On the Sentences, Three Books, Homilies, Talks of Instruction, On Solitude*

074. *Liber benedictus / Book of Divine Consolation*

This book in German language was written between 1308 and 1314 and is dedicated to Queen Agnes of Hungary. The title is derived from the New Testament, 2 *Cor* 1:3: "Deus ··· Pater misericordiarum et Deus totius consolationis, qui consolatur nos in omni tribulatione nostra. (God ··· Father of mercies and the God of all consolation ···, who consoles us in all our affliction···)"

Eckhart analyzes the "tribulations" and the different kinds of depression or feelings of grief that are found in the human heart. Then he uses 30 examples and parables to show that for a Christian there is no situation in life that would be totally devoid of consolation or hope. Most of his stories are explanations of quotations from the Bible, but he occasionally also takes morals and mottos from the Stoics (especially Seneca) or other classical thinkers.

The consolation consists in the insight that there is no pure evil nor any pure suffering in the world. Any kind of suffering is temporary and will sooner or later lead to something good. However, any human being should realize that suffering is part of the human destiny, and this joyful acceptance of suffering will liberate and encourage the heart. The origin of suffering is that a person misses some beloved thing that has been taken away, and this should lead to the insight that one should not love the temporal world too much. Excessive dependence on material and temporal things will cause much suffering. One should give up one's own will and turn to God so as to share in the divine graces and find to a mystical union with the Lord. The final part of the book presents the actions and words (Werke und Worte) of wise people (weise Leute) who encountered calamities in their lives.

The mystical one-ness of all things is a central idea in Eckhart's thought, and this concept was inspired by the Neo-Platonism of Augustine and Dionysius Areopagita, but also by Jewish and Arabic philosophical tenets. God is the One, and as He is the Being,

中。这种受造界和神之间的合一导致"持续性的创造"(creatio continua)和"降生成人的永恒过程"(incarnatio continua)。神在人的临在也表现于"灵魂深处"(scintilla animae,亦译为"灵魂之火花")这样的概念;这个词来自 Hieronymus 和 Augustinus。然而,恰恰这些关于一切事物的"合一性"的美丽思考引起了"泛神论"的嫌疑并导致对 Eckhart 的指控,但他始终愿意修改他的说法。

He is present in all created beings. This unity of God and the creation leads to the concepts of "continuing creation" (creatio continua) and the "eternal process of incarnation" (incarnatio continua). The presence of God in man finds its expression in the idea of the "scintilla animae" ("depth of the soul", also "spark of the soul"), a term which is inherited from Jerome and Augustine. However, exactly these beautiful meditations on the one-ness of all things also aroused the suspicion of "pantheism" and led to the indictment of Eckhart, who was always ready to correct his formulations.

但丁（1265—1321）

意大利最伟大的诗人，1265 年生于 Florentia（Firenze）；他曾在本笃会的 S. Croce 隐修院和道明会的 S. Maria Novella 隐修院获得哲学和神学方面的教育，早年模仿 B. Latini 和 G. Cavalcanti 等人的诗。据说他 9 岁时首次见到 Beatrice，后来在他的 *Vita nuova* 中赞美她，而在 *Commedia* 中使她受光荣。这位女士后来与别人结婚，24 岁就去世了（1290 年）。Dante 于 1293 年结婚并有两个儿子和一个女儿。他曾参与反对 Ghibellini（教宗派）的斗争，1296 年后在 Florentia 任职，曾是该城的使者，尽力为 Florentia 的独立奋斗，但因此惹起 Bonifatius VIII 和 Charles de Valois 的敌意。皇帝派（Guelphi）于 1302 年被镇压，而 Dante 被驱逐，又被判死刑。他周游各地，到过 Verona、Bologna、Lucca、Padova，晚年在 Ravenna 生活并在此去世。

著作：《神曲》(《地狱篇》、《炼狱篇》、《天堂篇》)、《论俗语》(《论普通话的口才》)、《飨宴》、《新生活》、《帝制论》、《诗歌》

075.《神曲》

这部篇幅很长的诗（14233 行）写成于 Dante 在 1302 年被驱逐之后的二十年间，并且在他去世的前不久才完成。原书名只是 *Commedia*（"曲"），后来的人才称它为"神圣的"，即《神曲》。也许 Boccaccio 是第一个这样称呼的人。原书名的 commedia（"喜剧"）指从忧虑到喜乐的过程，也就是从地狱永罚到天堂永福的跨越。

从地狱到天堂的道路结构呈现出很多象征性的数字，就是 1, 3, 7, 9, 10。Dante 发明了一种新的诗行格律，所谓的 Terza rima，其尾韵的形式是 ABA BCB CDC 等。本著作分为三部分（Inferno 地狱，Purgatorio 炼狱，和 Paradiso 天堂），每一部分为 33 篇，加上一个序曲，共 100 篇。Gregorius Magnus 提出来的"七个罪宗"的理论为"地狱"和"炼狱"提供基本的区分结构，而诗人每次加上来世中的两个区域。Dante 的世界的地理学和结构符合某些神学和哲学概念，他结合 Aristoteles 的伦理学理论和基督宗教的教导。在 Dante 提到的 600 个人物中有 250 个属于古典神话学（那些文学中的人物也被视为历史上的人物），有 250 个历史人物（大部分属于当时的意大利社会），以及 80 个来自《圣经》的人物。

《神曲》的框架叙述是关于 Dante 自己的故事。他在 1300 年的圣周五（受难日）在一个森林中迷路，三只野兽威胁着他，一只豹子、一只狮子和一只狼（三种动物分别象征着放纵、暴力和欺骗）。通过 Beatrice 在天上的代祷，Vergilius 被派遣找到 Dante 并在来世中充当他们的导游，因为 Dante 的迷惑太严重，只有这种奇特的、惊人的景象能

Dante Alighieri

Opera: *Commedia (=Commedia divina, Inferno, Purgatorio, Paradiso), De vulgari eloquentia, Il convivio, La vita nuova, Monarchia, Rime*

Works: *The Divine Comedy (Hell, Purgatory, Paradise), Of Eloquence in the Vulgar Tongue, The Banquet, The New Life, The Monarchy, Poems*

075. *Commedia Divina / The Divine Comedy*

This long poem (14233 verses) was written in the two decades after Dante's exile in 1302 and was completed shortly before his death. The adjective "divine" was added by later generations, first perhaps by Boccaccio. The title "comedy" was used because the poem depicts a progress from grief to joy, from damnation to heavenly bliss.

The journey from Hell to Heaven is structured by an elaborate use of the symbolical numbers 1, 3, 7, 9, 10. Dante invented the Terza rima (a poetic form with rhymes in the sequence of aba bcb cdc…) for his work, which he divided into three parts (Inferno = Hell, Purgatorio = Purgatory, Paradiso = Heaven), each section having 33 cantos, added one prologue this makes 100 altogether. The seven mortal sins (a doctrine of Gregory the Great) create the main subdivisions of Hell and Purgatory, to which two more departments of the afterlife are added. The topography and architecture of Dante's world are worked out according to theological and philosophical concepts, combining Aristotelian ethical divisions and Christian doctrine. Among the 600 characters Dante mentions there are ca. 250 of classical mythology (literary characters taken to be historical), ca. 250 historical figures, mostly of contemporary Italian society, and ca. 80 biblical persons.

The framework of the poem is a narrative about Dante himself. He is lost in a forest on Good Friday of 1300, threatened by three beasts, a leopard, a lion, and a wolf (the animals symbolize incontinence, violence and fraud). Through the intercession of Beatrice in heaven Vergil has been sent to meet Dante and to guide him through the world after death, for he has strayed so far that only this spectacle can lead him to salvation. First Vergil leads him through Hell, an inverted cone descending ty terraces to its apex at the center of the earth, where Satan himself is confined. The ante-hell is a place

够引导他走向救恩。首先，Vergilius 带他走过地狱。地狱是一种漏斗形式的空间，他们一层一层往下去，终于在最低的地方见到魔鬼撒旦。在地狱的"前厅"（所谓 limbo）中有一些没有受洗的婴儿和一些没有作决定的人（比如 Caelestinus V 教宗，他于 1294 年退位，因此使 Dante 感到震惊）。在第一层地狱中居住的人是一些优秀的、道德的外教人（比如诗人 Homerus 和思想家 Plato）等，他们对人类都有一些贡献，但因为他们没有受洗入基督宗教，他们无法得救。在地狱中的罪人无法进行忏悔和补赎，他们在地狱中受的折磨都是人间生活的延续。他们的惩罚的严重性符合他们罪行的性质。先有"不节制、放纵"的罪（比如那些不合法的情人，如 Francesca da Rimini），接着有暴力罪行的人，最终有欺骗者的地狱（比如那些出卖朋友的人，如 Brutus 和 Judas Iscariot）。Dante 和部分地狱中的人谈话，并同情他们。在描述地狱最低的层次时，作者结合了《圣经》中的火焰和欧洲北方的冰，描述撒旦为持有三个头的，这样表明魔鬼歪曲和颠倒三位一体的神的形象。

在复活节主日，Dante 和 Vergilius 通过一个地下通道从地狱最低的部分直接达到炼狱的第一个层次。炼狱被描述为一座位于地球对面的山。在炼狱中的人最终都要得救，但他们的罪在炼狱的种种台阶上需要经过净化和消除。那些进入地狱的人必须放弃一切希望，但在炼狱中的灵魂们都希望将被拯救，所以他们很乐意地接受他们的补赎。他们的补赎行动包括祈祷、体力运动（比如"跑步为了克服懒惰"），守斋和忍受烟或火焰。各种补赎行动符合七"宗罪"，即：骄傲、嫉妒、愤怒、懒惰、吝啬、饕餮、私欲偏情。一旦某一个罪的负担被拿走，这个灵魂很轻快地升高到上一层。每一个台阶的补赎时间都取决于相关罪行的严重性。那些完全净化的灵魂们达到山顶，这就是"伊甸乐园"（亦称"人间天堂"），从那里再要升天。在那里，Vergilius 离开 Dante，而 Beatrice 成为他的新"导游"。

Dante 的天界结构来自 Aristoteles 的宇宙论：地球在中心，七个行星（从月亮到土星）围绕着地球。每一层高天有一个行星、一种天使、一个美德和一个知识领域。比如，第 4 层是"太阳天"，这是"神学家的天"，第 5 层是"火星天"，这是"神圣战士的天"，第 6 天是"木星天"即"正义统治者的天"（除了 David 和 Constantinus 皇帝以外还包括古罗马的 Traianus 皇帝），第 7 天是"隐修者的天"（其中的人物包括 St. Benedictus, St. Bernardus, Petrus Damianus）。Dante 和 Beatrice 一边升高，一边和路边的人谈话。在最高的天，圣人的群众被安排为如同环绕着花朵的叶子，而圣母 Maria 是天上的王后。现在熙笃会的神秘神学家 Bernardus de Clairvaux（1090—1153 年）成为 Dante 的导游者。神的形象是三个有共同中心的圆圈，在中心的位置有一个人的形象。Dante 最终见到上主的永恒光明，这个光明就是"推动着一层一层的天和一切星星的爱"（"L'amor che muove il sole e l'altre stelle", 33,145 参见 Aristoteles 的"不动的推动者"）。这种对"荣福直观"的描述结束整个《神曲》。

called limbo reserved for innocent unbaptized infants and for uncommitted people (like Pope Celestine V whose resignation in 1294 shocked Dante). The first circle of hell is populated by virtuous pagans (poets like Homer and thinkers like Plato) who made great contributions to mankind but cannot be saved since they are not baptized. The sinners in Hell are incapable of repentance, and their tormented existence in Hell is a continuation of their lives on earth. The severity of their punishment is appropriate to the sinfulness of their actions: first come the sins of incontinence (for example illicit lovers like Francesca da Rimini), then sins of violence, and finally sins of fraud (for example those who betrayed their friends like Brutus and Judas Iscariot). Dante is talking to some of the people in Hell and feels pity for them. The lowest pit of Hell combines the Biblical image of fire with Nordic ice, and Satan is given three heads, in this way he is a perverse image of the Trinity.

On the morning of Easter Sunday a subterranean channel leads Dante and Vergil from the nadir of Hell to the base of Purgatory, imagined as mountain on the opposite side of the earth. On the terraces of Purgatory the sins of those who are ultimately to be saved are cleansed away. All who enter Hell must leave hope behind, but the souls in Purgatory are destined for salvation, they gladly accept their penance. Their acts of penitence include prayers, physical exercises (e.g. running against sloth), fasting and enduring smoke or fire. The acts of penitence are arranged according to the seven cardinal sins: pride, envy, anger, sloth, avarice, gluttony, luxury (lust). As the burden of one sin is removed the soul easily rises to the next terrace. The length of the expiation is determined by the burden of the sin which is cleansed there. The completely purified souls reach the top of the mountain, which is the Garden of Eden (also called the "earthly Paradise"), from which the elect ascend into Heaven. Here Vergil leaves Dante, and from now on Beatrice guides him.

Aristotelian cosmology with the earth at the center surrounded by seven planets from moon to Saturn is the structure of Dante's Heaven. Each sphere of Heaven has its own planet and rank of angels, its special virtue and branch of knowledge. For example the fourth sphere is the sphere of the Sun, this is the Heaven of theologians, next comes the sphere of Mars, which is the Heaven of saintly warriors, the sixth sphere—the Heaven of Jupiter—is the Heaven of just rulers (besides King David and Emperor Constantine also including the Roman Emperor Trajanus!), and the following sphere of Saturnus is the Heaven of contemplatives (St. Benedict, St. Bernard, Petrus Damianus). As Dante and Beatrice ascend through the heavens, they stop to talk with those that they meet along the way. In the highest Heaven the host of saints is arranged like the petals of a rose, and the Virgin Mary reigns as queen. Now the Cistercian mystic Bernard of Clairvaux (1090—1153) becomes Dante's guide. God is depicted as three concentric circles of light with the figure of a man at the center. Finally Dante sees the eternal light of God, which is "the love that moves the heavens and the other stars" ("L'amor che muove il sole e l'altre stelle", 33,145; confer Aristotle's "unmoved mover"). This description of the "beatific vision of God" ends the poem.

下面有 *Commedia* 所描述的地狱、炼狱和天堂的结构：在地狱(inferno)之前有一种"灵薄狱"(limbo，亦译"古圣所"、"冥府")，在那里有那些不冷不热的、拒绝选择善或恶的灵魂。在跨越 Acheron 河后是第一层地狱，这里有那些具有德性的外教人，比如 Plato、Aristoteles、Homerus 等高尚的诗人、哲学家、英雄，他们都无法进入天堂。

在地狱第二层中有一些为不正当爱情和贪欲受惩罚的幽灵，强烈的风困扰着这些人，其中有 Semiramis、Dido、Cleopatra、Helena、Paris、Achilleus、Tristan 等人，还有一些当代的意大利人，比如 Francesca da Rimini 和他的爱人 Paolo。

地狱第三层属于那些犯下贪吃(饕餮)或不节制方面的罪的灵魂。

第四层中的幽灵的罪是贪财或挥霍行为。

在第五层的地狱中，一些人为他们的愤怒和失控的憎恨受惩罚。

在跨越 Styx 河后是"低层地狱"(Dis 城)的大门，一些堕落的天使守卫这个入口。地狱的第六层属于那些持异端邪说或因知识而自高自大的人。Farinata 和一些教派人士在这里受烈火的折磨。

在地狱第七层中有那些犯下暴力罪行的灵魂，比如这里有十个暴君，包括 Alexander Magnus、Dionysios de Syracusa、匈奴王 Attila 和 Ezzolino。一些野兽折磨他们。自杀是一种违反自己的暴行，而那些曾进行自杀的人在这里受一些树木的控制，他们无法行动。违反神的暴行是亵渎神的罪，同样受严厉的惩罚。那些违背自然本性的罪包括同性恋和不自然的性行为。

在第八层地狱有十个沟壑，其中与欺诈、谄媚、圣职买卖、魔术、偷窃、造假有关系的罪行受到惩罚。这些罪人的灵魂在这里受到各种形式的惩罚，其中一种是活埋。在这层地狱中有一些教宗，但希腊英雄 Odysseus 也在这里。

第九层地狱是地狱的顶点或最低下的一层，这是堕落天使 Lucifer 的领域，他被冻结在永恒的冰海中。在这个地狱中有背叛和出卖朋友的象征：杀害了自己弟兄的 Cain，还有 Ugolino、Judas Iscariot，他曾出卖了主，以及暗杀 Caesar 的 Brutus 和 Cassius。

所谓的"前炼狱"是属于那些在临终时忏悔的，但因懒惰或太匆忙无法完成告解的人。他们被排除在外，无法开始净化的过程。这个领域的守卫者是 Cato。炼狱的形状是一座山，这座山的目标是灵魂们的净化，每一个灵魂需要摆脱七个重罪(peccata)。Petrus 守卫炼狱的门，而进入炼狱有三个台阶：承认和宣告自己的罪(confessio)、忏悔(contritio)以及补赎(satisfactio)。当灵魂们进入炼狱时，一个天使在每一个灵魂的额头上写下七个"P"(代表 peccatum，罪)。

The following is an outline of the structure of Hell, Purgatory, and Heaven presented in the *Commedia:* Before the Inferno (Hell) there is the Limbo (ante-hell) for those who are lukewarm, who refused to choose right and wrong. Then, after crossing the Acheron River, comes the first circle of hell, reserved for virtuous pagans like Plato, Aristotle, Homer and noble poets, philosophers, and heroes, who are excluded from heaven.

In the second circle of hell the sins of illicit love and lust are punished by strong winds which toss the people around. Here we find Semiramis, Dido, Cleopatra, Helena, Paris, Achilles, and Tristan. Among the contemporary Italians in this hell are Francesca da Rimini and her lover Paolo.

In the third circle of hell sinners have to atone for the sins of gluttony and intemperance.

The fourth circle of hell is reserved for the sins of avarice or wasteful prodigy.

In the fifth circle of hell sinners suffer for their failure to control anger and wrath.

After crossing the Styx River there is the entrance to the city Dis (lower hell), guarded by fallen angels. The sixth circle of hell covers the sins of heresy and intellectual pride. Burning flames torture men like Farinata and sectarians.

The seventh circle of hell is reserved for the sins of violence. Here are ten tyrants, among them Alexander the Great, Dionysos of Syracuse, Attila, the leader of the Huns, and Ezzolino. They are tortured by beasts. Suicide is a sin of violence against oneself, and those who committed suicide are imprisoned in trees, they are unable to move. Blasphemy is harshly punished as a sin of violence against God, and sins against nature comprise homosexuality and sodomy.

In the eighth circle of hell there are 10 ditches dedicated to the punishment of the sins of fraud, namely flattery, simony, sorcery, theft, falsification. The souls of the sinners undergo different kinds of punishment, one of them is to be buried alive. In this hell there are some Popes, but also the Greek hero Odysseus.

The ninth circle of the hell is the nadir of hell, the realm of Lucifer, the fallen angel, who is frozen to an eternal sea of ice. Here are the symbols of betrayal and treason: Cain, who killed his brother, Ugolino, Judas Iscariot who betrayed the Lord, Brutus and Cassius, the murderers of Caesar.

The Ante-Purgatory is for people who repented before death, but who were too lazy, or preoccupied to confess their sins before death. They are excommunicated and cannot enter the process of purgation. Cato is the guardian of this realm. The Purgatory is a mountain for the purging of the souls, freeing them from the stains of the seven main sins (peccata). The gate of Purgatory is kept by Peter, and there are three steps to enter: confession of sins, contrition (feeling sorry for wrongdoing), and satisfaction. An angel inscribes seven "P" (for peccatum) on the soul's heads, as they enter the purgatory.

炼狱的最底层属于那些必须纠正骄傲(superbia)之罪的灵魂。他们需要扛一些石头,同时他们念"我们的天父"(Pater noster)。在一定的时间后,一位天使(即代表谦虚的天使)宣布"那些虚心的人是有福的",并擦掉灵魂额头上的一个"P"。

第二层属于嫉妒之罪(invidia)。在这里的灵魂必须祈祷呼吁诸圣徒的经文,并且被迫闭上他们的眼睛。在这里,"宽容的天使"宣布"怜悯人的人是有福的"并拿掉第二个"P"。

在第三层炼狱中人们为"愤怒之罪"(ira)作补赎。灵魂们需要忍耐,比如他们被烟熏一段时间,同时要念"上主的羔羊",这样他们祈求基督的平安(dona nobis pacem)。另外,"和平的天使"隆重地宣读说:"缔造和平的人是有福的。"

炼狱的第四层属于那些犯下懒惰罪过(acedia)的灵魂。他们需要学习热忱,所以他们被迫快速跑来跑去。最后"热忱的天使"宣布:"哀恸的人是有福的。"

有关贪婪和贪财的罪(avaritia)在第五层中被克服,在那里的灵魂们需要俯伏在地。当他们的净化过程完成时,"慷慨的天使"告诉他们:"饥渴慕义的人是有福的。"

在第六个层次中那些属于饕餮(gula)的罪行被治疗。通过守斋挨饿,灵魂们学习节制。"节制的天使"说:"温良的人是有福的。"

最后,炼狱第七层属于不正当爱情和欲望(luxuria)的纠正,其中的净化方式是烈火。灵魂们需要经过这个火焰,此后"纯洁的天使"告诉他们:"心里纯净的人是有福的。"

在炼狱后 Dante 跨越 Lethe 河并达到"人间的乐园"(Eden 伊甸园),在那里 Beatrice 出现。Dante 有两个神视,他看到一次隆重的游行,前面有7位手持火炬的人、有24位长老、4个动物(代表四个福音书的作者),后面有一个半狮半鹰的动物(gryphus,代表基督的人性和神性)。这个半狮半鹰拉一辆车(即教会),而7个美德陪伴着他。在第二个神视中,Dante 看到教会与德国帝国之间的搏斗。此后他上升到天界,他进入天上的乐园(Paradiso)。

最低的天界是"月亮的天",在这里有那些缺乏恒心的灵魂们,比如 Fredericus II 皇帝的母亲 Constantia。所谓的"守护天使"属于这个领域。

第二层天是"水星的天",在这里有一些缺乏正义感或雄心勃勃的人,比如 Justinianus 皇帝。这个境界的统治者是"总领天使"。

第三层天被称为"金星的天",这是那些缺乏节制的灵魂的领域,比如 Carolus Martellus 居住在这个层次中,而那些"宰治者"是这层的天使。

The lowest terrace of the Purgatory is reserved for correcting the sins of pride (superbia). Here the souls must carry stones and pray the Our Father (Pater noster). After some time an angel (the Angel of Humility) announces "Blessed are the poor in spirit" and wipes off one "P" from the forehead of the souls.

The second level is dedicated to the sin of envy (invidia). The souls pray the litany of the saints, having their eyelids shut. Here the Angel of Generosity announces "Blessed are the merciful" and takes away the second "P".

On the third stage the sins of anger (ira) are atoned for. The souls have to learn to endure smoke, and they pray the Agnus Dei, asking for Christ's peace (dona nobis pacem). Another angel, the Angel of Peace solemnly recites: "Blessed are the peacemakers."

The fourth part of the Purgatory is reserved for the sin of sloth (acedia). Here the souls are learning zeal by running, they are trained to rush around quickly. The Angel of Zeal announces: "Blessed are they who mourn."

The sins of avarice and greed (avaritia) are overcome in the fifth level, where the souls purify themselves by prostration. After the purgative process is finished the Angel of Liberality tells them: "Blessed are those who are hungry for justice."

On the sixth platform of the Purgatory the sin of gluttony (gula) is healed. The souls attain temperance through starvation. The Angel of Temperance says: "Blessed are the meek."

Finally the seventh part is dedicated to the cure of illicit love and lust (luxuria), which is done by a kind of purging fire. The souls must pass this fire, and then the Angel of Chastity tells them: "Blessed the pure of heart."

After the Purgatory Dante crosses the river Lethe and arrives at the Earthly Paradise (Eden), where Beatrice appears. Dante has two visions, one of them is a solemn procession of 7 torch-bearers, 24 elders, 4 animals (the four evangelists), and a griffin (a lion with eagle's wings, symbol for the two natures of Christ). The griffin pulls a chariot (the Church) and is accompanied by allegories of the seven virtues. In a second vision Dante sees the struggle between the Church and the Empire. Then he ascends to the heavenly spheres, to the Paradiso.

The lowest heavenly sphere is the Heaven of the Moon, here are those blessed souls who somehow lacked perseverance, for example Constance, the mother of Emperor Frederick II. The lunar heaven is the realm of the Guardian Angels.

The second heaven is the Heaven of Mercurius, dedicated to blessed souls deficient in justice or tainted by ambition, here we find Emperor Justinianus. The Archangels reign in this sphere.

The third heaven is called the Heaven of Venus, it is the heaven of those lacking temperance, for example Charles Martell is located here. This realm is controlled by the

所谓的"太阳天"是神学家们的住所,在此有 24 位学者,包括 Thomas Aquinas(他赞美圣 Franciscus)、Bonaventura(他赞美 Dominicus)、Chrysostomus、Albertus Magnus、Petrus Lombardus、Boethius、Siger de Brabant、Augustinus 等人。在这个天层中有所谓的"掌权者"(另一种精神力量或一种天使)。

"火星天"是第五层天,在这里有 9 位神圣的战士,比如 Josuah、Judas Maccabaeus、Carolus Magnus 和 Roland。这个天界献给勇气,所以统治它的天使被称为"德性"。

因为 Jupiter(木星)是正义的象征,"木星天"(第六层天)是义人的高天。Dante 罗列六位:David 王、Traianus 皇帝、Hiskia 王、Constantinus Magnus、Sicilia 的 Wilhelmus II 王以及 Ripheus。属于这种领域的天使是"统治者"。

第七层天是"土星天",它属于那些选择默观生活的人,其中最突出的人是 Benedictus、Petrus Damianus 和圣 Bernardus。属于这种天界的精神力量是"上座者"(参见 Col 1:16)。

第八层天是"恒星天"。Dante 从这里俯瞰地球,而 Petrus(代表信仰)、Jacobus(代表希望)以及 Johannes(代表爱慕)来审问他。符合这三个"神性美德"(即信、望、爱)的是 Cherubim 天使。

第九层天等于是第一天,它推动一切其他的天界(primum mobile),它符合 Aristoteles 的"第一天"。Dante 在此见到天使们的秩序,而被称为 Seraphim 的天使属于第九层天。

最后的和最高的天层是"净火天"(empyreum),它被描述为一种由三个圆圈组成的玫瑰(这是三位一体的神的象征)。在这里有上主和那些被拯救的灵魂们,如 Maria、Bernardus、Beatrice、《旧约》中的八位真福人士,即 Adam、Moses、Eva、Rahel、Sara、Rebekka、Judith、Ruth、Anna,还有七位属基督宗教的真福人士,即 Johannes、Petrus、Augustinus、Franciscus、Benedictus、Lucia 和 Beatrice。Bernardus 为 Dante 的缘故祈求 Maria,此后 Dante 看见不可言说的光明,即是上主,那种"推动太阳和一切星星的爱"。

076. 《论俗语》

这篇关于口语和书面语的论文写成于 1303—1305 年间。作者认为,意大利人的口语(所谓的 lingua volgare)在某些条件下也能够成为一个和古拉丁语一样优美和庄严的语言。

在开始,Dante 描述人类语言的起源、本性和历史发展。根据《圣经》的记载(参见

"Principalities".

The Heaven of the Sun is the seat of theologians, 24 of them are found here, among them Thomas Aquinas, who praises St. Francis, Bonaventure, who praises Dominicus, then Chrysostom, Albert the Great, Petrus Lombardus, Boethius, Siger of Brabant, Augustine and others. Here the "Powers" (another kind of spiritual forces or angels) reign.

The Heaven of Mars is the fifth heavenly sphere, it harbours 9 saintly warriors, among them Joshua, Judas Maccabeus, Charlemagne, and Roland. This heaven is dedicated to fortitude, and thus it is controlled by the angels called "Virtues".

As Jupiter is a symbol of Justice, the Heaven of Jupiter (the sixth sphere) is the heaven of the just. Dante lists six of them: King David, Emperor Trajan, Hiskia, Constantine the Great, Wilhelm II of Sicilia, and Ripheus. In this realm the "Dominations" reign.

The seventh heaven is the Heaven of Saturnus, dedicated to the contemplatives, outstanding among them are Benedict, Petrus Damianus, and St. Bernard. The spiritual powers of the "Thrones" are assigned to this sphere (conf. *Col* 1:16).

The eight sphere is the Heaven of the Fixed Stars. Here Dante looks down on the earth, and he is examined by Peter (symbol of faith), James (symbol of hope), and John (representing love). Corresponding to these three theological virtues are the angelic forces of the Cherubim.

The ninth heaven, the first heaven which moves the other heavens (primum mobile) corresponds to Aristotles' first heaven: here Dante has a vision of the angelic hierarchy. The Seraphim angels are assigned to this ninth heaven.

The Fiery Heaven (empyreum), is the highest and last sphere, it is depicted as a celestial rose of three intersecting circles (symbol of the Trinity). Here are God and the redeemed souls like Mary, Bernard, Beatrice, 8 blessed of the Old Testament: Adam, Moses, Eve, Rahel, Sarah, Rebekka, Judith, Ruth, Anna, and 7 blessed of the New Covenant (Christianity): John, Peter, Augustine, Francis, Benedict, Lucia, and Beatrice. Bernard prays to Mary on behalf of Dante, and then Dante sees the ineffable Light, God, the "Love that moves the sun and all the other stars".

076. *De vulgari eloquentia / Of Eloquence in the Vulgar Tongue*

This treatise concerning spoken and literal language was written in 1303—1305 and tries to show that the colloquial Italian language (lingua volgare) can under certain conditions reach the beauty and dignity of classical Latin.

Dante begins with a general treatise on the origin, nature and history of human language. According to the Bible (*Gen* 2:20) Adam created a primordial language which developed into Hebrew and became a higher literary language. After the Babylonian

Gen 2:20),Adam(亚当)创造了一种最原始的语言,它成为后来的希伯来语这种高级的文学语言。在巴比伦的语言混乱后(参见 *Gen* 11),人类失去了 Eden 乐园中那种稳定不变和普遍适用的共同语言。此后只有犹太人能说希伯来语,而世界其他民族分裂为许多地方性的口语,这些地方语阻碍跨越地区的沟通,而且它们始终在变化当中。其中一部分的语言也发展成为文学语言。Dante 首次描述和分析欧洲(南部)的语言。他区分希腊地区、罗曼地区和格尔曼/日耳曼地区的语言。罗曼语系分为法语(普罗旺斯语)、西班牙语和意大利语,而意大利语又分为 14 种不同的方言:威尼斯语、西西里语、托斯卡尼亚语等等。

语言的逐渐分裂和众多地方语言的形成也意味着沟通与合一的消失和破裂。然而,一种与此相反的趋势是恢复"原始语言"的努力,这种倾向的目标是在种种语言中实现秩序和稳定性。这些努力导致一种"人定的"、高级的语言的形成(就是 grammatica"语法"或 locutio secundaria"第二层的语言"),它在人们的"自然语言"(locutio vulgaris"俗语")以外存在。这就是但丁关于"两种语言"的伟大理论:在婴儿时期,人们通过模仿学习"自然语言",它是"没有任何规律的"(sine omni regula),而那种"人定的语言"的语法规则需要长期的学习才能掌握。因为"第二种语言"有固定的语法规则,人们能够普遍地理解它,而它的语法形成某一种不可变的语言特性,它超越时间和地点(inalterabilis locutionis identitas diversis temporibus atque locis)。

对欧洲来说,拉丁语是这种普遍被理解的语言的理想标准,而通过拉丁语人们能够和古代的伟大诗人(antiquorum auctoritates)进行沟通或与其他地区的人对话。Dante 称古罗马的诗人 Vergilius、Horatius 和 Ovidius 为"规律性的诗人"(poetae regulares)。他们的拉丁语能够提供一个基础,而根据这种基础意大利语也能够逐渐成为一种具有语法规律的文学语言和诗的语言(所谓的 volgare illustre)。Dante 认为,最接近古罗马作者的优美文风(bello stile)的方言是 Tuscania 的方言(即他家乡 Florentia 城的方言)。实际上,在他的杰作《神曲》后,Tuscania 的方言逐渐成为意大利统一语言的基础。

confusion (conf. *Gen* 11), mankind has lost the language of Eden, a stable, unchanging and universal language. Now only the Jews could speak Hebrew, whereas the rest of the world was split up into many colloquial idioms that impede translocal communicantion and whose usage constantly changes. Some of those spoken languages developed into literary languages. Dante is the first to describe and analyze the languages of (Southern) Europe. He distinguishes Greek, Roman and German languages. The Roman languages branched out into French (Provencal), Spanish and Italian, and Italian again has 14 different dialects: Venetian, Sicilian, Tuscan etc.

The progressive split into a diversity of languages and dialects implies the ongoing disintegration and destruction of communication and unity. However, there is also a contrary tendency to bring order and constancy into the languages, namely the tendency to revive the ideal of the "primordial language". These efforts lead to the emergence of an "artificial" higher language (grammatica, or "locutio secundaria") beside the "natural" speech of the people ("locutio vulgaris"). This is Dante's great theory of the "two languages": the "natural" speech of the people is learned by pure imitation in infancy, "sine omni regula" (without any rule), whereas the grammar rules of the "artificial" language are only known by time-consuming study. Because the secondary artificial language has fix rules, it can be generally understood, and the grammar shapes a certain immutable identity of the language which transcends time and space ("inalterabilis locutionis identitas diversis temporibus atque locis").

In Europe Latin is the ideal example of such a generally understood literary language which enables us to communicate with the great thinkers of antiquity ("antiquorum auctoritates") or with people from other countries. The Roman poets Vergil, Horace and Ovid are called "poetae regulares" by Dante, and their Latin should provide the basis according to which the Italian language could emerge as a literary poetic language with grammar rules (the "volgare illustre"). Dante decides that the Tuscan dialect (=the dialect of his home city Florence) is closest to the noble style ("bello stile") of the old Roman authors. Indeed, after his masterpiece, the *Comedia Divina*, the Tuscan dialect became more and more the basis for a unified Italian literary language.

第六篇

中世纪晚期和文艺复兴的开端
The Late Middle Ages and the Beginnings of the Renaissance
(1320—1450 AD)

• *Knight, Death, and the Devil*

利尔的尼古拉斯(1270—1349)

生于法国 Normandie 地区 Evreux 附近的 Lyre,后在 Paris 学习,入方济各会,1308—1319 年间和 1326—1349 年间在 Paris 大学任神学教授。1319 年他当选为法国省方济各会的省会长,于 1324 年又任 Burgundia 省的省会长。他算是中世纪最伟大的圣经学家之一,他的荣称是 doctor planus"简明的博士"和 doctor utilis"有用的博士"。

著作:《全部〈圣经〉注解集》(5 册,中世纪最标准的释经书)

077.《全部〈圣经〉注解集》

本著作的另一个书名是 *Postillae perpetuae in vetus et novum Testamentum*(《关于〈旧约〉和〈新约〉的持续注解》)。它成书于 1322 年到 1331 年间,后来是第一部被印刷的《圣经注解》,曾于 1471 年和 1472 年在罗马问世。根据一个通俗说法,Martin Luther 和其他的改革者都深深受了这位方济各会学者著作的影响:Si Lyra non lyrasset, Lutherus non saltasset ("如果 Lyra 没有弹琴,Luther 也不能跳舞",或译 "如果 Luther 没有 Lyra 的研究,他也无法写成他自己的《圣经》译本")。Lyra 的伟大著作具有深远的影响,甚至为作者赢得了"现代圣经解释学之奠基人"的美名以及"有用博士"的荣称。然而,在评价 Lyra 的贡献时也必须考虑到经院传统和前经院时期的圣经解释学。

在前言中作者说自己要专门研究《圣经》文献文字上的意义,他仅仅偶尔会说明《圣经》文献的神秘意义。这样,他对整部《圣经》编写了一部注经学的著作,但他也参考了早一些的书,尤其引用 Thomas Aquinas 的著作。他也阅读犹太人学者的著作,比如 Rabbi Salomon(亦称"Rashi",1040—1105 年)的研究。Lyra 对古希伯来语有相当好的掌握,因此他能够根据希伯来文的《旧约》进行研究。 他编写这部注解的一个动机是他要向犹太人证明这一点:哪怕只是从字面上来看《旧约》也会发现《旧约》的文献指向基督和教会。根据中世纪的圣经学,神圣的文献中隐藏着四层意义:Littera gesta docet, quid credas allegoria, moralis quid agas, quo tendas anagogia.("文字指出发生过的事实,寓意告诉你应相信什么,比喻性诠释指示你应做什么,未来性的诠释教导你往哪里去。")Lyra 认为,寓意和灵性的解释有时候不太可靠,因此他更注重文献的字面意义。

Nicolaus de Lyra / Nicolaus of Lyra

Opera: *Postilla litteralis super totam Bibliam I-V*
Works: *Literal Explanation of the Bible*

077. *Postilla litteralis super totam Bibliam / Literal Explanation of the Bible*

This work is also known under the title *Postillæ perpetuae in vetus et novum Testamentum* (*Continuing Commentary Notes on the Old and New Testaments*). It was written between 1322 and 1331 and later became the first printed commentary on the Bible, since it was published in Rome in 1471 and 1472. A proverb claims that Martin Luther and the other reformers were deeply influenced by the work of the Franciscan scholar: "Si Lyra non lyrasset, Lutherus non saltasset" ("If Lyra would not have set the tone, Luther would not have been able to dance", i.e. Luther depended on Lyra to complete his translation of the Bible). Lyra's voluminous work became quite popular and earned for its author the praise of being the founder of modern exegesis as well as the title "Doctor utilis". However, his contribution must be seen in the context of the scholastic and pre-scholastic tradition of Biblical science.

In the prologue the author states that he intends to concentrate on the literal meaning of Biblical texts and only occasionally will expound the mystical significance of the Scriptures. Thus he presents an exegetical commentary to the whole Bible, based on earlier authors, especially Thomas Aquinas. He also consults the commentaries of Jewish scholars, for example the works of Rabbi Salomon (also known as "Rashi", 1040—1105). Lyra knew Hebrew quite well and could base his observations on the Hebrew text of the Old Testament. One of his motives to write the commentary was to demonstrate to the Jews that even a literal understanding of the text of the Old Testament would point to Christ and the Church. The medieval exegesis knew four layers of meaning hidden in the sacred texts: "Littera gesta docet, quid credas allegoria, moralis quid agas, quo tendas (= quid speras) anagogia." ("The text teaches you facts, allegory what you should believe, moral interpretation gives you advice for your actions, and anagogical interpretation tells you where you will go (=what you hope for)".) Lyra knew that the symbolic and spiritual interpretations were sometimes too poetic and unreliable, thus he paid more attention to the literal meaning of the text.

威廉·奥康(1285—1350)

约于 1285 年出生在英国 Ockham(Surrey 地区),于 1306 年进入 OFM(方济各会),在 London 学习逻辑学,大约 1310 年后在 Oxford 学习哲学和神学,1317 年在 London 任教,1324 年因 Oxford 大学校长 Lutterell 的阴谋被派到 Avignon 教廷,其教导被怀疑不正确;由于特殊的历史条件,他在 4 年"软禁"后离开 Avignon,因此被开除教籍;Occam 前往德国皇帝 Ludovicus Bavarus 的宫廷,曾向德国皇帝说:"请你用宝剑保护我,我将以我的笔头保护你。(Tu me defendas gladio, ego te defendam calamo.)"因为他与教廷有冲突。在皇帝去世后,Occam 试图重新与教廷和好。

著作:《论皇帝和教宗的权力》、《对话集》、《关于传统知识的金书》、《物理学注集》、《杂论》、《语录注集》、《逻辑学大全》、《自然哲学大全》、《论教宗的权威》、《论皇帝的权力》

078. 《语录注集》

Occam 在 1317 年和 1323 年间编写了这部重要的注解集,其中谈论一些哲学和神学的观点。他的解释表明作者是一个很特殊的唯名论者。

唯名论的种种理论都与认识论有关系。那些经院哲学家(比如 Thomas Aquinas)经常认为感官经验是一种物质因并导致对某事物的本质(本性,即 essentia、species、ratio aeterna)的理解。对 Occam 来说,经验并不会引发对事物的"本质"的了解,他甚至认为"本性"是一个多余的、形而上学的附加物,它既不是"在事物之前",也不是"在事物内"(ante rem, in re)。那些理念和普遍的概念"仅仅是在心灵中,而不是在事物当中"(Sent. 1, 2, 7)。这些普遍的概念仅仅是一种一般使用的"符号"(signum)。这些符号来自人们的约定,它们甚至是某种"虚构的东西"(quoddam fictum),它们仅仅是一种"声音"(vox, Sent. 1, 2, 7,参见 Roscellinus 关于这些"声音"的教导)。在真实的世界中没有普遍概念,因为我们通过直觉来认识真实的事物。对 Occam 来说,一个普遍的概念是一个代表真实的事物的思想性代替物,被称为 terminus(术语)。因此,属 Occam 学派的人后来更多地被称为 terministae(术语论者),而不是"唯名论者"或"概念论者"。

拒绝那些超越现象的直接表现的普遍根源和普遍性的解释(比如拒绝 Aristoteles 的"形式"和"物质"、"本体"和"属性"、"本质"和"存在"、"目的因"等等),这是"思想经济"的原则,而这种对形而上学思想的反感被称为"Occam 剃刀"。如果没有需要就不应增加概念(Entia non sunt multiplicanda sine necessitate.如无需要勿增实体)。Occam

Occam / William of Ockham

Opera: *De imperatorum ac pontificum potestate, Dialogus inter magistrum et discipulum, Expositio aurea super totam artem veterem, Expositio in libros Physicorum, Quodlibeta septem, Sententiae (=Ordinatio), Summa Logicae, Summula philosophiae naturalis, Super potestate pontificis, Tractatus de potestate imperiali*

Works: *On the Power of Emperors and Popes, Dialogue, Golden Book on the Whole Traditional Scholarship, Commentary to the Books of Physics, Mixed Treatises, Sentences, Sum of Logic, Sum of the Philosophy of Nature, On the Power of the Pope, Treatise concerning Imperial Power*

078. *Sententiae / Sentences*

Between 1317 and 1323 Occam wrote this monumental commentary to philosophical and theological sentences. The explanations of the statements show that he is a nominalist of a special kind.

The theories of nominalism are connected to the analysis of human understanding. The scholastic philosophers (for example Thomas Aquinas) usually saw sensual experience as the material cause which leads to insight into the essence (essentia, species, ratio aeterna) of a thing. For Occam experience does not lead to the insight into the nature of a thing, he even thinks the "species" is a superfluous metaphysical insertion, which is neither before nor in the things (ante rem, in re). Ideas and universal concepts are "only in the soul and not in the things" (*Sent.* 1, 2, 7). These universal concepts are just a sign (signum) commonly used. These signs are based on convention and they are even "something fictive" (quoddam fictum), they are only a "sound" (vox, *Sent.* 1, 2, 7, confer Roscellinus' teaching of the "voces"). The universal has no existence in the world of reality, because the real things are known to us by intuitive knowledge, not by abstraction. For Occam a universal is a mental substitute for a real thing, it is a "term" (terminus). Thus the adherents of Occam's school were later called "terminists" (terministae) rather than "nominalists" or "conceptualists".

The rejection of general causes and explanations that go beyond the immediate behavior of the phenomena (such as Aristotle's distinctions between matter and form, substance and accident, essence and existence, final causes etc.) is a principle of the economy of thought, the "Law of Parsimony", and this unwillingness to accept universal metaphysical ideas is called "Occam's razor". "Only if it is necessary one should add new entities." (Entia non sunt multiplicanda sine necessitate). Occam believes that we can

认为我们只能理解个别的事物,他甚至说我们无法作出普遍的判断。只有"Sokrates 是 Sokrates"这样的句子才是确切对的。无论如何,Occam 也想理解客观真理,而他接受"本体"和"品质"这些范畴,虽然他强调"数量"和"关系"概念的主观性,因此准备了现代的主观主义思维。这种主观主义和怀疑主义限制了人的理解的范围并后来促进了 Locke 和 Hume 关于人性认识来源的理论的诞生。

如果没有普遍的理念,神的行动是比较自由的,因此 Occam 介绍了 potentia Dei absoluta(神的绝对权力)的概念。虽然神的权力因他所建立的秩序而受到限制(即所谓 potentia Dei ordinata),但神也完全可能创造另外一个宇宙秩序。这种理论针对某种希腊的必然论——在 Aristoteles 的思想中有很多必然论因素,比如地心说——并保卫一切万物的偶然性;因为一切事物都是被创造的,而不是先天就有的。在伦理学的领域中,这种理解强调神的意志。神愿意支持"善",不是因为它是"善",而因为神愿意这样。对 Thomas 来说,自然法是永恒的、不可变更的,但在 Occam 眼中,Moses 的法律可以被另一套规定取代,只要神愿意这样做就可以。因为 Occam 的部分例子非常极端,很多人解释他的思想为一种道德上的实证主义。Occam 的思路后来影响 Gabriel Biel、Descartes 和 Kant,而 Biel 的学生 Luther 曾说:"Ich bin von Ockham's Schule(我属于 Occam 学派)。"

only understand singular things, he even asserts that we cannot make general judgments. Only the sentence "Socrates is Socrates" is certainly correct. However, also Occam wants to understand objective truth, and he accepts the transcendence of the categories of substance and quality, although he emphasizes the subjectivity of the categories of quantity and relation, thus preparing modern subjectivism. This subjectivism and skepticism limited the horizon of human understanding and later influenced the theories of Locke and Hume on the origin of human understanding.

If there are no universal ideas, the actions of God are more free, and thus Occam presents the idea of a potentia Dei absoluta (God's absolute power). Although God's power is limited by the order He set up (potentia Dei ordinata), but He could also have made a very different order of the universe. This doctrine opposes a certain Greek necessitarianism—there are many necessitarian elements in Aristotle's thought, for example geocentrism—and protects the contingency of all things, since all things are created and not apriori. In the area of ethics this understanding emphasizes God's will. God wills the good not because it is good but because He wants it so. For Thomas the law of nature was eternal and immovable, but for Occam the Mosaic Law could be replaced by some other regulation if God would want that. Some of Occam's examples are extreme, and many people consequently interpreted his thought as a kind of moral positivism. He influenced Gabriel Biel, Descartes and Kant, and Biel's student Luther said once "Ich bin von Ockham's Schule" ("I am of Occam's school").

布里吉特(约 1303—1373)

瑞典 Uppsala, Finstad 贵族人,1343 年后守寡,入熙笃会修道,曾经验许多神视,1346 年创立隐修院 Vadstena 和修女团体,1349 年后在意大利罗马;圣人,瑞典国的主保圣人。

著作:《诸神视》

079. 《诸神视》

Birgitta 的 *Revelationes* 分为七卷,大概是来自斯勘的纳维亚的最重要的中世纪文献。Birgitta 的瑞典神师(Petrus Olavi, Matthias de Linkoeping)将她的神视译成拉丁语,而西班牙的 Alfonso 主教(他在晚年是 Birgitta 的友人)校订了这个文献。Birgitta 要求他编写这部著作的第一个版本。Birgitta 生于一个贵族家庭,她结婚并生了八个小孩。她成为瑞典女王 Blancha 的家庭教师并在社会和政治生活中有一定的经验。她曾与丈夫一起去西班牙的 Santiago 朝圣(1341—1342 年),此后她与丈夫退隐到一个 Cistercienses(熙笃会)隐修院团体。1344 年她的丈夫去世,而她开始参与政治活动,因为一些神视和声音推动她这样做。她试图在法国和英国的冲突中缔造和平。1346 年她在 Vadstena(瑞典)创立了一个修女团体,而这个团体后来是由她的女儿管理的。1349 年 Birgitta 前往意大利,因为她想在罗马过 1350 年的禧年,此后她生活在罗马。很多人来拜访这位圣洁的女士,要与她交谈。

Revelationes 包含 600 多个神视的报告。在 *Revelationes* 的大部分叙事中,Birgitta 叙述上主、耶稣基督、童贞玛利亚或其他圣人曾经向 Birgitta 显现,并和她谈过话。在另一些文献中,Birgitta 聆听别人如何与圣人谈话,比如第 5 卷主要是一位持异端的隐修者与耶稣基督的对话。另一些故事描述一个灵魂的搏斗:魔鬼控诉某一个罪人,但护守天使想方设法来保护这个灵魂。一些文献是向别人写的信,其中包括一些具有深度的心理学观察和洞见。

贯穿着 *Revelationes* 的主题是对教会纪律下降的谴责。因为很多贵族人士利用隐修院来享受一种安宁的退隐生活,他们并没有准备过一种刻苦的克修生活,所以在很多地方的隐修院走向世俗化。Birgitta 敢于公开批评隐修者、司铎、主教,她甚至谴责了教宗。她劝勉教宗从 Avignon 回到罗马来。

Birgitta / Bridget of Sweden

Opera: *Revelationes*
Works: *Revelations (Visions)*

079. *Revelationes / Revelations*

The seven books of Birgittas's *Revelations* are probably the most important medieval text from Skandinavia. Her spiritual advisors from Sweden (Petrus Olavi, Matthias von Linkoeping) translated her narratives into Latin, and the Spanish Bishop Alphonse, a close friend of Birgitta in her last years, corrected the text. Birgitta had ordered him to edit the first version of the book. Birgitta was born into a noble family, she married and had eight children. She became the tutor of the Swedish queen Blancha and had experience in social and political life. After a pilgrimage to Santiago (Spain) in 1341/1342, she and her husband retreated to a Cistercian community. Her husband died in 1344, and Birgitta—motivated by visions and voices she heard—became politically involved, she tried to promote peace between France and England. In 1346 she founded a sister congregation in Vadstena (Sweden), which was later directed by her daughter. In 1349 she travelled to Italy in order to spend the jubilee year of 1350 in Rome and stayed in Rome for the rest of her life. Many visitors came to talk to this saintly woman.

The *Revelations* contain reports of more than 600 visions. In most of the stories in the *Revelations*, Birgitta narrates how God, Jesus Christ, the Virgin Mary or other Saints have revealed themselves to her and talked to her. In some other texts Birgitta listens to the dialogues of other people with the divine, for example book five is mainly a conversation between a heretic monk and Jesus Christ. Other narratives tell of the struggle for a soul: the devil accuses the sinner, but the guardian angel fights to protect the soul. Some messages or letters to other people contain penetrating insights and illuminating analyses of the psychology of a certain person.

The general theme pervading the *Revelations* is a critique of the decline of Church discipline. Monastic life has become secularized in many places, because many aristocrats used monasteries to enjoy a kind of peaceful retirement and were not ready to lead a life of ascetic fervor. Birgitta is not ashamed to openly blame monks, priests, bishops, and even popes. She urges the return of the papacy from Avignon back to Rome.

彼特拉克(1304—1374)

Francesco Petracco(后来自称 Petrarca)生于意大利 Arezzo,家人于 1312 年移居到法国南部的 Avignon 地区。父亲要求 Petrarca 学习法律,送他到法国 Montpellier 和意大利 Bologna 学习法学,但儿子于 1326 年放弃了法学研究,于 1330 年接受了剃头礼(tonsura),大概也接受了"小品"(ordines minores),曾于 1330—1347 年间在 Avignon 为 Colonna 枢机主教工作,并于 1353—1361 年间为米兰的 Visconti 家族工作,但他追求的不是金钱或地位,而是学习和写作。在 1337—1352 年间他也经常退隐到 Avignon 附近的 Vaucluse 别墅,同时他去巴黎等地,曾在很多隐修院的图书馆中寻找古代的文献,尤其是 Cicero 的书信。他于 1337 年首次前往罗马,后来经常赞扬罗马历史的伟大,并于 1341 年在罗马接受了诗人的桂冠。据他自己的说法,他于 1327 年在一个教堂中见到了 Laura 女士并爱上了她,而 Laura 在 1348 年的鼠疫中去世,但有的学者认为,Laura 完全是虚构的。无论如何,Petrarca 的《歌集》围绕着对 Laura 的爱。诗人没有结婚,有时候过独处的生活,但因为他的名气很多贵族人士请他作客。他重新评价古代的修辞学、历史著作、道德哲学、书信与诗歌,因此成为人文主义和文艺复兴的代表人物。1350 年他结识 Boccaccio 并且劝他放弃世俗的追求而严肃研究古典文学和希腊语。

著作:《阿富利加》、《反驳蔑视意大利的人》、《论宗教生活的优雅》(《论宗教超脱》)、《两种不同命运之道》、《论自己和众人的无知》、《名人列传》、《论独身的生活》(《论孤独生活》)、《诗信集》、《无名信集》、《家人的信》、《Griseldis 的故事》、《去耶路撒冷和圣地的小游记》、《写给后人》、《回忆录》、《歌集》(《劳拉在世时之诗》、《劳拉死后之诗》)、《我的秘密》、《老年人之信》、《胜利》

080.《两种不同命运之道》

Petrarca 于 1354 年至 1366 年间写下了这部道德性著作。

作者认为幸福和灾祸都阻碍一个人的内在平安,因此他试图说明人们都不应该陷入一种欢欣鼓舞或垂头丧气的心态。第 1 卷包含 122 篇简短的对话,即喜乐(Letitia)、希望(Spes)和理性(Ratio)之间的对话。无论喜乐和希望认为什么东西是伟大的、值得追求的,理性都一一揭露这些价值的缺点:它们在很短的时间内都会消失。一切世俗的东西的空虚性给人们以启发和教训:人们不应该拥抱世俗的享受和空虚的希望。

在第 2 卷中,理性和痛苦(Dolor)及恐惧(Metus)进行讨论;后两者抱怨说人生中有太多灾难和挑战。在 132 个小对话中,理性提出很多论点说,人们不需要害怕任何

Petrarca / Petrarch

Opera: *Africa, Contra eum qui malidixit Italie, De otio religioso, De remediis utriusque fortunae, De sui ipsius et multorum ignorantia, De viris illustribus (Quorundam virorum illustrium epitoma), De vita solitaria, Epistolae metricae, Epistolae sine nomine, Familiares (=Epistolae familiares, =Familiarum rerum libri xxiv), Historia Griseldis, Itinerarium breve de Ianua usque ad Ierusalem et Terram sanctam, Posteritati, Rerum memorandarum libri, Rime (Canzoniere, Rime in vita di Laura, Rime in morte di Laura), Secretum meum (=De secreto conflictu curarum mearum), Seniles (Senilium rerum libri), Trionfi*

Works: *Africa, Against the Slanderer of Italy, On Religious Leisure, On the Remedy for Each Fate, On My Own and Many Other's Ignorance, On Famous Men, On Solitary Life, Metric Letters, Anonymous Letters, Family Matters, History of Griseldis, Short Itinerary of a Journey to Jerusalem and the Holy Land, To Posterity, Memories, Rime (Canzoniere, Poems for Laura in Life, Poems for Laura in Death), My Secret, Letters of Old Men, Triumphs*

080. *De remediis utriusque fortunae / On the Remedy for Each Fate*

Petrarch wrote this moral treatise between 1354 and 1366.

The author thinks that both happiness and calamity are obstacles to the inner peace of a person, thus he tries to show that no man should be caught up in a state of elation or depression. The first book contains 122 short dialogues between Joy (Letitia), Hope (Spes), and Reason (Ratio). Whatever Joy and Hope describe as great values and riches worth pursuing, Reason unmasks each of these values as something that will disappear soon. The vanity and emptiness of all earthly things should teach humans not to cling to worldly pleasures and vain hope.

In the second book Reason discusses with Pain and Fear who complain about the calamities and future challenges of life. In 132 short conversations Reason argues that it is not necessary to be afraid of any disaster or calamity. These evils are a "blessing in disguise", because their aim is to educate and purify a person and thus to lead him or her to God. Petrarch often quotes from the Church Fathers, from the Bible and from sec-

灾难与祸害。这些坏事都是"焉知非福"的现象,因为其目标是教导和净化人,这样才能引导他们走向神。Petrarca多次引用教父的著作、《圣经》和世俗文学(比如Cicero和Seneca的书),但他也加上来自自己生活体验的一些观察,这样本著作也成为一种具有很多自传因素的作品,其中表达作者的悲观主义和他远离世俗世界的态度。

081. 《歌集》

诗人Petrarca终其一生都在改写和重新排列这些以意大利语编写的、献给Laura的抒情诗。因为Laura在1348年的鼠疫中死去,所以《歌集》分为两个部分(《劳拉在世时之诗》、《劳拉死后之诗》),共有366首诗。大部分的诗歌是以sonnet(十四行诗)的形式写成的,这种诗的十四行雅韵符合abba abba cde cde的模式。

很多人曾经赞美这些诗歌的完美形式与恒久的吸引力。Petrarch很仔细地探讨了他情绪的微妙表现的方方面面。他的情感和诸感觉的来源是感官和灵魂之间的张力,即肉身和心灵之间的冲突,换言之就是爱情的肉身情感以及爱情的精神层面之间的张力。Petrarca并不反抗这种张力,他反而以多愁善感的忧郁描述这种冲突,他使用很清晰的、甜蜜的和哀叹的语言来表达这些感受。人们曾说Petrarca那种以自我为中心的情绪主义已经和很多中世纪关于爱情的概念相去甚远。诗歌的情感、想象世界和格律模式深深地影响了几百年的欧洲文学。因此,Petrarca和Laura这两个名字成了"受深邃灵修控制的热烈爱情"的象征。

ular literature (Cicero and Seneca), but he also adds some observations from his own life, thus making the work also a deeply autobiographical expression of his pessimism and detachment from the world.

081. *Rime / Canzoniere*

Throughout his whole life Petrarch kept writing and rearranging these poems for Laura in Italian language. Laura died in the plague of 1348, thus the poems are divided into two parts (*Poems for Laura in Life, Poems for Laura in Death*), a total of 366 poems. Most of the poems are in the form of the sonnet, which is a poem of 14 lines riming in this pattern: abba abba cde cde.

The perfect form and lasting appeal of the poems have been praised by many. Petrarch explores in detail all the delicate phenomena of his emotions. The origin of his feelings and sentiments is the tension between the senses and the soul, the flesh and the spirit, the sensuality of his love and the mystical and spiritual aspects of it. Petrarch does not fight against the conflict but describes it with tender melancholy in clear, sweet, plaintive tones. It has been observed that Petrarch's self-centered sentimentalism is already far away from many of the medieval concepts of love. The mood, imagery, and rime pattern of the poems deeply influenced European literary circles in the next centuries. Thus Petrarch and Laura became names that symbolized a passionate love constrained by deep spirituality.

薄伽丘（1313—1375）

生于 Paris，是一位 Florentia 银行家的私生子，童年在 Florentia，1328—1341 年在 Napoli 学习经济和教会法，同时从事商务活动；1330 年后他爱上了 Maria d'Aquino（称她为 Fiametta，火焰），同时开始写作。1341 年他回到 Florentia，因为其父处于经济困境；1348 年他的父亲和 Maria 都死去了，而《十日谈》表达出当时的思想危机。Boccaccio 因他的博学获得一定的名气，他也曾经以 Florentia 城使者的身份去德国觐见皇帝并前往 Avignon 觐见教宗。1350 年他第一次见到他很重视的 Petrarca 并听从这位学者的指导。此后 Boccaccio 决定要"放弃世俗的事物并追求永恒的价值"。他不再写意大利语的不正经的故事，只编写一些严肃的拉丁语著作，他越来越多地过一种严谨的、虔诚的宗教生活，搜集、抄写和研究古老的手抄本，并开始学习古希腊语（当时很少有意大利人学习希腊语）。他关于古代神话、名人的堕落以及名女的故事都深深地影响了文艺复兴运动。1373 年他开始公开地讲解 Dante 的 *Commedia*（他也写过第一部《但丁传》并首次称 *Commedia* 为 *Divina Commedia*《神曲》）。

著作：《牧歌》、《名人之堕落》、《名女列传》、《异教诸神谱系》（一种古代神话学的百科全书）、《论诸山、林、泉、湖、河、沼泽、海之名》（一种地理学百科全书）、《方济各·彼特拉克的生活与风度》、《十日谈》（100 个故事，包括诗歌）、《菲亚美达的哀歌》、《信简》、《科巴丘》、《菲洛柯洛》、《菲洛斯特拉斯》、《苔塞伊达》、《但丁传》（《但丁赞》）

082.《十日谈》

这部包含 100 篇意大利语故事的著作成书于 1349—1353 年。书名来自希腊语（deka 十，hēmera 日子）并指出叙述的结构：讲故事十天之久。几乎所有的故事都来自更早的传统，有的来自古典文学（比如 Apuleius 的 *Metamorphosae*），另一些来自中世纪法国的传说和民间故事。Boccaccio 改写了很多故事并添油加醋。后来他感觉到《十日谈》有伤风败俗的影响，因此很长时间他没有告诉 Petrarca 这部书的存在。另外，Boccaccio 的《名人之堕落》的思想很重视伦理道德，似乎完全是另一个人写的。在晚年的时候 Boccaccio 后悔曾经创作《十日谈》，他甚至想烧毁这部书。

Boccaccio 设计的叙述框架是危害了全欧洲的鼠疫（1348—1349 年）。作者在开始部分描述 Florentia 城由于瘟疫遭受的损失。因为所有人都害怕被传染，法律、宗教和道德的戒律都被悬置了。在这种环境中，十位年轻的 Florentia 人（七位女士，三个男士）决定要从城市中逃走并暂且居住在乡间的一个别墅里。在外面的世界遭受瘟疫的困扰时，这些年轻的贵族人士创造了一个优雅的小乐园，也是社会秩序和纪律的

Giovanni Boccaccio

Opera: *Bucolicum carmen, De casibus virorum illustrium, De claris mulieribus, De genealogiis deorum gentilium, De montibus, silvis, fontibus, lacubus, fluminibus, stagnis seu paludibus, et de nominibus maris, De vita et moribus Francisci Petrarchae, Decamerone, Elegia di Madonna Fiammetta (Fiammetta amorosa), Epistolae, Il Corbaccio (Laberinto d'amore), Il filocolo, Il filostrato, Teseida, Vita di Dante Alighieri (Tratello in laude di Dante)*

Works: *Bucolic Song, On the Fates of Famous Men (Fall of Princes), Concerning Famous Women (Forty-six lives), On the Genealogy of the Gods of the Gentiles, On Mountains, Forests, Springs, Lakes, Rivers, Swamps or Marshes and on the Names of the Sea, The Life and Manners of Franciscus Petrarca, Ten Days' Work (Decameron), Amorous Fiammetta, Letters, Corbaccio, A Pleasant Disport of Diuers Noble Personages, Il filostrato, Teseida, Life of Dante Alighieri*

082. *Decamerone / Ten Days' Work*

This collection of 100 short stories in Italian was compiled between 1349 and 1353. The title (Greek: "deka" = ten, "hēmera" = days) points to the setting of the narrative: ten days of storytelling. Almost all stories are taken from earlier traditions, some come from classical sources (e.g. Apuleius' *Metamorphoses*), others are taken from medieval French legends and fabliaux. Boccaccio changes many of the stories and flavours them according to his own taste. He must have felt the demoralizing impact of the *Decameron*, because for a long time he did not tell Petrarch about the book, and his *De casibus* is so obviously moralizing that it seems to be from another author. In his later years Boccaccio regretted having written the *Decameron*, he even wanted to burn it.

Boccaccio's framing device is the outbreak of the plague that struck Europe in 1348—1349. The opening passage describes the devastating effects of the plague on Florence. The fear of contagion leads to a suspension of all bonds of law, religion and morality. In this environment a group of ten young Florentines, seven ladies and three men, decide to flee the city and to temporarily move to a country house. As the deadly disease threatenes the world outside, these young aristocrats create a small paradise of refined idleness, a model of social order and discipline. For each day of their quarantine

典范。他们每天选择他们中间一个人当他们的领导。这些领导规定一天的吃饭时间，休息时间，并且决定哪天应该讲什么样的故事，因为这个团体的主要活动就是说故事。然而，因为每天的题目不是很具体，人们就讲各式各样的故事，有高尚的，也有粗鲁的，有悲剧性的，也有好笑的。第二天的故事是关于"那些在种种困难后得到意外的幸福"，第四天的故事应该是关于那些"因爱情而走向悲剧"的人，第八天的题目是"妇女陷害男人或男人陷害妇女的诡计"。最后一天的题目是"那些在爱情或其他方面表现慷慨和高尚态度的人"，而在这里有一些充满智慧的克己者，也有纯洁仰慕的例子。

所有故事都描述中世纪晚期那种多彩的生活，包括骑士、贵族女士、城民们、圣职人员、隐修者、农民、工匠和囚犯。关于男女恋爱的浪漫故事很多，但作者采取一种礼貌的、幽默的方式叙述这些情节。有时候述说这些故事的女士们脸红了，但这时听众开始大笑，而故事的叙述也得以继续。然而，该书的特殊因素是所有说故事的人的角度都是相当世俗化的。他们并不认为爱情是一种神圣的、神秘的或理想的事，反而从一个自然主义的角度去描述爱情。因此很多故事涉及婚外恋。在中世纪文学中老一套的人物是充满淫欲的司铎或隐修者，而 Boccaccio 也几次引用这些角色，又加上寻求爱情的修女。在另一方面 Boccaccio 也支持这样的观点：爱情可能是一种高尚的、提高素质的事，而爱情也应该离不开伦理道德，比如关于"鹰"的故事。

鹰的故事属于第五天(5,9)。Federigo 是一个年轻的 Florentia 贵族人士，他始终钦慕贵族女士 Monna Giovanna，而为了赢得她的青睐，他举办很多宴席和表演比赛。然而，Monna Giovanna 已经有了丈夫和一个儿子，她完全忽视一切献给她的礼物和以她的名义举行的活动。不久后 Federigo 耗尽了他的一切财富，因穷困被迫退隐到郊区的一个小农场，在那里他唯一的财产是一只鹰，他非常喜爱这只鹰。

基于命运的奇妙转折，Monna Giovanna 的丈夫突然生病，当他意识到他的生命快要结束时，他写下一份遗嘱，其中规定他的小儿子应该是唯一的继承人；如果儿子去世，Monna Giovanna 将要继承一切财产。在她的丈夫去世后，Monna Giovanna 遵循一个古老的风俗和儿子一起退居到郊区几个月；她居住的地方离 Federigo 的农场不远。她的儿子喜欢飞鸟并且很快成为 Federigo 和他的鹰的朋友。他几次见到这只具有魅力的鹰并且很希望拥有它，但他始终不敢向 Federigo 提出这事。有一天这个小男孩生病了，而 Monna Giovanna 尽可能地照顾他，但情况越来越严重。什么东西能帮助这个小男孩子战胜他的疾病呢？最终她的儿子说："妈妈，如果我能拥有 Federigo 的鹰，我想我的病很快就会好转的。"

犹豫片刻后，Monna Giovanna 决定第二天早上前往 Federigo 的农场。Federigo 非常惊讶地欢迎她，但 Monna Giovanna 不好意思直接向他要这只鹰，所以她先说她想回报 Federigo 多年的热切爱慕，今天要和他一起吃午餐。Federigo 感到非常高兴并带

they elect a leader from among them. The leaders lay down times for meals, recreation, and they decide on a theme for the stories to be told on that day, since storytelling is the central activity of the group. However, since the directives for the stories are rather general, all kinds of narratives are presented, some are refined, others rough, some are tragical, others are funny. The second day is dedicated to "those, who after struggling with many calamities arrive at an unexpected happy end", the fourth day should cover the fates of "those whose love found a sad end", the theme of the eighth day are "tricks which a woman plays on a man of a man plays on a woman". The last day treats those "who have shown magnanimity and nobility in love affairs or in other matters", and here are examples of wise abstention and pure admiration.

All stories describe the colourful life of the late Middle Ages, the knights, noble women, citizens, clergy, monks, farmers, craftsmen, and criminals. The numerous love stories and erotic adventures are told in a decent and humorous way. Sometimes the ladies who tell the stories blush themselves, but then all have a good laugh, and the narrative continues. However, what is special about the book is, that all storytellers adopt a very secular tone. They view love not as something sacred, mystical, or ideal, but describe love from a naturalist perspective. Thus there are many stories about adulterous relationships, and the medieval stock character of the lecherous priest or monk appears more than once, accompanied by lecherous nuns. On the other hand, Boccaccio also supports the view that love can be ennobling and should be joined with morality, as in the story of the falcon.

The story of the falcon is told on the fifth day (5,9). A young Florentine aristocrat, Federigo, admires a noble lady, Monna Giovanna, and in order to win her heart he arranges feasts and tournaments. However, Monna Giovanna who has a husband and a son, ignores all the feasts arranged in her name and all the presents sent to her. Soon Federigo has wasted all his wealth, and his poverty forces him to retreat to a small estate on the countryside, having nothing left besides a falcon which he cherishes deeply.

By a sudden turn of fate the husband of Monna Giovanna becomes very sick, and as he sees that he is close to death he writes a testament in which he orders that his little son should be the only heir, and if the son should die, Monna Giovanna should inherit all his riches. After the death of her husband, Monna Giovanna follows an old custom and retreats with her son to the countryside for a couple of months, to a place not far from Federigo's farm. Her son likes birds and soon becomes a friend of Federigo and his falcon. Having seen the graceful bird a few times he develops the ardent desire to possess it, but the boy never dares to tell Federigo about this. One day the boy falls sick, and Monna Giovanna cares for him as good as she can, but the situation seems to get worse. What could help the boy to recover his health? Finally the boy says: "Mother, if I just could have Federigo's falcon, I think I would recover soon."

After some hesitation Monna Giovanna decides to walk over to Federigo's farm on the next morning. Federigo greets her with great surprise, and as Monna Giovanna is ashamed to directly demand the falcon, she says that she wants to reward him for his

她进入他的房子和花园中。他想为 Monna Giovanna 准备一顿很好的午餐,但又发现他无法为她提供任何高级的食物。因为他很穷且他没有想到别的方法,他就杀死了他的鹰并要求仆人用鹰准备一顿美餐。两个人一起吃饭,但后来 Monna Giovanna 还是告诉 Federigo 她的儿子生病的事并且恳请 Federigo 让她带走他的鹰。当 Federigo 听到这些话时,他开始流泪并说他想提供一顿美餐,而他们两个人刚刚吃完了这只鹰。Monna Giovanna 感到失望,但同时她也佩服 Federigo 的慷慨。几天后她的儿子去世,而她的弟兄们劝 Monna Giovanna 再次结婚。当他们听说 Monna Giovanna 要和那位穷困的 Federigo 结婚时,他们一开始拒绝他,但因为他们也意识到这个人具有崇高的精神气质,他们最终同意。这样 Federigo 能与他所爱慕的女士结合并且享受长久、幸福的生活。

083. 《名人之堕落》

受 Petrarca 的 *De viris illustribus*(1338—1339 年)的启发,Boccaccio 在 1355—1360 年间写下了这部著作。书名已经暗示了作者的目标:他的故事都想说明这一点,任何一个依赖于他的好运气的人在临终时都会遭受失败和灾难。1350 年后 Boccaccio 放弃了轻浮的虚构而转向严肃的研究;与此转变相应,本著作不是以 Florentia 的意大利语写的,而是用拉丁语写成的。

作者 Boccaccio 虚构了一些历史性的或传奇中的男人(和几个妇女)来到他的房间并开始向他报告他们的灾难性遭遇。第一个人物是 Adam,此后有几个古代国王、一位埃及女王、希腊的英雄,比如 Atreus 和他的兄弟 Thyestes,罗马皇帝 Tiberius 和 Caligula 以及很多来自 12、13 世纪意大利的人物。这些故事的结局都表达这样的严肃教训:人的骄傲和世俗的成就都是暂时的、变化无常的,而每一个人都应该意识到自己权力的局限性。

几年后(1360—1362 年)Boccaccio 写了另一部著作,目标显然是弥补第一个文集的缺点。*The claris mulieribus*(《名女列传》)包含 104 个有名的妇女的传记,从 Eva 开始一直到意大利南部 Neapolis 的 Joanna 女王,她曾慷慨地支持了 Boccaccio 的文学作品。Boccaccio 并不赞美女性的美德,他更多地揭露她们的弱点和她们那种无法控制的欲望。他使用一些来自 Tacitus、Vergilius、Ovidius、Valerius Maximus 的文献,但他又多次加入自己虚构的情节,因为他的文学理想既是娱乐又是教训。

passionate love throughout all these years by having lunch together with him. Of course Federigo is overjoyed and leads her into his house and to the garden. As he wants to prepare a good meal for Monna Giovanna he discovers that he cannot offer her anything, and since he is poor and sees no other way he kills his falcon and asks the servant to prepare it for lunch. They enjoy their meal together, but after lunch Monna Giovanna finally tells him of the sickness of her son and entreats him to let her take the falcon to her son. As Federigo hears this, he tearfully tells her that he wanted to offer her a good lunch and that they just have eaten the falcon. Monna Giovanna is disappointed but also admires the generosity of Federigo. After a few days her son passes away, and her brothers persuade Monna Giovanna to remarry. As they hear that she would choose the poor Federigo, they object, but seeing the noble spirit of the man, they finally agree. Thus Federigo is united with the lady of his heart and enjoys a long, happy life.

083. *De casibus virorum illustrium / On the Fates of Famous Men*

Inspired by Petrarch's *De viris illustribus* (1338—1339), Boccaccio wrote this work in the years from 1355 to 1360. The title already reveals the intention of the author: his stories want to show that any successful man who trusts in his good fortune will face a disaster at the end of his life. In accordance with Boccaccio's turn from frivolous fiction to serious studies after 1350, this work is not written in the vernacular language of Florence but in Latin.

Boccaccio imagines that famous men (and some women) from history and legend come to his room and start to tell him their sad stories, so that he should remind the reader of their calamities and tragic fate. The first figure is Adam, then follow several kings of antiquity, a queen of Egypt, Greek heroes like Atreus and his brother Thyestes, the Roman emperors Tiberius and Caligula, and many famous men from Italy of the 12th and 13th century. All stories of these famous men lead to a rigid moral at the end: human pride and earthly success are transitory, and every man should realize the limits of his power.

Some years later (1360—1362) Boccaccio wrote a work that obviously should have complemented the first collection: *De claris mulieribus* (*On Famous Women*), containing 104 biographies of famous women, starting with Eve and leading up to Queen Joanna of Naples, the generous supporter of Boccaccio's literary efforts. Boccaccio is far from praising the virtues of women, he rather exposes their weaknesses and their untameable desire. He uses texts from Tacitus, Virgil, Ovid, and Valerius Maximus, but he often adds his own fictions since he wants both to entertain and to teach.

俄瑞斯梅的尼古拉斯(约 1320—1382)

生于法国北部的 Caen 地区,曾在 Paris 上学,于 1377 年成为 Lisieux 的主教。他为 Aristoteles 的许多著作写注,因此成为非常渊博的数学家、自然哲学家、物理学家和神学家。他曾被称为 14 世纪最伟大的科学家之一。

著作:《论诸比例》、《论天界运行的一致性》(天文学著作)、《诸品质和运行的条件》、《论货币的来源、本性、法律和变化》(早期的经济学著作)、《论诸力量的一致性和特殊性》(在力学方面提出新的观点)、《反驳占星术》、《论天界》、《论 Euklid 的几何学》、《论各事物的广度》、《论诸比例》;Nicolaus 的部分著作是用法语写成的。

084.《货币论》

本著作的全名是 *De origine, natura, iure et mutationibus monetarum*(《论货币的起源、本质、规律和变化》),它成书于 1360 年,1484 年首次印行,但后来多次被重印,尤其在 17 世纪。这部作品是独一无二的,是当时唯一的专门探讨国度经济问题的。因此,本著作为作者赢得了"中世纪唯一经济学家"的美名。原文是拉丁语,但 Oresme 也著有一个法语译本。

Oresme 抨击中世纪货币制度的种种缺陷,尤其是各地货币膨胀的问题。在前半部作者使用一种相当科学的方式来描述钱币的现象。任何一个高度组织的人类社会都需要钱币,而钱币的目标是促进贸易。贸易导致资源的公平分配,而在这个过程中钱财可能是正义与公道的表现。

本论文第二个部分分析不同类型的贬值现象。对于那些控制造币局的人来说,贬值可能有好处,但在另一方面整个社会将会因货币贬值而遭受损失。有的国王甚至会利用自己的铸币权来剥削他们的人民并为自己搜刮财富。Oresme 很尖锐地批评和控诉那些降低硬币中的金子或银子成份的行为,因为他们这样降低钱的"实质价值",而同时保持钱的"名义价值"。如果一种货币的实质价值不再符合其名义价值,那些拥有钱财的人实际上是被欺骗的。最终,钱并不属于国王,而属于人民——人民需要通过出售自然物品而获得钱财。钱是一种"不自然的财富"。Oresme 的观点对 17 世纪占主导地位的重商主义(mercantilism)理论具有相当大的影响。该理论认为黄金和白银决定一个国度的财富,所以要注意与他国进行贸易时不要输出太多金子或银子。

Nicolaus Oresmensis / Nicholas Oresme

Opera: *Algorismus proportionum, De commensurabilitate et incommensurabilitate motuum caeli, De configurationibus qualitatum et motuum, De origine monetarum (=De origine, natura, iure et mutationibus monetarum), De uniformitate et difformitate intensionum, Quaestio contra divinatores horoscopios, Quaestiones de sphaera, Quaestiones super geometriam Euclidis, Tractatus de latitudinibus formarum, Tractatus proportionum*

Works: *On Proportions, On the Commensurability of Heavenly Motions, On the Configurations of Qualities and Motions, The Origin of Money (=On the Origin, Nature, Law and Change of Currencies), On the Uniformity and Diversity of Forces, Against Diviners and Horoskopes, On the Spheres, On Euclid's Geometry, On the Latitude of Things, An Essay on Proportions*

084. *De origine monetarum / The Origin of Money*

The full title of this work is: *De origine, natura, iure et mutationibus monetarum (On the Origin, Nature, Law, and Change of Currencies)*, it was written in 1360 and printed in 1484 for the first time, but it saw many reprints, especially in the 17th century. The study is unique and at that time it was the only treatise specifically concerned with questions of national economy, thus the book earned the author the reputation of being "the only economist of the Middle Ages". The text is in Latin, but Oresme also made a French translation.

Oresme wanted to attack the many shortcomings of the medieval minting system, especially the constant inflation of currencies. In the first part of the book the author describes the phenomenon of money in a very scientific way. Any structured human society needs money, and the purpose of money is to facilitate trade. Trade aims at an equal distribution of resources, and money can be an expression of justice and fairness in the process.

The second part of the treatise analyzes different kinds of devaluations. The inflation of a currency or a coin can have advantages for those who control the mint bureau, but the society on the other hand will suffer from the results of currency devaluation. Some kings even may try to use their mint prerogatives in order to exploit their people and thus accumulate wealth for themselves. Oresme sharply criticizes and accuses these unjust rulers who diminish the amount of gold or silver of the coins and thus bring down the "material value" while keeping the "nominal value" of the currency. If the "material value" of a currency is no longer proportional to its "nominal value", then the owners of money are actually cheated. In the final analysis money does not belong to the kings but rather to the people who acquire money by selling natural goods. Money is "artificial wealth". Oresme's principles had considerable impact on the mercantilist theories of economy that prevailed in the 17th century: the wealth of a country is determined by the amount of gold that is available, and it is thus important not to lose the valuable metals by trading with other countries.

Oresme 还给 Aristoteles 的 *De Caelo*(《论天》)写过注,其中将宇宙比喻成一个钟表,而这个比喻意味着从 Aristoteles 那种有机的世界观向比较现代的宇宙论的伟大转变。那些引导每一个天体的精灵的"神圣的、活的原则"被放弃,取而代之是一种机械(钟表),而这个钟表曾经(由神)被创造,并获得了一个使它持续运动的 impetus(动力,惯性)。此后,machina mundi("世界机械")这个词在科学著作中成为普遍被使用的,比如 Nicolaus Cusanus 曾多次引用这个比喻。Oresme 已经表达了惯性定律,因为他相信神在某个时刻创造了宇宙,此后使它遵从某些机械性的规则。在数学的领域中,Oresme 发现了无理数。

In his commentary on Aristotle's *De Caelo* (*On the Heaven*), Oresme compares the universe to a clock, and this metaphor implies the great change from the organismic Aristotelian world view to a more modern view of the universe. The "holy and living principles" of the intelligences that were in charge of each celestial body were abandoned in favor of a mechanism (a clock) that was once created (by God) and received an impetus to continue its movement. Thus the expression "machina mundi" became popular in scientific writings, for example it is often mentioned in the works of Nicolaus of Cusa. Oresme already formulated the theory of impetus, based on his belief that God once created the universe and then let it follow certain mechanical rules. In the field of mathematics, Oresme discovered the irrational numbers.

威克利夫（约 1330—1384）

大约生于 1330 年，家庭背景不明，他曾在 Oxford 大学攻读哲学并任教，1360 年成为 Balliol College 的 magister artium（哲学老师）。他在教会任职并有一些收入，后来一直在 Lutterworth 教堂；他于 1363 年学习神学，1369 年后在 Oxford 的 Queen's College 和 Canterbury College 教授神学，于 1372 年获得神学博士学位，曾被提名为 Canterbury College 的院长，但因为当地的 OSB（本笃会）人士反对他，于 1370 年被迫退位。他的思想和著作于 1373 年第一次受谴责，而在 1375 年后他写下很多与传统信仰有冲突的著作，他反对教宗、隐修院制度、圣职人员的独身生活，重新解释圣事和对圣人的尊敬。教廷反驳他的观点，而 1382 年在 London 召开的主教会议谴责了他的教导。同年 Wyclif 第一次中风，1384 年在 Lutterworth 去世。

著作：《论基督及其敌人反基督》、《论世俗政权》、《论十诫》、《论神的统治》、《论教会》、《论感恩祭》、《论国君的任务》、《论基督的贫穷》、《论教宗的权威》、《论三位一体》、《论圣言》、《论〈圣经〉的真理》（认为《圣经》是信仰唯一的基础）、《奋斗中教会的镜子》、《福音书》、《全部〈圣经〉注解》、《存有大全》、《三论》（1382 年成书，是作者种种主张的总结），还有其他的著作。

085. 《论世俗政权》

这部著作的别名是 *Tractatus de civili dominio*，成书时间是 1374 年或 1375 年，作者当时在 Queen's College 任教。

Wyclif 认为基督主要是谦卑、贫穷和受苦的榜样，而在他的教导中他赞扬《福音书》这个层面。他用《圣经》关于早期教会的描述来与自己同时代教会生活进行对比。他认为组织完备的教会制度并没有很完善地表达《福音书》的理想。他抨击 Avignon 教廷和教宗并说教廷基本上违背了基督宗教的精神。教会不应该有任何财产。国王们和其他的世俗领导有义务去保护"lex evangelica"（"福音的律法"），他们应该帮助民众过一种效法基督的自由和仿效基督及使徒们的清贫生活。在一部后期写下的著作中（*De officio regis*, 1379）他甚至称国王为"vicarius Christi"（"基督的代表"），国王具有相当大的尊严并有义务去传播信仰。因此 Wyclif 允许世俗的统治者去没收教会财产，如果这种财产不被正当使用。

英国的贵族人士自然支持没收教会财产，所以他们也欢迎 Wyclif 的思想，但 Gregorius XI 教宗（1370—1378 年）于 1377 年 5 月谴责了 *De civilio dominio* 中 18 条主张。虽然如此，Wyclif 的教导在英国继续传播了几年。他发行更多的著作，其中采纳

Johannes Wyclif / Wiclif

Opera: *De Christo et suo adversario antichristo, De civili dominio, De decem praeceptis, De divino dominio, De ecclesia, De eucharistia, De officio regis, De paupertate Christi, De potestate papae, De trinitate, De verbi (=De incarnatione), De veritate sacrae Scripturae, Dialogus sive speculum ecclesiae militantis, Opus evangelicum, Postilla super totam Bibliam, Summa de ente, Trialogus*

Works: *On Christ and His Enemy the Antichrist, On Civil Power, On the Ten Commandments, On the Reign of God, The Church, The Eucharist, The Duty of a King, The Poverty of Christ, On the Authority of the Pope, On Trinity, On the Word, On the Truth of Scripture, Dialogue or Mirror of the Militant Church, The Gospel, Explanations of the Whole Bible, Sum of Being, Trialogus*

085. *De civili dominio / On Civil Power*

This work is also known under the title *Tractatus de civili dominio* and was written in 1374 or 1375 when the author taught at the Queen's College.

Wyclif sees in Christ mainly a model of humility, poverty and suffering, and in his teachings he extols this dimension of the gospel. He compares the Biblical descriptions of the life of the early Church with the ecclesiastical life of his own time and concludes that the established Church does not fully express the ideals of the gospel. He attacks the Papal court at Avignon as basically contradicting the spirit of Christianity and denies that the Church should have any possessions. Kings and other secular rulers have the duty to protect the "lex evangelica" (law of the Gospel), they should help the population to lead a life that imitates the freedom and poverty of Christ and the apostles. In a later work (*De officio regis*, 1379) he even adresses the king as "vicarius Christi" (representative of Christ), who enjoys considerable dignity and has the duty to spread the faith. Thus Wyclif allows secular rulers to confiscate Church property if that property is not used in an adequate way.

The English nobility which naturally favored secularization of Church property welcomed Wyclif's ideas, but Pope Gregory XI (1370—1378) condemned 18 sentences of *De civili dominio* in May 1377. However, the teachings of Wyclif continued to spread in England for some more years. He published more works in which he adopted a firm realism (against nominalism), Biblicism (with fundamentalist inclinations) and Augus-

一种坚定的共相主义(realismus,即与 nominalismus 对立的主张)、"圣经主义"(包括一些基要主义因素)和 Augustinus 主义来攻击当时的教会结构。他反对教会的圣统制(hierarchia)、反对教会财产,他又淡化了诸圣事的意义(参见他关于 transubstantiatio 的理论)。因为 Wyclif 始终坚持贫穷的理想,那些托钵会的修会(方济各会、道明会)在 1380 年之前支持他,而本笃会反对他,因为本笃会在英国有很多地产。Wyclif 的部分观点直接影响了 Jan Hus(1372—1415 年)在波希米亚的运动,另一些则被 16 世纪的新教神学家所发展,但英国圣公会后来并没有正式肯定 Wyclif 的教导。

tinianism in order to attack the structure of the Church of his day. He was opposed to the hierarchy of the Church and ecclesiastical property, he relativized the meaning of the sacraments (confer his theory of transubstantiation). Because he upheld the ideal of poverty, Wyclif was initially supported by the mendicant orders (Franciscans, Dominicans) before 1380, but the Benedictine order opposed him, since the Benedictines had much property in England. Some of Wyclif's tenets directly influenced the movement of Jan Hus (1372—1415) in Bohemia, others were developed by protestant theologians of the 16th century, but the mainstream of the Anglican Church did not officially confirm his teachings later on.

兰格朗(约1330—1400)

William Langland 大概来自英国的 Worcestershire，他可能在一所隐修院学校受过教育，后在 London 当小品圣职人员(cleric in minor orders)，生平不详。

著作：《耕者皮尔斯的梦》：中古英语头韵诗，序诗7章，描写人世生活和七大罪的表现；诗13章，通过 Do-wel(良好先生，普通信徒、农夫)、Do-bet(更好先生，为信仰受苦的人、拯救别人者)和 Do-best(完善先生，人间的天国、新的人类、圣神的光明)叙述基督徒在自知、信仰和博爱方面的进步。

086.《耕者皮尔斯的梦》

这部中古英语头韵诗一般被归于 William Langland。保存有几个版本，最短的长达2400行，最长的有8000行，都包含一些关于 Piers Plowman(耕者皮尔斯)的梦，而在第二个部分有关于"良好"、"更好"和"完善"的故事。

长诗一开始，Will("意愿")沉睡在山谷的小溪旁边。他梦见很多人聚集在一个很大的平原或集市上，而这些人来自社会各个阶层。其中一部分的人是抽象价值的化身。当"意愿"走近时，"教会女士"向他解释背后两个城堡的差别：山上的宏伟城堡属于 Truth(真理，即神)，而在山下的丑陋和恐怖的城堡里住着 False("虚假"，即魔鬼)。教会女士想把艳丽的 Lady Meed("报酬女士")嫁给"虚假"，而 Fickle-tongue("反复无常")和 Liar("撒谎")支持这个计划，只有 Theology("神学")先生提出反对。他向国王建议要安排"报酬女士"和 Conscience("良知")先生结婚。然而，"良知"坚决拒绝"报酬女士"，因此后者说明她的好处和积极贡献。最终国王也意识到"报酬女士"不是很可靠的，所以他说在政治上仅仅要依赖于"良知"和"理性"。

在第二个梦中"意愿"见到"良知"向集市上的群众讲道并劝他们改进他们的生活。结果是七个罪宗，即 Pride(骄傲)、Lechery(淫荡)、Envy(嫉妒)、Avarice(贪婪)、Sloth(懒惰)、Wrath(愤怒)和 Gluttony(贪吃)纷纷忏悔并努力寻求"真理"。因为通往"真理"的路很远，又不好认出，耕者皮尔斯被要求担任一个向导。通过农活、守斋和苦修生活他想指出通往"真理"的路。作者很明显要通过耕者皮尔斯的声音谴责当时的人的缺点和恶习，同时也揭露14世纪末的英国的社会问题。

在下一个梦境的开头出现两个方济各会修士。"意愿"想知道 Do-well("良好")在什么地方，而这两个修士回答："良好在我们这里。"然而，"意愿"不满意于这个回答，而当他遇到别人时，他就关于"良好"、"更好"和"完善"的意义获得很多不同的解释。那些很热切提供自己观点的人包括 Thought(思想)、Wit(智慧)、Dame Study(学习

Langland

Opera: *Piers Plowman*
Works: *Piers Plowman*

086. *Piers Plowman*

This alliterating poem in Middle English is usually attributed to William Langland. There are several versions of the poem, the shortest with a length of 2400 verses, the longest has 8000 verses. All of them contain dreams about Piers Plowman and in the second part the stories of "Do-well", "Do-better" and "Do-best".

The poem starts with "Will" who sleeps at a little creek in a valley. In a dream vision he sees a big field and a market place crowded with many people from all layers of society. Some of the people are personifications of abstract realities. As Will approaches the place, "Lady Holy Church" explains the differences between the two castles seen in the background: the noble castle on the mountain belongs to Truth (God), whereas the ugly and terrifying castle on the foot of the mountain is inhabitated by False (the devil). Lady Church plans to marry the beautiful Lady Meed (Reward) to "False". Figures like "Fickle-tongue" and "Liar" readily support this plan. Only Mr. "Theology" opposes this wedding and suggests to the King to arrange a marriage between Lady Meed and Mr. Conscience. However, Conscience resolutely rejects Lady Meed who now defends her usefulness and positive contribution. Finally the King also realizes that Lady Meed is not reliable and decides to reign only with the assistance of Conscience and Reason.

In a second dream Will observes how Conscience preaches to the many people on the market place and urges them to amend their ways. As a result Pride, Lechery, Envy, Avarice, Sloth, Wrath, and Gluttony (the seven cardinal sins) do repentance and try to seek Truth. Since the way to Truth is long and not easy to discern, Piers Plowman is asked to be a guide on this way. Through hard work on the fields, fasting, and ascetic life style he tries to show the people the way to Truth. It is clear that through the voice of Piers Plowman the author wants to castigate his contemporaries for their shortcomings and vices, at the same time he exposes the many social problems of late fourteenth-century England.

The next vision starts with two Franciscan friars. Will wants to know where "Do-well" lives, and they answer: "Do-well is with us." However, Will is not satisfied with this answer, and as he encounters many other people he gets many different explanations

夫人)、Clergy(圣职人员)和他的妻子 Dame Scripture(圣经夫人)。这些解释的基本观点是,"良好"是一个生活在世俗世界,但遵守基督宗教教导的人;"更好"已经超越了世俗的欲望和追求,而"思想"、"忍耐"和"仁爱"引导他,所以他能够帮助别人并引导他们走向"真理"。"完善"是宗教上的领导,比如一位主教或教宗,他致力于改进社会。

在另一个梦境中,"意愿"见到一个穷困的人骑驴进入耶路撒冷,而这个人很像耕者皮尔斯。此后他观望耶稣在十字架上受苦去世。他的苦难意味着灵魂们的得救,但神的四个女儿("怜悯"、"和平"、"真理"与"正义",参见 *Ps* 85:11)在这个问题上的意见不一致。"怜悯"与"和平"认为 Maria 之子是为了解放先知们和犹太人的祖先而来,使他们脱离黑暗的领域,但"真理"与"正义"认为不能放这些灵魂出去。突然耶稣出现在地狱的门口并释放他要解救的灵魂。此后四个姐妹彼此和好。此时"意愿"醒来并提醒他的妻子和女儿庆祝复活节。

在长诗的结尾部分耕者皮尔斯以理想教宗的形象出现,他体现出 Do-best("完善")的价值。他想推动教会改革,因为腐败和恶习在多方面困扰着信徒们的团体。"意愿"甚至梦见圣灵(圣神)的降临,而皮尔斯抵抗 Anti-Christ(反基督)。值得注意的是,在整篇长诗中,"真理"、"良好"、"更好"和"完善"始终都是被寻找和追求的价值,人们无法完全实践它们。

about the meaning of "Do-well", "Do-Better" and "Do-Best". Those who eagerly offer their views are Thought, Wit (Wisdom), Dame Study, Mr. Clergy and his wife Dame Scripture. Some common understanding seems to be that Do-well is a person who lives in the secular world but follows the teachings of Christianity. Do-better has already overcome secular passions and desires, he is guided by Thought, Patience, and Love. Thus Do-better is able to help other people and to guide them to the Truth. Do-best is a religious leader like a bishop or a pope, who endeavours to change society to the better.

In another dream vision Will sees a poor man riding a donkey into Jerusalem, and the man looks like Piers Plowman. Then he observes how Jesus suffers and dies on the cross. His suffering means the redemption of the souls, but concerning this issue the four daughters of God (Mercy, Peace, Truth, and Justice, confer *Ps* 85:11) are divided. Mercy and Peace think that the son of Mary came to free the prophets and Jewish ancestors from the realm of darkness, but Truth and Justice believe they must remain in hell. Then Jesus appears at the gate of hell and frees the souls he wants to save, whereupon the four sisters are reconciled again. At this point Will wakes up and reminds his wife and daughter to celebrate Easter.

In the final part of the poem Piers Plowman appears in the image of an ideal Pope, embodying the values of "Do-best". He wants to promote reforms within the Church, since the evil of corruption besets the community of the faithful. Will even sees in this dream the coming of the Holy Spirit and how Piers resists the Anti-Christ. It is remarkable that throughout the whole poem "Truth", "Do-well", "Do-better", and "Do-best" are always to be striven for, they are ideals that are never fully realized.

傅华萨(约 1333—1400)

约于 1333 年生于(法国)Brabant 地区的 Valenciennes,是一位学者、圣职人员、诗人和宫廷史官,曾在英国女王 Philippa de Hainaut 的宫廷生活,后成为法国 Guy II de Chatillon 的随身司铎,曾去苏格兰、意大利、西班牙旅行,曾为各地王家贵族服务。他于 1400 年在 Chimay de Hainaut 去世。

著作:《闻见录》、《含情脉脉的钟》(将人心比喻成一个钟表)、《梅利亚多尔》(一个骑士的恋爱传奇)以及众多诗篇。

087.《闻见录》

这部法语著作的全名是 Chroniques de France, d'Angleterre, d'Escoce, d'Espaigne, de Bretaigne, de Gascogne, de Flandres, et lieux circunuoisins(《法国、英国、苏格兰、西班牙、布列坦尼、加其孔、佛兰德和周围地区的历史》),共分为 4 卷,成书时间是 1373 年至 1400 年。

Froissart 描述英法"百年战争"(一般约定其年代为 1337 年到 1453 年)中的"伟大武功和壮举"。他颂扬骑士精神的理想和宫廷生活的优雅华丽,并且劝告读者应该仰慕骑士生活的荣誉。然而,由于很多社会性的和技术性的变化,骑士生活实际上在 14 世纪开始逐渐没落。由于战争的影响,一些公国或伯国突然变得繁荣富强,这使它们在文化生活上暂时占有主导地位。

作为一位圣职人员和编写历史的人,Froissart 似乎探访过所有重要的欧洲朝廷,而他也直接受自己环境的影响,比如第 4 卷是在巴伐利亚的 Albrecht 的朝廷写的。作者没有什么政治倾向,这一点可能使现代的读者感到奇怪,但当时的法国并不是一个统一的国度,而是许多独立小国的组合体。根据 Froissart 的说法在各方面都有很多精神崇高的战士,而他喜欢叙述他们的伟大交战和武艺。他的生动文笔是扣人心弦的,很多轶事和故事描述社会生活,比如一些婚礼和丧礼,这样他的著作成为描绘封建时代和宫廷生活最详细、最形象化的文献。

人们曾经观察到 Froissart 主要叙述他的资助人的宫廷的华丽奢侈,同时他忽略了对 14 世纪普通人民的艰苦生活的描述。他决定专门描绘英雄们的伟大并忽视了种种战役的受害者和他们苦难的根源。

Jean Froissart

Opera: *Chroniques, L'Horloge amoureux, Meliador*
Works: *Chronicles, The Clockwork of Love, Meliador*

087. *Chroniques / Chronicle*

The full title of this French work is *Chroniques de France, d'Angleterre, d'Escoce, d'Espaigne, de Bretaigne, de Gascogne, de Flandres, et lieux circunuoisins* (*Chronicle of France, England, Scotalnd, Spain, the Bretagne, the Gascogne, Flanders, and of the Surrounding Regions*). It is divided into 4 volumes and was written between 1373 and 1400.

Froissart describes the "honorable adventures and feats of arms" during the Hundred Years' War between France and England (conventionally set at 1337—1453). He extols the ideals of knighthood and the splendor of courtly life, and he also urges the reader to aspire to the glory of knightly life. However, the 14th century saw the slow decline of the knighthood due to many social and technological changes. Because of the wars some duchies or counties became suddenly very rich or influential and thus for a time were able to play a leading role in cultural life.

Being a cleric and chronicler, Froissart visited almost all important European courts, and he wrote under the direct influence of his environment, for example the fourth volume was written at the court of Albrecht of Bavaria. The author had no political inclinations, a fact which could puzzle modern readers, but in Froissart's day France was not a unified country but rather a conglomeration of independent small states. According to Froissart there were many honorable warriors and knights at all sides, and he delights in telling the great battles they fought. His captivating and colorful writing style, the many anecdotes and descriptions of social events like weddings and funerals make his work the most detailed and visualized document of feudal times and courtly ideals.

It has been observed that Froissart concentrates mainly on the courtly pageantry of his patrons while neglecting to look at the ordinary or dire life of the common people of the 14th century. He decides to exclusively portray heroic greatness and overlooks the victims of the numerous feuds and the causes of their sufferings.

杰弗里·乔叟（约 1343—1400）

约于 1342 年或 1343 年出生在 London，来自中产阶级家庭，他曾为 Ulster 的女伯爵服务，1359 年到法国参加围攻 Rheims 的战争，被敌人逮捕，但 Edward III 赎出他。1366 年 Chaucer 与 Philippa Pan 结婚，1367 年在宫廷任职。他于 1370 年开始写作，被视为早期英语文学的主要诗人，因为其首次创作了杰出的英语作品。他的著作受法国文学、Dante、Boccaccio 和 Alanus ab Insulis 等人的影响。

著作：《公爵夫人之书》、《声誉之宫》(2000 多行诗)、《殉情女子传》、《百鸟议会》(700 行诗)、《坎特伯雷故事集》(24 位朝圣者的故事，全部在去坎特伯雷的路上讲述，包括对骑士、隐修士、司铎的理想描述)、《哲学的慰藉》(Boethius 名著的翻译)、《特洛勒斯与克丽西德》(8000 多行诗)

088. 《坎特伯雷故事集》

这部未完成的杰作约成书于 1390 年至 1400 年间。它对中古英语诗歌的风格有很大贡献，因为作者多次使用雅韵，具有很丰富的词汇，又采取所谓的 enjambment 的方式(即一句话的思想跨越几行)。这样英语的诗歌变得更流畅，更富有表现力。故事本身受了 Boccaccio 的 *Decamerone* 的启发，但与 Boccaccio 的名著不同，Chaucer 的朝圣者多次打断对方的话，或他们评论别人的叙述。

他所叙述的是一个由 30 人组成的朝圣团，他们在 London 城的 Tobard Inn 聚集，将要去探访 Thomas Becket(1118—1170 年)在 Canterbury 的墓。在其著名的前言中 Chaucer 描述了春天，这个季节激发了人们去旅游的想法，所以作者已经暗示这些朝圣者的动机包括很多种世俗的和宗教性的因素。Chaucer 也加入这个朝圣团并叙述自己的观察。在开始他们同意每个人要说 4 个故事，但最终只有 20 个完整的和 2 个不完整的故事。

正如作者告诉我们，*Canterbury Tales* 的框架叙述，即向一个神圣地方的朝圣活动，是人生之旅的象征：
"人间不过是一条充满悲哀的大路，
我们都是来去匆匆的朝圣者，
死亡则是人间苦难的终结。"(1,2847)

这些朝圣者是一个好斗的磨坊主、一个厨师、一个来自 Oxford 的学者(他喜欢学习和教书)、Bath 的妻子(她是一个有吸引力的、健谈的女士并表达一些具有女权主义倾向的观点)、一个骑士和他的儿子(后者代表典型的宫殿爱人和乡间贵族)、一个

Geoffrey Chaucer

Works: *Book of the Duchess, House of Fame, Legend of Good Women, Parlement of Foules, The Canterbury Tales, The Consolation of Philosophy, Troilus and Criseyde*

088. *The Canterbury Tales*

This masterpiece was written between 1390 and 1400 and was left unfinished. It made a big contribution to Middle English poetic style by the rich use of rhyme, a wide vocabulary, and the device of enjambment (the carry-over of an idea from one line to the next), thus making English poetry more fluid and expressive. The narrative was inspired by Boccaccio's *Decamerone*, but in difference to Boccaccio's work, Chaucer's pilgrims frequently interrupt each other and comment on each other's stories.

The narrative is about a group of 30 pilgrims who meet at Tobard Inn, London, in order to set forth to visit the shrine of Thomas Becket (1118—1170) at Canterbury. In the famous prologue Chaucer describes the spring time which inspires people to travel, and thus he already suggests that there are different kinds of secular and religious motivations alive in the pilgrims. Chaucer joins the pilgrims and makes his own observations. Initially it is agreed that each of the pilgrims tells 4 stories, but finally there are only 20 complete and 2 incomplete narratives.

As the author tells us, the frame story of the *Canterbury Tales*, the pilgrimage to a sacred place is a symbol of the journey of life:
"This world nys but a thurghfare ful of wo,
And we been pilgrymes, passing to and fro.
Deeth is an ende of every worldly soore."
("This world is but a thoroughfare of woe,
And we are pilgrims, passing to and fro.
Death is the end of every worldly sore." 1, 2847)

The individual characters are a belligerent miller, a cook, a clerk from Oxford who likes to learn and to teach, the wife of Bath, who is an attractive and outspoken lady with feminist views, a knight and his son, the squire representing the typical courtly lover and

医生、一个律师、一个水手、一个商人、一个工匠和一个农夫。好几个人来自宗教领域：一个修女和一个具有宫廷贵族风范的修女院院长、一个隐修者、一个修士、一个牧灵人士、一个堂区司铎、还有一个以细小的声音推销赎罪券的人。在某种意义上他们的故事反映出他们的社会地位和他们的世界观。他们所叙述的故事来自不同的文学形式，包括骑士文学和浪漫情节（骑士）、动物寓言（修女和司铎）、所谓的 fabliau（一种讽刺性的、甚至淫秽的小故事，参见磨坊主和水手的故事）、圣人的传记（修女）、关于圣母的奇迹的报告（女院长）、一种布道稿（牧灵者）和关于婚姻生活的评论（Bath 的妻子）。其中有很多故事涉及男女关系和婚姻生活。一方面 Bath 的妻子认为妻子应该控制丈夫，但来自 Oxford 的学者要求妻子必须为丈夫服务。在骑士的故事中出现的 Emily 被形容为"比百合花更美，比五月更鲜艳"，而她唱歌就"和一个天使一样"。磨坊主描述一个被称为 Alison 的妇女，她"和一棵梨树一样美丽，她的脸与新铸的钱币一样明亮"。她"比羊毛还软"，唱歌就"像一只落在谷仓上的燕子"。

rural aristocrat, a physician, a lawyer, a shipman, a merchant, a craftsman, and a farmer. There are many figures from the world of religion: a nun and a prioress with courtly manners, a monk, a friar, a parson (=pastor), a priest, and a pardoner who sells indulgences with a feeble voice. Their narratives in some way reflect their social positions and their world views. The stories they tell are from different literary genres, they comprise chivalric romance (the knight), beast fable (the nun and the priest), fabliau (a cynical, satirical, even obscene story, told by the miller and the shipman), saint's life (nun), report of a miracle of the Virgin (prioress), sermon (parson) and comments on marriage life (wife of Bath). Many of the stories comment on the relationship of the sexes and on marriage life. Whereas the wife of Bath thinks that the wife should control her husband, the clerk from Oxford demands that a wife must serve the husband. In the tale of the knight a certain Emily is described as "fairer than the lily, fresher than May", who sings "like an angel", whereas the miller describes a woman named Alison as beautiful "like a pear tree, her face bright as a new-minted coin". She is "softer than wool" and "sings like a swallow sitting on a barn".

若望（约 1350—1414）

捷克 Saaz 人，诗人，曾当过律师或官员。

著作：《波希米亚的耕夫》（一个悼念妻子早逝的人与"死亡先生"的对话；死亡仅仅从理性的角度贬低人生的价值，但"耕夫"说，上主所创造的人是美善的。）

089.《波希米亚的耕夫》

本对话篇大概成书于 1400 年，其主角是死亡和妻子刚刚去世的耕夫。作者是一位波希米亚官员，他很熟悉文学传统（比如 Boethius 的《哲学的慰藉》）。Ackermann（"耕夫"）也许是"作者"或"抄写书本者"的意思（参见拉丁语的 arator）。

耕夫控诉死亡，因为死亡夺取了他的妻子 Margaretha，"她在我内心的花园中是喜乐的芬芳"。为这种盗窃行为，死亡应当受惩罚，因为那个妇女的年龄不大，而耕夫的生活从此将是忧愁悲伤的。"现在她死去了，哀哉！那年那天那时刻她走了哀哉！无耻的死亡，你去地狱吧！但愿上主烧毁你，你与魔鬼相似，你乱害无辜的人。"死亡出现，要为自己抗辩并否认他的行为是"盗窃"："最近我使一个高尚的妇女享受我的恩赐，她是您的妻子吗？"死亡强调人生的种种苦难和辛劳，以之替自己的"贡献"进行辩护。

在双方的辩论中，耕夫控诉死亡说他是无耻的。因为人是按照上主的肖像而创造的，所以杀人等于蔑视上主。在乐园中没有死亡，而死亡并不是美好创造界的一个部分。如果观看任何一个人的脸面（眼睛、耳朵、鼻子），如果意识到每一个人都有理性思考的能力，就能明白人是上主的杰作，是神所爱的受造物。"走开，死亡，你就是人类的敌人，你始终撒谎，始终讽刺。"此时死亡表达某种虚无主义。哪怕人是如此美丽的、聪明的、有尊严的，但他仍然无法回避死亡的网络。如果一切人都必须死去，那么一切知识、科学、哲学、物理学、医学和法学还有什么用处呢？人应该面对死亡，这样应该学习谦虚以及了解自己的局限性。

下个主题是夫妻生活。耕夫说婚姻及夫妻生活在神的眼中是一种非常美好的生活方式，而如果他的妻子没有死去，他将会过一个忠诚的、快乐的、勤劳的生活——但他的妻子已经走了。死亡回答说婚姻生活并不值得赞美，因为它像"雷霆和骤雨"，像"家中有蛇，有狐狸"。老婆们始终有抱怨的心情，无论丈夫太温和或太严厉，婚姻都是一个挑战，都是一种损失。还要赞美妇女们吗？耕夫谴责死亡说他是恨妇女的。他提醒死亡说，Boethius 曾受了一个妇女的启发教育：哲学也是一个妇女！一切人间的美

Johannes de Tepla / John of Saaz

Opera: *Der Ackermann aus Boehmen*
Works: *The Ploughman*

089. *Der Ackermann aus Boehmen / The Ploughman*

This dialog between Death and Ackermann who has lost his wife was probably written in 1400 by a Bohemian official, who knew the literary tradition (for example Boethius' *Consolation*) well. "Ackermann" (plowman) can also mean "scriptor" (conf. Latin arator), that is writer of books.

Ackermann accuses death of having taken away his wife Margaretha, "the flower of my joys in the garden of my heart." Death should be punished for this robbery, for the woman had to die young, and Ackermann's life will be sad and sorrowful now. "Now she is dead, gone for ever! Woe! Oh the year, the day, the hour when she left! You shameless death, go to hell! May God burn you, wipe you out, you have a devilish character, you harm innocent people at random." Death appears to his defence and denies that it was robbery: "Recently I granted my graces to a fine, respectable lady, was she your wife?" Death points to the toils and sorrows of life and in this way tries to defend his "contribution".

After some more arguing, Ackermann accuses death of being shameless: by killing human beings, he despises God, because humans are created in God's image. Death was not in paradise, he is not part of the good creation. A look at the human face (eyes, ear, nose) and the human ability of reasoning can show that man is the work beloved by God, man is His masterpiece. "Let go, Death, you are the enemy of humanity, you will only lie and mock." Now Death expresses a certain nihilism. Even if man is so beautiful, clever and dignified, he will still be caught by Death's net. What then is the use of all the sciences, of philosophy, physics, medicine and jurisprudence, if wise and unlearned, good and evil people must die in the same way? By facing death man should learn humility and the wisdom to know about one's limitations.

The next topic is the value of marital life. Ackermann says that marriage and marital life is a most beautiful form of human life before God, and for the rest of his life he would have led a loyal, happy, laborious life with his wife, who is dead now. Death replies that marriage life deserves no praise, since it is like "thunder and rain", marriage is like "snakes and foxes at home". Wives are always complaining, and no matter whether the husband is too mild or too harsh, marriage is always a challenge and a disadvantage. Should women deserve praise? Ackermann accuses Death of being a hater of

丽的顶峰就是一个高贵的、有节制的、纯洁的妇女。耕夫重复强调骑士和宫廷爱情的理想：在每一个奋斗和每一个战争中，"永恒女性"的因素将有最好的影响。"如果一个人想知道什么是美好的纪律和荣誉，他就应该向高尚的妇女们去学习。"因此"人类的保存、强化和增长都取决于妇女们的高贵精神"。

当耕夫和死亡都淋漓尽致地表达了自己的论点后，上主来宣布他的审判。原告（耕夫）在某种意义上是错误的，因为从他的话语可以听出来这一点：他认为他的妻子是属于自己的固定财产，但实际上她只是借给他的，是一种某一段时期赐给他的"封地"（和中世纪的"采邑"类似）。死亡夸耀自己的权力，这也是错误的，因为他的力量也同样仅仅是一种"采邑"。上主知道原告的谴责和呻吟是他的悲伤所引起的，因此要赐给他"荣耀"作为安慰。死亡是胜利者，因为每一个人都得死，但死亡的胜利不是全面的：人的身体属于黄土，但人的灵魂属于上主。这样，耕夫和死亡双方都应该意识到自己观点的局限性。

women, a misogynist. He reminds Death that Boethius was educated by a woman: philosophy! The crown of all earthly beauty is a woman, honorable, disciplined, chaste. He repeats the ideal of the knight and of courtly love: at each tournament and in each war the "Eternally Female" (das Ewig-Weibliche) will have the best effects. "If one wants to know what is good discipline and honor, let him learn from noble women." Therefore the "conservation, confirmation and all growth of mankind is dependent on the noble spirit of women."

After both sides, Ackermann and Death have at length expounded their arguments, God announces His judgment. The accuser (Ackermann) is wrong in a sense, because he talks as if his wife would have been his own possession, but in fact she was only a gift that was lent, a "Lehen" (like a feudal fiefdom) that was granted to him for some time. Death has boasted of his power, this is wrong, too, because his power is likewise only a "Lehen". God knows that sorrow has induced the accuser to his indictment and to his sighs, therefore he is granted "honor" as a consolation. Death is victorious, since man must die, but Death's victory is not complete: the human body belongs to the earth, but the human soul belongs to God. In this way both sides, Ackermann and the Death, should see their limitations of their tenets.

杰尔松(1363—1429)

生于法国北部 Rheims 地区的 Rethel,1377 年以来在 Paris 学习,师从 Peter d'Ailly,在大学里有重要的影响,1395 年成为 Paris 大学校长;在"教会大分裂"后(1378 年),他先持比较保守的看法并认为一个主教会议无法弹劾教宗,但他逐渐转向"大公会议派"(conciliarismus),于 1409 年参与 Pisa 主教会议,又于 1414 年与 Peter d'Ailly 一起参与 Constantia 的会议,在会议上有核心地位。因为他反对"杀死僭君是正义的"这样的主张,所以于 1419 年才被允许回国。Gerson 是最有影响力的神学家之一,大约写过 540 部著作,部分是拉丁语的,部分是法语的或由他译成法语的。很多于 1517 年之前进行的教会改革运动都与他的思想有关系。

著作:《神学的安慰》、《论善终》、《论教会和世俗权威的权柄》、《神秘神学》(主要的著作)、《论教会的合一》(反对教会的分裂);共有 540 部拉丁语的或法语的著作。

090.《神秘神学》

具有影响力的神学家 Gerson 的这部著作成书于 1402—1407 年间。因为其中的思想继承 Augustinus、Dionysios Areipagita、Gregorius Magnus、Bonaventura、Hugo de Sancto Victore 和其他新 Plato 主义思想家的传统,所以该书在神学和哲学上具有重要的影响。这部书曾被多次抄写,印行的版本也很多,它曾影响了 Nicolaus de Cues、Gabriel Biel 和 Martin Luther。

因为 Gerson 深深受唯名论的影响,他认为神秘神学(即"心灵的神学")能更完善地认识神,超过经院思想的逻辑方法(即"理智的神学")。因此,神秘体验成了可靠的知识的基础。

本书分为两个部分,即 *De mystica theologia speculativa*(《思辨性的神秘神学》)和 *De mystica theologia practica*(《论实践性的神秘神学》)。前面的部分探讨人心的六种精神能力并说明外向的思想(cogitatio)、专心默想(meditatio)和默观(contemplatio)的意义。神秘体验的目标应该是与神的合一。

在 *Mystica theologia practica*(《实践性神秘神学》)中,作者鼓励一切信徒等待神的召唤。因为神的意愿是拯救一切人,他赋予每一个人一种不可丧失的、恒久的渴望,即寻觅至高的、真正的幸福与喜乐的渴望。然而,不同的人通过不同的职业、不同的生活方式、不同的召唤而获得救恩;神的预先安排规定了这一切生活方式。那些愿意发展自己的精神生活的人应该阅读《圣经》或一些宗教书籍,他们应该去听教堂中的讲

Johannes Carlerius de Gerson / Jean Gerson

Opera: *Consolatio Theologiae, De arte moriendi, De iurisdictione spirituali et temporali, De mystica theologia, De unitate ecclesiae*
Works: *The Consolation of Theology, On a Good Death, On Ecclesiastical and Secular Powers, Mystical Theology, On the Unity of the Church*

090. *De mystica theologia / On Mystical Theology*

This work of the influential theologian Gerson was written during the years from 1402—1407. It had important theological and philosophical implications, since it follows the tradition of Augustine, Dionysius Areopagita, Gregory the Great, Bonaventure, Hugo of St.-Victor and other thinkers that were inspired by Neo-Platonism. The book was often copied and printed, it influenced Nicolaus of Cues, Gabriel Biel, and Martin Luther.

Since Gerson was deeply steeped in nominalism, he thought that mystical theology (the "theology of the heart") would better be able to know God than scholastic logical methods (the "theology of the intellect"). The reliability of knowledge is thus based on mystical experience.

The book is divided into two parts, namely *De mystica theologia speculativa* (*On Speculative Mystical Theology*), and *De mystica theologia practica* (*On Practical Mystical Theology*). The first part deals with the six mental powers of the soul and explains the meaning of extensive thought (cogitatio), concentrated reflection (meditatio), and contemplation (contemplatio). Union with God is the aim of mystical experiences.

In the *Practical Mystical Theology* the author exhorts all the faithful to wait for the calling of God. Because God's will is that all people are saved, He gave each person an indestructible and permanent desire to find highest and true happiness and beatitude. However, different people arrive at salvation through different vocations, different ways of life and different callings, all of which are ordained by God's providence. Those who want to develop their inner spiritual life should read the Bible or pious books, they should listen to sermons, celebrate the sacraments, pray in churches or kneel in silent

道,应该参与圣事,在教堂中作祈祷或跪在圣体柜前静默。他们需要信仰、希望和爱德(即所谓的"三项神学美德")。如果一个人想过一种默观式的生活他还需要加上一种特殊的内心的平安,而祈祷中的默想将会带来这种宁静。

adoration before the tabernacle. They need the virtues of faith, hope, and love (the tree "theological virtues"), and in order to lead contemplative life they additionally need a special inner peace which is attained through prayerful meditation.

托马斯·肯璧斯（约 1380—1471）

出生于德国 Cologne 地区的 Kempten，原名 Thomas Hemerken；于 1392 年到荷兰的 Deventer，在"共同生活兄弟会"那里接受教育，约于 1400 年加入 Windesheim（荷兰，在 Zwolle 附近）的奥古斯丁会，于 1413 年被祝圣司铎，在 Windesheim 的隐修院中工作、研究与抄书 70 年之久。

著作：《师主篇》(《轻世金书》、《尊主圣范》、《效法基督》；古今中外最有影响的灵修学著作之一，共有 5000 多版，译为 95 种语言）、《论三个圣愿》(论贫穷、谦逊和贞洁三德）、《心灵的提升以便寻求神》、《玫瑰花园》、《关于基督生活的祈祷和默想》、《灵魂的自语》

091. 《师主篇》

这部具有神秘神学色彩的劝勉是由 Thomas a Kempis 编写的，于 1470 年印行。然而也存在一些更早的版本，即 1424 年和 1444 年的版本，而部分学者曾认为这部书可能是由另一个作者写的，但大多数历史学家仍然肯定 Thomas 为作者。曾在 Deventer 创立了 Fratres vitae communis（"共同生活的兄弟会"）的 Gerhard Groote（1340—1384 年）的一部著作是 *De imitatione Christi*（《师主篇》）的基础。Thomas 仅仅改写了 Groote 的书并赋予它另一种形象，使它变得非常流行。在后来的 500 年中，这部书共有 5000 多种不同的版本和译本，它至今仍是最广为人知的灵修学著作之一。

全书分为四部分：1）关于灵修生活的实用性建议（Admonitiones ad spiritualem vitam utiles）；2）一些催促我们过灵性生活的考虑（Admonitiones ad interna trahentes）；3）论内心的安慰（De interna consolatione）；4）论圣体圣事，劝勉人善领圣体（De sacramento, exhortatio ad sacram communionem）。

第一部分鼓励读者放弃世俗的考虑、自私的追求、骄傲和不正当的欲望。如果一个人要在生活中效法基督的榜样，他必须远离各种诱惑，必须爱慕孤独生活、沉默和谦虚的精神。Ama nesciri!（"喜欢无名的状态吧！"1, 2.15）

第二部分是关于人心深处的指南，包含很多心理学上的洞见。我们应该很谦逊地服从他人，应该有一颗平安的心、纯洁的灵魂以及明确的目标。一个人应该不断准备纠正和谴责自己的错误，这样能获得内心的平安。Magnam habet cordis tranquilitatem, qui nec laudes curat nec vituperia（"既不关心赞美又不担心辱骂，这样的人在心灵上非常宁静"，2, 6, 16）。每一个人应该要感谢上主的恩典，甚至也要感谢神派来的诱惑和痛苦。跟随基督意味着爱慕他的十字架。In cruce salus, in cruce vita.

Thomas a Kempis

Opera: *De imitatione Christi, De tribus tabernaculis, Elevatio mentis ad inquirendum Deum, Hortulus rosarum, Orationes et meditationes de vita Christi, Soliloquium animae*

Works: *The Imitation of Christ, Three Tabernacles, The Elevation of the mind to the Search for God, A Garden of Roses, Prayers and Meditations on the Life of Christ, Monologue of the Soul*

091. *De imitatione Christi / The Imitation of Christ*

This mystical exhortation by Thomas a Kempis was published in 1470, however there are older versions from 1424 and 1444, and other authors have been suggested, although most historians agree that Thomas compiled the work. The most part of the book is based on a similar work by Gerhard Groote (1340—1384), the founder of the "Brethren of the Common Life" at Deventer. Thomas only rewrote Groote's book and brought it into the form by which it became so popular. In the next 500 years it went through more than 5000 editions in numerous languages and is still one of the most well-known books of spiritual edification.

The work is divided into four parts: 1, Practical advice about the spiritual life (Admonitiones ad spiritualem vitam utiles); 2, Considerations inviting us to live an interior life (Admonitiones ad interna trahentes); 3, On inward consolation (De interna consolatione), and 4, About the Blessed Sacrament: A devout encouragement to receive Holy Communion (De sacramento, exhortatio ad sacram communionem).

The first book encourages the reader to leave back secular concerns, egoistic pursuits, pride and immoderate passions. To take Christ as a model for life means to keep temptations at bay and to love solitude, silence and humility. "Ama nesciri!" ("Love to be not known!", 1,2,15)

The second book is a guide to the depths of the human soul and contains many psychological insights. We should submit ourselves humbly to others, have a peaceful mind, purity and a clear purpose. One should be ready to constantly correct and critizise oneself, this will lead to inner peace. "Magnam habet cordis tranquilitatem, qui nec laudes curat nec vituperia" ("He who does not care about praises or criticism will have great tranquility in his heart.", 2,6,16). One should be thankful for God's grace, even for the temptations and sufferings He sends. Following Christ also means to love His cross. "In cruce salus, in cruce vita. In cruce protectio ab hostibus". ("In the cross there is salva-

In cruce protectio ab hostibus（"在十字架中有救恩和生命。十字架保护人们不受敌人的侵害。"2,12,7）

第3卷描述上主在内心中对灵魂说话的方式。人们应该很谦卑地接受这些话。对于神的敬爱（amor devotionis）将要使一切世俗的事物转向神，这样给予人接受痛苦和诱惑的力量。对于神的敬爱会引导信徒的思想并且在充满困惑的时期也带给他喜乐。作者多次呼吁读者怀着非常谦虚的态度。这种谦虚的一个层面是反对过分知识化的心态。真正分享上主的种种恩典并在上主面前过一种谦虚的生活，这就比读很多书或理解《圣经》的一切章节更能拯救人。如果缺少上主，一切世俗的事物都是没有用的。因此一个信徒必须在两种生活方式中选择一种，要么选择自然，要么选择圣宠，选择自爱或爱他者，世俗的荣誉或谦卑。Dimitte omnia transitoria, quaere aeterna. Quid sunt omnia temporalia nisi seductoria?（"你应该放弃一切暂时的、人间的东西，应该寻觅永恒的。世俗的东西不都是诱惑吗？"3,1,12）

第4卷谈论上主在圣体圣事（弥撒中的圣饼和圣杯）中表达的爱。信徒们应该非常尊敬地接受圣体，因为在这些有形的记号中上主使自己临在于人间。经常接受这种"神圣的灵药"（medicina divina）可以使人远离罪恶并赋予他力量继续行善。作者的灵感更多的来自刻苦精神，而非神秘主义，但他并不支持极端的苦修措施。所谓的devotio moderna（"现代虔敬灵修"，"现代虔信派"）是一个新的灵修学上的运动，而其主要的特征是系统地研究默观（contemplatio）的方式、注意心理学观察，以及一种开放的和灵活的理性主义。这个新灵修运动的创始人是Gerhard Groote，而Thomas的名著成为其主要的代表作。

tion, life, and protection from the enemies." 2,12,7)

Book 3 describes the way God speaks inwardly to the soul. These words should be accepted humbly. The love of God ("divine love", "devotional mystical love", "amor devotionis") will orientate all secular things towards God and thus makes it possible to bear suffering and to face temptations. Love of God directs a believer's thoughts and gives joy even in a time of troubles. The exhortation to humility is repeated many times in this book. One feature of this humility is a kind of anti-intellectualism. Reading many books and understanding all texts of the Bible is not as salvific as truly sharing in God's graces and living humbly in the sight of God. All secular goods are useless without God; thus a believer must choose between two life-styles, between nature and grace, between self-fulfilment and love, between secular glory and humility. "Dimitte omnia transitoria, quaere aeterna. Quid sunt omnia temporalia nisi seductoria?" ("Do away with all temporal goods, look for the eternal. What are the temporal goods but means of temptation?" 3,1,12)

Book 4 dwells on the great love shown by God to man in the holy Sacrament of Communion (Bread and Wine at Mass). The faithful should receive Holy Communion with deep reverence, since in these visible signs God Himself is present among them. Receiving this "divine medicine" (medicina divina, 4,3) frequently can drag a man away from evil and gives him the strength to remain good. The author is inspired by asceticism rather than by mysticism, but he does not favour extreme austerity. The orderly study of the path to contemplation (contemplatio), psychological observations, and a kind of enlightened and inspired rationalism, these are the main features of the new spiritual movement called "devotio moderna". This movement was created by Gerhard Groote, and Thomas' masterpiece became its major work.

库撒的尼古拉(1401—1464)

于 1401 年生于德国 Cues 城的平民家庭，在 Deventer 的兄弟团体接受教育，后在几所大学求学，成为非常渊博的人文学者、哲学家、数学家、自然科学家、神学家和神秘学家。他曾经参与 Basel 的主教会议，但于 1437 年转向 Eugenius IV 教宗，致力于改革教会并成功地拉近德国与教廷之间的距离，于 1448 年被提名为枢机，1450 年成为 Brixen / Bressanone 的主教。他曾出使 Byzantion，也掌握了一点希腊语。教宗 Pius II 曾要求他编写一个旨在改进教会纪律的宏大计划。

著作：《论公教的和睦》、《论推理》、《论隐藏的神》、《论有学识的无知》、《论上主的和平》、《论观看上主》等

092.《论有学识的无知》

这部著作曾被称为"德国哲学最早的经典"，而它深深影响了文艺复兴时期的思想（比如 Giordano Bruno, Marsilio Ficino 等人），它给予 Leibnitz 和 Baader 很多灵感。成书时间是 1440 年，分为三部分；Nicolaus 在其中描述他关于神、世界和基督（即"新人"）的见解。Nicolaus 的基本观点（"对立相合"coincidentia oppositorum）始终带给他很多安慰，即他认为互相对立的原则是相反相合的或是平衡共存的。在他的生活中，Nicolaus 面对很多"对立现象"：在 Concilium Basilianum 的主教会议上他主张要与希腊教会合一；作为一位主教，他面对世俗权力的压力，而在他的哲学中他努力结合信仰和理性。

本书的书名表达其内容与 Sokrates、Augustinus 以及 Dionysios Areiopagita 的否定神学的关系。对 Nicolaus 来说，神是一切万物的综合（complicatio rerum），因此在神内一切东西都失去它们的差异性。相反的东西和对立的现象将要合一。Nicolaus 使用一些数学原理来说明他的观点。人的理性能够掌握一些有限的东西，但无限的存在（神，Nicolaus 称他为 maximum，即最大的）对有限的人心来说是无法理解的，正如一个多角形无法完全适当地描述一个完美的圆圈的外线（圆周）。因此，人心必须满足于"对神的不理解"（ignoratio Dei）。然而，人的理性知道人在理解上的无知，进而开始发现无限者的那种不可理解的复杂性——一切对立的东西都包括在这种无限的复杂性之内。在有限的空间中，一个圆圈和一条直线是不同的，但在一个无限的圆圈那里，这种差异将是无限微小的，所以一条直线和一个圆圈是一样的。

第 2 卷谈论世界，即神的丰富存在的一种具体显示和表达（explicatio Dei）。世界来自于神，并且通过神存在，又存在于神内。正如一切数字都来自"一"，世界的多样

Nicolaus Cusanus

Opera: *De concordantia catholica, De coniecturis, De Deo abscondido, De docta ignorantia, De pace fidei, De visione Dei*

Works: *On Catholic Concordance, On Conjectures, The Hidden God, On Learned Ignorance, The Peace of Faith, On the Vision of God*

092. *De docta ignorantia / On Learned Ignorance*

This work has been called "the first classic of German philosophy", and it profoundly influenced the thought of the Renaissance (Giordano Bruno, Marsilio Ficino etc.), it inspired Leibnitz and Baader. The book was written in 1440 and presents in 3 treatises Nicolaus' vision of God, the world, and Christ, the new man. Nicolaus' basic insight (coincidentia oppositorum) that brought much relief to him was the idea of the coincidence and mutual balance of opposite principles. Nicolaus faced many oppositions in his life: at the Council of Basle he promoted the union with the Greek churches; being a bishop he encountered the pressure of secular power, and in his philosophy he tried to combine faith and reason.

The title of the work shows the connections to Socrates, Augustine and to the negative theology of Dionysius Areopagita. For Nicolaus God is the combination of all things (complicatio rerum) and thus within God the things lose their differences. Opposites coincide. Nicolaus uses mathematical considerations to explain his speculation. Human intelligence can understand limited things, but the infinite being (God, whom Nicolaus calls the "maximum", the absolute greatest) is not comprehensible for the limited human mind, just like a polygon can never adequately describe the circumference of a perfect circle. Thus the human mind must be contented with an "ignorance of God" (ignoratio Dei). Reason however knows about the ignorance of human comprehension and in a second step gains insight into the unintelligible complicatedness of the infinite in which all opposites are contained. In the finite space, a circle and a straight line are different from each other, but in an infinite circle the difference would be infinitely slight so that a straight line and a circle would coincide.

The second book treats the world as a concrete unfolding of the richness of God (explicatio Dei). The world comes from God, it exists in God and through God. Like all numbers spring from the number one, the pluriformity of the world is from it's first ori-

性也来自第一个根源，即神（这种思路来自 Dionysios Areiopagita）。因此整个世界是一个整体（unum）并包含很多单元：在一切东西当中能够找到一切其他的东西（quodlibet in quolibet），因为神在一切中是一切。个别的事物分享（methexis）普遍的存在，因此两种现实共同存在，即整体和个别事物。因为 Nicolaus 使用"分享"（methexis）和"类比"（analogia）的概念，他的思想没有滑入泛神论——泛神论的思想混合创造主与创造界。在自然科学方面 Nicolaus 的思辨性考虑引发了一些新的观点。如果一切事物都是独特的而宇宙是无限的，地球可能不是宇宙的中心点，因为每一个地点都代表整体，所以在每一个点中整体也临在。因此 Nicolaus 是 Copernicus 的先驱。他想衡量一切事物的大小和重量（比如一些金属的比重），而这种努力建立在这样的考虑之上：虽然我们在这个世界中无法达到对于实物的完全准确衡量，但我们应该尽可能接近真理。

第 3 卷以基督和人生观为核心。人应该寻找通往绝对者的路。基督成为人要为人类开启找到神性的可能性，这样使人们真正实现他们的人性。在神秘主义的传统中，个人应该与无限者合一，但 Nicolaus（与 Eckhart 一样）同时也强调个人的自我的重要性。每一个人都是一个"小宇宙"，是一个独特的主体，而每一个人都拥有创造性、自由和意志力。个人的指导原则是他的理想自我，因此他能超越盲目的命运、随意性和偶然的局限性。这种纯粹的、理想的自我也参与理念的世界，这样发现自己的真正个性。

gin, God. (This train of thought is taken from Pseudo-Dionysius.) For this reason the world is a unity (unum) and contains many units: all things can be found in all other things (quodlibet in quolibet), because God is all in all things. Individual things share in the universal (methexis), and thus both realities co-exist, the whole and the singular. The concepts of participation and analogy prevent Nicolaus' system from sliding into pantheism which confuses the Creator and the creation. In the field of science, Nicolaus' speculations led to new approaches. If all things are unique and if the universe is infinite, then the earth may not be the center of the universe, because every place is a center in which the infinite whole is present. Thus Nicolaus is a precursor of Copernicus. His method of measuring and weighing all things (for example the specific gravity of metals) is based on this consideration: in this world we are unable to achieve perfect measurement of the reality, but we should try to approach the truth as far as possible.

The third book is centered on Christ and on the view of humanity. Man should find the way to the absolute. Christ became man to open up the possibility for us to find the divine and thus become truly human. In the mystical tradition the individual should become one with the infinite, but Nicolaus (like Eckhart) also emphasizes the ego of the individual. Every person is a microcosmos, a unique subject which possesses creativity, freedom, will. The individual is guided by the vision of his or her ideal ego, thus it transcends blind fate, arbitrariness, and contingent limitations. This pure, ideal self participates in the world of eternal ideas and so finds its true individuality.

贝萨里翁(1403—1474)

  Bessarion 出生在东方黑海地区 Trapezunt / Trebizond 城,也许在 1403 年(或 1395 年),他的名字是 Ioannes 或 Basilios。他在 Constantinopolis 受教育,在那里早与意大利人接触,1423 年成为隐修者,同时向 Georgios Gemistos Plethon 学习 Plato 思想;1437 年被任命为 Nikaia 的主教,因此于 1438 年赴意大利参与 Ferrara-Florentia 大公会议,会议上支持东方教会与罗马教会合一,虽然在东方只有少数信徒接受这种合一(即所谓 Greek Uniate Church 希腊合一教会)。Bessarion 留在意大利,1439 年提升为枢机主教,他在罗马的房子成为传播希腊知识的基地,因为他曾拥有当时最大的希腊语手抄本图书馆(800 多卷),后来将它献给威尼斯 San Marco 图书馆。他于 1455 年几乎被选教宗,后成为教宗的特使,曾于 1460—1461 年在德国宣传十字军运动。Bessarion 是一位杰出的人文主义者,著作等身,而且也慷慨地帮助穷人并在 1453 年前后照顾很多来自东方的希腊难民。

著作:《反驳柏拉图的诽谤者》、《回忆录》、《形而上学》;还有许多译著和讲演稿等。

093.《反驳柏拉图的诽谤者》

  这部哲学著作成书于 1464 年,分为 4 卷并拥护 Plato 思想的传统。Bessarion 本来并不反对 Aristoteles 主义,他自己将 Aristoteles 的 *Metaphysica* 译成拉丁语,这样他帮助了西欧的学者更全面地掌握 Aristoteles 的思想。Bessarion 的著作攻击 Georgios de Trapezunt——这位学者曾翻译了 Plato 的 *Nomoi* 并在注解中指出 Plato 思想的缺陷,同时又颂扬 Aristoteles 的思想。Bessarion 不能容忍伟大的 Plato 受到批评,所以他针对 Georgios 写了这部书,其中罗列他译文中的种种错误(共 259 处),又揭露 Georgios 的错误注解。正如 Bessarion 试图结合 Plato 主义和 Aristoteles 主义的思想,他也成为希腊语和拉丁语之间的桥梁。他掌握很优雅的文笔,因此意大利的杰出人文主义者 Lorenzo Valla(1407—1457 年)曾称他为"Latinorum Graecissimus, Graecorum Latinissimus"("在拉丁语学者中最希腊化的,而在希腊人中最拉丁化的")。

Bessarion

Opera: *In calumniatorem Platonis, Memorabilia, Metaphysica*
Works: *Against the Calumniator of Plato, Memorabilia, Metaphysics*

093. *In calumniatorem Platonis / Against the Calumniator of Plato*

    This philosophical work in 4 books was written in 1464 and is a defense of the Platonic tradition. Bessarion was not against Aristotelianism, he himself translated Aristotle's *Metaphysics* into Latin and thus helped the Western scholars to get a better grasp of Aristotelianism. Bessarion's work attacks George of Trebizond who translated the *Laws* of Plato and in his commentary pointed to the shortcomings of Plato's thought, while at the same time praising Aristotle. Bessarion could not tolerate that Plato's great genius suffered denigration and turned against George, listing up the many mistakes (259 altogether) found in his translation and exposing the erroneous comments George made. Just as Bessarion tried to reconcile Platonism and Aristotelianism he was also a bridge between the Greek and Latin languages. He could write in an elegant Latin style, for which he was dubbed "Latinorum Graecissimus, Graecorum Latinissimus" ("The most Greek among the Latinists, and the most Latin among the Greeks") by Lorenzo Valla (1407—1457), an outstanding Italian Humanist.

皮科罗米尼(1405—1464)

Enea Silvio de Piccolomini 于 1405 年生于意大利 Siena 附近的 Corsignano,来自贫穷的贵族家庭,曾在 Siena 和 Florentia 学习法学和古典文学,1432 年参与 Basel 会议并支持 Felix V 对立教宗,又与 Fredericus III 皇帝有良好关系,1443 年成为皇帝的秘书、外交官和诗人,也是"中欧地区人文主义运动的主导人"。在 1445 年 Piccolomini 接受 Eugenius IV 教宗,并于 1446 年被祝圣司铎。他影响皇帝促进教会的合一,因此于 1447 年成为主教,而于 1458 年甚至被选为教宗,取名 Pius II。他愿意抵抗土耳其人的侵略,但欧洲的国君不太支持他于 1459 年想组织的十字军运动。教宗的理想是一个在基督信仰内合一的欧洲。他是最有学问、最有才华的教宗之一,编写很多历史学著作、诗歌,还有一部爱情小说和一部自传。

著作:《亚洲》、《科吕西斯》、《论 Basel 大公会议的文献》、《回忆录》、《论孩子的教育》、《论德国的习俗、地理和现状》(Piccolomini 被认为是"辨别资料的国家史学"的奠基人)、《诸名人传》、《欧洲》、《欧里亚鲁斯和卢科莱西亚》(《两个情人的故事》)、《波希米亚史》、《奥地利史》、《关于大公会议权威之书》,还有许多讲演稿等文献。

094. 《回忆录》

这部分为 12 卷的自传写于 Piccolomini 晚年并覆盖 1463 年以前所发生的事。这是唯一的由一位中世纪教宗写的自传,也有相当高的历史价值。本著作后来经修改,于 1584 年出版,但原来的著作仍保存。

本书的书名模仿 Caesar 关于 Gallia 战争的报告,而作者也使用第三人称的叙述法。首先 Piccolomini 讲述他被选教宗之前所发生的事。他于 1405 年出生在 Siena 地区的贵族家庭,曾勤奋地学习以获得良好的人文主义教育。他以某一位枢机主教秘书的身份参与 Basel 的主教会议(1431—1437 年)。该会议旨在改革教会。他后来成为对立教宗 Felix V 的秘书。Felix 于 1439 年被选,而他拒绝将会议迁到 Ferrara 或 Florentia。奥地利的国王 Fredericus III(1440—1493 年)于 1442 年邀请 Piccolomini 到维也纳,使他成为皇家的"桂冠诗人"和自己的私人秘书。Piccolomini 能够促进一些德国公爵及皇帝与罗马的和好,他努力为教会的合一工作并于 1446 年被祝圣司铎。不久后他也成为主教并继续成功地在罗马与德国各国之间当中介人。他也准备 Fredericus 于 1452 年在罗马被加冕为神圣罗马帝国的皇帝。Piccolomini 又与 Aragonia 的国王 Alphonsus V(在 1442 年以后他也是意大利南部的王)进行谈判并劝勉他协助反抗土耳其人的十字军运动——在 1453 年土耳其人占领了 Constantinopolis 并威胁东欧地区。

Enea Silvio de Piccolomini

Opera: *Asia, Chrysis, Commentarii de gestis concilii Basiliensis, Commentarii rerum memorabilium, De liberorum educatione, De ritu, situ, moribus et conditione Germaniae, De viris illustribus, Europa, Euryalus et Lucretia* (sive *Historia de duobus amantibus*), *Historia Bohemica, Historia Friderici III* (*Historia Austriaca*), *Libellus dialogorum de concilii generalis auctoritate*

Works: History of Asia, Chrysis, Commentaries on the Acts of the Council in Basel, Commentaries on Memorable Events, Book on the Education of Children, On the Customs, Locations and Condition of Germany, Famous Men, Europe, Euryalus and Lucretia (The Tale of Two Lovers), History of Bohemia, History of Austria, Book on Discussions Concerning the Authority of A General Council

094. *Commentarii rerum memorabilium* / *Commentaries on Memorable Events*

This autobiography in 12 books was written during the last years of Piccolomini's life, covering the events up to the year 1463. It is the only autobiography of a Pope from the Middle Ages and of considerable historical value. The work was revised and published in 1584, but the original version has been preserved.

The title of the *Commentarii* imitates Caesar's report on his wars in Gaul, and like Caesar Piccolomini writes from the third-person perspective. First Piccolomini narrates the events before he was elected pope. He was born in 1405 into a noble family in the area of Siena and had to work hard to acquire a good humanistic education. As secretary to a cardinal he went to the Council of Basel (1431 to 1437) which aimed at Church reforms. He eventually became secretary to the antipope Felix V who was elected in 1439 and refused to transfer the council to Ferrara and Florence. In 1442 Emperor Frederick III (1440—1493) of Austria invited Piccolomini to Vienna and made him imperial poet laureate and his private secretary. Reconciling German princes and the Emperor with Rome, Piccolomini worked for the unity of the Church and received sacred orders in 1446. Soon he was made bishop and continued his successful mediation between Rome and the German states. He also prepared Frederick's coronation as Holy Roman Emperor in Rome in 1452. Piccolomini negotiated with Alfonso V, king of Aragon (since 1442 also king of Naples / Sicilia), and induced him to assist in the crusade against the Turks who captured Constantinople in 1453 and threatened to invade Eastern Europe.

第 2 到 12 卷叙述 Piccolomini 于 1458 年被选教宗以后的事。在他当选时他曾说"Aeneam rejicite, Piium accipite!"("请你们宽恕原先的 Enea 并接受现在的 Pius！"），并为自己取 Pius II 为名字。他是一位有远见的政治家和敏锐的观察者，在读者面前展示出他对世俗世界的种种兴趣，即他对历史、社会和大自然的关注。他的风格很典型地反映出文艺复兴时期的优雅华丽。他很生动地描述很多属于 quattrocento（早期文艺复兴时期）的杰出人物，比如 Poggio Bracciolini、Cosimo de'Medici 等人士。

Poggio Bracciolini（1380—1459）再次发现一些古典拉丁文献的手抄本，而他也是早期文艺复兴时期最杰出的学者之一。他将 Carolus 时代的小字体（参见 Alcuin）发展成今天被称为"罗马的"字体，即是当时普遍使用的字体。在 15 世纪下半叶的很多出版物中也多使用这种字体。Poggio 在瑞士的 St. Gallen、法国的 Cluny、德国的 Fulda、意大利的 Monte Cassino 等隐修院中发现了一些记载 Cicero、Quintilianus 等人的宝贵文献，并为了发现更多手抄本在英国花了四年的时间（1418—1423 年）。在晚年，Poggio 和另一位人文主义者 Lorenzo Valla（1407—1457 年）发生激烈冲突。Poggio 的著作包括 *Contra hypocritas*（《反驳伪君子们》）、*De avaritia*（《论吝啬》）、*De miseria humanae conditionis*（《论人生的可怜状态》）、*De nobilitate*（《论崇高》）、*De varietate fortunae*（《论命运之变》）、*Facetiae*（《故事杂集》）、*Historia tripartita*（《历史问题座谈三篇》）。

Cosimo de'Medici（意大利人称他为 Cosimo il Vecchio，1389—1464 年）发展了 Medici 家族的银行。他是当时最有钱的人。自从 1434 年以来他控制了 Florentia 市，这也是该城前所未有的繁荣的开端。Medici 家族在 Florentia 和 Toscana 的统治维持一百年（1434—1537 年）。Cosimo 组织建设很多教堂、小圣堂和宫殿。他在 1444 年建设了一所图书馆（后来被称 Bibliotheca Laurenziana），储存从外国引进的宝贵手抄本并向外人开放。在他雇佣的抄书家、作家、画家和雕塑家中有 Poggio、Marsilio Ficino、Donatello、Fra Angelico 等人。在 1439 年 Cosimo 支持大公主教会议从 Ferrara 迁到 Florentia 并欢迎那些来自东方的学者。在他 50 岁时 Cosimo 成为希腊语和希腊思想的勤奋敬佩者和学生，并在 Florentia 郊区的 Careggi 别墅中重新创立了 Plato 的学园。因此，希腊来的学人 Gemistus Plethon 和 Iohannes Bessarion 于 1442 年创立了 Accademia Platonica，旨在研究希腊文学和 Plato 的哲学。

当时另一个有影响的人物是 Francesco Sforza（1401—1466 年），一位 condottiere（雇佣军的将军），他曾一时为 Milano 的公爵 Filippo Maria Visconti 服务，后来与 Cosimo de'Medici 结约，并协助 Venetia 和 Florentia 镇压 Milano。在 1450 年他终于成为 Milano 的公爵，但仍然受 Venetia、Neapolis、Savoy 和 Montferrat 的攻击。然而，Sforza 能够巩固他的统治，而他的家族后来领导 Milano 近一百年。与意大利其他城市的领导者一样，他也大力支助美术。他尽力以豪华的艺术品美化 Milano 城。

Books 2 to 12 are an account of the developments after Piccolomini was elected Pope in 1458. With the famous words "Aeneam rejicite, Pium accipite!" ("Please forgive the pagan Enea and welcome Pius, the Pope!") he accepted the election of the cardinals and took the name Pius II for his pontificate. Being an astute politician and keen observer he displays before the reader his manifold interests in the secular world, in history, society, and nature. His style is typical for the elegance and refinement of the Renaissance. He vividly portrays many of the important figures of the quattrocento (early Renaissance period), for example Poggio Bracciolini, Cosimo de'Medici, and many others.

Poggio Bracciolini (1380—1459), the rediscoverer of classical Latin manuscripts and leading scholar of the early Renaissance, developed the Caroline minuscule (see Alcuin) into what is now called the "Roman" font, the script widely used by the copyists of his time. This letter type was also used for many printed editions in the second half of the 15th century. Poggio discovered precious manuscripts of works by Cicero, Quintilian and others in the libraries of the monasteries of St. Gall (Switzerland), Cluny (France), Fulda (Germany), Monte Cassino (Italy) and he spent 4 years in England in the hope to discover more documents (1418—1423). In his last years Poggio engaged in a bitter fight with Lorenzo Valla (1407—1457), another leading Humanist. Among Poggio's works are *Contra hypocritas* (*Against the Hypocrites*), *De avaritia* (*On Greed*), *De miseria humanae conditionis* (*The Misery of the Human Condition*), *De nobilitate* (*On Nobility*), *De varietate fortunae* (*On the Change of Fortune*), *Facetiae* (*Facets*), *Historia tripartita* (*On History*).

Cosimo de'Medici (Cosimo il Vecchio, 1389—1464) developed the bank of the Medici family and was the wealthiest man of his time. Since 1434 he controlled Florence and inaugurated an era of unprecedented prosperity. The rule of the Medici in Florence and Tuscany lasted from 1434 to 1537. Cosimo ordered the construction of many churches, chapels and palaces. In 1444 he built a library (later called Bibliotheca Laurenziana), furnished it with valuable manuscripts from abroad, and opened it to the public. Among the copyists, writers, painters and sculptors employed by him were Poggio, Marsilio Ficino, Donatello, Fra Angelico and others. In 1439 Cosimo facilitated the move of the ecumenical council from Ferrara to Florence and welcomed scholars from the East. At the age of 50 Cosimo became an assiduous admirer and student of Greek language and thought, and he recreated the ancient Academy of Plato in his villa of Careggi outside of Florence. Thus in 1442 the Greek scholars Gemistus Plethon and John Bessarion founded the Accademia Platonica for the study of Greek literature and Platonic philosophy.

Other influential people of that period were Francesco Sforza (1401—1466), a condottiere (commander of mercenaries), who served Filippo Maria Visconti, the Duke of Milan, for some time, then made a pact with Cosimo de'Medici and fought against Milan on the side of Venice and Florence. In 1450 he finally became duke of Milan himself, only to be threatened by Venice, Naples, Savoy, and Montferrat. However, Sforza managed to establish his dynasty that ruled Milan for nearly a century. Like the leaders of other Italian cities he was a patron of the arts and tried to embellish Milan with magnificent artefacts.

士兵和残暴的统治者 Sigismondo Malatesta(1417—1468 年)也曾资助一些作家和艺术家。他有时候被视为意大利式的"文艺复兴王子"的原型。Malatesta 家族在 Milano、Brescia、Bergamo 和 Rimini 有一些地产。在教会的大分裂结束后(1417 年后)他们的家族逐渐衰落。Sigismondo 不断率军打仗,所以教宗 Pius II 于 1416 年宣布要镇压他并将他开除教籍。

Sigismondo Malatesta (1417—1468), a soldier and cruel ruler was also a patron of writers and artists. He is sometimes regarded as the prototype of the Italian "Renaissance prince". The Malatesta clan is associated with their possessions in Milan, Brescia, Bergamo, and Rimini. After the end of the Great Schism (1417) they lost influence. Alarmed by Sigismondo's incessant warfare Pope Pius II launched a campaign against him and excommunicated him in 1461.

格雷邦（约 1420—1471）

他 1420 年生于法国 Le Mans，在 Paris 学习神学和哲学，后在 Notre-Dame 成为管风琴师与合唱团指导员。这位宗教剧作家晚年在 Le Mans 的 Saint-Julien 教堂的圣职团生活。

著作：《巴黎受难剧》、《宗徒行传》(与其弟兄 Simon 合著，62000 行，需要 494 个演员，描述早期教会的故事，一直到 Nero 皇帝之死；1536 年在 Bourges 的古罗马圆形剧场演出，表演时间为 40 天。)

095.《巴黎受难剧》

这部法语的苦难剧的别名是 *La Passion de nostre saulveur Jhesu Crist*（《我们救主耶稣基督的苦难》）。在 15、16 世纪欧洲人在各处演出很多法语的、拉丁语的、德语的或荷兰语的苦难剧（苦难曲），而 Greban 的苦难剧是其中比较有名的。他的剧首次于 1450 年在 Paris 演出，长达 34000 多行，需要 200 多演员，演剧的时间为 4 天。作者使用《福音书》、早期的苦难剧、Petrus Comestor 的 *Historia scholastica*、Thomas Aquinas 的 *Summa Theologiae*、Nicolaus de Lyra 的《圣经》研究以及 Jacobus de Voragine 的传奇。

前言说明苦难剧的目标和内容。苦难剧旨在推动听众在观看基督的死亡和复活后去悔改并转向神。前言也叙述 Lucifer 的堕落、Adam 的罪行、Cain 和 Abel 之间的致命冲突以及 Adam 和 Eva 的死亡。这是人类的悲惨命运，而这样的背景才能说明基督为什么需要被派遣来拯救人类。

苦难剧的第一天描述天堂上的情况。在这里有"上主的四个女儿"，即仁慈（Miséricorde）、真理（Vérité）、和平（Paix）与正义（Justice），他们谈论人类被拯救的可能性。正义认为罪人应该遭受永远的惩罚，但真理问永久的惩罚是否必要。这四个拟人化的人物转向神，而神决定要派遣自己的儿子来救人类。他直接差遣他的使者 Gabriel 到以色列，要他宣布救世主的诞生。此后观众看到耶稣在 Bethlehem 的诞生和他在 Nazareth 的童年。

在第 2 天 Ioannes Baptista 出现并讲道。他指向 Messiah，而他自己的门徒转向耶稣。此后耶稣的公开生活被描述。来自 Nazareth 的耶稣唤起人们的希望，他在犹太人的会堂中讲道或教导人，向穷人宣布福音并且治愈很多人的病。然而，犹太人的领导反对耶稣，他们逮捕他并嘲笑他。

Arnoul Greban

Opera: *Passion de Paris* (=*Le Mystere de Passion*), *Les Actes des Apotres*
Works: *Passion of Paris* (=*The Mystery of the Passion*), *The Acts of the Apostles*

095. *Passion de Paris / Passion of Paris*

This French passion play is also known under the title *La Passion de nostre saulveur Jhesu Crist*, and it is one of the more popular of many passion plays in French, Latin, German, and Dutch, that were performed in many places since the 15th and 16th centuries. Greban's play was first performed in Paris in 1450, it is 34574 verses long, requires more than 200 actors, and the performance lasts for 4 days. The author uses the gospel texts, earlier passion plays, the *Historia scholastica* of Petrus Comestor, the *Summa Theologiae* of Thomas Aquinas, the Bible studies of Nicolaus of Lyra and the legends of Jacobus de Voragine.

The prologue explains the aim and content of the passion play. It wants to move the audience to repent and turn to God when seeing the story of Christ's death and resurrection. The prologue also shows the fall of Lucifer, Adam's sin, the deadly conflict between Cain and Abel and the death of Adam and Eve. This story of the dire fate of mankind forms the background which explains why Christ needed to be sent to save humankind.

The first day of the *Passion* leads the frame narrative to the paradise. Here the allegories of Mercy (Miséricorde), Truth (Vérité), Peace (Paix) and Justice (Justice), the "four daughters of God", debate about a possible salvation of mankind. Justice pleads for eternal condemnation of the sinners, but Truth asks whether eternal punishment is really necessary. The allegories turn to God Who decides to save mankind by sacrificing His Son. Immediately He sends the messenger Gabriel to Israel to announce the birth of the Saviour. Then the play shows the birth of Jesus in Bethlehem and his childhood in Nazareth.

The second day starts with the preaching of John the Baptist. John points to the Messiah, and his own disciples are attracted by Jesus. Then follows a description of the public life of Jesus. The man from Nazareth awakens hope by preaching and teaching in the synagogues of the Jews, he brings the good news to the poor and heals many people. However, the leaders of the Jews oppose Jesus, they detain him and ridicule him.

第3天描述"苦难"，即耶稣的受难和充满痛苦的死亡。经过审问后，耶稣被鞭策、受侮辱并被强迫背自己的十字架。他三次在沉重的苦架下跌倒崩溃，又三次站起来为了完成圣父交给他的任务。在通往 Golgotha 的路上他遇到母亲 Maria——她与儿子一同受苦并见到他的痛苦死亡，因为她站在十字架的旁边。耶稣和 Maria 之间的对话表明作者非常尊敬 Maria。耶稣被钉上十字架，而这个苦架在 Golgotha 山上被立起来。

第4天演基督的复活。耶稣的门徒们发现墓穴是空的，而复活的基督向他们显现。此后他升天，过一段时间他派遣圣灵（圣神）到信徒们的心灵。最后的部分回应前言的内容：仁慈、真理、和平与正义的化身现在可以彼此和好，她们彼此拥抱，正如《圣经》*Psalmus* 85:11 所记载。最后叙述者呼吁观众一起唱 *Te Deum laudamus*（《上主，我们赞美你》）；这是苦难剧的典型结尾。

因为苦难剧有非常多的角色，它能够丰富地表达很多内在的张力和伴随着无辜的耶稣惨遭酷刑的悲剧性因素。比如，在橄榄园中耶稣面对自己的痛苦死亡，而这一幕包含圣父与正义之间的对话。神的仁慈将不会允许他的儿子遭受残酷的死亡，但正义深信这种苦难是必需的，所以神同意让这一切事发生。

The third day depicts the actual passion, namely the suffering of Jesus and his painful death. After being sentenced, Jesus is whipped, mocked, and forced to carry his own cross. Three times he stumbles and collapses under the weight of the heavy cross, and three times he stands up again to accomplish the task the Father has given to him. On the way to Golgotha he encounters his mother Mary who suffers with her son and witnesses his painful death, as she stands besides the cross. The dialogues between Jesus and Mary show that the author had a deep veneration for Mary. Jesus is nailed to the cross, and the cross is erected on the hill of Golgotha.

The fourth day shows the resurrection of Christ. The disciples discover that the tomb is empty, and the risen Lord appears to them. Then he ascends to heaven and some time later pours out the Holy Spirit into the hearts of the believers. The last part responds to the prologue and returns to the four allegories of Mercy, Truth, Peace and Justice who are now reconciled and embrace each other according to the Biblical verse of *Psalm* 85:11. Finally the narrator exhorts the audience to sing the *Te Deum laudamus*, which was the usual end of a passion play.

A play with so many roles gives ample opportunity to show the internal tensions and tragic elements which go along with the violent death of the innocent Jesus. For example the scene at the olive garden where Jesus is confronted with his future painful death contains a remarkable dialogue between God the Father and the allegory of Justice. God's mercy would not tolerate that His Son must suffer this cruel death, but Justice is convinced that this suffering is necessary, and thus God admits that the events run their course.

附 录
Appendix

- *Roman de Renard*

无名作者

096. 《古兰经》

《古兰经》是一部阿拉伯语的语录集，即神的先知 Muhammad（穆罕默德，公元 570—632 年）于 610 年后所获得的启示。其文本在 'Utman 哈里发的时代（644—656 年）被统一并成为伊斯兰教的神圣经典。《古兰经》亦称 al-kitab（书）、dikr（训诲）和 hikma（智慧）。《古兰经》的篇幅大约和《新约》一样。

'Abd Allah 的儿子 Muhammad 本来属于 Mekka 的贵族家庭。他于 595 年和 Khadijah 一位富有的寡妇结婚并开始经商。约于 610 年他第一次获得一些信息并认为这些话语直接来自神，将自己视为神的使者（rasul Allah）或先知（nabi）。不久有一批朋友随从他。他们的新信仰被称为 Islam（伊斯兰，即"皈依"[神的旨意]），而信徒称 Muslim（"皈依者"）。由于 Mekka 的商人给他压力，Muhammad 于 622 年迁居（阿语 hijrah，拉丁语 hegira）到绿洲 Medina。这个迁移事件后来成为伊斯兰教的元年（拉丁语的 Anno Hegirae, AH）。因为 Muhammad 的信仰强调平等与对穷人的照顾，他能够统一 Medina 的阿拉伯部落。经过多年抵抗 Mekka 派来的军队，Muhammad 的政治能力和军事才干使得他于 629 年率领他的追随者进入 Mekka，在那里的 Ka'bah（黑石圣所，与神向 Abraham / Ibrahim 的启示有关系）他们建立了他们的敬拜中心。不久后大部分的阿拉伯支派加入了这个新的宗教运动，而在几十年内他们组建了一个庞大的帝国，东边达印度，西边包括西班牙。

《古兰经》分为根据长短编排的 114 章（surah）：长的在放在前面，短的在后，但第一章是例外，因为它是一个很短的祈祷。那些来自 Mekka 阶段（即在 hijrah 之前）的章一般来说比较短，并比那些排在前面的长篇教导、规律和训诲更具强调语气。类似中世纪的《圣经》版本，《古兰经》的章和节都带有数号。每一章的章名来自该章中提到的词，比如"黄牛"、"蜜蜂"、"太阳"等，但章名一般不反映全章的内容。在每一章的开头有所谓的 Bismala（只有第 9 章没有）："bi-smi llahi r-rahmani r-rahim"（"奉至仁至慈的真主之名"）。《古兰经》表现为真主的话语，而神经常以第一人称复数（"我们"）发言。经常出现的"你应该说"（Qar）暗示 Muhammad 回应上面来的命令针对信徒说话。

伊斯兰教的信仰是严格的一神论。真主是天地万物的创造者，也是报应日的主，他是宽仁的、慈悲的、正义的、智慧的，并全知的。一切人必须遵守真主的规律并接受所发生的事为神的意愿。《古兰经》肯定 Abraham / Ibrahim（亚伯拉罕/易卜拉欣/伊布

Anonymus

096. *Qur'an / Koran*

The *Qur'an* is an Arabic collection of sayings which were revealed through God's prophet Muhammad (570—632 AD) during the last two decades of his life. A unified standard version of the text was produced in the era of Caliph 'Utman / Othman (644—656 AD) and became the holy book of the Islam. It is also called al-kitab (book), dikr (admonition) and hikma (wisdom). The *Qur'an* has approximately the length of the New Testament.

Muhammad, the son of 'Abd Allah, belonged a prominent family in Mecca. He married a rich widow, Khadijah, in 595 AD and became a merchant. He started to receive verbal messages that he believed came directly from God around the year 610 AD and viewed himself as messenger of God (rasul Allah) or prophet (nabi). Soon he gathered a group of followers. The new faith was called Islam ("surrender" [to the will of God]), and the adherents were named "Muslim" ("those who have surrendered"). Growing pressure from merchants in Mecca led to Muhammad's emigration (hijrah, Latin: hegira) to the oasis of Medina in the year 622 AD. The year of the move to Medina subsequently became the first year of the Islamic Era (Latin: Anno Hegirae, or: AH). In Medina the faith of Muhammad could unify the Arab tribes, since it emphasized equality and care for the poor. After a few precarious years of fights against Meccan armies, the political and military capability of Muhammad enabled him to victoriously lead his followers back to Mecca in 629 AD, where they established the center of worship at the Ka'bah (the black stone connected with God's revelation to Abraham). Soon most of the Arab tribes joined the new religious movement, and within a few decades they could build a huge empire that reached from Spain to India.

The *Qur'an* is divided into 114 chapters (surah), who are arranged according to length: the longer ones come in the beginning, except for the first surah which is a short prayer. The surahs stemming from the period at Mecca (before the hijrah) are usually shorter and more emphatic than the elaborate teachings, regulations, and admonitions of the chapters in the first part of the *Qur'an*. Similar to medieval Bible editions, the chapters and verses of the *Qur'an* are specified by numbers. The title of each surah is derived from a word mentioned in it, for example "The Cow", "The Bee", "The Sun", but these headings do generally no reflect the contents of the whole chapter. The "Bismala" is the opening phrase of every surah (except surah 9): "bi-smi llahi r-rahmani r-rahim" ("in the Name of Allah, most merciful and gracious"). The *Qur'an* appears as the speech of God who mostly speaks in the first person plural ("we"). The imperative "Say" (Qar) indicates that Muhammad is speaking to the faithful responding to a divine command.

The faith of the Islam is a strict monotheism. God, the Creator of Heaven and Earth and the Lord of the Day of Judgment is forgiving, compassionate, just, wise, knowing all

拉欣)、Joseph / Yusuf(约瑟/优素福)和犹太先知的信仰。Jesus / 'Isa(耶稣/尔撒)被称为"埋希哈/弥赛亚"(al-Masih,即救世主),即一位有灵气的先知,他是处女 Maryam(麦尔彦)之子,但也明确指出他不应该被称"上主之子",因为真主没有儿子。Moses / Musa(摩西/穆萨)《十诫》(Dekalogos)在 3 个章中被提到。《古兰经》的词汇大多来自阿拉伯语,但也有一些来自希伯来语和叙利亚语的词,这就表明 Muhammad 在一定程度上也继承了犹太人和基督宗教的传统。《古兰经》中的外来语包括 injil ("引支勒",来自希腊语的 evangelion《福音书》)和 tawrat / taurat("讨拉特",来自希伯来语的 tora《摩西律法》),和 Iblis("易卜劣厮",从希腊语的 diabolos"魔鬼")。

097. 《亚历山大传奇》

在中世纪描述 Alexander Magnus 的历史性著作(比如 Arrianos 的 *Anabasis Alexandrou*《亚历山大远征记》和 Quintus Curtius Rufus 的历史小说 *Historiae Alexandri Magni regis Macedoniae*《马其顿王亚历山大传》)的影响远远不如所谓的《亚历山大传奇》的影响大。《亚历山大传奇》是关于 Alexander 的传说的合集。在 12、13 世纪中,这部传奇的拉丁语、英语、法语和德语版本非常流行,但当古典知识在中世纪晚期被恢复时,历史性的资料更受尊重,而那些虚构的传奇则逐渐消失。

一切亚历山大传奇的主要来源是一部约于公元 200 年在 Alexandria 成书的希腊语史诗。这部著作错误地被归于历史学家 Kallisthenēs(约公元前 370—前 327 年),因此被称为 *Pseudo-Callisthenes*。该故事结合一些历史性资料、一部更早期的亚历山大传奇、Alexander 向他母亲 Olympias 以及向老师 Aristoteles 写的信、以及很多奇妙的和魔术式的因素,后者来自埃及、希腊和印度的神话传统。因此,Alexander 不仅仅与印度的智者(gymnosophistai)对话,他在印度也遇到 Amazonai 人。由于该著作夸大各种超自然的、超一般人的、玄妙的和奇特的因素,历史因素被忽略或被歪曲。东方地区的读者显然很喜欢这部希腊语的叙事,但 Julius Valerius Polemius 于公元 320 年作的拉丁语翻译(书名为 *Res gestae Alexandri Magni*)没有很大的影响。根据 *Pseudo-Callisthenes* 出现的译本或新版本很多,包括亚美尼亚语的、科普特语的、叙利亚语的、阿拉伯语的和埃塞俄比亚语的。这些东方的版本更多注重关于 Gog 和 Magog 的传说:Alexander 打败了 Gog 和 Magog 的野蛮民族,而这个故事出现在 *Qur'an*(《古兰经》)当中。埃塞俄比亚的版本 *Zena Eskender* 甚至描述 Alexander 为一位基督徒君王、先知和讲道者,他是崇高道德的典范,既非常贞洁,又照顾穷人。

在使用拉丁语的西方,《亚历山大传奇》的突破发生在 10 世纪。当时 Leo de Neapolis 将希腊语的传奇译成拉丁语;他的 *Historia de preliis*(《诸战争的历史》,译称为 *Nativitas et victoria Alexandri Magni*)成书于公元 950 年到 970 年间,而其通俗的拉丁语风格使得欧洲西北地区的人容易掌握该叙事。Leo 的译本是大多后来的版本的主要资料来源,其中比较著名的版本是 Alberich de Besancon 的 *Roman d'*

things. All men must observe Allah's laws and should accept what happens as the will of Allah. The *Qur'an* confirms the faith of Abraham (Ibrahim), Joseph (Yusuf), and the Jewish prophets. Jesus is presented as the Messiah (al-Masih), a powerful prophet born of the virgin Mary (Maryam), but it is explicitly stated that he should not be called the "Son of God", since God has no son. Some of Moses' commandments (the *Decalogue*) are mentioned in 3 surahs. The vocabulary of the *Qur'an* is mainly of Arabic origin, but there are borrowed words, mostly from Hebrew and Syriac, which shows that Muhammad was indebted to Judaism and Christianity. Some of the loan words found in the *Qur'an* are injil ("gospel", from Greek evangelion), taurat ("law", from the Hebrew torah), and Iblis ("devil", from Greek diabolos).

097. *Alexandreis*

During the Middle Ages the impact of the historical works describing the life of Alexander the Great, e.g. Arrian's *Anabasis Alexandrou* (*The Expedition of Alexander*) and Q. Curtius Rufus' historical novel *Historiae Alexandri Magni regis Macedoniae* (*History of Alexander the Great*), was eclipsed by the so-called "Alexander romance", a collection of legends about the career of Alexander. Latin, English, French, and German versions of this romance were hugely popular in the twelfth and thirteenth centuries, but with the revival of classical scholarship in the late Middle Ages the historical sources about Alexander gradually displaced the fabulous Alexander romances.

The main source of all Alexander romance literature is a Greek epic written in Alexandria around 200 AD. This work was wrongly attributed to the historian Callisthenes (ca. 370—327 BC) and is thus called "*Pseudo-Callisthenes*". The narrative combines historical biographical data, an earlier Alexander romance, Alexander's letters to his mother Olympias and to his teacher Aristotle with magical and miraculous elements from Egyptian, Greek, and Indian mythology. Thus Alexander not only has conversations with the Indian wise men (gymnosophistai), he also meets the Amazons in India. Since the supernatural, superhuman, miraculous and exotic is highlighted the historical facts are neglected or distorted. The credulous readership of the eastern regions welcomed this Greek narrative, whereas the Latin translation by Julius Valerius Polemius in 320 AD (title: *Res gestae Alexandri Magni*) did not have much influence. Based on this *Pseudo-Callisthenes* there appeared Armenian, Coptic, Syriac, Arabic, and Ethiopian versions. Eastern accounts of Alexander's miraculous career paid more attention to the legend about how Alexander captured the wild peoples of Gog and Magog, and one version of this story was included in the *Qur'an*. The Ethiopian version *Zena Eskender* even presents Alexander as Christian king, prophet and preacher, as a model of morality, an embodiment of chastity, and care for the poor.

In the Latin West the Alexander romance came to a breakthrough in the 10th century when a certain Leo of Naples translated the Greek romance into Latin. His *Historia de preliis* (*History of Battles;* also known as *Nativitas et victoria Alexandri Magni*) was written between 950 and 970 AD, and its popular Latin style made the theme easily accessible to the peoples of western and northern Europe. Leo's translation was the main source of most later versions, among which the more famous are Alberich de Besancon's *Roman d'Alexandre* (Old French, between 1120 and 1140), the *Alexanderlied* by

Alexandre（古法语，1120—1140 年间成书），Lamprecht der Pfaffe 的 *Alexanderlied*（德语，约 1150 年），Rudolf von Ems 的 *Alexander*（约于 1240 年）和西班牙语的 *El libro de Aleixandre*（13 世纪初期）。这些著作通常将 Alexander 描写为骑士精神的模范。

分为 10 卷的拉丁语 *Alexandreis* 成书于 1184 年，其作者是 Walter de Chatillon（约 1135—1200 年）。该著作一时非常流行，它甚至在学校中取代了 Vergilius 的书。Walter 的优雅拉丁语风格表明作者很熟悉 Vergilius、Lucanus 和 Ovidius 的著作。他关于 Alexander 的描述基本上依赖于 Curtius Rufus 的书，但他也承纳并创造性地发展《亚历山大传奇》中的传说因素。著作的目标是颂扬 Alexander 的胜利并叙述波斯王 Darius 和印度王 Porus 的失败。早在 12 岁时 Alexander 很喜欢武器，他直觉地抓住一把剑。Aristoteles 教导他如何作战以及如何领导一个国度，这样就为他将来统治全世界做了准备。Alexander 预知自己将来的光荣事绩，但同时也知道他将很年轻就要去世。他征服世界，但他也知道如何克服自己的欲望、骄傲和恐惧。他用一支箭杀死一只印度大象，但他也照顾受伤的敌人，即 Porus 王，并后来接受他加入自己的朋友圈子。Alexander 也同情那位可怜的 Darius 王——他面临挫折和灾难。

在 Walter 的 *Alexandreis* 中，神明们支持 Alexander 的计划：胜利的女神 Victoria 在战场上帮助这位英雄，而好运的女神 Fortuna 支持他的行动。然而，在征服了亚细亚后 Alexander 说这个世界对他来说太小，他渴望见到另外一个世界（alium orbem, alias terras），而这句话得罪了创造的女神 Natura，因为 Alexander 似乎想穿透 Natura 的一切隐秘地区，他可能甚至会征服阴府。魔鬼很担心 Alexander 可能就是那位将要冲进地狱的人。(这是暗示基督宗教的章节之一。)因此，黑暗的种种力量决定要毒死这位英雄，而命运的女神 Fatum 就结束 Alexander 的生命。最后几行指向整个故事的教训：我们应该和 Alexander 一样，不要追求物质财富和世俗的荣誉，而要思念永恒的价值和想到自己的死亡。

098. 《一千零一夜》

这部文集亦称《阿拉伯夜》，包括 200 多个童话故事、爱情故事、传奇、动物寓言、幽默轶事和教育性的比喻故事。文本的核心是一些来自 8 世纪印度的故事，它们在 9 世纪被译成波斯语，10 世纪又译成阿拉伯语。框架叙事是印度的，很多人名是伊朗的，但许多故事来自那些与阿拉伯商人有关系的地区，包括印度、伊朗、伊拉克、埃及、土耳其和拜占庭。故事中出现的历史人物（比如 Alexander 大帝和 Solomon 王）和物品（如咖啡、烟叶、火器）有时暗示某故事的来源，也反映东方在中世纪的航海路线与商贸情况。显而易见，阿拉伯人在中世纪的岁月里不断加上了一些新的故事。大约于 1450 年形成了今天的《一千零一夜》。Antoine Galland 完成了第一部欧洲语言的翻译（*Les Mille et Une Nuits*, 10 卷，1704—1712 年）。大约 100 年后，现代阿拉伯学的创始人之一 Silvestre de Sacy 开始从一种语文学的角度来分析该文集。

Lamprecht der Pfaffe (German, around 1150), *Alexander* by Rudolf of Ems (ca. 1240) and the Spanish *El libro de Aleixandre* from the early 13th century. These works usually portray Alexander as a model of knightly chivalry.

The Latin *Alexandreis* in 10 books by Walter of Chatillon (ca. 1135—1200) was written in 1184 and became so popular that at one time it replaced the lecture of Vergil in medieval schools. Walter's elegant Latin style reflects the familiarity with the works of Vergil, Lucan, and Ovid. His version of Alexander's life basically follows Curtius Rufus' account but also integrates and creatively develops the more legendary elements of the Alexander romance. The aim of the work is to glorify Alexander's victories and tell of the defeat of the Persian king Darius and the Indian king Porus. Already at the age of 12 Alexander is very interested in weapons, he intuitively grasps a sword. Aristotle teaches him how to lead a battle and how to govern a country, thus preparing him for future world domination. Alexander foresees his future glory but also knows about his early death. He conquers the world but also knows how to overcome his own desires, his pride and his fear. He kills an Indian elephant with one arrow, but he cares for his wounded enemy, king Porus, whom he accepts in the circle of his friends later on. Alexander also feels sympathy for the miserable king Darius who faces defeat and disaster.

In Walther's *Alexandreis* the gods support Alexander's plans: Victoria, the goddess of victory, assists the hero in battle, and Fortuna, the goddess of good luck, favors his undertakings. However, after having conquered Asia Alexander says that this world is too small for him, he aspires another world (alium orbem, alias terras), and this word offends Natura, the goddess of creation, since Alexander seemingly intends to penetrate all her secret regions, he might even conquer the underworld. The devil fears that Alexander might be the one who devastatingly would break into hell. (This is one of the allusions to Christianity in Walter's epic.) Thus the forces of darkness decide that the hero must die by poisoning, and Fatum (the goddess of fate) ends Alexander's life. The final verses point to the lesson of the whole story: like Alexander we should not strive to obtain material riches and worldly honor but should think of eternal values and of our death.

098. *Alf lailah wa-lailah / Thousand and One Nights*

This collection, also known as *Arabian Nights*, contains more than 200 fairytales, romances, legends, fables, humorous anecdotes and didactic parables. The text grew around a group of Indian tales from the 8th century that was translated into the Persian language in the 9th and into Arabic in the 10th century. The frame story is Indian, the names of many characters are Iranian, but the numerous tales come from many cultures that were in contact with the Arab traders, including India, Iran, Iraq, Egypt, Turkey, and Byzantium. The appearance of certain historical persons (Alexander the Great, King Solomon) and goods (like coffee, tobacco, and firearms) sheds some light on the origin of the narratives and on medieval seafaring and trade in the East. It is also easy to show that the Arabs added more stories throughout the Middle Ages. By about 1450 the work had assumed its present form. The first European translation was made by Antoine Galland (*Les Mille et Une Nuits*, 10 volumes, 1704—1712). Around 100 years later one of the founders of modern Arabic studies, Silvestre de Sacy, started to analyze the text from a philological perspective.

框架故事描述印度苏丹 Shahriar 憎恨一切妇女，因为他的第一个妻子在他外出的时候不忠于他。作为一种残酷的复仇，苏丹每天娶一个新的妻子，但第二天又命令杀死她。然而，苏丹的大臣的女儿 Shahrazad 想好了一个诡计来拯救自己和其他妇女的性命。她要求父亲将她嫁给苏丹并在婚礼那天的夜晚开始讲一篇扣人心弦的故事。她很巧妙地中止她的叙述但承诺第二个夜晚要继续讲这个故事。因为苏丹很想听听妻子连续讲的故事的结局，他每天延迟处死 Shahrazad 并最终放弃他原来的恐怖计划。

《一千零一夜》中比较著名的故事是"Aladdin 和他的神灯"、"Ali Baba 和四十大盗"以及"航海者 Sindbad"。Sindbad 描绘他在七次远游中所遇到的险情，而这些故事反映出 8、9 世纪来自 Basra 的伊拉克商人冒着相当大的风险与东印度群岛和中国进行贸易。Sindbad 的奇妙经历中的一些元素与其他文学传统有类似之处，比如巨鸟 roc（阿拉伯语 ruhh），它的蛋像一个很大的白色楼房。这个神奇的巨鸟在 Marco Polo 的报告中也出现。那条被误认为是一个岛屿的鲸鱼也出现在 Plinius 关于海里动物的描述中，而 Sindbad 在第三次旅途中提到的吃人的巨人也许和 *Odysseia* 中的 Kyklopes 巨人有关。那个居住在黑海以北的地区的 Skythes 民族的奇特丧礼仪事——他们活埋某位去世的人的亲戚——早已被一些希腊历史学家和圣 Hieronymus 所提到。有学者认为 Sindbad 故事的法语翻译对 18 世纪的英国惊险文学，如 Defoe 的 *Robinson Crusoe*（1719 年）和 Swift 的 *Guliver's Travels*（1726 年），产生了一定的影响。

099.《贝奥武夫》

本著作是现存的最古老的古英语英雄诗（西撒克逊方言），同时也是第一部日耳曼人的史诗，大约成书于 730—750 年间，共有 3183 行头韵式的诗行。其主题是与龙的搏斗，为亡者的哀悼，臣民的忠诚以及英雄的自我牺牲精神。

丹麦人的国王 Hrothgar 生活在一个靠近大海的山上宫殿。每天晚上一只被称为 Grendel 的海怪袭击宫殿的大厅；这个海怪是 Cain 的后裔。当那些听音乐或喝甜酒的英雄们睡眠在宫殿里时，海怪杀死或虏走他们。年轻的 Beowulf 从瑞典而来，他愿意帮助 Hrothgar 王。他是一个和蔼善良的人。他与 14 位英雄一起假装睡眠在大厅中，而当 Grendel 海怪出现时，他就杀掉这个怪物。然而几天后 Grendel 的母亲来替孩子报仇并且杀死国王的最好朋友。Beowulf 依赖于上主的保护并跳入充满蛇及海鬼的海洋。他在海底深处杀害这个困扰国家多年的怪物。全国的人都赞美他的英勇。在这个光荣的成就后 Beowulf 回国并且平安地领导自己的国家 50 年之久。

第二章描述 Beowulf 最后的壮举以及他的死亡。在 50 年的和平时期后出现一条吐气喷火的龙，它毁坏部分的国土，因为曾经有人窃取了它的财宝。国王以及 12 个最威武的大臣起程要杀死这条龙。然而，一个个的英雄都因害怕龙而逃跑。最后只剩

The frame tale recounts how the jealous Indian Sultan Shahriar loathes all womankind, because his first wife has been unfaithful during his absence. As a kind of cruel revenge the Sultan marries a new wife each day and has her killed the next morning. However, Shahrazad, the daughter of the Sultan's vizier, devises a trick to save herself and others. She insists that her father gives her in marriage to the Sultan and begins to tell a captivating story on her wedding night. She artfully leaves the story incomplete, promising to finish it the following night. As the Sultan is curious and eager to hear the outcome of her tales within tales, he delays the execution of Shahrazad from day to day and finally abandons his original intention to kill her.

Among the more famous stories of the *Arabian Nights* are "Aladdin and his magic lamp", "Ali Baba and Fourty Robbers", and "Sindbad the Sailor". The narratives of Sindbad who recounts his adventures on seven journeys reflect the life and experiences of Iraqi merchants from Basra who under considerable risk traded with the East Indies and China during the 8th and 9th centuries. Some elements found in Sindbad's miraculous adventures suggest parallels in the narratives of other literary traditions, as for example the huge roc (Arabic "ruhh") whose egg looks like a big white building. This mythical bird also appears in Marco Polo's report. The big whale that is mistaken for an island may also be found in Pliny's description of huge sea animals, and the cannibal giants mentioned in Sindbad's third voyage may be related to the Cyclopes of the *Odyssey*. Certain strange funeral rites of the Scythians, a people living in the reagions north of the Black Sea, who bury alive the relatives of a deceased person were earlier mentioned by Greek historians and by St. Jerome. It has been suggested that the French translation of the tales of Sindbad had a certain impact on English adventure stories of the 18th century like Defoe's *Robinson Crusoe* (1719) and Swift's *Gulliver's Travels* (1726).

099. *Beowulf*

This is the oldest extant heroic poem in Old English (West-Saxon dialect), and the first Germanic epic, written ca. 730—750 AD, in 3183 alliterating verses. The main themes are: dragon fight, mourning for the dead, vassal loyalty, heroic self-sacrifice.

Hrothgar, the king of the Danes, lives in a palace on a mountain close to the sea. His court hall is attacked every night by the sea monster Grendel, a descendant of Cain. Many of the heroes, who are slumbering in the palace after listening to the bards' songs or after drinking sweet wine, are carried off or killed by Grendel. The young Beowulf, described as peaceful and mild, comes from Sweden across the sea to help King Hrothgar. Together with fourteen heroes he pretends to sleep in the court hall, and when Grendel appears, he kills the monster. However, some days later Grendel's mother takes revenge, killing the king's best friend. Trusting in the help of God, Beowulf dives into the dark sea, which is full of snakes and demons. Under water he kills the monster which has vexed the country for so many years. The whole country praises his heroism. After this glorious achievement Beowulf returns and reigns in his own country for 50 years in peace and happiness.

The second chapter depicts Beowulf's last heroic deed and his death. After 50 years of peaceful rule, a fire-breathing dragon devastates a part of his country to take re-

下 Wiglaf，一个年轻的骑士，他要陪同国王一直到最后。经过一场很长的搏斗，Beowulf 杀死了这条龙，但他自己因龙喷的毒气而受致命伤。他在 Wiglaf 的手中逝世，但他知道他是为自己的百姓牺牲了性命，这种思想带给他安慰。他很平静地面对神圣的审判者。Beowulf 表达的是一个理想国王（基督徒王）的形象，这样的国王应该为国民交出自己的性命。

100. 《救世主》

本头韵诗大概完成于公元 830 年，长达 6000 行，它使用古撒克逊方言来叙述福音的故事。关于作者没有什么资料，但他必然和 Fulda 隐修院有某些关系。他用的文献主要是 Tatianos 的 *Diatessaron*（从中大约选择了一半的故事）以及 Hrabanus 的《马太福音注解》。

自从天使预报耶稣的诞生一直到耶稣的复活，本叙述呈现出某些日耳曼文化因素：基督被描述为一个具有权威的老师，一位强有力的君王和保护者，因此他不骑着驴子进入耶路撒冷。耶稣的门徒比较类似一些忠臣，一些围绕着他们的立法者的战士。"山中圣训"（《马太福音》5~7 章）的描述暗示日耳曼部落举行的聚会（所谓的"thing"）。人们服从国王的赏报将是天国。跟随基督是某种法律关系。然而，《圣经》的真正精神也被保持。比如，当 Petrus 想用剑来保卫耶稣时，耶稣谴责了他，而 Heliand 的叙述符合《福音书》的原文。耶稣被描述为和平之王、温良与谦逊的导师，他自己也准备忍受侮辱。下面的语句来自 Heliand 的开头："Tho ni uuas lang after thiu, tho uuaard is uuisbodo an Galilealand, Gabriel cuman, engil thes aloualdon, thar he ene idis uuisse, munilica magad: Maria uuas siu heten."（"不久后，使者 Gabriel 被派遣去 Galilea，他就是万事大父的天使，他知道在那个地方有一个纯洁的女子，她被称 Maria"。请注意头韵 "munilica magad"。）

101. 《罗兰之歌》

这是最著名的古法语史诗，早期口述故事的记载来自第 11 世纪末，也保存拉丁语、意大利语和冰岛语的版本。古德语的文本来自 1172 年，共有 9094 行。历史基础是在 Pyrenees（比利牛斯山脉）的 Roncesvalles / Roncevaux 于 778 年发生的事件：当时有一些巴斯克人突击法兰克人的军队。

老 Charlemagne 王在西班牙活动已经有七年，他想回到法兰克地区去。当他的军队从西班牙地区撤退时，Charlemagne 的侄子 Roland 和另一位忠臣——Roland 的朋友 Oliver——在断后部队服务。Roland 指挥这些断后兵。他忠诚于他的君主，但似乎太勇敢。他有一个军号，名称 Olifant，其声音在 30 里外还能听到。他的宝剑 Durandot 原来是一个天使送给 Charlemagne 的。Roland 的继父是 Ganelon，他本来以谈判者的

venge for a treasure that was stolen from it. The king and 12 of his most capable vassals set out to kill the monster. However, one after the other shies away from the dragon and flees. Finally only the young knight Wiglaf remains with the king. In a long fight Beowulf can kill the dragon, but he himself is hurt lethally by the poisonous flames of the dragon. He dies in Wiglaf's arms, satisfied in the knowledge to have given his life for the good of his people. With a calm heart he can face the divine judge. Beowulf provides the model of an ideal (Christian) king who gives his life for his people.

100. *Heliand*

Written around 830 AD, this alliterative poem of 6000 verses tells the story of the gospel in an Old Saxon dialect. The author is unknown, but he must have had some contact to the monastery of Fulda. His main sources were the translation of Tatian's *Diatessaron* (from which he carefully chose about half of the narratives) and Hrabanus' commentary on *Matthew*.

From the annunciation of Jesus' birth by the angel Gabriel until the resurrection of Jesus there are some Germanic elements present in the text: Christ is depicted as an authoritative teacher, a powerful king and protector, and therefore he does not enter Jerusalem on a donkey. His disciples are somewhat similar to vassals, warriors surrounding their lawgiver. The sermon on the mount (*Mt* 5~7) is described in a way that alludes to the assembly of a Germanic tribe ("thing"). The reward for loyalty to the king will be the kingdom of heaven. Following Christ is a kind of legal relationship. However, the true spirit of the Bible is clearly kept. For example, when Peter tries to defend Jesus with his sword, Jesus' reproach is given as in the original gospel. Jesus is presented as king of peace, the teacher of mildness and humility who even is ready to suffer humiliation himself. Here is a passage from the beginning of the *Heliand*: "Tho ni uuas lang after thiu, tho uuaard is uuisbodo an Galilealand, Gabriel cuman, engil thes aloualdon, thar he ene idis uuisse, munilica magad: Maria uuas siu heten." ("It was not long after this, when the messenger Gabriel, the angel of the Father of all, was sent into the land of Galilee. He knew that in that place there was the pure maid, who was called Mary." See the alliteration "munilica magad".)

101. *Chanson de Roland / The Song of Roland*

This song is the most famous among Old French epics. The first redactions of the orally transmitted story date from the late eleventh century, and there are also versions in Latin, Italian, Icelandic. The German version of 1172 has 9094 verses. The historical basis of the narrative is the skirmish of Roncesvalles / Roncevaux in the Pyrenees, where a part of the Frankish army was attacked by Basques in 778.

The old king Charlemagne wants to return to France after seven years of campaigns in Spain. As Charlemagne's army retreats, two of his vassals, his nephew Roland and Roland's close friend Oliver, are serving in the rear part of the Frankish army. Roland is in command of that part of the army. He is loyal but audacious. He possesses a horn

身份被派遣到阿拉伯人那里去，但他憎恨 Roland，甚至与穆斯林军一同要谋害 Roland 领导的部队。

当穆斯林军队攻击 Roland 的士兵时，他决定要勇敢地抵抗他们，而不要吹号通知 Charlemagne，向他求援助。不久后，很多法兰克士兵阵亡，而 Oliver 谴责他的朋友，因为他没有吹大号，但 Roland 仍然拒绝吹号，同时要求他的士兵们更坚定地抵抗。后来他自己也受了严重的创伤，这才最终吹响 Olifant 号，这样使国王转回来，派遣他的军队来克服和惩罚阿拉伯人。在临终时，Roland 躺在一棵杉树下，在身边有他的宝剑和号。他向 Oliver 告别，而那位陪同军队的 Turpin 主教为他作一种临终的祈祷。Roland 想到"甜蜜的法兰西亚"，他的家人以及他的君主 Charles 王。他宣告自己的罪，请上帝宽恕他，最后以一种封建仪式向神提交他的手套。Gabriel 天使接受他的手套，而 Michael 天使带他的灵魂走入天堂。在他去世时突然挂起一场暴风，太阳停滞不前（参见《圣经·旧约》*Jos* 10:13 中的故事！）一直到 Charlemagne 完全克服阿拉伯人的军队。

102. 《熙德之歌》

本诗是最著名的西班牙语的 chanson de geste（"英雄诗歌"），长达 3730 行，大约于 1140 年被记载。后来很多诗歌都赞扬 Cid（熙德）的美德。

那位启发了该著作的历史人物是 Castilia（卡斯蒂利亚）将军 Rodrigo（或 Ruy）Diaz de Vivar（1040—1099 年），他曾经在基督宗教和伊斯兰教之间的战争中支持双方。Rodrigo Diaz 在卡斯蒂利亚王 Ferdinando I 的朝廷长大，与卡斯蒂利亚和 Leon 的统治者 Alfonso 的侄女结婚。后来 Alfonso 王驱逐他，因为 Rodrigo 擅自攻击了 Toledo 的伊斯兰教王国。在几年的时间内，Rodrigo 为 Saragossa 的伊斯兰统治者服务，但于 1089 年他自己试图征服 Valencia 的伊斯兰教王国。他于 1099 年在 Valencia 去世。他是一位很著名的无所畏惧的战士、能干的将军、礼貌且狡猾的政客，因此成为一个国家英雄。"Cid"来自阿拉伯语，意思是"主人"，而英雄的另一个西班牙称号是 El Cid Campeador（奋斗者）。在这首诗中，他是国王的忠臣，一位非常勇敢的战士，也是骑士精神的模范。

103. 《列那狐传奇》

这部故事集的最早版本来自 1170 年左右，但关于 Renard 狐诡计的口述传教可能在 10 世纪已经出现在罗兰地区。保存有拉丁语、法语、德语、荷兰语及英语版本，而在 13 世纪这些故事形成了一个分为 27 组叙事的整体。故事中的主人翁是一些保持自己特征的动物，而这些动物也代表着某些人的性格和道德风度，比如狮王 Noble 可能代表贵族人士并暴露出权威人物的无能为力。Renard 是狡猾和奸诈的化身，而

named Olifant whose distinctive blast can be heard even 30 miles away. His sword Durandot was once given by an angel to Charlemagne. Ganelon, Roland's stepfather, was sent as negotiator to the Arabs, therefore he hates Roland. He even conspires with the Saracenes to attack the rear guard led by Roland.

As the Arab army attacks Roland and his men, he decides to fight instead of blowing the horn in order to get reinforcement from Charlemagne. Soon many Frankish soldiers fall, and Oliver reproaches his friend Roland for not blowing the horn, but Roland still hesitates and asks his men to fight bravely. Only when he is deadly wounded himself, he finally blows the Olifant-horn and induces the king to send his men to overcome and punish the Arabs. As Roland's death is near he lies down at a pine-tree, sword and horn at his side. He says farewell to Oliver, and the accompanying bishop Turpin prays a dying benediction. Roland thinks of "sweet Francia", his family and his King Charles. Then he confesses his guilt, asks God for mercy and with a feudal gesture offers his glove to his Lord God. The angel Gabriel receives his glove, and Michael carries his soul to heaven. There is a storm at his death, and the sun stands still (Biblical allusion, conf. *Jos* 10:13) until Charlemagne has destroyed all the Arab army.

102. *Poema de mio Cid / Poem of the Cid*

The most famous of the Spanish "chansons de geste" ("song of heroic deeds", compare the Chanson de Roland) is this poem of 3730 lines written around 1140 AD. Later on an extensive ballad literature in praise of the "Cid" developed.

The hero whose legend inspired the work was the general Rodrigo (or Ruy) Diaz de Vivar (1040—1099) from Castile, a daring figure who fought on both sides in the wars between Christianity and Islam. Rodrigo Diaz grew up at the court of Ferdinand I of Castile, and married a niece of Alfonso, king of Castile and Leon. Later he was exiled by Alfonso for making an unauthorized attack on the Moorish kingdom of Toledo. For a span of several years Rodrigo served the Moorish rulers of Saragossa, but in 1089 he set out on his own to conquer the Moorish kingdom of Valencia. He died in Valencia in 1099. His fame as daring warrier, able military leader, courteous and shrewd statesman turned him into a national hero. "Cid" is a corrupted form of the Arabic word for "lord", and the hero was also known under the name of "El Cid Campeador" ("the Fighter"). In the poem he is a loyal vassal of the king, a man of tremendous courage, and a model of chivalry.

103. *Roman de Renard / Reynard the Fox*

The earliest version of this collection of tales comes from the time around 1170, but the cycle about the tricks of Reynard the fox may have appeared in Lorraine already in the tenth century. There are Latin, French, German, Dutch, and English editions, and in the 13th century the tales were organized in a series of 27 narratives. The characters in the stories are animals who keep some of their natural traits but otherwise represent certain human types or moral attitudes, for example Noble the Lion may represent the nobility, exposing the ineptitude of authority, Reynard stands for guile and shrewdness, Isengrim the Wolf for the arrogant abuse of power. Having no clear intention besides entertainment

狼 Isengrim 代表掌权者的傲慢。这些故事除了消遣以外没有很明确的目的,也许它们是一些民间传统的产物。和其他的 fabliaux(讽刺性故事)一样,这些动物故事没一个明显的"教训",他们仅仅描述聪明狡猾人的胜利,并有时候讽刺上阶层的人和圣职人员。

故事的核心是狡猾狐狸 Renard 的诡计以及他的残暴对手狼 Isengrim。因为一切动物都指控狐狸的无耻罪行,狮王 Noble 开庭要审理案件并惩罚 Renard。狮王派遣 Briand 熊出去寻找并逮捕 Renard 狐,使他接受应有的惩罚。Briand 熊既勇敢又粗壮,他知道 Renard 的狡猾并向王承诺狐狸的欺骗手段或阿谀奉承都不会让他上当。然而,一到 Renard 的居所,狐狸告诉熊一个蜂蜜多的地方,马上 Briand 满脑子想的都是吃蜂蜜的事。Renard 假装不愿意耽误到法院受审,但最后同意熊的请求。Renard 将熊带到某一棵可能有蜂蜜的树。树干被裂开,而当贪婪的熊在树上找蜜时,Renard 拿掉卡在那里的楔子。因此熊被压住,只能哀叹他的天真。住在附近的人们抓住熊并痛打他一顿,但熊还能逃跑并悲伤地向狮王报告狐狸如何欺骗了他。

不久后 Renard 被捕,上了法庭。因为所有的动物都谴责他的无数罪行,他的雄辩也没有用。狮王 Noble 判处他死刑。当他们走向绞刑架时,狐狸说他忏悔自己的罪恶,并透露说自己有大量的财宝,而这个消息立马改变贪婪国王的意图,宣布 Renard 无罪并使他成为宫廷的顾问。野兔和公羊去取 Renard 将要献给国王的财宝,但 Renard 用诡计杀死野兔,又吃掉兔子并让公羊把兔头带给国王。Renard 再次被迫前往法庭为自己辩护,而且又靠三寸之舌让国王相信他的无罪。只有狼 Isengrim 不相信 Renard 的谎言并仍然试图逮捕狐狸。当狼与狐狸在冬天过一个池塘时,Renard 说狼可以在冰上打个洞并使用他的尾巴当诱饵,这样可以很容易捕获池里的鱼。狼 Isengrim 希望获得一顿好餐,将尾巴探入冰水中并等待一会。Renard 劝狼不要动,要耐心等待。最终狼发现永远不会有鱼咬住他的尾巴,但那时他已经被冻住了,走不了。狡猾的诡计再次战胜了体力的优越性。

104. 《布拉纳歌集》

在 1803 年很多德国隐修院被解散。当时人们在巴代利亚的 Benediktbeuren 隐修院找到了一部很古老的拉丁手抄本。该诗歌集于 1847 年出版,它包含一些来自 12、13 世纪的诗歌,并被称为 Carmina Burana(即"来自 Benediktbeuren 的歌")。后来人们广泛地使用这个名称指中世纪的拉丁语诗歌或"流浪艺人"(vagantes)的文学作品。*Carmina Burana* 的著作包括道德的讽刺诗、赞美春天、青春、爱情、葡萄酒与世俗享受的诗歌。大部分的诗歌是拉丁语写的,也有一些轮流使用拉丁语和本地语言,这样创造了一些拉—德和拉—法诗歌。手抄本中的行首字是以优美的风格写的,书中还有一些小型的图画,其中最有名的描绘"命运女神之轮子"。在英国发现的 *Carmina Cantabrigensia*(《剑桥歌集》)是类似的著作,共有 50 首诗。这些诗歌大概是 11 世纪在

the stories are possibly the product of popular traditions. As is typical for these so-called fabliaux (satirical stories), the beast fables do not point to a moral, they just show the triumph of wit and guile and sometimes satirize the upper classes and the clergy.

The stories are centered on the cunning tricks of Reynard the Fox and the struggles with his cruel rival Isengrim the Wolf. King Noble the Lion holds a court to punish Reynard, because all animals keep complaining about the many shameless crimes of the fox. The king sends Briand the Bear to bring Reynard to court so as to receive his proper punishment. Briand the Bear is strong and fearless, he knows about the shrewd tricks of Reynard and promises to the king that he will not fall prey to the allurements of the fox. However, as he comes to Reynard's domicile to detain him, the fox tells about a place where one could easily get honey, and soon Briand can only think of the sweet delicacy. Reynard pretends to be eager to go to court first, but finally he answers the pleas of the bear. Reynard leads the Bear to a certain tree where the honey might be. The tree has been wedged apart, and as the greedy bear looks for the honey in the tree, Reynard removes the wedge. Now the bear is caught in the tree and can only lament his naivety. As the people from the neighborhood arrive the bear gets his blows but can escape. He returns to the king and tearfully reports how he was cheated by the fox.

Some time later Reynard is brought to court. Since all the animals are condemning his countless crimes, his eloquent defence cannot save him. King Noble the Lion decides that he must be hanged. On the way to his execution the fox says that he regrets all his sins, but at the same time he also mentions that he possesses a treasure of great value, and this information changes the greedy king's intention so much, that he not only announces Reynard to be innocent but also raises him to the status of an advisor at court. As the Rabbit and the Goat go to bring Reynard's treasure to the king, Reynard uses a trick to kill the Rabbit, devours the victim and asks the Goat to send the Rabbit's head back to the King. Again Reynard has to go to court to defend himself for his crime, and again his nimble tongue can convince the King that he is innocent. Only Isengrim the Wolf is not deceived by Reynard's lies and tries to detain the fox. As the Wolf and the Fox pass by a pond in the winter season, Reynard says that it would be easy to get the fish out of the pond, if only the Wolf would make a hole in the ice and use his tail as bait for the fish. Inspired by the hope for a good meal Isengrim lets his tail into the cold water and waits for a while. Reynard persuades him not to move for some time and to wait patiently, but as the Wolf discovers that no fish will ever bite into his tail he is already frozen to the ice and cannot escape. Once again guile has triumphed over physical strength.

104. *Carmina Burana* / *Carmina Burana*

In the year 1803 when many monasteries in Germany were dissolved, an old Latin manuscript was found in the monastery of Benediktbeuren in Bavaria. This collection of poetry from the 12th and 13th centuries was published in 1847 and called "Carmina Burana" ("Songs from Benediktbeuren"). Later this term was used to denote medieval Latin poetry or "goliardic poetry" in general. Among the poems found in the *Carmina Burana* are moral satires, songs in praise of spring, youth, love, wine, and the enjoyment of life. Most of the songs are in Latin, others are mixing Latin with alternating lines in the vernacular, thus creating Latin-German and Latin-French poems. The initial letters

德国写的,后来英国人抄录它们。

关于这些诗歌的作者没有很多资料,连作者的名字都没有。其中最有名的人是所谓的 Archipoeta,一位德国诗人,其原名无法考证。他的号是"Golias",而根据他的名称人们广泛指这些作者为 goliards。Archipoeta 来自下层贵族,他决定要当一个学者并开始学习神学,后在意大利的 Salerno 研究医学,再到 Paris 学习语文和修辞学。他谙悉古典文学,经常引用 Horatius、Ovidius 和 Vergilius 的语句。因为 Colonia 的总主教 Rainald von Dassel(1159—1167 年)是他的主保,他的一切著作都提到这位总主教(Electus Coloniae)。Archipoeta 最著名的诗大概是他的 *Confessio*(《告解》),其中替自己的生活辩护,同时控诉自己的罪(喜欢女孩子、赌博与喝酒),又因这些恶习而自豪,因为这些世俗的追求帮助他写更好的诗。另一个属于该派的诗人是 Walter de Chatillon(约 1135—1200 年),他曾经在 Paris 和 Rheims 学习,后来在英国的 Henricus II 王那里任职,但被迫离开英国,因为他支持 Thomas Beckett。他去 Bolonia 学习法律,最终在法国的 Amiens 大教堂中当圣职人员。他的名著是关于 Alexander Magnus 的拉丁史诗,即 *Alexandreis*。

Carmina Burana 的作者都是拉丁语的大师,他们使用很多来自文学和神学传统的资料,他们很熟悉古希腊和罗马的神话,也多次引用古典诗人,同时利用来自《圣经》的资料或改写一些来自拉丁礼仪的 sequentia(宗教赞美歌)。*Carmina Burana* 的诗人很奇妙地使用行尾韵、行中韵以及头韵法,比如这两行:Feror ego veluti—sine nauta navis, ut per vias aeris—vaga fertur avis("我流浪去各地,好比一条没有舵手的船,如同一只随风而飞的鸟。")这些诗歌的重音用法符合基督教的诗歌传统,即在古代晚期形成的模式。因此,他们仅仅看重词语的重音,并忽略音的长短。一行的后半部分保留自然的重音,但前面的部分有时候使用一些不符合散文用法的重音分配法。与宗教赞美歌及宫廷诗歌一样,*Carmina Burana* 的诗歌是配音乐唱的,这样协调了歌词的重音。

105. 《尼伯龙根之歌》

这个分为 39"回"的英雄史诗长 9516 行(2000 多小段),约于 1200 年用古高德语写成(作者大概是奥地利人,因为他对维也纳和帕骚之间的地区作了比较详细的描述)。

勃艮第王 Gunther("战争—军队")、Gernot("长矛—斗士")和 Giselher("箭—军队")的美丽妹妹是 Kriemhild("面具—战争")。她在梦中见到两只老鹰,它们杀死她培养的一只鹰(鹰经常代表爱人)。来自"低地"(荷兰地区)的王子 Siegfried("胜利—保护")向往这位美女。他想去 Worms 的宫廷,向 Gunther 求娶 Kriemhild。Gunther 的忠信封臣是 Hagen("围帐"),他叙述关于 Siegfried 的事:这个英雄获得了 Nibelung 地

in the manuscript are written in an elaborate style, some verses are adorned with miniature paintings, among which the picture of Fortune's wheel is the most famous. A similar work are the *Carmina Cantabrigensia* (*Cambridge Songs*), a collection of 50 songs. These poems were probably written in Germany in the 11th century and later copied in England.

Not much is known about the authors of these songs and poems, we do not even know their names. The most famous among them is the "Archipoeta", a German whose original name is unknown. His cognomen "Golias" was extended to the school of poets: they are called "goliards". The Archipoeta came from the lower ranks of the aristocracy and decided to become a scholar. He studied some theology, medicine in Salerno (Italy), grammar and rhetoric in Paris. Well acquainted with classical poetry he often uses phrases coined by Horace, Ovid, or Virgil. As he was patronized by the archbishop of Cologne, Rainald von Dassel (1159—1167), all his works mention the archbishop (Electus Coloniae). His most famous work is probably the *Confession of Golias*, an autobiographical apologia, in which he at the same time confesses his sins (desire for women, gambling, and wine) and boasts of them, since these worldly pursuits help him to write even better poetry. Another poet belonging to the school of goliards is Walter of Chatillon (ca. 1135—1200), who studied in Paris and Rheims, held a post in England under Henry II but left the country because he sided with Thomas Beckett. He went to Bologna to study law and finally became a canon of Amiens cathedral. His most famous work is a Latin epic on Alexander the Great, the *Alexandreis*.

The authors of the *Carmina Burana* are masters of the Latin language, they use literary and theological sources, they are well acquainted with the deities of Greek and Roman mythology and frequently cite the classical Latin poets, but they also quote from the Bible or parody sequences from the Latin liturgy. The poets of the *Carmina Burana* masterfully employ end rhyme and internal rhyme as well as alliteration, see for example these verses: "Feror ego veluti—sine nauta navis, ut per vias aeris—vaga fertur avis." (I wander around like a ship without helmsman, like a homeless bird that is carried around by the winds.) The use of accent follows the style of Christian hymns which emerged in late antiquity, thus the verses are organized in terms of accent, and the length of syllables is neglected. The last half of a verse preserves the natural accentuation, whereas words in the first part of a verse are sometimes accentuated in a way different from the use of these words in a prose text. Similar to sequences and courtly lyrics, the songs of the *Carmina Burana* were usually accompanied by music which harmonized the accentuations.

105. *Nibelungenlied / Song of the Nibelungs*

This heroic epic in 39 "adventures" (Aventiuren) and more than 2000 stanzas (9516 verses) was written ca. 1200 in old high German. The author was probably a native of Austria who knew the area between Vienna and Passau well.

Kriemhild ("mask-fight"), the beautiful sister of the Burgundian Kings Gunther ("fight-army"), Gernot ("spear-fighter") and Giselher ("arrow-army"), sees a vision in a dream: two eagles kill the hawk she raised (a hawk often symbolizes a lover). Siegfried ("victory-protection"), a prince from the "Niderlanden" (Netherlands, lower Rhine area), hears of Kriemhild's beauty. He plans to go to Worms to the court of King

精(矮子)的宝藏,具有力气的Balmung宝剑以及Alberich矮子的隐身帽。Hagen说,Siegfried曾经杀了一条龙,后在龙的血液中洗浴,所以他的皮肤刀枪不入。当Siegfried来到勃艮第的城市时,他们很尊敬地接待他,而年轻的Kriemhild对他一见钟情。然而,Gunther王要求Siegfried先帮助他对付丹麦人,又请他协助他赢得冰岛的女王Brunhild("武甲—战争")的爱情。Siegfried说,如果他将来获得Kriemhild为妻,他愿意帮助国王。

那个具有战士风格的Brunhild女王要求每一个求婚者参加一些比武或运动竞赛。只有一个在掷石块或掷长矛方面能超过她的男人将可以当他的丈夫。Siegfried戴上他的隐身帽,这样帮助他的主人Gunther在竞赛中战胜那位坚强的女王。她跟着他们回到Worms城,在那里他们庆祝两对夫妻的婚姻:Gunther—Brunhild和Siegfried—Kriemhild。然而,在当天晚上,Brunhild拒绝他的丈夫接近她,甚至将他捆绑起来挂在墙上。Gunther只得又请Siegfried帮助他,而在第二天夜里Siegfried戴上隐身帽并与Gunther一起压住Brunhild。现在这个女战士屈服于她的丈夫Gunther。在搏斗当中,Siegfried偷偷地拿走了Brunhild的腰带和戒指,后来将这些东西送给自己的妻子Kriemhild当礼物,又告诉她关于它们的事。婚后,Siegfried回到他的家乡Xanten,和他的妻子当王。

过了十年,Brunhild女王邀请Siegfried和Kriemhild来到Worms参加一个节庆。在比武赛场和在教堂门前,这两位女王开始吵架,最后Kriemhild控诉Brunhild说她在结婚之前与Siegfried有关系,她又出示腰带和戒指作证据。这种侮辱也使Gunther和Siegfried之间的关系转变。Hagen从一开始对Siegfried怀着敌意,现在他利用这次冲突来找机会去杀害Siegfried。他说将来有计划进行一些征服撒克逊人或丹麦人的战争。Hagen向Kriemhild说他一定要保护Siegfried,所以请她说出Siegfried的"保护层"是否能够很全面的保护。Kriemhild天真地说出他丈夫的致命弱点:在Siegfried的肩胛骨中间有一点,因为当他在龙血中洗澡时,一片橡树叶子落到那里。她甚至在丈夫的衣服上标出这个容易受伤的部位。

Hagen为了除掉Siegfried组织了一次打猎活动。在此之前,Kriemhild在梦中见到一些沾满血的花。在狩猎会中,Siegfried有一次在泉边喝水,而Hagen趁机从后面刺杀Siegfried。他们将他的尸体放在Kriemhild的卧室前,从此她的哀叹和控诉唠叨不绝。她感觉是Hagen杀死了Siegfried。当Hagen站在Siegfried的棺材边时,死者的伤口又开始出血,这就更使Kriemhild认定是谁杀死了丈夫。在Siegfried的葬礼后,她仍然留在Worms。4年后,Hagen劝勉Gunther要与Kriemhild和好。她也命令将尼伯龙根的宝藏带到Worms,并很慷慨地将宝库中的一些财富分给别人,但Hagen担心她的报复,所以拿到了宝藏的钥匙后,他将整个宝藏沉入莱茵河,这样夺取了Kriemhild的权力和幸福。

Gunther to ask for Kriemhild's hand. Hagen ("enclosure") of Tronje, the brave vassal of Gunther, reports that Siegfried has gained the treasure of the dwarf Nibelung (Niflung) together with the mighty sword Balmung and has obtained a magic hood (a cloak of invisibility) from the dwarf Alberich. Hagen also knows that Siegfried has killed a dragon and after a bath in the dragon's blood he has become invulnerable. When Siegfried arrives at the Burgundian court, he is received with due respect, and the young Kriemhild loves him at first sight, but Gunther asks Siegfried first to help him in the war against the Danes and then to win the hand of queen Brunhild ("armour-fight") in Iceland. Siegfried agrees under the condition that Kriemhild will become his wife.

The warrior-like Brunhild asks every suitor to undergo some martial and athletic tests. She will only marry a man who can outdo her in the competitions of throwing stones and hurling javelins. Hidden by his cloak of invisibility, Siegfried can secretly help Gunther to win the competition, and they lead the mighty queen back to Worms. There they celebrate a double wedding (Siegfried—Kriemhild, and Gunther—Brunhild). In the wedding night Brunhild refuses to let her husband consummate their marriage, she even binds him and hangs him unto a nail in the wall. Gunther asks Siegfried to help him again, and in the next night the invisible Siegfried helps Gunther to subdue Brunhild, who now submits to Gunther. In the fight Siegfried takes away the girdle and ring from Brunhild, which he later presents to his wife Kriemhild, not without telling her the story about them. After the wedding Siegfried returns to his home Xanten to reign there with his wife.

After ten years Brunhild invites Siegfried and Kriemhild to a festival in Worms. At the tournament and at the door of the church the two queens start a quarrel, in which Kriemhild charges Brunhild that she had a premarital affair with Siegfried and even shows the girdle and the ring as a proof. This insult brings estrangement between Gunther and Siegfried. Hagen has always been inimical to Siegfried and now uses the conflict to find a way to kill Siegfried. He tells of future wars against the Saxons and Danes. Under the pretext of protecting Siegfried, Hagen asks Kriemhild whether his invulnerability is complete. Kriemhild unwittingly reveals that there is a spot between his shoulderblades, where an oak-leaf fell when he bathed in the dragon's blood. She even marks the vulnerable spot on her husband's dress.

Hagen organizes a hunting party in order to trap Siegfried. The night before Kriemhild has a dream in which she sees flowers wet with blood. At the hunt Hagen stabs Siegfried in the back as he stoops down to drink water from a spring. Hagen and his men place Siegfried's dead body in front of Kriemhild's bedchamber, and from now on her mournings and accusations find no end. She feels that Hagen killed Siegfried, and her suspicion is confirmed as the wounds of Siegfried start to bleed again in the moment when Hagen approaches the bier. After Siegfried's funeral she remains in Worms and after four years Hagen persuades Gunther to be reconciled with her. She also orders the Nibelungen-treasure to be brought to Worms and distributes generously from it until Hagen who fears her revenge obtains the keys to the treasure, sinks it in the Rhine and so deprives Kriemhild of all her power and happiness.

第20到39"回"包含这个故事的后半部分。匈奴人的王Etzel(即Attila,他是历史上的人物,453年去世)的妻子Helche去世,所以他寻找一个新的对象。他派遣他的封臣Ruediger去Worms向Kriemhild求婚。Gunther和他的弟兄们支持这种婚姻,因为Kriemhild这样会远离他们——她的哀叹对他们来说始终是一种控诉。Kriemhild要求Ruediger发誓要在任何敌人面前保护她,此后她决定接受Etzel,虽然他不是基督徒(他被描述为一个诚实并应该受尊敬的人)。Kriemhild起程去匈奴人的王宫(即维也纳以东的Etzelenburg)。实际上,Kriemhild想利用Etzel来完成她的报复,她特别憎恨Hagen,因为他杀害了她的丈夫又夺取了她的宝藏。

13年后,Kriemhild使Etzel王邀请勃艮第人来参加一个节庆。Hagen有一个不好的预感,但那三个弟兄不理他的警告。Ruediger陪同他们沿着Danubius(多瑙河)去Etzel的宫廷,但在那里只有Giselher受到Kriemhild的热切欢迎,因为他是最小的,对于Siegfried的死亡他是无辜的。Kriemhild向其他的客人公开表示敌意,暗中挑起一些冲突。当贵族们在宫廷的大厅中吃饭时,Kriemhild使匈奴人在Etzel的弟兄Blodelin的领导下突击和杀死勃艮第的骑士们——他们在Dankwart的率领下陪同了Gunther王。Dankwart是Hagen的弟兄,他能够逃脱危险并跑到大厅,满身血痕地报告这个欺骗性的大屠杀。那些勃艮第贵族们并没有根据骑士礼貌在餐桌上脱掉了他们的武装。Hagen马上杀死Kriemhild和Etzel所生的儿子Orte,这样在大厅中发起战斗。Dietrich(即Theodoricus,历史上是东哥特人在意大利的王,493—526年)当时也在匈奴人的宫廷中。他和Ruediger,Etzel及Kriemhild能够离开大厅,此后Hagen封锁大厅所有的门。

大厅中的混战导致一切匈奴人都被杀。后来那些正在Etzel王宫中住的丹麦公爵和图林根公爵的士兵们也被杀。Kriemhild命令要从四方烧大厅。她想进行残酷的报仇并要求Ruediger兑现他的诺言。他面对一种无法解决的冲突(保护他的客人或忠于原先的誓词),后来与匈奴人一起攻击勃艮第人,但不久后阵亡。最终,除了Gunther和Hagen以外,一切勃艮第人都被杀。那位强大的战士Dietrich王克服他们,将他们两个捆绑起来并将他们交给Kriemhild。她问Hagen宝藏的所在地,但Hagen说只要他的主人中还有一个人活着,他就不会说出这事。Kriemhild马上命令人斩下Gunther的头,但Hagen仍然嘲笑她说:"现在只有上帝和我知道这个宝藏在哪里,而你这个魔鬼式的女人永远不会知道。"Kriemhild很愤怒,她见到Hagen的剑实际上就是Siegfried的宝剑Balmung,她拉出剑,一下砍下他的头。Etzel王大声哀叹说,像Hagen那样的英雄要被一个妇女杀死。这又使Dietrich王的战友Hildebrand感到气愤,他举剑将Kriemhild一剑刺死。

106. 《英国大宪章》

《英国大宪章》全名为《种种自由权利的宪章,即约翰内斯王与诸男爵之间关于教

The chapters ("aventiure") 20 to 39 contain the second part of the story. Etzel (Attila, the historical date of his death is the year 453), king of the Huns, is looking for a wife after the death of his first wife Helche. He sends his vassal Margrave Ruediger to Worms to ask for Kriemhild's hand. Gunther and his brothers welcome the match as a means to rid themselves of a sister whom they have cheated and whose mourning is a constant reproach. Kriemhild makes Ruediger swear that he will take revenge on anyone who harms Kriemhild, and now she decides to accept the pagan Etzel, who is portrayed as an honest and honorable man. Kriemhild travels to the Huns' court (Etzelenburg, east of Vienna), planning to use Etzel in her vengeance against the hated Hagen who killed her husband and seized her treasure.

After 13 years Kriemhild persuades King Etzel to invite the Burgundians to a feast. Hagen has a premonition of doom, but the three brothers do not heed his warnings. Ruediger accompanies them downward along the Danube river to Etzel's court, where Kriemhild receives only Giselher cordially since he is the youngest of the three brothers and innocent of Siefried's death. She treats the others with barely concealed enmity and provokes hostilities. As the kings have a meal in the palace hall, Kriemhild orders that the Burgundian knights who accompany King Gunther under Dankwart's command are suddenly attacked and killed by the Huns under Etzel's brother Blodelin. Dankwart, the brother of Hagen, enters the hall, soaked in blood, reporting the treacherous slaughter. The Burgundian nobles at the table have defied knightly politeness and kept their weapons at hand while eating. Hagen now kills Kriemhild's and Etzel's little son Orte and triggers a fight in the hall. King Dietrich of Bern (Theodoric the Great, historical king of the Ostrogothic kingdom in Italy 493—526) has been living in exile at the Huns' court. He and Ruediger together with Etzel and Kriemhild manage to retreat from the hall before Hagen orders to shut all the doors of the palace hall.

The result of the fierce fighting in the palace is that all Huns in the hall are killed, later also the knights of the Danish and Thuringian dukes who reside at Etzel's court. Kriemhild orders to set fire at all four corners of the palace hall. She wants bloody revenge and now asks Ruediger to keep his oath. He faces an insoluble conflict of loyalties (protection of his guests or keeping his former oath) and falls fighting on the side of the Huns. Finally Gunther and Hagen are the only Burgundian survivors. The great warrior King Dietrich overwhelms them, binds them and hands them over to Kriemhild. She asks Hagen about the treasure. Hagen answers that he has sworn not to reveal the place of the treasure as long as one of his masters is alive. Kriemhild immediately orders Gunther to be beheaded, but Hagen only laughs at her: "Now only God and myself know about the treasure, and you devilish woman will never find out." Kriemhild is furious, she sees that Hagen's sword is in fact Siegfried's sword Balmung, draws it and personally lops off Hagen's head. King Etzel sighs that a hero like Hagen should fall through the hand of a woman, and the enraged Hildebrand, armor-bearer of Dietrich, kills Kriemhild with a stroke of his sword.

106. *Magna Charta Libertatum / Great Charter of English Liberties*

The Charta is entitled *Magna Charta Libertatum, seu concordia inter regem Johannem et Barones pro concessione libertatum Ecclesiae et regni Angliae* (*The Great Char-*

会和政府的种种权利的契约》。自从 Wilhelmus（征服者威廉，1066—1087 年）的儿子 Henricus I（亨利一世，1100—1135 年）以来，很多英国国王签订了一些文献，其中保证教会和贵族各种权利。在 Johannes I（"失国者"约翰内斯一世，1199—1216 年）的时期，那些男爵都担心管理制度的中央化以及罗马法在国王法院的影响逐渐增加。另一方面，国王受法国 Philippus de Anjou（菲利普·安茹）的压力，并于 1204 年失去了诺曼底地区。Johannes 王也与教宗 Innocens III（依诺森三世，1198—1216 年）发生冲突，而教宗曾经绝罚了他。英国国王迫切地需要男爵们的（财力）支持。那位于 1207 年被祝圣为 Canterbury（坎特伯雷）总主教的 Stephanus Langton（兰顿）——当时国王也不同意他当总主教——与英国的男爵们利用了当时的情况并共同拟订这个《宪章》，在 Windsor 附近的 Runnymede 将它提交给国王。英国国王四天后（1215 年 6 月 15 日）签名同意。

这部《宪章》共 63 条，大部分内容澄清管理问题、各种贸易权利和封臣贵族们的特殊权利。从宪法思想的历史来看，第 39 条、40 条和 61 条有特别深远的意义。第 39 条规定："任何自由的人都不可以被逮捕、不可以入狱、不可以夺取他的财产、不可以驱逐他或以任何方式损害他（……）除非与他同等的人依法审判他或根据当地的法律。"

第 40 条规定："我们（指国王）不向任何人卖法律权利，不拒绝任何人他应有的权利和公道，也不延迟他的合法权利。"国王在后来的几百年当中曾经多次违背了这些原则，但它们至少首次表达"法律的统治"，而且说连国王和宫廷的法院也必须遵守法律的规定。

第 61 条甚至说，如果国王不遵守法律和契约，臣民们有权利不服从他。如果 25 个贵族中多数的人觉得国王没有完成他的任务，他们可以占领王家的地产，直到国王为他的违法行为提供赔偿。《英国大宪章》准备了后来的宪法文献的路：1628 年有 *Petition of Rights*，1679 年的 *Habeas Corpus Acts* 和 1689 年的 *Bill of Rights*。

107. 《黄金诏书》

文献的名称 Bulla aurea 来自书上的黄金封记（拉丁语：bulla）。这道敕令分为 31 章，由德国皇帝 Carolus IV 和选帝候分别颁布于 Nuremberg 的帝国议会（1356 年 1 月）和 Metz 的帝国议会（1356 年 12 月）。文献第一次规定德国国王的选举程序，并澄清七位选帝侯的地位。一直到 Napoleon 的时代，*Bulla aurea* 是神圣罗马帝国中最重要的宪法文献。

七位选帝侯是 Mainz、Trier 和 Cologne 的总主教（Erzbischof）、Rhein 的伯爵（Pfalzgraf）、Sachsen-Wittenberg 的公爵、Brandenburg 的边疆伯爵（Markgraf）和波希米亚的王。自从 1257 年以来这几个选帝侯获得了越来越大的影响力，而他们的共同目

ter of Liberties, or contract between King John and the Barons about the Rights granted to the Church and the Government of England*). Since Henry I （1100—1135）, the son of William the Conqueror （1066—1087）, many English kings had signed documents in which they promised to protect the rights of the nobility and of the Church. Under King John I （"Lackland", 1199—1216） the barons were worried about the centralization of the administration and the increasing influence of Roman Law at the royal court. The king was under pressure since he had lost the Normandy to the French King Philipp of Anjou （1204）. He had a conflict with Pope Innocens III （1198—1216）, who excommunicated King John. The king needed the （financial） support of the barons. Stephen Langton, who had been ordained Archbishop of Canterbury in 1207 against King John's will, and the barons used the situation and drafted a Charter which was presented to the King in Runnymede （at Windsor）. The king signed it after four days （June 15th, 1215）.

The 63 articles of the document try to regulate questions in the areas of administration, trade rights and certain feudal rights of the King's vassals. The articles 39, 40 and 61 are held to be of special importance in the history of constitutional law. Art. 39: Nullus liber homo capiatur, vel imprisonetur, aut disseisiatur, aut utlagetur, aut exuletur, aut aliquo modo destruatur [⋯] nisi per legale iudicium parium suorum vel per legem terrae. (No free man shall be arrested or imprisoned or disseised or outlawed or exiled or in any way victimized [⋯] except by the lawful judgment of his peers or by the law of the land.)

Art. 40: Nulli vendemus, nulli negabimus, aut differimus, rectum aut iustitiam. (To no one will we sell, to no one will we refuse or delay right or justice.) Of course, these principles were often not kept in the subsequent centuries, but they formulate for the first time the rule of law in a way that even the king an royal courts must abide by the law.

Article 61 even entitles the subjects of the king to refuse obedience if the king does not observe the law and keep the contract. If a majority of 25 nobles decides that the king has not kept his obligations, they may occupy royal lands until the king grants recompensation for his violation of the law. The Magna Charta prepared the way for later constitutional laws embodied in the *Petition of Rights* of 1628, the *Habeas Corpus Acts* of 1679 and the *Bill of Rights* of 1689.

107. *Bulla aurea / Golden Bull*

The name "Golden Bull" comes from the golden seal （in Latin "bulla"） of the document. This decree, consisting of 31 chapters, was issued by emperor Charles IV of Germany and the electors （Kurfuersten） at the diets of Nuremberg （January 1356） and Metz （December 1356）. The document regulated for the first time the election process of the German King and clarified the position of the seven electors. The *Golden Bull* remained the most important constitutional law of the Holy Roman Empire until the era of Napoleon.

The seven electors were the archbishops （Erzbishof）, of Mainz, Trier, and Cologne, the count palatine （Pfalzgraf） of the Rhine, the duke of Saxony （Herzog von Sachsen-Wittenberg）, the margrave （Markgraf） of Brandenburg, and the king of Bohemia. Since 1257 this group of electors wielded growing influence, and their common aim was to pre-

标是阻碍任何一个强有力的、普遍被接受的王朝的出现。因此他们连续选择一些来自不同贵族的统治者；这个现象被称为"跳动式的选举"：来自 Habsburg 王朝的 Rudolphus（1273—1291 年），来自 Nassau 的 Adolphus（1292—1298 年），Albrecht I（1298—1308 年），Henricus VII（1208—1313 年）和 Bavaria 的 Ludovicus（1314—1347 年）。这些皇帝们都无法建立一个皇朝。Carolus IV（1347—1378 年）皇帝要求选帝侯们选他的儿子 Wenzel，但选帝侯们后来弹劾那位无能的皇帝并提名 Pfalz 的 Ruprecht 当皇帝（1400—1410 年），又选择匈牙利王 Sigismund（1410—1437 年），他是 Wenzel 的弟弟。

《黄金诏书》规定七个选帝侯是选择德国皇帝的正规权威，并肯定多数投票原则。选帝侯们也获得了很多特权，他们被允许参与帝国的政治，他们的领土被宣布为"不可分割的"，而"领土之主"（domini terrae）的头衔带给他们几乎无限的司法权。选帝侯们可以向犹太人收税，他们垄断盐和矿物，甚至可以自己铸币。

《黄金诏书》也包含很多涉及复仇权和"大地和平"的规定。所谓的"大地和平"（pax terrae, Landfrieden）由德国皇帝或帝国议会宣布，其目标是镇压地区性的纷争。根据 Landfrieden 要求有关人士要宣誓保持和平。那些侵犯和平的人要遭受严厉的惩罚。这个规定一直到 1806 年有效并影响了德国公共刑法的形成。"大地和平"的根基是 Treuga Dei（神的和平）的传统，并可以限制于某些地区、某些事物（如教堂、墓地）或某些人（圣职人员、妇女）。最早的"大地和平"事件之一是 Henricus IV 于 1103 年为全帝国宣布的和平。

《黄金诏书》部分涉及德国国王选举的规定反映一些关于教宗选举的类似规定："选帝侯们或他们的代表在发誓后应该开始选举；在他们多数人为基督教世界选择了世俗的元首——即一位罗马王和将来的皇帝——之前，他们不得离开 Frankfurt 城。但如果他们在发誓后 30 天仍未选出国王，他们只能吃面包喝水并绝不得离开城市……但当他们或多数人在那里作出选择时，这个选择必须被尊敬，就像全部一致的选举一样。"

108.《每一个人》

这出宗教戏剧的主题是富裕的人面临死亡。保存的文本很多，荷兰语的版本（Elkerlijk）来自第 15 世纪。下面的提要符合 Hugo von Hofmannsthal 于 1911 年写的德语本，它的基础文献是 Hans Sachs 于 1549 年的德语本（*Comedi von dem reichen Sterbenden, der Hecastus genannt*《被称为每一个人的富有人面临死亡》）

前言的背景是天堂。上主要审判人类尤其是那些过着充满罪恶的生活的人或始终忽视耶稣在十字架的救恩的人。上主委派"死亡"去人间并把 Everyman（"每一个人"）带到审判的宝座面前，要他为自己的生活作报告和解释。

vent the emergence of a powerful imperial dynasty that would be universally accepted. Thus they successively nominated rulers from different aristocratic families, a phenomenon called "jumping elections": Rudolf of Habsburg (1273—1291), Adolf of Nassau (1292—1298), Albrecht I. (1298—1308), Henry VII. (1308—1313) and Louis the Bavarian (1314—1347). None of these emperors was able to establish an imperial dynasty. Charles IV (1347—1378) forced the election of his son Wenzel, but the electors later deposed Wenzel because of his lack of capability, and they nominated Ruprecht von der Pfalz (1400—1410) and then Sigismund (1410—1437), the king of Hungary, who was a brother of Wenzel.

The *Golden Bull* stated that the college of the seven electors was the authoritative body to choose the German emperor and confirmed the principle of majority vote. The electors received ample privileges, they could participate in the government of the empire, their lands were declared to be indivisible, and the title "domini terrae" (Lord of the Land) implied almost unlimited jurisdictive powers. The electors were entitled to tax Jews, they had the monopoly of salt and minerals and even could mint their own coins.

The *Golden Bull* also contained numerous stipulations concerning the limitations of feuds and the "Landfrieden". The Landfrieden (pax terrae, Peace of the Land) was a law promulgated by the German king or Emperor or by the Diet which aimed at the suppression of local feuds. The Landfrieden demanded that the people concerned swore an oath to keep peace. Those who broke the peace law were punished severely. This regulation was effective until 1806 and influenced the formation of the German public criminal law. The Landfrieden was rooted in the tradition of the Treuga Dei (Truce of God) and could be limited to certain regions, objects (churches, graveyards) or persons (clergy, women). One of the earliest cases was the Landfrieden proclaimed for the whole empire by Emperor Henry IV in 1103.

Some of the regulations of the *Golden Bull* that are concerned with the election of the German king somehow reflect similar stipulations for papal elections: "After the electors or their representatives have taken the oath, they shall begin the election and must not leave the city of Frankfurt before the majority of them has elected a secular head of the world or a head for Christendom, namely a Roman king and future emperor. But if they have not done so after 30 days counted from the day of swearing the oath, they should only receive water and bread and must by no means leave the city… But when they or a majority of them have made a choice at that designated place, then this election must be respected in the same way as a choice that is made unanimously and without objection."

108. *Elkerlijk / Everyman / Jedermann*

This mystery play of the rich man facing death has many different versions. The Dutch version (*Elkerlijk*) is from the 15th century. This abstract is following the famous modern German version of Hugo von Hofmannsthal from 1911 (*Jedermann*) is based on Hans Sachs' version of 1549 (*Comedi von dem reichen Sterbenden, der Hecastus genannt*).

The prologue is taking place in Heaven. God wants to hold judgment, especially on

本剧的第一个部分显示出那位富裕的 Everyman，他享受他的财富和奢侈的生活。他很自信、自豪、骄傲，并且公开宣称他对钱财的爱就等于是对最高的神的崇拜。然而,当他遇到一个穷困的邻居以及一个欠他钱的仆人时,他也感到生活中有一些悲哀的因素。另一个增多 Everyman 的忧愁的是他的母亲：她劝勉自己的儿子并提醒他说上主要求人怀有爱心，上主给予了一些许诺，使 Everyman 心情忧郁。此时他的情人上台，一团歌手和朋友围绕着她。他们为了使 Everyman 愉快创造一个充满喜乐的气氛并准备一个宴席。然而，无论是他们的娱乐活动还是甜美的葡萄酒，都无法带给 Everyman 真正的喜乐和幸福。他预先感觉到不久后会发生一件很严重的事。

在种种娱乐和嬉笑中死亡突然出现并要求 Everyman 随着他到上主宝座那里去。Everyman 恳求死亡饶恕他，但死亡的态度坚定不移。死亡仅仅愿意给予 Everyman 一个小小的迟延，这样 Everyman 能够找一个陪同他去上帝的朋友。Everyman 转向那些和他一起生活多年的人：他的一位老朋友、他的两个表弟，但他们都不愿意陪伴他走他最后的路。他的情人以及宴席的客人一旦见到死亡的到来，他们马上就逃跑了。在最后的道路上，Everyman 至少想有一点安慰和鼓励，所以他请人把他的银箱带进来。银箱被打开，而 Mammon——钱财之神（参见《圣经》*Lk* 16:9）——从箱子中走来。他的话带给 Everyman 一个冲击性的启示，因为他直截了当地告诉 Everyman 关于他的钱的真实情况：Everyman 始终认为自己的钱和自己的财产使他成为一个小的神灵，但 Mammon 说他从一开始控制了 Everyman 的灵魂，这样实际上使他成为钱财的傀儡。Everyman 是一个奴隶，他要为他的主人 Mammon 效劳，而不是反过来。

当 Everyman 走近坟墓时，一切朋友都放弃了他。（在一些版本中，这些朋友也包括"美丽"、"力量"、"能力"和"五个感官"。）留下来的只有"善行"和"信仰"（在一些版本中还有"忏悔"）。然而，"善行"很脆弱，她似乎无法保护他不受魔鬼打击。此时"信仰"开启 Everyman 的心胸，使他意识到上主已经通过耶稣的十字架而拯救了罪人们。只有在 Everyman 的皈依后，他的"善行"——在"信仰"的协助下——有足够的力量来保护他不受魔鬼的干扰。死亡回来并再次要求 Everyman 去见上帝。他和"善行"一起走入坟墓，而"信仰"说一些安慰的话。众天使唱的"哈利路亚"声暗示他获得了拯救。

those people who are living a sinful life and constantly disregard the salvation brought by Jesus' death on the cross. God orders Death to go and to bring Everyman to the throne of judgment to give an account of his life.

The first part of the play shows the rich Everyman who enjoys his riches and luxury. He is confident, self-assured, proud, and he openly declares that his love for money is like the veneration of the highest god. However, the encounter with a poor neighbor and his servant who owes him money bring some sadness into his life. Another person that increases Everyman's worries is his mother; she admonishes her son and reminds him of God's commandment of love and of His promises. Everyman is in a gloomy mood as his love appears, surrounded by a group of singers and friends. They create a joyful atmosphere and organize a banquet to cheer Everyman up. However, neither their entertainment nor the good wine can make him really happy. He has an inkling that something serious will happen soon.

In the midst of all merrymaking Death suddenly appears and asks Everyman to follow him to God's throne. Everyman pleads for mercy, but Death cannot be moved. The only thing Death is ready to grant Everyman is a short delay, so that Everyman may find a friend to accompany him to the throne of God. Now Everyman turns to those people who have lived with him for so many years, his old friend, his two cousins, but none of them wants to be with him on his last journey. His love and the other guests have already run away when they saw Death coming. Everyman wants at least to feel some assurance on his last way, so he orders his treasure box to be brought in. The box is opened and Mammon—the god of money (conf. Bible, *Lk* 16:9)—rises from the treasury. His words are a shocking revelation for Everyman, because he plainly tells Everyman the truth about his money: Everyman always has been thinking that his possessions and his money made him something like a minor god, but Mammon explains that in fact he has from the beginning controlled Everyman's soul and so totally enslaved him. Everyman is the slave in lord Mammon's service, and not the other way round.

All friends have deserted Everyman as he approaches the grave. (In some versions these friends also include "Beauty", "Strength", "Discretion", and the "Five Senses".) "Good Deeds" and "Faith" (in some versions: "Penitence") are the only true friends who stay with him, but "Good Deeds" is very weak and frail and will hardly be able to protect him from the devil. Now Faith opens Everyman's heart so that he realizes that God has already saved sinners through Jesus' cross. Only after Everyman's conversion his "Good Deeds" are strong enough to protect him—with Faith's help—from the devil. Death returns to claim Everyman, and together with "Good Deeds" he enters his tomb, consoled by the words of Faith. The alleluja singing of angels is a sign that he is saved.

拉丁语—英语—德语（法语、意大利语等）—汉语索引
Latin–English–German(French, Italian etc.)–Chinese Index

拉丁语 =L、希腊语 =Gr、英语 =E、德语 =D、法语 =F、意大利语 =It、西班牙语 =Sp。拉丁语和英语的写法多数是一样的。外文中的 ē 和 ō 指希腊语的长 ē 和长 ō。根源符号"<"表示某词的来源。"？"表示不确定的解释。"=>"意为"请查阅……"

Latin=L, Greek=Gr, English=E, German=D, French=F, Italian=It, Spanish=Sp. Sometimes the spelling of the Latin and English version of a name is the same. ē and ō denote the Greek letters Eta(long e) and Omega(long o). The symbol "<" signifies the origin of a word or name. "?" sinifies doubtful or uncertain explanations. "=>" means "Please check..."

A

Aachen, (Aquisgranum), F: Aix-la-Chapelle, E: Aachen, town in NW Germany, near the Dutch and Belgian borders; Charlemagne made the city his northern capital; some medieval German kings were crowned there 亚琛

Abaelardus, Petrus, E: Peter Abelard, D: Petrus Abaelard, 1079—1142, French dialectician, theologian, teacher, who spread the scholastic method, author of *Sic et non* and other works. => logica, theologia 阿伯拉尔/阿贝拉德, 见 Bernardus (opposed Abelard's views), Petrus Venerabilis (received him in Cluny), Petrus Lombardus (his student), Otto Frisingensis (his student), Johannes Saresberiensis (his student)

abbas, E: abbot, D: Abt, superior of a monastery; the abbot was usually elected by the monks of his community; after the 9th century many monasteries in western Europe possessed lands, and the abbot had to fulfill the obligations of a feudal lord. 隐修院长, 见 Adamnan, Aldhelmus, Hrabanus Maurus, Walahfridus, Abaelardus, Petrus Venerabilis, Joachim

Abbasidae, E: Abbasids, D: Abbasiden, an Islamic dynasty established by Abu-l-Abbas as-Saffah who ended Omayyad rule in 750. Baghdad became the new capital in 762, and the dynasty reached its height during the rule of Harun al-Rashid (786—809). After 900 a decline set in, and real power rested with the military commanders (sultans) of the Buwayhids and the Seljuk Turks. In 1258 Baghdad was destroyed by Hulagu (=> Mongols) 阿拔斯王朝

abbreviator, E: abbreviator, D: Abbreviator; secretary of the Roman Curia who drafted documents (using many abbreviations); the number of these clerks increased from the fourteenth century, as the business of the Curia expanded. 教廷秘书

Abel, the second son of Adam and Eve, who was killed by his brother => Cain. In medieval times he was regarded as a type of Christ because of the purity of his life, his sacrifice and his death. 亚伯

Abelard => Abaelardus

Abraham, E, D: Abraham; a person from the Old Testament, symbol of faith 亚巴郎/亚伯拉罕, 见 Alanus, *Anticlaudianus* (Abraham among the blessed in Heaven), Joachim, *Liber figurarum* (the first era starts with Abraham), Appendix, *Qur'an* (Ibrahim)

Abraham eremita, E: *Abraham the Hermit*, a play by Hrotsvita《隐修者亚巴郎》, 见 Hrotsvita

Absalon, +1201; Archbishop of Lund (1177), administrator, statesman, military leader, and patron of Saxo Grammaticus; Absalon built a castle on the place that was to become the city of Copenhagen 阿布撒伦, 见 Saxo Grammaticus, *Gesta Danorum*

abstractio, E: abstraction, D: Abstraktion; 抽象, 见 Thomas Aquinas, *Summa theologiae* (we abstract from the material world and arrive at basic principles)

Academia Platonica, It: Accademia Platonica, E: Platonic Academy; an institution dedicated to the study of Greek literature and thought, founded by Bessarion and Gemistus Plethon in 1442 in Florence and financed by the Medici family 柏拉图

学院,见 Piccolomini, *Commentarii*

accidens, E: accident, D: Akzidenz; an attribute or quality that is not essential and must inhere in another entity as a subject. Medieval thinkers used this term to explain the transubstantiation, when the accidents (the color of the host) remain the same after the words of consecration change the substance of the bread into the Body of Christ.属性,偶然性

Acco, E: Acre, F: Acre, D: Akkon, (Akkon-Ptolemais); ancient Syrian seaport, taken by the Arabs in 638; it was conquered during the first crusade and from 1190 to 1291 was controlled by the Knights Hospitalers; in 1291 it fell to the Moslems of Egypt which led to the loss of Christian possessions along the coast.阿克,见 Rubruk

acedia, E: sloth, D: Traegheit; one of the cardinal sins 懒惰,见 Dante, *Commedia* (Purgatorio)

Ackermann => *Der Ackermann aus Boehmen*

Acre = Acco

actio, E: action, D: Aktivitaet; active life, often opposed to contemplative life 行动,见 Hildegardis, *Causae et curae*

actus, E: act, D: Akt; a metaphysical principle; => potentia 实现,见 Thomas Aquinas, *Summa theologiae*

Adalbertus, E, D: Adalbert, + 1072, Archbishop of Hamburg-Bremen (from 1043), most outstanding of the prince-bishops of Bremen; He shared power with Anno of Cologne in 1062 and served as regent for the young Henry IV from 1064 to 1066. 阿达伯特

Adalbertus, E: Albert, D: Adalbert, Slav: Woitjech, Hung: Bela, St., 956—997, Bishop of Prague in 983; his reforms evoked opposition, and he was exiled, thus he served as adviser to Otto III, then went to do missionary work in Hungary, Poland, Prussia, "Apostle of Prussia", was martyred there in 997.阿达尔伯特

Adam, <Hebr: Adam, E: Adam, D: Adam; the first man, symbol of fallen and frail mankind 亚当,见 Hildegardis, *Causae et curae*

Adamnanus de Iona, E: Adamnan, Adomnain, Eunan, St., 624—704, Irish abbot and scholar in Hy (Iona), who urged the Irish to accept the Roman liturgy and calendar; the result of the Synod of Tara which he convened in 697, was a law which forbade women and children to be made prisoners of war. His most important work is a biography of St. Columba.阿达梅南,见 *Vita Columbae*

Adelardus, E, D: Adelard of Bath, +1145, English Benedictine scholar, one of the first to translate Arabic and Greek scientific writings into Latin. He traveled widely in the Mediterranean Sea.阿德拉尔

Adelheid, E: Adelaide, D: Adelheid; St., 931—999, widow of the Italian king Lothair, she appealed to Otto I to save her from Berengar, margrave of Ivrea, who had seized the crown and put her in prison. Otto rescued and married her. She was crowned Empress in 962 and served as regent for her grandson Otto III. She supported monastic reforms. 阿德莱德

Ado, monk, then Archbishop of Vienne, historian, + 875 阿多

Adolphus de Nassau, E: Adolph, D: Adolf von Nassau; German Emperor 1292—1298 阿多夫,见 *Bulla aurea*

Admomnain = Adamnanus de Iona

adoptianismus, theory that Christ as man is the "adopted" son of the Father; in 794 and 798 the theory was formally condemned as heresy. 嗣子说

adoratio, E: adoration, D: Anbetung; => Deus, unio mystica 敬拜,见 Bernardus, *De diligendo Deo* (selfless adoration)

Adrianus => Hadrianus

Adso Dervensis, E: Adso of Montier-en-Der, Adso of Toul, D: Adso von Toul, ca. 920—992, abbot of Montier-en-Der (France), friend of Gerbert, scholar and author 阿德索,见 *De ortu et tempore Antichristi*

aedificatio animi, E: edifying literature, D: Erbauungsliteratur; encouraging or consoling spiritual texts 灵修文学,见 Thomas a Kempis, *De imitatione Christi*

Aegidius Romanus, I: Egidio di Roma, E: Giles of Rome, D: Aegidius von Rom; Augustinian monk, +1316, first Augustinian master in theology at Paris, "doctor fundatissimus", author of a treatise on papal power, *De summi Pontificis Potestate* (1302), which may have inspired Pope Boniface VIII's *Unam Sanctam.* 艾吉丢

aegritudo, E: disease, sickness, D: Krankheit; => dolor, fatum, miseria 疾病,见 Hildegardis, *Causae et curae*, Hartmann, *Der arme Heinrich*, Innocens III, *De miseria humanae conditionis*, Boccaccio, *De-*

camerone, Thomas de Celano, *Vita Sancti Francisci* (a disease changed Francis' mind)

Aeneas, Bishop of Paris, +870 艾内亚斯

aenigma = enigma

Aethelbert = Ethelbert

Aetius, +454, the last great general of the Roman empire in the west; in his youth he was a hostage of the Visigoths, then of the Huns. He led the Roman army against German invasions, crushing the Burgundian kingdom with the help of Hunnish auxiliaries in 436. Most importantly, he defeated the Huns under Attila at Chalons (France) in 451, relying on the help of Visigoths and Franks. 艾提乌斯, 见 Attila

aevum medium => medium aevum

Agapetus II, Pope 946—955, he asked Otto I to come to Rome to restore law and order. 阿格佩图斯

Agathias, +582, chronicler in Byzantium 阿格提阿斯

Agatho, St., Pope 678—681, originally a monk of Sicily; he urged the condemnation of monotheletism and asked the English and Celtic churches to accept the Roman liturgy. 阿加托

Agnes de Poitou–Burgund, +1077, daughter of William, duke of Aquitaine, wife of Henry III, king of Germany, she was Empress 1056—1062 and regent for her son Henry IV. Her last years she spent in a monastery in Italy. 阿格内斯

Agnes de Bohemia, Agnes of Bohemia, Bl., +1282, daughter of Ottocar I, instead of marrying Frederick II of Germany she became a Clarissan sister in the convent in Prague which she had founded, she also supported the "Stelliferi" congregation. 阿格内斯

Agobardus, E, D: Agobard, +840, Archbishop of Lyon (816) who in his many writings on liturgical, juridical, and political issues attacked Adoptionism, witchcraft, trial by ordeal, and excessive veneration of images. 阿格巴德

agricultura, E: agriculture, D: Landwirtschaft; => planta 农业, 见 Hugo, *Didascalicon*, Langland, *Piers Plowman*, Chaucer, *Canterbury* Tales (farmer), Johannes de Tepla, *Der Ackermann* (arator could mean writer)

Ailly, Peter d', French theologian, 1351—1420, rector of Paris University, Archbishop of Cambrai, cardinal, scholar, prolific writer, exponent of nominalism and Church reform. One of his cosmographical books encouraged Columbus to sail westward in order to reach India. 阿伊, 见 Gerson

Aistulf, King of Lombards 749—756, who seized Ravenna in 751 and wanted to capture Rome, but was defeated by Pepin III who succurred Pope Stephen II. Pepin handed over Aistulf's conquered regions to the Pope (Donation of Pepin). 艾斯图尔夫

Al Farabi, Al-Farabi, ca. 875—950; Muslim scholar of Turkish parentage; he studied at Baghdad and wrote on logic, ethics, mathematics, chemistry, politics, and music; he tried to harmonize the views of Aristotle and Plato 阿尔法拉比, 见 Avicenna

Aladdin, E: Aladdin of the wonderful lamp, D: Aladin, a figure of the *Thousand and One Nights*; when the lamp was rubbed a spirit appeared who carried out every wish of the lamp's owner. 阿拉丁, 见 *Alf lailah wa lailah*

Alamanni, E: Alemans, D: Alemannen; the Alemannic people, a Germanic tribe living in the area of the Main and in Switzerland; In 495 Clovis defeated them, and they were absorbed into the Frankish kingdom. 阿勒曼尼人

Alanus ab Insulis, F: Alain de Lille, E: Alan of Lille, D: Alanus; 1128—1202, French Cistercian lay brother, encyclopedic scholar ("doctor universalis"), preacher, theologian, canonist, scientist, poet, and educator, who taught in Paris, then entered the abbey of Citeaux. 阿兰, 见 *Anticlaudianus*

Alberich, (Elberich), a dwarf appearing in the *Nibelungenlied*, Siegfried took from him the magic cloak of invisibility 阿尔贝克, 见 Appendix, *Nibelungenlied*

Albericus, E: Alberic, D: Alberich; Abbot of Citeaux 1099—1109, successor of Robert de Molesme 阿尔伯瑞克

Albericus de Besancon, F: Alberic de Briancon, E: Alberic de Besancon; French writer, author of the *Roman d'Alexandre* (ca. 1120—1140) 阿尔贝瑞克, 见 *Alexandreis*

Albericus II de Spoleto, E: Alberic, D: Alberich; +954, duke of Spoleto, son of Alberic I and Marozia, bearing the title Princeps Romanorum 932—954, he dominated papal policies and nominated four Popes; he supported monastic reforms. 阿尔伯瑞克

Alberti, Leone Battista, 1404—1472, Italian author,

artist, musician, philosopher, and architect. 阿尔贝蒂

Albertus de Behaim, E: Albert of Behaim, D: Albert von Behaim; + 1260, member of the Curia under Innocent III, he became a leader of the papal pary in Germany and was the legate of Pope Gregory IX. His letters are of great historical value. 阿尔伯特

Albertus de Buxhoevden, E: Albert I of Riga, D: Albert von Riga; canon in Bremen, successful missionary in Livonia 1200—1229, founder and first bishop of Riga. 阿尔伯特

Albertus de Jerusalem, E, D: Albert, St., +1214, bishop of Bobbio, papal legate, who was appionted Patriarch of Jerusalem, he approved the Carmelites in 1210. 阿尔伯特

Albertus Magnus, E: Albert the Great, D: Albert der Grosse; 1193—1280, a German Dominican, theologian, philosopher, scientist, who studied at Paris, taught there and at Cologne where he became the teacher of St. Thomas Aquinas; in 1260 he became bishop of Regensburg; in 1277 he went to Paris trying to avert the condemnation of Aristotelian views; he was interested in experimentation and observation and contributed significantly to the growth of medieval science 阿尔伯特, 见 *Summa de creaturis*, Dante, *Commedia* (placed in the Heaven of the Sun)

Albertus Saxonius, E: Albert of Sachsen, D: Albert von Helmstedt; German theologian, 1316—1390, nominalist philosopher and scientist, who taught at Paris and was rector there; he became first rector of the University of Vienna (1365), and Bishop of Halberstadt; author of *De latitudinibus formarum, Demonstrationes de quadratura circuli, Insolubilia, Logica Albertutii*, and many other works on mathematical and logical questions. Later logicians adopted his distinction of "a priori" and "a posteriori". 阿尔伯特

Albi, city in Languedoc, the stronghold of Catharism; => Albigenses 阿尔比

Albigenses, E: Albigensians, D: Albigenser; a branch of the Cathari, heretic sect in the 12th and 13th centuries, they promoted a "pure" life style; salvation was seen as emancipation from the needs of the body; one of their centers of influence was the town of Albi and the surrounding area in southern France; they spread fast and were persecuted; the Fourth Lateran Council of 1215 condemned their teachings; the cruel "Albigensian Crusade" 1208—1229 under Simon de Montfort (+1218) and Louis VIII ended the cultural brilliance of Languedoc and broke Albigensian resistance. 阿尔比派

Albornoz, Gil Alvarez Carrillo de, +1367, Cardinal from Spain, he restored papal rule in Italy 1353—1367 and has been praised as "second founder of the Papal States". 阿尔伯诺兹

Albrecht I de Austria, E: Albert, D: Albrecht; Duke of Austria, son of Rudolph of Habsburg, King of Germany 1298—1308. He consolidated the position of the house of Habsburg in central Europe 阿尔布瑞克特, 见 *Bulla aurea*

Albrecht II de Austria, E: Albert II, D: Albrecht; Duke of Austria, King of Germany 1438—1439, also elected king of Hungary and of Bohemia in 1438. By his marriage with Elizabeth, daughter of Emperor Sigismund, he united the Habsburg and the Luxemburg dynasties, two of the most powerful dynasties in Germany. 阿尔布瑞克特

Alcuinus, (Alkuin, Alchuine, Alcuin), 730—804, theologian, educator, calligrapher, originally from York he became an eminent scholar at Charlemagne's court 阿尔库因, 见 *De pontificus et sanctis*

Aldhelmus, E: Aldhelm, 639—709, Abbot of Malmesbury, first bishop of Sherborne (from 705), "Father of Anglo-Latin poetry", leading scholar and author of works on secular and religious learning. 阿尔德海姆, 见 *De laudibus, Epistola ad A circium*

Alemanni = Alamanni

Alexander, E: Alexander the Great, D: Alexander der Grosse; 356—323 BC, Macedonian king and conqueror, => magus 亚历山大, 见 Dante, *Commedia* (placed in the seventh circle of Hell), *Alexandreis*

Alexander II, Pope 1061—1073, originally Anselm, Bishop of Lucca; he kept Hildebrand as one of his advisers and continued the reforms of his predecessors, sent legates to Lombardy, France, Spain, and England. 亚历山大二世

Alexander III, Pope 1159—1181, originally Cardinal Roland Bandinelli, teacher of canon law; Frederick I Barbarossa refused to recognize Alexander as Pope and forced him into an exile, which he spent in France. For 17 years he was under pressure from emperor Frederick I, but managed to negotiate a settlement with him in 1177. In 1179 the Pope convened the Third Lateran Council. 亚历山大三世

Alexander IV, Pope 1254—1261, pursued an anti-Staufer policy and was driven from Rome. In vain he tried to unite Europe against the threat of the Mongols who had overrun Hungary. 亚历山大四世

Alexander V, Pope 1409—1410, orig. Petrus Philargi, Archbishop in Milan, elected by the council of Pisa to end Church division, he died 10 months after his election. 亚历山大五世

Alexander VI, Pope 1492—1503, a Spaniard, born Rodrigo Borgia from Valencia. As nephew of Pope Callistus III he entered upon a fast career, became bishop of Valencia at the age of 27 and despite a low moral reputation was elected Pope. He was a capable politician, first in alliance with Spain against France, after 1498 as an ally of France. In 1493 he drew the "Line of Demarkation" and granted to Spain all lands to the west and south in the Atlantic that were not held by another Christian power. Alexander was influenced by the ruthless policies of his son Cesare and is sometimes depicted as the "worst of the Renaissance popes". 亚历山大六世

Alexander de Hales, E: Alexander of Hales, D: Alexander von Hales; +1245, "Doctor irrefragibilis", English Franciscan, encyclopedic scholar, founder of the early Franciscan School of scholastic thought. He introduced the practice of lecturing on the *Sentences* of Peter Lombard rather than on the Bible directly, thus giving the study of theology a more systematic approach, which profoundly influenced the development of that science. 亚历山大, 见 Petrus Lombardus, *Sententiae* (chosen as textbook by Alexander in 1222)

Alexandreis, E: *Alexander romance*, a work by Walter of Chatillon, written in 1184《亚历山大传奇》, 见附录

Alexiani, E: Alexians, Cellites, Alexius-brothers, D: Alexianer; an order of laymen founded in the time of the plague (1349) in Holland for the care of the sick, burial of the dead, and education of children. They were sometimes charged of heresy and confused with the Lollards in England. 阿雷克修会

Alexias, E: *Alexiad*, a work by Anna Comnene《阿历史塞亚斯》, 见 Anna Comnene

Alexius I Comnenus, Gr: Alexios Komnēnos, E: Alexius, D: Alexius; Emperor in Byzanz 1081—1118, father of Anna Comnene; he asked the Pope for assistance against the Seljuk Turks in 1094 and so indirectly triggered the crusades. He managed to prevent Robert Guiscard and his Normans from conquering Greece and reestablished Byzantine rule over a large part of Asia Minor. 阿雷克休斯, 见 Malmesburiensis, *Gesta regum Anglorum*, Anna Komnene, *Alexias*

Alexius, St., semi-legendary saint of the fifth century; the biography of Alexius moved many (among them Waldes) to lead a radical Christian life 阿雷克修斯, 见 Jacobus de Voragine, *Legenda aurea*

Alf lailah wa-lailah, E: *Thousand and One Nights*, a medieval collection of tales《一千零一夜》, 见 Appendix

Alfonso => Alphonsus

Alfredus Magnus, E: Alfred the Great, D: Alfred der Grosse; King of England 871—901, founder of the English monarchy, who managed to push back the Danes to the northeastern part of England. He was a supporter of the Church, of monastic reforms, studies, and urged translations from Latin into English. => Anglia 阿尔弗烈德

Alger de Liege, theological author, ca. 1121 阿格尔

allegoria, Gr: allēgoria, E: allegory, D: Allegorie; a literary device in which characters stand for abstract ideas, so that the literal sense suggests a deeper symbolic sense; medieval literature often uses women to express ideas like "justice", "grace" etc. => filiae Dei, sorores, 隐寓, 见 Alanus, *Anticlaudianus*, Lullus, *Blanquerna*(allegories of Memory, Will, Intellect), Nicolaus de Lyra, *Postilla* (littera gesta docet, quid credas allegoria)

alliteratio, E: alliteration, D: Alliteration; the repetition of the same consonant sounds or of different vowel sounds at the beginning of words or in stressed syllables; many medieval vernacular epics were written in this style 头韵诗, 见 Appendix, *Beowulf, Heliand, Nibelungenlied*

Alphonsus V, Sp: Alfonso, E: Alphonse, D: Alfons; King of Aragon, since 1442 also King of Sicily 阿方索, 见 Piccolomini, *Commentarii*

Alphonsus I, Sp: Alfonso, E: Alphonse, D: Alfons;

King of Asturia (N Spain) 739—757 阿方索

Alphonsus VI, Sp: Alfonso, E: Alphonse, D: Alfons; King of Leon–Castile who conquered Toledo in 1085 阿方索

Alphonsus VIII, Sp: Alfonso, E: Alphonse, D: Alfons; King of Castile who defeated the Muslims decisively in 1212 at Navas de Tolosa 阿方索

Alphonsus IX, Sp: Alfonso de Leon, E: Alphonse, D: Alfons; King of Leon (Spain), ca. 1200 阿方索

Alphonsus X, Sp: Alfonso el Sabio, E: Alphonse the Wise, D: Alfons der Weise; King of Castile and Leon 1252—1284 阿方索

Alphonsus I, Sp: Alfonso, E: Alphonse, D: Alfons; + 1185, King of Portugal who was able to recover Lisbon from the Muslims in 1147 (with the help of British and German crusaders). 阿方索

Alsatia, E: Alsace, D: Elsass; a region on the west bank of the upper Rhine, occupied by Alemanni, then conquered by Clovis in 496 AD. The Treaty of Verdun assigned Alsace to Lothair, and in 925 it became part of the duchy of Swabia, thus was in close connection to the imperial power of the House of Hohenstaufen. During the 13th century most cities in Alsace became free imperial cities. 阿尔萨斯

altare, E: altar, D: Altar; the central place of worship in churches, originally made of stone with the remains of martyrs buried beneath. The large churches of the Middle Ages had side altars accommodating the big number of priests, and in the late Middle Ages altars were decorated with tabernacles (where sacred vessels and host rested). The altarpiece (also called "retable"), a structure above the altare covered with paintings and sculptures, can be traced back at least to the 11th century. 祭坛

Altmannus, E, D: Altmann, +1091, Bishop of Passau, a vigorous monastic reformer, who courageously opposed Henry IV in the struggle over lay investiture. 阿尔特曼

Alvarus de Cordova, E: Alvare of Cordoba, supporter of Christian zealots in Spain around 858. 阿尔瓦汝斯

Alvarus Pelagius, Sp: Alvaro Pelayo, +1350, a Spanish Franciscan, who became Bishop of Silves (Portugal), author of a work on the Church (1332) in which he defended papal authority against the views of Marsilius of Padua. 阿尔瓦鲁斯

Amalarius, E: Amalarius of Metz, + 850, Bishop of Metz, author of an important book on the interpretation of liturgy (*De ecclesiasticis officiis*, 830). 阿马拉留斯

Amalricus de Bena, F: Amaury de Chartres, E: Amalric of Bene, + 1207, theologian in Paris with pantheist and anti-clerical tendencies, his adherents (Amalricans) were discovered in 1209 and suppressed. 阿马尔里克

Amandus, St., +676, born in Aquitaine, he became a missionary itinerary bishop in northern France and is known as the "Apostle of Flanders". 阿曼都斯

Ambrosius, E: Ambrose, D: Ambrosius, St., ca. 330—397 AD, Bishop of Milan, important Latin Father of the Church 安波罗修斯，见 Otfrid, *Evangelienbuch*

Amfortas, (=Anfortas), king of the castle of the Grail 安弗塔斯，见 Wolfram, *Parzival*

Amled, E: Hamlet, D: Amled; a figure of Danish mythology; Amled pretended to be mad in order to deceive his uncle who had killed his father and usurped the throne. 哈姆莱特，见 Saxo Grammaticus, *Gesta Danorum*

amor, E: love, D: Liebe; one of the mental powers, also (since Augustine) symbol of the Holy Spirit; => virtutes theologicae 爱，爱德，见 Anselmus, *Monologion*, Bernardus, *De diligendo Deo* (intelligitur in quantum amatur; the steps of divine love), Chretien, *Erec et Enide* (perfect love includes charity), Maimonides, *More nevukhim* (amor Dei intellectualis), Hartmann, *Der arme Heinrich* (selfless love), Snorri Sturluson, *Edda* (Brynhild commits suicide so as to be united with Sigurd), Guillaume de Lorris, *Roman de la rose* (gap between immoral naturalism and courtly ideals of love), Bonaventura, *Itinerarium*, Raimundus Lullus, *Blanquerna*, (book of the Lover and the Beloved), Gertrudis, *Legatus divinae pietatis* (love between chaste spouses), Dante, *Commedia* (God is the love which moves the universe; spiritualized love of Beatrice), Petrarch, *Rime* (partly spiritualized, partly sensual longing for Laura)

Anacletus II, Antipope 1130—1138 阿纳克雷图斯

analogia entis, E: analogy of being, D: Analogie des Seins; 存有类比，见 Thomas Aquinas, *Summa theologiae* (analogia creaturae ad Deum)

Anastasius III, Pope 911—913 阿纳斯塔修斯

Anastasius IV, Pope 1153—1154 阿纳斯塔修斯

Anastasius, made Patriarch of Constantinople by Emperor Leo in 730 because he supported iconoclasm 阿纳斯塔修斯

Anastasius Bibliothecarius, scholar, cardinal priest, papal candidate in 855; translator of synod acts from Greek into Latin 阿纳斯塔修斯

Andreas, Gr: Andreias, E: Andrew, D: Andreas, one of the apostles 安德烈, 见 Nestorius, *Povest'* (Andrew supposedly visited Russia and introduced Christianity)

Andreas II, King of Hungary, father of St. Elisabeth of Thuringia who joined the crusade of 1217 安德烈

Andronicus, Emperor of Byzanz 1282—1328, opposed to Church union 安德洛尼克

Angela de Foligno, St., 1248—1309, Italian visionary, who lived a monastic life in Assisi since 1285, her mystic experiences are recorded in the *Memoriale* (*Memorial*) 安格拉

Angelico, Fra, Italian painter, +1455, famous for a style of heavenly purity and beauty 安杰利克, 见 Piccolomini, *Commentarii*

angelus, E: angel, D: Engel, a Biblical motive, in the philosophical world view of the scholastics the angels were created immaterial substances 天使, 见 Walahfridus, *Visio Wettini* (a guardian angel leads Wetti to hell and purgatory), Alanus, *Anticlaudianus* (angelic choirs), Albertus, *Summa de creaturis* 4, Dante, *Commedia* (angels in Purgatory, choirs of angels in Heaven)

Angelus Domini, E: Angel of the Lord, D: Engel des Herrn, Christian prayer since the 13th ct., very popular since the 17th ct. 主的天使

Anglia, E: England, D: England; the island was influenced by Roman culture since 55 BC, but Roman rule collapsed in the early fifth century, and the Angles, Saxons and Jutes moved in to rule the land. Christian missionaries came first from Ireland (St. Columba), and some time later a group of monks was sent by Gregory the Great in 597 AD. At the Synod of Whitby (664 AD) also the representatives of the Celtic church agreed to accept Roman liturgical usages and calendar. Archbishop Theodore of Canterbury (669—690) fostered theological education, and England became one of the leading centers of scholarship in the Middle Ages. Alfred the Great (871—899) controlled most of southern and central England, whereas Danes ruled the northeastern part of the country, esp. during the reign of Canute (1016—1035). In 1066 the conquest of William the Conqueror brought feudal institutions to England, and Henry II (1154—1189) secured a system of justice unequalled by any other people of medieval Europe. King John limited his royal prerogatives in the *Magna Carta* (1215). The 14th century saw the evolution of the parliament, the decline of serfdom, expansion of trade and industry, the Hundred Years' War with France (1337—1453), the Black Death (1348—1350). During the late Middle Ages the struggle between the landed aristocracy and the crown hardly ever ceased. => lingua Anglica 英国, 见 Adamnanus, Aldhelmus, Beda, *Historia Ecclesiastica gentis Anglorum*, Bonifatius, *Epistulae*, Malmesburiensis, *Gesta regum Anglorum*, Galfredus de Monmouth, *Historia regum Britanniae*, Wyclif, *De civili dominio*

Anglosaxoni, E: Anglosaxons, D: Angelsachsen; the Germanic tribes (Angles and Saxons) who emigrated to England around 450 AD; they were called in to protect the natives after the Roman armies had left in 410 AD, but they soon conquered a great part of England and established their own kingdoms; => Northumbria 安格鲁-撒克逊人, 见 Malmesbury, *Gesta regum Anglorum*

anima, Gr: psychē, E: soul, D: Seele; the self, the heart, also called "inner man" (homo interior), the spiritual core of a person; => *De anima*, corpus 心灵, 灵魂, 见 Bernardus, *De diligendo Deo* (a self-centered sould is bent, anima curva), Johannes Saresberiensis, *Policraticus* (the soul of the state is religion), Averroes, *De anima* (no personal immortality of the individual human soul), Alanus, *Anticlaudianus* (only God can create a human soul), Albertus, *Summa de creaturis* 2 (the vegetative, sensitive, and spiritual soul), *De unitate intellectus* (against Averroes' monopsychism), Bonaventura, *Itinerarium mentis in Deum*, Thomas Aquinas, *Summa theol.* (soul is the forma corporis), Eckhart, *Buch der goettlichen Troestungen* (scintilla animae), Gerson, *De mystica theologia* (reflects the mental powers of the soul)

animalia, E: animals, D: Tiere, often with symbolic

meaning in medieval literature; => eques 动物, 见 Aldhelmus, *Epistola ad Acircium* (riddles about animals), Beda, *Historia* (our life is like a sparrow flying through a room), Cynewulf, *Helena* (symbolic animals), Wolfram von Eschenbach, *Parzival* (not allowed to kill sparrows), Snorri Sturluson, *Edda* (symbol animals of Odin are the wolf and the raven), Vincentius Bellovacensi, *Speculum maius* (the *Speculum naturale* describes the animals), Fredericus II, *De arte venandi cum avibus* (the first scientific ornithological work), Thomas Aquinas, *Summa theologiae* II.II. 64 (discussion of the killing of animals), Boccaccio, *Decamerone* (story of the falcon), Appendix, *Roman de la Renard*

Anna Comnena, Gr: Anna Komnēnē, E: Anna Comnene, D: Anna Komnena; 1083—1148, daughter of Alexius I, emperor in Byzantium; she wrote the epic poem *Alexiad* in a convent.阿纳·康尼纳, 见 *Alexias*

annatae, (annalia), E: annates, D: Annaten; payment from the first annual income of a newly appointed Church office holder. These taxes were payed to bishops and abbots since the 11th century. Since the 14th century annates were attributed to the Roman Curia.年税

anno Domini, E: A.D., D: nach Christus; the common chronology of Latin Christian authors since Dionysius Exiguus and Bede 主年, 见 Beda, *Historia*

Anno Coloniensis, E: Anno (Hanno) of Cologne, D: Anno von Koeln, St., + 1075, being the Archbishop of Cologne, he was imperial chancellor and served for a time as regent during the minority of young Henry IV. He implemented monastic reforms. 安诺

Anonymus de York, ca. 1120, a writer from York whose 31 tractates defend royal power and limit Papal authority to the spiritual realm 无名人士

Anselmus Cantuarensis, E: Anselm of Canterbury, D: Anselm von Canterbury, 1033—1109; born in Aosta (Italy), he became Benedictine monk and abbot in Bec (Normandy), then Archbishop of Canterbury (1093—1109); theologian and philosopher, ("Father of Scholasticism"), who sought the support of reason for the explanation of theological tenets. He was exiled twice, but concluded an agreement with Henry I in 1107 安瑟伦, 见 *Cur Deus homo, Monologion, Proslogion*

Anselmus de Laon, E: Anselm of Laon, D: Anselm von Laon, +1117, French theologian, author, one of the early scholastics, teacher of Abelard. Anselm endorsed the doctrine of realism, => universalia.安瑟伦, 见 Abaelardus

Anselmus de Lucca = Alexander II

Ansgarius, E: Ansgar, Anskar, D: Ansgar; St., ca. 801—865, monk of Corbie, teacher at Corvey, he was engaged in missionary work in Denmark and Sweden, the "Apostle of the North". He became the first Archbishop of the see of Hamburg-Bremen and could convert King Haarik of Denmark and King Olaf of Sweden.安加略/安斯加尔

Anthony => Antonius

Antichristus, Gr: antichristos, E: Antichrist, D: Antichrist, the eschatological enemy of Christianity who was sometimes expected to come very soon. Medieval images of the Antichrist, who strives for the domination of the whole world, were based on *Rev* 11:7 and 2 *Thess* 2:8-10; => eschatologia 反基督/敌基督, 见 Johannes Damascenus, *Pēgē gnōseōs*, Adso Dervensis, *De ortu et tempore Antichristi*, Otto Frisingensis, *Chronica*, Joachim, *Liber figurarum*, Langland, *Piers Plowman*

Anticlaudianus, E: *Anticlaudianus*, a work by Alain de Lille《反克劳蒂安》,见 Alanus ab Insulis

Antiochia, E: Antioch, D: Antiochia, ancient capital of Syria, the third city of the Roman empire, it fell to the Persians in 538 AD, to the Arabs in 637, but was recovered for Byzantium in 969 by Nicephorus II. In 1085 it was captured by the Seljuk Turks, but a crusading army restored Christian rule in 1097. In 1268 the Mamluk sultan of Egypt took control of the city, and in 1401 it was sacked and totally destroyed by the Mongols led by Timur the Lame.

Antipapa, E: antipope, D: Gegenpapst, one who claimed to be Pope or was installed as Pope by his adherents, in opposition to a pontiff canonically elected and accepted by the Church. During the time of the Western Schism (1378—1415) it was difficult to identify the legitimate Pope.对立教宗

Antonius de Padua, E: Anthony, D: Antonius, St., + 1231, born in Lisbon, he became a Franciscan, taught at Bologna, Montpellier, and Toulouse and was famous as preacher (against heresies) and worker of miracles. He is a popular saint. 帕多瓦

的安托尼乌斯

Antoniti, E: Antonians, Antonites, D: Antoniter, the Hospital Brothers of St. Anthony, a medical congregation of lay brothers, founded in 1095 by Gaston de Dauphine. 安托尼医疗会

Antwerp, town in Flanders, an important port since the 11th century. Following the decline of Bruges and Ghent in the late Middle Ages, Antwerp slowly became the leading commercial and financial center of the Netherlands, and even of western Europe. Famous are the Cathedral of Notre Dame and the old guild houses. 安特卫普

apocalypsis, E: revelation, D: Apokalypse; the revelation of hidden wisdom, esp. in the last book of the New Testament (Apocalypsis Johannis). Apocalyptic literature grew out of the Jewish expectation of the Messiah. When the Christian expectation of a soon return of Christ lost its sense of urgency, apocalyptic writings became less popular. Some medieval authors revived apocalyptic imagery, sentiments and symbols. => Antichristus 启示, 见 Joachim, *Liber figurarum*

apostasia, E: apostasy, D: Apostasie; the renouncing of the faith 背信, 背教, 见 Hrotsvita, *Theophilus*

apostolic life = vita apostolica

apostolica successio, E: apostolic succession, D: apostolische Sukzession; the doctrine that the authority of Jesus was and is passed down in an unbroken line from the apostles to their successors, the bishops, especially to the Bishop of Rome, the Pope. 宗徒传承/使徒传统

Apostolici, E: Apostolic Brethren, D: Apostelbrueder, a congregation founded by Segarelli in 1260, it spread in Italy and Spain. They were inspired by the Franciscan ideals of poverty, but some extreme tenets led to their later suppression. 宗徒/使徒弟兄会

apostolus, Gr: apostolos, E: apostle, D: Apostel; title of the twelve friends of Jesus who spread the faith in the first century; they founded and directed local churches in many places; the bishops are regarded to be the successors of the apostles (successio apostolica); => Andreas, Jacobus, Johannes, Paulus, Petrus 使徒/宗徒

apparitio, E: apparition, D: Erscheinung; 显现, 见 visio

appellatio, E: appeal to Rome, D: Appellationsrecht, Berufung; the right of any bishop to appeal to Rome, denied by nationalist rulers (e.g. in England and France) 申诉权

Aquitania, E: Aquitaine, D: Aquitanien; region in southwestern France, which was overrun by the Visigoths around 400 AD, then controlled by the Franks (since 507). It became a duchy of William of Auvergne in the late ninth century and was under the English Crown from 1152 until the end of the Hundred Years' War (1450). 阿奎塔尼亚

Arabes, E: Arabs, D: Araber, the people who accepted the religion of Muhammad in the 7th century and expanded rapidly to the western regions, threatening to control the Mediterranean. The first literary monument of Arabic prose is the *Qur'an*, usually considered the best piece of literature of the Arabic language in regard to style and eloquence. The Arabic numerals are of ancient Hindu origin, came to Baghdad soon after 800 AD, were known in Spain in the tenth century, but only since the 15th century they were in general use in Western Europe. => *Qur'an*, Avicenna, Averroes, crusades, Islam 阿拉伯人, 见 Paulus Diaconus, *Historia Langobard.*, Albertus (open to Arab thinkers), Appendix, *Chanson de Roland* (fight against the Arabs)

Arabian Nights => *Alf lailah wa-lailah*

Aragonia, E: Aragon, D: Aragonien, the region east of Navarre, controlled by the Franks until Ramiro I of Aragon (+1063) established an independent kingdom there. Aragon expanded under Alfonso I (1104—1134), united with Catalonia in 1150, but lost possessions in France following the Battle of Muret (1213), when Pedro II was defeated in the Albigensian Crusade. Aragon acquired the kingdom of Valencia (1238), Sicily (1282), Sardinia (1320), and Alfonso V conquered Naples (1442). The marriage of Ferdinand II of Aragon to Isabella of Castile in 1469 united the two kingdoms into one Spain. 阿拉贡

arbor, E: tree, D: Baum; symbol of spiritual realities 树木, 见 Hugo, *De fructibus* (tree of virtues), Joachim, *Liber figurarum* (genealogical trees)

Arbues, Petrus, Sp: Pedro de Arbues, Augustinian canon, inquisitor of Aragon, known for his harshness, he was attacked and murdered in 1485 in the church of Zaragossa. 阿尔布斯

Arc, Joan of => Jeanne d'Arc

archidiaconus, E: archdeacon; D: Erzdiakon; important ecclesiastical official, who served in the administration of a diocese. The office disappeared in the late Middle Ages.总执事

archidioecesis, E: archdiocese, D: Erzdioezese; the province under the jurisdiction of an archbishop. The archdiocese as a jurisdictional area distinct from the diocese may be traced back to the 3rd century.总教区

Archipoeta, E: Archpoet, D: "Erzdichter"; a title given to a composer of goliardic verse; the patron of the Archpoet was Rainald of Dassel (1159—1167) (sometimes identified with the Archpoet himself).诗圣,见 Appendix, *Carmina Burana*

archipresbyter, E: archpriest, D: Erzpriester; a priest who represented a college of presbyters or represented the bishop; this ecclesiastical office can be traced to the 4th century AD.总司铎

architectura, E: architecture, D: Architectur; Medieval architecture was mainly shaped by the different ecclesiastical architectural styles (Romanesque, Gothic, Renaissance).教堂建筑风格

Arethas de Caesarea, E: Arethas of Caesarea, 849—932, disciple of Photius, later Archbishop of Caesarea in Cappadocia, one of the most accomplished theologians and exegetes of his age. 阿瑞塔斯

Argenteuil, Abbey of, a Benedictine abbey near Versailles, founded for women around 670. Heloise studied there and became abbess of the cloister. 阿根特尔

argumentum, E: argument, D: Argument => probatio

Argyropoulos, Ioannes, E: John Argyropoulos, +1487, Greek scholar, delegate at the Council of Ferrara–Florence (1438—1439), later in Florence and Rome, known for his translation of Aristotle's works.阿格若普洛斯

Arialdus de Milano, It: Arialdo, a leader of the Patarenes who denounced simony and immorality, he was killed in Milan in 1066.阿瑞阿尔都斯

Arianismus, E: Arianism, D: Arianismus, a non-orthodox Christian teaching originating from the early 4th century 亚略主义,见 Paulus Diaconus, *Historia Langobardorum* (Lombards were Arianists)

Aristoteles, Greek philosopher, +322 BC, whose works profoundly influenced scholasticism, especially since the time of Albertus Magnus and Thomas Aquinas 亚里士多德,见 Johannes Damascenus, *Pēgē gnōseōs*, Avicenna, *Kitab*, Otto Frisingensis, *Chronica* (some familiarity with Aristotelian works), Averroes, *De anima*, Alanus, *Anticlaudianus*, Maimonides, *More nevukhim* (tries to reconcile philosophy and Jewish faith), Fredericus II, *De arte venandi* (challenges Aristotle's authority), Albertus, *Summa de creaturis* (integration of Aristotelianism into the Christian world view), Thomas Aquinas, *Summa theologiae*, Oresmensis (moves away from the organistic universe to a "machina mundi")

arithmetica, E: arithmetic, D: Arithmetik; the mathematical science of numbers, one of the seven liberal arts. Influenced by the manuals of Boethius and Cassiodorus, the Middle Ages were much interested in the symbolic value of numbers. 算数学, 见 Hrabanus, *De institutione cler.*, (arithmetics helps to understand the mystical numbers in some Biblical texts)

Arles, city in Provence on the Rhone delta, the leading city of Gaul in the late Roman empire, and the site of church councils, the first of them convoked by Constantine I in 314 AD (clarifying questions concerning the date of Easter and Donatism). The Kingdom of Arles emerged in 934 with the union of the kingdoms of Provence and Burgundy (=> Burgundium) 阿尔

Armagh, a county in north Ireland, where, according to tradition, St. Patrick built a church and a monastery ca. 450 AD. Thus Armagh became the religious center of Ireland, and its abbot also served as bishop.阿玛格

Arme Heinrich => *Der arme Heinrich*

Armenia, E: Armenia, D: Armenien; a kingdom of eastern Asia Minor, said to be the oldest Christian state (since 294 AD). From the third century Byzantium and the Persians fought to control it, later the White Huns, Khazars, Arabs, Turks, and Mongols invaded the area. A period of autonomy (885 to 1046) was ended by Byzantine rule, followed by the invasion of the Seljuk Turks. Armenian refugees set up Lesser Armenia in Cilicia around 1080, which fell to the Mamluks of Egypt in 1375.Armenian Christians (monophysites) were united with the Roman Church in 1439. The translation of the Bible into Armenian in the fifth century established the the standards for the classical Armenian language. The works of Aristotle were translated into Armenian, and their outstanding poet is Catholicos Narses IV (+ 1172), prelate of Lesser Armenia.亚美尼亚

Arnaldus Amalrici, F: Arnaud-Amaury, E: Arnold of Citeaux, +1225, Cistercian monk, abbot several monasteries, finally abbot of Citeaux and abbot general of the order. As papal legate in the war against the Albigenses he led an army against adherents of the sect in 1209. He was appointed Archbishop of Narbonne.阿纳德

Arnaldus de Villanova, F: Arnaud de Vilanova, + 1311, eminent physician of the Middle Ages, teacher at Montpellier, he translated medical works from the Arabic.阿纳德

Arnoldus de Brescia, E: Arnold of Brescia, D: Arnold von Brescia; 1100—1155, student at Paris (influenced by Abaelard), Augustinian and prior of a monastery in Brescia, he advocated the return to the poverty of apostolic times, was banished from Italy in 1139, condemned by the Council of Sens (1141), he seized control of Rome and governed it with the support of a "republican" faction. A senate was organized after the model of ancient Rome. He was executed after Frederick I Barbarossa had been called in for help.布雷西亚的阿诺德

Arnulf de Carinthia, + 899, East Frankish ruler of Carinthia, which he received from his father, king of Bavaria. Arnulf was elected king of the Franks in 887, he defeated the Vikings and liberated Rome from the pressure of the duke of Spoleto. Pope Formosus crowned Arnulf in 896.阿尔努夫

Arpad, 840—907, the first grand prince of the Magyars (Hungarians), who lead his people from southern Russia to the region of Hungary in 895. His dynasty ruled Hungary until 1301.阿尔帕德

ars dictaminis, E: the art of dictation, D: Schreibkunst; the medieval art of the composition of letters, mostly stylistic exercises of notaries, scribes or teachers of rhetoric.写信的艺术

Ars magna, E: *The Great Art*, a work by Ramon Lull 《宏大的技术》,见 Raimundus Lullus

ars medica, E: medical knowledge, D: Heilkunst; => aegritudo, medicina 医学,见 Hildegardis, *Causae et curae*, Hartmann, *Der arme Heinrich*, Vincentius Bellovacensis, *Speculum maius* (uses Arab medical sources)

ars moriendi, E: the art of dying, D: die Kunst eines guten Todes; a genre of medieval (mostly devotional) literature dealing with death, especially the struggle between good and evil spirits over the soul of a dying person.善终的艺术,见 *Elkerlijk*

ars praedicandi, E: the art of preaching, D: die Kunst des Predigens; a literary genre regarding the rhetorical and spiritual matters of good preaching 讲道的技艺

ars venandi => *De arte venandi*

artes liberales, E: seven liberal arts, D: die sieben freien Kuenste, the "trivium" (grammatica, dialectica, rhetorica) and the "quadrivium" (geometria, arithmetica, astronomia, musica), the basis of medieval higher education; => encyclopaedia, scientia; grammatica, dialectica, rhetorica, geometria, arithmetica, astronomia, musica 七个自由学科/三学四艺,见 Hugo, *Didascalicon* (division into artes theoreticae, practicae, mechanicae, and logica), Alanus, *Anticlaudianus* (the seven liberal arts are depicted as virgins building a chariot for the journey to Heaven)

Artus, E: Arthur, D: Artus; a figure of Celtic legend, probably a local chieftain who defended the Britons against the invading Saxons; later he was depicted as a king of peace, who gathered many knights around his "Round Table". 亚瑟王,见 Galfredus Monemuthensis, *Historia regum Britanniae*, Chretien, *Erec et Enide*, Wolfram von Eschenbach, *Parzival*

Ascelino, E: Ascellion (Asselino, Anselmo, Ascelin), +1254, Italian Dominican who was sent as legate to Persia by Pope Innocent IV in 1245. Though he could not convert the Mongol khan Melik Saleh, Ascelino preached in Persia and returned to Europe in 1248.阿塞林诺

Asgaard,(Asgard), the dwelling place of the gods in Nordic folklore, usually identified with Valhalla 阿斯格德,见 *Edda*

Ash Wednesday => Cinerum

Asserus Ioannes, E: John Asser (Asker); +909, a learned monk who was invited by Alfred the Great to help educating both court and country. Asser was appointed bishop of Sherborne and assisted the king's translation projects.阿塞尔

assidere, E: assize, D: Sitzung; meetings of vassals or of a court, and the decrees following such meetings 会议,决议

Assisi, town of Umbria, central Italy, famous as the home of St. Francis 阿西西

Astrolabius, the illegal son of Abaelard 阿斯特若拉比乌斯, 见 Abaelardus

astrologia, E: astrology, D: Astrologie; popular in the late Middle Ages, but always opposed by the Church. => astronomia 占星术

astronomia, E: astronomy, D: Astronomie; one of the seven liberal arts. The basis of medieval astronomy was the geocentric system of Ptolemy, although the awareness of its inadequacies grew steadily. Until the 13th century Muslim astronomers had a leading position. Astronomy was needed for nautical purposes and calendrical computation, thus it was always supported by the Church. The studies of Omar Khayyam (+1132), Grosseteste (+1253), and Roger Bacon (+1292) led up to the reform of 1582 (Gregorian Calendar). One of the scientists proposing the earth's daily rotation was Oresme (+1382). 天文学, 见 Hrabanus, *De institutione cler.* (astronomy important for the computation of the date of Easter)

asylum, Gr: a-sylon, E: right to asylum, D: Asyl; the right of ancient Hebrew and Greek origin to hide in a church or other sanctuary. This right was recognized by most sects and by Islam. Thus churches and their adjacent buildings became places of refuge for criminals and for those persecuted by state officials. 避难权

Athenae, E: Athens, D: Athen; important cultural center in Greece, captured but not sacked by the Visigoths in 395, it remained a provincial capital until it passed into French hands after 1204 and experienced a time of relative prosperity. In 1311 Athens was devastated by Catalan raiders, and in 1388 it came under the rule of an aristocrat from Florence who ruled Corinth at that time. After a few decades of development the city fell to the Ottoman Turks in 1458. 雅典

Athos, Mount; a mountain in N Greece at the end of the Chalcidic peninsula. Hermits lived there perhaps since the fourth century. The first organized community of monks (called Lavra), was set up by St. Athanasius Athonitus in 963. His rule emulated the one of St. Basil. The spirituality of hesychasm developed at Mount Athos. 阿托斯山, 圣山

Attila, E: Attila, D: Atli, Etzel, Attila; +453; king of the Huns (=> Hunni); who led a huge army (of German and Slavic mercenaries) from his headquarters to Gaul but was defeated by Aetius' army of Visigoths, Burgundians and Franks in 451 AD. Attila threatened to invade Rome but was persuaded to retreat after a conference with Pope Leo I and a delegation of Roman senators. 阿提拉, 见 Ekkehard, *Waltharii poiesis*, Snorri Sturluson, *Edda*, Dante, *Commedia* (in the seventh circle of Hell), Appendix, *Nibelungenlied* (Etzel)

Atto of Vercelli, +961, Italian theologian and canonist, bishop of Vercelli. For several years he served Lothair II of France as chancellor. His writings and letters betray outstanding erudition. 阿托

auctoritates, E: authorities, D: Autoritaeten; for the scholastics the Bible and the writings of the Fathers of the Church were reliable authorities. Scholasticism tried to harmonize the various tenets of different authors. 权威, 权威性文献, 见 Abaelard, *Sic et non* (juxtaposition of authoritative sentences), Fredericus II, *De arte venandi* (challenges Aristotle's authority)

Augsburg, (L: Augusta Vindelicorum), town in Southern Germany, the provincial capital of the Roman province of Raetia, it was occupied by the Franks in 536 and became a bishopric around 600. Charlemagne invested the bishop with the authority of a count, but in 1276 the city became a free imperial city. The trade with linen and cloth made Augsburg prosperous. 奥格斯堡

Augusta Vindelicorum => Augsburg

Augustinus, Aurelius, E: Augustine, D: Augustin, St., 354—430 AD, the most influential Latin theologian of antiquity. Platonic-Augustinian thought had great impact, particularly on early scholasticism and mysticism. 奥古斯丁, 见 Hrabanus, *De institutione cler.*, Bernardus, *De diligendo Deo*, Petrus Lombardus, *Sententiae*, Otto Frisingensis, *Chronica* (imitates Augustine's "two cities"), Thomas Aquinas, *Summa theologiae* (the observation of the outside world is distinct from Augustine's interiority), Dante, *Commedia* (placed in the Heaven of the Sun)

Augustinus Cantuarensis, E: Augustine of Canterbury, D: Augustin; +604, a Benedictine monk sent to England in 597, he could convert Ethelbert, king of Kent, and established his bishopric at Canterbury, the capital of Kent. 奥古斯丁, 见 Beda, *Historia*

Augustini Canonici, E: Canons Regular of St. Augustine, D: Augustiner Chorherren; canons living according to Augustine's rule; members of a semi-monastic community. Since around 1050 the order became popular, because Pope Gregory VII encouraged priests living in collegiate churches to observe monastic regulations with regard to celibacy, obedience, and poverty. 奥古斯丁圣职团

Augustini Eremiti, E: Augustine-hermits = Ordo Sancti Augustini 奥古斯丁隐修士

Augustini Regula, E: Rule of St. Augustine, D: Augustinerregel; the monastic rule combined from Augustine's writings. This rule was applied since the 7th ct. to create monastic communities. Many communities of canons lived according to it, especially since the 12th ct. 奥古斯丁会规

aurum, E: gold, D: Gold; symbol of wealth, => divitiae 黄金, 见 Bernardus, *De consideratione*

Austrasia, eastern part of the Frankish kingdom (east of the Maas River); the main cities were Raims and Metz. 奥斯瑞西亚

Austria, E: Austria, D: Oesterreich; a region in the area of the upper Danube, inhabitated by Germanic tribes, then civilized by the Romans who established the provinces Noricum and Pannonia in the area. The Bavarians occupied the region in the sixth century, and after defeating the Avars Charlemagne incorporated the land into his kingdom. Otto I organized the region as "eastern border area" (Ostmark, Ostarrichi) in 976 and gave it to the Margraves of the house of Babenberg (until 1246). Then Ottocar II of Bohemia tried to annex the region but in 1278 Rudolph of Habsburg (1273—1291) defeated him and consolidated the rule of his dynasty which lasted until 1919. In 1363 the Habsburgs acquired Tyrol, and in 1382 Trieste, and they controlled the ecclesiastical states of Salzburg, Trent, and Brixen. After Rudolph many German kings belonged to the house of Habsburg. => Albrecht, Maximilian, Rudolph 奥地利, 见 Otto Frisingensis, Appendix, *Nibelungenlied*

Ava, (Ave), a poetess of the early twelfth century, author of spiritual literature, the first German poetess known by name. 阿瓦

Avalon, the Isle of the Saints in old Celtic or Welsh mythology, also the place where King Arthur recuperated from his wounds. 阿瓦伦, 见 Galfridus, *Historia regum Britanniae*

Avari, E: Avars, D: Avaren; Asiatic nomads who invaded Russia and the Balkans after 550. They subjugated many Slavic groups and established their state between the Danube and the Carpathians (in Pannonia). They attempted to capture Byzantium in 626 but failed. Having raided many regions in central Europe, Charlemagne substantially weakened their power after 791, and the Magyars absorbed their collapsing kingdom. 阿瓦尔人

avaritia, E: avarice, greed, D: Habsucht, Gier; => concupiscentia, desiderium, peccatum 贪婪, 见 Innocens III, *De miseria humanae conditionis* (human greed brings about calamity), Dante, *Commedia* (Purgatorio)

Ave Maria, E: Hail Mary, D: Gegruesset seist du, Maria; a popular prayer based on Biblical texts. 圣母经

Averroes, Arab: Ibn Rushd, E: Averroes; 1126—1198, Arab philosopher, interpreter of Aristotelianism, he deeply influenced scholastic thought 阿威罗伊, 见 *Tafsir kitab an-nafs*, Albertus, *Summa de creaturis*

Averroismus, E: (Latin) Averroism; a school of philosophy following Aristoteles' views as interpreted by Averroes. Having its center at the University of Paris, the movement accepted such unorthodox tenets as the eternity of matter and of the world, saw present life as the final destiny of human existence, and wanted to philosophize apart from theological considerations. Their leading exponent was Siger of Brabant. Averroism was first condemned in 1270. 阿威罗伊主义

Avicenna, Ibn Sina, E: Avicenna, ca. 980—1037, Persian philosopher, whose voluminous Arabic and Persian works incorporated a large measure of Greek thought and influenced medicine, philosophy, and mystical thought. 阿维森纳, 见 *Kitab as-sifa*, Albertus, *Summa de creaturis*

Avignon, town on the lower Rhone (France), a bishopric in the fifth century, ruled by the counts of Toulouse and Provence in the 12th century. The town became the papal residence from 1309 to 1367, and from 1370 to 1376; the move of the Roman Curia to France ("Babylon Captivity") was caused by the unstable situation in Rome, the election of a French cardinal as Pope (Clement V), and continuing difficulties with Philip IV who suppressed the Templars. The Popes of the period were generally qualified men. The criticism heaped upon the alleged luxury and corruption of the Avignonese papacy came mainly from churchmen in foreign countries who resisted the growing centralization and expansion of papal administration. 阿维尼翁, 见 Occam (fled from Avignon), Birgitta, *Revelationes* (urged the return of the papacy to Rome), Petrarca (served a cardinal at Avignon for 17 years), Wyclif, *De civili dominio* (attacks on papacy in Avignon)

avis, E: bird, D: Vogel => animalia

Azo, (Azolius, Azolinus), It: Azzone; ca. 1190—1220, teacher of law at Bologna, author of a popular commentary on the *Codex* and *Institutes* of Justinian. 阿佐, 见 Bracton, Gratianus

azyma, unleavened bread used for liturgical purposes; some authors in the Eastern Church accused Latin Christians of being "azymites". 无酵饼

B

Babenberg, the ruling house of Austria in the period from 976—1246. The Babenbergs consolidated their power in central Europe, inherited Styria in 1192, but lost their lands to Ottocar II of Bohemia after Frederick II of Babenberg had died without heir in 1246. 巴本贝格王朝

Babylon, Babel, E: Babylon, Babel, D: Babylon, Babel; city in Mesopotamia, sometimes seen as a center of anti-Christian forces, => Antichristus; the term "Babylonian captivity" was used to stigmatize the residence of the Popes at Avignon (already applied by Petrarch). 巴比伦, 见 Adso, *De ortu et tempore Antichristi*, Cosmas Pragensis, *Chronica* (starts with the dispersion of mankind after Babylon), Maimonides, *More nevukhim* (after the exile in Babylon the Jews neglected philosophy), Vincentius Bellovacensis, *Speculum maius* (contains a history of Babylon), Dante, *De vulgari eloquentia* (a common language of mankind before Babylon)

baccalaureus, E: bachelor, D: Bakkalaureus; a page, member of the lower clergy, younger member of a trade union, or a graduate from a medieval university (baccalaureus artium, B.A.). 巴卡劳瑞斯

Baco, Rogerius, E: Roger Bacon, D: Roger Bacon, 1214—1294, British Franciscan, talented but controversial teacher at Paris and Oxford, scholar of natural sciences and of the languages. 罗杰尔·培根, 见 *Opus maius*

Baghdad, (Bagdad), city on the Tigris, which became the capital of the newly established Abbasid caliphate in 762 AD. Within a century Baghdad became the largest city of the Islamic world, and during the reign of Harun al-Rashid (768—809) many scholars and artists lived in the city. The Mongols destroyed the city in 1258 (Hulagu), and in 1393 and 1401 (Timur the Lame). 巴格达, 见 *Alf lailah wa-lailah*

Bailli, E: bailiff, local royal administrative official in Normandy, England, and southern Italy, later also employed by the French kings from the 12th century. 官吏

Balduinus I, E: Baldwin of Flanders, D: Balduin; +1204; a count of Flanders and one of the leaders of the Fourth Crusade (1202—1204), Baldwin was chosen to be Emperor of Constantinople, when the city fell to the Crusaders and Venetians. 巴尔度因

Balduinus II, E: Baldwin II, D: Balduin II; Latin Emperor of Constantinople from 1237 to 1261, he traveled to many courts in Western Europe to ask for military and financial help for his realm in the East. In 1261 he was overthrown and fled to Italy. 巴尔度因

Balduinus I, E: Baldwin, D: Balduin; one of the leaders of the First Crusade (1096—1099), he founded the county of Edessa and was elected King of Jerusalem (1100—1118) to succeed his brother Godfrey of Bouillon. 巴尔度因

Balduinus II, E: Baldwin, D: Balduin; a cousin of Baldwin I, he was King of Jerusalem from 1118 to 1131, secured the aid of the fleets of Genoa and Venice, and he helped the rulers of the Crusading states of Antioch, Edessa, and Tripoli. He supported the establishment of the Templars (Order of Knights Templars) and Hospitallers. 巴尔度因

Baldur, the Norse god of light, sun and spring, a son of Freya 巴尔杜, 见 Snorri Sturluson, *Edda*

ballad, a light, simple song, or a narrative poem, sung by common people; ballads are sometimes also called "lays". 民歌, 民谣

Balliol, (Baliol), famous Scottish family of Norman ancestry; John Balliol (+1269) was an English baron and founded the Balliol College of Oxford in 1263. His son John Balliol (+1344) was king of Scotland from 1292 to 1296. Edward Balliol ruled Scotland from 1332 to 1356.巴流

Balmung, Siegfried's sword 巴尔蒙, 见 Appendix, *Nibelungenlied*

Bamberg, city in Bavaria, seat of a bishop since 1007. In the 13th century its bishops had the position of princes of the empire. Henry II and his wife Kunigunde are buried in the cathedral of Bamberg.班贝格

bandidi, E: bandits, It: Bravi; men who had become outlaws and who banded into associations, especially in Italy in the 13th and 14th centuries.邦会

Bandinelli, Roland = Alexander III

banna, E: ban, D: Bann; a proclamation (of a royal decree or of a condemnation by the Church).宣布

baptismus, E: baptism, D: Taufe; Christian sacrament of initiation, connected with the rite of pouring water on the head of the new Christian. The sacrament cleansed the person of original sin, qualified for eternal salvatiion, and made him or her an official member of the Church. Christian churches had baptismal fonts or baptisteries (baptisterium), the latter often decorated with artifacts like the baptistery of Florence (bronze doors). 洗礼

Bar Sauma, Rabban, +1294, Nestorian prelate whose diary is a unique historical source; born in Beijing he became a monk in China, then served in an ecclesiastical capacity in Armenia. The Mongol ruler of Persia sent him to western Europe to form an alliance with Christian kings against the Moslems in Syria and Palestine. Bar Sauma was received at courts in Rome, Paris, London, and Constantinople.巴扫玛

Barbarossa = Fredericus I Barbarossa

Barcelona, city of northeastern Spain, founded by Carthaginians (Hamilcar Barca), it fell to Rome after the Second Punic War, was captured by Visigoths in 415 and Saracens in 713, but since 801 belonged to Charlemagne's kingdom. Since 1000 Barcelona was the capital of Catalonia but united with Aragon in 1137, and the city became a rich and powerful trade harbor, rivaling Venice and Genoa. The university of Barcelona was formally chartered in 1450.巴塞罗纳

Bardas, Cesar Bardas, +865, the brother of the Empress Theodora, he supported her restoration of the veneration of images; he was regent for his nephew Emperor Michael III (842—867), helped defeat the Avars, and encouraged the mission work of Cyril and Method, but he was finally murdered.巴达斯

Barlaam et Joasaph, E: *Barlaam and Josaphat*, a work by John of Damascus《巴兰和约沙法特》,见 Ioannes Damaskenos

Barlaam of Calabria, +1350, a Greek monk and scholar who was sent to Avignon in 1339 in order to negotiate questions concerning the schism of the Latin and Greek churches. He joined the Latin church, was even appointed bishop, and taught Petrarch some Greek.巴兰

Baron, D: Baron, a vassal (in England and France) who served as a member of the king's great council 男爵

Bascia, E: Basque, D: Baskenland; an area in the north of Spain; the Basques converted to Christianity before the 5th century, they became vassals of Charlemagne but attacked the rearguard of his army at Roncesvalles in 778 (=> Song of Roland). In 824 the kingdom of Navarre was founded at Pamplona. This kingdom was annexed by Ferdinand II of Aragon in 1513. 巴斯克地区

Basileia, E: Basel, Basle, F: Basle, D: Basel; town in Switzerland, originally a Celtic settlement, then a Roman military post, it became the seat of a bishop in the fifth century, was occupied by the Alamanni, then by the Franks (until 912), and after that belonged to the kingdom of Burgundy. In 1006 Basel passed under German rule, and in 1250 it became an independent city. In 1502 Basel joined the Swiss confederation. The city was place of an ecumenical council (1431—1437), which was recognized by the Pope in 1433 but moved to Ferrara in 1437. The remaining participants of the Council of Basel became schismatic in 1438. In 1449 the men at Basel rescinded their election of the Antipope Felix V and announced their submission to Rome. The University of Basel (the first university in Switzerland) was founded in 1460 by Pope Pius II 巴塞尔, 见 Piccolomini, *Commentarii*

Basilius I, Gr: Basilios, E: Basil; Emperor of Byzanz 867—886, the founder of the Macedonian dynasty (867—1056)巴西略/巴西流斯

Basilius II, Gr: Basilios, E: Basil; "Bulgaroktonos", Emperor of Byzanz 976—1025, the most successful of the Macedonian emperors. He gave his sister Anna in marriage to Vladimir of Kiev (989) and thus prepared the conversion of Russia. 巴西略/巴西流斯

Basilius II = Vasilius

Bavaria, E: Bavaria, D: Bayern, a region in southern Germany. The Bavarii were a branch of the Suebi and related to the Marcomanni. In the 8th century St. Boniface and Celtic monks converted the population. During the era of Duke Odilo (737—748) the dioceses of Salzburg and Regensburg were established. Charlemagne deposed Duke Tassilo III and annexed the area. In 976 the Ostmark (Austria) was separated from Bavaria. Styria was ceded to Austria in 1180, when Emperor Frederick I Barbarossa decided to give Bavaria to the house of Wittelsbach, which ruled until 1918. 巴伐利亚，见 Eginhardus, *Vita Caroli* (wars in Bavaria in 787 AD)

Bavarii, Baiuvarii, Bavarians, a Germanic tribe 巴伐利亚人

Bayern = Bavaria

beatitudo, E: bliss, happiness, D: Seligkeit, Glueck; => miseria 幸福，真福，见 Innocens III, *De miseria* (many things impair the happiness of life)

Beatrice, E, D: Beatrice; a Florentine woman idealized by Dante; she died in 1290 at the age of 24. 贝亚特瑞斯，见 Dante, *Commedia* (symbol of purity and beatitude)

beatus, E: blessed, D: Selige; a blessed or saintly person; the souls of the blessed are thought to be in Heaven 真福，见 Alanus, *Anticlaudianus*

Beauvais, a town of northern France, settlement since Roman times and later ravaged by the Northmen, it was in English hands for much of the Hundred Years' War. 博韦，见 Vincentius Bellovacensis

Bec, Benedictine monastery in Normandy, founded in 1034, its most famous abbots were Lanfranc and Anselm of Canterbury.贝基，见 Anselmus

Becket, Thomas, E, D: Thomas Becket (Beckett); St., 1118—1170, England's most famous medieval martyr. Being the son of a Norman merchant, Becket became Henry II's chancellor in 1154, and Henry supported his election as Archbishop of Canterbury in 1162, but Becket resigned the office of chancellor and objected to Henry's manifold restraints of the English Church (Diet of Clarendon 1164). He was forced to flee to France but abided firmly by his principles. He was killed by four knights after his return. 托马斯·贝克特，见 Johannes Saresberiensis (wrote Becket's biography), Chaucer, *Canterbury Tales*

Beda Venerabilis, E: Bede, Beda, Baeda the Venerable, D: Beda; St., 672—732; monk and teacher in Jarrow (England), the most important precursor of the Carolingian Renaissance. Possibly he was the most learned man of his age (he knew Greek and perhaps Hebrew). Except for the translation of the Gospel of St. John into Anglo-Saxon, all his writings are in Latin. The author of the *Ecclesiastical History of England* is sometimes called the "first modern historian", because he cited the sources of his information. 比德/伯达/贝达，见 *Historia ecclesiastica*, Malmesburiensis, *Gesta regum Anglorum*

Begardi, E: Beghards, D: Begharden; pious communities of men, often fullers, dyers, and weavers, dedicated themselves to prayer and social work but took no formal monastic vows. They were popular in the Low Countries since 1220.贝格哈德会

Beguinae, (mulieres religiosae), E: Beguines, D: Beginen; communities of pious women since the end of the 12th century, who lived and prayed together but did not take religious vows. They were free to own property, to leave and to marry. They were most numerous in the Low Countries and the Rhineland. Like the Beghards they were sometimes charged of heresy, and the Council of Vienne condemned some of their teaching in 1311. 贝居因会

Beijing, (Cambaluc, Hanbali, Peking), important city in China, especially since the Mongol era. Mission activities of the Catholic Church in Beijing started after 1294 北京，见 Marco Polo, Rubruck

Bela I, King of Hungary 1061—1063, a cousin of St. Stephan.贝洛

Bela IV, King of Hungary 1235—1270, who suffered a defeat at the hands of the Mongols in 1241 but could resist a second invasion in 1261.贝洛

Belgium, E: Belgium, D: Belgien; the region where the Belgae lived at Roman times. In the third century the Franks occupied the area, and the medieval history of Belgium was linked to the duchies of Lorraine, Brabant, Luxemburg, and the bishopric of Liege. Since the 15th century the dukes of Burgundy controlled Belgium. 比利时，见 Ghent, Bruges

Belgrade, a city on the Danube, it was a Roman military camp and became a bishopric in the fourth century. It was occupied in turn by Avars, Slavs, Bulgars, Byzantium, Serbs, Hungarians, and in 1521 fell to the Turks after warding off a Turkish attack in 1456.贝尔格莱德

Benedictini = Ordo Sancti Benedicti

Benedictus III, E:Benedict, D: Benedikt; Pope 855—858 本笃/本尼狄克

Benedictus VIII, E: Benedict, D: Benedikt; Pope 1012—1024; in alliance with Genoa and Pisa he could drive the Saracens from Italy and Sardinia. 本笃/本尼狄克

Benedictus IX, E:Benedict, D: Benedikt, Pope 1032—1044.本笃/本尼狄克

Benedictus XI, E: Benedict, D: Benedikt; Pope 1303—1304, a Dominican who adopted a more conciliatory policy toward Philip IV of France.本笃/本尼狄克

Benedictus XII, E: Benedict, D: Benedikt; Pope 1334—1342, originally a French Cistercian, Bishop of Pamiers. During his pontificate he made efforts to reform the Cistercians and Benedictines. Residing in Avignon he began the construction of a papal palace there. 本笃/本尼狄克

Benedictus XIII, E: Benedict, D: Benedikt; Pope 1394—1423, former Cardinal Peter of Luna (Spain), who took part in the election of Urban VI in 1378 but later supported the Avignonese pope Clement VII. After Clement's death he himself was elected by the cardinals in Avignon (1394). He fled to Aragon (Spain) and refused to unite with the Roman faction.本笃/本尼狄克

Benedictus de Aniane, E: Benedict of Aniane, D: Benedikt; +821; monastic reformer, Abbot of the monastery at Aniane (southern France). Benedict became councillor of Louis the Pious and supervised the monasteries of the empire. In 817 he summoned the abbots to Aachen, where a modification of the Benedictine rule was generally accepted. 本笃/本尼狄克

Benedictus de Nursia, E: Benedict of Nursia, D: Benedikt; St., 480—547, Italian monk, founder of the Benedictine Order; around 529 he established the mother house of the order at Monte Cassino, south of Rome. His influential rule outlines the monk's activities throughout the day.本笃/本尼狄克，见 Paulus Diaconus, *Historia Langobardorum*, Dante, *Commedia* (placed in the Heaven of Saturnus)

beneficium, E: benefice, D: Benefizium; an estate or piece of land given by a king, nobleman, bishop, or monastery, to a bishop or monastery or a member of the aristocracy. 赠送的地产

Benevento, town in southern Italy. Around 665 occupied it was by the Lombards, in 787 conquered by Charlemagne. 贝内文托，见 Paulus Diaconus, *Historia Lang.*, Eginhardus, *Vita Caroli*

Benoit（F）= Benedictus

Beowulf, the oldest extant Old English heroic poem from ca. 750 AD.《贝奥武夫》，见 Appendix

Berengarius I, E: Berengar, D: Berengar, grandson of Louis the Pious, Margrave of Friaul, he controlled Italy (888—924) and was crowned Emperor in 915 by the Pope following his victorious campaigns against the Saracens.贝伦格尔

Berengarius II, E: Berengar, D: Berengar; +966; Margrave of Ivrea, who made himself king of Italy 950—963. In 963 he rebelled against the suzerainty of Otto I of Germany and threatened Pope John XII. The latter appealed to Otto who captured Berengar. 贝伦格尔

Berengarius de Tours, E: Berengar, D: Berengar, +1088; archdeacon of Angers cathedral, scholasticus at Tours. Based on the views of Ratramnus of Corbie he questioned the doctrine of transubstantiation but later retracted his views and died at piece with the Church.贝伦格尔

Berlin, city in Germany, founded around 1230 by Margrave John I and Otto III of Brandenburg. Since 1470 it served as the residence of the elector of Brandenburg.柏林

Bernardinus de Siena, It: Bernardino, E: Bernardine; St., +1444, Italian Franciscan, student of the Bible, but also of the classics, of canon law, and theology, he became a famous popular preacher and a very influential force for reform in Italy. 伯尔纳丁

Bernardus de Clairvaux, E: Bernard, D: Bernhard; 1091—1153, Saint, Abbot of Clairvaux, the "second founder" of the Cistercians, he was a theologian, mystic ("Doctor mellifluus"), politician, and the most influential Church authority in his age; => Abaelard, Petrus Venerabilis 伯尔纳德, 见 Bernard, *De consideratione*, *De diligendo Deo*, Dante, *Commedia* (placed in the Heaven of Saturnus)

Bernardus Guidonis, E: Bernard Guy, ca. 1261—1331, French Dominican, in charge of the inquisition from 1307—1324, author of a book on the procedures of the inquisition, the *Practica inquisitionis*. 伯尔纳德

Bernoldus, E: Bernold of Constance, +1100, monk in Constance at St. Blasien., scholastic author and canonist. 贝尔诺德

Bernwardus, E, D: Bernward, Bishop of Hildesheim (Germany), +1022, patron of artists. 伯恩瓦德

Bertholdus de Calabria, E: Berthold, founder of the Carmelites, he lived as hermit at Mount Carmel 1156—1195. 贝尔托德

Bertholdus de Regensburg, E: Berthold, D: Berthold; +1272, a Franciscan preacher, the most renowned preacher of medieval Germany; traveling through Germany, Switzerland, Bohemia, and Hungary he held Latin and German sermons, emphasizing moral living more than doctrine. 贝尔托德

Besancon, town in the county of Burgundy (France), place of the imperial diet of Besancon 1157. The university was founded around 1422. 贝桑松

Bessarion, Johannes, E: John Bessarion, D: Johannes Bessarion; 1403—1474, Byzantine scholar and theologian. Being Metropolit of Nicaea, he accompanied the Greek delegation to the Council of Ferrara Florence and supported the union of the Latin and Greek churches. He was made cardinal in 1439, taught Greek, translated works from Greek into Latin, collected manuscripts and helped other Humanists in their efforts. 贝萨里翁, 见 *In calumniatorem Platonis*

Bestiarium, E: Bestiary, D: Tierkunde; a collection of descriptions of animals; medieval bestiaries combined elements from the *Physiologus*, Aristotle, Pliny, and mythology. 动物画册, 见 Fredericus II, *De arte venandi*

Bibars, Sultan of Egypt and Syria, 1260—1277 比巴尔

Biblia, (Sanctae Scripturae), E: Bible, Holy Bible, D: Bibel; the most important book of the Middle Ages, copied, edited, studied, interpreted, printed after 1450, edited in multilingual versions by Ximenes and others; first German printed versions from 1466《圣经》, 见 Hrabanus, *De institutione clericorum*, Otfried de Weissenburg, *Evangelienbuch*, Cosmas Pragensis, *Chronica* (starts from the tower of Babylon), Nestorius, *Povest'* (starts from the time of Noah and his sons), Abaelardus, *Sic et non* (discussion of Biblical statements), Petrus Lombardus, *Sententiae* (many Biblical quotations), Vincentius Bellovacensis, *Speculum maius* (Biblical orientation of history; arrangement of contents according to "six days"), Rogerius Baco, *Opus maius* (exhorts the study of Biblical languages), Dante, *Commedia* (80 Biblical persons mentioned), Langland, *Piers Plowman* (allegory as Dame Scripture)

Biblia exposita, E: interpretation of the Bible, D: Erklaerungen der Bibel, Exegesis, => sensus allegoricus 解经方式, 圣经诠释学, 见 Hrabanus, *De institutione*, Otfrid, *Evangelienbuch* (spiritaliter, moraliter, mystice), Thomas Aquinas, *Summa theologiae* I.1,10 (a Biblical expression can have different layers of meaning, sensus allegoricus, moralis, mysticus), Nicolaus de Lyra, *Postilla*, Wycliffe, *De civili dominio* (emphasizing the "lex evangelica")

Biblia in versis, E: versified Bibles, D: Reimbibeln, versifications of Biblical texts 用诗体编写的《圣经》, 见 Otfried, *Evangelienbuch*

Biblia pauperum, E: Bible of the poor, D: Armenbibel, pictoral version of Biblical themes, especially popular in the 14th and 15th centuries. These Bibles first appeared in Bavaria and Austria in the 13th century. 穷人的《圣经》

Biblia prohibitiva, E: forbidden Bible, D: verbotene Bibel. Since the 13th century Church authorities issued local prohibitions to translate the Bible into the colloquial language, motivated by the abuse of Biblical texts by heretic sects. 被禁止的《圣经》, 见 Wycliffe

bibliotheca, E: library, D: Bibliothek; since late antiquity (Cassiodorus) monks started to copy books and compile small libraries. Alcuin told his monks that "it is better to copy books than to cultivate vines." Monastic scriptoria (writing rooms) exchanged books and manuscripts, and the monasteries of Fulda, Lorsch, Bobbio, Reichenau, St. Gall and Monte Cassino had thousand or more volumes. The cathedral schools of the eleventh century set up even bigger libraries, famous among them were Reims, Paris, Orleans, Chartres, Tours, and Laon. The humanists of Italy (Petrarch and others) were avid collectors of old manuscripts and of Greek texts, and soon the Vatican and Laurentian libraries appeared.图书馆

Biel, Gabriel, ca. 1420—1495, German theologian, famous professor in Tuebingen, "doctor catholicus", exponent of Occamism, he profoundly influenced M. Luther. He also wrote a work on economic theory. 比尔,见 Occam

Birgitta, E: Brigida, Brigitta, Bridget, D: Brigitte; St., 1303—1373, Swedish visionary, patron saint of Sweden. She was the daughter of a provincial governor, married and had eight children, entered the Cistercian order after becoming a widow. She founded a monastery in Wadstena in 1346, thus becoming the foundress of the Brigittine Sisters (Birgittines). She went to Rome to obtain papal confirmation of the order and lived an ascetic life in Rome after 1349, devoting her energies to works of charity, reform of the Church and to the return of the papacy to Rome. Her Revelations gave rise to disputes.布里吉特,见 Birgitta

Birgittines, a congregation of sisters founded by Birgitta in 1346 in Wadstena, they also accepted deacons and priests in their communities 布里吉特修女会,见 Birgitta

Bishop = episcopus

Blanquerna, E: *Blanquerna,* an utopian educational novel by Raimond Lull.《巴奎纳》,见 Raimundus Lullus

blasphemia, E: blasphemy, D: Blasphemy; 亵渎神,见 Dante, *Commedia*(blasphemists placed in Hell)

Blemmida Nicephorus, Gr: Nikēphoros Blemmydēs, +1272, a learned monk, teacher, author, founder of a monastery near Ephesus, who devoted much effort to ending the schism between the Greek and Latin churches.布雷米达

Bobbio, monastery in North Italy, founded by Columban in 612; it became a center of learning and was first granted the privilege of exemption (in 628). Decline set in after 1000. 博比欧

Boccaccio, Giovanni, E, D: Boccaccio; 1313—1375, son of a Florentine merchant, he was trained in Naples, then returned to Florence; he was writing the *Decameron* when Petrarch urged him to turn to classical studies. After that he devoted his time to the study of Greek and Roman mythology and became one of the earliest humanists. He was the first who tried to systematically study Greek language and literature. 薄伽丘,见 *Decamerone, De casibus virorum illustrium*

Boethius, 480—524, Roman philosopher, translator, politician who wrote the famous *De consolatione philosophiae* before his execution.波伊提乌斯/鲍埃蒂,见 Dante, *Commedia* (placed in the Heaven of the Sun)

Bogomili, E: Bogomils, D: Bogomilen; members of a sect on the Balkans, possibly developed from the Pauliciani in the 9th, 10th centuries, characterized by ascetic dualism. They were quite influential in Bulgaria and Bosnia, then they moved to the West, where they were called Cathari or Patarini. => Cathari 波格米勒派

Bogoris => Boris

Bohemi, Slavic people of central Europe 波希米亚人

Bohemia, E: Bohemia, D: Boehmen; region in central Europe, occupied by German tribes (Marcomanni), until ca. 600 AD when the Slavs settled in the area. Cyril and Methodius spread Christianity in the ninth century, and Otto I of Germany (936—973) incorporated the land into his kingdom. Ottocar I (died 1230) was the first to secure the title of king. In 1306 the house of Luxemburg took over the crown after the dynasty of the Przemyslides had become extinct. Charles IV was king of Germany from 1346 to 1378 and enlarged the capital Prague. German influence led to a nationalist movement. => Carolus IV, Hus 波希米亚,见 Cosmas Pragensis, *Chronica Bohemorum,* Johannes de Tepla, *Der Ackermann aus Boehmen*

Boleslaw, name of Bohemian Dukes 波列斯拉夫

Boleslaw I, Count of Bohemia 929—967, killed his brother Wenzel but accepted the feudal authority of Otto I in 950 波列斯拉夫

Boleslaw II, "the Pious", Count of Bohemia 967—999, supporter of the Church 波列斯拉夫

Boleslaw I Chrobry, Duke of Poland 992—1025, son of Miesko, he was the most powerful of the early Polish rulers and controlled Slovakia, Silesia, Lusatia, Moravia, Pomerania, Ruthenia, and temporarily even Bohemia. In 1000 he could obtain the elevation of Gniezno to the rank of a metropolitan see and thus freed the church of Poland from German control. Soon after his death some of the regions he had conquered fell away. 波列斯拉夫

Boleslaw II, King of Poland 1058—1079, son of Casimir I. He seized Slovakia from Hungary and held Kiev for some time but murdered Stanislaus, the bishop of Cracow and was excommunicated by Pope Gregory VII. 波列斯拉夫

Boleslaw III, King of Poland 1102—1138, who signed a treaty with Emperor Lothair II by which he received Pomerania and Ruegen as fiefs of the empire (1135). 波列斯拉夫

Bolonia, (=Bononia), E: Bologna, D: Bologna; a city of north-central Italy, originally an Etruscan town it became a Roman colony around 200 BC; Bologna's famed university (of one of the oldest universities of Europe) was originally founded as law school in 425 AD and (after a long interruption) chartered by Frederick I Barbarossa in 1158. Since the 12th century it attracted law students from all of Europe. Bologna joined the Lombard League in 1167 and resisted Papal rule, but Cardinal Albornoz asserted Papal rights in 1360, and since the time of Pope Julius II (1503—1513) the city was fully incorporated into the Papal States. => jus canonicum 博洛尼亚, 见 Gratianus, Innocens

Bonaventura, It: Giovanni Fidanza, E: Bonaventure; St., 1221—1274, Italian Franciscan, he studied in Paris under Alexander of Hales, taught there until 1257, then became superior general of the Franciscans (1257—1274), even has been honored as the second founder of the order in a time of trials; one of the leading mystical theologians, he emphasized that the faith must always lead reason in the search for truth. 波纳文都拉, 见 *Itinerarium mentis in Deum*

Bonifatius, E: Boniface (=Winfried, Wynfrieth), D: Bonifatius, St.; 673—754, the most important Anglo-Saxon missionary among the Germanic tribes, "Apostle of Germany", reformer of the Frankish church, he was consecrated bishop in 722 and given broad episcopal authority over Germany by the Pope; since 744 he was archbishop of Mainz, founded many monasteries, and was finally martyred in Frisia. 博尼法修斯/波尼法奇乌斯/卜尼法斯, 见 *Epistulae*

Bonifatius IV, E: Boniface, D: Bonifaz; Pope 608—615; he converted the Pantheon in Rome into a church. 博尼法奇乌斯, 见 Paulus Diaconus, *Historia*

Bonifatius VIII, E: Boniface, D: Bonifaz; Pope 1294—1303, original name: Benedict Gaetani; his struggle against the French king and against the Colonna clan prepared the exile in Avignon. His bull *Unam sanctam* emphasized papal authority. He instituted the celebration of the Holy Year in 1300 and expanded canon law with his *Liber Sextus*. 博尼法奇乌斯/博尼法修/卜尼法斯

Bonifatius IX, E: Boniface, D: Bonifaz; Pope 1389—1404, he resided in Rome, but failed to achieve Church unity. 博尼法奇乌斯/博尼法修/卜尼法斯

Bononia = Bolonia

bonum, E: good, D: das Gute, ein Gut; 善, 见 Thomas Aquinas, *Summa theologiae* II.I. 94,2 (realized first by practical reason)

Bordeaux, port city in southwestern France, a bishopric since the fourth century, it was seized by the Visigoths in 418 and by the Franks in 507. After destruction by the Normans in 848 it was rebuilt. Most of its wine export went to England, and it was an English possession for most of the time from 1154 until 1453. 波尔多

Boris, (=Bogoris), Duke of Bulgaria, 852—889, baptized in 864. He accepted missionaries from Constantinople and rejected those from the West. His son Vladimir wanted to revive paganism, but he returned to power and replaced Vladimir with his other son Symeon. Boris died in 907 and was later canonized by the Eastern Church. 鲍里斯, 见 Photios

Borussia = Prussia

Bourges, city of central France, capital of Roman Aquitania, it became the capital of the duchy of Berry. The "Pragmatic Sanction of Bourges" (1438) restricted papal power in France. 布尔日

Brabant, originally a Frankish county between the Maas and Scheldt, Brabant was attached to Lower Lorraine in 870, became a duchy in 1190, fell to Burgundy in 1390 and to the Habsburgs in 1477. 布拉班特

Bracciolini, Poggio = Poggio Bracciolini

Bracton, Henricus, E: Henry de Bracton (Bratton), E: Heinrich von Bracton; ca. 1200—1268, priest, chancellor of the diocese of Exeter, royal justice since 1248 and member of the king's council; his *De legibus et consuetudinibus Angliae* is the most authoritative medieval book on English law. 布拉克顿, 见 *De legibus et consuetudinibus Angliae*

Bradwardin, Thomas de, E: Thomas of Bradwardine, 1290—1349, English theologian, philosopher, and mathematician, chancellor of Oxford, Archbishop of Canterbury (1349), exponent of Augustinian thought. 布拉德瓦丁

Braga, city in northern Portugal, capital of a state of the Suebi in the fifth century, occupied by Visigoths in 485 and by Saracens around 720 but regained by Ferdinand I of Castile-Leon in 1040. It was the residence of the king of Portugal from 1093 to 1147. 波拉格

Bramante, 1444—1514, Italian artist who made a plan to rebuild St. Peter's Church in Rome. 布拉曼特

Brandenburg, city and margravate of Germany; Henry I conquered the region in 928 and subdued the west Slavonic Hevelli tribe. Albert the Bear rebuilt the town, invited German peasants to settle there, founded monasteries and in 1140 assumed the title of margrave. Later the prince of Brandenburg became one of the seven eledtors. => *Bulla aurea* 勃兰登堡

Bremen, city near the mouth of the Weser (Germany), a bishopric since 787. After the Vikings had destroyed Hamburg in 845, Bremen became an archbishop's seat and had jurisdiction over all Scandinavia and Iceland. 不来梅

Bretislav, name of Bohemian kings in the 11th century 布瑞提斯拉夫, 见 Cosmas Pragensis, *Chronica Bohemorum*

breviarium = liturgia horarum

Brigantia, D: Bregenz, town in W Austria, 布雷根茨

Brigitta, Brigida = Birgitta

Britannia, E: Britanny, D: Britannien; the nortwestern peninsula of France which was occupied by Bretons (Britons) from England in the fifth century. In the tenth century it became a duchy. It took a rather neutral course during the Hundred Years' War, but in 1499 the region passed under French authority. => Anglia 不列颠, 见 Brutus

Briti, Britanni, E: Brites, D: Briten, the inhabitants of England 布列提人, 见 Beda, *Historia* (Lucius, king of the Britanni wants to convert to Christianity at the end of the 2nd century AD)

Brothers = Fratres

Brothers of Common Life = Fratres vitae communis

Bruges, a rich commercial center of Flanders, called the "Venice of the North". Being a center of wool trade it lived through a period of cultural splendor and passed under the rule of the duke of Burgundy in 1382. 布鲁日

Brugman de Kempis, +1473, German Franciscan, famous preacher 布鲁格曼

Brunelleschi, Filippo, Italian artist, 1377—1446, architect and sculptor of Florence who tried to revive classical art forms as opposed to Gothic. 布鲁内莱吉

Brunhild, (Brunhilde, Brynhild), a heroic woman from Old Norse literature, the wife of King Gunther in the *Nibelungenlied* 布伦希尔德, 见 Snorri Sturluson, *Edda*, Appendix, *Nibelungenlied*

Bruni, Leonardo, +1444; Italian humanist scholar. He translated Greek classics and wrote biographies of Dante, Petrarch, and Boccaccio. 布鲁尼

Bruno, St., +1101; teacher at Rheims, founder of the Carthusians, first community in La Chartreuse in 1084; he died in La Torre, Calabria. 布鲁诺/布汝诺

Bruno de Colonia, D: Bruno von Koeln; St., +965; brother of Otto the Great and his chancellor from 940; in 953 he became archbishop of Cologne. He reformed monasteries and supported learning. 布鲁诺/布汝诺

Bruno de Querfurt, (Brun, Bruns), St. +1009, Bishop of Querfurt, student of St. Romuald, he accompanied Otto III to Rome in 997, decided to becam a missionary, worked among the Petchenegs north of the Black Sea and in Prussia. He and his 18 companions were martyred in 1009. 布鲁诺/布汝诺

Brutus, E: Brutus, D: Brutus; a common Roman name 布鲁图斯, 见 Galfredus, *Historia regum Britanniae* (Aeneas' descendant Brutus allegedly gives his name to Britain), Dante, *Commedia* (Brutus placed in Hell for his murder of Caeser)

Bruxellium, F: Bruxelles, E: Brussels, D: Bruessel; first noted in 966, it became the principal city of Brabant in the 14th century. 布鲁塞尔

Bryennius, E: Nicephorus Bryennius, D: Nikephoros Bryennios, 1062—1138, husband of Anna Comnene, general, statesman, and historian. 布里恩尼乌斯, 见 Anna Komnene

Brynhild, legendary queen, rescued by Sigurd; => Brunhild 布伦希德, 见 Snorri Sturluson, *Edda*

Budapest, city on the Danube, capital of Hungary,

re-founded by Magyar invaders in the ninth century. It was destroyed by the Mongols in 1241, but Bela IV erected a royal residence a few years later.布达佩斯

Bulgaria, E: Bulgaria, D: Bulgarien; a country in the west-central Balkans, in antiquity the area of the Roman provinces of Moesia and Thracia. The Bulgars, a Turko-Mongol people appeared around 550 AD and expelled the local Slavic tribes. In 681 Byzantium recognized a Bulgar state, and the first great Bulgarian leader Krum (+814) even laid siege to Constantinople. Boris I (852—889) accepted Christianity and welcomed missionaries from the Greek Church. The Mongols devastated northern Bulgaria in the 1240s, and in 1393 the country became part of the Ottoman empire. 保加利亚

Bulla aurea, E: *Golden Bull*, D: *Goldene Bulle*; a decree in 31 chapters issued by Charles IV of Germany in 1356; it designated seven electors to choose the future kings of Germany《黄金诏书》, 见 Appendix, *Bulla aurea*

Burchard of Worms, + 1025, Bishop of Worms, author of a collection of the ecclesiastical law. 布克哈德

Burdinus de Praga = Gregorius VIII

Burgos, city in north-central Spain, founded in 884 as a fortress agains the Moors. Around 1000 it became the first capital of Castile until the royal residence was moved to Toledo in 1087. Burgos was the home and burial place of Diaz de Vivar (el Cid).布尔格斯, 见 *Poema de mio Cid*

Burgundia, E: Burgundy, D: Burgund; the east German tribe of the Burgundi settled in the Main valley around 300 AD, then moved southward to the Rhone. In 436 they were defeated by a Roman army under Aetius, but under their king Gundobad (474—516) they overran the Provence. They became Christians, and in 534 their kingdom fell to the Franks. Boso, the ruler of Viennois (879—888), reestablished the kingdom of Burgundy, and then it included territories stretching from Autun to the Provence.勃艮第,见 *Nibelungenlied*

Burgundia, E: Duchy of Burgundy, D: Herzogtum Burgund; the area around Autun, Troyes, and Langres (northern France) was ruled by Capetian rulers from the 10th to the 14th century. In 1482 it fell under the rule of the French king.勃艮第公国

Buridanus, Johannes, F: Jean Buridan, E: John Buridan; ca. 1300—1358, French theologian, philosopher, scientist, rector of the University of Paris, he wrote Commentaries to Aristotle's works, was critical of the latter's necessitarianism and thus formulated the law of inertia.布里但

Byzantium, (=Constantinopolis), Gr: Byzantion, E: Byzantium, D: Byzanz; After Constantine had established Byzantion as the new capital of the Eastern Roman Empire (thus renamed Constantinople), the separation of the two parts of the empire was completed after the death of Emperor Theodosius in 395. Under his two sons (Honorius in the West, and Arcadius in the East) the two parts of the empire went separate ways. Since the fourth century the eastern emperors believed that the stability of their regimes depended on theological unity. Justinian (527—565) could recover Italy, north Africa, and part of Spain from the German tribes who had conquered these regions. Slavic, Germanic and Hunnic tribes became a threat similar to the pressure from the Persians in the East. Emperor Heraclius (610—641) could defeat the Persians but the Arabs destroyed his army in 636 at Yarmuk. Soon Syria, Egypt, and north Africa fell to the Moslems, who besieged Constantinople in 674—878 and in 717—718. In 726 Emperor Leo III condemned the cult of icons, thus straining the relations to Rome. The Bulgars inflicted a great defeat upon Byzantium in 811, but the rule of Basil II (976—1025) renewed the power of the empire, which then included much of Syria, southern Italy, the Balkans, Armenia, and the islands of Crete and Cyprus. The disastrous victory of the Seljuk Turks at Manzikert in 1071 brought decline to Byzantium, and in the same year the Normans expelled the Greeks from Bari, the last Byzantine foothold in Italy. Emperor Alexius Comnenus turned to Pope Urban II for help, and thus the First Crusade (1096) was organized. However, Crusaders did not cooperate with Byzantium, while Venice and Genoa exploited both sides for their own commercial ends. In 1204 the knights of the Fourth Crusade and Venice captured Constantinople and founded the "Latin Empire of Constantinople" (1204—1261). Michael Palaeologus VIII regained possession of the capital in 1261, and the dynasty of the Palaeologi ruled the empire until 1453. The Turks invaded the Balkans in 1354, destroyed Serbian power at Kossovo in 1389 and in 1396 routed a crusading army under Sigismund at Nicopolis. The Mongols under Timur the Lame defeated the Turks at Angora (1402) which kept off the Turks for a few more decades. In May 1453 the Turkis army entered Byzantium, and the city became Istanbul. 拜占庭, 见 Paulus Diaconus, *Hist. Lang.*, Photius, *Myrobiblion*, Nestorius, *Povest'* (stresses independence from Byzanz), Anna Comnene, *Alexias* (about Alexius Comnenus)

C

Caballerus, Sp: caballero, F: chevalier, E: knight, D: Ritter; => eques

Caedwalla, king of Wessex, 685—689, who did while on a pilgrimage to Rome. 凯德瓦拉, 见 Beda, *Historia Ecclesiastica*

Caedmon, friar in Whitby, ca. 630—680, author of Biblical poetry in Anglosaxon language 凯德蒙

Caelestinus = Coelestinus

caelibatus = coelibatus

caelum, E: heaven, D: Himmel; medieval literature combined Christian, classical, and neo-platonic elements to describe the heavenly spheres; => empyreum 天, 上天, 天界, 见 Alanus, *Anticlaudianus* (journey through the heavenly spheres), Dante, *Commedia* (detailed description of the Paradise and the inhabitants of the different layers of Heaven)

Caena Domini, E: Last Supper, D: das letzte Abendmahl; 最后晚餐

Caerularius = Cerularius

Caesarius de Heisterbach, + ca. 1240, German Cistercian monk, hagiographer, historian. 切撒留斯

Cain, E: Cain, D: Kain; according to *Genesis* 4 Cain killed his brother Abel 加音, 见 Wolfram, *Parzival* (Parzival he killed his relative Ither and realizes his guilt), Dante, *Commedia* (placed in the lowest part of Hell), Appendix, *Beowulf* (sea monster is a descendant of Cain)

calamitas => miseria

Caliph, the successors of Muhammad, especially the four Orthodox Caliphs Abu Bakr (632—634), Omar, Othman, and Ali. The Omayyad caliphs made Damascus their capital (until 750), and the Abbasids reigned in Baghdad until the Mongol invasion in 1258, when the caliphate came to an end. 哈里发

Calixtus II, E: Callistus, D: Calixt; Pope 1119—1124, originally Guido, Archbishop of Vienne, in whose pontificate the agreement on the investiture issue (Concordate of Worms 1122) was accomplished 卡里斯图斯, 见 Gregorius VII

Calixtus III, E: Callistus, D: Calixt; Pope 1455—1458, originally Alonso de Borja (Borgia) from Spain, he organized resistance against the Turks and achieved a naval victory over the Turkish fleet in 1457, but he also cultivated political nepotism. 卡里斯图斯

calligraphia, Gr: kalle graphe, E: calligraphy, D: Kalligraphie; throughout the early Middle Ages most calligraphy was produced in monastic scriptoria. 书法, 见 Columba, Alcuin

Camaldoli, (<Campus Maldoli), Camaldolensi, E: Camaldoleses, D: Kamaldulenser; a congregation that developed in the 11th century from a monastery founded by St. Romuald in 1012 in Italy. They observed the rule of St. Benedict but reduced community life. 卡马尔多里(会), 见 Gratianus

Cambaluc = Beijing

Cambridge, an ancient town about 50 miles north of London. A castle was built by William the Conqueror and monasteries were founded some time later. The university may have originated from a secession of teachers from Oxford in 1209. Seven colleges were founded in the 13th century. 剑桥

Canon Law => jus canonicum, codex iuris canonici

Canonici regulares Augustini => Augustini canonici

canonicus, E: canon, D: Kanoniker; a clergyman who belonged to a cathedral chapter or collegiate church. Those who observed a written rule (usually the Rule of St. Augustine) were called regular canons (canonici regulares); those who held personal property and lived in their own houses were called secular canons (canonici saeculares). Gregory VII urged the clergy to live in regular communities which thus became popular in the 11th century. 圣职团员, 见 Petrarca, Wyclif

canonissae regulares, E: regular canonesses, D: Kanonissen; regular women canons. In the early Middle Ages any pious woman, virgin or widow, who served in the Church, could be called canoness, if she observed certain rules prescribed by the bishop. Since the 8th century "secular canonesses" lived in convents but had the right to leave the cloister at times, whereas "regular canonesses" took vows of celibacy and poverty. The eleventh century saw a great rise of communities of regular canonesses, esp. the Canonesses Regular of St. Augustine.女士社祷团体

canonista, E: canonist, canon law expert, D: Kirchenrechtler; medieval scholar who wrote commentaries on papal decrees, => ius canonicum, legistae 教会法学家,见 Gratianus

canonizatio, E: canonization, D: Heiligsprechung; the formal announcement (by the Pope) that a person can be officially commemorated as Saint in the Church. Martyrs were publicly honored as Saints in the early church, and local bishops supported or rejected the veneration of outstanding witnesses in their dioceses. The first historically documented canonization occurred in 993 when Pope John XV proclaimed Ulrich of Augsburg a Saint, which was intended to hold for all Christians. Decretals of the 13th century restricted canonization to the official Church.宣布为圣人/圣徒

Canossa, city in Tuscany, location of the castle of Countess Mathilda, where Henry IV received forgiveness from Gregory VII in January 1077. Canossa became a symbol of papal dominance and imperial submission.卡诺撒,见 Gregorius VII

Canterbury => Cantuaria

Canterbury Tales, a work by Chaucer, considered to be the most important piece of English literature of the late Middel Ages.《坎特伯雷故事集》,见 Chaucer

Canticum canticorum, E: *Song of Songs,* a book of the Old Testament which inspired many allegorical interpretations.《雅歌》,见 Bernardus Claravallensis, *De diligendo Deo,* Raimundus Lullus, *Blanquerna* (esp. *Libre d'Amic e Amat*)

Cantuaria, E: Canterbury, D: Canterbury; city in Kent founded by the Romans. It was the capital of the kings of Kent, and since ca. 600 AD (arrival of Augustine the monk) it is the residence of archbishops. Many major political and religious events of medieval England were enacted in this city. Due to the tomb of Thomas Becket (murdered in 1170) it became the most popular pilgrim destination of England and one among the ten economically most important towns on the island. 坎特伯雷,见 Lanfrancus, Anselmus, Johannes Saresberensis, Chaucer, *Canterbury Tales* (the frame story is a group of pilgrims on the way to Canterbury)

Canutus Magnus, E: Canute the Great (Cnut), D: Knut der Grosse; King of Denmark and England (1018—1035). In 1028 he became king of Norway. He generously supported the Church and made a pilgrimage to Rome in 1026. 克努特,见 Saxo Grammaticus, *Gesta Danorum*

Canutus Sanctus, E: Canute the Saint, +1086, king (1080—1086) and patron Saint of Denmark. He built many churches and raised the status of his bishops.克努特

capitulare, orders issued by Charlemagne, the first in 769 法令集,见 Walahfridus, *Liber de cultura hortorum* (influenced by *Capitulare de villis*)

Capetii, E: Capetians, D: Kapetinger; the royal family which ruled France from 987 until 1328. The most famous Capetian kings were Louis VI, Louis VII, Philip II, Louis IX, and Philip IV. 卡佩提安王朝

capitulum cathedralis, E: chapter of a cathedral; D: Domkapitel; the clergymen at a cathedral church who enjoyed certain rights 大堂圣职团

cardinalis, E: cardinal, D: Kardinal; member of a group of clerics (deacons, priests, bishops) who had leading functions in the Church of Rome; they elected the Pope; their number varied from 15 to 70 in the Middle Ages. The nomination of French cardinals led to schismatic situations in the late 14th century. 枢机,见 Bernardus, *De consideratione* (the Pope should select able people to be cardinals)

caritas, E: charity, D: Naechstenliebe; => sacrificium 博爱,见 Chretien, *Erec et Enide,* Hartmann, *Der arme Heinrich,* Wolfram, *Parzival* (not showing sympathy for a sick person counted as sin of omission, => Amfortas), Thomas de Celano, *Vita Sancti Francisci* (Francis' compassion for the poor), Jacobus de Voragine, *Legenda aurea* (St. Nicholas, model of Christian charity), Appendix, *Elkerlijk* (good deeds)

Carlo => Carolo

Carmelitae, (Ordo Fratrum B. Mariae Virginis de Monte Carmelo), E: Brothers of the Blessed Virgin Mary of Mount Carmel, D: Karmeliten; an ascetic monastic congregation created by St.

Berthold in 1156 in Palestine. Albert of Vercelli, Bishop of Jerusalem, made a simple and ascetic rule for them in 1209. They received papal recognition in 1216 as a mendicant order of friars, but in 1247 the original rule was modified to enable the members to join in active apostolate. 加尔默罗会, 圣衣会

Carmina Burana, E: *Carmina Burana*, a collection of Latin poetry from the 12th and 13th centuries《布拉纳歌集》, 见 Appendix, *Carmina Burana*

Carolingii, E: Carolingians, D: Karolinger; a short-lived dynasty founded by Carolus Magnus 卡洛琳/加洛琳王朝

Carolomannus, E: Carloman, D: Karlmann, son of Carolus Martellus, he retired from politics in 747 in order to become a monk in Italy and died in 754. 卡洛曼, 见 Eginhardus, *Vita Caroli*

Carolus Magnus, F: Charlemagne, E: Charles the Great, D: Karl der Grosse; 742—814; son of Pepin III, king of the Franks 768—814, he subjugated the Saxons, conquered Lombardy and destroyed the kingdom of the Avars; his reign stretched from the Pyrenees to the Elbe and Oder, and in 800 he was crowned emperor by Pope Leo III in Rome. He promoted studies (Latin) and education, supported missions and used the feudal system of counts and margraves to rule his huge country. 查理大帝/卡尔大帝/查理曼, 见 Paulus Diaconus, *Hist. Lang.*, Eginhardus, *Vita Caroli*, Notkerus Balbulus, *Gesta Caroli Magni*, Dante, *Commedia* (placed in the Heaven of Mars), Appendix, *Chanson de Roland*

Carolus Martellus, E: Charles Martel, D: Karl Martell; leader of the Franks 714—741, he victoriously led the Frankish army against Frisians, Saxons, Alemanni, Bavarians, and Aquitanians. Most importantly, he defeated a Muslim army in Tours and Poitiers (France) in 732. He helped St. Boniface and other missionaries to spread the faith among the German tribes east of the Rhine. His son Pepin III became the first Carolingian king. 查理·马特, 见 Bonifatius (supported by Martell), Eginhardus, *Vita Caroli*, Dante, *Commedia* (placed in the Heaven of Venus)

Carolus II Glaber, E: Charles the Bald, D: Karl der Kahle; King of the West Franks, 843—877, who received the western third of the Carolingian empire in the division of Verdun 843. He was crowned Emperor in 875 by Pope John VIII. 卡若卢斯

Carolus III Crassus, E: Charles III the Fat, D: Karl der Dicke; king of Italy and Alamannia 876—887. He was crowned Emperor in 881, became king of the East Franks, and in 884 king of the West Franks. He was too weak to defend his huge kingdom against the Saracens in Italy and against the Viking who attacked Paris (886). His death in 888 marked the final dissolution of the Carolingian empire. 卡若卢斯

Carolus IV, E: Charles of Luxemburg, D: Karl; German Emperor 1346—1378, crowned in Rom in 1355; founder of the University of Prague; issuing the *Bulla aurea* (*Golden Bull*, 1356) he clarified the procedure of the election of the German King; he also wrote an autobiography. 卡若卢斯/卡尔/查理, 见 *Bulla aurea*

Carolus VI, F: Charles, E: Charles (the Mad), D: Karl, King of France 1380—1422. His years of minority reign and (after 1392) periods of insanity led to a division of France. His brother Louis, Duke of Orleans, and his uncle Philip, Duke of Burgundy contended for power, the latter faction even concluded the Treaty of Troyes (1420) with England. 查理

Carolus VII, F: Charles, E: Charles, D: Karl; King of France 1422—1461, who was crowned at Reims in 1429 after the military successes brought about by Joan of Arc. He ended the Hundred Years' War and approved the Pragmatic Sanction of Bourges (1438), in which he affirmed the liberties of the Gallican Church. 查理

Carolus I de Anjou, E: Charles of Anjou, D: Karl; King of Naples and Sicily 1265—1285. He was the brother of Louis IX of France and wanted to create a Mediterranean empire, but thw Sicilians drove him from the island (Sicilian Vespers, 1282). 查理

Carolus II de Anjou, E: Charles of Anjou, D: Karl; King of Naples 1285—1309 查理

carrus, E: chariot, D: Wagen; 车, 见 Alanus, *Anticlaudianus* (the seven liberal arts build a chariot), Dante, *Commedia* (vision of animals drawing a chariot)

Cartusii, E: Carthusian Order, D: Karthaeuser; an ascetic order founded in 1084 by St. Bruno in Chartreuse (north of Grenoble). Despite the harshness of its rule the order counted around 200 communities in 1500.加都西会

Casimirus III, E: Casimir, D: Kasimir; King of Poland 1333—1370, the last of the Piast dynasty. He gained Galicia, codified the laws, founded the University of Cracow (1364) and made concessions to the Polish aristocracy.卡西米尔

Castel Sant'Angelo, Castle in Rome, built as mausoleum for Emperor Hadrian in the 130s, later in papal possession, often used as a place of refuge when enemy forces invaded Rome. 圣安杰罗城堡,见 Gregorius VII

castellum, (castra), E: castle, D: Burg, Schloss; fortified structures have existed since the paleolithicum; stone castles appeared in England with the Normans, and in the 12th century they became universal in western Europe. Before the use of artillery (since 1400) castles were practically invincible and thus gave the landholding aristocracy a powerful position when they were challenged by royal pressure. => Grail 碉堡,见 Wolfram, *Parzival* (castle of the Grail)

Castilia, E: Castile, D: Kastilien; the kingdom in the center of the Spanish peninsula which the kings of the Asturias and Leon gradually recovered from the Saracens. After 900 Burgos was established as capital. From 1029 to 1188 Castile was under Leon's suzerainty. Later the marriage of Isabella and Ferdinand (1469) led to the emergence of modern Spain. => Hispania 卡斯蒂利亚,见 Appendix, *Poema de mio Cid*

castitas, E: chastity, D: Keuschheit; the ideal of medieval monks, nuns and clergymen; => coelibatus, virginitas 贞洁,见 Hrotsvita, *Abraham eremita*, Guillaume de Lorris, *Roman de la rose* (Nature disparages chastity), Jacobus de Voragine, *Legenda aurea* (Lucia, model of chastity; she remained pure like light even in an immodest environment)

Catalonia, contry of northeastern Spain, united with Aragon in 1137.加泰隆,见 Lullus

Cathari, E: Cathars, (Albigenses), D: Katharer; a dualist heretic sect especially popular in northern Italy and southern France, in the 12th and 13th centuries, the adherents demanded ascetic renunciation of the world and were perceived as danger to society, thus suppressed by church and state; => Bogomili 清洁派,见 Bernardus (he opposed them), Joachim, *Liber figurarum* (influence on the movement)

Catharina de Siena, E: Catherine, D: Katharina; St.; 1347—1380; she was a famous Italian visionary and tried to reconcile the Pope and the city of Florence (around 1376). 锡耶纳的加大利纳

cathedra, E: cathedral, D: Kathedrale; the church of a diocese, where the bishop had his throne (cathedra).大教堂

Catholica Ecclesia, E: Catholic Church, D: Katholische Kirche; derived from the Greek word 'katholikos' (universal); the expression was adopted in the second century by the mainstream Church in opposition to sectarian Christian groups.大公教会

causa, E: cause, D: Grund; the Aristotelian concepts of causa formalis, causa materialis, causa efficiens, causa finalis were often used by scholastic writers, especially by Thomists.原因,见 Thomas Aquinas, *Summa Theologiae* I.2 (God is the prima causa of all things)

causa primordialis => idea

Causae et curae, E: *Causes and Cures*, a medical work by Hildegard of Bingen《诸病因和治疗》,见 Hildegardis

Celestine => Coelestinus

celibacy => coelibatus

celsitudo, E: highness, majesty, D: Groesse, Hoheit; 崇高,见 Bernardus, *De diligendo Deo* (greatness of the human heart)

Cerularius, Michael, Gr: Kērullarios, E: Caerularius; Patriarch of Constantinople 1043—1058, he was bitterly anti-Latin and attacked the use of unleavened bread in the Eucharist. His intolerance, combined with the stubbornness of Cardinal Humbert led to the Schism of 1054. Isaac I Comnenus exiled Cerularius in 1058.凯卢拉利乌斯/克汝拉瑞斯

Cesarini, Julianus, Italian Cardinal, president of the Synod of Basel since 1431, he left for Ferrara in 1437 切撒瑞尼,见 Piccolomini

Chanson de Roland, E: *Song of Roland*, the most famous of medieval epics (chansons de geste)《罗兰之歌》,见 Appendix, *Chanson de Roland*

Chansons de Geste, Old French epics of the twelfth and thirteenth centuries.古法语史诗

Charles = Carolus

Chartres, a city of northern France SW of Paris, was sacked by the Burgundians (ca. 600) and

Vikings (in 858). In 1286 it passed under direct royal control. Its famous cathedral was begun in 1195 and completed around 1230. Chartres was a center of academic life since the era of bishop Fulbert (1006—1028). Famous scholars in the 12th century were Bernard and his brother Thierry, and Gilbert de la Porree. 沙特尔/夏特尔，见 Johannes Saresberiensis (studied here)

Chartreuse 见 Cartusii

Chaucer, Geoffrey, 1343—1400, English poet, he served as courtier, diplomat, and member of parliament. Translator of Boethius' *Consolation of Philosophy*, he is most famous for the *Canterbury Tales*.乔叟，见 *Canterbury Tales*

Cheltchizki, Peter, E: Chelcicky, 1390—1460, lay Hussite theologian and political writer. His views led to the formation of the Bohemian Brothers.海尔奇茨基

chevalerie, (<L: caballus), E: chivalry, D: Ritterlichkeit; => eques 骑士的精神

chiliasmus => millenarismus

China => Sina

Chretien de Troyes, E: Chre(s)tien of Troyes, D: Chretien de Troyes; ca. 1135—1190, French trouvere who wrote the earliest surviving Arthurian romances;克里帝安·德·特鲁瓦，见 *Erec et Enide*

Christologia, E: christology, D: Christologie, the teachings concerning Jesus Christ, => incarnatio 基督论，见 Anselmus, *Cur Deus homo*

Christus, Gr: Christos, E: Christ, D: Christus, Jesus Christ, the son of God, => Jesus, Trinitas 基督，见 Anselmus, *Cur Deus homo*, (=> incarnatio), Joachim, *Liber figurarum* (the "age of Christ"), Nicolaus Cusanus, *De docta ignorantia* 3

Chrodegang, Bishop of Metz, +766; he became archbishop of Metz and was chancellor to Charles Martel and Pepin III. He wrote a rule for canonical life and gathered his cathedral clergy every day to read a chapter of it (thus the name "chapter" for such gatherings).赫洛德冈

Chronica (*sive Historia de duabus civitatibus*), E: *Chronicle or a History of the Two Cities*, a work by Otto of Freising《编年史或两个社会的历史》，见 Otto Frisingensis

Chronicon, E: *Chronicle*, a world history by Herman the Lame《编年史》，见 Hermannus Contractus

Chroniques, E: *Chronicle*, a work by Froissart《闻见录》，见 Froissart

chronologia, E: chronology, D: Chronologie; the commonly used chronology of the Latin Middle Ages was the birth of Christ; the Jewish chronology started with the creation of the world. Dionysius Exiguus (ca. 500—540) first used the birth of Christ as the base year of the Christian calendar, but the Greek world adopted this calendar only in the 15th century, and Russia only at the time of Peter the Great. Another kind of chronology used in the Middle Ages was the indiction cycle of 15 years counted from the accession of Emperor Constantine in 312.年代学，见 Beda, *Historia* (popularizes the anno Domini, AD. chronology), Nestorius, *Povest'* (starting with the year 5508 BC, the creation of the world)

Chrysoloras, Manuel, + 1415, Byzantine scholar, teacher of Greek in Florence since 1396 and in other Italian cities, author of a Greek grammar (the first of its kind), translator of Homer's works. He wanted to end the schism of the Latin and Greek churches and died at the Council of Constance. 克里索罗拉

Chur, L: Curia, E, D: Chur; town and diocese in Switzerland.库尔

Cid => Rodrigo Diaz de Vivar, Appendix, *Poema de mio Cid*

Cimabue, Giovanni, It: Cenni Di Pepi; 1240—1303, Italian painter of the Florentine school. His style marks the transition from the strictly formalized Byzantine style to the freer expression of the 14th century. 契马布埃

Cinerum, E: Ash Wednesday, D: Aschermittwoch, a day of fasting, also the first day of Lent when the priest signed the foreheads of the faithful with ashes in order to remind them of doing penance. The rite can be traced back to at least the 8th century.圣灰日

circulus, E: circle, D: Kreis; symbol of perfection 圆圈，见 Joachim, *Liber figurarum* (three inter-penetrating circles as symbol of the Trinity)

Cistercians = Ordo Cisterciensium

Cistercium, F: Citeaux, a monastery in the area of Dijon, founded in 1098 by Robert of Molesme, it became the mother house of the Cistercian Order.熙笃，见 Bernardus

Civitas Dei, E: City of God, D: Gottesstaat; the ideal model of society, inspired by Augustine's thought. This political view was very influential in the

Middle Ages.上主之城/上帝之城

Clara, E: Clare, D: Klara; a lady from Assisi who founded a sisters community in 1212 together with St. Francis 加拉, 见 Thomas de Celano, *Vita Sancti Francisci*

Claravallis, F: Clairvaux, E, D: Clairvaux, a monastery in Champagne, France, founded by St. Bernard in 1115 (who was thus called "Bernard of Clairvaux"), during the next three centuries Clairvaux became the mother house of some 350 Cistercian abbeys.明谷, 见 Bernardus

Clarendon, diet of Clarendon of 1164, which was an attempt of Henry II to control the Church in England. The Constitutions of Clarendon placed restrictions on ecclesiastical judges and Church courts. Becket rejected these constitutions.克拉任顿

Clemens II, E: Clement, D: Klemens; Pope 1046—1047, originally Bishop Suidger of Bamberg (since 1040), who crowned Henry III Roman Emperor in 1046 and started a series of reforms. 克雷孟/革利免

Clemens III, E: Clement, D: Klemens; a Roman who was Pope from 1187—1191, in the chaotic situation he could return to Rome and sign a contract with the Romans; he worked hard for the success of the Third Crusade.克雷孟/革利免

Clemens IV, E: Clement, D: Klemens; a native of France he became lawyer and councillor of Louis IX, archbishop of Narbonne in 1259 and was elected Pope (in office from 1265 to 1268). He accepted Charles de Anjou as King of southern Italy and confirmed him as king of Naples. He encouraged crusades against the Moors in Spain.克雷孟/革利免, 见 Rogerius Baco

Clemens V, E: Clement, D: Klemens; originally Bertrand de Got, born in France, who became archbishop of Bordeaux in 1299 and was elected Pope (1305—1314). After his election he remained in France and moved the Roman Curia to Avignon in 1309. He yielded to the pressure of Philip IV and ordered the suppression of the Templars in 1312. Founding universities in Orleans (1306) and Perugia (1308) he advanced scholarship, especially the study of medicine and Oriental languages.克雷孟/革利免, 见 Petrarca

Clemens VI, E: Clement, D: Klemens; a French Benedictine abbot, he was Pope from 1342—1352 and bought Avignon and the surrounding area from Johanna I of Naples in 1348; he continued the centralization of the Church administration and practised nepotism, but he was generous to the poor and protected the Jews who were blamed for the plague of 1348.克雷孟/革利免

Clemens VII, E: Clement, D: Klemens; originally Robert of Geneve, a cousin of the king of France, he became archbishop of Cambrai in 1368 and cardinal in 1371. He led the move to declare invalid the election of Pope Urban VI and was elected by the other cardinals, thus he became antipope in Avignon (1378—1394), enjoying the adherence of France, Castile, Aragon, Navarre, Scotland and some parts of Italy.克雷孟/革利免

clementia, E: clemency, mildness, D: Milde, Toleranz; => temperantia 温和/容忍, 见 Petrus Venerabilis (tolerant), Wolfram, *Parzival* (a knight should spare his enemies), Thomas de Celano, *Dies irae* (mercy for sinners)

clerici, E: clergy, D: Klerus, a collective term for men in the holy orders (bishops, priests, deacons) who hold offices in the Church, as distinguished from the unordained believers, who are called laity (laici) 圣职人员, 见 Hrabanus, *De institutione clericorum* (a handbook for the clergy), Joachim, *Liber figurarum* (proclaimed the end of the "clerical age"), Boccaccio, *Decamerone* (stock criticism of clergy), Lullus, *Blanquerna* (ideal image of clergy), Langland, *Piers Plowman*, (critical of clergy), Chaucer, *Canterbury Tales* (clerk from Oxford)

Clermont, Synod of, Synod in France in 1095, where Pope Urban II exhorted Christians to organize the first crusade 克莱尔孟

clerus, Gr: klēros, E: clergyman, D: Klerus, Kleriker => clerici

clock => horologium

Clovis, E: Clovis, D: Chlodwig (Ludwig, Ludovicus); king of the Franks 481—511, founder of the Merovingian kingdom.克洛维

Cluny, (=Clugny, Cluniacum), E: Cluny, a monastery in Burgundy, founded in 909 AD, it became the central house of the first monastic order, a congregation of several hundred monasteries especially in Gaul; it was the center of monastic reforms in the 10th and 11th centuries; respected abbots were Odo, Odilo, Hugo, and Petrus Venerabilis; it was destroyed during the French Revolution.克吕

尼,见 Petrus Venerabilis

Codex iuris canonici, E: Canon law, D: Kirchenrecht; the body of rules governing the morals and organization of the Church, based on papal and synodal documents and edited in different collections since the 11th century. 教会法,见 Gratianus

Coelestinus III, E: Celestine, D: Coelestin; Pope 1191—1198, who was confronted with Emperor Henry VI. 切来斯提努斯

Coelestinus V, E: Celestine, D: Coelestin; Italian monk, hermit on Mt. Morrone, he was known for his piety, became elected Pope in 1294, but this "angelic Pope" came under French influence and (upon the suggestion of the cardinals) willingly resigned from office after 5 months; Boniface VIII kept him in honorable confinement to prevent political intrigue. 切来斯提努斯,见 Dante, *Commedia* (placed in the ante-hell)

Coelestini-Eremiti, a congregation of hermits founded in Italy by Pope Coelestinus V. 切来斯提努斯隐修者

coelibatus, E: celibacy, D: Zoelibat; the state of being unmarried, which was required of the clergy in the major orders (bishop, priest, deacon, subdeacon) in the Roman Church and of bishops in the Eastern Church; celibacy was an old tradition but particularly reinforced since the 12th century. => virginitas 独身制度,见 Aldhelmus, *De laudibus virginitatis*, Guillaume de Lorris, *Roman de la rose* (Nature disparages celibacy)

coelum => caelum

Cola di Rienzo, (Nicolaus di Laurentius), +1354; Italian demagogue who wanted to restore Roman glory, he made himself "tribune" in Rome in 1347 and 1353, but was killed in 1354; Petrarch supported him for some time. 科拉·里恩佐

Colombini, Johannes, Bl., +1367, Italian monk, founder of the Jesuati in Siena. 科隆比尼

Colonia, E: Cologne, D: Koeln, city on the Rhine from Roman times, it was occupied by the Franks ca. 400 AD and served as the residence of the Merovingian kings of Austrasia since 561. Since 785 the arch-bishop of Cologne had much influence on political affairs in Germany and in 1356 was reconfirmed as one of the seven imperial electors. In 1288 the city acquired a charter of self-government. The huge cathedral was begun in 1248, but when the Gothic style fell into disrepute, construction was interrupted in 1510, and the completion of the church had to wait until 1880. The four mendicant orders (Dominicans, Franciscans, Augustinians, Carmelites) had established their "studia generalia" before the city's university received its charter from the Pope in 1388. 科隆,见 Albertus Magnus

Colonna, Roman aristocratic family, which had connections to the imperial party; they violently opposed Pope Boniface VIII after 1297. 科罗纳

Colonna, Sciarra, a member of the Colonna family who helped to imprison Pope Boniface VIII in 1303. 科罗纳

Columba, (=Columcille), E: Columba, the Elder Columba, D: Kolumban; Irish monk, ca. 521—597 AD; he founded the monastery of Hy (Iona) around 560 AD 科伦班,见 Adamnanus, *Vita Columbae*

Columbanus, E: Columba, Columban, D: Kolumban, St.; Irish missionary in the area of France, Germany and Switzerland from 591 to 615; he became the founder of Bobbio. 高隆班/科伦巴,见 Adamnanus, *Vita Columbae*

Columella, E: Columella, ca. 10—70 AD, author of a work on agriculture, *De re rustica*, in 12 books, written around 60 AD 科卢梅拉,见 Walahfridus, *Liber de cultura hortorum*

comes, E: count, D: Graf; a title of military and civil officials since the the fourth century, the "count" was an advisor to the king in the Merovingian aristocracy. During the feudal period the count belonged to the upper aristocratic class. Within his county he exercised almost unlimited powers (officially in the name of the king) over law, finances, and defense. Counts were sometimes vassals of dukes, but often were just as powerful as a duke. Some German bishops held a countship. 伯爵,见 feudalismus

Commedia divina, E: *The Divine Comedy*, a long poem by Dante, describing the descent to Hell, the journey through Purgatory and the saints in Heaven. 《神曲》,见 Dante

commenda, E: commend, D: Kommende, concessions of (Church) property. The practice of commendation since the seventh and eighth centuries implied vassalage and contributed to the development of feudalism. 教会财产转让制度

Commentarii rerum memorabilium, E: Reports about

Remarkable Events, an autobiography by Enea Piccolomini (Pius II)《回忆录》,见 Piccolomini

common law, L: lex communis; the legal principles and procedures that became universal (common) in England after the reforms of Henry II (1154—1189); sources of common law were custom, Roman law, and policies adopted by the crown. Itinerant (royal) justices observed procedures set down by the crown and kept records of their judgments for the instruction of other justices, thereby creating a legal traditon that had more flexibility than continental Roman law.普通法,见 Bracton, *De legibus et consuetudinibus Angliae*

Comnene => Alexius I Komnenos, Anna Komnene

conciliarismus, E: conciliarism, D: Konziliarismus; the doctrine that the supreme authority in the church is embodied in a general or ecumenical council; this thinking was especially influential after the Great Schism (1378—1414) and at the Councils of Constance (1414—1418) and Basel (1431—1439). 大公会议理论

concilium, (synodus), E: council, D: Konzil; an ecclesiastical meeting; 1) meeting of bishops with their archbishop or metropolitan ("provincial council"); 2) meeting of a bishop with his diocesan clergy ("diocesan synod"); 3) meeting of all bishops (at least in principle) under the Pope ("ecumenical council").主教会议,见 Gregorius VII, *Dictatus Papae* 16 (only the Pope can convoke ecumenical councils)

concilium oecumenicum, E: ecumenical council, D: oekumenisches Konzil; a meeting of all bishops (at least in theory) under the auspices of the Pope.大公会议

Concordatum, Concordata, E: concordate, D: Konkordat; an agreement between the Apostolic See and a nation.政教协定

Concordatum Vindobonense, E: Concordate of Vienna, D: Wiener Konkordat; an agreement of 1448, it regulated the rights of the Catholic Church in Germany until 1803. 维也纳政教协定

Concordatum Wormatianum, (=Pactum Calixtinum), E: Concordate of Worms, D: Wormser Konkordat; an agreement between the Emperor and the Pope concluded in 1122, it regulated the question of lay investiture and formally ended the "Investiture Controversy".沃尔姆斯协约,见 Gratianus

concordia, E: concord, harmony, D: Einigkeit, Harmonie; 和睦,见 Alanus, *Anticlaudianus* (Concord is one of the heavenly sisters)

Concordia discordantium canonum, E: *Concordance of Canons,* a work on canon law by Gratian.《教会法汇编》,见 Gratianus

concupiscentia, E: concupiscence, desire, D: Begier, Verlangen; => avaritia 欲望,见 Hildegardis, *Causae et curae* (positive view of procreation), Dante, *Commedia* (sins of illicit love are punished in Hell)

conditio humana, E: the (limits of the) human situation, D: die Begrenztheit des Menschen; 人生的局限性,见 Innocens III, *De miseria humanae conditionis*, Petrarca, *Secretum meum*

Condwiramur, (L: conducimur), the wife of Parzival. 孔迪拉姆尔,见 Wolfram, *Parzival*

confirmatio, E: confirmation, D: Firmung, sacrament of the Church.坚振(圣事)

confraternitates, E: pious brotherhoods, D: Gebetsverbruederungen; popular prayer communities since the 8th century who commemorated the living and deceased members or benefactors of a monastery.祈祷联会

Conradinus, son of Conrad IV, 1252—1268, the last Staufer.康拉丁

Conradus II, E: Conrad, D: Konrad, German King 1024—1039, father of Henry III. He strengthened German monarchy and obtained Burgundy (the Kingdom of Arles) when his wife Gisela inherited the country (1032). 康拉德,见 Wipo, *Gesta Chuonradi II*

Conradus III, E: Conrad, D: Konrad, rival king under Lothair III, then German King 1138—1152, he was supported by the Church party, but was never crowned emperor.康拉德

Conradus IV, E: Conrad, D: Konrad, German King 1250—1254, one of the last Staufer kings, opposed by the Popes, he died at the age of 26.康拉德

Conradus, E: Conrad, D: Konrad, Duke of Masovia (Poland), who invited the Teutonic Knights in 1226. 康拉德

Conradus de Gelnhausen, E: Conrad, D: Konrad von Gelnhausen; +1390; German professor at Paris, he suggested a council to solve the division in the Church (1379, 1380).康拉德

Conradus de Hochstaden, E: Conrad, D: Konrad, Archbishop of Cologne, started the construction of the famous cathedral in 1248.康拉德

Conradus de Constantia, E: Conrad, D: Konrad, Bishop of Constance, +975.康拉德

Conradus de Marburg, E: Conrad, D: Konrad, German cleric, confessional priest of St. Elisabeth of Thuringia, first inquisitor of Germany since 1227, he was killed in 1233 because of his rigidity.康拉德

Conradus de Megenberg, E: Conrad, D: Konrad, + 1374; German author, canonist, who left us with German and Latin works.康拉德

conscientia, E: conscience, D: Gewissen; 良心, 见 Langland, *Piers Plowman*(allegory of Conscience)

consideratio, E: consideration, D: Bedenken, Nachdenken; 反省, 见 Bernardus, *De consideratione* (recollection of the heart in the search for God)

consolatio, E: consolation, D: Trost, Troestung; 安慰, 见 Eckhart, *Buch der goettlichen Troestungen* (Deus consolationis), Petrarca, *De remediis utriusque fortunae*

Constantia, E: Constance, D: Konstanze; +1198, daughter of Roger II of Sicily and heiress of the kingdom of Sicily; married to Henry VI (son of Frederick Barbarossa) she was the mother of Frederick II and served as regent for her son until her death. 康斯坦西亚, 见 Dante, *Commedia* (placed in the Heaven of the Moon)

Constantia, E: Constance, D: Konstanz, town in Southern Germany close to the Swiss border, where an ecumenical council was held from 1414 to 1418 in an effort to resolve the Western Schism. The council also condemned Wyclif and his writings and tried John Jus for heresy.康斯坦茨

Constantinopolis, Gr: Konstantinou polis, E: Constantinople, D: Konstantinopel, 君士坦丁堡, 见 Byzantium

Constantinus = Cyrillus

Constantinus Africanus, E: Constantine the African, D: Konstantinus Africanus; ca. 1030—1087, a merchant, physician and scholar from Africa who retired to Monte Cassino where he translated a number of Arabic works into Latin; his medical translations helped establish Salerno's reputation as medical center 君士坦丁, 见 ars medica

Constantinus Magnus, E: Constantine the Great, D: Konstantin der Grosse; ca. 285—337 AD, Roman emperor who issued the Edict of Milan which brought freedom for Christianity in 313 AD; he moved the capital to the East (Constantinople); in the Middle Ages it was widely believed that he had entrusted Italy to the care of the Popes ("Donation of Constantine") 君士坦丁大帝/康斯坦丁, 见 Cynewulf, *Elene* (Constantine sends his mother Helena to Israel to find the cross of Christ), Dante, *Commedia* (placed in the Heaven of the just rulers)

Constantinus V Copronymus, E: Constantine; D: Konstantin; Emperor of Byzanz 741—775, son of Leo III and a ruthless iconoclast, he organized a synod in Constantinople in 754. As he was unable to protect Rome against the Lombards, the Popes turned to the Franks for help.君士坦丁

Constantinus VI, E: Constantine, D: Konstantin; Emperor of Byzanz 780—802; since he divorced his wife and married his mistress he lost popularity and lived his last years in captivity.君士坦丁

Constantinus IX, E: Constantine, D: Konstantin, "Monomachus", Emperor of Byzanz 1042—1054, he invited Roman delegates to Constantinople but could not prevent the permanent schism of 1054. 君士坦丁

Constantinus XI, E: Constantine, D: Konstantin; "Palaeologus", Emperor of Byzanz 1448—1453, an able and courageous leader he could not ensure Western support against the Ottoman Turks. He tried to renew unity with the Roman Church. On May 29th 1453 he fell fighting with his troops when his capital was captured.君士坦丁

consummatio, E: consummation, the idea that all things will return to God at the end of time 万物归于神, 见 Eriugena, *De divisione naturae*

contemplatio, E: contemplation, D: Kontemplation; a spiritual attitude of envisioning divine realities; => spiritualia 默观, 见 Bernardus, *De diligendo Deo*, Hildegardis, *Causae et curae*, Bonaventura, *Itinerarium mentis in Deum*, Raimundus Lullus, *Blanquerna*(search for solitude), Gerson, *De mystica theologia*, Thomas a Kempis, *De imitatione Christi*

Contra Saracenos, E: *Against the Saracenes*, a treatise by Peter the Venerable《反驳萨拉森人》, 见 Petrus Venerabilis

conversi, E: converted laymen, converts, D: Konversen; 1) persons entering a monastery as an adult, in distinction to oblates (oblati), who entered as children; 2) lay brothers living and working in a monastery 皈依者

conversio, E: conversion, D: Bekehrung, a mental and spiritual shift towards the Christian faith, a central theme in medieval literature 皈依, 见 Johannes Damascenus, *Barlaam et Joasaph*, Beda, *Historia ecclesiastica* (conversion of Edwin; Pope Gregory recommends slow conversion methods), Cynewulf, *Elene* (conversion of Judas), Hrotsvita, *Abraham eremita*, Thomas de Celano, *Vita Sancti Francisci* (conversion of St. Francis)

Copenhagen, (Copenhavn), D: Kopenhagen; capital and largest city of Denmark, a trading center since the 11th century. First noted in 1032, it enjoyed rapid growth after Bishop Absalon of Roskilde had erected a castle in 1167. The city remained under the rule of the bishop of Roskilde until 1417 and became the Danish capital in 1445. 哥本哈根, 见 Saxo Grammaticus

Cor sacrum, E: Sacred heart, D: Heiliges Herz (Jesu); venerated by Christians 圣心, 耶稣圣心, 见 Gertrudis, *Legatus divinae pietatis*

Corbie, important Benedictine monastery in the western part of the Frankish kingdom near Amiens (France). Founded in 662 it was famous for its school and library and played a role in the adoption of the Carolingian minuscule. 科尔比

Corbinianus, E: Corbinian, D: Korbinian; St., died ca. 725; missionary in Bavaria, founder of the mission in Freising. 科尔比尼安

Cordoba, (Cordova), E, D: Cordoba; a city of southern Spain, northeast of Seville; established by Carthaginians, it was ruled by Romans, (since the Second Punic War 210 BC), by Visigoths (in the fifth century AD), and by Arabs (from 765 to 1031). Being the capital of the caliphate of Cordoba in the 10th century, it was possibly the most populous city in the Western world at that time and had a library with (allegedly) 400,000 volumes. 科尔多瓦, 见 Averroes, Moses Maimonides

corona, E: crown, D: Krone, since Charlemagne's times Frankish and German kings tried to go to Rome for coronation. 加冕, 见 Eginhardus, *Vita Caroli* 28 (coronation in 800 AD)

corpus, E: body, D: Koerper; => anima, medica ars 身体, 见 Hildegardis, *Causae et curae* (psychosomatic correlations, health care), Johannes Saresberiensis, *Policraticus* (human body is a symbol of the state)

corpus juris canonici => jus canonum

corpus juris civilis, E: Code of Civil Law, D: Kodex des Zivilrechts; the codification of Roman law carried out by Emperor Justinian (527—565). 民法大全, 见 Bologna

Corvey, D: Korvey, close to Hoexter at the Weser (Germany), important Benedictine monastery, founded in 822. 科尔维

Cosimo de'Medici => Medici

Cosmas Pragensis, E: Cosmas of Prague, D: Kosmas von Prag, ca. 1045—1125, author of the first chronicle of Bohemia 布拉格的科斯玛斯, 见 *Chronica Bohemorum*

cosmos => universum

count => comes

courtly love => curialis amor

Cracovia, E: Cracow, Krakow, D: Krakau; a city on the Vistula in Poland. In c. 1000 Boleslaw I seized it from the Czechs and made it a bishopric. The city was destroyed by the Mongols in 1241, but it was rebuilt and served as capital of Poland since 1320. The second oldest university of central Europe was founded in Cracow in 1364 by Casimir the Great. 克拉科夫, 见 Cosmas Pragensis, *Chronica Bohemorum*

creatio, E: creation, D: Schoepfung; the Christian belief that God created all things; 创造, 见 Hildegardis, *Causae et curae*, Alanus, *Anticlaudianus* (creation of a perfect man), Maimonides, *More nevukhim* (creatio ex nihilo), Thomas de Celano, *Vita sancti Francisci* (creation spirituality), Albertus, *Summa de creaturis*, Eckhart, *Buch der Troestungen* (creatio continua)

creatura, E: creature, D: Kreatur, Geschoepf; 受造物, 见 Hildegardis, *Causae et curae* (a sick person is always a creature)

credimus, credere => fides

Crescentii, members of the Roman Crescentia family who caused unrest in Rome in the years from 973—1000 克瑞申蒂

Creta, E: Crete, D: Kreta; island between Greece and Egypt, part of the Byzantine empire until the 9th ct., seized by Arabs in 826, reconquered by Nicephorus in 961, occupied by Venice in 1204 (then known as Candia), finally captured by the Turks in 1669. 克里特

Croatia, area at the Adria, roughly the roman porvince of Pannonia. The Croats, a south Slavic people settled there in the seventh ct., and they were converted to Christianity in the ninth ct. In 925 their first king, Tomislav, was crowned by the Pope, but Byzantine rule over Dalmatia was established at the end of the tenth century. Under Peter Kresimir (1058—1074) Croatia reached the height of its power and adhered to the roman rite. After that period Hungary and Byzantium conquered the greater part of Croatia.克罗地亚

crucigeri, E: crusaders, D: Kreuzfahrer, knights and nobles from Western Europe who undertook eight military expeditions between 1096 and 1271 to win or hold the Holy Land against Muslim rulers; the crusaders often sewed the cross on their clothing. They established four crusader states (Edessa, Antioch, Tripolis, Jerusalem), but by 1291 all had fallen back to Muslim rule.十字军, 见 Malmesburiensis, *Gesta regum Anglorum* (the last part gives an account of the first crusade), Anna Komnene, *Alexias*, Bernardus (supported the second crusade in 1146), Petrus Venerabilis, *Contra Saracenos* (critical of the crusades), Hartmann (perhaps took part in the crusade of 1189)

crusaders => crucigeri

crux Christi, E: the cross of Christ, D: das Kreuz Christi; sign of suffering and salvation, the cross of Christ was much venerated in the Middle Ages; => crucigeri 基督的十字架, 见 Cynewulf, *Elene* (Helena finds the cross in Jerusalem), Thomas a Kempis, *De imitatione Christi* (In cruce salus), Greban, *Passion de Paris*

culpa, E: guilt, D: Schuld; => peccatum 罪责, 见 Hartmann, *Der arme Heinrich* (is blind to his failure), Wolfram, *Parzival*(is slowly ready to face his guilt)

Cunegundis, E: Cunegunde, D: Kunigunde, St., German Empress, +1040.库尼贡德

Cunibertus, E: Cunibert, D: Kunibert, St. bishop of Cologne, +663.库尼贝图斯

Cupido, E: Cupid, D: Cupid; the god of love 爱神, 见 Guillaume de Lorris, *Roman de la rose*

Cur Deus homo, E: *Why Was God Made Man?* a theological treatise by Anselm of Canterbury; => incarnatio《上主为什么降生成人？》,见 Anselmus

curia, E: court; D: Hof, Gerichtshof; the king's court (curia regis) was the large assembly of the king's vassals that convened in ceremonial sessions usually at Christmas, Easter, and Pentecost. This assembly was the central governing body, it elected the king's successor, met as court of justice, decided financial matters and advised the king on legislative, military, and political matters.法院, 见 Hrotsvita, *Dulcitius* (interrogation), Bracton, *De legibus*

Curia Romana, E: Roman Curia, D: Kurie, the central administrative institution of the Roman Church, the legal and financial administration system under the Pope which developed in the Middle Ages, especially since the 12th century.教廷/罗马教廷

curialis amor, E: courtly love, D: hoefische Liebe; the love between a man and a woman as described by the troubadours during the 12th and 13th centuries. The lovers emphasized manners fitting for a noble society, which did not always exclude gratification of carnal desires. A vassal had to respect the Lady of his lord, and true love was seen as the source of all virtue.宫廷式的爱, 见 Chretiens de Troyes

Cynewulf, (=Kynewulf), ca. 750—800, poet from England, possibly from Northumbria, author of *Helena* (=*Elene*), *Juliana* and other works 基涅武甫, 见 *Elene*

Cyrillus, Gr: Kyrillos, E: Cyril, D: Kyrill, St.; 827—869, Cyrillus (original name: Constantine) was a Greek missionary in central Europe, who together with his brother Methodius invented an early form of the "Cyrillic" alphabet. They worked in Moravia, where they encountered hostility from Bavarian bishops, but they were supported by Rome. 济利禄/区利罗/基利洛斯

D

Dagobertus I, E, D: Dagobert; king of Gaul 629—639, the last powerful king of the Merovingian dynasty.达格贝特

d'Ailly = Ailly

Damascus, Gr: Damaskos, E: Damascus, D: Damaskus; one of the oldest cities of the world, it was an important commercial center on the road from Egypt to Persia. In 635 it fell to the Arabs and served as the capital of the Omayyad caliphs from 661 to 750. In 1076 it was seized by the Seljuk Turks, in 1260 by the Mongols, and in 1401 by Timur the Lame. Since 1516 it was controlled by the Ottoman Turks.大马士格

Damasus II, Pope in 1048 for 23 days, originally Bishop Poppo of Brixen 达马苏斯

Damiani = Petrus Damiani

Danes, E: Danes, E: Daenen, the inhabitants of Denmark, => Copenhagen, England 丹麦人, 见 Eginhardus, *Vita Caroli*（wars against the Danes in 810）, Saxo Grammaticus, *Gesta Danorum*（the first history of Denmark）, Appendix, *Nibelungenlied*（wars against the Danes）

Dante Alighieri, 1265—1321, Italian poet, scholar, political theorist, member of an aristocratic family of Florence who opposed French and papal influence in his home town and thus supported imperial power; the last twenty years of his life he spent in exile; he authored *De vulgari eloquentia*, but it was the *Commedia*（since Boccaccio called "*Divina*"）that made him immortal. 但丁, 见 *Commedia Divina*

David de Augsburg, + 1272, Franciscan preacher, author of German and Latin spititual writings. He was the first to write spirituality in German. 达味/大卫

David de Dinant, + after 1206, Aristotelian teacher in Paris with pantheist tendencies, which were condemned in 1210. 达味/大卫

De anima, E: *On the Soul*, a work by Averroes, => *Tafsir kitab an-nafs*

De arte venandi cum avibus, E: *On Falconry*, the first scientific work on ornithology, written by Frederick II around 1245.《论用鸟去打猎》, 见 Fredericus II

De casibus virorum illustrium, E: *On the Fates of Famous Men*, a work by Boccaccio《名人之堕落》, 见 Boccaccio

De civili dominio, E: *On Civil Power*, a treatise by Wyclif《论世俗政权》, 见 Wycliffe

De consideratione, E: *On Consideration*, a work by Bernard of Clairvaux; => memoria, Papa《论反省》, 见 Bernardus

De contemptu mundi = *De miseria humanae conditionis*

De cultu hortorum = *Liber de cultura hortorum*

De diligendo Deo, E: *On Divine Love*, a work by Bernard《论爱神》, 见 Bernardus

De docta ignorantia, E: *On Learned Ignorance*, a philosophical treatise by Nicholas of Cusa《论有学识的无知》, 见 Nicolaus Cusanus

De imitatione Christi, E: *The Imitation of Christ*, an ascetical work by Thomas a Kempis《师主篇》, 见 Thomas a Kempis

De institutione clericorum, E: *The Formation of Clerics*, a compendium on the education of priests by Hrabanus《论教士的培养》, 见 Hrabanus

De laudibus virginitatis, E: *Praises of Virginity*, a work by Aldhelm《赞美独身生活》, 见 Aldhelmus

De legibus et consuetudinibus Angliae, E: *On the Laws and Customs of England*, a work on English law by Henry de Bracton《英格兰的法律与习惯》, 见 Bracton

De miseria humanae conditionis, E: *On the Misery of Human Life*, a work by Innocent III《论人生的悲惨情况》, 见 Innocens

De mystica theologia, E: *On Mystical Theology*, a theological treatise by Jean Gerson《神秘神学》, 见 Gerson

De octo vitiis principalibus, E: *On the Eight Capital Sins*, a moral poem by Herman the Lame《八宗罪》, 见 Hermannus Contractus

De origine monetarum, E: *The Origin of Money*, a work by Nicolaus Oresme《货币论》, 见 Oresmensis

De ortu et tempore Antichristi, E: *On the Birth and Time of the Antichrist*, a narrative by Adso Dervensis《论反基督的诞生和时期》, 见 Adso

De remediis utriusque fortunae, E: *On the Remedy for Each Fate*, a moral treatise by Petrarch《两种不同命运之道》, 见 Petrarca

De vulgari eloquentia, E: *Of Eloquence in the Vulgar Tongue*, a treatise by Dante《论俗语》, 见 Dante

Decamerone, E: *Decameron*, a collection of tales by Boccaccio《十日谈》, 见 Boccaccio

decretum, E: decretal, D: Dekret; a papal letter or an excerpt from one which rules on a point of Canon Law. 宗座文件, 见 Gratianus, *Concordantia discordantium canonum*

decuma, E: tithe, D: Zehnte; the tenth part of（agricultural）products, given to the Church. 什一税

Denis, St.,（Gr: Dionysios Areiopagita）, patron of France, semilegendary first bishop of Paris who was martyred in the third century. His relics were translated to St. Denis（near Paris）. 圣迪那

Denmark => Danes, Copenhagen

Der Ackermann aus Boehmen, E: *The Ploughman*, a work by John of Saaz《波希米亚的耕夫》, 见 Johannes de Tepla

Der arme Heinrich, E: *Poor Henry*, an epic in Middle High German by Hartmann von Aue《可怜的

亨利》，见 Hartmann

Deschamps, Eustache, 1346—1406, French influenced by Machaut, author of *L'Art de dictier* (*The Art of Versification*, 1392), the first work on the style of French poetry.德尚

desiderium, E: desire, D: Verlangen, Sehnsucht; => avaritia, concupiscentia

Desiderius de Tuscia, King of the Lombards 757—774.德西得留斯

Deus, Gr: theos, E: God, D: Gott, the central entity of Christian faith, according to the Bible the Creator of the universe, who sent His Son (Jesus Christ) to save the world; => theologia, Trinitas 神，上帝，天主，见 Eriugena, *De divisione naturae* (God = natura creans non creata), Anselmus, *Prologion* (ontological proof of God's existence, =>probatio), Bernardus, *De diligendo Deo* (emphasizes God's love for mankind and how He deserves boundless adoration), Alanus, *Anticlaudianus* (God creates the soul of man), Maimonides, *More nevukhim* (rejection of anthropomorphism and positive statements about God; God is "first cause"), Wolfram, *Parzival* (rebellion against God), Thomas Aquinas, *Summa theologiae* I (proofs of the existence of God), Occam, *Sententiae* (potentia Dei absoluta), Nicolaus Cusanus, *De docta ignorantia* (God is the complicatio rerum, the coincidentia oppositorum), Appendix, *Elkerlijk*

Deusdedit, Cardinal, + 1100, Benedictine monk from St. Martin (Limoges), author of a collection of canon law which upheld the authority of the church against the claims of secular rulers. 德乌斯德迪特

Deutsche Theologie, E: *German Theology*, a book on spirituality, written ca. 1400, by an unknown author《德国神学》

Deventer, town in the Netherlands, founded in the eight century. It was a known center of learning and of the mystical movement of the "devotio moderna", a kind of Christian humanism in the 15th century. 德文特尔，见 Groote, Thomas a Kempis

Devotio moderna, E: New Piety, D: Neue Froemmigkeit; the religious renewal of the late Middle Ages which sought union with God through prayer, a simple life, and works of charity. It was much inspired by Gerhard Groote and Thomas a Kempis and found many followers, especially in the Low Countries and Germany. 新灵修，见 Thomas a Kempis, *De imitatione Christi*

diabolus, Gr: diabolos ("subverter"), E: devil, D: Teufel; the Evil One who tries to lead the faithful away from God, often depicted in medieval literature; => Antichristus, Lucifer, Satan 魔鬼，见 Hrotsvita, *Theophilus*, Alanus, *Anticlaudianus* (diabolic forces), Dante, *Commedia* (depiction of the devil)

diaconus, E: deacon, D: Diakon; clergyman holding the holy order just below the priesthood; the word is derived from the Greek diakonia = service. Deaconesses who had helped with adult baptisms became rare in the medieval Church.执事

dialectica, E: dialectical method, D: die dialektische Methode; logical reasoning as an instrument to explain the faith, employed much in the age of scholasticism since Abelard 逻辑学，辩论派，见 Abaelard, *Sic et non* (the first consistent use of the dialectical method)

Dictatus Papae, E: *The Dictate of the Pope*, a document by Gregory VII composed in 1075, containing the specific demands concerning the relation of spiritual and secular power and of ecclesiastical freedom from lay control《教宗敕令》，见 Gregorius VII

Didascalicon, E: *Didascalicon*, an encyclopedia by Hugh of St-Victor《学问之阶》，见 Hugo

Dies irae, E: *Day of Wrath*, a poem by Thomas de Celano《末日来临》，见 Thomas de Celano

Dietrich von Bern, a heroic figure in German epic, esp. in the *Nibelungenlied*, related to Theodoric, king of the Ostrogoths (died in 526)迪特瑞克，见 Appendix, *Nibelungenlied*

Dietrich de Niem, E: Theodoric of Nieheim, 1340—1418, German theologian, who served at the Curia in Rome, an exponent of conciliarism.迪特瑞克

diligere, E: love, D: lieben; => amor 爱，见 Bernardus, *De diligendo Deo*

dioecesis, E: diocese, D: Dioezese; the ecclesiastical division of territory under the supervision of a bishop; in the 14th century the Western Church had around 500 dioceses. 教区，见 episcopus

dioecesis, synodus, E: diocesan synod, D: Dioezesansynode; a meeting of the clergy of a diocese.教区会议

Dionysius Areopagita, E: Dionysius the Areopagite,

D: Dionysius Areopagita; ca. 500 AD, an author of very influential theological texts combining Neo-Platonism and Christian faith; according to medieval tradition a disciple of St. Paul who heard him at the Areopagus in Athens. 伪丢尼修斯，见 Eriugena

Dionysius de Ryckel, E: Dionysius the Carthusian, Denys van Leeuwen; +1471, Belgian Carthusian, mystical author, called "doctor ecstaticus". 狄奥尼修斯

disciplina, E: discipline, D: Zucht; => moderatio, temperantia 纪律，见 Wolfram, *Parzival*

Divina commedia = *Commedia*

divitiae, E: riches, wealth, D: Reichtum; the value system of the Old Testament appreciates secular wealth, but Cistercians and Franciscans followed the spirituality of the New Testament, they extolled poverty and opposed material wealth. 财富，见 Bernardus, *De consideratione* (opposes papal luxuries), Appendix, *Elkerlijk* (personification of wealth, => Mammon)

docta ignorantia, E: learned ignorance, D: gelehrte Unwissenheit; an idea proposed by late medieval mystics as a way to understand God. 有学识的无知，见 Nicolaus Cusanus

Doctor angelicus = Thomas Aquinas
Doctor authenticus = Gregorius de Rimini
Doctor catholicus = Biel
Doctor christianissimus = Gerson
Doctor communis = Thomas Aquinas
Doctor ecstaticus = Dionysius de Ryckel
Doctor fundatissimus = Aegidius Romanus
Doctor invincibilis = Occam
Doctor irrefragabilis = Alexander de Hales
Doctor mellifluus = Bernardus Claravallensis
Doctor modernus = Durandus de St. Pourcain
Doctor planus et utilis = Nicolaus de Lyra
Doctor profundus = Bradwardin
Doctor subtilis = Duns Scotus
Doctor universalis = Albertus Magnus, Alanus ab Insulis

dolor, E: pain, suffering, D: Schmerz, Leid; => aegritudo, miseria 痛苦，见 *Barlaam et Joasaph* (encounter with suffering leads to conversion), Eckhart, *Buch der goettlichen Troestungen* (there is hope in any suffering), Petrarca, *De remediis utriusque fortunae* (Reason talking to the allegory of Pain), Greban, *Passion de Paris*

Dominicani, (=Ordo Fratrum Praedicatorum, OP), E: Dominicans, D: Dominicaner; a congregation founded by St. Dominic in 1216 mainly for preaching the gospel and orthodox faith in order to save people from the influence of heresies. 道明会/多明我会，见 Vincentius Bellovacensis, Thomas Aquinas, Jacobus de Voragine

Dominicus, E: Dominic, D: Dominikus; St., 1170—1221, born in Castile (Spain) Dominic became the founder of the Dominican Order. 圣道明/多明我，见 Dominicani

Dominicus Gundissalinus = Gundissalinus

Dominus terrae, E: Lord of the Land, D: Landesherr; the title of the seven electors who enjoyed almost unlimited powers in their regions. 领土之主，见 *Bulla aurea*

Donatello, 1386—1466, Italian artist 多那太罗

Donatio Constantini 见 Constantinus Magnus

draco, E: dragon, D: Drache; in medieval literature usually a symbol of evil forces or of apocalyptical changes; => Fafnir, Midgard 毒蛇，见 Joachim, *Liber figurarum*, Appendix, *Beowulf* (the hero kills a dragon)

dualismus, E: dualism, D: Dualismus; the view that the universe is drawn into a struggle between a good and an evil power; groups holding dualistic views included the Cathars (Albigenses). 二元论

Duerer, Albrecht, 1471—1528, German painter who chose religious motives; hoping for church reforms he sympathized with Luther. 丢勒

Duke = dux

Dulcitius, E: *Dulcitius*, a play by Hrotsvita 《杜启修斯》，见 Hrotsvita

Dungal, Irish monk in St. Denis, ca. 825, opponent of iconoclasm. 顿伽勒

Duns Scotus, E: John Duns Scottus, D: Duns Scotus; Bl., 1265—1308, Franciscan scholar, "doctor subtilis", educated at Paris and Oxford, he became the exponent of a kind of Augustinian voluntarism, author of *De primo principio* (The First Principle), *Opus Oxoniense* (Work of Oxford), etc. 邓斯·司各脱

Dunstan, St. 908—988, Archbishop of Canterbury since 959, successful reformer of the Church. 邓斯坦

Durandot, the name of Roland's sword 杜兰多特，见 Appendix, *Chanson de Roland*

Durandus de St. Pourcain, +1334, a Dominican theologian, philosopher, bishop of Limoux (France). 迪朗都斯

Durandus, Wilhelm, Bishop of Mende, +1296, author of a compendium on liturgy.迪朗都斯

Durer = Duerer

dux, E: duke, F: duc, D: Herzog, Fuerst; a feudal title; a duke was subject to the king (rex) but above the counts (comes). In England the title was reserved for members of the royal family until the era of Richard II (1377—1399). In France a duc ranked below a royal prince. 公爵, 见 feudalismus

E

Eadmer, (Edmer), 1055—1124, monk in Canterbury, theologian, author of the first defense of the doctrine of the Immaculate Conception.埃德梅尔

Easter => resurrectio

Ebner, Margarete, + 1351; German Dominican sister, mystic.厄布内尔

Eboracum, E: York, city about 200 miles north of London, a fortress in Roman times; It was first mentioned as episcopal see in 314 (Council of Arles). In 735 it achieved the rank of an archdiocese. Egbert, a pupil of Bede, founded the cathedral school which became one of the cultural centers in the West. 约克, 见 Alcuin, *De pontificibus et sanctis Eboracensis ecclesiae*

Ecclesia, E: the Church, D: Kirche; the Christian community traditionally led by bishops and the Pope in Rome. In the Middle Ages this institution had a pervasive influence on thought, literature, arts, politics, and social life.教会, 见 Beda, *Historia Ecclesiastica*, Bernardus, *De consideratione* (the Pope may ask the Emperor to protect the Church), Hildegardis (her theology includes ecclesiology), Johannes Saresberiensis, *Policraticus* (the Church is the soul of the state), Joachim, *Liber figurarum* (the era of the Son is the period of the Church, Israel is a prefiguration of the Church), Langland, *Piers Plowman* (allegory of Lady Church)

ecclesia propria, E: private church, proprietary church, D: Eigenkirche; a church owned by a landlord or a monastery; in the Middle Ages many rural churches were founded by the owner of the land and remained under the control of his family, especially in Germany.私有教堂

Echternach, monastery West of Trier, founded by Willibrord in 698. It served as a basis for Irish and Anglo-Saxon missionaries and scholars coming to the continent. It had a famous school and scriptorium.厄克特纳克

Eckhart, Meister, E: Eckehart, Eckart, D: Eckhart; 1260—1327, German Dominican scholar, studied at Paris and Cologne, he was provincial of his congregation in Saxony and a teacher of theology at Paris and Strasbourg, acquired fame as spiritual director and preacher and is considered the most important exponent of German mystical speculation; his works were sometimes misinterpreted from a pantheistic point of view, which led to condemnations. Tauler and Seuse (Suso) were his disciples.艾克哈特, 见 *Buch der goettlichen Troestungen*

economia, E: economy, D: Wirtschaft; => moneta 经济, 见 Oresmensis, *De origine monetarum*

ecstasis, E: ecstatic experience, D: Ekstase; the trance or rapture associated with mystic or prophetic exaltation; the experience of a mystical union with God. 精神超拔, 见 Bernardus, *De diligendo Deo*

ecumenical council = concilium oecumenicum

Edda, E: *Edda*, a collection of Old Norse poems (*Elder Edda*); a manual of Icelandic poetry (*Younger Edda* or *Prose Edda*) written by Snorri Sturluson in the 13th century.《埃达》, 见 Snorri Sturluson

Eden, E: Eden, D: Eden, => Paradisium

Edessa, ancient city on the upper Euphrates, an important stronghold of Nestorianism. The city fell to the Arabs in 639 but was ruled by Christians between the First and Second Crusade (1099—1144).埃得撒

Edinburgh, city in Scotland, twice destroyed by the English (1341 and 1385). It developed into the capital of Scotland during the reign of James II (1437—1460).埃丁堡

Edmundus I, E: Edmund, D: Edmund; king of England 939—946 who recovered the northern part of England from the Norse invaders.埃德蒙

Eduardus Confessor, E: Edward the Confessor, D: Eduard der Bekenner; king of England 1042—1066, the last Anglo-Saxon king of England, who built Westminster Abbey. During his reign a split between the Anglo-Saxon faction and the Norman faction arose.爱德华

Eduardus I, E: Edward, D: Eduard; King of England

1272—1307. He conquered Wales and claimed suzerainty over Scotland. He regularly summoned the Parliament and reformed the legislation. He did not respond to the prohibitions of Boniface VIII about taxing clergymen.爱德华

Eduardus II, E: Edward, D: Eduard; King of England 1307—1327.爱德华

Eduardus III, E: Edward, D: Eduard; King of England, 1327—1377. He defeated the French at Crecy (1346), but the war with France continued to trouble his reign. He stopped to pay taxes to Rome.爱德华

educare, educatio, E: education, D: Erziehung, => artes, schola 教育,见 Eginhardus, *Vita Caroli* 19 (education of Charlemagne's children), Hrabanus, *De institutione clericorum*, Notkerus, *Gesta Caroli Magni* (Charlemagne emphasizing education), Wolfram von Eschenbach, *Parzival* (Herzeloyde's instructions, reflections on the education of a knight), Rogerius Baco, *Opus maius* (aims at the reform of the education system)

Eduinus, E: Edwin, D: Edwin; +632; king of Northumbria who converted to Christianity around 626 AD.艾德温,见 Beda, *Historia ecclesiastica*, Alcuin, *De pontificibus*

Edwin = Eduinus

Egbertus, E: Egbert, D: Egbert; king of Wessex 802—839 AD. He defeated the Danes in 838.艾格贝特,见 Malmesburiensis, *Gesta regum Anglorum*

Eginhardus, E: Einhard, D: Einhard, ca. 770—840, German monk, educated in Fulda, later he became abbot of Seligenstadt and adviser of Louis the Pious. He was a scholar, architect and the biographer of Charlemagne.艾因哈德,见 *Vita Caroli Magni*

Eichstaett, diocese in Germany 艾希施泰特

Eigenkirche = ecclesia propria

Einhard = Eginhardus

Einsiedeln, im portant Benedictine monastery in Switzerland, founded in 934 on the site of the cell of Meinrad (+861). In 1274 the abbot was made a prince of the Holy Roman Empire.艾恩西得尔恩

Ekkehard I, E: Ekkehard the Elder, ca. 910—973, monk in St. Gallen, poet, possibly the author of the *Waltharius*.艾克哈德,见 *Waltharii poiesis*,

Ekkehard II, + 990, monk in St. Gallen, poet.艾克哈德

Ekkehard IV, +1060, monk in St. Gallen, historian.艾克哈德

elector, E: elector, D: Kurfuerst; name given to one of the seven princes who elected the new king of Germany; Charles IV confirmed their authority in his *Golden Bull* of 1356.选帝侯,见 *Bulla aurea*

Elena, E: *Helena*, an epic poem by Cynewulf《埃琳娜》,见 Cynewulf

Elias de Cortona, E: Elias of Cortona, +1253; Italian friar, minister general of the Franciscan Order (1221—1227 and 1232—1239). He was harsh toward the Spiritual Franciscans and was deposed in 1239.厄里亚斯

Eligius, St., +660; Bishop of Noyon-Tournay, master of the mint under Dagobert I. He worked as missionary in Flanders, founded monasteries and ransomed captives.厄利基乌斯

Elipandus, Archbishop of Toledo, +802, the main exponent of the Adoptionist heresy in Spain. Because of the Arab rule in Spain he could not be removed from office.埃利班多斯

Elisabeth de Schoenau, E: Elizabeth of Schoenau; +1164; Abbess of the Benedictine monastery at Schoenau, mystic. Her brother recorded her visions. 伊丽沙白/依撒伯尔

Elisabeth de Thuringia, E: Elizabeth of Thuringia (Elizabeth of Hungary), St., +1231, daughter of King Andrew II of Hungary, wife of Louis of Thuringia, she selflessly helped the poor, founded a hospital at Marburg and became a popular saint, usually depicted carrying red roses. 伊丽沙白/依撒伯尔

Elkerlijk, E: *Everyman*, D: *Jedermann*, a play of the rich man who faces death.《每一个人》,见 Appendix, *Elkerlijk*

Elsass = Alsatia

Emmeram, (=Heimrham), +715, St., itinerary Bishop of Poitiers, he founded a monastery in Regensburg.圣艾梅兰

empyreum, E: empyreum, fiery heaven, D: Feuerhimmel, Empyreum; => caelum 净火天,见 Alanus, *Anticlaudianus*, Albertus, *Summa de creaturis*, Dante, *Commedia* (the highest and last sphere of Heaven)

enchiridion => manuale

encyclopaedia, E: encyclopedia, D: Enzyklopaedie, big collections or handbooks were compiled by classical scholars, and this tradition continued in the Middle Ages; in imitation of the =>Suda, the arrangement according to the alphabet gradually supplanted the topical order. 百科全书, 见 Plinius, *Historia nat.*, Augustinus, *De doctrina christiana*, Isidorus, *Etymologiae*, Hrabanus, *De universo*, Photios, *Myrobiblion*, Hugo, *Didascalicon*, Vincentius Bellovacensis, *Speculum maius* (a huge compilation, only surpassed in the 18th century), Thomas, *Summa theologiae*

Engelbertus, E, D: Engelbert, + 1331, scholarly abbot of the monastery at Admont, author of a work on the Roman Empire (1308).恩格伯尔特

Engelbert de Colonia, Archbishop of Cologne, regent of Germany 1220—1225.恩格尔伯特

England => Anglia

enigma, E: enigma, riddle, D: Raetsel; 谜语, 见 Aldhelmus, *Epistola ad Acircium*

ens => esse

entia => esse

Enzio, +1272, son of Frederick II, made king of Sardinia in 1238.恩西欧

epic = epos

episcopus, Gr: episkopos, E: bishop, D: Bischof, a consecrated church officer, usually the head of a diocese with spiritual authority over the other clergy and laity in that diocese. According to tradition, a bishop is a successor to the apostles. The election, nomination, investiture of a bishop or the right of approval were an important issue in negotiations between secular and religious power in the Middle Ages.主教, 见 Cynewulf, *Elene* (Judas becomes bishop of Jerusalem), Gregorius VII, *Dictatus Papae* 2 (only the Pope can depose and reinstate bishops), Anselmus (archbishop of Canterbury), Cosmas Pragensis (secretary of the bishop of Prague), Jacobus de Voragine, Raimundus Lullus, *Blanquerna*, Oresmensis (bishop of Lisieux)

Epistola ad Acircium, E: *Letter to Acircius*, by Aldhelm《致阿基求斯的信》, 见 Aldhelmus

Epistolae obscurorum virorum, E: *Letters of obscure men*, D: *Dunkelmaennerbriefe*, satirical letters written in 1515《无名人书信集》

Epistulae, E: *Letters*, by Boniface《信集》, 见 Bonifatius

epos, E: epic poetry, D: epische Dichtung; the oldest pieces of literature in the vernacular languages of the medieval peoples were heroic epics, most of them bearing the marks of Christian influence.英雄史诗, 见 Appendix, *Beowulf*, *Poema de mio Cid*, *Chanson de Roland*, *Nibelungenlied*

eques, (caballerus), E: knight, D: Ritter, Fr: chevalier, Sp: caballero; a medieval tenant obliged to give military service to a feudal landholder; a noble gentleman-soldier, trained as a page and squire, then raised to a privileged status; medieval literature often depicts the knight-errant, who wanders in search of adventures to prove his chivalry; => honos, pugna; => Artus, Erec, Parzifal 骑士, 见 Chretien, *Erec et Enide*, Wolfram von Eschenbach, *Parzival* (the education of a knight, superiority of spiritual motives, the wanderings of a knight-errant), Froissart, *Chroniques* (extols knightly virtue), Chaucer, *Canterbury Tales* (knight telling a chivalric romance), Appendix, *Beowulf* (faithfulness of vassals), *Poema de mio Cid* (chivalry), *Chanson de Roland* (loyalty to the king)

Erasmus, Desiderius (Roterodamus), E: Erasmus of Rotterdam, D: Erasmus von Rotterdam; 1466—1536, Dutch humanist scholar who promoted Latin and Greek studies, editor of a Greek New Testament (1517) and of patristic literature, he supported church reforms but later rejected Luther's views. => renasci 伊拉斯谟/埃拉斯莫

Erec et Enide, E: *Erec*, a work by Chretien of Troyes《艾莱克与艾尼德》, 见 Chretien de Troyes

eremita, E: hermit, D: Eremit => monachus

Eric IX, E: Erik, D: Erich; St., +1160; King of Sweden ca. 1150—1160. He propagated Christianity in Sweden, then in Finland 1156—1157. He is the patron saint of Sweden. 埃里克, 见 Saxo Grammaticus, *Gesta Danorum*

Eriugena = Johannes Scotus Eriugena

Eruditionis didascalicae libri septem, E: *Seven Books of Scholarly Teaching* = Didascalicon

eschatologia, E: eschatology, D: Eschatology; the Christian doctrines concerning the "last things" (death, resurrection, judgment, eternal reward or punishment); => Antichristus 终末论/末世论, 见 Hildegardis (her theology includes eschatology), Otto Frisingensis, Chronica (the last part covers eschatological issues), Innocens III, *De miseria conditionis humanae*, Thomas de Celano, *Dies irae*

esse, E: being, D: Sein; => analogia entis 存在, 是, 见 Occam, *Sententiae* (Entia non sunt multiplicanda sine necessitate. Occam's razor)

Este, E: Este, House of, D: Este; the aristocratic family of Ferrara, founded by Alberto Azzo (+1097). The House of Este was connected with Bavaria and the Guelfs.埃斯特

Estonia, E: Estonia, D: Estland; the Estonians are mentioned by Tacitus. Missionaries arrived there in the 12th century, when Albert of Buxhoevden, the bishop of Livonia organized the Knights of the Sword (1199) and moved his see to Riga. From 1237 to 1561 the Teutonic Knights controlled much of Livonia and Estonia.爱沙尼亚

Ethelbertus, E: Ethelbert, Aethelbert, D: Ethelbert, St., king of Kent 560—616, the Anglo-Saxon king who welcomed the missionary monks sent by Rome in 597. He was baptized and persuaded the kings of Essex and East Anglia to accept the new faith.埃特贝特

Etzel => Attila

Eugenicus, Gr: Eugenikos, E: Eugenicus; +1445; Archbishop of Ephesus who opposed the union of the Greek and Latin churches at the Council of Ferrara-Florence 1439.尤金尼库斯

Eugenius I, E: Eugenius, D: Eugen; St., Pope 654—657 尤金尼乌斯

Eugenius II, E: Eugenius, D: Eugen; Pope 824—827. He fought against iconoclasm.尤金尼乌斯

Eugenius III, E: Eugen III, D: Eugen III; Pope 1145—1153, orig. Bernardo Pignatelli, he entered the Cistercian Order, became a student of St. Bernhard; after becoming Pope he had to reside outside of Rome due to the activities of Arnold of Brescia.尤金尼乌斯, 见 Bernardus, *De considerations*

Eugenius IV, Pope 1431—1447, orig. Gabriel Condulmer, a pious Augustinian monk, also a patron of art and literature. He recognized the Council of Basel in 1433, but moved the synod to Ferrara in 1437, thus weakening conciliarism. He could persuade the Greek embassy to accept the reunion of the Latin and Greek churches, though most of the delegates from the East repudiated the union upon their return.尤金尼乌斯

Euthymius Zigabenus, +1118, monk and author in Constantinople. His work on heresies provides precious material concerning the Bogomils. 优提米乌斯

Eva, (=Heva), E: Eve, D: Eva; the first woman, often depicted in medieval art. 夏娃/厄娃, 见 Hildegardis, *Causae et curae*

Evangelienbuch, E: *Book of the Gospels*, a work by Otfrid of Weissenburg《福音之书》, 见 Otfrid

Everyman => *Elkerlijk*

Ewald, St., Anglo-Saxon missionary, martyred ca. 820 (?) 厄瓦德

Exarchatus Ravenna, E: exarchate, D: Exarchat; After Byzantium recovered Ravenna from the Vandals and Ostrogoths, this area (also called "Romagna") was called "exarchate". The Greek governor resided here. Ravenna was occupied by the Lombards in 751, then in 754 by Pippin who made it a donation to the Holy See, which was reconfirmed by Charlemagne in 774; throughout the Middle Ages the Romagna was considered part of the Papal lands.拉文纳教省

excommunicatio, E: excommunication, D: Exkommunikation; the formal exclusion of a person from the communion of the Church. In the Middle Ages excommunication had serious social and legal consequences, especially for a king, since his subjects were no longer bound to obey him.绝罚, 见 Gregorius VII, *Dictatus Papae*, Appendix, *Magna Charta*

exemptio, E: exemption, D: Exemption, the immunity from local (diocesan) authority or special privileges of a monastery; exempted monasteries were directly affiliated to Rome.豁免权

Exeter, town in England. In the local monastery Winfried-Bonifatius was educated (ca. 700).埃克塞特, 见 Bonifatius

experientia, E: experience, D: Erfahrung, 经验, 见 Walahfridus, *Liber de cultura hortorum* (experience of gardening), Fredericus, *De arte venandi cum avibus* (experiments with falcons), Albertus (saw the importance of experiments), Rogierus Baco, *Opus maius* (emphasizes experiments)

exspectantiae, E: expectancies, expectatives, D: Exspektanzen; benefices promised (usually by the Pope); the benefices were conferred when they became vacant. The practice started in the 12th century and involved payment for candidacy for an ecclesiastical office.候选金

Eyck, Jan van, +1441, Dutch painter, greatest artist of the early Netherlands school, court painter of Philip the Good, duke of Burgundy. Together with his older brother Hubert van Eyck (+1426) he painted the altarpiece of Ghent.爱克

Ezzelino da Romano, +1259, son-in-law of Emperor

Frederick II, lord of Verona, Vicenza, and Padua, holding power from 1236 to 1259 in northern Italy, feared for his despotism. He was excommunicated by Pope Innocent IV in 1254; Dante placed him in hell with the tyrants. 艾佐林诺, 见 Dante, *Commedia*

F

fabliaux, E: fabliau, a humorous story in verse, popular in the 12th and 13th centuries; the fabliau usually was a coarse satire exposing the weaknesses of clerks, burghers, peasants, and women. 讽刺故事, 见 Boccaccio, *Decamerone*, Appendix, *Roman de Renard*

fabula, E: fable, D: Fabel; story about animals that took on the character of men. Like Aesop's fables the medieval stories often contained a moral. The *Romance of Renard the Fox* is often classified as fable although no moral is found there. 动物叙事

Fafnir, the dragon slain by Sigurd; => draco 法弗尼尔, 见 Snorri Sturluson, *Edda*

fama, E: fame, D: Ruf, Ansehen; 名声, 见 Alanus, *Anticlaudianus* (allegory of fame)

Farabi => Al Farabi

fasting = ieiunium

fatum, E: fate, D: Geschick; => aegritudo, providentia 命运, 见 Hartmann, *Der arme Heinrich* (unable to understand his fate)

Felix V, originally Amadeus VIII of Savoy, antipope chosen by the conciliarists at Basel (1439—1449). He had dwindling support, submitted to Pope Nicholas V in 1449 and was the last of the antipopes. 菲理克斯

femina, E: woman, D: Frau; the position of women in medieval society was improved by the ecclesiastical emphasis on monogamy; the ideal of chaste motherhood was seen in the life of Mary (=> Maria); noble women often went to nunneries; female authors => Birgitta, Gertrudis, Hildegardis, Hrotsvita; => allegoria, sorores 妇女, 见 Hrotsvita, *Dulcitius* (three Christian women bravely face martyrdom, contrasted to the vice of a man), Guillaume de Lorris, *Roman de la rose* (women's vices exposed by the Old Woman), Rubruk, *Itinerarium* (description of the life of Mongol women), Boccaccio, *Decamerone* (role of noble women), *De claris mulieribus* (100 biographies of famous women from Eve to a contemporary Italian Queen), Chaucer, *Canterbury Tales* (wife of Bath, nun, prioress), Johannes de Tepla, *Der Ackermann* (death is a misogynist, whereas Ackermann defends the nobility of women)

Ferdinandus II, Sp: Fernando, E: Ferdinand, + 1516, King of Aragon, he married Isabella of Castile (1469), expelled Muslims from Grenada in 1492, forced Jews in Spain to be baptized. He financed Columbus's journey to America, and in 1494 Spain and Portugal divided the New World between themselves (Treaty of Tordesillas). 斐迪南

Ferdinandus III, Sp: Fernando, E: Ferdinand the Saint, King of Castile 1217—1252, who conquered Cordoba and Sevilla, where he restored Christian rule. He was the founder of the University of Salamanca (1239). 斐迪南

Ferdinandus I, Sp: Fernando, It: Don Ferrante, E: Ferdinand; son of Alfonso V of Aragon, King of Naples 1458—1494. He extended his rule over southern Italy, fought against his uncle Pope Sixtus IV. He also promoted humanism, commerce, and industry in Naples. 斐迪南

Ferrara, town in northern Italy (area of the Po delta), it was captured by the Lombards in 753, but came under Papal rule in 774, in the tenth century fell to the margrave of Tuscany. Later it was ruled by the House of Este. The ecumenical council of Ferrara-Florence took place in 1438—1442. 费拉拉

Ferrer, Vincentius, E: Vincent Ferrer, D: Vinzenz Ferrer; St., ca. 1350—1419, Dominican of Valencia (Spain), teacher of theology at Valencia and influential preacher, who travelled for many years through Spain, Italy, Switzerland, and the Low Countries to preach moral reform and penance. For some time he supported Benedict XIII and the Avignonese faction. 味增爵·菲雷

festum ecclesiae, E: feast day, D: Festtag; some feast-days of the Church were a local custom and became feasts of the whole Church, when approved by Papal decision. 教会节日

Festum Corpus Christi, E: Feast of the Holy Body of Christ, D: Fronleichnam; the feast celebrating the Holy Body of Christ, it began as a local tradition and was made a universal feast in 1264 by Urban IV. 耶稣圣体节

Festum fatuorum, E: festival of fools, D: Narrenfest; a medieval custom celebrated on the first of January.愚人节

Festum orthodoxiae, E: feastday of Orthodoxy, D: Fest der Orthodoxie; introduced by the Greek Church after 843 when the iconoclasm movement was over.正统信仰的节日

Festum Sanctissimae Trinitatis, E: Feast of the Holy Trinity, D: Dreifaltigkeitsfest; proclaimed in 1334 as feast of the universal Church 圣三节

feudalismus, E: feudalism; D: Feudalismus; the feudal system of the Middle Ages was both political and economic, it provided services for the nobility and protection for the weak; although there existed different forms of exploitation, it was in the interest of the local aristocracy to support and protect their subjects. The nobility was divided into many ranks, => rex, dux, comes 封建制度，见 Oresme, *De origine monetarum*

feudum, (<fidelitas), E: fiefdom, D: Lehen, Lehngut, a value (usually a piece of land) entrusted to a vassal, the origin of the word "feudalism". => fidelitas 采邑，封地，见 Johannes de Tepla, *Der Ackermann aus Boehmen* (life is just a "fiefdom")

Ficino, Marsilio, Italian humanist scholar, +1499, director of the Plato-Academy in Florence. He translated works of Plato, Plotinus and other Greek authors.菲奇诺

fidelitas, E: loyalty (of a vassal), D: triuwe, Treue (eines Belehnten), in medieval feudalism the king demanded loyalty from his vassals; medieval literature often describes the conflict between loyalty and friendship 忠信，见 Ekkehard, *Waltharii poiesis*, Gregorius VII, *Dictatus Papae* 27 (the Pope can absolve from the oath of loyalty), Anonymus, *Nibelungenlied*, Wolfram, *Parzival* (God's triuwe)

fides, Gr. pistis, E: faith, D: Glaube, 1) the Christian teachings that are believed ("fides quae"), 2) the trust in God's providence, a basic Christian virtue ("fides qua"); => virtutes theologicae 信仰,信德, 见 Anselmus (fides quaerens intellectum)

Fiesole, Giovanni da = Fra Angelico

figura, E: figure, symbol, metaphor, D: Figur, Symbol, Metapher; => allegoria 形象，见 Joachim, *Liber figurarum*

Filelfo, Francesco, Italian scholar who went to the East to learn Greek, ca. 1400 菲雷夫

filia, E: daughter, D: Tochter; => allegoria 女儿，见 Hermannus, *De octo vitiis principalibus* (sins are "daughters" of pride), Langland, *Piers Plowman* (God's four daughters: Mercy, Peace, Truth, Justice), Greban, *Passion de Paris* (conflicting views of the four daughters of God)

Filioque, E: "and from the Son", D: "und vom Sohn"; a formula in the creed claiming that the Holy Spirit proceeds from the Father "and from the Son", opposed by the Eastern Church, but accepted by Eastern delegates at the Council of Ferrara/ Florence of 1439."及由圣子"/"由圣子", 见 Photios, *Logos peri tēs tou Hagiou Pneumatos mystagōgias*

Finlandia, E: Finland, D: Finnland, mission work probably started in the eleventh century; Sweden had annexed most of the region by 1250.芬兰

Flagellantes, E: Flagellants, D: Flagellanten; rigid groups of believers or reformers who used whips to beat themselves as a sign of penitence, especially after the outbreak of epidemic diseases in the 13th and 14th centuries. Other factors explaining the popularity of the flagellants are apocalyptic thought (Joachim of Fiore, Spiritual Franciscans) and the miseries of the Hundred Years' War. A Papal bull of 1349 tried to suppress them. 鞭笞运动,鞭笞己身派

Flandria, E: Flanders, D: Flandern; a county since the 9th century, this region around Bruges asserted its independence in 1302 (battle of Courtrai) against Philipp IV of France. In 1369 it came under Burgundian control and in 1482 Flanders fell to the Habsburgs.佛兰德(比利时)

Flodoartus, E: Flodoard, D: Flodoart; +966, French priest, historian, and Latin poet at Reims.弗罗多特

Florentia, It: Firenze, E: Florence, D: Florenz; a city of central Italy, originally an Etruscan settlement, then under Roman rule; after the collapse of the Roman Empire in the fifth century the city was captured by the Goths, the Byzantine Empire, the Lombards, but during the reign of Charlemagne Florence revived. Under Countess Matilda of Tuscany the city repelled a siege by Henry IV in 1082 and acquired increasing autonomy in the twelfth century but was caught in the struggle between Guelf and Ghibelline factions, alliances of aristocratic families, and conflicting interests of guilds and banking houses. Since its first appearance in 1252 the gold florin became Europe's most depe ndable currency. Construction of the city's cathedral started in 1294. The rule of Cosimo de' Medici in 1434 inaugurated a period of relative peace. The Ecumenical Council of Ferrara was moved to Florence in 1439. The powerful city-state became a center of humanist learning already in the 14th century, but especially under Lorenzo the Magnificent (died in 1492). From 1492 to his execution in 1498 the Dominican friar and demagogue Savonarola held sway in the city, but after him the Medici returned to power. The Tuscan dialect became the basis for modern Italian. 佛罗伦萨, 见 Dante, Boccaccio, Medici, Piccolomini

flores, E: flowers, D: Blumen, symbolic value of flowers, => lilium, rosa 花, 见 Walahfridus, *Liber de cultura hortorum*, Thomas de Celano, *Vita sancti Francisci* (treating them like rational beings), Guillaume de Lorris, *Roman de la rose*

Flotte, Petrus, +1302; adviser of Philip IV of France; he wrote an anti-papal Pseudo-bull in 1302.佛洛特

Fontevrault, L: Fons Ebraldi, E, D: Fontevrault; Congregation of Fontevrault (ca. 20 km southeast of Saumur, France), founded in 1100 by Robert of Arbrissel, supported by Henry II of England, who is buried in the abbey. The double monastery was headed by an abbess and became the mother house of communities in France, England, and Spain. It was dissolved in the time of the French Revolution.冯特沃

Formosus, Bishop of Porto, Pope 891—896, who encouraged missionary activity in England and north Chermany. After his death Lambert of Spoleto, whose control of Rome Formosus had opposed, had Formosus condemned in a postmortal trial.福尔摩苏斯

fortitudo, E: courage, strength, D: Mut; one of the four cardinal virtues, => virtutes cardinales 勇气, 见 Wolfram, *Parzival*

Francesca da Rimini, +1284, daughter of the ruler of Ravenna, who became the wife of Gianciotto Malatesta of Rimini in 1275. She had an affair with Paolo, her brother-in-law and was thus placed in the circle of the immoral by Dante.弗兰切斯卡, 见 Dante, *Commedia*

Francesca da Roma, E: Frances of Rome, D: Franziska von Rom, St., +1440, a noble-woman of Rome, co-founder of the Oblates of St. Frances of Rome (originally "Oblates of Olivetan Benedictines") in 1433. This community focused on the help for the poor.方济加

Franci, E: Franks, D: Franken; a German tribe first noted 258 AD; In the fifth century the Franks on the lower Rhine came to be known as the Salian Franks, those in the area of Cologne and farther north as the Ripuarian branch of the tribe. The Franks were defeated by the Roman general Aetius in the 430s, but after Aetius' death (454) they became independent, and Clovis I (481—511) united them under the leadership of the Merovingians. In 751 Pepin deposed the last Merovingian and founded the new Frankish dynasty of the Carolingians. => Carolus Magnus 法兰克人, 见 Appendix, *Chanson de Roland*

Francia, F, E: France, D: Frankreich; for the early history => Franci. The Treaty of Verdun (843) divided the Carolingian empire into three parts, assigning the western section to Charles the Bald, who died in 877. In 987 the feudal lords of France elected Hugh Capet their king. His granduncle had saved Paris from the Vikings in 885, and Hugh established a dynasty which ruled France until 1316. The stable growth of royal power is in a marked difference to the disruptions which German monarchs faced. The divorced wife of King Louis VII (1137—1180), Eleanor of Aquitaine, married Henry II of England, which gave the English king possession of the western half of France, including Normandy, Anjou, and Flanders. However, Philip II Augustus (1180—1223) recovered Normandy and Anjou for France, and he defeated Otto IV of Germany, the ally of king John of England, in 1214. From the early thirteenth century France was the leading country of Western Europe. The saintly king Louis IX (1226—1270) gained much popular support, but his grandson Philip IV the Fair (1285—1314) employed a series of harsh measures to expand royal revenues, including the suppression of the Knights Templars and the humiliation of Pope Boniface VIII. After the outbreak of the Hundred Years' War the further consolidation of central power was halted, but at the end of the Middle Ages Louis XI (1461—1483) reconfirmed the rule of the king who controlled the whole country.

Franciscani, (=Ordo Fratrum Minorum, OFM), E: Franciscans, minorites; D: Franziskaner, Minoriten; a congregation founded by St. Francis of Assisi, confirmed by Pope Innocens in 1209, it spread fast across Europe, but due to the controversy about poverty it soon split into "spirituals" and "conventuals", => Bonaventura; the Franciscan school of thought (a kind of Augustinianism) rejected some rationalistic traits. 方济各会, 见 Joachim, *Liber figurarum* (influenced spiritual Franciscans), Wycliffe, *De civili dominio* (initially welcomed by Franciscans)

Franciscus, It: Francesco, E: Francis of Assisi, D: Franz von Assisi; St., 1181—1226, Italian monk with a new approach to religious life; he was famous for his spirit of poverty and humility, his charitable attitude to the poor and to nature; he founded the Franciscans (=> Franciscani) and was canonized in 1228.方济各/法兰西斯/弗朗西斯, 见 Thomas de Celano, *Vita Sancti Francisci*, Dante, *Commedia* (Francis placed in the highest Heaven)

Franciscus de Retz, E: Francis of Retz, +1427; Austrian Dominican, preacher, professor, reformer. 方济各/法兰西斯

Frankfurt, E: Frankfurt; town in Germany, first mentioned in 793. It became the capital of the East Franks. In 1356 it was designated as the place of the election of the king of Germany (=> *Bulla aurea*).法兰克福

Franko de Colonia, ca. 1200—1250; German musician, originator of mensural and figural notation theory.法兰克

Franks = Franci

frater, E: friar, D: Bruder, Frater; Gr: adelphos; the term applied to Christians by St. Paul, later used for any monk, but since the 13th century restricted to members of the Mendicant orders.弟兄

Fraticelli, name of extreme Franciscan sects in the late Middle Ages. They were influenced by Joachim's thought and held that Pope John XXII was guilty of heresy when he condemned their views concerning poverty. Some groups of the Fraticelli returned to orthodoxy, others suffered persecution.弗拉提切利

Fratres Apostolici = Apostolici

Fratres de Ponte, E: Bridge-Building Brotherhood, D: Brueckenbrueder; lay association with the aim to build bridges. One such brotherhood was founded at Avignon in 1181, another at Lyons in 1184. They disappeared in the 15th ct.修桥弟兄会

Fratres devoti = Fratres vitae communis

Fratres militiae Christi, E: Knights of the Sword, D: Schwertbrueder; a congregation founded in 1202 (or 1199) by Bishop Albert in Riga (Estonia), they merged with the Teutonic Knights in 1237.基督士兵弟兄会

Fratres Minimi, E: Order of the Minims; mendicant order with strict Franciscan rule, founded by Francis de Paula in Calabria in 1460.最小的弟兄会

Fratres vitae communis, Fratres devoti; E: Brothers of Common Life; D: Fraterherren; a community devoted to education and prayer, organized by Gerhard Groote after 1374.共同生活弟兄会

Fredericus I Barbarossa, E: Frederick; D: Friedrich; King of Germany 1152—1190. His father was a Hohenstaufen, his mother a Guelf, and he became the greatest German monarch of medieval Germany. His main rival was Henry the Lion, duke of Bavaria and Saxony. He went to Italy 6 times, hoping to control the cities of north Italy. He executed Arnold of Brescia and was crowned Emperor in Rome in 1155. After the Lombard League defeated him in 1176 at Legnano, he was reconciled to Pope Alexander in 1177. In 1186 his son Henry (VI) married Constance, the heiress of the kingdom of Sicily. He died on the Third Crusade in Asia Minor.红胡子腓特烈

Fredericus II, E: Frederick, D: Friedrich; 1194-1250, German King and Emperor 1215-1250, son of the Staufer Henry VI, educated in Apulia (Italy), under the guardianship of Innocent III, crowned Emperor in 1220. He founded of the University of Naples in 1224, went on crusade in 1228, but tried to control Italy and came in conflict with the Popes; he was banned 1227—1230 and 1239, 1245. Frederick was a poet, linguist, statesman, and a scientist. His book on falconry is unique.腓特烈

Fredericus III, E: Frederick, D: Friedrich von Habsburg, German King and Emperor 1440—1493, he accepted Pope Eugen in 1445, signed the Concordate of Vienna in 1448; he was the last German Emperor crowned in Rome (1452). His support for Pope Eugenius IV helped the papacy to overcome conciliarism. His son Maximilian married Mary of Burgundy and thus won the Low Countries for the Habsburgs' empire. 腓特烈, 见 Piccolomini, *Commentarii*

Fredericus III, E: Frederick, D: Friedrich; King of Aragon and Sicilia 1296—1337, son of Peter III of Aragon. 腓特烈

Fredericus de Lothringia, (=Pope Stephanus IX) 腓特烈

Fredericus de Austria, E: Frederick the Handsome, D: Friedrich der Schoene, +1330, duke of Austria, candidate to become German King in 1314. 腓特烈

Freising, Roman settlement, then a town of Bavaria, in 739 Boniface made it a bishop's see and established the diocese. The brewery was founded in 1040 and is one of the world's oldest. 弗赖辛

Freya, (Freia, Frija, Frea, Frigga, Frigg), a Nordic goddess of love and marriage, the wife of Odin (Wodan) and mother of Baldur. 佛瑞亚, 见 Snorri Sturluson, *Edda*

friar => frater

Frigg = Freya

Frisia, E: Frisia, D: Friesland; The Frisian people lived in the area of north Germany and Holland. They formed a powerful kingdom in the seventh century under King Radbod but came under the domination of the Franks in the following century. Boniface was martyred in the area in 754. 弗里西亚/弗里斯兰, 弗里斯兰人

Fritzlar, town in Hessen (Germany), the monastery was founded by Boniface in 723. The town became a favorite residence of the kings of Germany. 弗利茨拉尔

Friuli, E, D: Friaul, district in north Italy, which was controlled by Carinthia, Aquileia, and Venice. 弗利奥尔

Froissart, Jean, E, D: Froissart, ca. 1333—1400, French chronicler, whose *Chronicle* is an informative survey of the political events of western Europe from 1325 to 1400. 傅华萨, 见 *Chroniques*

Fulbertus, E: Fulbert of Chartres, D: Fulbert, St.; ca. 970—1029, teacher in the cathedral school of Chartres, he made it one of the leading centers of scholarship in western Europe. He became Bishop of Chartres in 1006. 夫尔贝特

Fulda, German town; the Benedictine monastery of Fulda was founded by Boniface (or his disciple Sturmius) in 744 AD. Being Boniface's burial place, the abbey became an intellectual and cultural center, especially during the abbacy of Rabanus Maurus (+856) and throughout the Middle Ages. In the 13th century the abbot of Fulda became a prince of the German Empire. 富尔达, 见 Eginhardus (he was educated there), Hrabanus, Otfrid de Weissenburg, Walahfridus

Furiae, E: the Furies, D: Furien; goddesses of revenge 报复女神, 见 Alanus, *Anticlaudianus* (Allecto)

G

Gabriel, E, D: Gabriel; an archangel who announced the future birth of Christ to Mary (Luke 1:18ff). His trumpet will announce the Last Judgment. According to Islam, the *Qur'an* was revealed to Muhammad by Gabriel. 佳伯尔, 见 Appendix, *Heliand*, *Chanson de Roland* (Gabriel receives Roland's glove), Appendix, *Qur'an*

Gaetani, Benedictus = Bonifatius VIII

Gahmuret, the father of Parzival 伽姆瑞特, 见 Wolfram von Eschenbach, *Parzival*

Galfredus Monemuthensis, E: Geoffrey of Monmouth, D: Gottfried von Monmouth; 1100—1154, English chronicler, whose work is a source of Arthurian legend. 蒙默恩的杰弗里, 见 *Historia regum Britanniae*

Gallen, St., E: St. Gall; D: St. Gallen; monastery in Switzerland, founded by St. Gall (Gallus) in 615, it became one of the leading centers of culture and scholarship in the time of the "Ottonian Renaissance", ca. 930—1000. 圣伽伦隐修院, 见 Ekkehard

Gallia, Gallicanismus, E: Gaul, Gallicanism, D: Gallien, Gallikanismus; special privileges and rights of the French king over the Church in France like nomination of bishops. 高卢主义

Gallus, E: Gall, D: Gallus; St. companion of Columbanus, missionary in Switzerland ca. 612—630, founder of the monastery St. Gallen; => Columbanus, Gallen 圣加卢斯/圣伽伦

Gallus Anonymus, +1120 (?); Benedictine monk and oldest chronicler of Poland. His chronicle was written in Cracow around 1115. 伽卢斯

Gandersheim, Benedictine monastery in Germany, founded as a house for canonesses in 856. 甘德斯海姆, 见 Hrotsvita Gandeshemensis

Ganelon, (Gano), stepfather of Roland, whose treason lead to Roland's death 甘内隆, 见 Appendix,

Chanson de Roland

Gaunilo, monk of Marmoutier, who argued with Anselmus, ca. 1100 高尼罗，见 Anselmus, *Proslogion*

Gawain, E: Gawain, D: Gawan, Gawein; one of the Arthurian knights; => Artus 格温，见 Galfredus Monemuthensis, *Historia regum Britanniae*, Wolfram, *Parzival* (fight between Parzival and Gawan)

Geismar, place in German, where Bonifatius felled the oak of Donar (724), symbol of pagan superstition.格斯马尔

Gelasius II, Pope, 1118—1119, who banned Henry V of Germany and died in Cluny.葛拉西乌斯

Gemisthos Plethon = Plethon

genealogia, E: genealogy, D: Genealogie; a table of descent from an ancestor, a family tree 家族史，家谱，见 Joachim, *Liber figurarum*

Gennadius II Scholarius, +1 472; monk, adviser to Emperor John VIII Palaelogus at the Council of Ferrara-Florence. He had endorsed Church unity, but after his return opposed it, was made patriarch of Constantinople after 1453, retired to a monastery in 1466. He admired Aristotle and translated Thomas of Aquinas into Greek.格纳丢斯

Genoa, D: Genua; seaport in northwestern Italy which expanded since the 10th century and shared with Venice the commercial leadership during the time of the crusades. In 1250 the city declared independence. The Black Death of 1348 ushered in a slow decline.热那亚，见 Jacobus de Voragine

Gent => Ghent

gentiles, E: gentiles, heathens, D: Voelker, Heiden; a Biblical concept denoting the non-Christian peoples 外帮人，见 Thomas Aquinas, *Summa contra gentiles*

Geoffrey of Monmouth = Galfredus

geometria, E: geometry, D: Geometrie; one of the seven liberal arts. It was concerned mainly with the measurement of land. 几何学，见 Hrabanus, *De inst. cler.* (geometry is useful for the construction of religious buildings)

Georgius, Gr: Geōrgios, E: George, D: Georg; the name of a martyr whose cult became popular in the sixth century. He is the patron saint of England, Portugal, Aragon, Lithuania and of many cities. The story of his slaying a dragon first appeared in the 12th century. 乔治，见 Jacobus de Voragine, *Legenda aurea*

Gerardus de Cremona, E: Gerard of Cremona, D: Gerhard von Cremona; +1187; he studied a Toledo and translated many works from Arabic into Latin, among these Ptolemy's *Almagest* and commentaries to Aristotle's works. 格拉德

Gerbert de Aurillac = Silvester II

Gerhoh de Reichersberg, +1169; provost in Reichersberg (Austria), theologian, author, supporter of the Gregorian reforms. He opposed violence against heretics.格尔霍

Germani, E: Germans, D: Germanen; after 375 AD. German tribes overran the Roman empire; they had no script but often mixed with the local Roman population, and they accepted the Christian faith. Around the year 500 the Visigoths, Burgundians and, Salian Franks wrote down their laws. The earliest Frankish code, the Lex Salica was compiled in 508 AD. by order of King Clovis I. However, crude Germanic institutions like the ordeal usually replaced the more refined Roman judicial procedures. 日耳曼人，见 Appendix, *Heliand* (Germanic elements in the gospel)

Germanus, + 733 (?), Patriarch of Constantinople (715), deposed in 730 for his defense of sacred images.格尔曼努斯

Gernot, one of the Burgundian princes in the *Nibelungenlied* 格尔诺特，见 Appendix

Gershom, Ben Judah, E: Rabbi Gershom (Gerson); +1040; Jewish scholar, rector of the rabbinical academy in Mainz and founder of Talmudic studies in France and Germany. His legal decisions helped to organize the life of the Jews in Europe. 格尔松

Gerson, Johannes, F: Jean Charlier de Gerson, 1363—1429, French theologian, chancellor of the University of Paris, a well-known orator, poet, humanist, and outstanding author of works in the French tongue. He wrote several hundred books. His moderation and dedication brought him the title "doctor Christianissimus". He headed the French delegation at the Council of Constance (1414—1418).杰尔松，见 *De mystica theologia*

Gertrudis Magna, E: Gertrude the Great, D: Gertrude die Grosse; 1256—1302, nun and mystic in the Cistercian convent of Helfta (Germany). She worked as copyist and composed several treatises. She is famous for her mystical theology, her *Messenger of Divine Love* helped popularize the devotion to the Sacred Heart of Jesus.格尔特儒德，见 *Legatus divinae pietatis*

Gesta Caroli Magni imperatoris, E: *The Deeds of Charles the Great*, D: *Die Taten Karls des Grossen*, a popular work by Notker the Stammerer《查理大帝言行录》，见 Notkerus Balbulus

Gesta Chuonradi II imperatoris, E: *Biography of Emperor Conrad II*, a historical work by Wipo《康拉德二世皇帝传》，见 Wipo

Gesta Danorum, E: *Danish History*, the first history of Denmark《丹麦史》，见 Saxo Grammaticus

Gesta regum Anglorum, E: *History of English Kings*, a historical compilation by Wilhelm of Malmesbury《英国史》，见 Malmesbury

Ghent, E: Ghent, D: Gent; one of the leading cities of Flanders 根特

Ghibellini, E: Ghibellines, D: Waiblinge; pro-imperial faction in Italy, opposed to the Guelphi (Welfs); they supported a certain influence of the German Emperor (Frederick II 1215—1250) in Italy.吉伯林派

Gilbertus, E: Gilbert of Sempringham, D: Gilbert; St., +1189, founder of the English Order of Gilbertines around 1140. The Gilbertines were organized in double monasteries and formed the only exclusively English religious order of the Middle Ages.格尔贝特

Gilbertus de la Porree, F: Gilbert, E: Gilbert; +1154, French scholar, teacher at Chartres and Paris, since 1142 Bishop of Poitiers, controversial for his teaching on the Trinity.格尔贝特，见 Johannes Saresberiensis (his student)

Giotto di Bondone, Italian painter, 1267—1337, sometimes honored as the "father of modern painting" for his use of light and shadow and the creation of natural and individual figures. He worked in many Italian cities and was very influential.乔托

Giselher, one of the princes at the Burgundian court 吉塞赫尔，见 Appendix, *Nibelungenlied*

gladius, E: sword, D: Schwert; symbol of power, => potestas 剑，见 Bernardus, *De consideratione*

Glasgow, city in Scotland, see of a bishop in 1115. Its university was founded in 1451 by a charter of Pope Nicholas V.格拉斯高

Gnesnia, Gniezno, D: Gnesen; city of Poland, established in the 8th century. In 1000 it became the first Polish archdiocese, the place of coronation for Polish kings, and the capital of the Piast state (Poland).格涅兹诺

Gog et Magog, E: Gog and Magog; nations which under the leadership of Satan will try to destroy the kingdom of God (*Rev.* 20:8), sometimes thought to be wild peoples from the steppes of Asia; => Antichristus 哥格和马哥格，见 Appendix, *Alexandreis*

Golden Bull => *Bulla aurea*

goliardi, E: goliards, D: Goliarden; composers of secular Latin lyrics of the 12th and 13th centuries; they were wandering scholars and clerks from Germany, France, and England. The most extensive collection of goliardic poems is the *Carmina Burana*, => Archipoeta, Rainald of Dassel, Walter of Chatillon 格里亚德诗人，见 Appendix, *Carmina Burana*

Good Friday => passio

Gorze, monastery in Germany 格尔泽

Gothica Ars, E: Gothic art, D: gotische Kunst; the period from ca. 1150 to 1400 in the history of art. Gothic art originated in the area of Paris and spread to most countries of western Europe. The use of the pointed arch and the flying buttress changed the low and dark Romanesque church into an edifice of lofty naves, elaborate vaults and huge stained-glass windows. Gothic script arose in north France in the eleventh century.哥特艺术风格

Gottesfrieden = Treuga Dei

Gottfridus de Bouillon, E: Godfrey of Bouillon, D: Gottfried; +1100; a count of Lorraine who led crusaders in 1096. In 1099 he had a major role in the capture of Jerusalem but he rejected the title "King of Jerusalem", since he felt only Christ deserved this title.戈特夫里德

Gottfridus de Fontaines, E: Godfrey of Fontaines, D: Gottfried; +1306; Parisian theologian who opposed the presence of the friars at the university.戈特夫里德

Gottschalk, (Godescale), ca. 804—869, Benedictine monk, poet, the first Saxon theologian, exponent of strict predestination. He was condemned by the council of Mainz held in 848.格特沙尔克/戈特沙克/哥特沙耳克

Graecia, E: Greece, D: Griechenland; After the death of Theodosius (395 AD) the peninsula of Greece suffered from repeated raids by Goths, Huns,

Avars, Slavs, and Bulgars. The Macedonian rulers of Byzantium controlled the area from 867 to 1025. After that the Turks and Normans appeared, and during the Fourth Crusade (1202—1204) Venice established its rule in Greece. In 1456 The Ottoman Turks seized all of the peninsula.希腊,见 Byzantium

Grail, L: lapis ex caelis, lapis electrix, D: Gral; a mysterious life-giving chalice or stone kept in the castle of the Grail ("Munsalvesche" according to Wolfram's *Parzival*), => medicina 圣杯,见 Wolfram, *Parzival*

grammatica, E: grammar, D: Grammatik; the most important of the seven arts until the scholastics of the 12th century placed more emphasis upon dialectic (logic). Donatus' textbook from the fourth century was most commonly used; grammar studies included selected readings of ancient authors. 语法,语文学,见 Dante, *De vulgari eloquentia* (grammar rules shape immutable identity of the language)

Grammaticus => Saxo Grammaticus

Gran, (Esztergom), archdiocese in Hungary, established ca. 1010.格兰

Grandmont, Order of; a religious order founded in the area of Limoges by St. Stephen of Muret in 1076. The monks lived by a very austere rule. It disappeared in the French Revolution.格兰德蒙

Gratianus, E: Gratian, D: Gratian; + ca. 1159; canonist of the 12th century, author of an important early collection of Canon Law (*Decretum Gratiani*, ca. 1140), therefore called "Father of Canon Law".格拉提安,见 Gratianus

Greban, Arnoul, ca. 1420—1471, French scholar and musician, author of religious plays. 格雷邦,见 *Passion de Paris*

Greece => Graecia

Gregorius I Magnus, E: Gregory, D: Gregor; St. Gregory the Great, Pope 590—604, important organizer of the church in Rome, author, supporter of the monastic movement; he sent the first missionaries to Britain; his works profoundly influenced the Middle Ages. 大额我略/贵格利/格列高利,见 Adamnanus, Beda, *Historia*, Paulus Diaconus, *Historia Lang.*, Bernardus, *De consideratione* (Gregory as a model Pope)

Gregorius II, E: Gregory, D: Gregor; Pope 715—731, he warned the emperor of Constantinople not to promote iconoclasm.额我略/贵格利

Gregorius III, E: Gregory, D: Gregor; Pope 731—741, he approached Karl Martell in 739 for protection against the Lombards.额我略/贵格利

Gregorius IV, E: Gregory, D: Gregor; Pope 827—844, he was invited by King Lothair in 833 to come to Germany to decide quarrels in the royal family.额我略/贵格利

Gregorius V, E: Gregory, D: Gregor; Pope 996—999, originally Bruno of Carinthia and grand-grandson of Otto the Great, he crowned Otto III in 996.额我略/贵格利

Gregorius VI, E: Gregory, D: Gregor; Antipope 1012. 额我略/贵格利

Gregorius VII, E: Gregory, D: Gregor; Pope 1073—1085, originally monk Hildebrand, papal legate and active in the Curia since Leo IX (1049—1054); he was an ardent Church reformer, opposed lay investiture and fought for the independence of the Church, deposed Emperor Henry IV in 1076 but absolved him in Jan 1077 at Canossa. His *Dictatus Papae* claims the supremacy of the Pope also in secular matters. 额我略/贵格利七世,见 *Dictatus Papae*

Gregorius VIII, E: Gregory, D: Gregor; Pope 1187, whose pontificate lasted only 8 weeks. 额我略/贵格利

Gregorius VIII, E: Gregory, D: Gregor; Antipope Burdinus 1118—1121.额我略/贵格利

Gregorius IX, E: Gregory, D: Gregor; Pope 1227—1241, originally Ugolino de Ostia, canonist (*Decretales Gregorii*), supporter of the Franciscans; he banned Frederick II in 1227 and in 1239 and faced severe pressure from the emperor. 额我略/贵格利,见 Thomas de Celano, *Vita Sancti Francisci* (written in answer to Pope Gregory's request)

Gregorius X, E: Gregory, D: Gregor; St., Pope 1271—1276, originally Theobaldo Visconti from Piacenza; he worked for the reunion of Eastern and Western Church at the ecumenical council at Lyon in 1274.额我略/贵格利

Gregorius XI, E: Gregory, D: Gregor; Pope 1370—1378, the last French Pope, he responded to Catharina of Siena's appeals and returned from Avignon to Rome, taking quarters in the Vatican (instead of the Lateran). 额我略/贵格利

Gregorius XII, E: Gregory, D: Gregor; Pope 1406—

1415, originally Angelo Corrario, he wanted first to achieve Church unity but did not retire from office after the election of Alexander V at Pisa in 1409.额我略/贵格利

Gregorius Asbesta, Gr. Grēgorios, E: Gregory, D: Gregor; Archbishop of Syracuse, banned by Ignatius, he ordained Photius in 858. 额我略/贵格利

Gregorius Palamas, Gr. Grēgorios, E: Gregory, D: Gregor, 1296—1359, main exponent of the contemplative practices of Hesychasm, monk at Mt. Athos, author of ascetical works.额我略/贵格利

Gregorius de Rimini, E: Gregory, D: Gregor; +1358, Italian Augustinian scholar, theologian, "doctor authenticus". He taught at Paris, Bologna, Perugia. 额我略/贵格利

Gregorius Turonensis, E: Gregory of Tours, ca. 538—594 AD, Latin historian, author of the *Historia Francorum* 格列高利，见 Paulus Diaconus, *Historia Langobardorum*

griffin, gryphus, E: griffin, D: Greif; a legendary animal of the ancient and medieval literary tradition; it was thought to have the body of a lion, the head of an eagle, and wings 半狮半鹰，见 Dante, *Commedia* (the features of the two animals reflect the two natures of Christ)

Griseldis, Griselda, a woman humbly enduring the harsh treatment of her husband 格瑞西德，见 Boccaccio, *Decamerone* 10.10

Groote, Gerhardus, E: Gerhard Groote, 1340—1384, founder of the Brothers of common life. He came from Deventer, studied at Cologne, Paris, and Prague and became preacher in the diocese of Utrecht. His disciples at Deventer and Zwolle founded the Brethren of Common Life. Making mystical spirituality more practical, balanced, and methodical, he became the father of the movement known as "devotio moderna". 格劳特，见 Thomas a Kempis, *De imitiatione Christi*

Grosseteste, Robertus, (=Grosso Capitis), E: Robert the Greathead, D: Robert Grosseteste; 1175—1253; Franciscan scholar who studied at Oxford, Paris; he was the first chancellor of Oxford University and became Bishop of Lincoln 1235—1253; urging the study of Arabic, Greek, and mathematics, he wrote works on optics and calendar reform. Being a zealous bishop, he invited Franciscans to come to Lincoln. 格劳斯泰特，见 Rogerius Baco

gryphus => griffin

Gualbertus, Johannes = Johannes Gualbertus

Guarino de Verona, +1460; Italian scholar who went to Constantinople to learn Greek. He translated and edited Greek and Latin classics.挂瑞诺

Gudrun, the daughter of King Giuki (Gunther), married to Sigurd.古德润，见 Snorri Sturluson, *Edda*

Guelphi et Ghibellini, E: Guelfs and Ghibellines, D: Welfen und Waiblinge; two opposed factions in Italy in the 13th century. One supported the Bavarian Welfs (=Guelphi), the other the Waiblinge (=Ghibellini). Guelfs had papalist inclinations, Ghibellines demanded equality between Pope and emperor or a certain political influence of the emperor in (northern) Italy.归尔甫派和吉伯林派，见 Dante (favored imperial intervention and tried to keep Florence free from papal influence)

Guido de Spoleto, (Wido), Emperor 891—894 古多/维多

Guido de Arezzo, E: Guido of Arezzo, +1050; a Benedictine monk, musician at Arezzo, he is known for the introduction of modern musical notation.古多

Guido de Vienne (=Calixtus II, 1119—1124), Archbishop of Vienne 古多

Guigo, Fr: Guiguese du Chastel; +1137; Carthusian Prior, author of the Carthusian Rule.古依格

Guilelmus = Wilhelmus

Guillaume de Lorris, E: William Lorris, D: Wilhelm von Lorris, 1213—1237, author of the first part of the *Roman de la Rose*.罗里斯，见 *Le Roman de la rose*

gula, E: gluttony, D: Essgier; => vitium 饕餮，见 Dante, *Commedia* (in Purgatory fasting helps to correct the sins of gluttony)

Gundissalinus, Dominicus, (Gundisalvi); archdeacon in Toledo, translator of Arab Aristotelian works, 12th century.多米尼库斯

Guntharius, E: Gunther, D: Gunther; the king of Burgundy, perhaps related to Gundahar, king of Burgundy 412—436 AD. 贡特尔，见 Ekkehard, *Waltharii poiesis*, Snorri Sturluson, *Edda* (Giuki = Gunther, father of Gudrun), Appendix, *Nibelungenlied* (brother of Kriemhild, husband of Brunhild)

Gunther, Archbishop of Cologne ca. 860 巩特尔

Guenther, hermit, +1045; missionary in Bohemia 翁特尔

Guenther de Schwarzenburg, count of Thurningia, royal candidate in 1348 巩特尔

Gurnemanz, the uncle of Parzival who taught him courtly manners 古尔内曼斯, 见 Wolfram, *Parzival*

Gutenberg, Johann, +1468; the inventor of the printing press with movable metal types around 1445. The first book to be printed was the so-called "Gutenberg Bibel". 古腾贝格

H

Habsburg, House of Hapsburg / Habsburg, Austrian royal (imperial) dynasty in power from 1278 to 1919. Rudolf IV, count of Habsburg, was elected king of Germany in 1273, thus ending the Interregnum. From 1438 through modern times, the Emperors of the Holy Roman Empire came from the House of Habsburg. 哈布斯堡王朝

Hadith, the sacred tradition based upon Muhammand's words not preserved in the *Qur'an*. 圣训, 见 *Qur'an*

Hadrianus I, E: Adrian, D: Hadrian; Pope 772—795, from Roman nobility; facing pressure from the Lombards he turned to the Frankish king and received Charlemagne in Rome in 774; Adrian requested the Byzantine empres Irene to summon the Second Council of Nicaea (787) to suppress iconoclasm. 哈德良

Hadrianus II, E: Adrian, D: Hadrian; Pope 867—872, who appointed Methodius archbishop of Pannonia and banned Photius. 哈德良

Hadrianus III, E: Adrian, D: Hadrian; Pope 884—885. His brief pontificate was marred by factional strife in Rome. 哈德良

Hadrianus IV, E: Adrian, D: Hadrian; Pope 1154—1159, the only Pope from England, originally Nicolaus Breakspear; he went to Skandinavia as papal legate in 1152 and crowned Frederick I Barbarossa in 1155 but later supported the cities of north Italy to block the extension of imperial power south of the Alps, thus he faced increasing pressure from Frederick I. 哈德良

haeresia, E: heresy, D: Haeresie; a teaching contradicting the orthodox Christian faith. Some heretics directly attacked the clergy of the official Church. 异端, 见 Johannes Damascenus, *Pēgē gnōseōs*

haereticus, E: heretic, D: Haeretiker; a person who obstinately holds to a view that is contrary to one or more of the fundamental beliefs of the Church; the obstinate holding to the error when instructed by a properly constituted authority was punished severely 持异端者

Hagen, (Hagano), one of the heroes of Burgundy, a loyal vassal of king Gunther; => Gunther 哈根, 见 Ekkehard, *Waltharius*, Appendix, *Nibelungenlied*

hagiographia, E: hagiography, D: Hagiographie; historical or edifying literature about Christian saints, for example *martyrologia*. 关于圣人/圣徒的文学, 见 Jacobus de Voragine, *Legenda aurea*

Haimo, Bishop of Halberstadt, historian, exegete, +853. 海莫

Hakon, (Haakon), King of Norway 938—961 哈孔

Hamburg, city on the lower Elbe (Germany); it began as a fortress constructed by Charlemagne and had a church in 811. In 834 it became the seat of an archbishop and the center of missions in northern Europe. Destroyed several times by the Vikings it prospered since the 11th ct. and became a principal member of the Hanseatic League, an association of merchants and towns of north Germany. 汉堡/不来梅

Hamlet => Amled

Harald, E: Harald Bluetooth, D: Harald Blauzahn; King of Denmark, who accepted Christianity around 860. 哈拉尔, 见 Saxo Grammaticus, *Gesta Danorum*

Harding, Stephanus, E: Stephen Harding, D: Stefan Harding; the third abbot of Citeaux, 1109—1134, author of the constitutions *Charta caritatis* of 1119. 哈丁, 见 Ordo Cisterciensium

Harold II, King of England, defeated by William the Conqueror in 1066. => William 哈拉尔

Hartmann von Aue, E: Hartmann of Aue; ca. 1150—1220, German minnesinger (poet). 哈特曼, 见 *Der arme Heinrich*

Harun Al-Rashid, Abbassid caliph, 786—809, who ruled Islam during a very prosperous era. At his luxurious court at Baghdad he patronized poets, artists, philosophers and scientists. 河伦

Hastings, site of the battle by which William the Conqueror defeated the Anglosaxons under Harold II in 1066. Harold fell and William was consequently crowned king of England. 哈斯丁斯, 见 Malmesburiensis, *Gesta regum Anglorum*

Hedwigis, Pol. Jadwiga, +1399, Polish queen, daughter of Louis I of Hungary. In 1386 she married Jagiello of Lithuania. She restored the regions of Lvov and Galich to Poland.赫德维

Hegira, Hidjra, Higra, Hejira, the emigration of Muhammad from Mecca to Medina in September 622. This year serves as base year of the Muslim calendar.希吉勒

Heidelberg, city on the Neckar（Germany）; the university（the oldest in Germany）was founded in 1386.海德堡

Helena = Elena

Helfta, monastery of Cistercian nuns near Eisleben （Saxony）, founded in 1228. It was a place of spiritual education, home of the authors Mechtildis and Gertrudis, and during the era of Abbess Gertrude of Hackeborn（1251—1292）it was the center of German mysticism.赫尔弗塔

Heliand, a poem based on Tatian's harmony of the Gospels. It was written in Old Saxon language, ca. 830.《救世主》,见 Appendix

Heloise, 1098—1164, pupil and lover of Abelard, later abbess of Argenteul and of Le Paraclet, which Abelard had founded.埃洛伊兹,见 Abaelardus

德国国王：

Henricus I, E: Henry the Fowler, D: Heinrich I, duke of Saxony, German King 919—936, he was the father of Otto I.亨利

Henricus II Pius, E: Henry the Saint, D: Heinrich der Heilige, St.; King of Germany 1002—1024; he generously supported or founded churches, was crowned emperor in 1014 by Benedict VIII.亨利

Henricus III, E: Henry III, D: Heinrich III, King of Germany 1039—1056, Emperor in 1046, one of the most powerful German kings of the Middle Ages. He tried to restore order in the Church in Rome, held a synod at Sutri 1046 and supported the German Pope Clement II. 亨利，见 Wipo, *Gesta Chuonradi*（dedicated to Henry III）

Henricus IV, E: Henry IV, D: Heinrich IV, 1050—1106, German King since 1056, in power since 1066, he tried to depose Pope Gregory VII at a synod in Worms in 1076, was excommunicated but absolved again at Canossa in Jan. 1077; he overcame the opposition of the German nobles, invaded Rome and was crowned emperor in 1084. 亨利四世,见 Otto Frisingensis, *Chronica*（critical of Henry's excommunication）

Henricus V, E: Henry V, D: Heinrich V, German King 1106—1125, he forced his coronation in Rome in 1111.亨利

Henricus VI, E: Henry VI, D: Heinrich VI, King of Germany 1190—1197, son of Barbarossa. He married Constance of Naples –Sicilia, thus acquired control over southern Italy and Sicily. He held Richard I of England captive from 1192 to 1194 and released him only on payment of an enormous sum. Henry died on a crusade.亨利

Henricus VII, E: Henry VII, Henry of Luxemburg, D: Heinrich VII; King of Germany 1308—1313, crowned emperor in 1312.亨利,见 *Bulla aurea*

Henricus（VII）, E: Henry, D: Heinrich, son of Frederick II, who had him elected king of Germany in 1220. He opposed his father in 1234, led a revolt but was defeated, probably committed suicide in 1235.亨利

英国国王：

Henricus I Beauclerc, E: Henry, D: Heinrich; King of England 1100—1135, he arranged an agreement with Anselm of Canterbury concerning the investiture issue.亨利

Henricus II, E: Henry of Anjou –Plantagenet, D: Heinrich II; King of England 1154—1189, married to Eleanor of Aquitaine, whom he kept confined from 1173. His empire included England, Normandy, Anjou, Brittany, and Aquitaine. He developed the system of royal courts and tried to control the Church（Diet of Clarendon 1164）. First he was a friend of Thomas Becket, the Archbishop of Canterbury, later he opposed him and suggested his murder. 亨利二世,见 Johannes Saresberensis, *Policraticus*

Henricus III, E: Henry, D: Heinrich; 1216—1272, King of England, who confirmed the *Magna Charta*.亨利

Henricus IV, E: Henry, D: Heinrich; King of England 1399—1413; He directed a revolt that led to the murder of Richard II and remained an usurper in the eyes of many. He started to suppress Wycliffe's movement in 1400.亨利

巴伐利亚王：

Henricus Leo, E: Henry the Lion, D: Heinrich der Loewe; +1195; Duke of Saxony and Bavaria, the most powerful of the German dukes. He led the Welf faction in Germany and opposed the Hohenstaufens. Because he refused to support

Frederick Barbarossa against the Lombard League in 1176 (Battle of Legnano) he was deprived of his fiefs and returned to his private lands Brunswick and Lueneburg..亨利

其它：

Henricus de Ghent, E: Henry of Ghent, D: Heinrich; +1293, philosopher and theologian, called "doctor solemnis", he was professor at Paris, an exponent of Augustinism and thus opposed Thomas.亨利

Henricus de Langenstein, E: Henry; D: Heinrich (Heinbuch), +1397, German author, philosopher, theologian, vice rector of the University of Paris and one of the founders of the University of Vienna. He authored the first Hebrew grammar in the German language. He suggested a council to end the division of the Church (1379, 1380).亨利

Henricus de Lausanne, E: Henry of Lausanne, D: Heinrich von Lausanne; +1145; a heretic agitator against the Church in the Provence (France). He insisted on absolute poverty for all churchmen. 亨利

Henricus Suso, E: Henry Seuse, D: Heinrich Seuse = Suso

Henricus de Veldeke, E: Henry of Veldeke, D: Heinrich von Veldeke; 1140—1210, author of German courtly love poetry; his main work is the *Eneide*.亨利，见 Hartmann

Heraclius, Gr: Hērakleios, E: Heraclius; Emperor of Constantinople 610—641, who recovered Asia Minor, Armenia, and Syria from the Persians but was defeated by Muslim forces in 636.赫拉克留斯

herba, E: herbs, D: Kraeuter 花草，见 Walahfridus, *Liber de cultura hortorum*

Hercules, Gr: Hēraklēs, E: Heracles, hero in Greek mythology, model of hard work 赫拉克勒斯，见 Aldhelmus, *De laudibus* (Heracles compared to Samson)

Heriger de Lobbes, + 1007, abbot and director of a school at the monastery of Lobbes (Laubach) in Germany. Author of theological and mathematical treatises.赫瑞格尔

Hermannus Contractus, E: Herman the Lame, D: Hermann von Reichenau; 1015—1054, son of a count in Swabia, educated at Reichenau he became monk in Reichenau. Although crippled from birth he was one of the most erudite scholars and poets of his time.赫尔曼，见 *Chronicon, De octo vitiis*

Hermannus de Salza, E: Herman of Salza, D: Hermann von Salza; Hochmeister (grand master) of the Teutonic Knights 1210—1239. Frederick II assigned him in 1226 to conquer and convert the regions occupied by the Prussians. Herman tried to reconcile the Emperor and the Pope.赫尔曼

hermeneutica, ars, E: hermeneutics, D: Hermeneutik => interpretatio

Herzeloyde, the mother of Parzival 赫尔则罗德，见 Wolfram von Eschenbach, *Parzival*

Hesychasmus, E: hesychasm, D: Hesychasmus; A kind of monastic quietism in the monasteries of Mt. Athos and on Mt. Sinai. Interior tranquility was sought through a suppression of all thought, the repetition of a short prayer and control of breathing. The most influential and controversial exponent was Gregorius Palamas (+1359). Hesychasm never spread to the West.宁静派/静修主义

Hexen = malificae

Heynlin de Stein, Johannes Heynlin de Lapide, E: John Heynlin of Stein; 1428—1496, German theologian belonging to the school of realism. He was rector of the University of Paris and one of the founders of the first printing press in Paris (1470).海恩林

hierarchia, E: hierarchy, D: Hierarchie, the sacred order of leadership within the Church 圣统制，见 Hrabanus, *De institutione*

Hieronymus, E: Jerome, D: Hieronymus; 347—420 AD, eminent Biblical scholar of late antiquity who translated the Bible into Latin (Vulgate)热罗尼莫/哲罗姆，见 Hrabanus, *De institutione cler.*, Photios, *Logos*

Hlerosolyma = Jerusalem

Hildebrand, Germanic name, in German epic the faithful armorbearer of Dietrich of Bern. In the *Hildebrandslied* from ca. 820 Hildebrand faces his son Hadubrand, who fails to recognize the father, in battle. Hildebrand was the name of Pope Gregory VII 希尔德布兰德，见 Appendix, *Nibelungenlied*

Hildegardis, E: Hildegarde, D: Hildegard; St., 1098-1179, German Benedictine sister in Disibodenberg, then abbess in Bingen, respected author of medical and spiritual literature. She kept correspondence with kiings, popes, prelates, and saints. => Bernardus 希尔德加德，见 *Causae et curae*

Hiltgunt, (Hildegund), the bride of Walter of Aquitania 希尔德贡特, 见 *Waltharii poiesis*

Hincmarus, E: Hincmar, D: Hinkmar; Archbishop of Rheims 845—882, counsellor of Charles II, author of treatises on canonical, pastoral, political, philosophical, and historical subjects. He condemned the divorce of Lothair II of Lorraine and imprisoned Gottschalk.安克马尔

Hirsau, monastery near Stuttgart (Germany) founded in 830. It became a base of Gregorian reforms after 1070.希尔骚

Hispania, Sp: Espania, E: Spain, D: Spanien; => Castilia 西班牙, 见 Eginhardus, *Vita Caroli* (campaign in Spain in 778 AD)

historia, E: history, D: Geschichte; medieval authors started to compile histories of their own nations or regions and of local churches or monasteries. Lifes of saints were very popular, but sometimes semi-legendary. => chronologia 历史, 见 Beda, Paulus Diaconus, Notkerus Balbulus, Wipo, Hermannus Contractus, Cosmas Pragensis, Nestorius, Malmesburiensis, Anna Komnene, Galfredus Monemuthensis, Otto Frisingensis, Joachim (three ages), Saxo Grammaticus, Vincentius Bellovacensis, *Speculum maius* (the *Speculum historiale* is a world history), Rubruk, Jacobus de Voragine, Froissart, Piccolomini

Historia ecclesiastica gentis Anglorum, E: *Ecclesiastical History of England*, the earliest work on the history of England《英格兰教会史》, 见 Beda Venerabilis

Historia Langobardorum, E: *History of the Lombards*, a work by Paulus Diaconus《隆巴德人的历史》

Historia regum Britanniae, E: *History of the Kings of Britain*, a work by Geoffrey of Monmouth《不列颠诸王纪》, 见 Galfredus

Hohenstaufen, aristocratic family of Swabia (Germany) founded by Count Frederick of Bueren (+ 1105) who married Agnes, the daughter of Henry IV. After the death of Henry V in 1125 the Salian possessions fell to the Hohenstaufens, and from 1138 to 1254 this family occupied the German throne. Powerful rulers were Frederick I Barbarossa (1152—1190) and Frederick II (1212—1250).霍亨斯陶芬

Hohenzollern, aristocratic family of Swabia (Germany), since 1192 in possession of Nuremberg, they received the margravate of Brandenburg in 1415.霍亨佐伦

Holy Roman Empire => Imperium Romanum

homicidium, E: homicide, D: Toetung; => vita 杀人, 见 Thomas Aquinas, *Summa theologiae* II.II. 64 (discussion of the lawfulness of homicide in self-defence etc.)

homilia, homiliarium = praedicare

homoteleuton, E: rhyme, D: Reim; in the Middle Ages the poets developed rhyme poetry which gradually substituted the metric poetry of antiquity.尾韵诗, 见 Otfried, *Evangelienbuch*

honor, E: honor, D: Ehre; in medieval literature the self-esteem of the knight is often depicted; => eques 自尊, 荣誉, 见 Chretien, *Erec et Enide*, Hartmann, *Der arme Heinrich* (loss of honor)

Honorius II, antipope 1061—1071, originally Cadalus, Bishop of Parma.霍诺利乌斯

Honorius II, Pope 1124—1130, originally Bishop Lambert of Ostia, who kept contact with King Lothair.霍诺利乌斯

Honorius III, Pope 1216—1227, originally Cardinal Savelli; he approved the Franciscan, Dominican, and Carmelite Orders and crowned Frederick II in 1220. Aware of Frederick's political ambitions he urged him to lead a crusade against the Turks. 霍诺利乌斯

Honorius IV, Pope 1285—1287, from the Roman Savelli family.霍诺利乌斯

Honorius Augustodunensis, E: Honorius of Autun, ca. 1100—1156, monk in Regensburg and encylopedic writer, exponent of a kind of Christian Platonism.霍诺利乌斯

honos = honor

Horarium, Fr.: Livres d'heures; E: office of the hours, D: Stundenbuch; prayer books flourishig in the 14th and 15th centuries; see: liturgia horarum. 日课, 祈祷本

horologium, E: clock, D: Uhrwerk; possibly Boethius invented the first wheel clock (after 500 AD). The first weight-driven clock is reported to have been built by Pacificus, a ninth-century archdeacon of Verona. Pope Sylvester II may have constructed a mechanical clock around 996. Many cathedral spires, monastery churches and public square had mechanical clocks since the 12th century.钟表, 见 machina

Hortulus animae, E: *Garden of the Soul*; D: *Seelengaertlein*, popular spiritual book in the late Middle Ages.灵魂之花园

hortus, E: garden, D: Garten 花园，见 Walahfridus, *Liber de cultura hortorum*

Hospitaliter = Antoniti

Hospitaliti, E: Knights Hospitallers, D: Johanniter, Malteser; knight order, founded 1119 in Jerusalem, mainly concerned with medical services; their hospitals were model institutions; since 1310 their main center was Rhodus, and from 1530—1798 their headquarters were at Malta; Reformation and secularization after 1800 brought severe losses for them.医院骑士团

Hospitaliti de Spiritu Sancto, E: Hospitallers of the Holy Spirit, D: Taubenbrueder; founded ca. 1180 by Guido de Montpellier, they cared for the Hospital S. Spirito in Sassia in Rome after 1204.圣神医务会

hospitium, E: hospital, D: Spital; In the early Christian communities deacons cared for the sick. Basil founded one of the first hospitals near Caesarea in the 4th century. Individual parishes and cathedrals began to set up institutions for the care of the sick during the Middle Ages, but the main factor in this development were the monastic orders organized for nursing since the twelfth century, such as the Order of the Holy Spirit（Hospitaliti de Sancto Spiritu）, the Knights Hospitallers, and the Antonines.医院

hostia, E: Host, D: Hostie; the Holy Bread, Body of Christ 圣饼/基督圣体，见 *Parzival*

Hrabanus, (=Rabanus), E: Hraban, D: Hrabanus Maurus, 784—856, German Benedictine monk, Abbot of Fulda, important educator and author 拉班努，见 *De institutione clericorum*, Appendix, *Heliand*（dependent on Hrabanus）

Hrotsvita, (Roswitha), ca. 935—975, a German nun in Gandersheim, author of several Latin works.赫若斯维塔，见 *Abraham eremita, Dulcitius, Theophilus*

Hucbaldus, E: Hugbald, D: Hukbald; + ca. 930; monk of St.-Amand in Flanders, he introduced polyphony.胡克巴德

Hugo Capet, E: Hugh Capet, D: Hugo Capet; +996; This duke of the Franks（956）was elected King of France（987）and so became the founder of the Capetian Dynasty.胡格/雨果

Hugo de St. Cher, E: Hugh of Saint-Cher, +1264; French Dominican, scholar, cardinal; organizer of scholarly institutions to correct Bible（Vulgate）editions, author of the first Bible concordance.胡格/雨果

Hugo de Cluny, E: Hugh the Great, E: Hugo von Cluny; St., +1109; Abbot in Cluny 1049—1109 who upheld the ideal of St. Benedict and supported Church reforms; he was an advisor of Gregory VII.胡格/雨果，见 Cluny

Hugo de Payens, one of eight French knights who founded the Templars in Jerusalem in 1119.胡格/雨果

Hugo de St. Victor, E: Hugh of St. Victor, D: Hugo von St. Victor; 1096—1141, German monk who moved to the newly founded Abbey of St.-Victor in Paris in 1115, where he became the leading master at the abbey. He was an influential scholar and mystic, even praised as "the second Augustine". => St. Victor 胡格/雨果，见 *Didascalicon*

Humanismus, E: Humanism, D: Humanismus; the revival of classical studies and poetry in Europe. Jerome first felt the tension between the beauty of non-Christian literature and the faith. Medieval scholars selectively used the classics. Italian scholars since Petrarca（+1374）, emphasized the intrinsic value of any natural human experience. Many of the Renaissance Popes were outstanding humanist scholars themselves. Humanism was conducive to Biblical studies but had some harmful influence due to a naturalist world view and the satirizing of clergy and Church institutions（see Boccaccio, Erasmus）.人文主义

Humbertus de Silva Candida, E: Humbert of Silva-Candida; D: Humbert; +1061, monk in Moyenmoutier（Lorraine）, since 1050 Bishop of Silva Candida and cardinal; influential legate in Constantinople in 1054.亨伯特

Humiliati, E: Humiliati, D: Humiliaten; a pious lay movement among cloth producers in Milan and N Italy; many of them joined the Waldenses, the rest was reorganized in 1201 as religious order with a Third Order.卑微派

humilitas, E: humility, D: Demut; the virtue opposed to pride, => superbia 谦卑，见 Hugo, *De fructibus carnis et spiritus*（humility is the root of all virtues）, Thomas a Kempis, *De imitatione Christi*（humility and anti-intellectualism）

Hungaria, E: Hungary, D: Ungarn; the ancestors of the Hungarians were the Magyars（Madyars）, a Finno-Ugric people living at the Volga and the mouth of the Don. Around 880 AD they moved into the region of the middle Danube and raided western areas as far as France until Otto I defeated them at the Lechfeld in 855. In 975 their ruler Geza was baptized, and his son St. Stephen who was crowned king in 1000, established the civil and ecclesiastical structure of medieval Hungary. In 1241 the country was ravaged by the Mongols, and the battle of Nicopolis (1396) destroyed the army of Emperor Sigismund, which implied the loss of Serbia and Dalmatia. Janos Hunyadi led the country in a time of Turkish aggression, and his son Matthias Corvinus was elected king (1458—1490). 匈牙利, 见 Stephanus

Hunni, E: Huns, D: Hunnen; a nomadic tribe from central Asia. Having invaded China the Huns moved to the west and arrived in the area north of the Black Sea ca. 375 AD, subjugating the Alans and Ostrogoths and causing the Visigoths to flee westward across the Danube. Until 450 the Huns settled in what became later Hungary, but in 451 their leader Attila led the Huns to destroy the kingdom of Burgundy. They also threatened to sack Rome. In Gaul an army of Romans, Visigoths, and Franks under Aetius defeated them at Chalons (Gaul), and in 453 Attila died, thus invoking the early decline of Hunnic power. => Attila 匈奴人, 见 Cynewulf, *Elene*, Eginhardus, *Vita Caroli* (wars against Huns, 797—799), Ekkehard, *Waltharii poiesis*, Snorri Sturluson, *Edda*

Hunyadi, Johannes, (Janos Hunyadi), E: John Hunyadi, +1456; Hungarian regent, 1387—1456, he defeated the Turks in 1456, which saved Hungary from falling to the Turks. His son Matthias Corvinus was elected King of Hungary (1458—1490). 匈雅提

Hus, (**Huss**), Jan, E: John Hus, D: Johann Hus; 1372—1415, Bohemian reformer, national leader and heretic. He studied at Prague and taught theology at the university, even became rector in 1409. He was influenced by Wyclif's ideas and was excommunicated in 1412. He was sentenced at the Council of Constance, and his death at the stake made him a national martyr. Some of his treatises are in Czech, most in Latin. 胡斯, 见 Wycliffe

Hy = Iona

I

Ibn Rushd = Averroes

Ibn Sina = Avicenna

iconoclasmus, Gr: eikōn-klasma (breaking of icons), E: iconoclasm, D: Bildersturm; the destruction of icons; a campaign in the Greek Church to remove religious images (edict of Emperor Leo III in 726) or to destroy them (edict of 730), which remained the policy of Byzantine emperors between 725 and 842; it led to fierce struggles in the 8th and 9th century, and aggravated the tensions between East and West. The destruction of icons was condemned by most believers in the east and in the west. 破坏圣像运动/反圣像运动/捣毁圣像运动/圣像破坏之争, 见 Johannes Damascenus, *Pēgē gnōseōs,*

idea, Gr: eidos, idea, L: idea, ratio aeterna, forma, causa primordialis, prototypa, species; E: idea, eternal form, species, D: Idee, Urbild; according to the traditon of Plato, the intelligible world is the world of ideas, and all things are created through the ideas 理念, 见 Eriugena, *De divisione naturae*, Anselmus, *Proslogion* (idea of God), Alanus, *Anticlaudianus* (the ideas an elements of all things are at the palace of God in Heaven), Thomas Aquinas, *Summa theologiae* I.84,6 (sensual perception is needed in addition to rationes aeternae; universal ideas exist ante rem, in re, post rem), Occam, *Sententiae* ("species" is only a "sign" in the soul and not in the things)

ieiunium, => jejunium

Ignatius, Gr: Ignatios, E: Ignatius, D: Ignatius; Patriarch at Byzantium 847—858, 867—877, rival of Photius. He was deposed in 858 but reinstated in 867. 伊格纳提乌斯, 见 Photios

ignis, E: fire, D: Feuer; => aqua, empyreum, scintilla animae 火, 见 Alanus, *Anticlaudianus* (empyreum), Snorri Sturluson, *Edda* (Brynhild is surrounded by a circle of fire, the Waberlohe)

ignorantia, E: ignorance, D: Unwissenheit; => sapientia 无知, 见 Wolfram, *Parzival* (the "fool"), Nicolaus Cusanus, *De docta ignorantia*

imagines, E: images, icons, D: Bilder, sacred images; => iconoclasmus 圣像, 圣像争论, 见 Bonaventura, *Itinerarium mentis in Deum* (imaginatio)

imago Dei, E: the image of God, D: Bild Gottes; according to the Bible man is created in the image of God and thus always tries to recover this original self. 神的肖像, 见 Bernardus, *De diligendo Deo* (man is created ad imaginem Dei)

Imitatio Christi, E: *Imitation of Christ*, D: *Die Nachfolge Christi*, a very popular spiritual book by Thomas a Kempis, written ca. 1420《师主篇》/《效法基督》,见 Thomas a Kempis

imperator, E: emperor, D: Kaiser, the title of German kings since the time of Charlemagne who was crowned in Rome in 800 AD (however not as leader of the "Holy Roman Empire", an expression used only since ca. 1200); the emperor was supposed to get papal support (=> corona) and was accepted by medieval kings in northern Europe as the highest secular authority, although his actual power was very limited, since he was elected by the "electors" (Kurfuersten, seven German dukes); from the 14th to the 16th centuries the emperor convoked and presided the "imperial diet" (Reichstag), where the nobles of the empire met. => *Bulla aurea* (position of the electors), Carolus Magnus, Carolus IV, Conradus II, Fredericus II, Henricus IV 皇帝,见 Notkerus, *Gesta Caroli Magni imperatoris*, Wipo, *Gesta Chuonradi II imperatoris* (emperor = "vicarius Christi" in an "imperium Christianum"), Gregorius VII, *Dictatus Papae* 12 (the Pope may depose emperors), Bernardus, *De consideratione* (the pope may ask the emperor to defend the Church)

Imperium Romanum Sanctum, E: Holy Roman Empire, D: Heiliges Roemisches Reich (Deutscher Nation); the institution that originated in the year 800 when Pope Leo III crowned Charlemagne and proclaimed him "Emperor of the Romans". Throughout the Middle Ages German kings tried to go to Rome to be crowned by the Pope, but they also used their imperial title to justify territorial claims in Italy. Since the coronation of Otto I in 962 the paternalistic attitude of German kings created controversies. 神圣罗马帝国

In calumniatorem Platonis, E: *Against the Calumniator of Plato*, a work by Bessarion《反驳柏拉图的诽谤者》,见 Bessarion

incarnatio, E: incarnation, D: Inkarnation, the theological tenet that God became man in the person of Jesus Christ 神降生成人/道成肉身,见 Anselmus, *Cur Deus homo*, Bernardus, *De diligendo Deo* (incarnation as a sign of love), Thomas Aquinas, *Summa contra gentiles* (explanation by rational means), Eckhart, *Buch der goettlichen Troestungen* (incarnatio continua)

inclusae, E: recluses, D: Inklusen; monks or nuns who led a life immured in a small cell.封闭隐修者

India, E: India, D: Indien; => China 印度,见 *Alexandreis* (Alexander in India)

indulgentiae, E: indulgences, D: Ablass; Indulgences were a practice in the Church life of the late Middle Ages, usually understood as doing penance or giving alms in support of the deceased ("remissio sive indulgentia a poena et culpa"); this pious practice helped to build magnificent churches but also gave rise to misuse and superstition. 大赦,罪罚的赦免,见 Chaucer, *Canterbury Tales* (a pardoner selling indulgences)

infernum, (tartarus), E: hell, the underworld, D: Hoelle; according to Christian tradition the place where the condemned souls receive their punishment. => diabolus 地狱,见 Walahfridus, *Visio Wettini*, Alanus, *Anticlaudianus* (evil powers from hell attack man), Dante, *Commedia* (inferno)

infinitum, E: infinite, D: Unendlichkeit; 无限,见 Thomas Aquinas, *Summa contra gentiles* (only an infinite object can satisfy man)

Ingolstadt, a city in upper Bavaria, first mentioned in 806 AD, it became the residence of the dukes of Bavaria in 1392; the University of Ingolstadt, was authorized by Pope Pius II in 1458 (as studium generale) and became a center of Humanism. 因格尔施塔特

Innocens II, E: Innocent, D: Innozenz; Pope 1130—1143, originally Cardinal Gregory, faced opposition from Antipope Anacletus II, he fled to France and was supported by St. Bernard.依诺森

Innocens III, E: Innocent, D: Innozenz; Pope 1198—1216, originally Lothar Segni, one of the most influential Popes in history, expert of canon law, he confirmed the new mendicant orders and organized the 4th Lateran council in 1215. He could persuade John of England to accept Stephen Langton as archbishop of Canterbury and demanded that Philip II Augustus took back his wife Ingeborg. He hoped that all Christian kings would accept his position as overlord, thus he might be able to prevent wars among them and to enhance the success of a crusade against the Turks. 依诺森,见 *De miseria humanae conditionis*

Innocens IV, E: Innocent, D: Innozenz; Pope 1243—1254, originally Sinibald Fieschi, avoided Frederick II and went to Lyon (1244—1251), where he held a synod in 1244.依诺森

Innocens V, E: Innocent, D: Innozenz; Bl., Pope 1276, who worked for the union with the Greek Church.依诺森

Innocens VI, E: Innocent; D: Innozenz; Pope 1352—1362, he resided in Avignon, reorganized the Curia and directed Cardinal Albornoz to bring order to the Papal States.依诺森

Innocens VII, E: Innocent, D: Innozenz; Pope 1404—1406. He could not resolve the Western Schism. 依诺森

inquisitio, E: inquisition, D: Inquisition; an ecclesiastical institution (court) to systematically find and punish heretics, in response to the spread of sects (Cathars, Albigensians, Waldensians) after 1180. The inquisition was supported by the Lateran Council of 1215 and by Emperor Frederick II. It was notorious for reviving the means of torture used by Roman Law in antiquity. The inquisition court was active only in France, Italy, and parts of Germany. After a peak in the second half of the 13th century it generally ceased to operate in the early 14th century. The inquisition in Spain after 1478 was of a different kind and aimed at the suppression of Jews and Muslims. => Eckhart, Judaei, malefica, persecutio 宗教裁判所/异端裁判所

institutio, E: education, D: Erziehung, => educatio

intellectus, E: intellect, understanding, D: Intellekt, Verstehen; one of the mental powers, also symbol of the Second Divine Person (Christ) 理智,理解能力,见 Anselmus, *Monologion, Proslogion* (fides quaerens intellectum), Avicenna, *Kitab* (intelligentia agens, intelligentia materialis), Bernardus, *De diligendo Deo* (intelligitur in quantum amatur), Averroes, *Tafsir* (intellectus agens, intellectus materialis), Maimonides, *More nevukhim* (amor Dei intellectualis), Bonaventura, *Itinerarium* (intellectus, intelligentia), Thomas Aquinas, *Summa theologiae* (intellectus agens, the cause of insight), Raimundus Lullus, *Ars magna* (credere and intellegere)

interdictum, E: interdict, D: Interdikt; the prohibition of sacramental actions except baptism and extreme unction. Interdicts were first imposed on churches of a city, then on entire dioceses, and from the 12th century on whole countries. Interdicts were used as political tool by some Popes, for example by Innocent III who tried to force King John to accept Stephen Langton as archbishop of Canterbury and placed England under an interdict from 1208 to 1213.禁罚

interpretatio, E: interpretation, D: Auslegung; the explanation of texts, especially of Biblical documents; => Biblia exposita 解释,诠释学,见 Abaelardus, *Sic et non* (hermeneutical rules for the discernment of truth), Nicolaus de Lyra, *Postilla* (different layers of meaning in the text)

investitura, E: investiture, D: Investitur; the act of formally putting someone into an office or a landholding; the ceremony of handing over regal rights to a (Church) official, usually performed by handing over the bishop's ring and crozier or similar symbols; Church reformers in the 11th and 12th centuries opposed lay rulers (kings) who invested clergy with the symbols of their positions, => Investiture Controversy 授权礼/授职礼/叙任仪式,见 Gratianus, *Concordantia discordantium canonum*

investiturae controversio, E: Investiture Controversy, D: Investiturstreit; conflict over the right of lay people (kings) to bestow powers to a bishop, (see Gregory VII), resolved by the Concordat of Worms in 1122.授权之争/主教任命权之争/叙任权之争,见 Gratianus, *Concordantia discordantium canonum*

invidia, E: envy, D: Neid; one of the cardinal sins; => vitium 嫉妒,见 Dante, *Commedia* (Purgatorio)

Ioachim = Joachim

Ioannes = Johannes

Iona, (=Hy, Io, Eo), a monastery founded 560 AD at the west coast of Scotland. It became the cultural basis of Irish missions. Iona had a leadership position within the Celtic church until the Synod of Whitby (664) favored the Roman liturgy and customs and opposed the Celtic tradition. Iona was destroyed by Vikings in 986. 伊奥纳,见 *Columba*

ira, E: wrath, D: Zorn; one of the cardinal sins, => vitium 愤怒,见 Dante, *Commedia* (in Purgatory praying the Agnus Dei corrects the sins of wrath)

Ireland, (Eire, Hibernia), D: Irland; St. Patrick converted the island after 432, and Irish culture enjoyed a Golden Age from 500—800. In this period the monasteries and the work of missionaries such as Columba and Columban were of central importance. In the 9th and 10th centuries the island was attacked by Vikings. After that English immigrants grew in numbers and influence, which led to a revolt (1315) led by Edward Bruce, brother of Robert I Bruce, king of Scotland. English influence weakened somewhat during the 14th century.爱尔兰, 见 Adamnanus, Aldhelmus, Columba, Columbanus, Eriugena

Irene, E: Irene, D: Irene; +803, byzantine Empress 780—802. Ruling as regent for her young son Constantine VI she tried to correct the iconoclastic policy of former emperors.伊任内

Irnerius, +1130, law teacher in Bologna, founder of a "Roman School of Law" in 1084. He introduced closses to expound Roman law. 伊内利乌斯, 见 Gratianus

ironia, E: irony, humor, D: Ironie, Humor; 讽刺, 见 Hrotsvita, *Dulcitius*, Anonymus, *Carmina Burana*

Isaac II Angelus, Byzantine emperor 1185—1195 and 1203—1204. In 1195 his brother Alexius III deposed and blinded him. The Crusaders put him back on the throne in July 1203 only to dethrone him again.依撒克

Isabella de Castilia, E: Isabella I of Castile, D: Isabella von Kastilien; +1504. Queen of Castile 1474—1504, she married Ferdinand of Aragon and united the two kingdoms (1479).伊莎贝拉

Isidorus, Sp: Isidoro, E: Isidore, 560—636, Archbishop of Sevilla, the "Last Latin Father", important compiler, author of *Etymologiae*, => encyclopaedia 伊西多尔, 见 Hrabanus, *De institutione cler.*

Isidorus, Gr: Isidoros, E: Isidore of Kiev; +1464. Abbot of the convent of Demetrius in Byzantium he became Metropolitan of Kiev and thus participated in the Council of Ferrara 1438, where he advocated the union with Rome. He was arrested after his return and later moved to Rome.伊西多尔

Islam, the religion founded by the Arab prophet Muhammad (570—632) in Medina and Mecca; the believers of this religion are called Muslim (= Moslem); the expansion of Islam effected the (forced) conversion of large Christian areas in northern Africa and Asia Minor, it caused long-term conflicts, especially in Spain, and eventually led to the crusades; => crucigeri, *Qur'an* 伊斯兰/穆斯林, 见 Johannes Damascenus, *Pēgē gnōseōs*, Malmesburiensis, *Gesta regum Anglorum* (report on the first crusade), Bernardus, *De consideratione* (Christians may resist violence), Petrus Venerabilis, *Contra Saracenos* (the first serious discussion of the Islamic faith by a Christian), Otto Frisingensis, *Chronica* (search for an objective view of Islam), Raimundus Lullus, *Blanquerna* (parts of it influenced Sufi mysticism)

Italia, E: Italy, D: Italien; The death of Emperor Theodosius in 395 brought about the final split of the Roman empire. Under Emperor Honorius, the son of Theodosius, Stilicho commanded the army and for a time prevented the Visigoths from invading Italy, but in 410 they sacked Rome. In 476 the last emperor, Romulus Augustulus was deposed by Odoacer. Odoacer's rule in Italy lasted until 493 when Theodoric, king of the Ostrogoths set up his own kingdom, that succumbed to the armies of Byzantium in 555. Already in 568 the Lombards invaded the northern part of Italy, and since then Italy remained a divided country until the late 19th century. As the power of Byzantium declined the Lombards tried to seize more regions, occupied Ravenna in 751, and even threatened Rome. The Pope appealed to the Franks for help, and in 756 Pepin III handed over to the Pope the administration of Rome, the exarchate of Ravenna, and the region of Pentapolis (the so-called Donation of Pepin). In 774 Charlemagne terminated Lombard rule in Italy, but the stability of his kingdom did not last long. Saracens and Magyars raided parts of Italy, and local dukes and margraves fought for control of Italy. In 951 Otto I, king of Germany, forced Berengar, king of Lombardy, to accept his suzerainty and had himself crowned Roman emperor. In the eleventh century the papacy implemented reforms and acquired new authority so that Pope Gregory VII was able to resist the ambitions of the German ruler Henry IV. Popes often allied themselves with the cities of Lombardy (north Italy) whose wealth and power increased steadily. The Normans were another power to thwart German infringements. They expelled the Saracens from Sicily and southern Italy. In 1084 they rescued Pope Gregory VII. From 1154 to 1250 Frederick I Barbarossa and Frederick II tried to gain more control of Italy, but the cities of Lombardy and the papacy combined to keep the

German kings at bay. However, after the invasion of Charles of Anjou who ruled Sicily from 1268, Aragon seized control of Sicily in 1282, and the papacy faced ever more aggressive powers, including the cities of the north: Milan, Florence, Genoa, and Venice. The absence of the papacy during much of the 14th century brought new confusion, but the end of the Western Schism and the stabilization of papal rule in the 1430s century went hand in hand with the Renaissance. Rome was rebuilt and its authority renewed. At the same time the influence of Genoa and Venice declined with the rise of overseas trade.意大利

Itinerarium ad partes orientales, E: *A Journey to the East,* a report by Rubruk《东方游记》, 见 Rubruk

Itinerarium mentis in Deum, E: *The Mind's Road to God,* a mystical work by Bonaventure《灵魂迈向天主的路程》

ius = jus

Ivan III, (Vasilievich), E: Ivan, D: Iwan; +1505, Czar of Russia 1462—1505. As duke of Moscow he conquered regions east of the Dnieper, forced out the Mongols and united all Russia under his rule. As he married Sophia, niece of Constantine XI, the last of the Byzantine emperors, he claimed the position of Roman Caesar for himself ("Czar").伊凡

Ivo de Chartres, F: Yves, 1040—1115, Bishop of Chartres, important writer and canonist.伊夫

J

Jacobus de Vitry, +1240, Cardinal, hagiographer 雅各伯

Jacobus de Voragine, It: Jacopo de Varazze, E: Jacob of Voragine; +1298, Italian Dominican, provincial of the Lombardy and Archbishop of Genua (1292), famous hagiographer, author of the immensely popular *Legenda aurea,* a collection of lives of the the saints. 雅各伯/雅各, 见 *Legenda aurea*

Jacopone da Todi, +1306, Franciscan poet who wrote spiritual poems but also attacked Pope Boniface VIII for his views on poverty.雅各布尼

Jadwiga = Hedwigis

Jagiello, (Jagello), +1434, grand duke of Lithuania. In 1386 he married Jadwiga, queen of Poland, was baptized and became king of Poland as Ladislaus II. He defeated the Teutonic Knights in 1410.雅各洛

Jaroslaw = Yaroslaw

Jean de Meun, E: John of Meun, D: Johannes de Meun; ca. 1255—1305, author of the second part of the *Roman de la rose.* 让·德·孟, 见 *Roman de la rose*

Jeanne d'Arc, (F), E: Joan d'Arc, D: Johanna von Orleans, 1412—1431, French national hero, responding to visions she helped to liberate Orleans but later fell into English hands, she was sentenced and burned in 1431 but was declared innocent in 1456. She was canonized (proclaimed a Saint) in 1920. 冉·达克/贞德, 见 sancti

jejunium, E: fasting, D: Fasten, Fasttage; fasting on Fridays, Saturdays, in the Quadrages (season of Lent) 守斋期/守斋日, 见 Hrabanus, *De institutione cler.*

Jerusalem, (Hierosolyma), E: Jerusalem, D: Jerusalem; the city where Christ was crucified, important pilgrim destination in the Middle Ages. Jerusalem was captured by Muslim forces in the seventh century, but from 1099 to 1244 it was under the control of Christian crusaders.耶路撒冷, 见 Cynewulf, *Elene*

Jesuati, lay congregation founded 1360 in Siena for the care of the sick, later called "Apostolic Clerics of St. Jerome"; the community was dissolved in 1668.耶稣阿提会

Jesus, E, D: Jesus; the central figure of Christianity. His teachings, death and resurrection were widely believed to be the salvation of humankind. Medieval culture sometimes highlighted the human aspect of Jesus' life, for example St. Francis started the tradition of imagining Jesus' birth in a manger, and since the 13th century the pain Jesus suffered at his crucifixion was shown in artifacts. => cor sacrum, Deus, dolor, ecclesia 耶稣, 见 Anselmus, *Cur Deus homo*, Gertrudis (sacred Heart veneration), Langland, *Piers Plowman* (Jesus' suffering), Thomas a Kempis, *Imitation Christi*, Greban, *Passion de Paris*, Appendix, *Heliand*

Joachim de Flore, E: Joachim of Fiore, D: Joachim; 1130—1202, Italian monk, founder of the congregation of the Florenses 约亚敬, 见 *Liber figurarum*

Joan of Arc = Jeanne d'Arc

Joasaph = Josaphat

Johanna, legendary female pope, proven to be a later

fiction.约翰纳

Johanna I, E: Joan, Joanna, D: Johanna; Queen of Naples 1342—1382, she sold Avignon to the Pope in 1348.约翰纳

Johanna II, Queen of Naples 1414—1435.约翰纳

Johannes = Ioannes / John / Hannes / Jean / Juan / Joao / Ivan / Jan / Giovanni 约翰内斯=约翰/若望/汉斯/让/胡安/若安/伊凡/杨/乔凡尼

教宗：

Johannes VIII, E: John, D: Johann; Pope 872—882, talented and energetic, he crowned two emperors but received little support from them 约翰内斯

Johannes X–XIX, E: John, D: Johann; Popes 914—1032, who had to face the power struggles of Roman clans (like the Crescentii) and the influence of German kings (like Otto I–III) 约翰内斯

Johannes XXI, E: John, D: Johann, Pope 1276—1278, originally Petrus Hispanus, born in Lisben, outstanding logician and medical expert, professor in Paris and Siena, cardinal in 1273 约翰内斯

Johannes XXII, E: John, D: Johann; Pope 1316—1334, originally Jacob Duese from Cahors, the most influential of the Avignon Popes, talented and diligent, but too much influenced by France. He developed the administration system of the Curia. 约翰内斯

Johannes XXIII, E: John, D: Johann; Pope 1410—1415, originally Bishop Cossa, he had political interests, elected by the synod in Pisa; he tried to flee from the council of Constance, where he was deposed.约翰内斯

政治领导：

Johannes VIII Palaeologus, Gr: Iōannēs, E: John, D: Johann; Emperor of Constantinople 1425—1448, he promoted Church union and was participant in the Council of Ferrara in 1438.约翰内斯

Johannes, E: John Lackland, D: Johann ohne Land; King of England 1199—1216. During his reign the English lost most of their possessions in France, the nobility rose against John, thus he was forced to sign the *Magna Carta*; => Philippus II Augustus; Innocens III（失土王）约翰内斯，见 *Magna Charta Libertatum*

其他：

Johannes de Brienne, E: John, D: Johann; King of Jerusalem, leader of a crusade to Egypt 1218—1221.约翰内斯

Johannes Presbyter, E: Prester John, D: Priesterkoenig Johannes; mythical priest–king in the East. 约翰内斯

Johannes Buridanus => Buridanus

Johannes de Capestrano, E: John Capistran, D: Johann Capistran; St., Italian Franciscan, +1456, popular preacher against the Hussites and against the Turks 1451—1456.约翰内斯

Johannes Capreolus, +1444, French Dominican theologian, "Thomistarum princeps". 约翰内斯

Johannes Damascenus, E: John of Damascus, Gr: Ioannes Damaskenos, 650—753, monk in the Sabas –Monastery at Jerusalem 715—749, most influential Greek theologian of his century, author of *Fountain of Wisdom*, precursor of scholasticism 大马士革的约翰内斯，见 *Barlaam et Joasaph, Pēgē gnōseōs*

Johannes Gualbertus, E: John Gualbert, D: Johann Gualbert; St., +1073; monk in Italy, founder of a monastery in Vallombrosa （1038） and of the Vallombrosian Congregation.约翰内斯

Johannes de Matha, E: John of Matha, D: Johann von Matha; St. founder of the Trinitarians in 1213; this order tried to ransom Christians held captive in Moslem countries. 约翰内斯

Johannes de Montecorvino, It: Giovanni di Montecorvino, E: John of Monte Corvino; +1328; Italian Franciscan, successful missionary in China under the Mongols; in 1307 he became the first Bishop of Beijing (Cambalic). 约翰内斯/孟高维诺，见 Marco Polo

Johannes Nepomuk = Johannes de Pomuk

Johannes de Neumarkt, E: John of Neumarkt; D: Johann von Neumarkt; +1380, Bishop of Leitomischl and Olomouc, chancellor of Charles IV and humanist scholar.约翰内斯

Johannes Nider, 见 Nider

Johannes de Parma, It: Giovanni, E: John, D: Johann; +1289; Italian scholar, general of the Franciscans 1247—1257, being a supporter of Joachim's spiritualism, he was charged with heresy and retired from active life. 约翰内斯

Johannes de Piano del Carpine, It: Giovanni de Pianocarpini, E: John; +1252; Italian Franciscan who was sent to the Mongols （Karakorum） by Pope Innocent IV and left a valuable account of his mission (1245—1247).约翰内斯

Johannes de Pomuk, E: John of Nepomuk, D: Jo–

hannes Nepomuk; St., +1393; canon and vicar general in Prague, doctor of canon law. He was popular pastor the queen's confessor. Because he refused to break the confessional secret he was tortured to death by King Wenceslaus in 1393. 约翰内斯

Johannes Quidort, E: John Quidort of Paris, D: Johann Quidort; +1306; Dominican writer in Paris who supported separation of powers in 1302. 约翰内斯

Johannes Scotus Eriugena, E: John Scottus Erigena, Irish scholar ca. 810—877; translator, director of the court school of Charles the Bald, one of the leading thinkers in the 9th century. 艾利基纳/艾留金那, 见 *De divisione naturae*

Johannes de Tepla, E: John of Saaz, D: Johannes Tepla; ca. 1350—1414, official in Prague, author of the *Ackermann*, a dialogue with Death. 约翰内斯, 见 *Der Ackermann aus Boehmen*

Johannes Veccus, E: John, D: Johann; Patriarch of Constantinople, supporter of Church union, he was forced to resign after 1282. 约翰内斯

Johanniter = Hospitaller

Jordanus de Saxonia, E: Jordan of Saxony, D: Jordan von Sachsen; St., +1237; German Dominican, second general superior of the order (1222—1237). He authored a history of the order and started the tradition of singing the *Salve Regina* at the evening prayer. 约达努斯

Josaphat, Joasaph, Gr: Ioasaph, Arab: Judasaf, Sanskrit: Bodhisattva, a prince who converts to Christianity, in fact a version of the conversion of the Buddha. 约沙法特, 见 Johannes Damascenus, *Barlaam et Joasaph*

Josephus, E: Joseph, D: Josef; St., Christian saint, foster-father of Jesus, venerated since the later Middle Ages together with Anna, the mother of Mary. 若瑟/约瑟夫

Josephus, E: Joseph, D: Josef; Patriarch of Constantinople 1267—1275 and 1282—1283. He opposed the efforts of Emperor Michael VIII Palaeologus towards union with the papacy and was later reinstated as patriarch (1282). 若瑟/约瑟夫

jubilaeum, E: Jubilee year, D: Jubilaeumsjahr; since 1300 the Popes announced jubilee years which were celebrated with pilgrimages to Rome; indulgences were granted. 大禧年

Judaei, E: Jews, D: Juden; since the first century AD a tension between Jews and Christians emerged; after the destruction of Jerusalem in 70 AD the Jews were dispersed all over the world and suffered from discrimination. Under Islam Jews were excluded from public office and paid a tax, but in Moorish Spain Jews enjoyed freedom and moved into high government positions. In the late 14th century Jews in Spain suffered from persecution and were forced into ghettoes, the first in Europe. Many Jews converted but secretly kept their tradition (the so-called Marranos). The Spanish inquisition was revived in 1478 to suppress the Marranos, many of whom were killed or forced to leave the country (1492). Jews were bankers of some medieval kings since they were exemt from certain Christian prohibitions concerning money lending and usury. Thus medieval kings often protected Jews. There were no persecutions of Jews in the Papal States or in Avignon, and Rome is the only big city of Europe where the Jewish community lived undisturbed from antiquity to modern times. Persecutions of Jews happened sporadically, especially severe during the first and second crusade (1095, 1146) and during the time of the plague (1348—1350). Jews were expelled from England in 1290, later from France, Portugal and some parts of Germany. Vicious calumnies (such as "ritual murderers") were endangering Jews throughout the period. Some humanists promoted Jewish studies (Pico della Mirandola, Reuchlin); => lingua Hebraica 犹太人, 见 Cynewulf, *Elene*, Adso, *De ortu et tempore Antichristi* (persecution of Jews), Maimonides, *More nevukhim*, Nicolaus de Lyra, *Postilla* (consults the works of Rabbi Salomon)

judex, E: judge, D: Richter; => lex 审判官,法官, 见 Gregorius VII, *Dictatus Papae* 18, 19 (the Pope is a kind of supreme judge but may be judged by nobody), Bracton, Thomas de Celano, *Dies irae* (the divine judgment), Johannes de Tepla, *Ackermann* (God judges between Ackermann and the Death)

Juliana de Norwich, E: Julian of Norwich, 1342—1416, English recluse and mystic who lived outside the walls of St. Julian's church in Norwich after being healed by visions in 1373, author of *Revelations of Divine Love*, a famous work of spirituality in the English tongue. 尤利安纳/朱利安

jurispurdentia, E: jurisprudence, D: Jurisprudenz; => lex

jus canonum, E: canon law, ecclesiastical law, D: Kirchenrecht; the discipline of canon law was established in the 12th century; many medieval Popes were experts in this field, e.g. Innocent III and Boniface VIII, => canonistae 教会法, 见 Gratianus, *Concordantia*, Innocens III ("pater juris", author of *Compilatio tertia*)

Justinianus I Magnus, E: Justinian I (the Great), D: Justinianus; 483—565 AD, Emperor of Byzantium 527—565, who defended his empire against the Persians in the East and reconquered former Roman territories in Africa, Italy, and Spain. He ordered the codification of the law of ancient Rome (Justinian code, *Codex iuris civilis*), and this code was rediscovered by Italian lawyers in the 11th century, => Irnerius, legistae 尤斯廷尼安, 见 Gratianus, *Concordantia discordantium canonum*, Dante, *Commedia* (placed in the Heaven of Mercury)

justitia, E: justice, D: Gerechtigkeit; one of the cardinal virtues 正义, 见 Dante, *Commedia* (the Heaven of Jupiter is the place of just rulers), Oresmensis, *De origine monetarum* (money can be an expression of justice)

justitiarius, E: justiciar, D: Justiziar; chief adviser to the English king, head of the royal judicial system. The office was introduced by William the Conqueror. 王室法官, 见 Bracton

juvenis, E: youth, D: Jugend, Jugendlicher; 青年, 见 Alanus, *Anticlaudianus* (the new man "Juvenis")

K

K = C

Kant, Immanuel, 1724—1804, German idealist philosopher, author of *Critique of Pure Reason* 康德, 见 Anselmus, *Proslogion* (Kant rejected the ontological proof), Averroes (similarities to Kant)

Karakorum, city in Outer Mongolia, founded by Genghis Khan in 1220 as capital for his empire. Khubilai Khan destroyed the city in 1267 and moved the court to Cambaluc (Peking). 和林, 见 Rubruk, *Itinerarium*

Karl = Karolus = Carolus

Katharer, Katharoi = Cathari

Kempis = Thomas a Kempis

Kiev = Kiovia

Kilianus, E: Kilian, Killena, D: Kilian, St., +689, Irish Bishop, missionary in Thuringia and Franconia, he was martyred. 基利安努斯

Kiovia, E: Kiova, Kiev, D: Kiew; important city on the middle Dnieper; founded in the 8th century, it was captured by Varangians from Novgorod in 864 and in 882 became the capital of the first major state in Russia. The metropolitan diocese was established in 1039; around 1150 it was a large trade city, second only to Constantinople, in 1240 it was ruined by the Mongols and paid tribute to the Golden Horde until 1320, but Ivan III recovered it for Russia in 1471. 基辅, 见 Nestorius, *Povest'*

Kircher, Athanasius, 1602—1680, German Jesuit who was inspired by Lull's works. 基歇尔, 见 Raimundus Lullus, *Ars magna*

Klosterneuburg, a monastery near Vienna (Austria), established by Leopold III around 1100, since 1133 it is under the direction of Augustinians; it possesses a large library of important manuscripts. 克洛斯特内堡, 见 Otto Frisingensis

knight => eques

Knut = Canutus

Koeln = Colonia

Koenigsberg, a city in East Prussia, founded by the Teutonic Order in 1255. Its name comes from king Ottocar II of Bohemia who had carried out a crusade in the area. 柯尼斯堡

Konrad = Conradus

Koran = Qur'an

Kriemhild, (=Krimhilt, Kriemhilde), wife of Siegfried; she avenged the death of her husband by destroying the entire clan of his murderers. 克里木希尔特, 见 Appendix, *Nibelungenlied*

Kublai Khan, (Khubilai, Kubla), 1215—1294, the grandson of Genghis Khan, who moved the capital from Karakorum to Yanjing (Cambaluc = Beijing) in 1264, completed the conquest of China (1279), founded the Yuan Dynasty of China, but failed to conquer Japan. => Mongoli 忽必烈, 见 Marco Polo

Kunigunde = Cunigundis

L

La Commedia divina => Commedia

labor, E: labor, hard work, D: Arbeit; physical work was demanded from Benedictine monks, and ecclesiastical teaching encouraged daily work 劳动,

见 Langland, *Piers Plowman* (hard work is the way to truth)

lacrimarum vallis, E: vale of tears, D: Tal der Traenen, an expression denoting the sorrows of this earthly life.泪谷,见 Innocens III, *De miseria*

Ladislaus, E: Ladislas, King of Naples 1386—1414, who sacked Rome and expelled Pope John XXII in 1413.拉迪斯劳

laicus, Gr: laikos ("common"), E: lay person, D: Laie; a Christian who does not live in holy orders. 平信徒,见 laicus frater

laicus frater, E: lay brother, D: Laienbruder; also called "conversus", who lived and worked in monasteries.平信徒修士,见 Franciscus

Lambertus, (Lampbert), + ca. 1080, monk Hersfeld, Hessen, Germany, author of a universal history.兰贝图斯

Lamprecht der Pfaffe, German poet, author of the *Alexanderlied* (ca. 1120—1130) 兰普瑞希特,见 *Alexandreis*

Lancelot, one of the knights at Arthur's Round table, the lover of Guinevere and father of Galahad, introduced to romance literature by Chretien de Troyes. 兰斯洛特, 见 Galfredus Monemuthensis, *Historia regum Britanniae*, Chretien de Troyes

Lanfrancus, E: Lanfranc, D: Lanfrank, ca. 1010—1089, Italian monk, Prior of Bec in the Normandy, Archbishop of Canterbury 1070—1089, scholastic theologian; he turned Bec into a great spiritual and intellectual center and worked with William the Conqueror in implementing church reforms in order to check simony and concubinage. 兰弗朗克, 见 Anselmus, Malmesburiensis, *Gesta regum Anglorum*

Langland, William, ca. 1330—1400, author of the alliterative poem *The Vision Concerning Piers Plowman*, one of the most important pieces of literature in late medieval England. 兰格朗,见 *Piers Plowman*

Langobardi, E: Lombards, D: Langobarden, Germanic tribe which invaded Italy in 568; they controlled northern Italy and occupied the exarchate Ravenna in 751; as they threatened Rome, the Popes appealed to the Franks for help; their capital Pavia was destroyed by Charlemagne in 774. 伦巴第人,见 Paulus Diaconus, *Historia Langobardorum*, Eginhardus, *Vita Caroli* (wars against the Lombards, 773—781)

Langton, Stephanus, +1228; theologian at Paris, Biblical scholar, writer; he became Archbishop of Canterbury in 1207 against King John's will and was instrumental in drafting the *Magna Carta*. 兰顿,见 Appendix, *Magna Charta Libertatum*

Lateranus, E, D: Lateran, a papal palace in Rome, old episcopal church of the Pope, many synods were held there, for example the Synod of 769, Synod of 1059, Synod of 1060, Council of 1123, Council of 1139, Council of 1179, Council of 1215 (the biggest ecclesiastical conference of the Middle Ages, => Innocens III); Council of 1512—1517.拉特兰

laura, (lavra), a colony of anchorites (hermits) who occupied their own cells but came together for liturgical celebrations. The oldest lauras probably were those in fourth-century Palestine. Others existed near Kiev (Russia).隐修者团体

Laura, the woman who inspired Petrarch's poets, possibly only a fiction. She allegedly died in the plague of 1348.劳拉,见 Petrarca, *Rime*

Lear => Leir

Lech, river in the border area between Germany and Austria. In the battle at the Lechfeld Otto I defeated the Magyars (Hungarians) in 955, which ended their marauding.莱希河

legatus, E: legate, D: Legat, Gesandter; clerics whom the Pope sent to foreign countries to represent the Holy See. From the ninth century more formal legations appeared. The *legati a latere* of the eleventh century often superseded the authority of the local hierarchy.大使,特使,见 Gregorius VII

Legatus divinae pietatis, E: *Messenger of Divine Love*, a work by Gertrude the Great《神爱的使者》,见 Gertrudis

Legenda aurea, E: *Golden Legend*, a collection of saints' lives by Jacobus de Voragine《金传》,见 Jacobus de Voragine

leges => lex

legistae, E: legal experts, D: Legisten; scholars who wrote commentaries (glossae) to the *Code of Civil Law,* => canonistae 法学家,见 Gratianus, Irnerius

Leir, (=Lear), (< Irish: Ler = "ocean"), D: Lear; legendary Irish king who divided the reign between his three daughters, was deceived by two of them, but the youngest saved him 李尔,见 Galfredus Monemuthensis, *Historia regum Britanniae*

Leo III, St., Pope 795—816, who fled to Germany

(Paderborn) in 799. He crowned Charlemagne in 800 in Rome, which marked the beginning of the "Holy Roman Empire" (so called since the 13th century). 利奥/莱奥

Leo IV, St., Pope 847—855, he built a wall around St. Peter's, the "Leonine City", against the threat of Saracen attacks. 利奥/莱奥

Leo V–VIII, Popes in the period from 903 to 965 who had to face power struggles of Roman factions. 利奥/莱奥

Leo IX, St., Pope 1049—1054; originally Bruno, from Alsatian nobility, Bishop of Toul; he was an effective reformer of the Church through the nomination of talented cardinals. He sent out legates to the different kings of Western Europe. 利奥/莱奥

Leo III, Isaurus, Byzantine Emperor 717—741, a Syrian peasant by birth, who became a general and could beat off a dangerous Arab attack on Constantinople in 717, driving the Muslims out of Asia Minor. He launched the policy of iconoclasm in 726, and his edict of 730 ordered the destruction of images. His *Ecloga* of 726 replaced the *Corpus Juris Civilis* in the courts of the empire. 利奥/莱奥

Leo V, Byzantine Emperor 813—820, who renewed iconoclasm. He was murdered. 利奥/莱奥

Leo VI, E: Leo the Wise; Byzantine Emperor 886—912, who lost Sicily to the Saracens and deposed Photius; his fourth marriage in 906 triggered the Tetragamy controversy. 利奥/莱奥

Leo de Neapolis, E: Leo of Neapolis, ca. 920—970, the translator of the Alexander romance. 利奥, 见 *Alexandreis*

León, kingdom of northwestern Spain from 909 AD. It was joined to Castile in 1037, gained independence in 1157 again, but was finally united with Castile in 1230. 莱昂

Leonardus Pisanus, It: Leonardo Pisano, E: Leonard of Pisa, +1230, mathematician known for introducing the Hindu-Arabic numerals and the zero to Western Europe. 利奥纳多

Leopoldus de Austria III, E: Leopold, D: Leopold (Luitpold); St., Margrave of Austria 1095—1136, married Agnes, daughter of Hery IV of Germany, among his sons were Bishop Otto of Freising and Archbishop Conrad II of Salzburg. He founded several (Cistercian) monasteries and laid the basis for Austria's future prosperity. 利奥波德, 见 Otto Frisingensis

Leopoldus de Austria V, E: Leopold, D: Leopold; Duke of Austria 1177—1194, rival of King Richard Coeur de Lion. 利奥波德

lex, E: law, D: Gesetz; => jus, jus canonicum 法律, 见 Adamnanus (author of *Lex innocentium*), Eginhardus, *Vita Caroli* 29 (Charlemagne ordered codification of laws), Gratianus, *Concordantia* (=> jus canonicum), Joachim, *Liber figurarum* (the age of the Father is the age of the Law), Maimonides, *More nevukhim* (philosophical inquiry will not undermine the Law of the Jews, the Tora), Bracton, *De legibus et consuetudinibus Angliae*, Thomas Aquinas, *Summa theologiae* (discusses many legal questions, confirms the stable law of nature; => homicidium), Occam, *Sententiae* (his voluntarist tendencies suggest moral positivism), Wyclif, *De civili dominio* (emphasizes the "lex evangelica"), Chaucer, *Canterbury Tales* (lawyer)

Lex Salica, E: Salic Law, D: Salisches Recht, one of the early Germanic law codes, it was written down in Latin around 510 AD under the order of Clovis, founder of the Merovingian dynasty; being mainly a penal code, one of its most famous civil law stipulations barred daughters from inheriting lands. 萨利卡法典

liber, E: book, D: Buch; 书本, 见 Thomas de Celano, *Dies irae* (book of Conscience)

Liber de cultura hortorum, E: *On the Cultivation of Gardens*, a work by Walafried Strabo 《园艺之书》, 见 Walahfridus

Liber figurarum, E: *Book of Symbols*, a work by Joachim de Fiore 《象征之书》, 见 Joachim

Libre d'Amic e Amat, E: *The Book of the Lover and the Beloved*, a work by Raymond Lull 《关于怀爱者和爱人之书》, 见 Raimundus Lullus

Libussa, semi-legendary wife of Przemysl, the first king of Bohemia 里布萨, 见 Cosmas, *Chronica Bohemorum*

Liege, (L: Legia, Leodium), E: Liege, D: Luettich; city in the Low Countries, see of a bishop since the eight century. It was an independent principality ruled by prince-bishops and subject to the Holy Roman emperor. 列日

lilium, E: lily, D: Lilie, a flower, symbol of faith 百合花, 见 Walahfridus, *Liber de cultura hortorum*, (Christ combined the values of the lily and of the rose)

limbo, E: limbo, ante-hell, D: Limbo; a place or state assigned to souls without faith who were excluded from both the pains of hell and the bliss of heaven. 灵薄狱, 见 Dante, *Commedia*

lingua, E: language, D: Sprache; the common academic language of the Middle Ages and of the Renaissance was Latin; => interpretatio, translatio 语言, 见 Eginhardus, *Vita Caroli* (Charles tries to learn foreign languages), Nestorius, *Povest'* (Vladimir Monomachus thinks that a ruler must learn foreign languages), Dante, *De vulgari eloquentia*

lingua Anglica, E: English language, D: Englisch; => Juliana de Norwich 英语, 见 Appendix, *Beowulf* (oldest extant poem in Old English), Langland, *Piers Plowman*, Chaucer, *Canterbury Tales*

lingua Arabica, E: Arabic, D: Arabisch; learned by some medieval scholars and translators 阿拉伯语, 见 Constantinus Africanus, Vincentius Bellovacensis, *Speculum maius* (use of Arab sources), Raimundus Lullus, Raimundus de Penafort, Appendix, *Poema de mio Cid* ("Cid" is the Arabic word for "lord")

lingua Francorum, E: French, D: Franzoesisch; 法语, 见 Chretien de Troyes, Albericus de Besancon, *Roman d'Alexandre*, Vincentius Bellovacensis (his *Great Mirror* was translated into French in 1328)

lingua Germanica, E: German languge, D: Deutsch; 德语, 见 Eginhardus, *Vita Caroli* 29 (recording of German hymns), Otfrid, *Evangelienbuch* (written in vernacular "theotisce"), Hartmann (model of Middle High German), Mechtildis de Magdeburga (works in Low German), Appendix, *Heliand* (Old Saxon dialect, from ca. 830 AD)

lingua Graeca, E: Greek language, D: Griechisch; almost forgotten in the Latin West after the 6th century 希腊语, 见 Eginhardus, *Vita Caroli* (Charles tried to learn it), Eriugena (translator from Greek into Latin), Rogerius Baco, *Opus maius* (urges study of Greek), Bessarion (teacher of Greek in Italy, praised as "Latinorum Graecissimus, Graecorum Latinissimus")

lingua Hebraica, E: Hebrew, D: Hebraeisch 希伯来语, 见 Otfrid, *Evangelienbuch* (one of the "noble tongues"), Maimonides, *More nevukhim* (translated from Arabic into Hebrew and Latin), Rogerius Baco, *Opus maius* (urges the study of Hebrew), Nicolaus de Lyra, *Postilla* (the author knew Hebrew well)

lingua Hispanica, E: Spanish, D: Spanisch; 西班牙语, 见 *Alexandreis* (*El libro de Aleixandre*)

lingua Italiana, E: Italian, D: Italienisch; 意大利语, 见 Dante, *De vulgari eloquentia*, Boccaccio, *De casibus virorum illustrium* (his turn to serious writing implied the shift from Italian to Latin)

lingua Latina, E: Latin language, D: Latein; medieval Latin was the common academic language of western Europe, although not the mother tongue of Franks, Anglo-saxons or Celts; Latin became the normative language for the emerging vernacular literatures of France, Italy, Spain, England, Germany etc. The origins of medieval Latin are found in the vulgar Latin spoken by the people of the declining Roman empire, which St. Jerome had employed in his *Vulgata*. Compared to classical Latin medieval Latin had a simpler grammar and sentence structure, because it neglected literary refinement, but it was in general use and had an ever growing vocabulary. Renaissance scholars tried to purify Latin and thus treated medieval Latin with less respect. => translatio 拉丁语, 见 Eginhardus, *Vita Caroli* (Charles' proficiency in Latin), Otfrid, *Evangelienbuch* (similarities between Latin and German), Saxo Grammaticus, *Gesta Danorum* (chose Latin to write local history), Dante, *De vulgari eloquentia* (Latin is the common language which facilitates communication with the antiquorum auctoritates)

lingua Russica, E: Russian language, D: Russisch; the earliest chronicle in Old Russian language is from the 11th century 俄罗斯语, 见 Nestorius, *Povest'*

Lioba, St., + 782, relative of St. Boniface, Benedictine nun, she became abbess in Tauberbischofsheim and founded several convents in Germany. 利欧巴

Lissabon, Port: Lisboa, E: Lisbon; capital of Portugal. From the fourth century it was an episcopal see. After having been occupied by Alans, Sueves, and Visigoths, the Moors seized Lisbon in 712. Alfonso I captured it in 1147, and Alfonso III moved his residence from Coimbra to Lisbon in 1256. The university was founded in 1290. 里斯本

Lithuania, E: Lithuania, D: Litauen; country in the region between Poland and the Dnieper. The grand duke Mindaugas accepted baptism in 1251. In 1386 grand duke Jagiello married Jadwiga, the heiress of Poland and defeated the Teutonic Knights several decades later (1410). Casimir IV king of Poland and Lithuania (1447—1492) forced the Teutonic Knights to cede Pomerania in 1466, but the grand duke of Moscow Ivan III (1462—1505) took away the lands east of the Dnieper. 立陶宛

Liutprand, King of the Lombards 712—744; he expelled the Byzantines from Italy and expanded the Lombard empire. 留特布兰德, 见 Paulus Diaconus, *Hist. Lang.*,

Liutprand, (Liudprand), +972; Bishop of Cremona, historian. 留特布兰德

Livonia, E: Livland, country in north-eastern Europe, mission activities started in the 12th century. The Livonians were baptized through the efforts of Bishop Albert of Riga, who founded the Livonian Knights of the Sword in 1202. The Teutonic Knights also helped in the mission work. 里夫尼亚

Lobbes, D: Laubach, monastery in Germany 罗贝斯

logica, Gr: dialektikē, E: logic, D: Logik, the art of thinking and speaking correctly, especially emphasized by the scholastics since Abaelard; => philosophia 逻辑学, 见 Aristoteles, Hrabanus, *De institutione cler.*, (emphasizes dialectica), Avicenna, *Kitab*, Abaelardus, *Sic et non*, Petrus Hispanus, *Summulae logicales*, Thomas Aquinas (his discussions are steeped in logical thinking), Raimundus Lullus, *Ars magna* (logical combinations of words and numbers)

Loki, a Norse god of the underworld who creates discord among the gods and is punished for his wickedness 罗克, 见 Snorri Sturluson, *Edda*

Lollardi, adherents of Wyclif, who were suppressed after 1382. 罗拉迪人, 见 Wyclif

Lombards = Langobardi

London, (L: Londinum), E: London, D: London, the main city of England, first a Celtic settlement, known as Londinium under the Romans. Ethelbert, king of Kent founded St. Paul's Cathedral (around 600). After the Danes occupied the city (871), Alfred the Great restored it to the English (886). London was England's effective capital since 1180, and in 1191 Richard granted it a charter. 伦敦, 见 Galfredus Monemuthensis, *Historia regum Britanniae* (origin of the name "London", originally named "Troia nova")

Loreto, famous pilgrim destination in Italy since the 14th century 罗瑞托

Lorraine = Lotharingia

Lotharingia, E: Lorraine, D: Lothringen; duchy in the border area between Germany and France. Charles the Bald, king of the West Franks, and Louis, king of the East Franks, divided the area between them in 870. Otto I gave it the status of a duchy (939). Lower Lorraine included most of the Netherlands at that time. After 1250 French influence prevailed for some time. 洛林

Lotharius, E: Lothair, D: Lothar; son of Louis the Pious, Co-Emperor 817—843. 洛塔尔

Lotharius II, E: Lothair, D: Lothar; German king 855—869 in control of Lorraine (between the French and the German part of the Frankish empire). 洛塔尔

Lotharius III, E: Lothair, D: Lothar; Lothair of Supplinburg, Saxon Duke, King of Germany 1125—1137, he supported Innocens II, was crowned Emperor in Rome in 1133. 洛塔尔

Lotharius II, It: Lotario; Italian king 948—950. 洛塔尔

Louis => Ludovicus

Lublin, city in Galicia (Poland), founded in the tenth century. 卢布林

Lucia, E: Lucia, D: Luzia; a popular saint and martyr, model of chastity. 路齐亚, 见 Jacobus de Voragine, *Legenda aurea*, Dante, *Commedia* (Lucia placed in the highest Heaven)

Lucifer, E: Lucifer, D: Luzifer; originally the name of the morning star, later associated with the Satan; => Diabolus, Satan

Lucius II, Pope 1144—1145. 卢修斯/路齐乌斯

Lucius III, Pope 1181—1185, who could reside in Rome only for a few months due to republican tendencies of Roman nobles. 卢修斯/路齐乌斯

Ludolphus de Saxonia, E: Ludolph of Saxony, D: Ludolph von Sachsen; +1378, Carthusian from Strasbourg, author of a *Vita Christi*. 鲁多夫

路易, 德国王:

Ludovicus I Pius, E: Louis the Pious, D: Ludwig der Fromme, son and successor of Charlemagne, Emperor 814—840, he divided the Frankish empire among his sons Lothair, Peopin, Louis, and Charles. 路易一世(虔诚者), 见 Eginhardus, *Vita Caroli*, 30, (coronation of Louis)

Ludovicus II, E: Louis, D: Ludwig, son of Lothair I, king of Italy 844—875, anointed and crowned Emperor in 850. He could stop Saracen invasions of Italy. 路易

Ludovicus III, E: Louis, D: Ludwig, +928; King of the Provence, crowned Emperor in 901. 路易

Ludovicus Infans, E: Louis the Child, D: Ludwig das Kind, German king (only seven years old) 900—911, last of the east-Frankish Carolingians. 路易

Ludovicus Teutonicus, E: Louis the German, D: Ludwig der Deutsche, ruler of the Eastern part of the Frankish empire 843—876. 路易

Ludovicus IV Bavarus, E: Louis the Bavarian, D: Ludwig der Bayer; king of Germany 1314—1348, Holy Roman Emperor (1328), member of the house of Wittelsbach; Pope John XXII refused to confirm his election, thus he criticized the Avignonese papacy and was banned by the Pope in 1324; Louis provided a haven for critics of the pope as Marsilius of Padua and William of Occam. In 1328 he invaded Rome and had himself crowned by Sciarra Colonna. 巴伐利亚人路易，见 *Bulla aurea*, Occam

路易，法国王：

Ludovicus II, F: Louis, E: Louis the Stammerer, D: Ludwig; King of France 877—879. 路易

Ludovicus VII, F: Louis, E: Louis, D: Ludwig; King of France 1137—1180, one of the leaders of the Second Crusade (1147—1149). He annulled his marriage to Eleanor of Aquitaine, who subsequently married Henry of Anjou, the duke of Normandy, who became King of England. Thus Aquitaine fell to England until the end of the Hundred Years' War. 路易

Ludovicus IX Sanctus, F: Louis le Saint, E: Louis the Saint, D: Ludwig der Heilige; St., King of France 1226—1270, model of a Christian ruler who led an ascetic life and died on a crusade in Tunis. He was peace-loving and just, persuaded Henry III of England to abandon claims on Normandy and stabilized the frontier with Aragon. He was a devout Christian but did not support the Pope in his struggle with Frederick II of Germany. 圣王路易九世，见 Vincentius Bellovacensis, Rubruk

Ludovicus XI, F: Louis, D: Ludwig, King of France 1461—1483 路易

Luettich = Liege

Lullus / Lull / Llull => Raimundus Lullus

lumen => lux

Lund, city in south Sweden, the archdiocese was established in 1104, and it was in charge of Denmark, Sweden, Iceland, Greenland. 隆德

Lupoldus de Bebenburg, +1363; Bishop of Bamberg, canonist, adviser to Emperor Charles IV. 鲁波德

Lupus de Ferrieres, E: Lupus of Ferrieres; +862; humanist and theologian, since 840 abbot of Ferrieres. He was an enthusiastic collector of manuscripts, some of which he copied and annotated. 卢普斯

Luther, Martin, E, D: Martin Luther, 1483—1546, German reformer, translator of the Bible. 路德，见 Nicolaus de Lyra (Luther relied on his studies), Occam ("I am of Occam's school")

lux, (lumen), E: light, D: Licht; symbol of wisdom, also of God, => optica 光明，见 Alanus, *Anticlaudianus* (symbol of the Trinity), Roger Baco, *Opus maius* (interest in optics), Thomas Aquinas, *Summa theologiae* (lumen naturale = natural reason), Dante, *Commedia* (light, symbol of the Trinity)

Luxemburg, E: Luxemburg, Duchy of; Luxemburg became a county in the eleventh century and a duchy in 1354 and fell to the Habsburgs in 1477. 卢森堡

Luxeuil, the abbey of Luxeuil (France) was founded by St. Columban around 590. It became a Benedictine monastery, was sacked by Arabs in 732 and by Normans in 888. 卢修，见 Columban

luxuria, E: lust, lechery, D: Wollust; sin against modesty and self-control in sexual matters; one of the cardinal sins; => vitia 淫荡，迷色，见 Hrotsvita, *Dulcitius*, Dante, *Commedia* (Purgatory cures the sins of lust)

Lyons, L: Lugdunum, E: Lyons, D: Lyon; town in southern France, see of a bishop from the second century. In 470 it became the capital of the Burgundians. In 1032 the city became a part of the kingdom of Germany, but in 1312 it fell to France. It was the place of the 13th and 14th ecumenical council (1245 and 1274). The Council of 1274 confirmed the union of the Latin and Greek churches. A Greek delegation accepted this union but was rejected in Constantinople. 里昂

M

Macbeth, king of Scotland 1040—1057, who slew

Duncan I in a battle but was in turn killed by Kuncen's son Malcolm. He made a pilgrimage to Rome in 1050.麦克白

Machaut, Guillaume de, 1300—1377, French poet and composer, priest at the cathedral of Reims, he worked for some time at the French court and authored *Voir-Dit*. 马肖

machina, E: machine, D: Maschine; medieval technical devices were manifold, the outstanding invention of the 9th century was the weight-driven clock, possibly first in Verona, Italy. Pope Sylvester II may have invented a mechanical clock around 1000, and many cathedrals and monasteries in the 12th century had clocks which struck the hours. 机械,见 Oresmensis (machina mundi, the breakthrough towards a mechanist world view)

Maerlant, Jacob van, + 1300, Flemish poet, the first Dutch author. One of his didactic poems was modeled after the encyclopedia of Vincent of Beauvais. 马艾兰

Magdalenae Sorores, E: Sisters of Magdalene, D: Magdalenen; established to do penitence or to care for former prostitutes, established by Rudolf of Hildesheim at Metz in 1226.玛达勒纳修女会,见 Hrotsvita, *Abraham eremita*

Magdeburg, town in Germany, archdiocese since 967.马格德堡

Magna Charta Libertatum, (*Magna Carta*), E: *Great Chart of Liberties*; document protecting civil rights, signed by King John in 1215 under special circumstances; => Innocens III, John Lackland《英国大宪章》,见 Petrus III de Aragon (issued a similar document in 1283), Appendix, *Magna Charta*

Magog => Gog

magus, E: wise man, wizard, D: Magier; the Middle Ages admired the erudition, wisdom or seemingly superhuman abilities (prophecy, healing powers etc.) of certain individuals, often attributing miracles to them; late antiquity thought Virgil to be a wise prophet; => malefica, sancti 智人,见 Beda, *Historia* (description of saints), Columba, Fredericus II, Merlin, Silvester II, Albertus Magnus (admired for his grasp of natural sciences), *Alexandreis* (Alexander as superhuman hero)

Maimonides, Moses, (Moses Ben Maimon), E: Maimonides; 1138—1204, Spanish-born Jewish philosopher and physician; his works influenced mystical thought; he tried to reconcile Aristotelian philosophy with Jewish theology. 迈蒙尼德,见 *More nevukhim*

Mainz, L: Moguntia, Fr: Mayence, E: Mainz; city on the middle Rhine, a bishop's see since 200 AD, it was seized by Alemanni, Vandals, Slavs, and Franks (in 500). St. Boniface worked here, and in 780 it became the see of an archbishop. Since the 10th century the the archbishop of Mainz had the right to crown the German king. Later the archbishop of Mainz was one of the electors of the German king. In 1244 the city received the status of a free city.美因茨

Malachias, E: Malachy, D: Malachias; +1148; Archbishop of Armagh (1132). He was papal legate for Ireland and introduced Roman liturgy and Cistercian monasteries to Ireland.马拉基亚

Malatesta, Sigsimondo, 1417—1468, Italian condottiere at Rimini, patron of arts and letters. 马拉特斯塔,见 Piccolomini, *Commentarii*

malefica, E: witch, D: Hexe; superstitious belief in the existence of witches and sorcery was long existent, but the persecution of witches at a large scale started only at the end of the 15th century. => magus; Sprenger 巫婆狂热,巫婆案

Malmesburiensis Guilelmus, E: William of Malmesbury, D: Wilhelm von Malmesbury, 1080—1142, English scholar, librarian of the Benedictine monastery at Malmesbury, the most notable English historian since Bede. 马梅斯布里,见 *Gesta regum Anglorum*

Malmesbury, Benedictine monastery in Wiltshire, Wessex, founded in 635 by Maidulf, whose pupil Aldhelm became its first abbot in 673. It was a center of learning but dissolved in 1539. 马尔梅斯堡,见 Aldhelmus

Malta, island south of Sicily, occupied by Vandals, Ostrogoths, Byzantium, and the Arabs (870). In 1091 the Normans expelled the Arabs, and in 1266 Charles of Anjou seized the island, but after the Sicilian Vespers in 1282 the island fell to the kingdom of Aragon. In 1530 the emperor Charles V gave the island to the Hospitallers (thus their name "Knights of Malta")马耳他

Mammon, a term of the New Testament (*Mt* 6:24-28) denoting money and the avaricious pursuit of wealth 马蒙,见 Appendix, *Elkerlijk* (personification of mammon)

Mandeville, Sir John, English writer around 1350, author of a travel report in Norman French (*The Voyage and Travels of Sir John Mandeville*) in which he tells of fantastic journeys to Africa, the Orient, even to the Valley of the Devils and to the realm of Prester John. 曼德维尔

Manegold de Lautenbach, +1103, Augustinian canon in Alsace, theological author, who wrote commentaries on Plato and Ovid. 马内格德

Manfredus, E: Manfred, D: Manfred; +1266, son of Frederick II, brother of Conrad IV, regent and King of Sicilia from 1258 to 1266. 曼弗雷德, 见 Fredericus II, *De arte venandi*

Manitius, Max, German scholar, whose magisterial work on the history of the literature of the Middle Ages (3 volumes) was published from 1911 to 1931. 马尼提乌斯

manorialism, (L: manere), Seigneurial System, D: herrschaftlicher Gutbesitz; The manor was usually a village community whose fields and woods belonged to the lord. The peasants had to work for the lord (corvee), but they also tilled their own plots of land which they had inherited from their parents. The rise of trade, towns, and capitalism (money circulation became popular in the 14th century) made it possible to replace labor services with a payment to the lord, and thus serfdom slowly disappeared. 地主制度

Manrique, Jorge, +1479, Spanish poet, author of an elegy on the death of his father, famous for its perfect verses and the sublimity of expression. 曼里克

Mantellati, a third order of women performing medical services, founded in the early 14th century by Juliana Falconieri. 曼特拉提

Mantua, city of Lombardy (Italy). The Synod of Mantua was held in 1062, and in 1115 Mantua achieved the status of a free city. 曼托瓦

manuale, E: handbook, manual, textbook, D: Handbuch, Lehrbuch; a handy compilation of essential texts introducing the reader to one area of knowledge 手册, 见 Hrabanus, *De institutione clericorum*, Gratianus, *Concordantia discordantium canonum*, Petrus Lombardus, *Sententiae* (textbook of theology)

Manuel I Comnenus, Byzantine emperor 1143—1180, who failed to support the Second Crusade (1147) and suffered a major defeat from the Turks in Asia Minor (1173). During his reign merchants from Venice, Genoa, and Pisa settled in Constantinople. 马努尔/曼努埃尔

Manuel II Palaeologus, Byzantine emperor 1391—1425, who repeatedly visited the West in order to get support against the Ottoman Turks who had surrounded his empire. King Sigismund's crusader army was destroyed at Nicopolis (1396), but Timur the Lame defeated the Turks at Angora in 1402, thus granting the Byzantine empire a few more years. Manuel was a patron of humanists. 马努尔/曼努埃尔

Mankizert, (Armenia), site of a decisive battle between Seljuk Turks and a large Byzantine army (1071). The defeat of the Byzantines led to the conquest of Asia Minor and ultimately to the First Crusade (1096). 曼克择特

Marco Polo => Polo, Marco

Margareta, E: Margaret, D: Margarete; +1412, queen of Denmark, Norway, and Sweden. From 1376 she ruled Denmark in the name of her son Olaf, since 1380 she served as regent in Norway. In 1397 Denmark, Norway, and Sweden recognized her grandnephew and adopted son Eric of Pomerania as joint king of their contries, but Margaret exercised royal authority until her death. 玛格丽特

Margareta Maultasch, E: Margaret of Carinthia, +1369; Duchess of Tyrol, married to the son of Louis the Bavarian in 1342. She thwarted the plan of Emperor Louis IV to deprive her of Tyrol. 玛格丽特

Margareta, E: Margaret, D: Margarete, St., Queen of Scotland 1069—1093, wife of Malcolm III. She influenced her husband to implement reforms. Being advised by Lanfranc she introduced Roman liturgy to Scotland. 玛格丽特

Maria, E: Mary, D: Maria; the mother of Jesus, traditionally respected and venerated by Christians; in medieval literature she often intercedes for the sinners 玛利亚/马丽亚, 见 Walahfridus, *Visio Wettini*, Hrotsvita, *Theophilus* (Mary saves the man), Hermannus Contractus, *Salve Regina* (Mary, the "mother of mercy"), Bernardus (veneration of Mary), Alanus, *Anticlaudianus* (Mary among the blessed in Heaven), Dante, *Commedia* (Mary in highest Heaven), Appendix, *Heliand* (angel Gabriel sent to Mary)

Marianus Scottus, +1081; Irish monk, who founded a monastery at Regensburg in 1075, the origin of the "Schottenmoenche". He was known as an excellent calligrapher. 斯格托

Marie de France, +1190, earliest known French poetess, author of lays (lais) and fables. 玛丽

Marignolli, Giovanni de', +1357; Franciscan member of an embassy which Pope Benedict XII set to the court of the great khan in China in 1338. He reached Beijing in 1342 and remained there for four years. In 1353 he reached Avignon and authored an itinerary. 马利诺里

Marinus I, Pope 882—884. He conducted discussions with the Patriarch of Byzantium, Photius. 马瑞努斯

Marinus II, Pope 942—946 马瑞努斯

Marozia, member of the powerful Crescentii family, daughter of Theophylact. She was married to Alberic I of Spoleto, Guido of Tuscany, then to Hugh of the Provence. As "Senatrix and Patricia" she supported her son John XI (Pope 931—935) and influenced papal policies. 马若基亚

Marrano, Marranos, converted Jews in Spain and Portugal who secretly supported their old religion; they were perceived as dangerous and suppressed by the Spanish Inquisition (after 1480). 马拉诺

Marsilius de Inghen, +1396; German theologian, nominalist, rector of the University of Paris, then first rector of the University of Heidelberg. 马尔西留

Marsilius de Padua, It: Marsilio, 1270—1343, Italian theologian, professor at Paris, then writer for Louis IV; critical of papal power and of many traditional tenets. 马尔西留

Martinus IV, E, D: Martin, Pope 1281—1285, originally Simon de Brion, chancellor of Louis IX of France. As Pope he was under French influence, supporting the policies of Charles of Anjou, the king of Sicily. 马尔提努斯/马丁

Martinus V, E, D: Martin, Pope 1417—1431, orig. Odo Colonna, elected in Constance, the first pope universally accepted after the Great Schism. He convoked the synods of Pavia (1423) and Basel (1431) and tried to organize crusades against the Turks. 马尔提努斯/马丁

Martinus Polonus, E: Martin of Troppau, D: Martin von Troppau; +1278, Dominican of Prague, archbishop of Gnesen, author of a history of the popes and the German emperors. 马尔提努斯/马丁

martyium, E: martyrdom, E: Martyrium, the witness of a Christian who is killed for his or her faith 殉道, 见 Hrotsvita, *Dulcitius*

martyrologium, E: martyrology, D: Martyrologium; lists or records of martyrs; => hagiographia, vita 殉道士列传

Mary = Maria

Masaccio, Tommaso Giovanni di, +1428, Italian painter, famous for his naturalistic use of light. 马萨乔

mater, E: mother, D: Mutter; 母亲, 见 Hermannus, *De octo vitiis principalibus* (pride is the mother of all vices), Wolfram, *Parzival* (Herzeloyde's motherly care)

Mater misericordiae, E: mother of mercy, => Maria

materia, E: matter, D: Materie; a philosophical principle, => creatio, forma 物质, 见 Albertus, *Summa de creaturis* (matter, the passive indifferentiated principle of all things), Thomas Aquinas, *Summa theologiae* (matter is the principle of individuation)

mathematica, E: mathematics, D: Mathematik; one of the => artes 数学, 见 Oresmensis (discovered the irrational numbers), Nicolaus Cusanus (uses mathematical examples to explain his speculations)

Mathilda de Tuscia, Countess of Tuscany, 1040—1115, supporter of the papacy and of law studies, received Gregory VII in her castle in Canossa in 1077. She resisted Henry IV who deposed her and came to terms with Henry V in 1110. 玛蒂尔达

matrimonium, E: marriage, matrimony, D: Eheleben; 婚姻, 见 Raimundus Lullus, *Blanquerna* (starts with the ideal of marital life), Johannes de Tepla, *Der Ackermann* (death is skeptical of the joys of marital life)

Matthaeus Parisiensis, E: Matthew of Paris, +1259, monk of St. Albans, one of the leading English chroniclers of the Middle Ages, author of the *Chronica Maiora*. 玛迪亚

Matthias Corvinus, King of Hungary 1458—1490, through his wife also king of Bohemia (1469—1478). He patronized scholars and artists, founded the University of Bratislava (Pozsony) and the first printing press of Hungary, but after his death the Turks overran his reign. 玛迪亚·科维努斯

maze => mensura, moderatio

Mecca, E: Mecca, D: Mekka, the birthplace of

Muhammad, the Holy City of Islam.麦加, 见 Islam, *Qur'an*

Mechtildis de Hackeborn, E: Mechthild, D: Mechthild von Hackeborn; St., + 1299, Cistercian sister in the convent of Helfta near Eisleben (Germany), author of works on mystical theology (*Liber specialis gratiae*). She was a friend of Gertrude the Great. 梅希特尔德, 见 Gertrudis

Mechtildis de Magdeburga, E: Mechthild, D: Mechthild von Magdeburg, ca. 1207—1282, of noble Saxon ancestry, Cistercian Sister in Helfta, friend of Mechtild of Hackeborn and Gertrude the Great, author of a mystical work in Low German (*Das fliessende Licht der Gottheit*), spiritual poems and admonitions.梅希特尔德, 见 Gertrudis

Mecklenburg, German duchy on the southern Baltic shore, there were early Germans settlements, but in ca. 600 the region was taken over by Wends; Henry the Lion (+1195) reestablished German rule; missionary activity started around 920. 梅克伦堡

medica ars => medicina

Medici, wealthy and influential family of Florence, which dominated that city from the 1420s to the 1490s.美第奇

Medici, Cosimo de, 1389—1464, Florentine banker, who secured the Medici's control of Florence; he was a humanist, patron of the arts and helped to found and finance the Accademia Platonica in 1442.美第奇, 见 Piccolomini, *Commentarii*

Medici, Lorenzo de, I: Il Magnifico, E: Lorenzo the Magnificent, +1492, Italian maecen of arts, leader of the Republic of Florence 1469—1492, maintaining a balance of power among Milan, Venice, Naples, and Florence; he escaped the assassination of 1478 and had some of his rivals executed, therefore he was banned by the Pope.美第奇

Medici, Giuliano de, Italian politician, who was murdered in the Dome of Florence in 1478.美第奇

medicina, E: medicine, D: Medizin, especially herbal medicine; => ars medica 药品, 见 Walahfridus, *Liber de cultura hortorum*, Hildegardis, *Causae et curae*, Wolfram, *Parzival* (healing powers of the Grail), Thomas a Kempis, *De imitatione Christi* (communion is a medicina divina)

Medina, a large oasis north of Mecca to which Muhammad fled in 622. His tomb is in Medina.麦地那, 见 *Qur'an*

Mediolanum => Milano

meditatio, E: meditation, D: Meditation, Betrachtung; silent contemplation of spiritual realities 默想, 见 Hugo, *Didascalicon* (the last book entitled *De meditatione*), Gerson, *De mystica theologia*

Medium aevum, E: Middle Ages, D: Mittelalter, the period of European history extending from the end of classical antiquity (ca. 600 AD) to the Renaissance (ca. 1450). The first half of the Middle Ages is sometimes called "the Dark Ages" because of the collapse of the international trade and administration system of the Roman Empire, the invasion of barbarian tribes (most of them Germanic), and the beginnings of the somewhat oppressive feudal system. During the second half of the Middle Ages many institutions of the modern world emerged: schools and universities, big cities with their own city governments, transportation and communication systems, a prosperous, independent middle class of merchants and artisans, the separation of temporal and spiritual power, legal codes and institutions. During the whole period the Church was main force working for learning, trans-national communication, morals, social order and the transmission of culture in general, thus much of medieval literature is shaped and inspired by ecclesiastical beliefs. => Renasci 中世纪, 见 Joachim, *Liber figurarum* (division of history into three ages)

Meister Eckhart => Eckhart

memoria, E: memory, D: Gedaechtnis, one of the mental powers, since Augustine symbol of God the Father; => mens 记忆力, 见 Anselmus, *Monologion*, Bernardus, *De consideratione* (remember the great models of antiquity), Snorri Sturluson, *Edda* (Sigurd suffers a loss of memory through a magic potion)

mendicantes, E: mendicant orders, D: Bettelorden; mainly the Franciscan and Dominican friars who decided to work among the people, combining contemplative and apostolic vocations. The Council of Lyons (1274) approved the four orders of Franciscans, Dominicans, Augustinians, and Carmelites. The zeal and popularity of the Mendicants aroused some hostility from the secular clergy.托钵修会, 见 Thomas de Celano, *Vita Sancti Francisci*

Mendoza, Pedro Gonzales de, +1495; Archbishop of

Toledo, adviser to Ferdinand and Isabella of Spain, he was a humanist and patron of scholars. 孟多撒

mens, E: mind, D: Geist; => anima 心灵, 见 Bonaventura, *Itinerarium mentis in Deum* (apex mentis), Thomas Aquinas, *Summa theologiae* I.16,6 (human mind can reflect the truth)

mensura, E: measure, D: Mass, maze; => numerus 衡量, 尺度, 见 Bernardus, *De diligendo Deo* (sine modo diligere), Nicolaus Cusanus, *De docta ignorantia* (try to measure all things)

mercator, E: trader, merchant, D: Haendler; medieval trade increased steadily after the 9th century, influenced by Venice, the crusades, the reconquista in Spain, leading to the trade with overseas regions after 1492 商人, 见 Marco Polo, Oresmensis, *De origine monetarum* (influence on mercantilism)

Mercedarii, E: Mercendarians => Ordo B. Mariae Virg. de mercede redemptionis captivorum

Merlin, a magician and seer in Arthurian literature. Political prophecies were ascribed to him. => magus 梅尔林, 见 Geoffrey Monmouth, *Historia regum Britanniae*

Merovingiani, E: Merovingians, D: Merowinger, the Merovingian dynasty ruled the Franks from 481 AD to 751 AD and was followed by the Carolingians; their king Clovis accepted Christianity in 496 AD.梅洛温格人, 见 Eginhardus, *Vita Caroli*

Methodius, E: Method, D: Methodius, St., 825—885, from a noble family in Salonici, he was sent to Moravia by Photius in 863; as missionary in central Europe (together with Cyrillus) he translated the Bible and liturgical texts into the local Slavic language; after a visit to Rome in 867 he was made Archbishop of Pannonia but was opposed by the bishops of Salzburg and Passau who claimed Pannonia as their area.美多迪乌斯/梅托丢/麦托丢斯, 见 Photios

metropolita, E: Metropolitan, D: Metropolit, an archbishop in one of the larger cities of the Roman provinces; the metropolitan exercised authority over suffragan bishops. Metropolitans were usually archbishops and sometimes also primates. 大主教

metrum, E: metre, D: Versmass; important in Latin poetry. One of the most widely used meter was the hexameter.诗律, 韵律, 见 Aldhelmus, *Epistola ad Acircium*

Metz, town in Upper Lorraine (now France). It was a Roman fortress, suffered sacking by Attila in 451, became the capital of Austrasia around 535 and fell to Lothair in the division of the Carolingian empire. In the 13th century it acquired the status of an imperial city. The church St. Pierre-aux-Nonnains is the oldest in France and dates from the fourth century.梅斯

Michael II, Emperor of Byzantium 820—829, founder of the Amorian Dynasty, who pursued a moderate policy regarding iconoclasm.弥格尔/米迦勒

Michael III, Emperor of Byzantium 842, 856—867, who influenced Bulgaria to accept missionaries. He deposed Ignatius as patriarch and so triggered the Photian schism. In 866 he arranged the murder of his uncle and co-emperor Bardas and was murdered himself in 867.弥格尔/米迦勒

Michael VIII Palaeologus, Byzantine Emperor 1259—1282, founder of the dynasty of the Palaeologi. In 1261 he captured Byzantium from the Latins and Venetians. Accepting the Church union proclaimed by the Council of Lyons (1274) he made peace with the papacy and tried to avoid French aggression by supporting the overthrow of the Angevin rule in Sicily (1282). During his reign the Turks seized much of Asia Minor. 弥格尔/米迦勒

Michael Cerularius = Cerularius

Michele de Cesena, E: Michael of Cesena, D: Michael von Cesena; +1342; Italian doctor of theology, general superior of the Franciscans (1316), who supported Louis the Bavarian after 1323, when Pope John XXII condemned his views regarding the absolute poverty of Christ and the apostles. 弥格尔/米迦勒

Middle Ages => Medium Aevum

Midgard, a huge dragon in Norse mythology 米德格德, 见 Snorri Sturluson, *Edda*

Mieczyslaw I, / Miesko, Duke of Poland, 960—992, who married the Christian daughter of Boleslaw I of Bohemia and was baptized in 966. His land was soon led to Latin Christendom by Bohemian and German missionaries. Miesko donated his land to the Pope in 990 and received it back as fiefdom, which meant more independence from Germany.梅士科一世

migratio, E: migration (of peoples), D: Voelkerwanderung; the movement of nations especially in central Europe from the late fourth to the sixth century. The migrations were triggered by the Huns who threatened the Ostrogoths in the area north of the Black Sea (375). Most of the migrating people were of Germanic origin, among them the Visigoths, who sacked Rome in 410, the Vandals, Burgundians, Franks, Angles, Saxons, and the Lombards who occupied northern Italy in 568. In 955 Otto I defeated the Madyars, thus ending their invasions. Some scholars use this date to denote the end of the period called the "Migration of Peoples".民族大迁移

Milano, E, D: Milan; city of Celtic origin north of the Po. From the time of Diocletian it was an imperial city but suffered from the invasions of Huns (452), Ostrogoths (493) and Byzantine armies during Justinian's reign (534—562). The trade revival stimulated by the crusades brought prosperity for Milan. Frederick I Barbarossa seized and sacked the city in 1162, but it was quickly rebuilt and headed the Lombard League. In 1277 the family of the Visconti took control of the city, and in 1395 Galeazzo Visconti was granted the title "Duke of Milan" by the Holy Roman Emperor. Francesco Sforza married the daughter of the last Visconti duke and was made duke himself (1447). The construction of the cathedral (Duomo) began in 1386, and it was completed five centuries later.米兰

millennarismus, (=chiliasmus), E: millenarism, chiliasm, D: Endzeitdenken, Chiliasmus; the idea that Christ would return soon and begin a reign of 1000 years.千年主义,见 Joachim, *Liber figurarum*

Minimi = Fratres Minimi

Minnesinger, the German troubadour or lyric poet of the twelfth and thirteenth centuries who sang of courtly love (Minne). He composed both words and music and performed his songs in the open court. The most famous Minnesinger was Walther von der Vogelweide (+1230).宫廷抒情诗人

Minorites = Ordo Fratrum Minorum, Franciscani

minuscula, E: minuscule, D: Minuskel, a writing style using small and big letters, first used in the Carolingian period (around 780), later developed by Poggio and other humanist scholars. 小字体,见 Alcuinus

miraculum, E: miracle, D: Wunder, esp. the miracles Jesus worked; => mysteria 奇迹,见 Otfrid, *Evangelienbuch*

miseria, E: misery, D: Elend, Not; the people in the Middle Ages were aware of the calamities of life; => aegritudo 悲惨情况,见 Innocens, *De miseria*, Petrarca, *De remediis utriiusque fortunae*, Boccaccio, *Decamerone* (consolation in the plague of 1348)

missio, E: mission, evangelization, E: Mission; the efforts to spread the gospel or introduce Christian teachings to other people. By 500 AD most of the peoples who occupied the territories surrounding the Mediterranean Sea, had accepted Christianity, and missionaries were converting the semicivilized peoples in the north. The missionary movement corresponded roughly with the spread of civilization, since the missionaries needed literature and schools to instruct the heathen peoples. Monasteries were both cultural centers and mission outposts. Outstanding missionaries were Patrick, Columba, Columban, Boniface, Cyril and Methodius, Ansgar, Lullus, Francis of Assisi, and Dominic. 传教,见 Adamnanus, *Vita Columbae*, Beda, *Historia ecclesiastica* (mission efforts and methods of Pope Gregory the Great), Bonifatius, *Epistolae*, Bernardus, *De consideratione* (mission is a duty of the Pope), Thomas de Celano, *Vita Sancti Francisci* (Francis wanted to convert Muslims)

moderatio, E: moderation, D: Maessigkeit; => temperantia

modernitas, E: modernity, D: Modernitaet; the word "modernus" was first used by Pope Gelasius (492—496 AD), and the Walahfrid Strabo called the age of Charlemagne a "saeculum modernum"; many elements of "modernity" can be found in the Middle Ages; => scientia 现代性,见 Petrus Venerabilis, *Contra Saracenos* (dialogue with Islam), Hildegardis, *Causae et curae* (modern approach to sexuality), Thomas a Kempis, *De imitatione Christi* (devotio moderna)

modus, E: mode, measure, D: Art, Mass; 方式,程度,见 Bernardus, *De diligendo Deo* (diligere sine modo)

Mohammed => Muhammad

Molay, Jacobus de, General of the Templars, unjustly arrested and accused in 1307, forced to a "confession", he was executed in 1314 摩莱,见 Philippus IV

Mombaer, Johannes, Mauburnus, Dutch mystic, +

1501 蒙巴尔

monachus, E: monk, D: Moench; male member of a monastic community who kept the rule of their order, which usually meant to live by the vows of chastity, poverty, and obedience. The word "friar" implies a combination of contemplation with a- postolic work (as in the case of the Franciscans). Many of the medieval scholars were monks, especially Benedictines. 隐修者，见 Abaelardus, Adamnanus, Aldhelm, Adso Dervensis, Beda (wrote about his monastic life), Columban, Columbanus, Hermannus Contractus, Joachim, *Liber figurarum* (expected the arrival of a monastic age), Paulus Diaconus

monasteria mixta, E: combined monasteries; D: Doppelkloester, monasteries where women communities were living close to male religious communities 男女共同修道的隐修院, 见 Heloise (Le Paraclet), Hildegardis (Disibodenberg)

monasterium, <Gr. monos "alone", E: monastery, D: Kloster; the origins of monasticism are related to Anthony of Egypt, Pachomius, Basil of Caesarea in the East and Jerome, Martin of Tours, Augustine of Hippo, John Cassian, and Benedict of Nursia in the West. Many authors of the Middle Ages lived in monasteries or founded monastic communities. Famous monasteries are: Bobbio, Citeaux, Clairvaux, Cluny, Fulda, Helfta, Iona, Malmesbury, Monte Cassino, Reichenau. The mendicant orders of the 13th century combined the contemplative spirit of the cloister with an active apostolate. Through the copying of manuscripts monks preserved learning, they maintained schools and staffed universities. The spirit of monasticism enriched the life of the secular clergy and of lay society. 隐修院，见 Adamnanus, Aldhelm, Adso Dervensis, Beda, Columban, Columbanus, Hermannus Contractus, Malmesburiensis, Paulus Diaconus, Petrarca

moneta, E: money, D: Geld; In the 13th century Venice and Florence began to mint gold coins (florins and ducats) which stabilized the monetary system in western Europe and aided the expansion of trade and industry in the later Middle Ages. 钱财，见 Oresmensis, *De origine monetarum*

Mongoli, E: Mongols, D: Mongolen; an ethnic group in Central Asia, also known as Tartars (=Tatars). In 1206 their leader Temugin assumed the title Genghis Khan and welded the Mongols and some Turkish tribes into a powerful confederation. Under Genghis' son Ogadai and under his grandson Batu the Mongols conquered Russia (with the exception of Novgorod), then Hungary during the years from 1223 to 1241. After 1251 Mangu and his brothers Hulagu and Kublai continued to enlarge the huge empire of the Mongols. Hulagu invaded Persia, destroyed Baghdad (1258) and defeated the last of the Abbasid caliphs. He captured Damascus and Antioch. Kublai succeeded as great Khan in 1260 and conquered south China and Burma. The huge multi-lingual empire lacked unity and was replaced by the Ming Dynasty in 1368. => Johannes de Monte Corvino 蒙古人，见 Fredericus II, *De arte venandi*, Rubruk, *Itinerarium ad partes orientales* (the most reliable source concerning Mongols at that time), Marco Polo (possibly a high official under Mongol rule)

Monologion, E: *Monologion*, the earliest "scholastic" treatise, an inquiry into the rationality of faith by Anselm《独白篇》，见 Anselmus

Monte Cassino, oldest Benedictine monastery in Italy, founded in 529, important library and center of studies. It was destroyed by the Lombards in 581 and by the Saracens in 883. During the 11th century Monte Cassino reached the peak of its influence. 卡西诺山隐修院，见 Paulus Diaconus

Monte Corvino = Johannes de Montecorvino

Montpellier, E, D: Montpellier; a city of southern France near Marseilles, founded in the 8th century, it became the seat of a famous medical university, founded in 1220 and confirmed by the Pope in 1289. 蒙彼利埃，见 Alanus (teacher in Montpellier)

Moravia, E: Moravia, D: Maehren; the region east of Bohemia, occupied by the Moravians, a branch of the West Slavs c. 550 AD. In 863 the missionaries Cyril and Methodius came to Moravia. Magyars invaded the country after 900 but were driven out by Otto I in 955. In 1029 the region was incorporated into Bohemia. 摩拉维亚

More nevukhim, E: *Guide of the Perplexed*, a philosophical work by Moses Maimonides《迷途指津》，见 Maimonides

Moriscos 见 Marranos

mors, E: death, D: Tod; => aegritudo, miseria 死亡,

见 Ioannes Damaskenos, *Barlaam* (experience of death), Eginhardus, *Vita Caroli Magni* (death and funeral of Charles), Innocens III, *De miseria humanae conditionis*, Wolfram, *Parzival* (unknowingly causing the death of his mother), Thomas de Celano, *Dies irae*, Gertrudis, *Legatus divinae pietatis* (she writes about preparation for death), Boccaccio, *Decamerone* (inspired by the fear of Black Death), Johannes de Tepla, *Der Ackermann aus Boehmen*, Greban, *Passion de Paris*, Appendix, *Chanson de Roland* (heroic death), *Elkerlijk* (the rich man must die)

Moscovia, E: Moscow, D: Moskau; city of central Russia, first noted in 1147. The first Kremlin (citadel) was erected in 1156. The Mongols plundered the settlement in 1238 and again in 1293 and 1382. In 1328 the metropolitan see of the Russian Church was moved from Kiev to Moscow. Russian rulers opposed Church unity in 1441, proclaimed independence from Byzanz in 1459. Ivan III, the Grand Duke of Moscow, married Zoe (the niece of the last Greek Emperor Constantine XI) in 1472, and thereafter Moscow was called "the Third Rome." Tartar dominion ended in 1480.莫斯科

Moses, E: Moses, D: Mose; in the Old Testament the prophet and lawgiver who led the Israelites out of Egypt.梅瑟/摩西, 见 Maimonides, *More nevukhim* (Moses achieved union with God)

Moses Maimonides => Maimonides

motus, E: move, movement, D: Bewegung; 运动, 见 Thomas Aquinas, *Summa theologiae* (one of the arguments for the existence of God)

Mozarabs, Christians in Spain under Arab rule (from the 9th to the 15th century), who adapted their customs to Moorish ways. 莫扎勒布/摩尔人统治下的西班牙基督徒

Munich, (L: Monachium), E: Munich, D: Muenchen; the main city of Bavaria (Germany), originally a settlement near the monastery of Tegernsee (whence the name). From 1255 it was the home of the Wittelsbach family. The University of Munich was founded iin 1472.慕尼黑

Munster, (L: Monasterium), E: Muenster, D: Muenster; city in Westphalia (Germany). The local diocese was founded around 800 AD.明斯特

Muhammad, E: Mohammed, D: Mohammed; 570—632, founder of Islam, who led a life of prayer and preaching. In 622 he moved from Mecca to Medina where his faith spread fast. In 630 he returned to Mecca which became subsequently the center of the religion of Islam.穆罕默德, 见 Appendix, *Qur'an*

Musae, E: the Muses, D: die Musen, usually personalized allegories in medieval literature 文艺女神, 见 Hermannus Contractus, *De octo vitiis principalibus*

musica, Gr: mousikē, E: music, D: Musik; one of the seven liberal arts. Medieval music originated from plain songs or chants of liturgical singing from the first centuries of the Christian era. Many-voiced polyphony emerged as a result of developments between the ninth and thirteenth centuries. The invention of musical notation is attributed to Guido of Arezzo (+1050). => organum 音乐, 见 Eginhardus, *Vita Caroli* (Charles used to listen to music during meals), Hrabanus, *De institutione cler.*, (music essential for liturgy), Johannes Saresberiensis, *Policraticus* (music at court)

Muslim => Islam

mysteria, (<ministeria), E: mystery plays, D: Mysterienspiele; plays performed during the late Middle Ages and early Renaissance usually centered on the Bible ("Biblical plays"), the life of saints ("miracle plays") or moral issues "moral plays"); they developed from an elaboration of the trope (tropus, for example the Easter trope), a short dialogical song during liturgical celebrations; mystery plays were performed outdoor on stages built on large wagons ("pageants") and usually presented in groups or cycles. => passio 宗教戏剧, 见 *Elkerlijk*

mystica, E: mystic, D: Mystik; special religious experiences (voices or visions) and literature about these spiritual experiences; mysticism flourished since the 12th century. Important authors are Bernard of Clairvaux, Francis of Assisi, Bonaventure, Catherine of Siena, Mechtildis, Hildegard, Gertrude the Great, Birgitta of Sweden. => unio mystica 神秘主义/神秘神学/神秘文学, 见 Bonaventura, *Itinerarium mentis in Deum*, Gerson, *De mystica theologia*

N

Nantes, E, D: Nantes, a city of western France. In 936 it fell to the dukes of Brittany after being captured by Norse raiders.南特, 见 Chretien, *Erec et Enide* (coronation at Nantes)

Naples => Neapolis

Narbonne, a French seaport on the Mediterranean, capital of the Visigoths in 413 AD, it was conquered by the Arab invaders in 719 but reclaimed by Pepin III in 759; at the end of the 13th century the Jews were expelled which led to the city's decline.纳博讷

natura, E: nature, D: Natur;=> scientia naturae 自然本性, 见 Eriugena, *De divisione naturae* (natura creans non creata), Alanus, *Anticlaudianus* (allegory of nature creates a new man), Guillaume de Lorris, *Roman de la rose* (Nature reconciles Reason and Cupid), Thomas Aquinas, *Summa theologiae* (use of the lumen naturale; philosophy and politics are "natural")

navis, E: ship, D: Schiff, symbol for the community, for the Church 船, 见 Bonifatius, *Epistolae* 78

Neapolis, E: Naples, D: Neapel; city in Italy, founded by Greeks, it was a duchy under Byzantine rule at Justinian's time, but became independent in the 9th century and fought against Saracen invaders until 1087. In 1139 Roger II of Sicily annexed Naples, and from 1194 to 1266 it was ruled by the German Hohenstaufen. Frederick II founded the University of Naples in 1224 as the first state institution of higher learning in the Western world. Charles of Anjou controlled Naples after 1266. In 1282 Sicily fell to Aragon, but Naples followed only in 1442. 那波里/那布勒斯, 见 Fredericus II, Thomas Aquinas (educated there)

Nennius, E, D: Nennius, a Celtic author around 800 AD, author of *Historia Britonum* 内尼乌斯, 见 Galfredus, *Historia regum Britanniae*

neoplatonismus => Plato

Nestorius, E: Nestor, D: Nestor, ca. 1050—1114; Russian monk in Kiev, the "Father of Russian Historiography" 涅斯托尔, 见 *Povest' vremennych let*

Nestoriani, E: Nestorians, Syrian Church of the East, D: Nestorianische Kirche; the followers of Nestorius (+451) who were forced to leave the Byzantine empire after 486; their communities were established in Persia, Central Asia, India and China but suffered under the Mongol invasions. Their liturgical language was Syriac. 聂斯托利派/东叙利亚教会, 见 Rubruk, *Itinerarium ad partes orientales* (Christians in 15 cities of China)

Netter, Thomas, 1370—1431, English Carmelite and theologian who refuted Wycliffe. He was given the title "doctor praestantissimus". 内特, 见 Wycliffe

Neustria, northwestern part of the Frankish kingdom. The region included the cities of Paris, Soissons, and Tours. In the seventh century Neustria fought against Austrasia.诺斯提瑞亚

Nibelungenlied, E: *Song of the Nibelungs*, a heroic epic in Old High German from ca. 1200 AD.《尼伯龙根之歌》, 见 Snorri Sturluson, *Edda* (stories of the Volsungs)

Nicaea, Gr: Nikaia, D: Nizaea; The place of the Council of Nicaea (787), the Seventh Ecumenical Council, which was convoked by Empress Irene and condemned the position of the iconoclasts. 尼西亚会议

Nicephorus, Gr: Nikēphoros, E: Nicephorus, +829; theologian and historian, Patriarch of Constantinople (806). Being an opponent of iconoclasm he was exiled in 815.尼克弗若斯

Nicephorus I, Gr: Nikēphoros, E: Nicephorus; Byzantine Emperor 802—811, who was slain in a battle with the Bulgars.尼克弗若斯

Nicephorus Bryennius => Bryennius

Nicolaus I, E: Nicholas, D: Nikolaus; St., Pope 858—867, from a noble Roman family, he became the most outstanding Pope between 600 and 1070, directed church life in Italy, France, Germany, sent missionaries to Pannonia (Methodius) but faced resistance from Constantinople (Photius). He forced Lothair II, king of Lorraine, to take back his first wife whom he had divorced. 尼苛劳/尼哥拉/尼古劳斯, 见 Photius

Nicolaus II, E: Nicholas, D: Nikolaus; Pope 1058—1061, originally Gerhard, Bishop of Florence (1045), who decreed on the order of the election of the Pope and promoted reforms (Synod in the Lateran, 1059), thus preparing the Gregorian reform of the Church. 尼苛劳/尼哥拉

Nicolaus III, E: Nicholas, D: Nikolaus; Pope 1277—1280, from the Roman Orsini family, he established the Vatican as the permanent papal residence. He could reconcile Franciscan Conventuals and Spirituals and obtained some political achievements but was prone to nepotism. 尼苛劳/尼哥拉

Nicolaus IV, E: Nicholas, D: Nikolaus; Pope 1288—

1292, former Franciscan general, close ally of the Colonna family and therefore opposed to the Orsini. As Pope he supported the claims of the house of Anjou in Sicily against Aragon. He sent missionaries to Ethiopia, Persia, and China. => Monte Corvino 尼苛劳/尼哥拉

Nicolaus V, E: Nicholas, D: Nikolaus; Pope 1447—1455, orig. Thomas Parentucelli, bishop of Bologna (1443). As papal legate he made a successful plea for the recognition of Eugenius IV at the Diet of Frankfurt. His diplomatic skill and tolerance won him the support of the Princes of western Europe, thus the antipope Felix submitted in 1449. He became the first of the "Renaissance Popes" by supporting building activities in Rome, founding the Vatican Library and financing scholars and artists. 尼苛劳/尼哥拉

Nicolaus V, E: Nicholas, D: Nikolaus, this Franciscan friar advanced to the papacy through the support of Emperor Louis IV of Bavaria and was an antipope from 1328—1330 but submitted to Pope John XXII in 1330 尼苛劳/尼哥拉

Nicolaus Cusanus, E: Nicholas of Cues, D: Nikolaus von Kues; 1401—1464, German doctor of canon law, delegate at the Council of Basel (1431—1438), papal legate in Constantinople (1437), cardinal (1448), bishop of Bressanone / Brixen (1450). He was a humanist scholar and promoter of Church unity. Siding with conciliarism in the beginning (he authored *De concordantia catholica*), he left the Council of Basel in 1437 in support of the Pope 尼苛劳/尼哥拉, 见 *De docta ignorantia*

Nicolaus de Dinkelsbuehl, E: Nicholas, D: Nikolaus; +1433, professor of theology in Vienna, rector of the university, he was a famous preacher and theological author. 尼苛劳/尼哥拉

Nicolaus de Fluehe, E: Nicholas of Flue, D: Nikolaus von der Fluehe, St., +1487, Swiss hermit, who had been married and served as judge before; he was widely known to be a man of peace and universal brotherhood. 尼苛劳/尼哥拉

Nicolaus de Lyra, E: Nicholas of Lyra, D: Nikolaus von Lyra; ca. 1270—1349, French Biblical scholar, professor in Paris, author of the *Postilla* (a literal exegesis of the Bible), he could read Hebrew and enjoyed considerable fame as Biblical scholar. 尼苛劳/尼哥拉, 见 *Postilla litteralis super totam Bibliam*

Nicolaus Mysticus, a nephew of Photius, Patriarch of Constantinople, blamed Emperor Leo VI, was deposed but restituted in 911. 尼苛劳/尼哥拉

Nicolas Oresmensis => Oresme

Nider, Johannes, +1438, a German Dominican who attended the councils of Constance and Basel, he taught at Vienna and promoted reforms within the Dominican order; author of the *Formicarius*, a work containing information about the Church at his time. 尼德尔

Nogaret, Wilhelmus, F: Guillaume de Nogaret, E: Nogaret; +1313, French chancellor of Philipp IV. He was an aggressive advocate of royal power and organized the capture of Pope Boniface VIII in Sept. 1303. He also directed the king's attack on the Knights Templars. 诺加雷

Nolasci = Ordo B. Marae Virgine de mercede redemptionis captivorum

nominalismus, E: nominalism, D: Nominalismus; the view that universal ideas only exist "nominally" and not apart from the thing itself. This school of thought was increasingly influential since the 12th century. The nominalists opposed the realists and the Platonic view that general ideas exist from all eternity and thus precede physical objects in time (ante rem); the nominalists thought that general ideas come only after the things (post rem). => universalia 唯名论, 见 Petrus Hispanus, *Summulae logicales*, Wyclif, *De civili dominio* (firm opponent of nominalism), Gerson, *De mystica theologia* (his theology of the heart was influenced by nominalism)

Nomokanon, the legal code of the Greek Orthodox Church, attributed to Photius, but probably older. 教会法典

nonna, E: nun, sister; D: Nonne, Schwester; communities of nuns emerged in many places since late antiquity; most educated women in the Middle Ages were nuns; => Birgitta, Gertrudis, Hildegardis, Hrotsvita 修女, 见 Aldhelmus, *De laudibus*, Thomas de Celano, *Vita Sancti Francisci* (Francis helped to found the "Sisters of St. Clare")

Norbertus, E: Norbert of Xanten, D: Norbert, St., +1134; Archbishop of Magdeburg 1126—1134. He founded of a monastery at Premontre near Laon in 1120, which became the mother-house of the Premonstratensians. 诺贝特

Normandia, E: Normandy, D: Normandie; the region in northwestern France that Charles the Simple handed over to Rollo and his Normans in 911. It was under English rule from 1066 to 1204 and for some a period during the Hundred Years' War, but in 1450 it finally fell to France.诺曼底

Normanni, E: Norsemen, Normans, Vikings, D: Normannen, Wikinger; seafaring Scandinavian tribes who raided the coasts of northern and western Europe (England, France) and even of southern Europe from the 8th to the 10th century.诺曼人，见 Saxo Grammaticus, *Gesta Danorum* (contains mythology of the Vikings)

Northumbria, E: Northumberland, D: Northumbrien; one of the Anglo-Saxon kingdoms in England, it was established around 600 AD. After 620 King Edwin introduced Christianity.诺森伯兰, 见 Aldhelmus, *Epistola ad Acircium*, Beda, *Historia* (dedicated to king Ceowulf), Alcuinus (of noble Northumbrian descent)

Norway, the Viking state of Norway started to accept Christianity during the reign of the kings Harald I (+940), Hakon (Haakon I, +960) and Olaf Trygvason (Olaf I, +999). King Olaf II (1015—1030) completed the conversion of the country. 挪威

Notkerus Balbulus, E: Notker the Stammerer, D: Notker der Stammler, ca. 840—912, monk of St. Gall, librarian, poet, composer. 诺特克尔，见 *Gesta Caroli Magni*

Notker Labeo, Notker Teutonicus, E, D: Notker Labeo; +1022, monk of St. Gall, writer and teacher, translator of Latin works into German.诺特克尔

Notker de Liege, [Notker of Luettich], Bishop of Liege, founder of a school, +1008 诺特克尔

Novgorod, D: Nowgorod, ancient settlement in northwest Russia, first mentioned in 862 when the Varangians under Rurik seized the place. It enjoyed independence until Ivan III captured the city in 1456.诺夫哥罗德

numerus, E: number, D: Nummer; the mystical meaning of numbers was often contemplated in medieval literature; => mathematica 数字，见 Aldhelmus, *Epistola ad Acircium*, Dante, *Commedia* (symbolic use of numbers), Nicolaus Cusanus, *De docta ignorantia* (all numbers spring from number one, thus the whole world is created by God)

O

oblatus, E: oblate, D: Oblate; a child offered to a monastery by his/ her parents to be educated there; the practice is already mentioned in the *Rule* of St. Benedict. => conversi 被奉献者，见 Beda (he was an oblate)

Occam, Wilhelmus de, E: William of Occam, D: Wilhelm von Ockham; 1295—1349, English Franciscan who studied at Oxford, and lectured on theology; as he was an exponent of nominalism, he was inclined to deny the rationality of faith and had to go to Avignon to defend himself in 1326. In 1328 he fled from Avignon to the court of Louis IV the Bavarian, where he wrote against the temporal power of the papacy, accepted the fallibility of the Pope and argued for the supremacy of a general council in matters of faith. 奥康的威廉，见 *Sententiae*

octo vitia principalia => De octo vitiis principalibus

Oderic = Odoricus

Odilo, E: Odilo of Cluny, D: Odilo, St., Abbot of Cluny 994—1048, called "Archangel of the Monks". He cared for the poor, enforced the regulations concerning the Truce of God and was highly respected by Popes and kings. He introduced the feast of the commemoration of the deceased.欧迪罗，见 Cluny

Odin, (=Wotan), one of the main Germanic gods, origin of the word "Wednesday"欧丁，见 Cynewulf, *Elene*, Snorri Sturluson, *Edda*

Odo, E, D: Odo, St., +942, Abbot of Cluny 927—942, and one of the organizers of the Cluniac reform movement. 欧多/奥多，见 Cluny

Odoricus de Pordenone, E: Odoric, D: Oderich, St., 1286—1331, Italian Franciscan missionary who worked for more than 30 years in the Balkans, Persia, Terbizond, and in Beijing (China). 和理德，见 Monte Corvino

Odysseus, E, D: Odysseus; figure of Greek mythology, symbol of inventiveness and shrewdness 奥德修斯，见 Alanus, *Anticlaudianus*, Dante, *Commedia* (placed in the inferno)

Olaf Haraldson, E: Olaf the Saint, D: Olaf der Heilige; patron saint of Norway; King of Norway and Sweden 1014—1030, who promoted Christianity in Norway with the help of Anglo-Saxon missionaries. 奥拉夫

Olaf Trygvason, King of Sweden and Norway 995—

999 who was baptized in England.奥拉夫

Olifant, the magic horn of Roland 欧里凡，见 *Chanson de Roland*

Oliver, figure in *the Song of Roland* 欧里维，见 *Chanson de Roland*

omnipotentia (**Dei**), E: omnipotence, D: Allmacht (Gottes); => Deus, theologia 全能，见 Maimonides, *More nevukhim*（divine omnipotence does not exclude himan freedom and responsibility）

ontologia, E: ontology, D: Ontologie, the discipline exploring being 本体论，见 Anselmus, *Proslogion*（ontological proof）

operatio, E: action, D: Tat; 行动，见 Hildegardis（writes about God's action in history）

optica, E: optics, D: Optik; => lux 光学，见 Grosseteste, Rogerius Baco, *Opus maius*

Opus maior, E: *Greater Work*, a work by Roger Bacon《伟大著作》，见 Rogerius Baco

oratio => prex

ordalium, ordalicium, E: ordeal, D: Gottesurteil; the pagan custom to find out the guilt of a person by submitting him/her to some test, or to a duel. The outcome was seen as "decision of God." The Fourth Lateran Council (1215) forbade the clergy to take part in ordeals, and the legal procedures of Henry II (1154—1189) brought an end to the use of ordeals in England.神的裁判

ordines, E: sacrament of holy orders, D: Weihen; the grades of the Christian ministry; the so-called minor orders were porter, acolyte, lector, exorcist; the major orders were subdeacon, deacon, priest, bishop.品位/小品/圣秩圣事

Ordo Beatae Mariae Virginis de mercede redemptionis captivorum, E: Mercedarians, Nolasci, D: Mercedarier; a congregation founded in 1222 by Perter Nolasco with the aim of ransoming slaves or Christians held captive by Moslems.慈母会

Ordo Cisterciensium, OCist, E: Cistercians, D: Zisterzienser; a monastic order based on the Benedictine tradition, it began as a reform movement in 1098, flourished in the 12th and 13th centuries, in particular through the influence of St. Bernard of Clairvaux. They promoted a return to the strict, more literal observance of Benedict's Rule. The mother house of many affiliated monasteries was in Citeaux.熙笃会，见 Bernardus, Gertrudis, Otto Frisingiensis, Alanus ab Insulis

Ordo Fratrum Minorum, OFM = Franciscani

Ordo Hospitalis = Hospitaller

Ordo Praedicatorum, OP = Dominicani

Ordo Sancti Augustini, OSA, E: Hermits of St. Augustine, D: Augustinermoenche; a monastic congregation founded in the 13th century in central Italy and Lombardy. Inspired by St. Augustine they constituted a union of semi-eremitical communities. Papal approval was given in 1244 and 1256, obliging them to keep a rule similar to that of the Dominicans. Together with the Franciscans, Dominicans, and Carmelites, they were one of the four mendicant congregations accepted by the Council of Lyon 1274.圣奥古斯丁会

Ordo Sancti Benedicti, OSB, E: Benedictines; D: Benediktiner; a monastic order founded in 529 AD in Italy by Benedict of Nursia through his Rule (*Regula*), hugely influential for the establishment of monastic culture, education and scholarship. Many of the scholars of the early Middle Ages were Benedictines.本笃会/本尼狄克修会，见 Beda, Bonifatius, Paulus Diaconus

Ordo Sanctissimae Trinitatis de redemptione captivorum, E: Trinitarians, D: Trinitarier; an order founded in 1198 by St. Johannes de Matha and St. Felix de Valois. The main aims of the order were the freeing of captives and medical services. 圣三会，

Ordo Teutonicus, E: Teutonic Knights, German Order; D: Deutschorden; a military religious order originally founded as a hospital established by German merchants in Acre in 1190. Approved as an order of knights, priests and lay brothers in 1199 by Pope Innocent III, they first fought against the Saracens in Syria and Palestine but since 1226 were mostly active in eastern Europe, where they established their own state in Pomerania and Prussia. Poland and Lithuania united in 1386 to resist the Teutonic Knights and in 1466 limited the order to its possessions in East Prussia. 条顿骑士团

Oresmensis, Nicolaus, F: Nicole Oresme, E: Nicholas Oresme, D: Nikolaus Oresme; +1382, a founder of modern science and mathematics. He studied theology and was ordained Bishop of Lisieux (1377), translated works of Aristotle into French and wrote on theology, nature, mathematics, economics, politics. His De coelo et mundo anticipated Copernicus, and his studies in analytical geometry contained the discoveries which made Galileo and Descartes famous. 俄瑞斯梅，见 *De origine monetarum*

organum, E: organ, D: Orgel; musical instrument used in churches, possibly developed from instruments that Byzantium sent to the Franks in 757 and 812; by the thirteenth century organs were common in many of the larger parish churches in Europe.管风琴

Orleans, F: Orléans, E, D: Orleans; a city of north-central France; it withstood Attila's Huns in 451 and became an intellectual center due to the nearby abbey of Fleury. In the tenth and eleventh centuries Orleans served as the real capital of France. The University of Orleans was founded by Pope Clement V in 1305. In 1429 Joan of Arc led troops to lift the English siege of the city.奥尔良，见 Alanus (educated there)

Orthodoxia, festum = Festum Orthodoxiae

osculatio pedum, E: kiss of the feet, D: Fusskuss; an expression of respect, sometimes performed when greeting the Pope.亲脚礼，见 Gregorius, *Dictatus Papae*

Otfried de Weissenburg, ca. 800—879, monk in Fulda (Germany), author of a *Book of the Gospels* 奥特弗里德，见 *Evangelienbuch*

Othmarus, E: Otmar, D: Othmar, St., ca. 700, abbot of St. Gall 欧特马尔

Otloh, Othlo, +1070, Monk in St. Emmeram, Regensburg, author of theological literature 欧特罗

Otto I Magnus, E: Otto the Great, D: Otto der Crosse; King of Germany 936—973, he defeated the Magyars in 955 and was crowned Emperor in Rome in 962. He confirmed the position of the Pope in Italy but at the same time controlled the papacy.奥托

Otto II, E, D: Otto; King of Germany 973—983, who fought against the Saracens in Italy and died in Rome at the age of 28.奥托

Otto III, E, D: Otto; King of Germany (983) and Roman Emperor 996—1002, who influenced the papal election in 996 and was crowned emperor the same year. He founded archdioceses in Poland and Hungary. Having settled down in Rome in 998 he was forced to flee that city in 1001 together with Pope Silvester II.奥托

Otto IV de Brunsvic, E: Otto IV, D: Otto von Braunschweig, +1218; King of Germany 1208—1215, he was crowned Emperor in 1209.奥托

Otto Frisingensis, E: Otto of Freising, D: Otto von Freising; 1111—1158, son of Leopold III of Austria, bishop and historian 奥托，见 *Chronica sive Historia*

Ottonian Renaissance, D: Ottonische Renaissance; the revival of culture and learning during the reigns of Otto I, II, and III of Germany (the tenth century). The monastic and cathedral schools of Passau, Regensburg, Magdeburg, Corvey and Gandersheim were the main centers of the movement.奥托文艺复兴，见 Hrotsvit of Gandersheim

Oxonia, Oxford, a city on the upper Thames, mentioned as Oxenford in 912. The university was established in the 13th century as one of the earliest universities of Europe, it emphasized philosophy of nature and sciences. Its first chancellor was Robert Grosseteste (from 1215 until 1235). 牛津大学，见 Petrus Lombardus, *Sententiae* (used as textbook in Oxford)

P

Padua, city in northeast Italy, destroyed by the Lombards in 601 but became a commercial and cultural center. The University of Padua (Italy) was founded in 1222 by masters and students who came from Bologna.帕多瓦

paenitentia = poenitentia

pagani, E: pagans, D: Heiden; literally people who live in remote villages (pagus) and have not contact with (Christian) culture; in the Middle Ages the term denoted non-Christians 外教人，见 Hrabanus, *De institutione cler.* (discussion of pagan literature and its censorship)

Palaeologus, Gr: Palaiologos, E: Palaeologus; the name of the ruling dynasty of the Byzantine Empire from 1261 to 1453. The emperors included Michael VIII (1261—1282), Andronicus II (1282—1328), Manuel II Palaeologus (1391—1425), Johannes VII (1425—1448) and Constantine XI (1448—1453).帕来欧罗格斯

pallium, E: pallium, D: Pallium, honorary white stole sent to archbishops. Archbishops were not entitled to exercise certain powers until the pallium had been received from Rome. 白羊尾披肩带，见 Bonifatius, *Epistulae* 28 (the pallium sent to Boniface)

Pantheon, Gr: Pantheon, E: Pantheon; a temple dedicated "to all gods", it was turned into a church in the era of Pope Boniface IV （608—615 AD） 万神殿, 见 Paulus Diaconus, *Hist*.

pantheismus, E: pantheism, D: Pantheismus; the confusion of Creator and creation; some medieval mystic theologicans emphasized the union of the soul with God and were accused of pantheism. 泛神论, 见 Eckhart, Nicolaus Cusanus, *De docta ignorantia* (analogy and the theory of participation prevent pantheism)

Papa, E: Pope, D: Papst; the word meaning "father" was originally a term for any bishop, but later became the exclusive title of the bishop of Rome, who as the successor of St. Peter was regarded as the chief Bishop of the Church. The Pope had dominant influence in the governance of the （Western）Church; after 1000 many Popes were scholars of law, and the struggle between the papacy and the kings of Germany over the question of lay investiture encouraged the development of secular law and canon law. As the Lombards threatened central Italy in the early eigth century, the papacy turned to the Franks for help. In 754 Pepin III responded to Pope Stephen II's appeal for help, drove the Lombards from Rome and turned the city and the exarchate of Ravenna over to the Pope （the so-called Donation of Pepin）, which created the temporal power of the papacy in central Italy （a fact that was changed only in the second half of the 19th century）. During the era of Innocent III （1198—1216）the influence of the papacy reached a peak, but the 14th century brought decline and the disaster of the Great Schism of the western Church. => Gregorius Magnus, Gregorius VII, Innocens III, Petrus Hispanus, Piccolomini 教宗/教皇, 见 Carolus Magnus （crowned in Rome）, Gregorius VII, *Dictatus Papae*, （special privileges of the Pope）, Bernardus, *De consideratione* （handbook for an ecclesiastical leader）, Lullus, *Blanquerna* (description of an ideal Pope), Dante （placed his hope in the emperor and resisted papal influence in Florence）, Wyclif, *De civili dominio* （attacks on the papacy）, Langland, *Piers Plowman* （image of an ideal Pope）

Paradisium, E: Paradise, D: Paradies; the Garden of Eden （see Bible, *Gen* 2）, => caelum 天堂, 见 Dante, *Commedia* （after the Earthly Paradise, Eden, comes the eternal Heavenly Paradise）, *De vulgari eloquentia* （the language of Eden was a stable and universal language）

Parcifal => Parzival

Paris, （<Lutetia Parisiorum）, E: Paris, D: Paris, first a Celtic settlement, Paris was known as Lutetia Parisiorum in Roman times. According to tradition St. Denis （+258 AD）was the first bishop of the local church. In 508 AD Clovis made Paris his capital, but after 800 it was sacked by the Vikings, and only when the Capetians made the city their capital （in 987）the town grew in importance. The beginning of the construction of the cathedral of Notre Dame was in 1163, and in the same period Paris became a center of studies, its famous university was formally chartered in 1200, it emphasized philosophical studies （the artes）, but also had faculties of theology, law, and medicine. The president of the university was an important （theological）authority, especially during the period of the ecclesiastical split around 1400. => St. Victor 巴黎大学, 见 Abaelardus （teacher at Notre-Dame）, Petrus Lombardus, *Sententiae* （textbook in Paris since 1222）, Alanus （teacher in Paris）, Gerson （president of the university）

parliament, （<L: parabola, parlare）, D: Parlament; the English legislative body that emerged from the council which the king usually convened once or twice every year. During the 13th century the representation became broader and was accepted as proper. Kings needed the support of local nobles for subsidies, especially during the Hundred Years' War against France. The parliament limited the power of the king and since the 14th century shared in the crown's responsibility for enacting legislation. In the same period the lords and commoners started to meet separately, thus forming the House of Lords and the House of Commons. 议会, 国会, 见 Beda, *Historia* （meeting of nobles）, Appendix, *Magna Charta*

parodia, E: parody, D: Parodie; satires and parodies ridiculing Church and clergy were common in the later Middle Ages. 讽刺, 见 Boccaccio, *Decamerone*, Appendix, *Roman de Renard*

Parzival, （=Parcifal）, E: Perceval, D: Parzival; a hero of Arthurian legend 帕齐法尔, 见 Galfredus Monemuthensis, *Historia regum Britanniae*

Parzival, E: *Parzival* (*Perceval*), a novel in Old High German by Wolfram von Eschenbach. The central theme is Parzival's search for the Holy Grail.《帕齐法尔》，见 Wolfram

Pascalis I, Pope 817—824, who crowned King Lothair I in 823.帕斯卡利斯

Pascalis II, Pope 1099—1118, a Benedictine abbot and cardinal. He opposed lay investiture and for a time was taken prisoner by Emperor Henry V in 1111.帕斯卡利斯

Pascha, E: Easter, D: Ostern, => resurrectio

Paschasius Radbertus, St., +860, Benedictine theologian, Abbot of Corbie, who produced the first longer doctrinal treatment of the Eucharist, in which he affirmed the real presence of Christ in the Eucharist (transubstantiation).帕斯卡修斯

Passau, city and diocese in Bavaria. It grew from Celtic origins and became a bishop's see in 739 by St. Boniface. The bishops of Passau were very influential since the 9th century.帕骚

passio, E: passion, D: Passion, esp. the passion of Christ, remembered every year on Good Friday 受难，苦难，见 Otfrid, *Evangelienbuch*, Wolfram, *Parzival* (he is carrying arms on Good Friday), Dante, *Commedia* (Dante gets lost in a forest on Good Friday), Greban, *Passion de Paris*

Passion de Paris, E: *Passion of Paris*, a French passion play by Arnoul Greban《巴黎受难剧》，见 Greban

Pastor angelicus, Papa angelicus, E: Angelic Shepherd, Angelic Pope; D: Engelhirt, Engelpapst; the expectation of Joachim of Fiore and the Spiritual Franciscans that a saintly person would appear and restore the holiness of the early Church.天使般的牧者，见 Joachim

Pataria, E: Patarenes, D: Patarener; a lay movement in Milan (and some other cities of north Italy) after 1050. They demanded ecclesiastical reforms, wanted to raise moral standards among the clergy and suppress simony. The enthusiasm of the First Crusade (1096) absorbed the zeal of these reformers, and the movement only reappeared in the late 12th century, when the name Patarenes was equal to "heretics" and "Cathars".帕塔利亚

Pater ecclesiae, E: Father of the Church, D: Kirchenvater; those Christian authors who defended the orthodox faith in late antiquity 教父，见 Johannes Damascenus, *Pēgē Gnōseōs* (the compilation earned him the title "Last father of the Church"), Abaelardus, *Sic et non* (sentences from the Fathers), Petrus Lombardus, *Sententiae*

Patricius, E: Patrick, D: Patrick; St., ca. 385—461, the apostle of Ireland who started his successful mission work in Ireland in the year 432 AD; => Columba 帕特里克

Patricius Romanorum, E: patron of Rome, D: Patron der Roemer; the title of Pepin confirmed by the Pope in 754, later of Charlemagne. 罗马人的保护者

Patrimonium Petri, E: Legacy of Peter, D: Erbgut Petri; estates (mainly in central Italy) under the administration of the Popes. The "Donation of Pepin" (756) confirmed the political authority of the Pope in these areas.圣伯多禄/彼得的遗产

patrologia, E: patristic literature, patristic studies, D: Patrologie; the tradition of the Fathers of the Church, => Pater ecclesiae 教父学

Paulani = Fratres Minimi

Paulinus de Aquileia, E: Paulinus of Aquileia; +802, theologian and scholar at Charlemagne's academy, later appointed patriarch of Aquileia. 保利努斯

Paulus, Gr: Paulos, E: Paul, D: Paulus; St., one of the Apostles and a fervent missionary, who was martyred at Rome in 64 or 67. His letters (New Testament) inspired the theology of later ages. 保禄/保罗，见 Alanus, *Anticlaudianus* (Paul among the blessed in Heaven)

Paulus I, E: Paul, D: Paulus; Pope 757—767, who continued to develop the relationships to the Franks.保福/保罗

Paulus II, E: Paul, D: Paulus; Pope 1464—1471, originally Cardinal Barbo, who tried to counteract Turkish aggression; he also suppressed the Roman Academy.保福/保罗

Paulus Diaconus, E: Paul the Deacon, ca. 720—799, historian; he was from Lombard nobility and became a monk in Monte Cassino, later a member of Charlemagne's academy.保福/保罗，见 *Historia Longobardorum*

paupertas, E: poverty, D: Armut; => divitiae, mendicantes 贫穷，见 Thomas de Celano, *Vita Sancti Francisci* (the vocation to live in voluntary poverty), Jacobus de Voragine, *Legenda aurea* (St. Alexius, model of poverty), Wyclif, *De civili dominio* (upheld poverty)

Pavia, town in North Italy, capital of the Lombards until 774, place of synods（1160, 1423）帕维亚

pax, E: peace, D: Frieden; 和平, 见 Thomas a Kempis, *De imitate Christi*（inner peace）, Appendix, *Heliand*（Christ, the king of peace）, *Bulla aurea*（Landfriede）

Pax Dei => Treuga Dei

peccatum, E: sin, D: Suende; according to the Christian tradition and thought, word or action that is contradictory to God's will is sinful; sinners should confess their sins and do penitence for them, => poenitentia, purgatorium, vitium 罪, 见 Walahfridus, *Visio Wettini*, Anselmus, *Cur Deus homo*, Innocens III, *De miseria*（man is born in the bonds of sin）, Dante, *Commedia*（punishment in Hell for different kinds of sin; confession, contrition, and satisfaction are the steps to purge sins, => purgatory）, Langland, *Piers Plowman*（allegories of the seven cardinal sins）

Pēgē Gnōseōs, E: *Fountain of Wisdom*, a work by St. John of Damascus《智慧的泉源》

penitence = poenitentia

Pepin => Pippinus

Perceval => Parzival

peregrinatio, E: pilgrimage, D: Pilgerfahrt; a journey abroad or to a holy place for the purpose of worship, thanksgiving or doing penance（indulgences）. Christian pilgrimages started in the period of Constantine the Great whose mother Helena visited Jerusalem in 326, where she is believed to have discovered the True Cross. Throughout the Middle Ages the most famous pilgrim destinations were the Holy Land, the tombs of Saint Peter and Saint Paul at Rome and the shrine of St. James at Compostela（northern Spain）. After the murder of Thomas Becket（1170）Canterbury became England's most popular pilgrimage destination. Moslems are expected to visit the Kaaba in Mecca and the tomb of Muhammad in Medina. 朝圣, 见 Cynewulf, *Elena*; Chaucer, *The Canterbury Tales*

persecutio, E: persecution, D: Verfolgung; in the Roman empire Christians were persecuted before 313 AD. From the fourth century heretics or those resisting imperial policies were suppressed, especially in Byzantium（=> iconoclasm）. Radical heretic teachings that spread fast in western Europe since the 12th century produced fear and were suppressed by inquisition courts（=> inquisitio）. In many places Jews were persecuted sporadically（=> Judaei）. 迫害, 见 Hrotsvita, *Dulcitius*

pessimismus, E: pessimism, D: Pessimismus; => aegritudo, dolor, miseria, timor 悲观主义, 见 Innocens III, *De miseria conditio humanae*, Snorri Sturluson, *Edda*（main figures inevitably approach their doom）

pestilentia, E: pestilence, Black Death, D: Pest; => plaga

Petrarca, It: Francesco Petracco, E: Petrarch, D: Petrarca; 1304—1374, son of a Florentine exile, he studied at Montpellier and Bologna, but abandoned his legal career and devoted all time to classical studies, encouraging others（Boccaccio）to do the same. Being a scholar and poet he lived as a cleric of minor orders at the Papal court of Avignon for ca 18 years, later supported Cola di Rienzo（1347）and the return of the Pope to Rome. His love for Cicero and antiquity led to a certain depreciation of the "dark" Middle Ages.彼特拉克, 见 *De remediis utriusque fortunae*, *Rime*

Petrus, Gr: Petros, E: Peter, D: Peter; the leading figure within the group of Jesus' disciples. Peter founded and directed the church community of Rome, where he was martyred. Based on certain Biblical passages, the successor of Peter（as bishop of Rome）was seen as a general authority in matters of faith and morals. The Middle Ages developed the administration system of the Catholic Church under the leadership of the Roman curia. => Papa, cardinalis 伯铎禄/彼得, 见 Bernardus, *De consideratione*, Alanus, *Anticlaudianus*（Peter among the blessed in Heaven）, Dante, *Commedia*（Peter keeps the gate of Purgatory）, Appendix, *Heliand*（Peter rebuked for drawing the sword）

Petrus d'Ailly = Peter of Ailly 见 Ailly

Petrus Abaelardus = Abaelard

Petrus II de Aragon, Sp: Pedro, E: Peter; King of Aragon 1196—1213, count of Barcelona, he was crowned at Rome by Pope Innocent III, thus accepting the Pope as overlord. In 1212 he supported Alfonso VIII of Castile to push back the Moors at the battle of Las Navas de Tolosa. He made strict laws against heretics in 1197 but fought against Simon de Montfort, leader of the Albigensian Crusade. 伯多禄/彼得

Petrus III de Aragon, Sp: Pedro, E: Peter; King of Aragon 1276—1285, he married Constance, the daughter of Manfred, became King of Sicily (1282—1286) after the insurrection of Sicily against the Anjou-regime in 1282. In 1283 he granted his nobles and the towns of Aragon privileges similar to those of the *Magna Charta*. 伯多禄/彼得，见 *Magna Charta*

Petrus Aureoli, F: Pierre, E: Peter; +1322; Franciscan theologian, archbishop of Aix-en-Provence, an exponent of nominalism.伯多禄/彼得

Petrus de Castelnau, E: Peter; Cistercian, papal legate, whose murder in Toulouse in 1208 prompted Innocent III to proclaim the Albigensian Crusade.伯多禄/彼得

Petrus Comestor, E: Peter Comestor, D: Petrus Comestor; 1120—1178, chancellor of the cathedral school in Paris, author of the popular *Historia scholastica*, the standard work on the history of the Bible, covering the events from the Creation to the Acts of the Apostles. 伯多禄/彼得·科梅斯托，见 Petrus Lombardus, *Sententiae*

Petrus Damiani, It: Pietro, E: Peter, D: Petrus; St., ca. 1010—1072; Italian monk, prior of the Benedictine community at Fonte Avellana, which had adopted the strict rule of St. Romuald, the founder of the Camaldoleses. In 1057 Peter was made cardinal bishop of Ostia, and he served as papal legate in many European countries (France, Germany). His numerous letters, sermons, hymns, and treatises aim at the reform of the Church. He also wrote against the marriage of the clergy. => Gregory VII 伯多禄/彼得达米阿尼，见 Dante, *Commedia* (placed in the Heaven of Saturnus)

Petrus Hispanus, Sp: Pedro, E: Peter of Spain, 1210—1277, born in Portugal, he became professor in Paris and Siena, was famous for his medical knowledge, was made cardinal and elected Pope (Pope Johannes XXI 1276—1277) 伯多禄/彼得，见 *Summulae logicales*

Petrus Lombardus, E: Peter Lombard, D: Petrus Lombardus; 1100—1160, Italian scholar, teacher at the cathedral school of Notre Dame, Paris, in 1159 he was ordained Bishop of Paris; his famous collection of maxims of theology served as textbook in medieval universities until it was superseded by Aquina's *Summa theologiae*. 伦巴第人伯多禄/彼得，见 *Sententiarum libri quattuor*, Dante, *Commedia* (placed in the Heaven of the Sun)

Petrus de Luna = Pope Benedict XIII 伯多禄/彼得

Petrus Nolascus, Sp: Pedro, E: Peter; St., +1256, co-founder of the Mercedarians (founded 1222 at Barcelona). 伯多禄/彼得

Petrus de Pisa, It: Pietro, E: Peter; +799; Italian grammarian and scholar at Charlemagne's academy, possibly Charlemagne's Latin teacher. 伯多禄/彼得

Petrus Venerabilis, E: Peter the Venerable, D: Petrus der Ehrwuerdige; +1156, abbot of Cluny from 1122; he directed about 2000 Cluniac houses in western Europe and impressed many by his saintly and peace-loving attitude. "可敬的"伯多禄/彼得，见 *Contra Saracenos*

Philippus I, Fr: Philippe, E: Philip, D: Philipp; French king 1060—1108, who negotiated with Pope Urban II about investiture issues (1098). 菲利普

Philippus II Augustus, Fr: Philippe, E: Philip, D: Philipp; King of France 1180—1223, who greatly enlarged his domain by seizing Maine, Touraine, Anjou, Brittany, and Normandy from King John of England. In 1214 he defeated John's ally Otto IV of Germany. By permitting his vassals to crusade against the Albigenses in Languedoc he began to absorb Toulous into his reign. He enhanced royal authority in France, beautified Paries, chartered the University of Paris and embarked on the Third Crusade together with Richard I of England and Frederick I Barbarossa (1189—1192). Pope Innocent III turned against him when he divorced his wife Ingeborg, sister of the Danish king, and married Agnes of Meran.菲利普

Philippus IV, Fr: Philippe le Bel, E: Philip the Fair, King of France 1285—1314, an unscrupulous monarch whose humiliation of Pope Boniface VIII gave him more control of the Church in France. He expelled Jews, persecuted the Templars and confiscated their possessions. To bolster his attack on the papacy he (for the first time) convoked the estates general in 1302. 菲利普

Philippus VI, Fr. Philippe, E: Philip, King of France 1328—1350, whose reign saw the beginning of the Hundred Years' War (1337). He tried to negotiate between the Roman Curia and Louis the Bavarian in 1341.菲利普

Philippus de Suabia, E: Philip, D: Philipp; son of Frederick I Barbarossa, German king 1198—1208, who faced opposition from Otto IV and was murdered in 1208.菲利普

philosophia, E: philosophy, D: Philosophie, the earnest search for wisdom, accepted as a useful tool be medieval theologians; scholastic works call Aristotle the "Philosophus"; => dialectica, intellectus, logica, ratio 哲学, 见 Johannes Damascenus, *Pēgē Gnōseōs*, (philosophy, the handmaid of theology), Eriugena, *De divisione naturae* (philosophy and religion are the same), Avicenna, *Kitab* (Islamic "falsafah" marginalized by the orthodox "kalam"), Abaelard, *Sic et non*, Petrus Venerabilis, *Contra Saracenos* (philosophy has a mediating function), Maimonides, *More nevukhim* (Jews have always had philosophy), Albertus, *Summa de creaturis* (philosophy as independent science), Thomas Aquinas, *Summa contra gentiles* (faith described in terms of philosophy), *Summa theologiae* (philosophy is a science in its own right)

Photius, Gr: Phōtios, E: Photius, 810—897, Patriarch of Constantinople from 858 to 867 and from 877 to 886; he sent Cyril and Methodius to Moravia and broke off relations with Rome in 867; he was an eminent scholar, author of the *Bibliotheca* (*Myrobiblion*).佛提乌斯/傅丢斯, 见 *Myrobiblion*

Piccolomini, Enea Silvio de, (=Pius II), E, D: Enea Piccolomini; 1405—1464, one of the leading Humanists of his age, he attended the Council of Basel, supported conciliarism, entered imperial services and became court poet of Frederick III in Vienna. In 1445 he changed his position, was reconciled to Pope Eugenius IV and influenced the Emperor to foster the unity of the Church. He was ordained priest, then bishop, and in 1458 was elected Pope (Pius II). In his pontificate he organized resistance against the Turks, he also tried to tackle Church reforms.皮科罗米尼, 见 *Commentarii rerum memorabilium*

Picardia, E: Picardy, D: Pikardie; a province in northern France between Normandy and the Low Countries. Its capital was Amiens and came eventually under French control.彼卡迪

Piers Plowman, a poem by Langland《耕者皮尔斯梦》, 见 Langland

pilgrimage = peregrinatio

Pippinus, E: Pepin II, D: Pippin; father of Charles Martell, first a kind of administrator (Maiordomus) of the Merovingians, then Duke (Dux Francorum) 688—714. He was a supporter of Willibrord.丕平

Pippinus, E: Pepin the Short, D: Pippin; father of Charlemagne, king of the Franks 751—768, he received anointment from St. Boniface, was anointed by Pope Stephen II in 754, expelled the Lombards from Ravenna and donated the area to the Pope ("Donation of Pepin", 756).丕平

Pirminus, E, D: Pirmin, St., +753; an itinerary bishop, founder of the monastery in Reichenau. 皮尔明努斯

Pisa, town in Italy west of Florence, it became a commercial and industrial center in the 12th and 13th centuries, when its trade and influence was almost equal to Genoa and Venice. In 1284 Genoa destroyed Pisa's naval power in the sea battle of Meloria. The University of Pisa was recognized in 1343. The Council of Pisa (1409) convened in order to end the Western Schism.比萨

Pius II, Pope 1458—1464, originally Enea Silvio Piccolomini 比约/庇护, 见 Piccolomini

Placet, approval, a vote of assent; also the right of approval, usually the right of a king to approve (or disapprove) papal decisions or documents 批准权

plaga, E: bubonic plague, "black death", pestilence, D: Pest; The worst outbreak happened in 1347—1351, during these years the plague swept across Europe from Byzantium to Norway, possibly killing a third of the European population. It reappeared several times thereafter.鼠疫

planta, E: plants, D: Pflanzen; => arbor, flores, medicina 植物, 见 Vincentius of Beauvais, *Speculum maius* (the *Speculum naturale* describes many plants)

Plato, Gr: Platōn, E: Plato, D: Platon, 427—347 AD, Greek philosopher and author whose influence on medieval and Renaissance thought was profound; Neoplatonism developed in late antiquity and merged with Christian thought, especially in the works of Augustine, Dionysius Areopagita etc.柏拉图, 见 Hrabanus, *De institutione cler.*, Eriugena, Bernardus, *De diligendo Deo*, Alanus, *Anticlaudianus* (ascent to the light), Bonaventura (influenced by Plato), Thomas Aquinas, *Summa theol.* (combines Aristotelian and Platonic elements), Gerson, *De mystica theologia* (influenced by Plato), Bessarion, *In calumniatorem Platonis* (against George of Trebizond)

Plethon, Gemistos, + 1452, a Byzantine scholar who

promoted Platonism in Italy, he authored *Nomon syngraphe*, a political utopia. 普莱顿, 见 Piccolomini, *Commentarii*

Plinius, E: Pliny the Elder, D: Plinius, Gaius Plinius Secundus, 23—79 AD, compiler of the *Historia naturalis*, an encyclopedic work often quoted by medieval authors 普林尼, 见 Walahfridus, *De cult. hort.*

Podiebrad, Georg, Jiri of Podebrady; King of Bohemia 1458—1471, a former Hussite leader who was elected king by the Bohemian estates in 1458. He was supported by the moderate Hussites. When he refused to abolish the Compacts of Prague which recognized their privileged status, Pope Paul II excommunicated him in 1466. 波迪布拉德

Poema de mio Cid, E: *Poem of the Cid*, the most famous of the Spanish "chansons de geste"《熙德之歌》, 见 Appendix

poena => poenitentia

poenitentia, E: penitence, punishment for sins, D: Busse; penitential practices, usually fasting, praying, pilgrimages, giving alms or donating money to beneficial projects and churches; according to Christian doctrine, after their death sinners have to do penitence in purgatory in order to reach heaven. => satisfactio 忏悔/悔罪/补赎, 见 Walahfridus, *Visio Wettini*, Hartmann, *Der arme Heinrich* (suffering accepted as punishment), Thomas de Celano, *Vita Sancti Francisci* (a life of penitence and service)

poenitentiaria, an office at the Roman Curia 补赎法院

Poggio Bracciolini, 1380—1459, Italian humanist scholar, discoverer of Latin manuscripts. He translated Greek works into Latin. 波焦·布拉乔利尼, 见 Piccolomini, *Commentarii*

Poitiers, city in west-central France, whose first bishop was St. Hilary (+367). It was taken by the Visigoths, then in 507 by the Franks. In 732 Charles Martell stopped Arab invaders in a battle near Poitiers. Also in this place the "Black Prince" gained a victory over the French in 1356. 普瓦捷

Poland => Polonia

Policraticus, E: *Polycraticus*, a work by John of Salisbury《论政治》, 见 Johannes Saresberiensis

Polo, Marco, E, D: Marco Polo, 1254—1324, Venetian merchant who came to the court of Kublai Khan at Shangdu (near Beijing) in 1271, he was entrusted with several missions, and the Khan may even have appointed him governor of Yangzhou. In 1292 the Polos went back to Venice. Marco's report about China became very famous and helped to stir interest in the study of scientific geography. 马可·波罗

Polonia, E: Poland, D: Polen; state in east-central Europe, founded in the 9th and 10th centuries. The first prince in control of a united Poland was Miesko I (+992) who recognized the authority of Otto I of Germany and became a Christian. His son Boleslaw (992—1025) was the first to hold the title of king. In 1386 the Poles allied themselves with Lithuania and inflicted a defeat on the Teutonic Knights at Tannenberg in 1410 which restricted the expansion of the Knights. 波兰, 见 Cosmas, *Chronica* (Poland attacked by Bohemia under Duke Bretislav), Malmesburiensis, *Gesta regum Anglorum* (Silvester II supported the Polish king)

Pomerania, E: Pomerania, D: Pommern, border area between Germany and Poland at both sides of the Oder River. Mission activities were carried on since the 12th century. 波美拉尼亚

Pomponius Laetus, It: Julio Pomponio Leto, +1497, Italian humanist who founded the Roman Academy in the 1460s. 彭波尼乌斯

pontifex, E: pontifex, D: Pontifex, title of bishops and of the Pope. 彭提菲克斯, 见 Alcuin, *De pontificis et sanctis Eboracensis ecclesiae*

Pope => Papa

Portiuncula, chapel in Italy where St. Francis received his vocation; after 1270 the practice of "Portiuncula-indulgences" emerged. "小块教堂"

Portugal, once a part of the Roman empire, the area was overrun by Sueves and Visigoths in the fifth century and conquered by Muslims after 700. Ferdinand I of Castile seized the town of Coimbra in 1064 and thus started the process of the reconquista (reconquest). Important medieval rulers include Alfonso III (1248—1279), his son Diniz (1279—1325) who founded the University of Coimbra in 1290, and Henry the Navigator (+1460) who established a mariners' school at Cape St. Vincent. Thus Madeira and the Azores were colonized, Tangier was taken from Morocco (1471), and Vasco da Gama sailed to India

(1498). The fate of the Church in Portugal was in many ways dependent on the situation in Spain.葡萄牙

Posna, E: Poznan, D: Posen, a city of Poland, the first Polish diocese which was established in 968.波兹南

Postilla, commentaries on the Bible were called postilla, for example the one of Nicolaus of Lyra 波斯提亚

Postilla litteralis super totam Bibliam, E: *Literal Explanation of the Bible*, an exegetical work written in the 1320s by Nicholas of Lyra《全部〈圣经〉注解集》, 见 Nicolaus

potestas, potentia, E: power, D: Macht; the Middle Ages recognized the spiritual power of the Pope and the secular power of the Emperor, however the limits of these two powers also needed clarification. => imperator, Papa 权力, 见 Gregorius, *Dictatus Papae*, Bernardus, *De consideratione*, Occam, *Sententiae* (potentia Dei absoluta, potentia Dei ordinata; => voluntas)

Povest' vremennych let, E: *Tale of Bygone Years*, the first chronicle of Russian history《往年故事》, 见 Nestorius

praebenda, E: prebend, D: Pfruende; the part of the revenue of a church (income from the manor belonging to the church) that was given to a priest. The term might also denote a piece of property in general.教堂的固定收入

praedestinatio, E: predestination, D: Vorherbestimmung; the decision of God that certain souls will be saved and others damned. The controversy about predestination started with St. Augustine's critique of Pelagius' views.预定论

praedicare, E: preaching, D: Predigt; important means of spreading the gospel or of converting heretics; the Dominicans were founded as an "Order of Preachers". 讲道/布道, 见 Thomas de Celano, *Vita Sancti Francisci* (Francis led a community of lay preachers)

praedicatores, Ordo Praedicatorum = Dominicani

praelatus => praepositus

Praemonstratenses, E: Norbertines, Order of Premontre, D: Praemonstratenser; a congregation founded by St. Norbert in 1120 at Premontre (Laon); their dress is white.普雷蒙特会

praepositus, praelatus, E: prelate, D: Propst, Praelat; the superior of an ecclesiastical (canonical) community(圣职团的)长上

praescientia (Dei), E: foresight, prescience (of God), D: Vorherwissen, Vorsehung (Gottes); 预知, 见 Hildegardis (emphasizes God's prescience)

Praga, E: Prague, D: Prag, main city in Bohemia, founded in the 8th century, first mentioned in 928. The Diocese of Prague was established in 973. Prague had the first university in the German speaking countries (founded in 1348 by Charles IV) and became one of the leading cultural centers of Europe. => Bohemia 布拉格, 见 Cosmas Pragensis, *Chronica*

preces => prex

presbyter, E: priest, (<Gr: presbyter), D: Priester; a man who held an office in the Church, administering to the spiritual needs of the people under the guidance of a bishop. Many medieval authors were priests (or bishops).司铎/神父

prex, preces, E: prayer, D: Gebet; the verbal expressions of the adoration of God; many medieval texts are based on the prayers of the Bible.祈祷, 见 Hrotsvita, *Theophilus* (40 days of prayer), Dante, *Commedia* (in Purgatory the souls pray certain prayers to correct their sinful attitudes)

prima causa, E: the first cause, D: die erste Ursache 第一原因, 见 Eriugena, *De divisione naturae* (God is the first cause of the universe)

princeps episcopus, E: prince-bishop, D: Fuerstbischof; the name given to bishops in the Holy Roman empire who governed territories as secular princes, for example the archbishop of Cologne.侯爵主教

prior, the second in command after the abbot (in a Benedictine monastery); also the head of a religious community that did not have the legal status of a monastery.隐修院副院长

probatio, E: proof, D: Beweis; 证明, 见 Anselmus, *Proslogion* (ontological proof of the existence of God), Maimonides, *More nevukhim* (proofs of the existence of God), Thomas Aquinas, *Summa theologiae* (quinque viae)

prophetes, E: prophet, D: Prophet; especially the prophets of the Old Testament 先知, 见 Petrus Venerabilis, *Contra Saracenos* (Muhammad compared to the prophets of the Old Testament), Galfredus Monemuthensis, *Historia regum Britanniae* (Merlin' political prophecies)

Proprietary churches =>ecclesia propria

Proslogion, E: *Proslogion*, a theological treatise containing the ontological proof of the existence of God《对话篇》, 见 Anselmus

Provence, the oldest possession of ancient Rome north of the Alps which was given the name "Provincia" (the province). The area was occupied by the Burgundians, then by the Visigoths, Ostrogoths, Franks, and it was raided by Arabs from the eighth to the eleventh century. After 934 part of it was absorbed by Toulouse, and in 1246 it came under the control of the Angevin dynasty of Naples. Only in 1481 it fell under the direct authority of the French crown. 普罗旺斯

providentia, E: providence (of God), D: Vorsehung (Gottes); => Deus 预知，天佑, 见 Maimonides, *More nevukhim* (divine prescience and omnipotence does not exclude human freedom)

prudentia, E: prudence, D: Vorsicht, Besonnenheit; => allegoria 谨慎, 见 Alanus, *Anticlaudianus*

Prussia, (Pruzzia, Borussia), E: Prussia, D: Preussen; the area between the Vistula and the Memel. The most famous missionary working among the Prussians was Adalbert of Prague (martyred in 997). In 1230 the Polish duke of Mazovia invited the Teutonic Order to subjugate the people and conquer the area. The Teutonic Order held the region until forced to turn over the greater part of it to Poland in 1466 (Treaty of Torun). 普鲁士

Przemysl, one of the first kings of Bohemia 普施米斯勒, 见 Cosmas Pragensis, *Chronica Bohemorum*

Psellus, Michael, Gr: Psellos, E, D: Psellus, +1078; Byzantine polymath, erudite author, interested in the revival of classical learning. He was the first professor of philosophy in the newly founded University of Constantinople. 普塞鲁斯

Pseudo-Dionysius Areopagita, author of very influential theological texts, ca. 500; according to medieval tradition a disciple of St. Paul who heard him at the Areopagus in Athens 伪丢尼修斯

puer oblatus, => oblatus

pugna, E: fight, D: Kampf; motive of heroic literature; => eques 交战, 见 Ekkehard, *Waltharius*, Alanus, *Anticlaudianus* (fight of good and evil forces), Chretien, *Erec et Enide*

purgatorium, E: purgatory, D: Fegefeuer; the Christian concept that sinners are punished in some form for their sins after their death; after this purification process the souls can reach heaven. 炼狱, 见 Walahfridus, *Visio Wettini*, Dante, *Commedia* (detailed description of Purgatory)

Q

Quadragesima, forty days of fasting, season of lent 四旬斋期, 见 Hrabanus, *De institutione clericorum*

quadrivium, E: quadrivium, D: Quadrivium; the four arts of arithmetica, geometria, astronomia, musica, which formed the seven liberal arts together with the Trivium (grammatical, logica, rhetorica). 四科

quaestio, E: question, D: Frage, Quaestio; topics open to debate in scholastic treatises 论题, 见 Abaelardus, *Sic et non*

Quedlinburg, nunnery in Germany, founded in the 10th century, a place of education and culture. 奎德林堡

Quierzy, treaty of Quierzy from 754, a compactation between Pope and the Frankish King. 克尔西条约

Qur'an, E: *Koran*, D: *Koran*; the sacred book of the Islam 古兰经, 见 Appendix, *Qur'an*, Petrus Venerabilis, *Contra Saracenos* (suggested translation into Latin), *Alexandreis* (Alexander is mentioned in the *Qur'an*)

R

Rabanus Maurus => Hrabanus

Rachis, king of the Lombards, deposed by Austulf in 749. 拉赫斯

Raimundus Lullus, E: Ramon Lull, D: Raimund Lull; 1235—1316, a mystic of Catalonia, married and became a Franciscan Tertiar; on the advice of Raymond of Penafort he spent 9 years in Majorca to study Arabic and theology. He promoted mission among the Muslims and language studies. Being the author of ca. 300 works in Latin, Arab and Catalan, he influenced both Franciscan and Sufi mysticism. His Catalan prose and poetry established the literary norms of that language. 瑞孟多/赖孟多

Raimundus de Pennaforte, E: Raymond of Penafort, D: Raimund von Penafort; St., 1175—1275, Dominican scholar and canonist, general superior of his society 1238—1240, co-founder of the Mercedarians, he lectured at Bologna and at some time directed a school of Arabic and Hebrew studies in Spain for the conversion of Jews and Moors. 瑞孟多/赖孟多, 见 Thomas Aquinas,

Summa contra gentiles

Raimundus du Puy, E: Raymond of Puy, D: Raimund von Puy; Superior of the Hospitallers 1120—1160, he wrote a rule for them.瑞孟多/赖孟多

Raimundus de Sabunde, E: Raymond, D: Raimund; +1436; Spanish philosopher, theologian, physician, professor at the University of Barcelona. 瑞孟多/赖孟多

Raimundus VI, E: Raymond VI, +1222, Count of Toulouse, a supporter of the Albigenses. He and his ally Peter II of Aragon were defeated by Simon de Montfort at the battle of Muret (1213).瑞孟多/赖孟多

Rainaldus de Dassel, E: Rainald of Dassel, D: Rainald von Dassel; Chancellor of Frederick I 1156—1167, he influenced the anti-papal policy of the Emperor and was a patron of poems; sometimes he is identified with the Archipoeta 莱纳尔德, 见 Appendix, *Carmina Burana*

Rastislaw, Moravian King 846—870 拉斯提拉夫

Ratherius, E: Rather, D: Rather; +974; Bishop of Verona and Liege, an important author.拉特尔

Rathramnus, +ca.868, Benedictine monk in Corbie (Germany), whose writings on the figurative meaning of the Eucharist produced controversies. 拉特兰努斯

ratio, E: reason, D: Verstand, Vernunft, especially emphasized by scholastic philosophers and theologicans; => intellectus 理性, 见 Anselmus, *Cur Deus homo* (rational method with juridical overtones), Abaelardus, *Sic et non* (not promoting rationalism), Hildegardis (often uses the term "rationalitas"), Alanus, *Anticlaudianus* (allegory of reason), Guillaume de Lorris, *Roman de la rose* (argues against love), Bonaventura, *Itinerarium*, Petrarca, *De remediis utriusque fortunae* (allegory of Reason talking to Hope and Fear)

rationalitas => ratio

rationes aeternae => idea

Ravenna, E: Ravenna, city in northern Italy whose marshes offered protection. Thus it served as residence for Emperor Honorius (from 402), Odoacer, the Ostrogothic kings, and the exarch of Ravenna from 584 until the invasion of the Lombards in 751. In 756 Pepin III handed it over to the Pope. Treasures of early Christian art are found in the churches of Ravenna. 拉文纳, 见 Paulus Diaconus, *Historia Lang.* (almost occupied by the Lombards)

Raymond => Raimundus

realismus, E: realism, D: Realismus; the school of thought which maintained that universal ideas possess objective reality apart from individuals that embody the ideas. Nominalism dismissed these ideas as mere words or terms. Plato's thought effected that most scholastics were realists before the 13th century.实在论, 唯实论, 见 nominalismus

Regensburg, L: Regina castra, Ratisbon, E, D: Regensburg; celtic settlement at the Danube in Bavaria, it was a fortress (Regina castra) in Roman times. Since 530 AD it was the residence of the dukes of Bavaria, became a bishop's see in 739, and Louis the German used it as his capital in 827. In 1245 it became an imperial free city.雷根斯堡

Regina scientiarum, E: queen of the sciences, => scientia

Regino de Pruem, E: Regino of Pruem; +915; Abbot of Pruem (Eifel, Germany), historian, 瑞格诺

regnum, E: political power, reign, D: Herrschaft; => lex, rex, res publica 政权, 见 Johannes Saresberiensis, *Policraticus*

regula, E: rule, D: Regel; the documents that regulated the life of monastic communities, usually written by the founders of these communities.会规, 见 Thomas de Celano, *Vita Francisci* (Francis' rule)

regulares, E: regular clergy, D: Regularkleriker, canons, friars and other clergymen who lived in communities under a rule; => clerici regulares 有规律的圣职人员

Reichenau, Benedictine monastery in southern Germany, founded by Charles Martel in 724, famous for its book illuminations. 赖兴瑙, 见 Walafried Strabo, Hermannus Contractus

Reims => Remi

reliquiae, E: relic, D: Reliquien; an object venerated by believers because it was associated with a saint; the relics were often a part of the saint's body, a mantle or a book kept in a shrine (reliquary). 圣物/圣髑

Remi, E: Rheims, D: Reims; town and episcopal see northeast of Paris. It served as the residence of the rulers of Austrasia during Merovingian times. In 1179 its archbishop gained the right to crown the kings of France.兰斯

Renasci, It: rinascimento, E: Renaissance, D: Renaissance; the revival of classical learning, especially of classical Greek and Latin studies, sped by the fall of Constantinople in 1453 and the invention of book printing in Germany around 1455; the humanist scholars of the Renaissance aspired to an all-round development of man and extolled the beauty of all the experiences this world has to offer (spirit of "worldliness"). Early exponents were Petrarca and Boccaccio, but only in the 15th century the movement spread in northern Europe (Erasmus, Reuchlin). The same intellectual ferment also gave rise to the reformation. see: humanism 文艺复兴, 见 Johannes Saresberiensis, *Policraticus* (description of many aspects of life, love for classics), Alanus, *Anticlaudianus* (neglect of salvation through Christ), Dante, *Commedia* (position of classical literature, e.g. Vergilius), Petrarca, Boccaccio, Poggio, Medici

Rene, (L: Renatus), Fr: Rene d'Anjou, +1480; Duke of Anjou, whose daughter Margaret became the wife of Henry VI of England. In 1442 he was defeated by his rival for the crown of Naples, Alphonse V of Aragon. Rene was a patron of poets and musicians and one of the last champions of medieval chivalry.瑞内

requies, E: rest, inner peace, D: Ruhe; => hesychasmus 宁静, 见 Bonaventura, *Itinerarium* (requies datur intellectui)

res publica, E: republic, state, D: Republik, Staat; => rex

resurrectio, E: resurrection, D: Auferstehung; the resurrection of Christ is celebrated annually at Easter. Many medieval works reflect on the meaning of the resurrection.复活, 见 Dante, *Commedia*, Greban, *Passion*

Reuchlin, Johannes, German humanist scholar, Hebraist and Grecist, 1455—1522, author of the first textbook of classical Hebrew in Germany, *De rudimentis hebraicis* (1506). 瑞克林

revelatio, E: revelation, D: Apokalypse => apocalypsis

Revelationes, E: *Revelations*, a work containing the visions of Bridget of Sweden, the most important medieval text from Skandinavia《神视》, 见 Birgitta

rex, E: king, ruler, D: Koenig, Herrscher; in the Middle Ages the ruler of a country was a person who enjoyed ecclesiastical support (anointment, coronation), whereas there were no Biblical allusions for sanctions concerning the lower aristocracy; => feudalismus; 国王, 见 Nestorius, *Povest'* (autobiography of Grand Duke Vladimir Monomachus, the ideal of a Christian ruler), Johannes Saresberiensis, *Policraticus* (divine mandate of a ruler, theory of tyrannicide), Dante, *Commedia* (the Heaven of Jupiter is the place of saintly kings like David and Constantine), Wyclif, *De civili dominio* (emphasizes the power of the king, who is "vicarius Christi"), Appendix, *Beowulf* (ideal king), *Heliand* (Christ, the king of peace)

Rhenus, E: Rhine, D: Rhein, main river in Germany 莱茵河, 见 Ekkehard, *Waltharii poesis*

rhetorica, E: rhetoric, D: Rhetorik, the art of talking persuasively 修辞学, 见 Hrabanus, *De institutione cler.*

rhyme => homoteleuton

Richard I Coeur de Lion, E: Richard Lion-Heart, D: Richard Loewenherz; King of England, 1189—1199, one of the leaders of the Third Crusade (1189—1192), on his way back he was captured in Austria (1192) and ransomed in 1194. After his return he recovered the possessions in France that Philip II Augustus had seized.理查德

Richard II, E, D: Richard; King of England 1377—1299, married Anna of Luxemburg (the sister of the king of Bohemia) in 1382. His reign was marred by conflicts with the aristocracy, and finally he was murdered. 理查德

Richard de St. Victor, E, D: Richard, +1173; Scottish theologian and exegete, from 1162 prior of the abbey of St-Victor in Paris. He was an important mystical writer and had strong links with Hugh of St. Victor. 理查德, 见 Hugo de Sancto Victore

Riga, archdiocese of Riga, center of mission activities in the 12th and 13th centuries. It became the seat of an Archbishop in 1253 and a member of the Hanseatic League in 1282.里格

Rime, (***Canzoniere***), E: *Poems*, a collection of poems by Petrarch《歌集》, 见 Petrarca

Robertus, E: Robert => Rollo

Robertus Guiscard, E: Robert Guiscard, D: Robert Guiscard; ca. 1015—1085, Norman Duke, military leader who conquered Apulia and Calabria and then was enfeoffed by the Pope with Apulia,

Calabria, Sicilia in 1059. In 1071 he captured Bari, the last Byzantine foothold in Italy. In 1084 he returned from Greece to rescue Pope Gregory VII and drove the army of Henry IV out of Rome. 罗伯特, 见 Gregorius VII

Robertus de Arbrissel, E: Robert of Arbrissel, Bl., +1117; itinerary missionary and eminent preacher, he established the Order of Fontrevault in 1100. 罗伯特

Robertus de Molesme, E: Robert of Molesme, St., +1110; Benedictine abbot, who founded the reform monastery of Citeaux (Cistercium) in 1098. Together with Stephen Harding he is the founder of the Cistercian order. 罗伯特

Robertus de Sorbon, Robert of Sorbon, 1201—1274, chaplain of Louis the Saint, founder of a college called "Sorbonne", later the name of the University of Paris. 罗伯特

Rodericus, Sp: Rodrigo, E: Roderick, D: Roderich; +713; the last king of the Visigotones (Spain). He fought Franks and Burgundians when the Muslim forces crossed over from north Africa in 711. 若得瑞克/罗得里格

Rodericus Diaz, Sp, E: Rodrigo Diaz de Vivar; 1040—1099, born in Castile, who served Alfonso of Castile, was exiled, served Moorish rulers of Saragossa, finally died in Valencia. Being a symbol of military ability, chivalry, and generosity, he became a national hero of Spain. 罗德里格, 见 Appendix, *Poema de mio Cid*

Roger I, +1101, a Norman Duke who together with his older brother Robert Guiscard conquered Sicily from the Muslims in 1072 and in 1085 succeeded Robert as ruler of southern Italy. 罗杰/若格尔

Roger II, Norman Duke, 1101—1154, king of Sicily and southern Italy 1130—1154; he captured Naples and Capua and established a foothold in Tunisia and Tripoli that were under Arabic rule. He issued a new code of laws, centralized the government, fought against Byzantium, Venice, the papacy but also patronized science and art. His efficient rule has won him the praise to be the "first modern ruler". 罗杰/若格尔

Roger Bacon => Baco, Rogerius

Roland, E, D: Roland; semi-legendary nephew of Charlemagne who fought and fell in Spain 罗兰, 见 Appendix, *Chanson de Roland*, Dante, *Commedia* (placed him in Heaven),

Roland Bandinelli = Alexander III

Rollo, (Robertus), ca. 860—936, leader of the Normans (Vikings), he was pacified and baptized in 912, when he received the piece of land known as Normandy from Charles III the Simple. Rollo agreed to hold the region as a fief, although he independently founded a state with his men. 若罗

Roma, E: Rome, D: Rom, center of Western Christendom, traditional seat of the Pope; religious, cultural, political center of Italy; => Italia, Papa 罗马, 见 Photius (conflict with Rome), Gregorius VII, *Dictatus Papae* (special position of the Roman Church)

Romagna, the region east of Florence (Italy), which was usually part of the Papal States. 罗曼地区

Roman de la rose, E: *Romance of the Rose,* a work by Guillaume de Lorris and Jean de Meun《玫瑰传奇》, 见 Guillaume de Lorris

Roman de Renard, E: *Reynard the Fox,* a medieval collection of tales belonging to the genre of fabliaux《列那狐传奇》, 见 Appendix, *Roman de Renard*

romance, E: romance, D: Legende; => Alexandreis 传奇

Romualdus, E: Romuald, D: Romuald; St., +1027; Bishop of Ravenna, friend of Otto III, founder of Camaldoli in 1012, from which developed the Camaldolese Congregation. 若姆阿尔德

Roncesvalles, F: Roncevaux, a site in the Pyrenees where Basques attacked the Frankish army in 778. 荣塞沃, 见 Appendix, *Chanson de Roland*

rosa, E: rose, D: Rose, symbol of love or self-giving 玫瑰花, 见 Walahfridus, *Liber de cultura hortorum* (Christ combined the lily and the rose, faith and love), Guillaume de Lorris, *Roman de la rose* (symbol of love and of the lady)

Roscelinus, F: Roscelin de Compiegne, D: Roscellinus von Compiegne; 1050—1125, French theologian, exponent of nominalism, who taught that the universals are only "voices" (voces). 洛色林, 见 Occam

Roswitha, => Hrotsvita

Rubruk, Wilhelmus de Rubruquis, E: William Rubroeck (Ruysbroeck), D: Wilhelm von Rubruck; 1215—1270, a Franciscan from Flanders who traveled to the Mongol court in 1253—1255. 鲁布鲁克, 见 *Itinerarium ad partes orientales*

Rudolphus, E: Rudolph of Hapsburg, D: Rudolf von Habsburg; Duke of Austria, King of Germany 1273—1291, recognized by the Pope but not crowned Emperor. His major success was the defeat of Ottocar II of Bohemia in 1278, which enabled him to recover the imperial fiefs of Austria, Styria, and Carinthia. 鲁道夫/儒多尔夫, 见 *Bulla aurea*

Rudolphus IV, E: Rudolph, D: Rudolf der Stifter; Duke of Austria 1358—1365, founder of the University of Vienna in 1365. 鲁道夫

Rudolphus, E: Rudolf of Ems, D: Rudolf von Hohenems; +1250; an erudite poet of Middle High German, whose works reveal a high sense of moral responsibility. 鲁道夫

Rupertus, (Hrodbert), E, Rupert of Worms, D: Rupert, St.; +722; missionary in Salzburg (Austria). 儒佩特

Rupertus de Deutz, E: Rupert of Deutz, D: Rupert von Deutz; +1135; Benedictine Abbot, prolific writer, theologian, mystic. 儒佩特

Ruprecht I von der Pfalz, +1410, German Kurfuerst (elector), founder of the University of Heidelberg in 1368, King of Germany 1400—1410. 儒波瑞克特

Rurik, (Rjurik, Hrorekr), +879, a Viking (Varangian) leader of the tribe of the Rus; according to tradition he and his two brothers established the first Russian principality at Novgorod in 862. 留里克/儒瑞克

Rus, a Norman tribe which settled in Nowgorod and the Ukraine in ca. 850. => Rurik 儒斯人/罗斯人

Russia, early settlements were in the area of Kiova, the Mongol invasion of 1224 led to the establishment of a new center in Moscow; there were mission activities in the area of Kiova since the 10th century; Olga, the widow of Grandduke Igor, was baptized in 954; in 988 king Vladimir Svjatoslavic was baptized; => lingua Russica 俄罗斯, 见 Nestorius, *Povest'*

Rutebeuf, (Rutebuff), +1285, leading French lyric poet before Villon. 卢特贝夫

Ruysbroek, Johannes, Jan van Ruisbruk (Ruusbroec); Bl., 1293—1381, Flemish theologian, important mystic, unjustly accused of pantheism in 1402. 鲁伊斯布鲁克/鲁斯布鲁克

S

Sachsen = Saxones

sacramentum, E: sacrament, D: Sakrament; according to tradition there are seven Christian sacraments: baptism, confirmation, reconciliation (confession of sins), Holy Communion, sacrament of the sick, marriage, and priesthood. 圣事, 见 Ioannes Damaskenos, *Pēgē gnōseōs*, Hrabanus, *De institutione clericorum*, Hildegardis (her theology emphasizes the sacraments), Petrus Lombardus, *Sententiae*, Thomas Aquinas, *Summa contra gentiles* (explanation by means of reason), Wycliffe, (attacking traditional view of sacraments), Thomas a Kempis, *De imitatione Christi* 4 (exhortatio ad sacram communionem)

sacrificium, E: sacrifice, D: Opfer; => virtus 牺牲, 见 Anselmus, *Cur Deus homo* (God sacrifices His son), Hartmann, *Der arme Heinrich* (sacrifice of one's own life to save another person)

Saladin, Sultan, Salah Al-Din, +1193; Muslim leader, who in 1171 ended the rule of the Fatimids in Egypt and founded the dynasty of the Ayyubids. He ruled over Egypt, Damascus and Mesopotamia. In 1187 he destroyed a large Crusading army and held Jerusalem during the Third Crusade, but after negotiations with Richard I Lion-Heart permitted Christians the visitation of the Holy Places. Dante placed him in the circle of the inferno where virtuous unbelievers are found. 萨拉丁

Salamanca, city of Leon in west-central Spain. It was conquered by Arabs and recovered by Christians after 1087. Alfonso IX founded its famous university in 1227. 萨拉曼卡

Salerno, E: Salerno, a city of southern Italy, originally a Greek settlement, since 197 BC a Roman colony. In the ninth century its medical school became famous. Sometimes this institution is referred to as Europe's first university. 萨雷尔诺, 见 Hartmann, *Der arme Heinrich*

Salic Law => Lex Salica

Salier, Frankish dynasty of German Emperors (Conrad III, Henry III, IV), 1024—1125 撒里尔

Salisbury, a city of Wiltshire, England; the Diocese of Salisbury was founded in 1-58, and the famous Gothic cathedral was built between 1220 and 1260. 萨里斯堡

Salutati, Coluccio, +1406, Italian humanist scholar, who induced Manuel Chrysoloras to come to Florence in 1396. 撒鲁塔提

Salve Regina, a prayer text and religious song, popular

since ca. 1100, ascribed to Herman the Lame "母后万福"(祈祷经文),见 Hermannus Contractus

Salzburg, city and province of Austria which grew from the monastery of St. Peter erected around 690 by St. Rupert. In 739 St. Boniface made it a bishop's seat. In 1278 Rudolph II raised its ecclesiastical ruler (bishop) to the dignity of a prince of the Holy Roman Empire.萨尔茨堡

sancti, E: saints, D: Heilige; exemplary Christians, traditionally respected or formally proclaimed saints by the Church authorities ("canonization", first in 973); saints are commemorated or venerated by the believers; literature about them is called "hagiography". Famous saints from the Middle Ages are: Becket, Bernard of Clairvaux, Francis of Assisi, Joan d'Arc, Thomas Aquinas; => beatus, vita 圣人/圣徒,见 Thomas de Celano, *Vita sancti Francisci,* Jacobus de Voragine, *Legenda aurea* (miraculous stories about many popular saints, e.g. Nicolas, Alexius, Lucia, Silvester, Christopher, George)

Santiago de Compostela, a town in north-western Galicia (Spain), according to tradition the place where the body of St. James (Sant'Jago) was found. It became one of the most popular pilgrimage destinations of medieval Europe. 圣地亚哥

sapientia, E: wisdom, D: Weisheit; => allegory 智慧,见 Alanus, *Anticlaudianus* (wisdom appears as Phronesis and Sophia)

Satan, E: Satan, D: Satan; the devil, symbol of evil 恶魔,见 Dante, *Commedia* (depicted with three heads)

satisfactio, E: satisfaction, D: Genugtuung 补赎,见 Anselmus, *Cur Deus homo*

Saxo Grammaticus, E: Saxo Grammaticus, ca. 1150—1216, author of the *History of Denmark* 萨克索,见 *Gesta Danorum*

Saxones, E: Saxons, D: Sachsen, a people in northern Germany, some of their tribes migrated to England in the 5th century; the tribes in Germany were converted by force in Charlemagne's time 萨克森人,见 Alcuin, *De pontificibus* (their name is derived from saxum, "rock"), Eginhardus, *Vita Caroli* (wars against the Saxons)

Saxonia, E: Saxony, D: Sachsen; a region in Germany 萨克森地区

Scanderbeg, E: Scanderbeg, D: Skanderbeg; +1467; Duke of Albania, 1405—1467, originally George Castriota, an Albanian reared as a hostage and Muslim at the court of the Turkish sultan. In 1442 he abjured Islam and escaped to Albania, where he proclaimed himself prince. He repeatedly defeated the Turks from 1444 to 1466, went to Rome to ask for help but did not get much support.斯坎德倍

schisma, E: schism, D: Schisma; a formal split in the Church over a disagreement concerning a practice (not faith); the formal break between Roman Catholicism and the Greek Orthodox Church happened in 1054. The Great Schism of the Western Church (1378—1414) was the split in the Western Church between the Roman faction and the Avignon faction.教会分裂

schola, E: school, D: Schule; throughout the early centuries of the Middle Ages, monastery schools were the only place to receive high standard education.学校/隐修院学校

scholasticismus, E: scholasticism, D: Scholastik, studies and academic work combining faith and reason, especially from the 12th to the 15th century. Thomas Aquinas is usually regarded as the most outstanding exponent of scholasticism. The humanism of the Renaissance was opposed to the sober, logical and legalist methods of scholastic reasoning. 经院思想,见 Lanfrancus, Anselmus, Abaelardus, Hugo de Sancto Victore, Petrus Lombardus, Averroies, Alanus ab Insulis, Albertus Magnus, Petrus Hispanus, Rogerius Baco, Bonaventura, Thomas, Lullus, Occam

Schongauer, Martin, +1491, German painter 雄高尔

scientia, E: science, D: Wissenschaft; medieval authors made elaborate divisions of the sciences; => ars medica, artes liberales, juris prudentia, jus canonicum, logica, philosophia, scientia naturae, theologia 科学,学科,见 Johannes Damascenus, *Pēgē gnōseōs* (theology, the queen of sciences), Albertus, *Summa de creaturis* (philosophy as independent science), Bonaventura, *Itinerarium, De reductione artium ad theologiam* (science is love of God), Thomas Aquinas, *Summa theologiae* I.1 (analysis of the possibility of theology as a scientific discipline, distinction of speculative and practical science)

scientia naturae, E: natural science, physcial science, D: Naturwissenschaft(en); the Middle Ages were interested in the phenomena of nature and cultivated mathematics, astronomy, physics, chemistry, biology, botany, etc. 自然科学，见 Walahfridus, *De cultu hortorum*, Malmesburiensis, *Gesta regum Anglorum* （Silvester II, an outstanding mathematician）, Hugo, *Didascalicon* （artes mechanice = technical knowledge, e.g. weaving, forging, navigation, agriculture）, Vincentius Bellovacensis, *Speculum maius* （*Speculum naturale*, detailed description of the phenomena of nature）, Fredericus II, *De arte venandi* （the first scientific book of ornithology）, Albertus （broad knowledge of botany and other sciences）, Rogerius Baco, *Opus maius* （influenced by Grosseteste, interested in mathematics, astronomy, optics）, Oresmensis （one of the greatest scientists of the 14th century, he discovered the irrational numbers）

scientia practica, E: practical science, D: praktisches Wissen; 实践科学，见 Hugo, *Didascalicon*, （ethics, economy, politics count as practical sciences）, Vincentius Bellovacensis, *Speculum maius* （the *Speculum doctrinale* is a compilation of philosophy, poetry, law, politics）, Thomas Aquinas, *Summa theologiae* I.1 （theology, a practical science?）, Oresmensis, *De origine monetarum*

scintilla animae, E: spark of the soul, D: Seelenfunke; the depth of the soul 灵魂之火花，见 Eckhart, *Buch der goettlichen Troestungen*

Scriptura Sancta => Biblia

sensus, E: senses, sensual experience, D: Sinne, Sinnlichkeit; 感官，见 Bonaventura, *Itinerarium mentis in Deum*, Thomas Aquinas, *Summa contra gentiles* （insight starts from the senses, sacraments are tangible signs）, *Summa theologiae* I.1,9 （omnis cognitio a sensis habet initium）

sensus allegoricus, E: metaphorical sense, D: allegorische Bedeutung; => imago 比喻意义，见 Thomas Aquinas, *Summa Theologiae* I. 1,10 （discusses the different layers of meaning that a Biblical word can have）, Nicolaus de Lyra, *Postilla* （littera gesta docet, quid credas allegoria）

sententia, E: sentence, D: Sentenz; the scholastic way of discussing matters was to use sentences （statements, proposals） from the Bible or from ecclesiastical authors; many collections of theological sentences were compiled in the Middle Ages; => quaestio; scholasticismus 语句/命题/判断，见 Abaelardus, *Sic et non*,

Sententiae, E: *Sentences*, a work by William of Ockham《语录注集》，见 Occam

Sententiarum libri quattuor, E: *Sentences in Four Books*, a work by Peter Lombard《四部语录》，见 Petrus Lombardus

septem artes liberales => artes liberales

septem peccata => peccatum

Sergius I, St., Pope 687—701, he rejected the decrees of the Trullo Council （692） that were contrary to Roman practice, for example the marriage of priests. He supported Willibrord's mission. 塞尔吉乌斯

Sergius II, Pope 844—847 塞尔吉乌斯

Sergius III, Pope 904—911 塞尔吉乌斯

Sergius IV, Pope 1009—1012 塞尔吉乌斯

Sergius II, Patriarch of Constantinople 999—1019. 塞尔吉乌斯

Servatus Lupus => Lupus

Serviti, （Servi Beatae Mariae Virginis）, E: Servites, D: Serviten; an order founded in Florence by seven pious laymen in 1233; they accepted the rule of Augustine and developed also a branch of Servitian sisters. 圣仆会

servitudo, E: serfdom, D: Leibeigenschaft; from the 8th to the 14th century most peasants in western Europe were semifree farmers who worked on their lord's land and paid him certain dues. The money economy that developed in the late Middle Ages made it possible for the serf to substitute a certain money rent for his labor charge. 佃农，奴隶

Seuse = Suso

sexus, E: sexuality, D: Geschlechtlichkeit; => amor, concupiscentia, femina 性，见 Hildegardis, *Causae et curae* （positive view of sexuality）

Sforza, Francesco, 1401—1466, Italian mercenary leader, who became duke of Milan in 1450. 斯佛萨，见 Piccolomini, *Commentarii*

Shahrazd, a figure of the *Arabic Nights* 山鲁佐德，见 *Alf laila wa laila*

Sic et Non, E: *Yes and No*, a theological treatise by Abelard, example of the scholastic method of comparing different sentences concerning the same question;《是与否》，见 Abaelardus

Sicilia, E: Sicily, D: Sizilien; island at the SW end of Italy, it was under Greek influence, then it became a fiefdom of the Pope, was occupied by Muslims （in the ninth century）, reclaimed by Normans （in

1072, see Roger I), then it came under German (see Frederick II), French (Charles of Anjou ruled only from 1266 to 1282), and finally Spanish (Aragon) influence.西西里岛,见 Fredericus II

Siciliana Vespera, E: Sicilian Vespers, D: Sizilianische Vesper; an insurrection of the locals against the French on the Easter Monday of 1282, the Sicilians voted for Peter III of Aragon although Pope Martin IV supported the House of Anjou.西西里晚祷大屠杀

Siegfried, (=Sigurd, Seifried), hero of the *Nibelungenlied*, embodiment of all manly virtues, husband of Kriemhild but murdered by Hagen 西格弗里德,见 Appendix, *Nibelungenlied*

Siena, Italian city of Etruscan origin, because of its traditional rivalry with Florence it became the center of Tuscan Ghibellinism in opposition to the Guelf interests which controlled Florence. Siena prospered as a center of art throughout the later Middle Ages.锡耶纳

Siger de Brabant, E: Siger of Brabant, D: Siger von Brabant; +1282, teacher of theology at Paris, who examined tenets of Aristotle that could not be reconciled with Christianity, e.dh. the eternity of the world. He was accused of Averroism, splitting theological and philosophical truth. The Bishop of Paris condemned several of Siger's opinions.希格尔,见 Dante, *Commedia* (surprisingly placed in the Heaven of the Sun)

Sigmund de Luxemburg, E: Sigismund of Luxemburg, D: Siegmund von Luxemburg; +1437; son of Emperor Charles IV, king of Hungary (1387), king of Germany (1411) and king of Bohemia (1436), Holy Roman Emperor 1410—1437. His army suffered a devastating defeat at Nicopolis at the hands of the Ottoman Turks (1396). He convoked the Council of Constance (1414—1418), and approved the Compacts of Prague in 1436 to pacify the Hussites. 西格蒙德

significatio, E: meaning, D: Bedeutung; => veritas 意义,见 Abaelardus, *Sic et non* (words [voices] and their meaning [significatio]), Occam, *Sententiae* (universals are only a signum)

Sigune, a cousin of Parzival 西古纳,见 Wolfram, *Parzival*

Sigurd, (=Siegfried), the central hero of the Volsungs, => Siegfried 西尔古德,见 Snorri Sturluson, *Edda*

Silvester I, (Sylvester), St. Pope 314—335; according to medieval belief, Emperor Constantine had bestowed on him the rule over Italy and the western regions, which is known as "Donatio Constantini".西尔维斯特

Silvester II, E: Silvester II, D: Silvester II, Gerbert of Aurillac, Pope 999—1003, the first Frenchman to become Pope, who had been advisor of Otto III, archbishop of Ravenna; he was an eminent scholar; he had to flee from Rome in 1002. 西尔维斯特,见 Malmesburiensis, *Gesta regum Anglorum*

Simeon = Symeon

Simon de Montfort, E: Simon of Montfort; +1228; Count of Montfort, leader of the war against the Albigenses.西满/西门的孟福特

simonia, E: simony, D: Simonie, (derived from Simon the Magician, *Acts* 8:5-24), the buying or selling of Church offices or generally mingling the secular and sacred (see Investiture Controversy). It was one of the main problems of the medieval Church which needed reforms. One factor which led to simony was that ecclesiastical offices were linked to property rights in the feudal period (since ca. 800 AD). 圣职买卖/圣物交易,见 Dante, *Commedia* (simony is punished in the eight circle of Hell)

Sina, E: China, D: China; a huge country in Asia 中国,见 Joachim, *Liber figurarum* (influence on the "figurist" interpretation of Chinese culture), Rubruk, *Itinerarium ad partes orientales*, Marco Polo, *Il Milione*, Appendix, *Alf lailah wa-lailah* (stories about Persian traders in China and Southeast Asia)

Sindbad, a figure of the *Arabian Nights* 辛巴达,见 *Alf lailah wa lailah*

Sixtus IV, Pope 1471—1484, Francesco della Rovere, former general superior of the Franciscans. He was a generous supporter of arts and sciences and built the Sistina Chapel. Sixtus' image is tainted by nepotism.西克斯图斯

Slavi, E: Slavs, D: Slaven, indogermanic peoples who settled in the regions of Eastern Europe 斯拉夫人,见 Cosmas Pragensis, *Chronica Bohemorum* (tensions between Germans and Slavs)

Slavia, E: Slavic regions, D: Slavengebiete, => Bohemia, Hungaria, Moravia, Poland

Snorri Sturluson, 1179—1241, Icelandic historian, scholar, author of the *Edda* 斯诺里·斯图鲁松,见

Edda

Soissons, city of France on the Aisne river; it was the capital of the Roman province of Belgica.苏瓦松

sol, E: sun, D: Sonne; symbol of light, truth, and God 太阳,见 Thomas de Celano, *Vita sancti Francisci*

Sorbonne, college in Paris, founded by Robert de Sorbon; => Robert de Sorbon 索邦学院

soror, F: soeur, E: sister (nun), D: Schwester; => allegoria, femina, mater, nonna 姐妹,见 Hermannus, *De octo vitiis principalibus* (the vices are sisters), Cosmas Pragensis, *Chronica* (three daughters of Croccus), Alanus, *Anticlaudianus* (the "heavenly sisters" Concord, Youth, Reason…)

Sorores vitae communis, E: Sisters of the Common Life, D: Schwestern des gemeinsamen Lebens; a community founded by Groote in the 14th century; see Fratres vitae communis 共同生活的姐妹

Spain => Hispania

species, E: species, D: Art; => idea

speculatio, (speculum), E: speculation, meditation, D: Spekulation, Betrachtung; 默想,见 Bonaventura, *Itinerarium mentis in Deum* (find images of God within the soul), Thomas Aquinas, *Summa theol.* I.16,6 (the human soul mirrors truth, sicut in speculo)

Speculum maius, E: *The Great Mirror*, a work by Vincent de Beauvais《知识宝鉴》,见 Vincentius Bellovacensis

spes, E: hope, D: Hoffnung, one of the Christian virtues 希望,望德,见 Anselmus, *Monologion*, Hugo, *De fructibus*

spiritualia, E: spirituality, D: Spiritualitaet; attitudes and experiences towards the divine, especially the adoration of God; => amor, anima, Deus, ecstasis, fides, imago Dei, incarnatio, mystica, poenitentia, unio mystica, visio 灵修,见 Bernardus, *De diligendo Deo* (love of God in several stages), Hugo, *Didascalicon* (the last book is entitled *De meditatione*), Thomas de Celano, *Vita sancti Francisci* (creation spirituality), Bonaventura, *Itinerarium mentis in Deum*, Gertrudis, *Legatus divinae pietatis*, Gerson, *De mystica theologia*, Thomas a Kempis, *De imitatione Christi*

Spiritus Sanctus, E: the Holy Spirit, D: der Heilige Geist, the third person of the Trinity 圣灵/圣神,见 Photios, *Logos peri tēs tou Hagiou Pneumatos Mystagōgias*, Alanus, *Anticlaudianus* (Noys, the divine spirit, creates a human soul), Joachim, *Liber figurarum* (age of the Spirit expected to start in 1260 AD)

St. Victor => Victor, St.

status, E: state, D: Staat => res publica

Staufer, Hohenstaufen, German imperial family, esp. Frederick I Barbarossa and Frederick II 施陶费尔

Stephanus II, Pope 752—757, facing pressure from the Lombards he went to Ponthion (France) in 754 and secured the support of Pepin III. 斯特凡努斯

Stephanus III, Pope 768—772, he was worried about the cooperation between Franks and Lombards; he opposed the iconoclast movement in the East.斯特凡努斯

Stephanus V, Pope 885—891, who was under severe pressure from Spoleto 斯特凡努斯

Stephanus VI, VII, VIII, Popes in the 9th and 10th century who were exposed to the power struggles of Roman nobles.斯特凡努斯

Stephanus IX, Pope 1057—1058, originally Frederick of Lorraine, he was a reformer supported by Hildebrand. He nominated Petrus Damiani Bishop of Ostia and cardinal.斯特凡努斯

Stephanus, E: Stephen, D: Stephan, St., the first king of Hungary 997—1038. According to tradition he received his crown from Pope Sylvester II in 1000. He was decisive for the development of the Church in Hungary and pursued a pro-German policy.斯特凡努斯/斯德望/司提反,见 Malmesburiensis, *Gesta regum Anglorum* (Silvester II supported king Stephen)

Stephanus de Autun, +1140, Bishop of Autun, theologia; possibly the first to use the term "transsubstantiatio". 斯特凡努斯

Stephanus Harding = Harding

stigmata, E: stigmata, D: Stigmata; scars or sores resembling the crucifixion wounds of Christ; 五伤,见 Thomas de Celano, *Vita Sancti Francisci* (he received the stigmata during a vision)

Strabo => Walahfrid Strabo

Strasbourg, (L: Argentoratum), E: Strasbourg, D: Strassburg; a town in the border area between Germany and France; the diocese was probably founded in Roman times; strategically important it became a free imperial city in 1262, was occupied by France in 1681 and passed to Germany in 1871, only to be recovered by France in 1919. 斯特拉斯堡

Suda, (=Souda, Suida), E: Suda, a Byzantine literary encyclopedia from the late 10th century, => encyclopaedia 苏达, 见 Photios, *Myrobiblion*

Suetonius, E: Sueton, D: Sueton, 70—140 AD, author of *De vita Caesarum*, which became the model for medieval biographies 苏埃托尼乌斯, 见 Eginhardus, *Vita Caroli Magni*

Suger, +1151, Abbot and builder at St. Denis, Paris. 徐格

Suida => Suda

summa, E: summa, sum, D: Summa; a systematic presentation of some subject (theology, philosophy, canon law, ethics, etc.), used as textbook or reference book; a compendium by a scholastic author《大全》, 见 Johannes Damascenus, *Pēgē gnōseōs* (comprehensive explanation of the faith, model for later sums), Thomas Aquinas

Summa contra gentiles, E: *Summa Against the Heathen*, a work by Thomas Aquinas《反驳异教大全》, 见 Thomas Aquinas

Summa de creaturis, E: *Sum on Creation*, a work by Albert the Great《受造界大全》, 见 Albertus Magnus

Summa theologiae, E: *Sum of Theology*, a huge systematic and authoritative work by Thomas Aquinas, which deals with questions of theology, philosophy, ethics, and law《神学大全》, 见 Thomas Aquinas

Summulae logicales, E: *Small Logical Sums*, a work by Peter of Spain《逻辑学大全》, 见 Petrus Hispanus

superbia, E: pride, D: Stolz; feelings of superiority and lack of respect for others; => honor 骄傲, 见 Photios (disdain for westerners), Cosmas, *Chronica Bohemorum* (Germans look down on Slavs), Anna Komnene, *Alexias* (disdain for the knights from the west), Hartmann, *Der arme Heinrich*, Innocens III, *De miseria* (a work damping human pride), Dante, *Commedia* (in Purgatory the sins of pride are corrcted by carrying heavy stones)

superna, E: the things above, D: Hoeheres; spiritual values 高尚的价值, 见 Bernardus, *De diligendo Deo*

superstitio, E: superstition, D: Aberglaube; => magus 迷信, 见 Alexandreis

suppositio, E: suppositio, D: Supposition; the way in which a word represents something 指称, 见 Petrus Hispanus, *Summulae logicales*

Suso, Henricus, D: Heinrich Seuse, 1295—1366, German Dominican, mystic, theologian, student of Meister Eckhart. He preached to nuns and Friends of God in Switzerland and southern Germany. He authored *Das Buechlein der ewigen Weisheit* (*Little Book of Eternal Wisdom*, one of the finest pieces of German mysticism), *Das Buechlein der Wahrheit, Horologium Sapientiae*. 苏索

Sweden, originally a Viking state since the ninth century conducting raids along the rivers east of the Baltic into Russia; at the same time Frankish missionaries tried to penetrate the land; Olaf Skutkonung (993—1024) was the country's first Christian ruler. In 1164 Uppsala became the seat of an Archbishop. The Folkung dynasty was founded by King Waldemar in 1250, the nephew of Birger Magnusson. 瑞典, 见 Birgitta (national saint of Sweden)

symbolum => figura

Symeon Metaphrastes, +ca. 1000, most important hagiographer of Byzantium, editor of a collection of legends, *Menologion*. 西默盎/西面

Symeon, the "new theologian", 949—1022, Abbot in Constantinople, considered the greatest Greek mystical author. 西默盎/西面

synodus = concilium

T

Tafsir kitab an-nafs, L: *De anima*, E: *On the Soul*, a work by Averroes《论灵魂注》, 见 Averroes

Tankred de Lecce, Count of Lecce, half-brother of Constance, King of Sicily, Apulia and Capua 1190—1194. 坦克瑞德

Tartari, E: Tatars, Tartars, D: Tartaren; => Mongoli

Tartarus => infernum

Tauler, Johannes, 1300—1361, German Dominican, priest, influential mystic theologian, author of *Buch von der geistlichen Armut* (*The Book of Spiritual Poverty*), *Goettliche Lehren* (*Divine Teachings*). 陶勒尔

temperantia, E: temperance, D: Maessigung, Selbstkontrolle, maze; the ability to control one's desires, traditionally one of the four cardinal virtues 节制, 见 Hugo, *Didascalicon* (temperance, frugality, and purity are necessary for studies), Wolfram, *Parzival* (maze),

Tempier, Stephanus, E: Tempier; Bishop of Paris, he

condemned more than 200 Aristotelian tenets in 1270 and 1277, marking the turn to a more critical reception of Aristotelian tenets 坦皮耶，见 Averroes ("Latin Averroism" condemned)

Templarii, (=milites templi), E: Templars; D: Templerorden; a congregation of knights founded in 1119 in Jerusalem; soon they became quite rich, especially in France. They were unjustly accused and dissolved in the early 14th century, a victim of the ruthless greed of the French King Philip IV (1285—1314).圣殿骑士团，见 Wolfram, *Parzifal*

terminismus, E: terminism, D: Terminismus; the nominalism of the Late Middle Ages (under the influence of Occam) was called terminism, conceptism, or "via moderna"; => nominalismus 唯名论，见 Occam

tertiarii, E: Third Order, D: dritter Orden; lay people who are associated with an order, especially with the Franciscans.第三会

tertium aevum, E: the third age, D: die dritte Periode; => aevum 第三时期，见 Joachim, *Liber figurarum*

theatrum = mysteria

theocratia, E: theocracy, D: Theokratie; the theory that all power should be subjected to God or a religious leadership; one example might be the *Dictatus Papae* of Gregory VII. 神权政治

Theodora, Byzantine Empress, +862; wife of Emperor Theophilus (829—842) and mother of Michael III (842—867). As regent she convened a synod in 843 which ended iconoclasm. She is honored as a saint by the Greek Church.狄奥多拉

Theodora, wife of Theophylactus, "Senatrix", mother of Theodora the Younger, influenced papal policy in the time from 910—926.狄奥多拉

Theodoricus Magnus, E: Theodoric the Great, D: Theoderich der Grosse; king of the Ostrogoths 471—526; he led his people from Pannonia to Italy, defeated Odoacer at Ravenna in 493 and ruled Italy, preserving Roman culture. He employed Cassiodorus and Boethius but in the last period had Boethius executed for fear that he might cooperate with the Byzantine emperor in an attempt to recover Italy. In the *Nibelungenlied* Theodoric appears as Dietrich von Bern 特奥多瑞克，见 Appendix, *Nibelungenlied*

Theodorus, Gr: Theodōros, E: Theodore of Tarsus, D: Theodor; +690; a Greek monk who studied at Tarsus and Athens, then went to Rome, was sent to England and became Archbishop of Canterbury (669—690); he summoned the first important synod of the English church in Hertford in 672, and he established Canterbury as a center of culture and studies 特奥多尔，见 Beda, *Historia ecclesiastica*

Theodorus, Gr: Theodōros, E: Theodore the Studite, D: Theodor von Studios; +826, Abbot of Studios Monastery (Constantinople), who made the monastery a model of Byzantine monasticism. His courageous opposition to iconoclasm led twice to his exile.特奥多尔

Theodulfus, E: Theodulf of Orleans, +821; Gothic poet from Spain, Archbishop of Orleans (800), for some time scholar at Charlemagne's court.特欧多夫

theologia, E: theology, D: Theologie, the science concerned with divine matters, especially the reasonableness of the Christian faith 神学，见 Johannes Damascenus, *Pēgē gnōseōs* (philosophia as ancilla theologiae), Eriugena (affirmative, negative, transcendent theology), Anselmus (fides quaerens intellectum), Petrus Abaelardus, *Sic et non* (shaped the scholastic way of thinking), Petrus Lombardus, *Sententiae* (influential textbook of scholastic theology), Averroes (division of theological and philosophical truth), Alanus, *Anticlaudianus* (allegory of theology), Maimonides, *More nevukhim* (negative theology), Dante, *Commedia* (the Heaven of the Sun is the place of saintly theologians), Langland, *Piers Plowman* (allegory of theology), Gerson, *De mystica theologia* (theology of the heart),

Theophanu, Gr: Theophanou; +991; Byzantine princess, wife of Otto II, crowned Empress in 972. She served as regent during the early years of the reign of her son Otto III.狄奥法努

Theophilus, Byzantine emperor 829—842, an iconoclast; during his reign many areas of Asia Minor were lost to the Muslims.特欧菲卢斯

Theophilus, E: *Theophilus,* a work by Hrotsvita《德欧斐路斯》，见 Hrotsvita

Theophylactus, E: Theophylact; +926; consul and leader in Rome after 900, husband of Theodora, father of Marozia and Theodora the Younger. He also was the protector of Sergius III and other Popes of the era.狄奥菲拉克图斯

Thierry de Chartres, E: Thierry of Breton, D: Thierry von Chartres; +1156, head of the school of Chartres.提艾里

Thomas de Aquino, E: Thomas Aquinas, D: Thomas von Aquin, St., 1225—1274, born in Aquino (Italy), he was educated at Naples and Paris, followed his mentor, Albert the Great, to Cologne, then became the first Dominican to occupy the chair of theology in Paris, universally acclaimed for his erudition and piety; author of many works, esp. *Summa Theologiae* (partly translated into Chinese in the 1650s); He creatively combined Aristotelian thought and Christian theology. 托马斯/多默/多马,见 *Summa theologiae*

Thomas Becket = Becket

Thomas de Bradwardin = Bradwardin

Thomas de Celano, E: Thomas of Celano, 1190—1260; Italian author 托马斯·杰拉诺,见 *Vita Sancti Francisci*

Thomas a Kempis, E: Thomas a Kempis, D: Thomas von Kempis (Thomas Hemerken von Kempen); 1380—11471, German Augustinian living at Zwolle (Holland), author and copyist of theological literature, author (or compiler) of the Imitation of Christ (ca. 1420) 托马斯/多默/多马,见 *De imitatione Christi*

Thomas Netter (Waldensis), +1431; Carmelite theologian, the most outstanding opponent of Wycliffe's theories.托马斯

Thor, the Norse god of thunder, son of Odin, famed for his hammer.托尔,见 Snorri Sturluson, *Edda*

thronus, E: throne, D: Thron; the seat of a king; the heavenly throne of God was connected with the divine judgment, => judex 宝座,见 Thomas de Celano, *Dies irae,* Anonymus, *Elkerlijk*

Thuringia, E: Thuringia, D: Thueringen, region of Germany along the upper Weser. The natives were converted by St. Boniface, and Charlemagne founded the Thuringian march in 804. 图林根

Tiara, special crown ("helmet") of the Pope, first mentioned in a life of Pope Constantine I (708—715). 教宗冠/教皇三重冠

timor, E: fear, D: Furcht; => judex, mors 恐惧,见 Innocens III, *De miseria humanae conditionis,* Thomas de Celano, *Dies irae* (fear of the divine judgment), Petrarca, *De remediis utriusque fortunae* (Reason talking to Fear)

Tithe = decuma

Toledo, city in central Spain, capital of the Visigoths in the seventh century, it was seized by the Moslems in 711 and became the capital of a Moorish state from 1036. In 1085 Alfonso VI of Castile occupied the city and turned it into an important political and cultural center. Toledo was the see of a metropolitan in the fourth century, and in 1088 it acquired primatial rank.托莱多

Torquemada, Thomas, +1498; Spanish Dominican, in charge of the inquisition in Spain from 1483—1498; => inquisition 托尔克马达

tortura, E: torture, D: Folter; a means of forcing confessions at court, used in ancient Rome (especially in the case of slaves), prohibited by Pope Nicolaus I in 866 AD, but re-admitted by Innocens IV in 1252, partly as a result of the revival of Roman law. 拷打,虐待

translatio, E: translation, D: Uebersetzung; Latin was the common language of western Europe throughout the Middle Ages, but most authors were bilingual and could express the meaning of Latin texts in the local vernacular language. => lingua 翻译,见 Alfredus Magnus (translations from Latin into Old Englis h), Ioannes Damaskenos, *Barlaam et Joasaph* (translated into many languages), Eriugena (translations from Greek to Latin), Photius (bilingual), Avicenna (Latin translations), Petrus Venerabilis (urged translation of the *Qur'an*), Galfredus Monemuthensis (many translations), Averroes (only the Latin translation is extant), Moses Maimonides, *More nevukhim* (translated from Arabic into Hebrew, Latin), Vincentius, *Speculum maius* (trsl. into French), Rogerius Baco (urged studies of Greek and Hebrew), Albertus Magnus (urged translations from Greek into Latin), Raimundus Lullus (polyglot), Eckhart (books in Latin and German), Boccaccio (started to learn Greek), Oresmensis (translated his works from Latin into French), Wyclif (urged the translation of the Bible), Chaucer (translated the *Consolatio philosophiae*), Bessarion, *In calumniatorem Platonis,* (he exposed translation mistakes)

transubstantiatio, the theory of trans-substantiation, which means that the bread and wine turn into the true Body and Blood of Christ at Holy Eucharist. 体变说,见 Wycliffe, Paschasius, Stephanus de Autun

Treuga Dei, Pax Dei; E: Peace of God, D: Gottesfriede; a peace movement since the 10th century, inspired by the Church, which tried to forbid fighting on Sundays and during the main religious seasons and feasts (or at crusades). Several church councils of the 10th and 11th centuries proclaimed that holy places, the clergy, peasantry, travelers, and pilgrims should be safe and not suffer violence in wars. 神的和平/上主的和平

Trevrizent, literary figure in the *Parzival*, a hermit who explains to Parzival the mystery of the Grail and thus brings him back to his faith 特瑞弗瑞

Tridentinum < Trento

Trier, L: Augusta Treverorum, Fr: Treves; city west of the middle Rhine (Germany). It served as imperial capital after Diocletian's reorganization of the Roman empire. For a time it served as capital of Austrasia. Since the end of the twelfth century the Archbishop of Trier was one of the electors of the Emperor, which was confirmed by the Golden Bull of 1356. 特里尔, 见 Appendix, *Bulla aurea*

Trinitarii = Ordo Sanctissimae Trinitatis de redemptione captivorum

Trinitas, Sancta Trinitas, E: Holy Trinity, D: die Heilige Dreifaltigkeit, God the Father, Son and Holy Spirit; symbols of the Trinity: => circulus, lux 圣三, 三位一体, 见 Anselmus, *Monologion* (the three mental activites reflect the Trinity) Petrus Lombardus, *Sententiae*, Alanus, *Anticlaudianus* (Trinity as fountain, stream and river in one), Joachim, *Liber figurarum* (historical explanation of the Trinity), Dante, *Commedia* (concentric circles of light), Greban, *Passion de Paris* (justice demands that God's son must suffer, even if the Father's mercy would not agree)

Tristan, E: Tristan, D: Tristan, (Tristant, Tristrams); Celtic figure connected with Arthurian legend; according to some narratives he was enchanted by a fairy and since then suffered from the incurable wound of love; another tradition makes drink a love potion and fall in love with Isolde even to the extent that a separation would cause illness. 特里斯坦, 见 Galfredus Monemuthensis, *Historia regum Britanniae*, Dante, *Commedia* (placed in the second circle of Hell)

trivium, E: trivium, D: Trivium; the study of grammar, rhetoric and logic; together with the quadrivium, the trivium formed the "septem artes liberales", => artes liberales, quadrivium 三学/三个学科

Troia nova => London

troubadour, (<L trope), F: trovere, E: minnesinger, D: Minnesaenger; lyric poets in Provence, northern Italy and northern Spain in the 12th and 13th centuries; their songs about courtly love were composed in langue d'oc, they inspired French and German poetry; => trouvere 抒情诗人, 见 Hartmann

trouvère, (=trouveur), the type of poet-musicians of northern France in the 12th and 13th centuries who composed narrative works (chanson de geste) in langue d'oil 行吟诗人

Tuebingen, university of Tuebingen, place of nominalist (G. Biel) and realist (J. Heynlin) professors in the 15th century 图宾根

Tuscia, E: Tuscany, D: Toskana; a region of northwest Italy, inhabited by the Etruscans in ancient times; it was a grand duchy under the Medicis (1569—1860); => Florentia 托斯卡纳

Tusculani, Roman clan, influenced papal policies 1012—1050 托斯库拉尼

U

Ubertinus de Casale, E: Ubertino of Casale, +1329 (?), Franciscan writer, leader of the Franciscan Spirituals and critical of Pope Boniface VIII. 乌贝提努斯

Ugolino de Ostia = Gregorius IX

Ulricus, E: Ulric, D: Ulrich, St., +973; Bishop of Augsburg, who defended the city against the Hungarians in 955. He was the first German bishop have the right to mint money, and he was also the first person to be formally canonized by the Pope. 乌尔里克

Ultramontani, term for French bishops who were inclined to nationalism in the 14th century. 越山主义, "阿尔卑斯山脉以北的"

Unam Sanctam, Bull by Boniface VIII, 1302, emphasizing ecclesiastical power《唯一至圣(教会)》

unio mystica, E: mystical union, D: mystische Vereinigung; the unity of God and man experienced in some acts of contemplation; => spiritualia; 神秘的合一, 见 Bernardus, *De diligendo Deo* (like the mixture of water and wine; ecstasis), Bonaventura, *Itinerarium mentis in Deum*, Gertrudis, *Legatus divinae pietatis* (Christ, the divine Bridegroom), Eckhart, *Buch der goettlichen Troestungen* (mystical one-ness of all things)

unitas, E: unity, D: Einheit; 合一性, 见 Albertus, *De*

unitate intellectus contra Averroem

universalia, E: universals, D: Universalien; general ideas, => idea; the controversy of universals, the debate about the reality of universal ideas, which divided medieval philosophers into nominalists and realists, => nominalismus 共相之争, 见 Thomas Aquinas, *Summa theol.* I.45,1 (God as causa universalis)

universitas, E: university, D: Universitaet; the medieval universities emerged from monastery schools and cathedral schools in the 12th century. Philosophical and scientific works were translated from Arabic and Greek sources. This included the works of Aristotle, Galen, Ptolemy, Avicenna, Averroes, and the *Corpus Iuris Civilis*. The assimilation of this broad stream of knowledge into Christian thought was the intention of many medieval scholars. The early term for the university was "studium generale", after 1200 Popes or kings granted newly founded university charters, which contained certain privileges for the community "universitas" of teachers and students. Larger universities were organized into the four faculties of arts, law, medicine, and theology. At larger schools, especially at Paris, the students were divided into nations (nationes). After four years of study in the arts curriculum (trivium, quadrivium), the student received a bachelor's degree, two more years and a successfully defended thesis might lead to a master's degree. 大学, 见 Bonaventura, Thomas Aquinas

universum, Gr: kosmos, ta panta, E: universe, cosmos, D: Kosmos; medieval works often contemplate the handiwork of the Creator who has arranged all things "according to a certain number, measure, and weight" (*Wisdom* 11:20). => machina 宇宙, 见 Eriugena, *De divisione naturae*

Uppsala, E: Upsala, city to the northwest of Stockholm. It became an archdiocese in 1164. Swedish kings were crowned in the cathedral of Uppsala. The University of Uppsala was founded by Archbishop Ulfsson in 1477. 乌普萨拉

Urbanus II, Pope 1088—1099, from France, originally Cardinal Odo of Ostia, former abbot of Cluny, he continued the reforms of Gregory VII; in 1096 he responded to the pleas of Alexius I and preached the first crusade. 乌尔巴努斯, 见 Malmesburiensis, *Gesta regum Anglorum*

Urbanus III, Pope 1185—1187, formerly the archbishop of Milan. 乌尔巴努斯

Urbanus IV, Pope 1261—1264, of French descent, former Patriarch of Jerusalem, he nominated 6 French cardinals and offered the crown of Naples and Sicily to Charles de Anjou, thus influenced future papal policy. 乌尔巴努斯

Urbanus V, Bl. Pope 1362—1370, who tried to move the Curia from Avignon back to Rome. 乌尔巴努斯

Urbanus VI, Pope 1378—1389, orig. Bishop Prignano from Naples, was elected and properly installed in Rome, but the French cardinals withdrew from him later, thus causing a schism. 乌尔巴努斯

usura, E: usury, interest, D: Zinsen; since antiquity Christians and especially clergymen were not allowed to charge interests, Jews were excepted from this prohibition, and for this reason they often became money lenders. 利息/利润/高利贷

Uther Pendragon, E, D: Uther Pendragon; a legendary ruler of England, father of King Arthur 乌德·彭德瑞根, 见 Galfredus Monemuthensis, *Historia regum Britanniae*

Utraquisti, E: utraquists, D: Utraquisten; Christians who wanted to receive Christ in bread and wine in connection with the movement of Jan Hus 体血并领派

Utrecht, town and diocese in the Netherlands; Willibrord was the first Archbishop of Utrecht (695). The bishops of Utrecht had the position of princes of the Holy Roman Empire. Utrecht developed into a wealthy textile center. 乌得勒支

V

Valentinus, Pope in 827 瓦伦提努斯

Valla, Lorenzo, 1405—1457, Italian scholar, who became a priest and served as secretary to King Alfonso V of Aragon and Naples. In 1448 Pope Nicholas V gave him a papal secretaryship, although Valla had extolled the pleasures of the senses and exposed the doubtful authenticity of the "Donation of Constantine". The Pope commissioned him to translate Greek classics, including the *Iliad*. 瓦拉, 见 Bessarion, Piccolomini

Vallombrosa, Vallombrosani, E: Vallombrosans; monastery and congregation founded in 1038 by John Gualbert near Florence. By the end of the 12th century the order had more than 50 communities. 瓦伦布罗撒

Varangii, E: Varangians, D: Waraeger, a tribe of Norsemen who invaded the area of Kiev around 850. 瓦朗基人, 见 Nestorius, *Povest'*

Vasari, Giorgio, Italian scholar, 16th century, he was the first to use the term "Gothic art" 瓦撒瑞

Vassilius II, (Basilius, Wassilij, Vasily), Great Duke of Moskow 1425—1462, he opposed ecumenism after 1439. 瓦西里二世

Vaticana bibliotheca, E: Vatican library, D: Vatikanische Bibliothek; the library was established by Pope Nicholas V (1447—1455) and greatly enlarged by Pope Sixtus IV (1471—1484). 梵蒂冈图书馆

Vaticanus, E: Vatican, D: Vatikan, the hill of Rome where the church of St. Peter is located. The Vatican became the residence of the Popes, especially after 1380 when the Pope returned from Avignon. 梵蒂冈

venatio, E: hunting, D: Jagd; => avis 打猎, 见 Fredericus, *De arte venandi cum avibus*, Appendix, *Nibelungenlied* (Siegfried killed at a hunting party)

venerabilis, E: venerabile, D: ehrwuerdig; 可敬的, 见 Petrus Venerabilis

Venetia, E: Venice, D: Venedig; a city built on islands when the local tribe of the Veneti sought refuge from the Huns in 452 AD. The invasion of the Lombards in 568 increased this refugee population. The island was virtually autonomous although nominally under the Byzantine exarch of Ravenna. After ca. 950 Venice led the revival of trade which gave much incentive for the nascent economy of western Europe. In 1082 Alexius Comnenus granted Venice the right of free trade in his empire, because the city had assisted him against the Normans under Robert Guiscard. The crusades brought benefit to Venice but also to its rival city Genoa. Venice diverted the Fourth Crusade (1202—1204) to serve its own ends and profited from the loot of Constantinople. The rise of the Turks weakened Venetian supremacy in the eastern Mediterranean. The fall of Constantinople to the Turks in 1453 and the discovery of a sea route to India in 1498 irretrievably ended the dominant position of the city. 威尼斯, 见 Genua, Bessarion (donated his manuscripts to the San Marco Library of Venice)

Veni Creator Spiritus, E: *Come, Creator Spirit*, a breviary hymn honoring the Holy Spirit; it was written in the 9th century, probably by Rabanus Maurus《恳求圣神降临》, 见 Hrabanus

Venus, E, D: Venus, goddess of love 爱神, 见 Guillaume de Lorris, *Roman de la rose*

Verdun, town in NW France; the Carolingian Empire was divided by the Treaty of Verdun (843). 凡尔登

Vergilius, E: Virgil, D: Vergil, 70—19 BC, most famous Latin poet, often quoted in Medieval literature; since late antiquity Virgil was perceived as prophet, scholar and wise man with magic powers; => magus 维吉尔, 见 Adamnanus, Aldhelmus, Paulus Diaconus, Walahfridus, *De cultura hort.*, Ekkehard, *Waltharii poiesis*, Malmesburiensis, *Gesta regum Anglorum* (Silvester II, a wise man like Vergilius), Galfredus Monemuthensis, *Historia* (descendants of Aeneas are the founders of London), Dante, *Commedia* (guide through Hell and Purgatory), *De vulgari eloquentia* (together with Horace and Ovid, Virgil is one of the "poetae regulares")

veritas, E: truth, D: Wahrheit; scholastic teachers used the logical method to discern the truth of certain statements 真理, 见 Abaelardus, *Sic et non* (hermeneutic rules), Thomas Aquinas, *Summa theol.* I, 16, 1 (veritas est adaequatio rei et intellectus), Langland, *Piers Plowman* (allegory of truth)

Verona, city in northern Italy, the residence of the Ostrogothic ruler Theodoric, the Lombard king Alboin, and Charlemagne. In 1387 it fell to *Milan*, and in 1405 it was ruled by Venice. 维罗纳

Verrocchio, Andrea del, Italian artist, +1488 韦罗吉奥

vestimenta, E: vestments, dress, D: Kleider, Kleidung; 衣服, 见 Aldhelmus, *De laudibus* (garments of nuns)

via media, E: middle way, D: Mittelweg; 中间的道路, 见 Maimonides, *More nevukhim* (combines the Tora with Aristotle's "middle way")

Victor II, Pope 1055—1057, originally the chancellor of Henry III of Germany. Pope Victor implemented some reforms. 维克托

Victor III, Bl., Pope 1086—1087, abbot of Monte Cassino who mediated between the papacy and

Robert Guiscard, the Norman ruler of southern Italy. 维克托

Victor, St., F: St-Victor, E: St. Victor, a monastery and school in Paris, the congregation of St. Victor was founded in 1108 by William of Champeaux; => Hugo of St. Victor; Richard of St. Victor 维克托, 见 Hugo

Vienna => Vindobona

Vienne, a city on the left bank of the Rhone (southern France). In 879 it was the capital of Lower Burgundy and belonged to the Holy Roman Empire until France took possession of it in 1448. The ecumenical council of Vienne took place in 1311/1312.维恩, 见 Lullus

Villon, Francois, +1463, the leading lyric poet of medieval France. His life was a mixture of misery, remorse, and moral degradation.维庸

Vincentius Bellovacensis, E: Vincent de Beauvais, D: Vinzenz von Beauvais; ca. 1190—1264, French Dominican, author of the biggest encyclopedia before 1750, educator of King Louis' sons. 博韦的樊尚, 见 *Speculum maius*

Vincentius Ferrer 见 Ferrer

Vindobona, E: Vienna, D: Wien; a Celtic settlement, then a Roman fortress, Vienna became a possession of the Babenbergs around 1000 and became the capital of their dominion. In 1137 the town received a charter, and Rudolf of Habsburg recovered Vienna from Ottocar II, king of Bohemia. The University of Vienna was founded in 1365 by Archduke Rudolf IV.维也纳

vinum, E: wine, D: Wein; symbol of the divine nature of Christ 葡萄酒, 见 Bernardus, *De diligendo Deo* (mystical union with God is like a drop of water dissolved in wine)

violentia, E: violence, D: Gewalttat; => Treuga Dei 暴力, 见 Dante, *Commedia* (sins of violence)

Virgil = Vergilius

virginitas, E: virginity, D: Jungfraeulichkeit, the lifestyle of monks, nuns and celibate priests; virginity was often extolled as an evangelical ideal; => viriditas 贞洁, 见 Aldhelmus, *De laudibus virginitatis*, Hildegardis (writes about "virginitas"), Wolfram, *Parzival* (virgins and celibate knights in the Grail community)

virgo, E: virgin, D: Jungfrau; symbol of purity and youth; => allegoria, castitas, virginitas 贞女, 见 Alanus, *Anticlaudianus* (seven liberal arts are seven virgins)

viriditas, E: viridity, greenness, D: Frische, das Gruensein; a term associated with youthfulness, especially in Hildegard's writings 青春, 见 Hildegardis

virtus, E: virtus, D: Tugend, medieval literature often uses allegories of the virtues, especially of the four cardinal virtues (justice, prudence, fortitude, temperance) and the three theological virtues (faith, hope, love)美德, 见 Ekkehard, *Waltharii poiesis* (fortitude), Hugo, *Didascalicon* (cardinal virtues)

virtutes cardinales, E: cardinal virtues, D: Kardinaltugenden; central values, according to Plato and Cicero they are: justice, wisdom, courage, and temperance; => justitia, prudentia, fortitudo, temperantia 枢德, 见 Hugo, *De fructibus carnis et spiritus*

virtutes theologicae, E: theological virtues, D: theologische Tugenden; central values that are dependent on revelation, namely Christian faith, hope, and love, => fides, spes, caritas, amor 超性美德, 见 Hugo, *De fructibus carnis et spiritus*, Gerson, *De mystica theologia*

Visigothones, E: Visigoths, D: Westgoten; a tribe located north of the Black Sea, from where they moved to the West in 375 in order to escape the approaching Huns. Under Alarich they sacked Rome in 410. They established a kingdom in Spainin the sixth century, which was destroyed by Muslim forces in 711.西哥特人

visio, E: vision, D: Vision, the experience of somehow encountering God, Jesus or a saint; Biblical accounts of visions inspired medieval attitudes and mystical experiences; => contemplatio 神视, 见 Walahfridus, *Visio Wettini*(the first vision in lyric form), Hildegardis (she had many visions), Thomas de Celano, *Vita Francisci* (a vision confirmed his vocation to live in poverty), Gertrudis, *Legatus divinae pietatis* (visions or apparitions of Christ, Mary, saints)

visio beatifica, E: vision of God, D: Gottesschau, the blessed vision of God (after death), conf. the end of Dante's *Commedia*; there was a controversy in the 14th century whether the souls of the just would enjoy the vision of God only after the last judgment 真福荣观

Visio Wettini, E: *The Vision of Wetti*, a work by

Walafried, the first visio in lyric form《维提的神视》，见 Walahfridus

vita, E: life, D: Leben; 生命，见 mors

vita, E: biography, D: Lebensbeschreibung, Biographie; in the Middle Ages the biographies of the saints were particularly popular 传记，见 *Legenda aurea*, *Vita Caroli Magni*, etc.

vita apostolica, apostolic life, the way of life of the apostles, emphasizing lack of a stable home, poverty and preaching; this ideal became very influential, particularly in the 12th and 13th centuries, compare Mendicants 宗徒/使徒生活

Vita Caroli Magni, E: *Life of Charles the Great*, D: *Biografie Karls des Grossen*, a work by Einhard《查理大帝传》，见 Eginhardus

Vita Columbae, E: *Life of St. Columban*, a work by Adamnan《科伦班传》，见 Adamnan

Vita Merlini, E: *Life of Merlin*, a work by Geoffrey Monmouth《梅尔林传》，见 Galfredus Monemuthensis

Vita Sancti Francisci, E: *Life of Saint Francis*, a biography by Thomas of Celano《圣方济各传》，见 Thomas de Celano

vita sanctorum = hagiography

Vitalianus, E: Vitalian, Pope 657—672, he sent the monk Theodore to Canterbury and appointed him Archbishop.维塔利阿努斯

vitium, E: vice, D: Laster; especially the "seven captial sins" (pride, envy, wrath, sloth, lust, gluttony, avarice), => acedia, avaritia, gula, invidia, ira, luxuria, superbia 恶习，见 Ekkehard, *Waltharius* (Gunther's avarice and pride), Hermannus Contractus, *De octo vitiis principalibus* (Pride and her seven daughters), Dante, *Commedia* (seven cardinal sins)

Vittorino da Feltre, +1446, Italian humanist and outstanding paedagogue, sometimes called the "first modern schoolmaster".维托瑞欧

Vladimir I, E: Vladimir, D: Wladimir, St., Grand Duke of Kiev 980—1015, and prince of Novgorod; he was baptized in 988, married Anna, the sister of Emperor Basil II, erected many churches and monasteries and led his people to Christianity.弗拉基米尔，见 Nestorius, *Povest'*

Vocatus, E: overseer; D: Vogt, the administrator of a fiefdom or piece of property, often notorious for extracting unjust taxes.管理者

Volsung Saga, E: *Volsung Saga*, an Icelandic prose narrative from the 13th century; the central hero of the work is Sigurd (=Siegfried)《沃尔松歌》，见 *Edda*

voluntas, E: will, D: Wille, one of the mental powers 意愿，见 Anselmus, *Monologion*, Occam, *Sententiae* (emphasis on God's will, voluntarism), Langland, *Piers Plowman* (Will is the allegory of will)

vox, E: voice, D: Stimme, Schall; 声音，见 Abaelardus, *Sic et non* (the same words [voices] can have different meanings [significationes])

Vulgata, E: *Vulgate*, D: *Vulgata*; the authoritative Latin Bible translation of the Middle Ages, often copied, re-edited, improved (by adding numbers to each verse etc.) 拉丁通俗圣经译本，见 Rogerius Baco, *Opus maius* (urges revision of the text), Nicolaus de Lyra

W

Walahfridus Strabo, E: Walafried, D: Walafried; 808—849, Abbot of Reichenau, teacher of Charles the Bald, he was a poet, exeget, and a prolific writer. 瓦拉夫瑞德，见 *Liber de cultura hortorum*, *Visio Wettini*

Waldemar I, (Valdemar), King of Denmark, 1157—1182, he conquered Ruegen where he introduced Christianity in 1168. 瓦尔德马尔

Waldo, (Petrus Waldes), merchant from Lyon, + ca. 1217; founder of a pious but heretic movement after 1176, failed to get recognition from Alexander III in 1179 (Lateran Synod).瓦尔多

Waldenses, E: Waldenses, Waldensians, D: Waldenser; a heretic movement founded by Peter Waldo, influential in southern France and northern Italy after 1180.瓦尔多派，见 Joachim, *Liber figurarum* (influence on Waldenses)

Walter de Aquitania, E: Walter of Aquitania, the hero of the *Waltharii poiesis* 瓦尔塔，见 Ekkehard I

Walter de Chatillon, E: Walter of Chatillon, ca. 1135—1200, one of the goliards; author of the *Alexandreis* 瓦尔特，见 Appendix, *Alexandreis*, *Carmina Burana*

Waltharii poiesis, (=*Waltharius*), E: *Life of Waltharius*, the only extant Latin poem about a Germanic narrative《瓦尔塔里乌斯之诗》，见 Ekkehard I

Walther, Walther von der Vogelweide, 1170—1230; the leading German (or Austrian) minnesinger who extolled the ideal of mutual love. Some of his poems are moral, religious, political, and satirical.

瓦尔特,见 Hartmann

Welf, Welph, (Guelph, Welfen), noble family of Bavarian, Frankish origin, fought against the faction of the Hohenstaufen (Ghibellini), => Guelphi 威尔夫

Wenceslaus, D: Wenzel, son of Charles IV, King of Germany 1378—1400, he was deposed. 文策老/文西斯劳斯

Wenceslaus, D: Wenzel, St., +929, Duke of Bohemia, who tried to introduce Christianity but was murdered. 文策老/文西斯劳斯

Wendes, Wends, a Slavic tribe at the Elbe 温德人

Wenzel = Wenceslaus

Westgoten = Visigothones

Wiclif = Wycliffe

Wido = Guido

Widukind, (=Wittekind), +790 (?), leader of the Saxons in 782, he rejected Christianity. 维德金特

Wilfrith, (Wilfrid, Wilfried), St., +709; Abbot of Ripon who spent some years at Lyons and in Rome; he became Bishop of York, but was expelled from England in 678/79 and returned six years later. 威尔弗利得

Wilhelmus = Wilhelm = William = Guillaume

Wilhelmus, E: William, D: Wilhelm; King of Holland, proclaimed German King 1247—1256 but without influence. 威廉

Wilhelmus I, E: William the Conqueror, D: Wilhelm der Eroberer; King of England 1066—1087; son of Robert I, Duke of Normandy, in the battle of Hastings 1066 he defeated the last Anglo-Saxon King Harald II, succeeded to the English throne and established the rule of the Normans in Britain, introducint feudal institutions and customs. In 1086 he made a survey ("Domesday Book") of all property held in England. He supported the Church reforms directed by Archbishop Lanfranc and agreed to set up a separate system of ecclesiastical courts. 威廉,见 Malmesburiensis, *Gesta regum Anglorum*

Wilhelmus II Rufus, E: William the Red, D: Wilhelm der Rote; King of England 1087—1100, son of William I the Conqueror, he ruled with an iron hand; in 1097 he forced Anselm of Canterbury into exile. 威廉,见 Anselmus

Wilhelmus I, E: William, D: Wilhelm; King of Naples-Sicily 1154—1166, son of Roger II. 威廉

Wilhelmus II, E: William, D: Wilhelm; King of Sicily 1166—1189. 威廉,见 Dante, *Commedia* (placed in the Heaven of Jupiter)

Wilhelmus de Aquitania, E: William of Aquitania, D: Wilhelm von Aquitanien; Duke of Aquitania, he founded Cluny in 910. 威廉,见 Petrus Venerabilis

Wilhelmus de St. Amour, E: William of St. Amour, D: Wilhelm; opponent of mendicant professors at Paris University after 1252. 威廉

Wilhelmus de Champeaux, F: Guillaume de Champeaux, E: William of Champeaux, 1070—1122; French theologian, student of Anselm de Laon and Roscelin de Compiegne, exponent of extreme realism, thus attacked by his pupil Abelard; he became the founder of St. Victor in Paris (1108), was consecrated Bishop of Chalons (1113—1121). 威廉

Wilhelmus de Maleval, It: Guilelmo, E: William, D: Wilhelm; St., hermit in Italy, Siena, Maleval, he founded the Wilhelmites in 1156. 威廉

Wilhelmus Malmesburiensis => Malmesbury

Wilhelmus de Moerbeke, E: William of Moerbeke, D: Wilhelm von Moerbeke; +1286, Dominican of Ghent, studied in Cologne, helped St. Thomas Aquinas with the translation of Greek philosophical writings. He served as papal penitentary to several popes, became Archbishop of Thebes in 1278 and worked with much devotion for the reunion of the Greek and Latin churches. 威廉,见 Thomas Aquinas

Wilhelmus de Occam, E: William of Ockam = Occam

Wilhelmus de Rubruk / Rubruquis => Rubruk

Wilhelmus de St. Thierry, E: William of St-Thierry, D: Wilhelm von St. Thierry; +1149; French scholars, friend and biographer of St. Bernard, mystical author. 威廉,见 Anselmus, *Sic et non* (Abaelard's opponent)

William => Wilhelmus

William of Occam = Occam

Willibrordus, E: St. Willibrord,. 658—739, Anglo-Saxon missionary in Europe, called 'Apostle of Frisia' for his successful activities there, Archbishop of Utrecht in 695. "弗里西亚的宗徒/使徒",维利波德/威利布罗德,见 Beda, *Historia ecclesiastica*

Willigis, Archbishop of Mainz, chancellor of Otto I and II, +1011. 维利格斯

Winfrieth = Winfrid = Bonifatius
Wladimir = Vladimir
Wodan = Odin
Woitjech = Adalbertus
Wolfgang, St., 924—994, Bishop of Regensburg (972).沃尔夫冈,见 Regensburg
Wolfram von Eschenbach, E, D: Wolfram von Eschenbach; ca. 1170—1220, the leading German composer of courtly romances. 沃尔夫拉姆·冯·埃申巴赫,见 *Parzival*
Worms, (L: Wormatia), E, D: Worms; a city of southwest Germany on the Rhine River; originally a Celtic settlement it became a bishopric in the fourth century and was the center of the legendary kingdom of Burgund before the Huns and Aetius destroyed it in 436 AD. At the Diet of Worms (1521) Luther refused to recant his beliefs; => Concordatum Wormatianum 沃尔姆斯,见 Appendix, *Nibelungenlied*
Wotan = Odin
Wuerzburg, L: Herbipolis, E: Wuerzburg; city of Franconia; the episcopal see was created in 741. The bishop of Wuerzburg was a prince of the Holy Roman empire.维尔茨堡
Wycliffe, John, (=Wiclif, Wyclif, Wicliff); 1330—1384, English theologian, teacher at Oxford and royal clerk. He opposed much of traditional Catholicism (vows, indulgences, the papacy, the sacraments, transubstantiation) and caused much conflict but died peacefully. He wrote profusely on philosophical and theological questions and promoted the translation of the Bible into English. He influenced Hus and later reformers.威克利夫
Wynfrith = Bonifacius

X

Ximenes de Rada, Rodrigo, +1247, Archbishop of Toledo (1208), chief adviser of Ferdinand III of Castile. He protected Jews but advocated war against the Moors. He authored a chronicle of Spanish history.吉麦内兹

Y

Yaroslaw Mudry, E: Yaroslav the Wise, D: Jaroslav der Weise; Grand duke of Kiev 1019—1054, a supporter of Christianity. 雅罗斯拉夫,见 Nestorius, *Povest'*
York = Eboracum
Yves = Ivo

Z

Zacharias, Pope 741—752, a Greek from southern Italy, he managed to keep peace with the Lombards; he agreed that Pepin should be chosen king of the Franks (751). 扎卡利亚斯
Zehnte = Tithe
Zins = usura
Zizka, Johannes, (Jan Ziska), +1424; Bohemian general, one of the leaders in the Hussite Wars (1420—1431), who inflicted several defeats on the imperial armies. 西斯卡
Zoe, Byzantine empress, 1028—1050, wife of Romanus III, Michael IV, and Constantine IX.佐艾

出版后记

　　小说《红与黑》中有这样一段情节：主人公于连在贝藏松神学院考试的时候对答如流，眼看最后不拿第一就拿第二，与他作对的一位主考就心生一计，在问完关于圣哲罗姆和西塞罗的作品的问题后，话题一转谈到了贺拉斯、维吉尔等其他世俗作家。这时有些忘乎所以的于连热情洋溢地背诵和解释了贺拉斯的好几首颂歌，主考让于连得意了二十分钟后，突然变了脸，严厉责备于连不该把时间浪费在非宗教的作品上，以致脑子里塞满了没用甚至罪恶的想法。虽然主考的奸计即使在神学院里也被认为是卑鄙的，但是凭此将于连降为第一百九十八名也是让别人难以置喙的。吃了哑巴亏的于连恰好在几天之后有一次面见贝藏松主教的机会，没想到主教本人是位优秀的人文学者，他们大谈特谈维吉尔、贺拉斯、西塞罗，于连因此也得到主教格外的青睐，并且从主教那里获赠一套八卷烫金切口的塔西佗著作。这次谈话的内容传到神学院后，原来与于连作对的人也开始卑躬屈膝地讨好她，虽然他并不吃这一套。

　　我们且不论司汤达在这一峰回路转的桥段中寓涵了多少辛辣的讽刺和对命运的感慨，但从这个情节的表面来看，我们就能知道，在小说故事发生的那一年（1830年），世界远不像二十多年前黑格尔看到大败普鲁士的拿破仑时所做出的预言历史已经终结，仅在贝藏松神学院这样的一个世界的角落里，仅在一位乡下木匠的儿子于连身上，就上演着世俗精神与基督宗教传统相互对峙又相互渗透的吊诡剧目。我们是否有理由怀疑，向来我们所熟悉的文艺复兴、宗教改革、启蒙运动、法国大革命一路高歌猛进将新世界从中世纪的黑暗中催产出来会不会只是一种夸大其词的历史叙事？每一次向希腊罗马的回首是否真的绕过了中世纪？

　　弗里德里希·希尔在《欧洲思想史》中表达了一种希腊罗马、中世纪共同塑造了欧洲文化的观点：

　　　　古老欧洲的文化是各种辉煌形式组成的一个封闭世界。它的文化、科学与宗教信仰的传统都是遵照一个神圣的古代模式，以其最初一代创立人为最高权威，世代相传。这种古代的权威成为每次复兴运动、每次保守传统的革命的典范和模式。在这个贵族文化世界中的每个成员都有义务按这种权威的要求教育自己和别人。亚里士多德、柏拉图、普罗蒂诺和普罗克洛斯，西塞罗、塞内加、维吉尔、奥维德、贺拉斯、普鲁塔克和萨鲁斯特、希波克拉底和加仑、欧几里得、维特鲁威和托勒密，教父从奥古斯丁起到托马斯和苏亚雷斯以及正统的新教徒，这些都被接受为文化教育领域中的楷模。宇宙是神作为第一动因而治理的。留给人去做的只是按照外部世界中神定下来的模式,在世界内部(亦即第一层的人间世界)进行建设。

他尤其强调,中世纪对学习古典拉丁文、修辞学、研读古典著作的重视保障了欧洲经院文化和文学中的连贯性,这种连贯性又带来了欧洲思想上的一致性。同时,共同的贵族-市民政制使欧洲在政治与社会上保有一致性,欧洲思想史上创痕斑斑的的剧烈斗争也是在这种政制中进行的,这种世代相传的贵族政制的稳定性为思想领域的矛盾、争论、辩论提供了条件,也为各种思想能够抒发己见提供了贵族的宽容态度。

由此可见,中世纪在政治与文化领域中所形成的传统深刻影响着其后千年的欧洲,我们只有正视中世纪的遗产才能更好的了解现代世界,希望本卷提要能够引领读者对中世纪有一个最初的了解,吸引读者深入了解中世纪的方方面面。

世界图书出版公司北京公司

服务热线:133-6631-2326　139-1140-1220

服务信箱:teacher@hinabook.com

世图北京公司"大学堂"编辑部
2010 年 9 月

图书在版编目(CIP)数据

西方经典英汉提要.第3卷,中世纪经典100部/(奥)雷立柏著.—北京:世界图书出版公司北京公司,2010.10
ISBN 978-7-5100-2718-5

Ⅰ.①西… Ⅱ.①雷… Ⅲ.①著作—内容提要—西方国家—英、汉 Ⅳ.①Z835

中国版本图书馆 CIP 数据核字(2010)第 205787 号

西方经典英汉提要(卷三):中世纪经典100部

| 著　　者:(奥)雷立柏 | 筹划出版:银杏树下 | 责任编辑:张　鹏 |

出　　版:世界图书出版公司北京公司
发　　行:世界图书出版公司北京公司(北京朝内大街 137 号　邮编 100010)
销　　售:各地新华书店
印　　刷:北京盛兰兄弟印刷装订有限公司(北京市大兴区黄村镇西芦城　邮编 102612)
开　　本:787×1092 毫米　1/16
印　　张:29　插页 4
字　　数:580 千
版　　次:2010 年 12 月第 1 版
印　　次:2010 年 12 月第 1 次印刷

教师服务:teacher@hinabook.com　139-1140-1220
投稿邮箱:onebook@263.net
编辑咨询:133-6631-2326
营销咨询:133-6657-3072　010-8161-6534

ISBN 978-7-5100-2718-5/C·125　　　　　　　　　　　　定　价:50.00 元

(如存在文字不清、漏印、缺页、倒页、脱页等印装质量问题,请与承印厂联系调换。联系电话:010-61232263)

版权所有　翻印必究

韦洛克拉丁语教程
（插图第 6 版）

张卜天 译 （奥）雷立柏 审阅

雷立柏 彭小瑜 沈 弘 推荐

ISBN 978-7-5062-9310-5/G·323

定价：99.00 元　2009 年 4 月出版

为什么要学习拉丁语？

★ 拉丁语是了解欧洲文化的"大门"。无论是在文学、历史学、哲学、法学、宗教学、伦理学，还是心理学、医学、自然科学或教育学，西方许多经典著作都是用拉丁文写成的，要想深入了解西方文化，学习拉丁语是最好的途径之一。

★ 了解拉丁语有助于学习英语。60%的英语词汇都源于拉丁语。学过拉丁语的学生对 SAT 的词汇部分会更加得心应手。拥有较大词汇量也通常预示着管理方面的潜力和成功。

★ 在一个国家，古典语言是否受到足够的重视，是其综合实力的重要标志。像拉丁语这样一门重要的语言，目前在我国远没有受到应有的重视。但随着我国综合国力的增强，拉丁语越来越热，必定是大势所趋。

学习拉丁语，人必称"韦洛克"

听说韦洛克（Wheelock）的著名拉丁语教程将要在中国出版，我感到非常兴奋与欣慰。2002 年以来，我在北京教授拉丁语和古希腊语，但始终没有找到令我满意的拉丁语语法教材、文选和拉汉词典。《韦洛克拉丁语教程》终于能满足这个迫切需要。对学习西方哲学、文学、法律、历史或宗教的大学生和学者来说，这部教科书的出版是一件重大的事，因为拉丁语是一切西方知识的"大门"，而韦洛克也算是自学拉丁语的最好资料之一……我很高兴可以推荐它，希望它成为很多大学生的读物。

——雷立柏，奥地利古典学家，中国人民大学文学院教授

内容简介

《韦洛克拉丁语教程》是 20 世纪后半期以来英语世界最受欢迎的拉丁语教材，初版于 1956 年，很快就因其严密的组织结构、清晰的叙述讲解、循序渐进的设计安排、适中的难易程度以及其中收录的丰富的古代文献而被誉为"拉丁语学习的标准著作"，其"拉丁语学习首选教材"的地位无可撼动。

全书共分四十课，以简洁而不学究气的语言，系统讲解了拉丁语的基本词形、句法，并通过丰富的词汇学习、众多的英语词源研究、英拉句子互译和古典拉丁语作家原文赏读，来锻炼拉丁语学习者使用单词的灵活性和精确性，培养其观察、分析、判断和评价的能力，加强对语言形式、清晰性和美的感受；并通过探讨战争、友谊、未来、生老病死等发人深省的主题来学习古典作家的思想和技艺，分享他们的人文主义传统。

西方经典英汉提要

著者：(奥)雷立柏

(Ⅰ) 古希腊罗马经典 100 部(公元前 800 年到公元 150 年)
ISBN：978-7-5100-1155-9/H·1048
出版时间：2010 年 1 月　　定价：39.80 元

(Ⅱ) 古代晚期经典 100 部(公元 150 年到 650 年)
ISBN：978-7-5100-2068-1/H·1048
出版时间：2010 年 6 月　　定价：42.00 元

内容简介

　　自严复翻译西方政法诸书至今，汉语学界数代学人为窥西学堂奥，凭借个人禀赋和志趣选译西方经典，锱铢相累，可谓夥矣。然而，并不是每个人都有机会和能力直接阅读经典，另外，如果缺乏看待西方经典的整全视野和正确心态，启迪心智的经典读物也可能成为"毒物"。因此，一套优秀的辅助性读物就是必需的，这套《西方经典英汉提要》就是为此目的而写。

　　★ **外籍教授专为中国学生写作西方经典入门读物**：作者雷立柏为奥地利籍古典语文学家，在北京大学获得哲学博士学位，学贯中西，熟谙古希腊语、拉丁语、希伯来语、英语、德语、汉语等多种语言。在人民大学教授"拉丁语基础"、"古希腊语基础"、"拉丁语文学史"、"古希腊语文学史"等课程时，深感没有合适的教材可以使用，于是决定自己编写这套能够帮助学生学习西方经典文化的英汉提要。

　　★ **打破学科界限，西方经典著作一网打尽**：这套书并不依现代学术分科体系选取文献，而是以它们对西方智识传统的贡献为择取标准，优先录取那些提供了整全知识视野的"伟大叙事"，这种打破学科壁垒的做法将会使每一位读者从中获益，无论你是对文学、历史、哲学，还是对宗教、法学或艺术感兴趣。书中介绍的部分书籍尚无中译本，读者可以借助本提要先睹为快。

　　★ **注重语文学的写作方式，带领读者临近原汁原味的西方经典**：书中汉语提要部分的专名使用西文原文，一方面避免翻译不统一所引起的误解，另一方面有助于读者熟悉原典，便于读者进一步查阅原文和深入研究。书后附有关键词汇、人名、书名的多语索引，相当于一部小型的语文学词典，包含丰富的语文学知识，是初习古典语文学的学子不可多得的便利工具。

　　★ **中英双语简易流畅、朴实可读**。

小说鉴赏
（双语修订第3版）

(美)克林斯·布鲁克斯　罗伯特·潘·沃伦 著
主万　冯亦代　草婴　丰子恺　汝龙　等译
ISBN 978-7-5062-5475-5/C·10
定价：56.00元　2008年10月出版

　　这是美国新批评派学者布鲁克斯和沃伦合编的一部短篇小说鉴赏集，是新批评(the new criticism)理论观点和方法在小说批评与理论领域的体现。作者选用各种题材和多种风格的短篇小说，加以分析讨论和互相比较，提出鉴别好小说的一些原则，阐述小说的形成与发展过程，为我们提供了小说批评与赏析的范例；目的是为了加深读者对作品的理解，提高其鉴赏力，使读者更接近于成功小说的真谛。

　　作为新批评派细读式(close reading)批评和理论阐述的名著，本书帮助新批评派在美国大学的文学讲坛中确立了"文学批评"的地位，对文学教学与批评实践影响深远。它既是一本文学教科书，也是文学爱好者的自修读物。本书采用中英文对照模式，对于广大具有一定英语基础的文学爱好者和英语专业的师生来讲，它又是一部难得的英语阅读材料。

什么是好小说？如何理解小说？

　　★ **经典著作**　美国新批评派里程碑性质的著作，全世界大学都在使用的经典文学教科书，同时也被认为是最好的文学自修读物。两位作者站在世界文学的前沿，从内部到外部对小说进行研究，突破传统意义上的小说审美，是新批评理论观点和方法在小说批评与理论领域的全新体现。

　　★ **双语呈现**　既可欣赏信达雅致的中文译文，又能品味原汁原味的英文文献，中英双语对应呈现，使本书既是一部绝妙的小说读本和文学教材，同时又是一部难得的英语学习素材。

　　★ **权威著者**　本书作者布鲁克斯和沃伦同为新批评派的领军人物，耶鲁大学教授，著名文学评论家，享有世界声誉。沃伦曾两获普利策奖，是美国第一位桂冠诗人。二人共同创办了当时美国最有影响力的文学杂志《南方评论》。

　　★ **超强阵容**　顶级翻译团队，草婴、主万、汝龙、冯亦代、丰子恺、雨宁等均为我国重要的翻译名家。著名作家、小说理论家、北京大学中文系曹文轩教授，著名翻译家、《世界文学》主编李文俊审阅；海外著名华人女作家聂华苓女士倾力推荐。

大学堂(第一期)

筹划出版:银杏树下

"大学堂"开放给所有向往知识,崇尚科学,对宇宙和人生有所追问的人。

"大学堂"中展开一本本书,阐明各种传统和新兴的学科,导向真理和智慧。既有接引之台阶,又具深化之门径。无论何时,无论何地,请你把它翻开……

001.社会学与生活(插图修订第9版)　定价:68.00元
(美)理查德·谢弗 著　马戎 杨文山 审阅　刘鹤群 房智慧 译　赵旭东 译校
这是一部当今中国最需要的社会学高级普及读物。

001-02.社会学与生活(插图修订第9版·普及版)　定价:39.80元

001-03.社会学与生活(插图双语第10版)　定价:78.00元

002.小说鉴赏(双语修订第3版)　定价:56.00元
(美)布鲁克斯 沃伦 编著　主万 冯亦代 丰子恺 等译　聂华苓 推荐
什么是好小说？如何理解小说？

003.拍电影——现代影像制作教程(插图第6版)　定价:45.00元
(美)琳恩·格罗斯 拉里·沃德 著　廖澺苍 凌大发 译　焦雄屏 推荐
一本实用的影像制作教程。

004.认识电影(插图第11版)　定价:68.00元
(美)路易斯·贾内梯 著　(瑞典)英格玛·伯格曼 (日)黑泽明 等供图　焦雄屏 译
最畅销、最国际化的电影导论,远流版"电影馆"丛书的代表作。

005.中国近代史:1600—2000,中国的奋斗(第6版)　定价:66.00元
(美)徐中约 著　计秋枫 朱庆葆 译　茅家琦 钱乘旦 审校　徐中约 审定
英语世界及海外华人社会中最畅销的中国近代史用书。

006.经济学的思维方式(第11版)　定价:49.80元
(美)保罗·海恩 等著　马昕 陈宇 译　张维迎 审阅
(美)道格拉斯·诺斯 梁小民 熊秉元 推荐
经济学教材的革命——像经济学家一样思考。
本书是一部国际知名的经典经济学教科书,堪称经济学教育领域一部标尺性著作。

007.听音乐:音乐欣赏教程(插图第6版·赠配套光盘)　定价:78.00元
(美)罗杰·凯密恩 著　陈美鸾 总召集　王美珠 等译
陈佐湟 余志刚 杨燕迪 严宝瑜 推荐
2008年献给爱乐人的顶级有声读物,美国使用最广泛的音乐欣赏课程教材。

008.伦理学与生活(第9版)　定价:58.00元
(美)雅克·蒂洛　基思·克拉斯曼　**著**　程立显　刘建　**等译**　周辅成　**审阅**

美国最权威、最受欢迎的伦理学教材。

009.电影艺术——形式与风格(插图第8版)　定价:78.00元
(美)大卫·波德维尔　克莉丝汀·汤普森　**著**　曾伟祯　**译**　李安　焦雄屏　**推荐**

2008年度最重要的电影图书,最令人期待的大众艺术读品。

010.西方哲学史——从苏格拉底到萨特及其后(修订第8版)　定价:68.00元
(美)斯通普夫　菲泽　**著**　匡宏　邓晓芒　**等译**

邓晓芒　**翻译策划**　何兆武　**作序**　赵汀阳　**推荐**

一部既植根传统又向当代开放的哲学史,堪称当代西方哲学史的主流和典范之作。

011.现代世界史(插图第10版·上下册)　定价:88.00元
(美)R.R.帕尔默　乔·科尔顿　劳埃德·克莱默　**著**

何兆武　孙福生　董正华　陈少衡　**等译**　罗荣渠　何兆武　刘北成　**推荐**

世界现代史领域的殿堂级学术教科书,全世界几代学人透过他的眼睛看历史。
2002年被美国历史学会(AHA)评为"教科书的黄金标本"。

012.韦洛克拉丁语教程(插图修订第6版)　定价:99.00元
(美)弗雷德里克·M·韦洛克　**著**　理查德·拉弗勒　**修订**　张卜天　**译**

(奥)雷立柏　**审阅**　雷立柏　彭小瑜　沈弘　**推荐**

学习拉丁语,人必称"韦洛克"。
20世纪后半期以来英语世界最受欢迎的拉丁语教材。

013.认识商业(插图第8版)　定价:68.00元
(美)威廉·尼科尔斯　詹姆斯·麦克修　苏珊·麦克修　**著**　陈智凯　黄启瑞　**译**

魏杰　张维迎　汪丁丁　吴晓波　唐骏　**推荐**

汇集近代管理智识,积累百年管理实务、智慧与典范。
美国最畅销的商业入门教程,经济学意义上的商业普及教育。

014.中国文学史(上册)　定价:42.00元
龚鹏程　**著**

注重文学发展中多远异质成分的挖掘,尽力为读者还原一部真实的文学发展史。
历时两年,"天下第一才子"龚鹏程最新力作;下笔风流,嬉笑怒骂,弹指间旧说陈论灰飞烟灭。

（第二期）

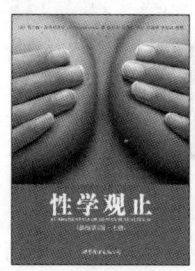 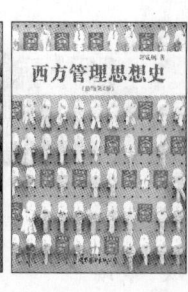    

015.性学观止（插图第6版） 定价:88.00元
（美）贺兰特·凯查杜里安 **著** 郎景和 赵伯仁 **审订** 江晓原 李银河 **推荐**
美国历史上第一部成功的性学教科书，作者特为中国读者撰写全新章节，讲述性与东方文化！

016.西方管理思想史（插图第4版） 定价:60.00元
郭咸纲 **著**
二十年磨炼，第一本成功的中文管理思想史读物最新版！
纵览管理思想演变，激赏古今杰出头脑。

017.意识形态:起源和影响（第10版） 定价:42.00元
（美）利昂·P·巴拉达特 **著** 张慧芝 张露璐 **译** 刘苏里 **推荐**
从历史的角度解析意识形态，着眼意识形态的实践特性。
以一视同仁的立场澄清政治立场的混乱。

018.简明逻辑学导论（第10版） 定价:78.00元
（美）帕特里克·赫尔利 **著** 陈波 **翻译策划** 陈波 宋文淦 熊立文 **等译**
北美最广泛使用、最受欢迎的逻辑导论型教材。

019.世界政治:走向新秩序?（插图第11版） 定价:68.00元
（美）查尔斯·W·凯格利 **著** 夏维勇 阮淑俊 **译** 倪世雄 **推荐**
呈现国际关系纷繁各象，剖解未来世界政治走向。

020.认识媒体（插图第2版） 定价:88.00
乔治·罗德曼 **著** 邓建国 **译** 刘香成 喻国明 展江 **作序推荐**
小百科书式的内容架构，从图书、报纸到广播、电视、互联网无所不包，让读者一次认识媒体。
……………

"大学堂"丛书部分备有教师手册、习题、PPT和章节提要等教学资料，欢迎采用丛书作为教材的教师来电来函索取。

诚挚欢迎读者为我们提供有价值的选题，同时也期待着具有翻译才华的读者加入我们，为进一步充实"大学堂"丛书，给读者提供更多、更好、更实用的图书共同努力。

联系人： 杜老师
邮　箱： marketing@hinabook.com
电　话： 133-6657-3072　139-1140-1220　　**传　真：** 010-6401-8116
地　址： 北京市朝内大街137号　世界图书出版公司北京公司　后浪公司（邮编100010）